GW00543746

Edited by Niall MacMonagle

Niall MacMonagle has taught English for the Leaving
Certificate for many years. A well-known literary
commentator on radio, he is the editor of several poetry
anthologies, including the best-selling *Windharp: Poems of
Ireland since 1916* (Penguin, 2015) and *TEXT: A Transition
Year English Reader*. He writes a weekly art column for the
Sunday Independent. In 2017, he was awarded a Doctorate
of Letters, *honoris causa*, by UCD, for services to literature.

'... until everything
was rainbow, rainbow, rainbow!'

Elizabeth Bishop

First published in 2021 by
The Celtic Press

Ground Floor – Block B, Liffey Valley Office Campus, Dublin 22

ISBN: 978-0-7144-2796-6

for John MacMonagle

Up Mayo!

essay
Poetry words
_____

→ radiates
→ awareness
→ the poet alerts the reader to ...
→ the poet draws the readers attention to ...
→ effectively communicates/portrays/conveys
→ relishes the beauty of ...
→ enters into the lives of others
→ we catch a glimpse into
→ this poem explores ...
→ this poem is a meditation on ...

Contents

William Butler Yeats (1865–1939)

Introduction

'Study is the resting place – poetry the adventure'

– Wallace Stevens

The Leaving Certificate student is already an experienced reader of poetry. For Junior Cycle, you were invited to read a great variety of poems on a wide range of subjects by many different poets. You will have realised that poets use language differently, that poetry is both challenging and rewarding, and in an age of soundbytes and mediaspeak it can hold its own and offer something unique and special; that poetry, in Allison Pearson's words, 'is not in the business of taking polaroids: it should be a long slow developer, raising images that we frame and keep'. You have also had experience of both seen and unseen poems. A similar challenge awaits you at Leaving Certificate level, but there are some important differences. Until now, you might have looked at three or four poems by different poets; in the Leaving Certificate, at Higher Level, you are being invited to read an interesting and representative sample of work by eight poets and you will also be given the opportunity to respond to unseen poetry.

It is worth remembering at the outset that the word for poet in English comes from the Greek word for maker. A good poem is language that has been carefully shaped and well made. Samuel Taylor Coleridge's definition of poetry in the nineteenth century as 'the best words in the best order' still holds. W. H. Auden has described poetry as 'memorable speech'. The *New Princeton Handbook of Poetic Terms* defines a poem as 'an instance of verbal art, a text set in verse, bound speech. More generally, a poem conveys heightened forms of perception, experience, meaning, or consciousness in heightened language, i.e., a heightened mode of discourse.'

But, whichever definition we accept, we will find definitions inadequate and less important than the unique and individual experience when we, as readers, allow ourselves to enter into the world of the poem that the poet has created for us on the page.

'The Voice You Hear When You Read Silently' by Thomas Lux reminds us of the unique, very private, pleasurable experience of reading poetry:

The Voice You Hear When You Read Silently

is not silent, it is a speaking–
out-loud voice in your head: it is spoken,
a voice is saying it
as you read. It's the writer's words,
of course, in a literary sense
his or her 'voice' but the sound
of that voice is the sound of your voice.
Not the sound your friends know
or the sound of a tape played back
but your voice
caught in the dark cathedral
of your skull, your voice heard
by an internal ear informed by internal abstracts
and what you know by feeling,
having felt. It is your voice
saying, for example, the word 'barn'
that the writer wrote
but the 'barn' you say
is a barn you know or knew. The voice
in your head, speaking as you read,
never says anything neutrally – some people
hated the barn they knew,
some people love the barn they know
so you hear the word loaded
and a sensory constellation
is lit: horse-gnawed stalls,
hayloft, black heat tape wrapping
a water pipe, a slippery
spilled chirr of oats from a split sack,
the bony, filthy haunches of cows . . .
And 'barn' is only a noun – no verb
or subject has entered into the sentence yet!
The voice you hear when you read to yourself
is the clearest voice: you speak it
speaking to you.

When we look at a poem for the very first time, we can appreciate and sense how that poem has been made and shaped. This does not only include its actual shape as printed text, though this in itself is extremely important; more importantly, it means that thought, idea, and feeling have been structured and the careful combination produces the living poem.

An open approach brings its own rewards. If we learn to understand how something complex works, then we are aware of its intricacies and can better admire the creative mind that made it possible. The Irish writer Michael Longley says that 'a poet makes the most complex and concentrated response that can be made with words to the total experience of living.' But he also admits that one of the things that studying literature taught him was 'the beauty of things difficult.'

It is an exciting challenge to stand before a painting and discover what it has to say to us, to listen to a piece of music and hear it for the first time, to read a poem unknown to us until that moment. And then to return to these works and to realise how our relationship with them changes and develops as we ourselves change and develop. As we grow and change, so does our response.

We can all remember instances and experiences which we found difficult and challenging initially, but with careful thought and an open, positive approach we gained insight and understanding. Stephen Booth puts it like this: 'Any reader superstitiously fearful that the magic of a poem will vanish with knowledge of its sources need not worry any more than a student of zoology need worry that gazelles will slow down if he investigates the reasons why they run so fast.' Helen Vendler also offers good advice when she says that a reader should not look at a poem 'as if you're looking at the text with a microscope from outside'. For Vendler, the close reader is 'someone who goes inside a room and describes the architecture. You speak from inside the poem as someone looking to see how the roof articulates with the walls and how the wall articulates with the floor. And where are the crossbeams that hold it up, and where are the windows that let light through?'

Poetry can sometimes be difficult and a challenge to understand. But if we reject challenges, our vocabulary, for example, would never grow; the enquiring mind would close down. We need challenges in our lives to sharpen our intellect and keep our minds from dozing off. Sometimes we fall into the trap of saying 'I like this poem because it is easy for me to understand' or 'Why doesn't the poet say what he or she wants to say in an easy-to-understand language?' If we adopt such a position, we are saying that we want a poetry that is at our level only, that if there is an unknown word or a difficult allusion, then the poem should be rejected. If we spoke down to little children throughout their childhood, they would never grow up. Most poetry is written by adults for other adults and as a Leaving Certificate student you are on the threshold of adulthood. Allow the poems in this antology to have their say and you will not be disappointed. And if you come upon a poem in a newspaper, magazine, book, the London Underground, the New York Subway or the DART, you should give that poem a chance. The poem might deserve it and so do you.

Some years ago, the Irish poet Paul Muldoon was asked to judge a poetry competition, in the north of Ireland, which was open to young people up to the age of eighteen. There were hundreds of entries and there were poems, short and long, on all the big subjects – famine, time, death, space travel, nuclear war. Muldoon awarded first prize to an eight-year old boy who wrote the following poem:

The Tortoise

The tortoise goes movey, movey.

There was 'consternation' when 'this little poem about a tiny little subject' was awarded the prize. Muldoon explains that a great deal of the consternation was in the minds of the school teachers in the audience: 'They were upset by the fact that there's no such word in the English language as "movey, m-o-v-e-y". I tried to point out that until recently that there'd been no such word as "movey", but there now certainly was such a word, and I would never again be able to think of a tortoise without seeing it go "movey, movey".' One teacher told Muldoon that the prize-winning poet was illiterate, forgetting that the same boy had an extraordinary fresh and alive imagination.

Consider the poem again. Say it aloud and its atmospheric rhythm is immediate:

The Tortoise

The tortoise goes movey, movey.

Professor Paul Muldoon now teaches creative writing at Princeton University and the first task he sets his students is to write a one-line poem that will change the way he looks at the world. When they have made their poem, he shows them 'The Tortoise', which, for him, does just that. It goes . . .

m-o-v-e-y, m-o-v-e-y.

There are many aspects to be considered when it comes to the poem on the page, but let us begin without any set ideas. Consider the following:

In a Station of the Metro

The apparition of these faces in the crowd;
Petals on a wet, black bough.

What have we here? A poem. How can we tell? One of the reasons we can identify it as poetry is by its physical arrangement on the page. Prose is presented within a right and left hand margin on the page, whereas poetry is written in lines, each one causing us to pause, however briefly, before we move on. When we read it through, we can sense a concentration and intensity, a focus, a way of looking, which is one of poetry's hallmarks. What have we here? Three lines, the first of them the title, then two lines separated by a semi-colon; twenty words in all. For accurate understanding, almost all you need is a dictionary: remember Elizabeth Bishop's advice: 'Use the dictionary. It's better than the critics'.

To ask 'What have we here?' is infinitely more rewarding than 'What is this poem about?' And this, I think, is by far the best way of approaching any text. 'What have I here?' means that I, in my own time, will interpret the poem. I will gradually build up an understanding of it in my own mind. A poem is not a static thing. It is in the poet Thomas Kinsella's words 'an orderly dynamic entity'. 'What is this poem about?' is an alienating way of looking at a text, implying as it does that there is only one way of looking at the poem and that I, as reader, must somehow crack some code.

We all bring different things to a text. My way of looking at a poem will be different from yours. The person who has walked Inniskeen Road on a July evening will read Patrick Kavanagh's poetry in a different light from the reader who has never been there. If you have been to Rathlin Island, on the north Antrim coast, then Derek Mahon's description of the place will have different resonances for you than for the person who has never seen the 'rock-face and cliff-top' of Rathlin, just as Emily Dickinson's poetry will be different for those who have been to Amherest, Massachusetts.

Similarly, if you have grown up on a farm you might find yourself reading Seamus Heaney's poetry from a different perspective to the urban dweller. One way is not necessarily better than the other. It is different. What does matter, however, is that interpretation and discussion of the text should be rooted in the text itself. There is such a thing as a wrong interpretation: one which does not take the details of the text into account.

In the short poem by Ezra Pound, the title – 'In a Station of the Metro' – gives us the setting of the poem.

In a Station of the Metro

The apparition of these faces in the crowd;
Petals on a wet, black bough.

We are in Paris, but the actual Metro stop is not named. The title is clinically factual; there is no word in the title to indicate an attitude or a tone. Yet the reader is immediately invited to imagine this particular scene: usually a crowded and very busy underground railway station. In many ways, it is a scene that sums up an aspect of twentieth-century life – urban, anonymous, busy, lacking individuality.

Then the first line of the poem itself speaks of the individual and separate faces in the crowd. Pound on seeing particular faces compares the event to that of experiencing an apparition. The faces are somehow supernatural or ghostly. In a world of concrete and steel, the human being is phantom-like. This is a sense impression. The poem for example has no verb. It is not so much concerned with making a definite statement as with capturing an immediate response to a situation at a particular moment in time.

The second and final line of the poem speaks about the natural world, petals on a tree. The tree itself is wet and black suggesting, perhaps, something unattractive; but the petals are wet too and therefore shiny. They stand out. There are many of them and yet each one is individual and unique. From the way the two lines are arranged on the page, and from the use of the connecting semi-colon, we can tell that Pound is making a link between the nameless faces of people moving through an underground station (with their bright faces) and the petals that stand out against the dull tree bough.

The train in the underground station is a hard, steel object and, it could be argued, bough-like in shape. The faces coming towards Pound are soft, living faces; the petals are soft against the hard surface of the tree, just as the faces are bright against the background of the Metro.

Ezra Pound has defined an image as 'an intellectual and emotional complex in an instant of time' and you can see how this poem is such an image. It captures the idea and the feeling, the intellectual and the emotional, and both are linked together within the one picture.

Pound himself has written of how he came to write this poem. He left the Metro at La Concorde and 'saw suddenly a beautiful face, and then another beautiful woman, and I tried all that day to find words for what this had meant to me, and I could not find any words that seemed to me worthy, or as lovely as that sudden emotion.' Later he wrote a thirty-line poem and destroyed it. Six months after that, he wrote a poem half that length; a year later, he made the haiku-like poem 'In a Station of the Metro'.

The above observations on this poem are far longer than the poem itself, but poetry is compression and intensity. So much is being said in such a short space that any discussion of a poem will require expansion and explanation. What is most important is that you feel comfortable and at ease with poetry. You speak the language in which it is written and this allows us to be closer to poetry and literature than any other art form; the words are ours already or, as we read, they become ours as well as the poet's. There may be no one single, definitive response, explanation or interpretation to a poem, but there are wrongheaded ones. Take care and then the private dialogue between you and the poem, the class discussion, the personal study of the text become rewarding and enriching experiences.

The philosophy behind this Leaving Certificate English course is 'knowledge made, not knowledge received'. In other words, you are expected to take an active, not a passive, part in the learning process. The knowledge, insight and understanding gained by you is more enjoyable and memorable than the knowledge presented to you by another. That is to say that if we had the time and inclination a library of books would educate us well if we were willing and enthusiastic readers. However, reality is otherwise. Most of us find a system and a structure, such as classroom and school, necessary, if not vital – initially at any rate. So we go to school and find ourselves in English class studying poems and poets and poetry.

Each year, young people worldwide study poetry in school. Poetry is an art form that exists in every known language. It is also known that only a small percentage of people continue to read poetry throughout their adult life, despite the fact that many enjoy it and remember it from school. But this is changing. Poetry readings now attract very large audiences. More poetry books are being sold; occasionally, poetry books even become best-sellers. *Birthday Letters* by Ted Hughes, for example, sold over 120,000 copies in one year, while 200,000 hardback copies of Seamus Heaney's translation of *Beowulf* were bought in 2000.

Silence and slow time are not things that we associate with the way we live today. Yet silence and slow time are probably the two most important things when it comes to the intensely private experience of reading poetry. There are specifically public poems as well of course. When President Mary McAleese was inaugurated, she quoted from Christopher Logue's poem 'Come to the Edge'. On 11 November 2004 in her Re-Inaugural speech, President McAleese ended with a quotation from a poem by Seamus Heaney, a poem which had been written especially to mark the expansion, six months earlier, of the European Union on 1 May: 'Move lips, move minds and make new meanings flare'. Michael D. Higgins, Ireland's ninth president, is himself a published poet. His *New and Selected Poems* was published in 2011.

Poetry does not offer easy answers or solutions, but it does allow us to experience emotions. It does not lessen our fear and confusions and anger, but it helps us to accept our anger, confusions and fears, and, in Richard Bernstein's words, we find in literature 'a difficult sort of comfort' because great literature 'refuses to provide comfort that is 'false' or 'saccharine''. Likewise, it heightens our experience of positive feelings and, at its best, is life-affirming.

In the film *Invictus*, Nelson Mandela, played by Morgan Freeman, tells the captain of the Springboks rugby team Francois Pienaar that his favourite poem is William Ernest Henley's 'Invictus'. When one remembers that Mandela was imprisoned for twenty-seven years for opposing apartheid, eighteen of which were spent on Robben Island, it is easy to see why such a poem sustained him during his imprisonment:

Invictus

Out of the night that covers me,
Black as the Pit from pole to pole,
I thank whatever gods may be
For my unconquerable soul.

In the fell clutch of circumstance
I have not winced nor cried aloud.
Under the bludgeonings of chance
My head is bloody but unbowed.

Beyond this place of wrath and tears
Looms but the horror of the shade,
And yet the menace of the years
Finds, and shall find me, unafraid.

It matters not how strait the gate,
How charged with punishments the scroll,
I am the master of my fate:
I am the captain of my soul.

William Ernest Henley (1849–1903)

This book provides you with the texts, the most important things of all. You may find the critical apparatus of some use, but absolutely nothing can replace the lively, engaged, discursive atmosphere in a classroom where poems and poets are discussed between teacher and student and student and student, or the careful reading of the poems and thinking done by you in private. It is hoped that you will return again and again to these wonderful poems and that long after you have left school, a poet's way of seeing, a poet's way of saying will remain with you. In an age such as ours, where we often demand and expect instant gratification, the reading and re-reading of poetry is sometimes viewed as an unusual and strange activity. It is also one of the most valuable, enriching and stimulating things you could do. And it can be, as Wallace Stevens reminds us, an adventure.

Niall MacMonagle

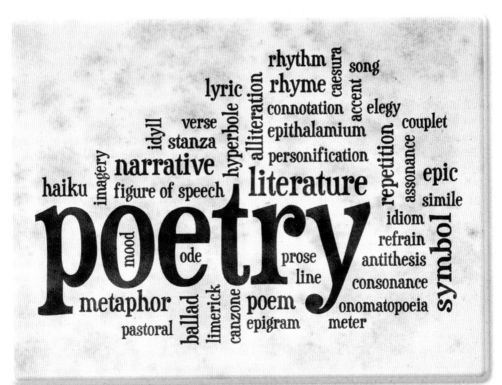

How To Use This Book

There are two compulsory poetry questions on **Paper II** of the Leaving Certificate English course: **Prescribed Poetry** and the **Unseen Poem**. Read the prescribed poems closely, preferably aloud. Then read the poems again (with the aid of the dictionary or glossary if necessary). Think about the poems and talk about the poems. Re-read the poems until you feel comfortable with them. There is no substitute for knowing the poems well; reading the poems and thinking about the poems is the most important of all. The questions beneath each poem will direct you towards some important aspects of the text. Later, you may wish to read the Biographical Notes and the Critical Commentary. These might help clarify your own thinking. Finally, you should find writing on the texts a very good way of finding out how much you understand.

There has been a long and interesting discussion regarding the relevance of biographical detail, glossary, background and so on to the poem. In 1929, I. A. Richards published an important and influential book called *Practical Criticism*. It was based on an experiment in which he gave his students at Cambridge a series of unsigned poems for comment. Such an exercise produced some misreadings, but in itself was valuable and promoted a close and careful reading of the poem. As a result, 'practical criticism' became a standard classroom exercise throughout the English-speaking world.

You might wish to adopt this method and, simply by ignoring the critical apparatus in this textbook, such an approach is possible. But the teaching of literature also allows for other approaches. If you met a person during the course of a long journey and that person withheld details regarding background, place of birth, nationality, religion, politics, influences, then your knowledge and understanding of the individual would be constrained and incomplete. So too with a poem. The more we know, the greater our understanding. Professor Declan Kiberd thinks that every text should have a context and that to stay with the 'practical criticism' approach is to become the ostrich that sticks its head in the sand and looks at one grain, then another and then attempts to make a connection between them.

For the Unseen Poetry question, you might find the response to 'A Blessing' by James Wright of interest. There is also an Appendix which includes an outline of various strategies when responding to any poem and a Glossary of Literary Terms.

Eight poets are prescribed for Higher Level. Students will be expected to have studied **at least six poems** by each poet.

American spelling has been retained where appropriate.

Prescribed Poets and Poems
at Higher Level
Part I

Elizabeth Bishop
(1911–1979)

Contents	Page

The Overview

These ten poems by Elizabeth Bishop reveal many of the most striking characteristics of her work: her eye for detail, her interest in travel and different places (Brazil; Nova Scotia; Worcester, Massachusetts), her apparently conversational tone, her command of internal rhyme, her use of repetition, her interest in strict poetic forms (the sonnet and the sestina), childhood memories, identity, loss.

The world which Bishop describes in her poetry is vivid and particular. Colm Tóibín says of Elizabeth Bishop that 'She began with the idea that little is known and that much is puzzling' (*On Elizabeth Bishop*, Princeton University Press, 2015). She is so intent on accurate description that often a detail is qualified and clarified within the poem. In Mexican-British poet Michael Schmidt's words, 'the voice affirms, hesitates, corrects itself; the image comes clear to us as it came clear to her, a process of adjusting perception until the thing is seen. Or the feeling is released.' For example, in 'The Fish' she tells us 'his gills were breathing in/ the terrible oxygen/ — the frightening gills,' fresh and crisp with blood,/ that can cut so badly' or that the eyes of the fish 'shifted a little', and then the more precise observation: ' — It was more like the tipping/ of an object toward the light'.

Bishop is a sympathetic observer and it has been remarked that she asks us 'to focus not on her but *with* her'. She looks at the fish, imagines its insides – 'the coarse white flesh/ packed in like feathers,/ the big bones and the little bones'; she sings hymns to the seal in 'At the Fishhouses'; she is concerned for the 'piercing cry/ and panic' of the armadillo; she finds love is present in the unlikely setting of a dirty filling station. When she uses 'I' in her poetry, it is never alienating or distancing. Somehow she makes the reader feel at ease. The poems as we read them are working out something.

The poetry is not always explicitly autobiographical but Bishop, an outsider for much of her life, writes indirectly in 'The Prodigal' of the outsider and later, in the explicitly autobiographical 'In the Waiting Room', she names herself ('you are an *Elizabeth*') and charts the sense of her child's mind realising her uniqueness and identity. 'Sestina' is also autobiographical, in that it tells of a home without a mother and father. Bishop only wrote about her childhood experiences late in life: 'Sestina', 'First Death in Nova Scotia', and 'In the Waiting Room' all date from when Bishop was in her fifties. She captures in them the confusion and complexities of childhood, its terror, panic and alienation. In 'First Death in Nova Scotia', she pieces together, as a child's mind would, the details, in order to understand them: 'Arthur's coffin was/ a little frosted cake,/ and the red-eyed loon eyed it/ from his white, frozen lake.'

Bishop preferred geography to history. It is significant that she remembers reading *National Geographic* in 'In the Waiting Room'. The title of her first book, *North & South*, contains the idea of opposites, but opposites that co-exist. Yet her descriptions of place are never just descriptions of place. Morality, history and politics are also evident in Bishop's landscapes. In 'Questions of Travel', Brazil and its otherness prompt Bishop to ask if it's right to watch strangers in another country. She dwells on the country's traditions ('In another country the clogs would all be tested'), religious influences ('a bamboo church of Jesuit baroque'), history ('the weak calligraphy of songbirds' cages').

Not only Bishop's eye but also her ear is finely attuned to the nuance of language. For example, she makes music in unusual and interesting rhyme patterns. In the closing lines of 'The Bight', the ear responds to sounds:

> and brings up a dripping **jawful** of marl.
> All the untidy activity continues,
> **awful** but cheer**ful**.

Rhyme (end rhyme, internal rhyme) and repetition are also used effectively. Bishop's tone is immediate ('Be careful with that match!'), often seemingly conversational ('There are too many waterfalls here'), relaxed ('He was curious about me. He was interested in music') or self-deprecating ('What childishness is it that while there's a breath of life/ in our bodies, we are determined to rush/ to see the sun the other way around?'). Bishop once wrote in a notebook that 'our nature consists in motion; complete rest is death.'

In Elizabeth Bishop's poetry, there is self-discovery, a sense of difference, moments of heightened awareness, a strong sense of here and now, an absence of any religious belief but a belief in the mystery of knowledge 'flowing and flown'. In 'At the Fishhouses', what begins as accurate and gradual description of landscape gives way to a downward movement towards the dark, cold centre of meaning, here imagined as deep beneath the ocean surface and something which we can never know or understand fully.

In Bishop, the act and the art of writing bring shape and order to experience. In 'Questions of Travel', she describes the traveller taking a notebook and writing. The use of 'we' in the poem and the way in which every traveller is contained in 'the traveller' allows everyone to enter into the experience. This record of thought and feeling is what Bishop herself does in her poems. She was interested in form: the sonnet and the sestina are very formal, but in other poems where the structure and rhythm may not be obvious at first, there is often a very fine command and control.

Biographical Notes

An only child, Elizabeth Bishop was born on 8 February 1911, in Worcester, Massachusetts, and her father died of Bright's disease the following October, when she was eight months old. Her mother was deeply affected by the death and spent the following five years in and out of nursing homes and mental hospitals, moving between Worcester, Boston, and Great Village, her hometown, in Nova Scotia, Canada. In 1916, when Elizabeth Bishop was five, her mother was permanently confined in Dartmouth Hospital in Nova Scotia and she never saw her again.

Bishop was brought up by relatives. First by her maternal grandparents in Nova Scotia (from spring 1916 to September 1917, returning every summer for two months until 1923), and later by relations in Massachusetts.

Bishop's Nova Scotia childhood is captured in 'First Death in Nova Scotia' and 'Sestina', both written when she was in her fifties. Though 'Sestina' describes childhood anxiety, Bishop, elsewhere, has spoken kindly of her grandparents who were simple, loving and conservative people. Her grandfather was a deacon in the Baptist church and her grandmother used to sing hymns to the young Elizabeth. These were her first introduction to poetry. Later she stayed with her father's relations in Worcester and her aunt Maud, her mother's sister, in Boston. It was here that she first read the Victorian poets and learnt many poems by heart during the many days she spent ill in bed. It was here too, at the age of eight, that Bishop began to write poetry and prose. Looking back, she described her early years with relatives as a time when she was 'always a sort of guest', adding, 'I think I've always felt like that.'

As a child she had weak lungs and suffered from eczema, bronchitis and asthma. These and other lung-related illnesses were to bother her for much of her adult life. Her wealthy paternal grandparents paid for Elizabeth to attend boarding school but Bishop, when she stayed with them, was always uncomfortable in their luxurious home and it was here that she first suffered asthma attacks.

In 1928, Elizabeth Bishop published her first poems in the school's literary magazine. She was seventeen. In her school essays from this time she wrote about things that were to matter to her for the rest of her life: her love of the sea, islands, the seashore, and the need to travel. When she was twelve, Bishop won a $5 gold piece, awarded by the American Legion for an essay on 'Americanism'.

The opening sentence was quoted by Bishop in 1961 and she said of it that it seems to have been prophetic, indicating directions taken later in life and work: 'From the icy regions of the frozen north to the waving palm trees of the burning south....'

After high school, in the autumn of 1930, Bishop went to Vassar intending to be a composer but, at Vassar, music meant that you had to perform in public once a month and this terrified her. She gave up the piano and majored in English literature instead. Her other subjects included music, history, religion, zoology and Greek.

On 16 March 1934, the Vassar College Librarian arranged for Bishop, a young and enthusiastic admirer of Marianne Moore ('I hadn't known poetry could be like that; I took to it immediately'), to meet the poet on the right-hand bench outside the reading-room of the New York Public Library. It was the beginning of an important literary friendship. Moore became Bishop's mentor. She was, says one of Bishop's biographers, 'the most important single influence on Elizabeth Bishop's poetic practice and career'. What has been called Moore's 'meticulous taste for fact' was certainly an influence. The seventeenth-century poet George Herbert, Protestant hymns, Cowper and Wordsworth are other important influences. Like Wordsworth's, many of her poems contain a solitary figure, but George Herbert (1593–1633) was the poet she admired most and it is thought that Herbert strongly influenced Bishop's purity of line.

She left Vassar in June 1934 (Bishop's mother had died that May) and, determined to be a writer, moved to New York. She kept a notebook and that summer her entries record several trips to the sea and anticipate many of her poems, including 'The Fish' and 'At the Fishhouses'.

In December 1934, Bishop was so ill with asthma that she spent two weeks in bed. Alone on New Year's Eve she sat on the floor of her apartment, a map of the North Atlantic before her, and she wrote her poem 'The Map'. It is the first poem in her first collection, *North & South*, first in *The Complete Poems*, and it marks her first real signature as a poet.

Between 1935 and 1951, Elizabeth Bishop led an unsettled, restless life. In the poet Andrew Motion's words, Bishop was 'energetically nomadic'. Mark Strand, the American poet, says that for Bishop there was 'always the possibility of finding a place for herself', adding that 'if we have a home why travel?' She travelled to Europe (Belgium, France, England, Spain, Ireland, Italy), visited North Africa, spent a year in Washington as poetry consultant at the Library of Congress, lived in Key West in Florida, lived in Mexico and New York, but from 1952 to 1971 she considered Brazil her home, where she lived with her partner Lota de Macedo Soares. They lived in Rio de Janeiro and Petropolis, and Bishop eventually bought a house of her own in Ouro Preto. It was an eighteenth-century colonial house and she named it Casa Mariana after Marianne Moore.

She gave very few readings: once in 1947 at Wellesley College, two months after her first book appeared, when she was sick for days in anticipation; again in Washington in 1949, when she was sick again. And then she didn't read publicly for twenty-six years. She survived on grants, fellowships and the generosity of friends and, when she returned to the United States from Brazil in 1970, she took a teaching post at Harvard and later at New York University. She returned permanently to the United States in 1972, living for a time in Seattle and San Francisco. She spent her final years in Boston.

Bishop won the Pulitzer Prize in 1956, the National Book Award in 1969, and the Neustadt International Prize for Literature in 1976, but, in Eavan Boland's words, Bishop 'disliked the swagger and visibility of literary life'. In an interview in 1978 Bishop remarked that 'There's nothing more embarrassing than being a poet really... There must be an awful core of ego somewhere for you to set yourself up to write poetry. I've never felt it, but it must be there'. Her friend, the American poet James Merrill, speaking of Elizabeth Bishop, spoke of her 'instinctive, modest, lifelong impersonations of an ordinary woman, someone who during the day did errands, went to the beach, would perhaps that evening jot a phrase or two inside the nightclub matchbook before returning to the dance floor. Thus the later glimpses of her playing – was it poker? – with Neruda in a Mexican hotel, or pingpong with Octavio Paz in Cambridge, or getting Robert Duncan high on grass – "for the first time" – in San Francisco, or teaching Frank Bidart the wildflowers in Maine.'

Elizabeth Bishop, always a traveller, spent the last years of her life in her native Massachusetts, where she taught at Harvard. She was alone in her apartment on Lewis Wharf when she died of a cerebral aneurysm on 6 October 1979.

Elizabeth Bishop disapproved of biography; she considered it 'finally just unpleasant'. In Eavan Boland's words, she was 'shy and hidden' and preferred to remain that way. 'Elizabeth Bishop was known for not wishing to be known' was how Ian Hamilton put it; and Marianne Moore said that Bishop was 'spectacular in being unspectacular'. 'The shy perfectionist with her painter's eye' is how the writer Derek Mahon described her. Helen Vendler thought Elizabeth Bishop 'A foreigner everywhere, and, perhaps, with everyone.' But the poems are born of the life, and biographical details can deepen our understanding and appreciation of the poems and our admiration for the poet.

In one of Elizabeth Bishop's finest poems, 'Crusoe in England', she imagines Robinson Crusoe lonely for his island and Friday; and, remembering his time there, she writes:

> The sun set in the sea; the same odd sun
> rose from the sea,
> and there was one of it and one of me.

Here we have the voice of Robinson Crusoe, and the voice of Bishop, and the voice of all other lonely, observing, travellers. It is significant that Bishop was attracted to a figure like Crusoe, an isolate, someone ill-at-ease having returned to society. Bishop's sexuality and her struggle with alcohol were part of her own sense of isolation. In a letter written in 1948 to Robert Lowell, she said 'When you write my epitaph, you must say I was the loneliest person who ever lived.' Her later work suggests a happier person, but her life was never uncomplicatedly happy.

One other thing – read Bishop's poem called 'Poem' sometime. It maps a reader's experience of the reading of poetry itself – that initial distance between reader and poem, possibly indifference, then the gradual, awakening recognition and the final realisation that both reader and poet share a common humanity.

Bishop's *The Complete Poems 1927–1972* contains just over 140 poems and some thirty of these are translations from French, Spanish and Portuguese. She wrote very slowly, very carefully, sometimes pinning bits of paper on her walls, leaving blank spaces ('with gaps / and empties for the unimagined phrases' is how Robert Lowell described it in a poem for her), waiting for the right word. Some of her poems were several years in the making. She worked on 'The Moose' for over twenty-five years, yet it seems effortless as all good poetry does. She writes a poetry which echoes the rhythms of natural speech and her rhymes are not always easy to detect. End rhymes and cross rhymes or slant rhymes create a special and effective music. And what Yeats says of all true poetry is true of Bishop:

> 'A line will take us hours maybe;
> Yet if it does not seem a moment's thought,
> Our stitching and unstitching has been naught.'

POEMS

Dates refer to the year of composition. The poems as they are printed here, are in the order in which they were written.

[handwritten: Narrative Poem / autobiographical]

The Fish

[handwritten: ← mundane and prosaic title]

[handwritten left margin: theme of belonging]
[handwritten left margin: taken from his home]

I caught a tremendous fish *[handwritten: pride]*
and held him beside the boat *[handwritten: dramatic moment]*
half out of water, with my hook *[handwritten: of uncertainty]*
fast in a corner of his mouth.
He didn't fight.   5
He hadn't fought at all.
He hung a grunting weight, *[handwritten: assonance conveys the weight]*
battered and venerable *[handwritten: personification — makes the fish]*
and homely. Here and there *[handwritten: out to be very respectable]*
his brown skin hung in strips   10
[handwritten left margin: simile] like ancient wallpaper,
and its pattern of darker brown
was like wallpaper:
shapes like full-blown roses
stained and lost through age.   15
He was speckled with barnacles,
fine rosettes of lime,
and infested *[handwritten: microscopic, Bishop's extreme]*
with tiny white sea-lice, *[handwritten: observation skills]*
and underneath two or three   20
rags of green weed hung down.
While his gills were breathing in
the terrible oxygen
— the frightening gills, *[handwritten: becomes more reflective]*
fresh and crisp with blood,   25
that can cut so badly — *[handwritten: observation goes so far that]*
I thought of the coarse white flesh *[handwritten: it goes inside the fish]*
packed in like feathers, *[handwritten: sensuous]*
the big bones and the little bones,
the dramatic reds and blacks   30
of his shiny entrails,
and the pink swim-bladder *[handwritten: describing ugly things]*
like a big peony. *[handwritten: as beautiful]*

[handwritten right margin: free verse → no stanzas]
[handwritten: emotion — feeling pity for the fish]

I looked into his eyes
which were far larger than mine   35
but shallower, and yellowed,
the irises backed and packed
with tarnished tinfoil
seen through the lenses
of old scratched isinglass.   40
They shifted a little, but not
to return my stare.
— It was more like the tipping
of an object toward the light.
I admired his sullen face,   45
the mechanism of his jaw,
and then I saw
that from his lower lip
— if you could call it a lip —
grim, wet, and weaponlike,   50
hung five old pieces of fish-line,
or four and a wire leader
with the swivel still attached,
with all their five big hooks
grown firmly in his mouth.   55
A green line, frayed at the end
where he broke it, two heavier lines,
and a fine black thread
still crimped from the strain and snap
when it broke and he got away.   60
Like medals with their ribbons
frayed and wavering,
a five-haired beard of wisdom
trailing from his aching jaw.
I stared and stared   65
and victory filled up
the little rented boat,
from the pool of bilge
where oil had spread a rainbow

[Handwritten annotations:]
Bishop starts to engage more with the fish
intimate, aware of the fish as a living creature
alliteration
fascination and wonder
human features
realises the fish is not human
symbol of the fish's past struggle
resiliant, fighter, survivor
the pain the fish has experienced
repetition adds drama before climax
* Epiphany
describing ugly things as beautiful

around the rusted engine 70
to the bailer rusted orange,
the sun-cracked thwarts,
the oarlocks on their strings,
the gunnels — until everything
was rainbow, rainbow, rainbow! *repetition – climax* 75
And I let the fish go. *drama*

Glossary

Line 1 tremendous: it may seem unnecessary to explain the word tremendous, but poets are attuned to the nuance of words and the dictionary is a vital companion for the reader of poetry. Tremendous does not only mean immense; more accurately, it means that which excites trembling or awe from the Latin *tremere* to tremble, tremble at; awe-inspiring.

Line 8 venerable: worthy of reverence, aged-looking.

Line 9 homely: familiar or plain/ugly (in American English).

Line 17 rosettes: rose shaped patterns – knots of radiating loops of ribbon or the like in concentric arrangement.

Line 25 crisp: firm.

Line 31 entrails: the internal parts of the fish.

Line 33 peony: a large showy crimson or white globular flower.

Line 40 isinglass: a whitish semi-transparent gelatin substance used for windows, originally got from the swim bladders of some freshwater fish.

Line 45 sullen: showing irritation or ill humour by a gloomy silence or reserve.

Line 52 leader: short piece of wire connecting fishhook and fishline.

Line 53 swivel: a ring or link that turns round on a pin or neck.

Line 54 five big hooks: Bonnie Costello, in her book *Elizabeth Bishop: Questions of Mastery*, says, 'Five wounds on a fish make him a Christ figure but the epiphany he brings the poet has nothing otherworldly about it.'

Line 59 crimped: shrunk and curled.

Line 68 bilge: filth that collects in the broadest part of the bottom of a boat.

Line 71 bailer: bucket for scooping water out of the boat.

Line 72 thwarts: the seats or benches for rowers.

Line 73 oarlocks: a rowlock – metal devices to hold the oars, attached by 'string' to the boat itself.

Line 74 gunnels: or gunwale – the upper edges of a boat's side.

> In a letter, Bishop wrote: 'With "The Fish", that's exactly how it happened. It was in Key West, and I did it just as the poem says. That was in 1938. Oh, but I did change one thing; the poem says he had five hooks hanging from his mouth, but actually he had only three. Sometimes a poem makes its own demands. But I always try to stick as much as possible to what really happened when I describe something in the poem.'

? Questions

1. Between the opening line, 'I caught a tremendous fish', and the poem's final line, 'And I let the fish go', is a detailed and interesting account of Bishop's response to the incident. How does the speaker feel about catching this 'tremendous fish'? Which words and phrases, in your opinion, best capture her feelings? Comment on Bishop's use of 'him' and 'he'.

2. How does the fish react when caught this time? How and why does the poet empathise with the fish?

3. Comment on Bishop's use of language. What is the effect of repetition? Which lines or images are particularly vivid? Discuss images such as 'ancient wallpaper' and 'big peony' and say what they contribute to the poem.

4. 'I looked into his eyes …', says the poet in line 34. What happens?

5. How would you describe the speaker's tone? Look particularly at lines such as '– It was more like …' or '– if you could call it …'

6. What do you think Bishop means by 'victory' in line 66? How would you describe the poet's mood in the closing line?

7. Does the ending of the poem come as a surprise? Give reasons for your answer. Why do you think the speaker 'let the fish go'? What does this poem say about power and control?

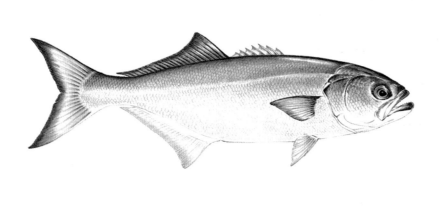

At the Fishhouses

Although it is a cold evening,
down by one of the fishhouses
an old man sits netting,
his net, in the gloaming almost invisible,
a dark purple-brown,   5
and his shuttle worn and polished.
The air smells so strong of codfish
it makes one's nose run and one's eyes water.
The five fishhouses have steeply peaked roofs
and narrow, cleated gangplanks slant up   10
to storerooms in the gables
for the wheelbarrows to be pushed up and down on.
All is silver: the heavy surface of the sea,
swelling slowly as if considering spilling over,
is opaque, but the silver of the benches,   15
the lobster pots, and masts, scattered
among the wild jagged rocks,
is of an apparent translucence
like the small old buildings with an emerald moss
growing on their shoreward walls.   20
The big fish tubs are completely lined
with layers of beautiful herring scales
and the wheelbarrows are similarly plastered
with creamy iridescent coats of mail,
with small iridescent flies crawling on them.   25
Up on the little slope behind the houses,
set in the sparse bright sprinkle of grass,
is an ancient wooden capstan,
cracked, with two long bleached handles
and some melancholy stains, like dried blood,   30
where the ironwork has rusted.
The old man accepts a Lucky Strike.
He was a friend of my grandfather.

We talk of the decline in the population
and of codfish and herring   35
while he waits for a herring boat to come in.
There are sequins on his vest and on his thumb.
He has scraped the scales, the principal beauty,
from unnumbered fish with that black old knife,
the blade of which is almost worn away.   40

Down at the water's edge, at the place
where they haul up the boats, up the long ramp
descending into the water, thin silver
tree trunks are laid horizontally
across the gray stones, down and down   45
at intervals of four or five feet.

Cold dark deep and absolutely clear,
element bearable to no mortal,
to fish and to seals . . . One seal particularly
I have seen here evening after evening.   50
He was curious about me. He was interested in music;
like me a believer in total immersion,
so I used to sing him Baptist hymns.
I also sang 'A Mighty Fortess Is Our God.'
He stood up in the water and regarded me   55
steadily, moving his head a little.
Then he would disappear, then suddenly emerge
almost in the same spot, with a sort of shrug
as if it were against his better judgment.
Cold dark deep and absolutely clear,   60
the clear gray icy water . . . Back, behind us,
the dignified tall firs begin.
Bluish, associating with their shadows,
a million Christmas trees stand
waiting for Christmas. The water seems suspended   65
above the rounded gray and blue-gray stones.

I have seen it over and over, the same sea, the same,
slightly, indifferently swinging above the stones,
icily free above the stones,
above the stones and then the world.   70
If you should dip your hand in,
your wrist would ache immediately,
your bones would begin to ache and your hand would burn
as if the water were a transmutation of fire
that feeds on stones and burns with a dark gray flame.   75
If you tasted it, it would first taste bitter,
then briny, then surely burn your tongue.
It is like what we imagine knowledge to be:
dark, salt, clear, moving, utterly free,
drawn from the cold hard mouth   80
of the world, derived from the rocky breasts
forever, flowing and drawn, and since
our knowledge is historical, flowing, and flown.

Glossary

Line 4 gloaming: twilight, dusk.

Line 6 shuttle: an instrument used for shooting the thread of the woof between the threads of the warp in weaving.

Line 10 cleated: having pieces of wood nailed on to give footing.

Line 10 gangplank: a long, narrow, movable wooden plank/walkway.

Line 15 opaque: dark, dull, cannot be seen through, not transparent.

Line 18 translucence: when light shines through.

Line 24 iridescent: coloured like the rainbow, glittering with changing colours.

Line 28 capstan: a machine with a cylindrical drum around which rope is wound and used for hauling.

Line 32 Lucky Strike: an American brand of cigarette.

Line 37 sequins: small, circular, thin, glittering, sparkling ornament on a dress.

Line 52 total immersion: a form of baptism practised by certain Christian groups.

Line 63 associating: uniting.

Line 74 transmutation: a change from one form into another.

Line 77 briny: very salty water.

Line 83 historical: pertaining to the course of events.

Questions

1. This poem begins with a particular place and then it becomes a poem which explores many complex and abstract ideas such as knowledge and meaning. Identify the words and phrases that allow the reader to picture the fishhouses in detail. Comment on Bishop's use of colour.

2. Can you suggest why Bishop has divided 'At the Fishhouses' into three sections? How would you sum up what is happening in each section? Which of the three sections is the most personal?

3. There are three solitary figures in the poem: the fisherman, the speaker and the seal. Imagine the poem without the fisherman and the seal and discuss what would be lost.

4. The poem moves from description towards meditation. Is it possible to identify where the poem becomes meditative or philosophical? Explain your answer.

5. 'Cold dark deep and absolutely clear,/the clear gray icy water . . .' (lines 60–61) refer not only to the ocean. What similarities, according to Bishop, are there between water and knowledge?

6. There are many religious references in the poem. Identify these and say whether you think the poem is religious or not.

7. What do you think Bishop means when she writes 'and then the world' (line 70)?

8. The poem ends with an image of knowledge. How would you describe Bishop's understanding of human experience as it is revealed to us in this poem?

The Bight
[On my birthday]

At low tide like this how sheer the water is.
White, crumbling ribs of marl protrude and glare
and the boats are dry, the pilings dry as matches.
Absorbing, rather than being absorbed,
the water in the bight doesn't wet anything,   5
the color of the gas flame turned as low as possible.
One can smell it turning to gas; if one were Baudelaire
one could probably hear it turning to marimba music.
The little ocher dredge at work off the end of the dock
already plays the dry perfectly off-beat claves.   10
The birds are outsize. Pelicans crash
into this peculiar gas unnecessarily hard,
it seems to me, like pickaxes,
rarely coming up with anything to show for it,
and going off with humorous elbowings.   15
Black-and-white man-of-war birds soar
on impalpable drafts
and open their tails like scissors on the curves
or tense them like wishbones, till they tremble.
The frowsy sponge boats keep coming in   20
with the obliging air of retrievers,
bristling with jackstraw gaffs and hooks
and decorated with bobbles of sponges.
There is a fence of chicken wire along the dock
where, glinting like little plowshares,   25
the blue-gray shark tails are hung up to dry
for the Chinese-restaurant trade.
Some of the little white boats are still piled up
against each other, or lie on their sides, stove in,
and not yet salvaged, if they ever will be,
        from the last bad storm,   30
like torn-open, unanswered letters.

The bight is littered with old correspondences.
Click. Click. Goes the dredge,
and brings up a dripping jawful of marl.
All the untidy activity continues,   35
awful but cheerful.

Glossary

Title The Bight: a bay formed by a bend in a coastline, a wide bay. The bight here is Garrison Bight in Key West, Florida.

Subtitle: 'on my birthday' – 8 February 1948 – Bishop was 37. Personal details in Elizabeth Bishop's poetry are rare and most often not explicitly expressed. By placing 'On my birthday' beneath a title that names a place, Bishop is suggesting both place and the passing of time.

Line 1 sheer: transparently thin; smooth, calm; bright.

Line 2 marl: deposit consisting of clay and lime.

Line 3 pilings: sharp posts or stakes, a heavy timber driven into the ground, especially under water, to form a foundation.

Line 7 Baudelaire: French poet (1821–1867).

Line 8 marimba: African xylophone adopted by Central Americans and Jazz musicians.

Line 9 ocher dredge: yellowish-brown machine used to scoop/draw up silt.

Line 10 claves: wooden percussion instruments; small wooden cylinders held in the hand and struck together to mark Latin American dance rhythm.

Line 16 man-of-war birds: the frigate-birds – large tropical sea bird with very long wings.

Line 17 impalpable: not perceivable by touch, imperceptible to the touch, not perceptible by the watching poet.

Line 17 drafts: currents of air.

Line 19 wishbones: forked bones in front of the breasts of some birds.

Line 20 frowsy: ill-smelling, offensive, unkempt.

Line 21 retrievers: dogs who have been trained to find and fetch.

Line 22 jackstraw: a short staff, usually set upon the bowsprit or at the bow of a ship on which the flag called the jack is hoisted.

Line 22 gaffs: hooks used especially for landing large fish.

Line 22 hooks: the hooks on a sponge-catching boat to hold the catch.

Line 25 plowshares: the part of a plough that cuts and turns the soil.

Line 27 Chinese-restaurant trade: shark tails are used in Chinese cooking. Shark-tail soup is a delicacy.

Line 29 stove in: broken — especially in the hull or lowermost portion.

Line 32 old correspondences: cf. line 7 — Baudelaire wrote a sonnet 'Correspondences' in which he speaks of man as one who, while wandering among Nature, wanders among symbols. Baudelaire says that the perfumes of Nature are as sweet as the sound of the oboe, as green as the prairies, as fresh as the caress of a child. Bishop responds in a similar way to the natural world in her poem. Baudelaire in his theory of correspondences promised connections or links by means of poetry between the physical and spiritual worlds.

> This is a Bishop poem which, like 'At the Fishhouses', begins with objective description and gradually gives way to a more personal, private world. The objective and subjective are side by side in the poem's title and subtitle. A bight is a public place; a birthday is personal and an occasion for thinking more intensely about oneself, one's birth, one's life and death. In the poem, Bishop is on her own; she celebrates her birthday by celebrating the bight. The poem overall may not seem that personal, but the choice of subject matter, the way of seeing, the words used, the mood conveyed, all convey Bishop's personal view.

? Questions

1. Like 'At the Fishhouses', this is another place poem. What is usually associated with a birthday? Why do you think Bishop included the detail of her birthday here? Does it alter the poem? Explain.

2. In many of her poems, Bishop describes in an atmospheric way a particular place. Discuss how she does that in 'The Bight'. Pay particular attention to lines 7 and 8.

3. Is Bishop enjoying what she sees? Support your answer by reference to the text. Does it matter that she is alone in the poem?

4. Consider all the action and movement described in the poem. What is the significance of the dredge? What do you think Bishop means by the phrase 'untidy activity' in the closing lines?

5. Some sentences here are four or five lines long; others consist of one word. Examine and discuss how the sentence length and sentence organisation contribute to the poem's movement.

6. Is the bight in any way symbolic?

The Prodigal

synesthesia

sensuous language

The brown enormous odor he lived by   *man is reduced to his odour*
was too close, with its breathing and thick hair,   *personify the*
for him to judge. The floor was rotten; the sty   *smell to emphasise*
                                                    its presence
was plastered halfway up with glass-smooth dung.
Light-lashed, self-righteous, above moving snouts,   *filth*   5
the pigs' eyes followed him, a cheerful stare –   *personification*
                                                  of the pigs, they
even to the sow that always ate her young –   *are his companions*
till, sickening, he leaned to scratch her head.   *(sense of*
                                                   home and
But sometimes mornings after drinking bouts   *belonging)*   10
(he hid the pints behind a two-by-four),
the sunrise glazed the barnyard mud with red;
the burning puddles seemed to reassure.   *parenthesis*
                                                   conveys his
And then he thought he almost might endure   *shame*
his exile yet another year or more.   *unsure*   *transfigures*
      suffering   *something ugly*
                                                 into beautiful

But evenings the first star came to warn.   15
The farmer whom he worked for came at dark
to shut the cows and horses in the barn
beneath their overhanging clouds of hay,
with pitchforks, faint forked lightnings, catching light,
safe and companionable as in the Ark.   20
The pigs stuck out their little feet and snored.
The lantern – like the sun, going away –
laid on the mud a pacing aureole.
Carrying a bucket along a slimy board,
he felt the bats' uncertain staggering flight,   25
his shuddering insights, beyond his control,
touching him. But it took him a long time
finally to make his mind up to go home.

📖 Glossary

Title: The poem was originally referred to by Bishop as 'Prodigal Son'.

The Prodigal: A reference to the story of the Prodigal Son in the Bible as told by St. Luke, Chapter 15: A certain man had two sons and the younger of them said to his father, Father, give me the portion of goods that falleth to me. And he divided unto them his living. And not many days after the younger son gathered all together and took his journey into a far country, and there wasted his substance with riotous living. And when he had spent all, there arose a mighty famine in that land; and he began to be in want. And he went and joined himself to a citizen of that country; and he sent him into his fields to feed swine. And he would fain have filled his belly with the husks that the swine did eat: and no man gave unto him. And when he came to himself, he said, How many hired servants of my father's have bread enough and to spare, and I perish with hunger! I will arise and go to my father, and will say unto him, Father, I have sinned against heaven, and before thee, and am no more worthy to be called thy son: make me as one of thy hired servants. And he arose, and came to his father. But when he was yet a great way off, his father saw him, and had compassion, and ran, and fell on his neck, and kissed him. (King James Version).

Title prodigal: wasteful, extravagant.

Line 2 close: stifling, unventilated, oppressive.

Line 10 two-by-four: timber with cross-section, 2 inches by 4 inches.

Line 20 companionable: happily together.

Line 23 aureole: the halo or celestial crown round the head of a pictured martyr or divine figure.

❓ Questions

1. What immediately comes to mind when the words 'prodigal' or 'prodigal son' are mentioned? (Bishop's original title was 'Prodigal Son'.)

2. Look at how the poem is organised and shaped (metre, line length, end-rhyme). Can you suggest a reason why Bishop chose this form?

3. How does Bishop imagine the life of the prodigal son in the first section of the poem? Is it all ugly and hopeless? Give reasons for your answer and quote from the text to support the points you make.

4. What is the effect of the use of 'But' in lines 9, 15 and 27?

5. Comment on the significance of 'sunrise', 'star', 'aureole' and the Biblical reference to the Ark.

6. What is meant by tone? How would you describe the tone in the opening lines? Is there a change of tone in the poem?

7. How do you respond and how do you think Bishop wanted her reader to respond to line 21: 'The pigs stuck out their little feet and snored' (a perfect example of an iambic pentameter)?

8. Comment on Bishop's choice of adjectives: 'enormous', 'glass-smooth', 'cheerful', 'overhanging', 'companionable', 'slimy', 'staggering', 'shuddering' and the power of the last word in the poem. Write a note on any four of these.

Filling Station

Oh, but it is dirty! *lighthearted, conversational tone*
– this little filling station,
oil-soaked, oil-permeated *repetition of "oil"*
to a disturbing, over-all
black translucency.   5
Be careful with that match! *humour*

Father wears a dirty,
oil-soaked monkey suit   *characature, sad*
that cuts him under the arms,
and several quick and saucy   10
and greasy sons assist him   *Sibilance conveys the*
(it's a family filling station),   *grease and dirt*
all quite thoroughly dirty.
                                        Bishop is observing more
              intrigued   *and more about the*
Do they live in the station?   *filling station.*
It has a cement porch   15
behind the pumps, and on it
a set of crushed and grease-
impregnated wickerwork;
on the wicker sofa
a dirty dog, quite comfy.   20

Some comic books provide
the only note of color –
of certain color. They lie
upon a big dim doily
draping a taboret   25
(part of the set), beside
a big hirsute begonia.

theme of "home" & family

[handwritten: wonder, fascination]

Why the extraneous plant?
Why the taboret?
Why, oh why, the doily?   30
[handwritten: conversational tone]
(Embroidered in daisy stitch
with marguerites, I think,
and heavy with gray crochet.)

[handwritten: repetition]   *[handwritten: assonance]*
Somebody embroidered the doily.
Somebody waters the plant,   35
[handwritten: humour]
or oils it, maybe. Somebody
arranges the rows of cans
so that they softly say: *[handwritten: Sibilance is calming]*
ESSO-SO-SO-SO   *[handwritten: and soft/soothing]*
to high-strung automobiles.   40
[handwritten: moment of epiphany] Somebody loves us all.

📖 Glossary

Line 5 translucency: shiny, glossy quality.

Line 8 monkey suit: dungarees, overalls.

Line 18 impregnated: saturated.

Line 24 doily: a small ornamented napkin, often laid under dishes (from Doily or Doiley, a famous haberdasher).

Line 25 taboret: a low seat usually without arms or back/a small drum.

Line 27 hirsute: shaggy, untrimmed.

Line 27 begonia: plant with pink flowers and remarkable unequal-sided coloured leaves.

Line 28 extraneous: of external origin, not belonging, not essential.

Line 31 daisy stitch: a design pattern.

Line 32 marguerites: ox-eye daisies.

Line 33 crochet: knitting done with hooked needle forming intertwined loops.

? Questions

1. What details immediately strike the reader on a first reading? Is this a typical or an atypical Bishop poem? Give reasons for your answer.

2. Lines 1 and 6 end with exclamation marks. How would you describe the tone of the opening stanza? Dismissive? Cautious? Both? Identify the other tones in the poem.

3. How does Bishop convince her reader that the place is indeed 'oil-soaked, oil-permeated' and 'grease-impregnated'?

4. Bishop has been described as a very accurate observer. Where in the poem is this evident? Quote from the poem in support of your answer.

5. Choose any stanza from the poem and show how Bishop creates an inner music in her use of language. Your answer should include a discussion of alliteration, assonance, slant or cross-rhyme.

6. Discuss Bishop's use of repetition in the poem, especially the repetition of 'why' and 'somebody'.

7. Were you surprised by the final line in the poem? How is the line justified within the context of the poem as a whole?

Questions of Travel

There are too many waterfalls here; the crowded streams
hurry too rapidly down to the sea,
and the pressure of so many clouds on the mountaintops
makes them spill over the sides in soft slow-motion,
turning to waterfalls under our very eyes.   5
— For if those streaks, those mile-long, shiny, tearstains,
aren't waterfalls yet,
in a quick age or so, as ages go here,
they probably will be.
But if the streams and clouds keep travelling, travelling,   10
the mountains look like the hulls of capsized ships,
slime-hung and barnacled.

Think of the long trip home.
Should we have stayed at home and thought of here?
Where should we be today?   15
Is it right to be watching strangers in a play
in this strangest of theatres?
What childishness is it that while there's a breath of life
in our bodies, we are determined to rush
to see the sun the other way around?   20
The tiniest green hummingbird in the world?
To stare at some inexplicable old stonework,
inexplicable and impenetrable,
at any view,
instantly seen and always, always delightful?   25
Oh, must we dream our dreams
and have them too?
And have we room
for one more folded sunset, still quite warm?

But surely it would have been a pity   30
not to have seen the trees along this road,
really exaggerated in their beauty,

not to have seen them gesturing
like noble pantomimists, robed in pink.
— Not to have had to stop for gas and heard   35
the sad, two-noted, wooden tune
of disparate wooden clogs
carelessly clacking over
a grease-stained filling-station floor.
(In another country the clogs would all be tested.   40
Each pair there would have identical pitch.)
— A pity not to have heard
the other, less primitive music of the fat brown bird
who sings above the broken gasoline pump
in a bamboo church of Jesuit baroque: 45
three towers, five silver crosses.
— Yes, a pity not to have pondered,
blurr'dly and inconclusively,
on what connection can exist for centuries
between the crudest wooden footwear   50
and, careful and finicky,
the whittled fantasies of wooden cages.
— Never to have studied history in
the weak calligraphy of songbirds' cages.
— And never to have had to listen to rain   55
so much like politicians' speeches:
two hours of unrelenting oratory
and then a sudden golden silence
in which the traveller takes a notebook, writes:

'Is it lack of imagination that makes us come
to imagined places, not just stay at home?   60
Or could Pascal have been not entirely right
about just sitting quietly in one's room?

Continent, city, country, society:
the choice is never wide and never free.
And here, or there . . . No. Should we have stayed at home, 65
wherever that may be?'

📖 Glossary

Title: Not only this particular poem but the title of Bishop's third collection.

Line 1 There: Brazil.

Line 11 hulls: framework or body of boats.

Line 22 inexplicable: unable to be explained.

Line 37 disparate: dissimilar, discordant.

Line 45 baroque: an exuberant kind of European architecture which the Jesuits in the seventeenth century introduced into Latin America.

Line 51 finicky: overdone.

Line 52 fantasies: fanciful design.

Line 54 calligraphy: a style of writing but here refers to the style of construction of the cages.

Line 57 unrelenting: persistent.

Line 57 oratory: public speaking.

Line 61 Pascal: French mathematician, physicist and philosopher (1623–1662) who in his *Pensées* wrote: 'I have often said that the sole cause of man's unhappiness is that he does not know how to stay quietly in his room'.

? Questions

1. In the opening section of the poem, Bishop describes a Brazilian landscape. How is a state of flux conveyed? How would you describe her response to it? Give reasons for your answer.

2. In the second section, she uses the pronoun 'we'. Who is she including here? Why is she uneasy about certain aspects of travel? Why does she think travel invasive and childish?

3. Which images do you find striking or interesting in the poem? Does the poem focus on the particular or the general or both? What is the effect of this?

4. 'But surely it would have been a pity ...' begins her justification for travel. Examine how she argues her point. Which details justify her point? Look at her use of the dash and repetition. Is the argument convincing? Why or why not? Is the speaker a sympathetic observer?

5. Bishop suggests that Pascal (line 61), who believed that 'the sole cause of man's unhappiness is that he does not know how to stay quietly in his room', might not have been entirely right. Which viewpoint would you agree with? Give reasons for your answer. Does Bishop put forward a convincing argument?

6. The poem's final italicised section takes the form of an entry in the traveller's notebook, written during 'a sudden golden silence'. What does the traveller conclude in this notebook entry? Why do you think the poem ends with a question mark?

· this poem is wonderful for its vivid imagery & sound effects

the story becomes more than the event itself (on a metaphorical level)

The Armadillo

For Robert Lowell *activist, pacifist → this poem is an indictment of war*

mankind's love of power

This is the time of year A — *tight rhyming scheme*
when almost every night B
the frail, illegal fire balloons appear. A — *l sounds – consonance have a soporific effect*
Climbing the mountain height, B
ascension
"frail" → juxtaposes "illegal" and "climbing"

rising toward a saint C — *aware she is an outsider, an observer* — *rhyming scheme*
still honored in these parts, D — *becomes more irregular*
the paper chambers flush and fill with light E — *tight assonance*
that comes and goes, like hearts. D — *rhythmical pulse* — *onomatopoeic*

5

conversational element = speaking voice
Once up against the sky it's hard — *simile*
to tell them from the stars — — *imbues them with life*
planets, that is — the tinted ones: *perspective*
Venus going down, or Mars, — *aware of the vastness of the universe*
love *war*

10

conversational thinking aloud
or the pale green one. With a wind, — *internal monologue*
they flare and falter, wobble and toss; — *this line is busy with verbs quickens the pace*
sibilance and consonance "t" sounds
but if it's still they steer between — *increases the danger*
the kite sticks of the Southern Cross, — *"wobble and toss" scared fall over*

15

present participle makes the action immediate and exciting
magical
receding, dwindling, solemnly
and steadily forsaking us, *(communal)*
change in the atmosphere
or, in the downdraft from a peak, — *captivated by this spectacle*
suddenly turning dangerous.

20

language becomes less poetic
Last night another big one fell. — *heavier words*
we had been looking up and now we're brought back down
birth
It splattered like an egg of fire
against the cliff behind the house. — *vivid imagery*
The flame ran down. We saw the pair — *immediacy*

the home is under threat
wisdom *home, belonging*
of owls who nest there flying up — *forced exile*
frantic panic
and up, their whirling black-and-white
stained bright pink underneath, until — *damage caused by mankind to nature*
they shrieked up out of sight. — *aural imagery*
vivid, painful, disturbing imagery
innocent victims

war can be glamourised

25

[handwritten top margin: wanton destruction = out of control]
[handwritten: invokes a sense of respect for the owl]

[handwritten left margin: short line energy saids]

The ancient owls' nest must have burned.
Hastily, all alone,   *[handwritten: home, sadness]*
a glistening armadillo left the scene,
rose-flecked, head down, tail down,   *[30]*

[handwritten right: all alone - protracted vowel sounds]

[handwritten left: beautiful description of blood]
and then a baby rabbit jumped out,   *[handwritten: baby = home, nest]*
short-eared, to our surprise.   *[handwritten: conversational quality, natural interjection]*
So soft!—a handful of intangible ash   *[35]*
with fixed, ignited eyes.   *[handwritten: interrupted life, untimely death → "eye" sound mimics a cry]*

[handwritten left: too good to be true]   *[handwritten: taking on the voices of the oppressed in the last stanza]*
Too pretty, dreamlike mimicry!   *[handwritten: confusion]*
[handwritten left: destruction] O falling fire and piercing cry
and panic, and a weak mailed fist   *[handwritten: language becomes much more serious, almost]*
clenched ignorant against the sky!   *[handwritten: shakespearean]*   *[40]*

[handwritten: epiphany: finding fault with herself - she was taken in by the beauty]

📖 Glossary

Title: the armadillo is a chiefly nocturnal, burrowing animal whose body is encased in bony plates. It is found in southern United States and in Latin America. When captured it rolls itself into a ball and while curled tight it is protected from everything except fire. It is pronounced 'armadeeo' in Spanish. When this poem was first published – in *The New Yorker* on 22 June 1957 – it was called 'The Armadillo – Brazil'. Her friend the American poet Robert Lowell, to whom the poem is dedicated, considered the title wrong at first but later thought 'The Armadillo' right: 'the little creature, given only five lines, runs off with the whole poem'.

Line 1 time of year: June, particularly 24 June which is St. John's Day. This is the shortest day of the year in the Southern Hemisphere, a holy day, and as part of the celebrations balloons are released on St. John's Night and the nights before and after. These were fire balloons and supposedly illegal. The house mentioned in the poem is the house in Petropolis which Bishop shared with Lota de Macedo Soares.

Line 13 the pale green one: the planet Uranus, perhaps.

Line 16 kite sticks: the kite-like formation of the constellation.

Line 16 Southern Cross: constellation visible only in the southern hemisphere.

Line 35 intangible: cannot be touched/cannot be grasped mentally.

Line 37 mimicry: imitating, imitative, especially for amusement.

[handwritten right: Does Bishop in the last stanza imply that the role of the poet is futile, all they do is use words and they can't protect the oppressed]

*[handwritten bottom: *Unlike other Bishop poems → usually Bishop describes ugly things as beautiful, but in this poem we move from beauty to ugliness]*

? Questions

1. The poem describes St. John's day, a religious feast in Brazil, and the practise of releasing fire balloons. Discuss how in the first five stanzas Bishop describes the balloons. Are they viewed as beautiful, or dangerous, or both?

2. Consider line length, stanza and rhyme. What is the effect of the short sentence at line 21 and the short line at line 30?

3. Does our attitude towards the fire balloons change when we read of the owls, the armadillo and the rabbit?

4. The balloons are described, at first, as 'paper chambers ... like hearts'. What does Bishop think of the balloons by the end of the poem? Where is this most evident?

5. Why do you think Bishop chose 'The Armadillo' as her title?

6. The armadillo and the other creatures have been interpreted symbolically as the oppressed, the victimised. Look particularly at lines 39–40. Do you think this is a valid interpretation? Give reasons for your answer.

7. What is being signalled, in your opinion, by the change to italics in the last stanza?

8. How would you describe the poet's tone? Does the tone change?

Strong sense of fate
& inevitability

WATER DOMINATES

ELIZABETH BISHOP

Poems

autobiographical yet she never uses the first person or possessive language

Sestina

bleak

Pathetic fallacy — bleak mood

cozy atmosphere inside until the last line

September rain falls on the house.
In the failing light, the old grandmother
sits in the kitchen with the child
beside the Little Marvel Stove,
reading the jokes from the almanac,
laughing and talking to hide her tears.

source of heat

6 words are at the end of every line of every stanza in a different order

5

"the child" → objective, inclusive of all children

magnify the tears

2nd stanza is more intense

She thinks that her equinoctial tears
and the rain that beats on the roof of the house
were both foretold by the almanac,
but only known to a grandmother.
The iron kettle sings on the stove.
She cuts some bread and says to the child,

more intense than "falls"

personification the almanac

hollow "o" sound

cold & clinical language - impersonal. "The Grandmother"

10

2 perspectives: adult vs child

Grandmother trying to care for the child

symbolism

child's view

child's grief internal

It's time for tea now; but the child
is watching the teakettle's small hard tears
dance like mad on the hot black stove,
the way the rain must dance on the house.
Tidying up, the old grandmother
hangs up the clever almanac

intensity of the child's grief and tension

15

monosyllabic, quick rhythm frantic plosives

personify the almanac

enjambment

the almanac is a predator

magical fantasy childlike imagination

absent father figure

on its string. Birdlike, the almanac
hovers half open above the child,
hovers above the old grandmother
and her teacup full of dark brown tears.
She shivers and says she thinks the house
feels chilly, and puts more wood in the stove.

the almanac has a prophetic role

20

poem becomes more sinister → fate

sibilance assonance "i" entrapment ↓ trapped by fate → trapped by the strict form of a sestina

the grandmother is unable to speak to the child and comfort them

It was to be, says the Marvel Stove.
I know what I know, says the almanac.
With crayons the child draws a rigid house
and a winding pathway. Then the child
puts in a man with buttons like tears
and shows it proudly to the grandmother.

teaming up with the almanac

25

the child is expressing herself (not through words) through art

30

the story of the poem is multi-layered
at the heart of the poem there's a deep sadness

45

[handwritten annotations: sound effects · rhythm (4) · iambic tetrameter · assonental patterning]

But secretly, while the grandmother
busies herself about the stove,
the little moons fall down like tears

[handwritten: the tears will allow the flowers to grow]

from between the pages of the almanac
into the flower bed the child

35

has carefully placed in the front of the house.

[handwritten: tears are restorative]

[handwritten: the tears will be planted and permanent]

Time to plant tears, says the almanac.
The grandmother sings to the marvellous stove
and the child draws another inscrutable house.

[handwritten: underpinning the poem is a sense of tragedy]

📖 Glossary

Title Sestina (meaning song of sixes): a rhymed or unrhymed poem with six stanzas of six lines and final triplet, each stanza having the same words to end its lines but in a different order. Lines may be of any length. The final three lines, the triplet, must introduce the six words which end the six preceding stanzas – in this instance, 'tears', 'child', 'almanac', 'stove', 'grandmother', 'house'. The sestina was supposedly invented by Arnaut Daniel in the twelfth century.

The order in which the end-words are re-used is prescribed by a set pattern which is very formal and it has been argued that such rules are so inhibiting that the poem becomes artificial and strained. But, on the other hand, if a poet chooses six key words or ideas or images, then they become vitally important throughout the poem and the accomplished poet can explore in great detail the important relation among all six. The six key words in Elizabeth Bishop's 'Sestina' are: house; grandmother; child; stove; almanac; tears, and many of these are highly charged, significant words in themselves. They become even more powerful in the context of what we know of Bishop's parents and early childhood. This poem was originally titled 'Early Sorrow'.

Line 5 almanac: a register of the days, weeks, months of the year, with astronomical events, anniversaries *et cetera*.

Line 7 equinoctial: at the time of the autumn equinox.

Line 37 inscrutable: that which cannot be searched into and understood.

Commenting on this poem, Paula Meehan says: 'Bishop's 'Sestina' is a masterclass in the artifice that conceals art. If you read it without preamble to a class of writing students they will invariably relate first to the narrative, to the simple kitchen imagery of a child drawing a house, the kettle on the stove, the almanac of rural life with its forecasts and market days and moon cycles. The writing students will be opened emotionally to the abyss of grief conjured by the mesmeric patterning, without necessarily knowing they are being coldly or craftily manipulated.'

? Questions

1. Having read the poem through a number of times, study the end word in every line. What is the effect of this? How does Bishop convey sorrow in 'Sestina'?

2. The sestina is a very strict poetic format. Try writing one yourself. What do you learn from the exercise?

3. The poem offers a view of the world from a child's perspective. What details are being pieced together in the child's mind? How can you tell that things are being seen from a child's point of view?

4. Of the six key words in the sestina, which would you consider more important? Give reasons for your choice.

5. The almanac becomes a sinister presence – it 'hovers'. What does this poem say about the passing of time? Why do you think Bishop uses the present tense throughout?

6. Choose any one example of very ordinary language (e.g. 'It's time for tea now') and one example of unusual language and comment on both.

7. What is the significance of the child's drawing in stanza 5? Why does the child draw 'another inscrutable house'?

8. What image of the grandmother emerges from the poem?

9. Discuss what is said and what is left unsaid in this poem.

Handwritten annotations (top): narrative poem · heavy / cold — cacophony \ hollow o sound · alliteration · loss of innocence · momentous occasion

First Death in Nova Scotia

Handwritten: overwhelming presence of cold in the poem

In the cold, cold parlor
my mother laid out Arthur
beneath the chromographs:
Edward, Prince of Wales,
with Princess Alexandra,
and King George with Queen Mary.   5
Below them on the table
stood a stuffed loon
shot and stuffed by Uncle
Arthur, Arthur's father.   10

Since Uncle Arthur fired
a bullet into him,
he hadn't said a word.
He kept his own counsel
on his white, frozen lake,   15
the marble-topped table.
His breast was deep and white,
cold and caressable:
his eyes were red glass,
much to be desired.   20

'Come,' said my mother,
'Come and say good-bye
to your little cousin Arthur.'
I was lifted up and given
one lily of the valley   25
to put in Arthur's hand.
Arthur's coffin was
a little frosted cake,
and the red-eyed loon eyed it
from his white, frozen lake.   30

Handwritten annotations throughout:
- accentuates the word "cold" · repetition · slows the rhythm and adds emphasis to the cold
- positioning the child is beneath the chromographs & are high and mighty
- Royal personages accentuate the child's helplessness · the child fixates on certain things (royal family) · is this to distract from what is happening?
- couples · couples · unity · togetherness
- death · repetition
- sibilance · the child is trying to evade emotion · trying to understand death → focusing on the loon
- silence · mortality
- personification → realm of fantasy (terrifying) · imagery, metaphor · motif of coldness · frozen = the child is rigid with fear
- yearning for comfort · cacophony → harsh and bitter and cold
- Importance of objects → child is trying to focus on anything other than her sadness/fear
- aware of her youth · assonance "i" · Sounds are dainty portray how small Arthur was
- metaphor · contrast — cake — celebration · malevolent · imagination
- the whole poem is cold

[handwritten: drawn out assonental patterns]

Arthur was very small. *[handwritten: simile]*
He was all white, like a doll *[handwritten: realm of fantasy]*
that hadn't been painted yet. *[handwritten: aware of childhood perspective]*
Jack Frost had started to paint him *[handwritten: child is attempting to comprehend death]*
the way he always painted   35
the Maple Leaf (Forever). *[handwritten: fragments from childhood]*
He had just begun on his hair, *[handwritten: ↳ learning the national]*
a few red strokes, and then *[handwritten: anthem, childrens]*
Jack Frost had dropped the brush *[handwritten: stories like Jack Frost]*
and left him white, forever.   40
[handwritten: ↳ repetition, realisation of the significance of death]

The gracious royal couples
were warm in red and ermine; *[handwritten: only reference to colour apart]*
their feet were well wrapped up *[handwritten: from white in the poem is]*
in the ladies' ermine trains. *[handwritten: red]*
They invited Arthur to be *[handwritten: child's fantasy]*   45
the smallest page at court.
But how could Arthur go, *[handwritten: "o" sounds are mournful and]*
clutching his tiny lily, *[handwritten: full of sorrow]*
with his eyes shut up so tight
and the roads deep in snow? *[handwritten: childhood lack of understanding]*
[handwritten: metaphor of a journey]

Glossary

Title First Death: not only does the phrase suggest Bishop's first experience of death, but also the death of the very first person to die in the province of Nova Scotia.

Line 3 chromographs: pictures obtained by means of chromo-lithography – a method of producing coloured pictures by using stones with different portions of the picture drawn upon them in inks of different colours, so arranged as to blend into the complete picture.

Line 4 Edward: (1841–1910) Prince of Wales, eldest son of Queen Victoria and Prince Albert, later Edward VII.

Line 5 Alexandra: beautiful Danish Princess who married Edward VII in 1863.

Line 6 King George with Queen Mary: George V (1865–1936) and Mary (1867–1953), Queen consort of George V.

Line 8 loon: bird, the great northern diver.

Line 14 kept his own counsel: keeps to oneself secret opinions or purposes.

Line 28 frosted: iced.

Line 36 Maple Leaf: symbol of Canada. 'Maple Leaf Forever' is a phrase from the Canadian national anthem.

Line 42 ermine: a white fur (from the stoat's winter coat in northern lands).

Line 46 page: a boy attendant.

'First Death in Nova Scotia' was first published in *The New Yorker*, 10 March 1962, and was included in her third collection, *Questions of Travel*, in the section entitled 'Elsewhere'. The poem remembers a moment in Bishop's childhood, but she didn't write the poem until she was in her fifties. Elsewhere, Bishop wrote of other early deaths, many of them in Nova Scotia.

'First Death in Nova Scotia' remembers the winter funeral of Bishop's cousin Arthur (whose real name was Frank) circa 1914, when Bishop was almost four. It was first published when Bishop was fifty-one.

? Questions

1. What is suggested by the title of this poem? How does it capture a child's experience, a child's way of thinking?

2. In this poem, Bishop is remembering a winter funeral of a cousin almost half a century before. What details of the experience are being remembered here? How does Bishop give the sense of a child's confused mind? In your answer, you should discuss the significance of repetitions, confusions and connections.

3. Religion plays no part in the death of little cousin Arthur as it is described in this poem. What is the significance of the royal personages? Consider the colours and their clothes in your answer, quoting from the text to support your answer.

4. Identify and list all the references that give the poem a chilling quality.

5. How would you describe the speaker's mood in the closing stanza? What details help to create that mood? Do you think death is seen here as mysterious and frightening?

6. Compare the speaker's view of 'my mother' and 'Uncle Arthur' with the other adults mentioned in the poem – the figures in the chromographs.

In the Waiting Room

In Worcester, Massachusetts,
I went with Aunt Consuelo
to keep her dentist's appointment
and sat and waited for her
in the dentist's waiting room.   5
It was winter. It got dark
early. The waiting room
was full of grown-up people,
arctics and overcoats,
lamps and magazines.   10
My aunt was inside
what seemed like a long time
and while I waited I read
the *National Geographic*
(I could read) and carefully   15
studied the photographs:
the inside of a volcano,
black, and full of ashes;
then it was spilling over
in rivulets of fire.   20
Osa and Martin Johnson
dressed in riding breeches,
laced boots, and pith helmets.
A dead man slung on a pole
— 'Long Pig,' the caption said.   25
Babies, with pointed heads
wound round and round with string;
black, naked women with necks
wound round and round with wire
like the necks of light bulbs.   30
Their breasts were horrifying.
I read it right straight through.
I was too shy to stop.
And then I looked at the cover:
the yellow margins, the date.   35

Suddenly, from inside,
came an *oh!* of pain
— Aunt Consuelo's voice —
not very loud or long.
I wasn't at all surprised;   40
even then I knew she was
a foolish, timid woman.
I might have been embarrassed,
but wasn't. What took me
completely by surprise   45
was that it was *me*:
my voice, in my mouth.
Without thinking at all
I was my foolish aunt,
I — we — were falling, falling,   50
our eyes glued to the cover
of the *National Geographic*,
February, 1918.

I said to myself: three days
and you'll be seven years old.   55
I was saying it to stop
the sensation of falling off
the round, turning world
into cold, blue-black space.
But I felt: you are an *I*,   60
you are an *Elizabeth*,
you are one of *them*.
Why should you be one, too?
I scarcely dared to look
to see what it was I was.   65
I gave a sidelong glance
— I couldn't look any higher —
at shadowy gray knees,
trousers and skirts and boots

and different pairs of hands 70
lying under the lamps.
I knew that nothing stranger
had ever happened, that nothing
stranger could ever happen.
Why should I be my aunt, 75
or me, or anyone?
What similarities –
boots, hands, the family voice
I felt in my throat, or even
the *National Geographic* 80
and those awful hanging breasts —
held us all together
or made us all just one?
How — I didn't know any
word for it — how 'unlikely'... 85
How had I come to be here,
like them, and overhear
a cry of pain that could have
got loud and worse but hadn't?

The waiting room was bright 90
and too hot. It was sliding
beneath a big black wave,
another, and another.

Then I was back in it.
The War was on. Outside, 95
in Worcester, Massachusetts,
were night and slush and cold,
and it was still the fifth
of February, 1918.

Glossary

Line 1 Worcester, Massachusetts: where Elizabeth Bishop was born on 8 February 1911.

Line 2 Consuelo: Aunt Florence in real life.

Line 9 arctics: an American expression for waterproof overshoes/galoshes.

Line 21 Osa and Martin Johnson: a well-known and popular husband and wife team of explorers and naturalists; Osa Johnson (1894–1953) and Martin Johnson (1894–1937) wrote several travel books.

Line 23 pith helmets: sun helmets made from dried pithy stemmed swamp plant.

Line 25 'Long Pig': the name given by Polynesian cannibals to a dead man to be eaten.

Line 53 February 1918: this poem, though first published in 1971, was written in 1967. She included it in a letter to her friend, the American poet Robert Lowell. The setting of the poem is precisely dated – 5 February 1918 – 'three days and you'll be seven years old' – she writes in lines 54–55. Bishop waited 49 years before she wrote about the experience.

Line 61 Elizabeth: this is the first poem in which Elizabeth Bishop names herself.

> Though it remembers and recalls a moment from 1918, Elizabeth Bishop did not write so directly about early childhood until she was in her fifties.

? Questions

1. What does the title suggest? Can it be interpreted in different ways?

2. Like 'First Death in Nova Scotia', 'In the Waiting Room' is a poem, also written in her fifies, where Elizabeth Bishop recalls a moment from early childhood, a very precise moment in this instance: 5 February 1918. What does the adult remember of her childhood in the opening lines of the poem?

3. Prompted by her reading of the *National Geographic*, the location of the poem shifts (at line 17) to an altogether different and unfamiliar world. Describe what the young Elizabeth Bishop reads and sees and discuss her reaction to it.

4. What does the young girl think of her aunt? Why? Consider the women in the poem – Aunt Consuelo, Osa Martin, the black, naked women, the women in the waiting room.

5. Why does Bishop write 'I — we — were falling, falling'. Why does she think that she becomes her foolish aunt? And why 'foolish'?

6. In the poem's third section, why does the speaker focus on herself?

7. In the poem as a whole, 'I' is used twenty-six times. Considering that in some of Bishop's poems the personal pronoun is never used, why is it used so often here?

8. What do you think is meant by lines 72–74: 'I knew that nothing stranger/ had ever happened, that nothing/ stranger could ever happen.'

9. Discuss this poem as an exploration of childhood and adulthood. Use the text to support your answer.

10. Of the ten poems by Elizabeth Bishop on your course, which one is your favourite? Which one do you admire most? Give reasons for your answer.

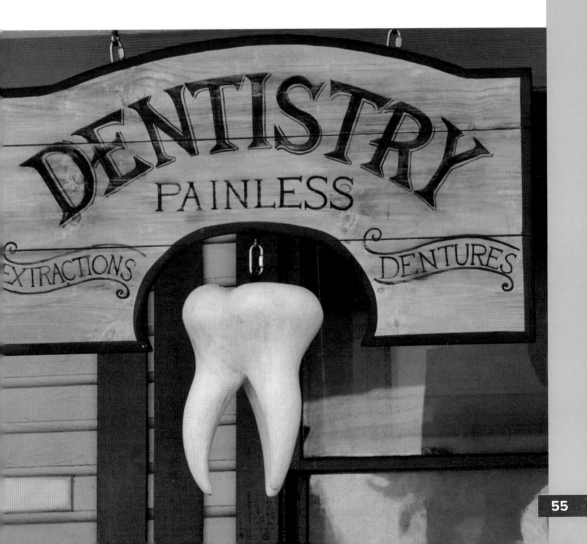

General Questions

A. 'Bishop, in her poetry, writes about the familiar and the unusual and does so in an interesting and unusual way.' Discuss this view, supporting your answer by relevant quotation from or reference to the poems by Elizabeth Bishop on your course.

B. 'The full complexity of childhood and adulthood is effectively evoked by Elizabeth Bishop in her poetry.' Discuss this view, supporting your answer by appropriate quotation from or reference to at least six of the poems by Bishop on your course.

C. 'In her poetry Elizabeth Bishop is a curious and sympathetic observer.' Discuss this view, supporting your answer by quotation from or reference to the poems by Bishop on your course.

D. 'In Elizabeth Bishop's poetry, description is never mere description; her poetry is a moral landscape, an emotional journey.' Discuss this statement, supporting your answer by relevant quotation or reference to the poems by Elizabeth Bishop on your course.

E. 'Bishop's poetry through both natural speech rhythms and formal patterns achieves an extraordinary immediacy and musical quality.' Discuss this view, supporting your answer by reference to the poems by Bishop on your course.

F. Discuss how Bishop uses images from Nature (water, fire, snow, for example) in her poetry, supporting your answer with reference to or quotation from the poems by Bishop on your course.

G. Randall Jarrell, the American poet, said of Elizabeth Bishop's work: 'all of her poems have written underneath, "I have seen it"'. Discuss what Bishop sees and explores in her poetry and how her descriptions and insights are vividly conveyed. You should refer to the poems on your course in your answer.

H. Bishop, according to Craig Raine, has 'a plain style in which the images appear like sovereigns'. Would you agree with this estimate of Elizabeth Bishop's poetry in the light of your reading the poetry by Bishop on your course? Support your answer with suitable quotation or reference to the poems.

I. Bishop herself said that 'I like painting probably better than I like poetry'. Discuss the painterly qualities of Elizabeth Bishop's work. In your answer you should refer to or quote from the poems by Bishop on your course.

J. 'Elizabeth Bishop's poems are not poems that begin with conclusions nor do they reach conclusions and yet we learn a great deal from them.' Would you agree with this statement? Support your answer by relevant quotation or reference to the poems by Bishop on your course.

K. Bishop, in her poetry, 'asks us to focus not on her but with her.' Would you agree with this statement? Support your answer with suitable quotations or reference to the poems by Bishop on your course.

Critical Commentary

The Fish

Elizabeth Bishop loved Florida and settled in Key West between 1939 and 1948. There Bishop discovered her love of fishing and, days after pulling in a sixty-pound amberjack, she began recording in her notebook descriptions which would later become part of her poem 'The Fish'. In Brett Millier's words, it is a poem of 'remarkable clarity and straightforwardness'. The form of the poem is the trimeter line interspersed at times by the dimeter. This is a form often suited to storytelling.

The fish of the poem is the enormous Caribbean jewfish which Bishop caught at Key West. Though the opening line is direct, 'I caught a tremendous fish', the adjective adds interest and excitement immediately. The fish isn't just described as 'large' or 'huge', though it is both. Instead, Bishop chooses the more powerfully subjective word 'tremendous', meaning immense and something that causes one to tremble. That first sentence is almost matter-of-fact:

> I caught a tremendous fish
> and held him beside the boat
> half out of water, with my hook
> fast in the corner of his mouth.

Yet it is 'my hook'. That detail, along with 'half out of water' (the fish is out of his element, between worlds) and 'fast', adds to the dramatic quality of the opening lines.

The focus shifts with the second sentence, line 5, 'He didn't fight', from Bishop to the fish, from fisher to the thing caught. Now we are told something about this fish and the personality which the poet attributes to it.

> He hadn't fought at all.

The fish submitted. The description of it as a 'grunting weight' is the first of many vivid pictures:

> He hung a grunting weight,
> battered and venerable
> and homely.

'Grunting', 'battered' and 'homely' (meaning, in American English, plain-looking) capture the exhausted and ugly state of the fish, but then Bishop's use of 'venerable' casts a different light on things. It means both aged looking and worthy of reverence.

Bishop is an extraordinary observer. The fish, once caught, is not just cast aside. She looks at it in great detail. Line 9 begins this thorough examination and observation of the fish:

> Here and there
> his brown skin hung in strips
> like ancient wallpaper:
> shapes like full-blown roses
> stained and lost through age.

Throughout the poem there is a very definite sense of Bishop as participant and observer: 'I caught', 'I thought', 'I looked', 'I stared and stared', but the poem is so much more than a matter-of-fact account of catching a fish. The fish intrigues her; it fascinates and frightens her, teaching her something about the fish and something about herself.

The simile in line 14, 'like full-blown roses', is a beautiful image, even if the shapes on the fish are 'stained and lost through age'. Here the fish becomes less 'homely' but, as Bishop looks more closely, a less attractive aspect of this fish is revealed:

> He was speckled with barnacles,
> fine rosettes of lime,
> and infested
> with tiny white sea-lice,
> and underneath two or three
> rags of green weed hung down.

These physical details are such that the texture (speckled, infested, rags) and the colours (lime, white, green) vividly help to create the complete picture.

The fish exists between the two elements of air and water: 'his gills were breathing in/the terrible oxygen'. The fish will die if its gills drink in the air, not water, and the gills are 'frightening': they are 'fresh and crisp with blood', they 'can cut so badly'.

In line 27, there is a shift in emphasis signalled by the phrase 'I thought'. Here Bishop imagines the insides of the fish, that aspect of the fish invisible to the fisherman or fisherwoman. By speaking now of

> the coarse white flesh
> packed in like feathers,
> the big bones and the little bones,
> the dramatic reds and blacks
> of his shiny entrails,
> and the pink swim-bladder
> like a big peony.

we have a sense of the whole fish, outside and inside. The image of the feathers, the use of 'little', the colours red, black and pink signal Bishop's sympathetic imaginative response.

The 'big peony' is a startling and beautiful image. The guts of a fish are not often viewed in this delicate, imaginative manner. And this peony image sends us back to line 14, where the fish's skin was also described in terms of flower imagery – the shapes of full-blown roses.

In some respects, the fish is familiar – his skin is compared to 'ancient wallpaper' – but the fish is also 'infested', 'coarse' and 'weapon-like'. She admires him, but she also recognises something disgusting in the fish. Yet the fish is ugly only to the careless observer; Bishop recognises that the fish is beautiful too.

When, in line 34, Bishop tells us that she 'looked into his eyes', a more immediate relationship between the poet and the fish is being established. The captor is now looking straight into the eyes of the captive. The eyes of the fish are then described in typical Bishop style: a style which seems objective at first but in fact reveals Bishop's unique and subjective eye. First, the eyes are described in terms of size, shape, colour:

> his eyes
> which were far larger than mine
> but shallower, and yellowed.

Then we are given more detailed imagery; the irises are

> backed and packed
> with tarnished tinfoil

and even this image is overlain with another image – the image of the irises

> seen through the lenses
> of old scratched isinglass.

The fish does not return her look, her stare. The eyes, we are told,

> shifted a little, but not
> to return my stare.

The fish not looking, not returning Bishop's stare, suggests the separateness, the independence, the dignity and yet the vulnerability of the fish. When the stronger captures the weak, it does not mean that the weaker one surrenders everything.

As in much of Bishop's poetry, the writing is such that, as we read through the poem, it is as if we are reading her thoughts directly as they are being formed.

The use of the dash at line 43 (she also uses the dash elsewhere in the poem at lines 24, 49 and 74) suggests a considered, explanatory addition; it indicates Bishop's attempt at getting it right. She has spoken of how the eyes shifted slightly and then we are given the further explanation or clarification:

> – It was more like the tipping
>   of an object toward the light.

'I caught' (line 1), 'I thought' (line 27) and 'I looked' (line 34) have already marked certain stages in the poem. Now, with line 45, we have a new development: Bishop tells us that

> I admired his sullen face,
> the mechanism of his jaw.

Sullen is not a quality usually or often admired, but Bishop attributes a resolute quality to the fish and senses a gloomy and unresponsive state. It is at this point that she mentions how she saw 'five pieces of fish-line', each one indicating a former struggle and unsuccessful catch. The struggle was powerful and determined, and the fish still bears the evidence to prove it:

> A green line, frayed at the end
> where he broke it, two heavier lines,
> and a fine black thread
> still crimped from the strain and snap
> when it broke and he got away.

Here the adjectives and the verbs achieve the convincing effect: frayed, broke, heavier, crimped, broke, got away – that of a long, determined struggle. This fish has had an interesting and vivid past.

Bishop is clearly impressed. She sees the hooks as victory medals, while the gut lines are like the ribbons attached to such medals and they form a five-haired beard of wisdom. The fish, personified, has survived the wars – in this instance the fight with the fisherman's hook.

Earlier in the poem (line 46), Bishop has spoken of 'the mechanism of his jaw'; in line 64 we read of the fish's aching jaw. Bishop has become more engaged with the plight of this tremendous, battered and venerable fish. There is also, of course, the sense of the fish as male, as conqueror – it has battled with the hook and won. Now it is well and truly caught, but Bishop, female, does not play conqueror, as the last line of the poem indicates.

All the details so far lead us to the poem's conclusion. The second last sentence begins with the line 'I stared and stared'. It is a moment of triumph and victory; Bishop speaks of how

> victory filled up
> the little rented boat.

Everything seems transformed. The boat is 'little' and 'rented': nothing remarkable there. The fish, however, was 'tremendous' and 'victory' seems to belong to Bishop for having caught the fish, but also to the fish itself for having survived five previous hooks.

She mentions no other person in this poem; Bishop, it would seem, is alone in the boat. One person in a little boat floating on the sea conjures up a small scene, but the feeling which she is experiencing is an expansive feeling, a feeling which begins within and spreads to embrace and include the very ordinary details of the boat. 'The 'pool of bilge', the 'rusted engine', 'the bailer', 'the sun-cracked thwarts', 'the oarlocks', 'the gunnels' are transformed. In the pool of bilge at the bottom of the boat, Bishop notices where oil had 'spread a rainbow'. And that rainbow spreads everywhere

> – until everywhere
> was rainbow, rainbow, rainbow!

The poem's final line is one of the shortest sentences in the poem. By the poem's end, we ask what has happened between line 1 ('I caught a tremendous fish') and line 76. 'And I let the fish go' is not surprising. The word 'and' suggests that everything has led to this conclusion.

Bishop's use of rhyme in the final couplet (rainbow/go; elsewhere in the poem she prefers to use internal rhymes) also adds to the mood of exultation with which the poem ends:

> – until everything
> was rainbow, rainbow, rainbow!
> And I let the fish go.

This is the moment of epiphany and revelation, a visionary moment. (An *epiphany* is an extraordinary moment of heightened awareness, insight and understanding.)

The poem not only describes the fish, but also tells us a great deal about Elizabeth Bishop. The poet Randall Jarrell admired this poem for its moral quality.

The speaker sets out to catch a fish: it is a battered creature and in the end the fish is let go. The fish has escaped the hook five other times – the 'five big hooks' have 'grown firmly in his mouth' to remind us, but this time it is literally being let off the hook. Bishop admires the fish for its individual self; as the American writer and literary critic David Kalstone observed, 'victory belongs both to the wild survivor and his human counterpart'.

Bishop's 'The Fish' can also be seen as an allegorical poem: in other words, it gives us a narrative that can be understood symbolically or at a level other than the literal or actual one. It is but one of several poems by Bishop which Andrew Motion has called 'arguifying, Metaphysical and fabling'. Between that opening and closing line, not only is there, in Craig Raine's words, an 'unhurried, methodical, humane' response to the fish but 'she pronounces a true but merciful verdict on our precarious existence'.

These closing lines can also be read as a reversal of the macho stance. American literature has memorable examples of the fisherman in search of the fish. Melville's great novel *Moby Dick* (1851) and Ernest Hemingway's *The Old Man and the Sea* (1952) reveal a man's determined and ambitious attempt to conquer. But this is not a poem about the fish that got away: 'I let the fish go'.

At The Fishhouses

There is almost something anti-poetic or non-poetic about the words 'At the Fishhouses'. But Elizabeth Bishop was to make and shape her poetry from what might be termed the very opposite of the traditional sources of poetic inspiration. 'Filling Station' and 'In the Waiting Room' are other such titles which suggest the apparently unpoetic. Fishhouses are functional buildings, reeking of fish. Fishhouses are also places linked with death in that all the fish stored and processed are dead. The fishhouses of the title are fishhouses on Cuttyhunk Island, Massachusetts, by the cold Atlantic, though the notebooks Bishop kept while at Lockeport Beach in Nova Scotia in 1946 also found their way into this poem.

The poem begins unassertively, almost apologetically:

> Although it is a cold evening
> down by one of the fishhouses
> an old man sits netting,
> his net, in the gloaming almost invisible,
> a dark purple-brown,
> and his shuttle worn and polished.

The only other person beside the poet is 'an old man'. He 'sits netting, / his net, in the gloaming almost invisible'. There are echoes of Wordsworth here, in that William Wordsworth often wrote about ordinary working people and the lives they lived against a background of 'the goings on of earth and sky'. The fisherman is a solitary figure. So too is Bishop.

The opening section of the poem describes the five fishhouses and her conversation with the old fisherman while he is waiting for a herring boat to come in. The language, though conversational, is also very musical. Within the opening lines, for example, are alliteration and internal rhyme, two of Bishop's favourite techniques. The long 'o' sound of 'although' is echoed in the word 'gloaming'; 'cold' and 'old' rhyme; the words 'brown', 'worn', 'strong', and 'run', together with 'sits', 'nets', 'purple' and 'polished', all add to this musical effect.

Feeling the cold, seeing the fisherman and smelling the codfish establish immediately a world created through the senses:

> The air smells so strong of codfish
> it makes one's nose run and one's eyes water

And again:

> The five fishhouses have steeply peaked roofs
> and narrow, cleated gangplanks slant up
> to storerooms in the gables
> for the wheelbarrows to be pushed up and down on.

These lines illustrate the music of poetry. In 'five' and 'fish. . .' the poet uses alliteration and assonance and the rhyming 'steep ly' and 'peak ed'; alliteration again with 'slant' and 'storerooms'. The 'up' of 'pushed up' echoes the 'up' at the end of the line two lines earlier and everything goes to create what seems both a very natural sounding utterance and a musical quality which is typical of Elizabeth Bishop.

The initial effect of the place on the poet is physical. Bishop, in lines 7 and 8, tells us that

> The air smells so strong of codfish
> it makes one's nose run and one's eyes water

but her use of 'one's' rather than 'my' makes it more impersonal. What the opening lines offer us is, according to Seamus Heaney, 'the slow-motion spectacle of a well-disciplined poetic imagination'. Everything is presented to us without fuss.

Line 13 announces that 'All is silver'. This is the cold opaque silver of the sea, the apparently translucent silver

of the benches
the lobster pots, and masts, scattered
among the wild jagged rocks.

Such detail is characteristic of Bishop. She watches everything closely. In many of her poems, she will begin with a description (a particular place, a particular time, an object) and from description, through imagination, she moves towards understanding and insight.

What Seamus Heaney called Bishop's 'lucid awareness' is clearly at work in lines 21 and following:

The big fish tubs are completely lined
with layers of beautiful herring scales
and the wheelbarrows are similarly plastered
with creamy iridescent coats of mail,
with small iridescent flies crawling on them.

Her eye picks out the tiny detail of the 'small iridescent flies' crawling on the silvered, rainbowed wheelbarrows. For Bishop there is a beauty here in the sensory details she describes. She uses the word 'beautiful' in line 22, and the 'creamy iridescent coats of mail' is an example of that beauty.

The poem's focus then moves, camera-like, from the minute, the flies in line 25, to the wide-angle shot captured in line 26:

Up on the little slope behind the houses,
set in the sparse bright sprinkle of grass,
is an ancient wooden capstan,
cracked, with two long bleached handles
and some melancholy stains, like dried blood,
where the ironwork has rusted.

The capstan, cracked and rusted, is a reminder of the work done over the years. This detail and precision is, yet again, giving us the exterior world. Bishop does not hurry us through the poem, though the poet's main preoccupation, or that which forms one of the poem's main themes (how to make sense of the world), is not yet arrived at.

Up until now, Bishop has been describing what she sees, but line 32 ('The old man accepts a Lucky Strike') marks the human encounter and conversation. Bishop enters into the poem in a more obvious way. The detail that the old man 'was a friend of my grandfather' creates a human and personal story. The final lines in this first section of 'At the Fishhouses' give the reader the factual, outward, public world:

> We talk of the decline in the population
> and of codfish and herring
> while he waits for a herring boat to come in.

And Bishop's own private observations:

> There are sequins on his vest and on his thumb.
> He has scraped the scales, the principal beauty,
> from unnumbered fish with that black old knife,
> the blade of which is almost worn away.

The old man in these four lines is described as expert at his task but one who is also coming to the end of his life. His 'blade is almost worn away'. The literary critic Bonnie Costello sees the fisherman as a divine agent. Bishop herself said of these four lines (37–40) that they came to her in a dream.

To see the fishscales as sequins is another example of Bishop's ability to bring a word with such specific connotations and associations (glittering ballgowns, glamour) and to give it a new life and appropriateness. The man, both times he is mentioned, is spoken of as old. The awareness of mortality is never explicitly stated, but, in the third section of the poem, Bishop confronts her own mortality.

Meanwhile, in the second section, lines 41–46, the picture is of the water's edge:

> Down at the water's edge, at the place
> where they haul up the boats, up the long ramp
> descending into the water, thin silver
> tree trunks are laid horizontally
> across the gray stones, down and down
> at intervals of four or five feet.

Bishop has shifted her focus from the details of the old man's hands (he is not mentioned again in the poem) and 'that black old knife' to that in-between world of land and sea:

> the place
> where they haul up the boats, up the long ramp
> descending into the water.

The phrase 'down and down' in line 45 suggests not only the angle of the tree trunks but the direction of the poem, in that Bishop, in the third and final section, goes deep beneath the surface of the moment, deep into her own consciousness and this leads her to a fuller understanding and awareness of her own aloneness and mortality.

Section 3 begins with the line:

> Cold dark deep and absolutely clear

Seamus Heaney refers to this line as 'a rhythmic heave which suggests that something other is about to happen'. Eavan Boland recognises its 'serious music', and we are reminded of its importance when the same line is repeated 13 lines later. The four adjectives present us with the chilling reality of the water of the North Atlantic, an 'element bearable to no mortal'. It is in this third section that the seal makes his appearance. In an earlier draft of this poem, Bishop speaks of seals; in the final draft of 'At the Fishhouses', the seal is solitary, just as the old man and Bishop herself are.

Bishop is drawn to this sea shore 'evening after evening', to this curious seal. In his element, the seal believes in total immersion and Bishop says that she too believes in it. Total immersion can refer to a baptism by water and this is why Bishop adds 'so I used to sing him Baptist hymns', but the phrase can also mean a state of deep absorption or involvement, a meaning which is also interesting in this context. The seal belongs to another world and a different world.

The seal appears in line 49 and disappears in 59, but it is more than a charming, distracting and delightful interlude.

> One seal particularly
> I have seen here evening after evening.
> He was curious about me. He was interested in music;
> Like me a believer in total immersion,
> so I used to sing him Baptist hymns.
> I also sang 'A Mighty Fortress Is Our God'.
> He stood up in the water and regarded me
> steadily, moving his head a little.
> Then he would disappear, then suddenly emerge
> almost in the same spot, with a sort of shrug
> as if it were against his better judgement.

Though Bishop here refers to religion and belief she finds no comfort or consolation there. God may be a fortress but one to which Bishop does not belong.

Seals belong to sea and land; they are often seen as ambiguous creatures. In the water, the seal is in its element, 'a believer in total immersion', and it allows Bishop to imagine more fully the element to which it belongs. Total immersion for Bishop is immersion of herself in knowledge, and what she imagines knowledge to be is this 'Cold, dark deep and absolutely clear' water before her.

Immediately after the seal disappears from the poem, Bishop repeats the line which began this third section:

> Cold dark deep and absolutely clear,

bringing us again to the more serious concerns of the poem, namely that, like the 'cold dark deep' water there are, in Eavan Boland's phrase, corresponding 'cold interiors of human knowledge'.

That passage in the poem from line 60 to the end marks a very different order of experience. The thinking within these lines is at a different level from the earlier part of the poem. Before Bishop is 'the clear gray icy water', like knowledge. Behind,

> ... Back, behind us,
> the dignified tall firs begin.
> Bluish, associating with their shadows,
> a million Christmas trees stand
> waiting for Christmas.

It has been suggested that the Christmas trees are behind her in more than one sense. These have been interpreted as the traces of Christianity which Bishop herself has put behind her. Here the Christmas trees are waiting not for Christ's birth, but to be cut down.

There is also the use of 'us' here, the only time Bishop uses it in the poem. The 'us' refers to Bishop, the seal and the old man, but it has been argued that she could also be including us, the readers, here.

It is only in this third section of 'At the Fishhouses' that Elizabeth Bishop uses the personal pronoun 'I'. What fascinates her and what makes her human is knowledge. She has seen the water 'over and over, the same sea' and it is

> icily free above the stones,
> above the stones and then the world.

The sea of knowledge is a familiar phrase. Bishop's sea of knowledge is cold, dark and painful.

The final section of the poem is more private and more difficult to grasp. Yet Bishop in this very passage speaks directly to the reader, using 'you' (line 71). The water is bitterly cold:

> If you should dip your hand in,
> Your wrist would ache immediately,
> your bones would begin to ache and your hand would burn
> as if the water were a transmutation of fire
> that feeds on stone and burns with a dark gray flame.
> If you tasted it, it would first taste bitter

> then briny, then surely burn your tongue.

Bishop herself makes her meaning clear. To dip into this bitterly cold water and to taste it

> is like what we imagine knowledge to be:
> dark, salt, clear, moving, utterly free.

Knowledge, the poet tells us, is 'drawn from the cold hard mouth / of the world, derived from the rocky breasts / forever'. Knowledge, in other words, hurts. The 'cold hard mouth' and 'the rocky breasts' are uncomfortable images. The source is part maternal, but Mother Nature here is cold and forbidding.

What began seemingly as an objective descriptive poem has become a personal and private poem. Yet, 'At the Fishhouses' is a poem in which the reader can enter into the experience and share the poet's understanding. When she writes 'It is like what we imagine knowledge to be', Bishop is speaking for herself, the reader and everyone.

What we know, our knowledge, is drawn from the past, but knowledge is also something which is ongoing, never static and flowing. Knowledge, as Bishop puts it in those closing lines, is

> forever, flowing and drawn, and since
> our knowledge is historical, flowing, and flown.

We have moments of insight and understanding that might enrich or unsettle us and we have witnessed one such moment in this poem. The moment is 'flowing', in that it belongs to the present, and it is 'flown', in that it becomes part of our past. As humans we are part of flux and we cannot hope to control or to stop it.

The poem ends with this heightened moment of insight. In *Elizabeth Bishop: An Oral Biography*, we learn that Bishop told her friend Frank Bidart that 'when she was writing it she hardly knew what she was writing, knew the words were right, and (at this she raised her arms as high straight above her head as she could) felt ten feet tall.'

The Bight

The poem begins with description and in fact most of the poem describes a place. Yet the poem is much more than a place-picture; it becomes a romantic meditation. The phrase 'it seems to me' (line 13) and the final line are the most personal, though in fact what Bishop chooses to describe and how she describes it reveals her personality everywhere.

The opening lines are both plain and sensuous, in that the bight is described in terms of sight, touch, smell and hearing. And though the place is neither remarkable nor beautiful, Bishop makes it interesting and almost beautiful through her choice and control of language.

The very first line – 'At low tide like this how sheer the water is' – achieves an immediacy with the phrase 'like this', and Bishop's sense of engagement or awe is expressed in the words 'how sheer the water is'. Here and elsewhere, Elizabeth Bishop often writes a line which is almost entirely composed of monosyllabic words (lines 1, 9, 16, 26, 33 are other examples in 'The Bight'). It is a spare, simple and strong style.

What is remarkable about these opening lines, and it is one of Bishop's identifying characteristics, is her ability to bring a particular place alive. Marl isn't just marl:

> White, crumbling ribs of marl protrude and glare

Details – the adjectives and verbs – give it a vivid presence.

The dry boats, the dry pilings and the water in the bight that doesn't wet anything create a very distinctive atmosphere. Bishop describes the colour of the water as 'the color of the gas flame turned as low as possible' and this accurate image is followed by the surreal when Bishop says:

> One can smell it turning to gas; if one were Baudelaire
> one could probably hear it turning to marimba music.

The use of 'one' here, not 'I', includes rather than excludes the reader, and yet the use of 'one' is more impersonal than 'I'. This imagined transformation of water 'turning to gas', 'turning to marimba music', involves the senses. Smell allows us to imagine water as gas; our sense of hearing can turn the water into vibrant jazzy sounds. As Bishop reminds us, this is a way of thinking or of viewing the world that can be found in Baudelaire's poetry. Unusual and marvellous connections are being made. Bishop herself, in lines 9 and 10, is now thinking in this way when she hears a Latin American dance music in the sounds of the dredging machine:

> The little ochre dredge at work off the end of the dock
> already plays the dry perfectly off-beat claves.

The poem is a busy one. There is a great deal of activity. Lines 11 to 19 describe the pelican and man-of-war birds. A phrase like 'humorous elbowings' catches the pelicans' movements; the man-of-war birds are also caught: they 'open their tails like scissors on the curves / or tense them like wishbones'.

The next section of the poem has sponge boats, the shark tails and the little white boats, but they are not simply listed. The sponge boats are 'frowsy', coming in 'with the obliging air of retrievers', and the words 'bristling' and 'decorated' give them energy; the shark tails are 'blue-gray' and are 'glinting like little plowshares'; and the damaged little white boats are 'like torn-open, unanswered letters'. In a letter to Robert Lowell, Bishop had written, 15 January 1948, that the harbour was a mess – boats piled up, some broken by a recent hurricane – and that it had reminded her a little of her desk. Here the image from the letter reappears in the poem, not as Bishop's untidy writing desk, but in the phrase 'old correspondences'.

'The bight is littered with old correspondences', but the personal detail of Bishop's own desk is made less personal and the word 'correspondences' also has the literary echo of Baudelaire's sonnet 'Correspondances'. The bight is not only a place that resembles a paper littered desk; it is also a place where interesting, unusual connections or correspondences can be found.

The poem ends with the sound of the dredger, first mentioned in line 9. The 'little ocher dredge' continues its digging. Bishop spoke of the pelicans crashing into the water and 'rarely coming up with anything to show for it'. The dredge comes up with something:

> Click. Click. Goes the **d**redge,
> and brings up a **d**ripping *jawful* of marl.
> All the untidy activity continues,
> *awful* but cheer*ful*.

The sounds here are spot on. First, the mechanical sharpness of the 'Click. Click.', each one given a definition of its own with those full stops. The sound contained in the phrase 'a dripping jawful of marl' is the sound of heavy wetness. And the movement of that line – 'and brings up a dripping jawful of marl' is awkward and staggered, just as the dredger's digger would be as it gouges out, scoops and lifts up the clayey, limey wet soil. Apart from rhythm and individual sounds, there is another music also, which Bishop captures in the use of alliteration, assonance and cross or slant rhyme. Look again. Listen.

> Click. Click. Goes the **d**redge,
> and brings up a **d**ripping *jawful* of marl.
> All the untidy activity continues,
> *awful* but cheer*ful*.

The second last line in the poem refers to all that is going on before her in the bight, but it could also be read as a description of life itself. Life goes on, but life can be random, chaotic, disorganised. It is a poem that she associates with her thirty-seventh birthday, and every birthday is a moment of natural reflection on the passing of time and the nature of one's life.

That famous last line, 'awful but cheerful', sums up much about Elizabeth Bishop. Towards the end of her life she herself asked that those words be inscribed on her tombstone in the Bishop family plot in Worcester, Massachusetts. The accepted and most usual meaning for 'awful' is 'very bad, terrible, unattractive', but there is also its original meaning of 'inspiring awe, solemnly impressive'. This bight and its untidy activity are not conventionally pretty. It has, of course, been the inspiration for this very poem. The first and more common interpretation of the word is probably the more valid in the context of the 'untidy activity' in the preceding line. Bishop has clearly enjoyed observing. Life does go on and it can be both 'awful' and 'cheerful'. Bishop does say 'awful but cheerful', suggesting perhaps that the birds, the 'frowsy sponge boats' and the dredger all continue their activity with good humour, as we should and must. It is perhaps the only way to go on.

The Prodigal

It is worth asking at the outset why Bishop should be drawn to such a figure as the prodigal; she often felt like an outsider, someone away from home, and, like the prodigal son of the poem, she also engaged in drinking bouts.

The structure of the poem consists of a double sonnet and the irregular but ordered rhyming scheme is as follows: abacdbcedfeggf

A different sound rhyme and a different rhyming scheme is used in stanza 2: abacdbecfedfdgh. An identical rhyming scheme is used in the first six lines of each stanza. The American literary critic David Kalstone spoke of 'two nicely rhymed sonnets' and how the 'air of sanity' in the poem is what makes it frightening, 'its ease and attractiveness only just keeping down panic and fear'.

The poem, though based on the biblical story of the Prodigal Son, chooses to focus on the lowest and ugliest part of that man's life – his time minding pigs. The ugliness and unpleasantness is presented immediately in the opening line: 'The brown enormous odor' captures the colour and the impact of the stench. This is the world he knows now. It is 'too close', too close for comfort, and so close that he does not judge. Not judging in this context could mean he has lost all sense of a world other than this one. It could also mean that this man does not judge – in other words, he is not thinking whether he deserves this life or not. Later there will come a time when he will judge it wise or best to go home and ask his father for forgiveness, but Bishop is suggesting at this point that the world of the pigs is so overwhelming that he does not judge. The phrase 'he lived by' in line 1 can mean that the prodigal son lived next to this horrible smell or it could also be interpreted to mean that he lived by it in the sense that it allows him to survive. The presence of the pigs is there before us in the two details 'breathing and thick hair'.

The first part of the poem brings us within the pig shed. 'The floor was rotten; the sty / was plastered halfway up with glass-smooth dung.' The vivid ugliness of 'glass-smooth' is all the more effective in that 'glass-smooth' is more often associated with the surface of a calm, beautiful lake. That the dung is 'halfway' up the wall reminds us of its prevalence and liquid state.

Lines 5 to 8 focus on the pigs themselves, their heads, more specifically their eyes, their snouts. As everywhere in Bishop, the observations are exact: the eyes are 'light-lashed' and 'self-righteous'. Who gives the 'cheerful stare' – the pigs or the prodigal? The dash at the end of line 6 suggests that the stare belongs to the pigs' eyes and that the pigs even stare in a cheerful manner at the 'sow that always ate her young'. The 'always' is frightening. Whether it is intentional or not, line 7 does prompt the reader to consider this sow's behaviour towards its offspring and the comparison between that and the subsequent attitude of the father towards his prodigal son.

The pigs follow their carer and, even though he feels sickened by it all, something eventually ('till' – line 8) in the prodigal causes him to offer a gesture of comfort or affection:

> sickening, he leaned to scratch her head.

In line 9, we are given a sense of the prodigal's meaningless life and secret drinking bouts but something else, something other, is also introduced. Bishop reminds us that there is a world beyond the pigsty. There is the sunrise, and the morning sun transforms the ordinary and everyday. In this instance, the barnyard mud is glazed with red. Earlier in line 4 we read that the ugly smelly pigsty walls were glazed with dung; here the mud and the puddles are made beautiful by the sunrise and, seeing them, the heart seems to be reassured.

Such a moment of passing beauty sustains him in his suffering and loneliness and exile:

> And then he thought he almost might endure
> his exile yet another year or more.

The use of 'But' at the beginning of line 9 indicates hope. And Bishop also uses 'but' to begin the second section of 'The Prodigal', this time to signal a change of direction.

> But evenings the first star came to warn.

Perhaps Bishop is using 'star' here as a signal of fate or destiny. If it is spoken of in terms of warning then the prodigal is being told that he must act or make decisions. Then follows such a comforting picture of order and safety (the farmer tending to his cows and horses and seeing that they are safe for the night) that

Bishop speaks of it in terms of it being

> safe and companionable as in the Ark.

Lines 18 and 19 give only some details of the inside of the barn in lantern light:

> beneath their overhanging clouds of hay,
> with pitchforks, faint forked lightnings, catching light,
> yet these few details allow the reader of the poem to picture it clearly.

'Clouds of hay' and the words 'safe and companionable' suggest warmth and a dry place, a contrast with the wet, dung-covered pigsty where the prodigal works. Line 21 is one sentence. It returns us to the world of the pigs and gives us both their vulnerability – 'their little feet' – and their ugly side – they snored.

The farmer shuts the barn door and goes home, but Bishop, imagining the life of the prodigal, never speaks of him as having a home separate from the animals. The farmer's lantern is observed: its light 'laid on the mud' forms a moving or 'pacing aureole', and this interpretation of light on mud is similar to the earlier lines in which the early morning sun colours the mud and puddles. The lantern light becomes an aureole or halo and this too, like the glazed mud in stanza 1, sustains him.

We are given another very vivid description of the prodigal at work before the poem ends. It is as if the time spent among the pigs is so long and the drudgery so great that Bishop returns to it again to remind us of its awfulness. With

> Carrying a bucket along a slimy board,
> he felt the bats' uncertain staggering flight

we are once again in the wet and smelly dark. The prodigal's private, inner self is spoken of in terms of 'shuddering insights'. We know from the biblical story what he is thinking, what conclusions he is reaching. These insights are 'beyond his control, / touching him'. This is the disturbed, aware Prodigal Son. But Elizabeth Bishop does not give us a simple, quick ending. St. Luke says 'And when he came to himself. . .'. Bishops charts the journey towards that difficult decision with words such as 'shuddering', 'touching him' and the final sentence in the poem. Here again she uses 'But' with great effect; it wasn't an easy or sudden decision:

> But it took him a long time
> finally to make his mind up to go home.

The final word resonates particularly because the word does not hark back to an obvious rhyme and because of what it implies within the poem as a whole. The loner, outsider, exile is returning to the place where he will be forgiven and loved.

Our knowing the ending of this biblical story adds to the poem's effect. However, our knowing that Bishop's mother was confined to a hospital for the insane and that Bishop herself grew up never having a home to go to also adds to the poem's power and effect.

In a letter to Robert Lowell, dated 23 November 1955, Bishop herself said that in 'The Prodigal' the technique was like a spiritual exercise of the Jesuits – where one thinks in great detail about how the thing happened. In another letter to U. T. and Joseph Summers, dated 19 October 1967, she tells of how 'The Prodigal' suggested itself. It 'was suggested to me when one of my aunt's stepsons offered me a drink of rum, in the pigsties, at about nine in the morning, when I was visiting her in Nova Scotia'.

Filling Station

'Oh, but it is dirty!' There is no introduction, no explanation. The title sets the scene and there is an immediacy in that opening line. The 'Oh' is spontaneous, the word 'dirty' given extra force with that exclamation mark. In this, as in many of Bishop's poems, we begin with a place and Bishop's description of it but, by the end of the poem, the experience has expanded to include wider, deeper issues. It is a poem that moves towards a wonderful and, in the end, an unsurprising last line.

The place is black, glistening and disturbing because it can also be dangerous:

> oil-soaked, oil permeated
> to a disturbing, over-all
> black translucency.
> Be careful with that match!

That final line in stanza 1 – 'Be careful with that match!' – is very ordinary and everyday. It certainly isn't a line one might associate with the language of poetry, but poetry is the living, speaking voice of the time. This opening stanza combines a language that is exact ('black translucency', for example) with an equally effective the language which may seem throwaway or commonplace, but which in the context of the poem is perfectly right.

A masculine place, usually, the filling station is given a human and domestic dimension in the second stanza. Father and sons give it a family feeling, as do details later in the poem such as the wicker sofa, the dog, the doily. The word 'dirty' occurs in the first three stanzas. The place is dirty, the father dirty, the sons dirty; the dog is a 'dirty dog'.

The dirt is fascinating. Every aspect of it is noted: the father's clothes are so black they resemble an

> oil-soaked monkey suit
> that cuts him under the arms

The 'several quick and saucy' sons are 'greasy'. 'All', Bishop tells us, is 'quite thoroughly dirty'.

Stanza 3 draws us in further with the question 'Do they live in the station?'

The comic books are the only things which seem to have retained their original, 'certain color'. Bishop's humorous eye suggests that the plant is oiled, not watered; the doily is 'dim', yet the plant on the doily-covered taboret fascinates her. The doily is improbable and unexpected, totally unnecessary, it could be argued, and it is dirty:

> Why, oh why, the doily?

This question is both simple and crucial. The doily reminds us that there are such things as creativity, grace, manners; it is a gesture towards elegance. Filling stations are naturally oily and dirty, and we've already seen how the father, the sons, the furniture and the dog are filthy. The doily is not as fresh as the day it was made, but it was created to decorate and to enhance. It was also most likely embroidered and crocheted by a woman, which may be another interesting consideration. A woman brought something special to this place and it is a woman who is reminding us of this in the very act of writing the poem.

The cans of oil have also been attended to in a special way:

> Somebody
> arranges the rows of cans
> so that they softly say:
> ESSO—SO—SO—SO
> to high-strung automobiles.

Whoever embroidered the doily, whoever waters the plant, whoever arranges the oil cans, is a 'somebody' never named. There is, it would seem, always someone doing small, almost unnoticeable little acts of kindness or acts which reflect our ability as humans to care, to shape, to bring order or to create. They are not always named and they do not need to be named, but the world is a better place because of them. Andrew Motion thinks the filling station 'the small theatre for a degraded life which stubbornly refuses to give up the effort to decorate and enjoy'. No matter where we live, we try to make it home.

The oil cans so arranged say musically and comfortingly 'SO-SO-SO', which was, according to Bishop herself, a phrase used to calm and soothe horses. This little detail adds a further interesting perspective to the poem. 'High-strung' automobiles refers to the tension and busyness of the cars' occupants more than the cars themselves, but the 'so-so-so' is doubly effective in that it was once used to comfort horses and now the phrase is read by those who sit in automobiles whose power is often described in terms of horse-power. The word 'high-strung' is also applied to thoroughbred horses; Bishop is describing the cars in terms of horses.

The last line is astonishing and wonderful and totally justified.

> Somebody loves us all.

It is a short sentence, a line complete in itself and gains the power of proverb. It is a wise, true, and marvellously comforting thought with which to end, all the more effective and powerful when we see how the dirty filling station, observed closely, reveals this truth and makes possible this insight.

Questions of Travel

The poem begins with the description of a place and its climate, movement and flux. Unlike, say, the opening lines of 'At the Fishhouses', Bishop's presence is more evident:

> 'There are too many waterfalls here'

This gives both a sense of the landscape and her opinion of it. Bishop speaks of her travels in the opening section. There are clouds and mountain tops and movement. A scientist would talk about the hydrological cycle, but Bishop, a poet, sees it differently. She is clearly engaged with the 'too many waterfalls'; the water is described as 'those streaks, those mile-long, shiny, tearstains' becoming waterfalls. This is what she sees on her travels, and she even imagines more and more water falling and waterfalls:

> the pressure of so many clouds on the mountaintops
> makes them spill over the sides in soft slow-motion,
> turning to waterfalls under our very eyes.

Not only is Bishop the traveller, the 'streams and clouds' (line 10) 'keep travelling, travelling' too. It is as if the mind cannot take everything in. This first section ends with yet another example of how Elizabeth Bishop can make us see:

> the mountains look like the hulls of capsized ships,
> slime-hung and barnacled.

In section 2, Bishop's mood, her preoccupation, becomes more complex and philosophical. Should we travel? Why do we travel? What if we were to stay at home? What right have we to be here in a strange, foreign place?

Section 2 is made up of nine sentences, eight of which end with question marks, and these questions become the questions of travel. First, there is the invitation to

> Think of the long trip home.

and then the sequence of eight questions.

> Should we have stayed at home and thought of here?
> Where should we be today?
> Is it right to be watching strangers in a play
> in this strangest of theatres?
> What childishness is it that while there's a breath of life
> in our bodies, we are determined to rush
> to see the sun the other way around?
> The tiniest green hummingbird in the world?
> To stare at some inexplicable old stonework,
> inexplicable and impenetrable,
> at any view,
> instantly seen and always, always delightful?

Bishop is clearly intrigued by the whole concept of travel and is disoriented and a little uneasy about it. She wonders, in line 18, if it is childishness that causes us 'to rush / to see the sun the other way round?' (Brazil being below the Equator). Her focus has been on landscape and the natural world, but people and their work are also included. The people are 'strangers in a play'; the old stonework is 'inexplicable'. Bishop is in a place and yet feels separate and outside of it.

The American academic Brett Millier thinks that 'Questions of Travel' is concerned with 'the limitations of one's knowledge and understanding of a foreign culture'. It is a poem that admits to difference: the view may be 'inexplicable and impenetrable', yet the traveller is forever looking. To the questions

> Oh, must we dream our dreams
> and have them, too?
> And have we room
> for one more folded sunset, still quite warm?

the answers are implied but never given. The traveller did not stay at home and think or dream of here. The dream became a reality. There is a human need to see for oneself. The traveller has not grown weary of collecting sunsets. The image is that of folded, ironed clothes being packed away in a suitcase.

Bishop reinforces this viewpoint in the third section, which begins:

> But surely it would have been a pity
> not to have seen the trees along the road,
> really exaggerated in their beauty,
> not to have seen them gesturing
> like noble pantomimists, robed in pink.

Here Bishop is clearly enthralled and captivated, as a child is at the pantomime. She notices and delights in the tiniest of details, such as the clacking sounds of the petrol pump attendant's clogs:

> the sad, two-noted, wooden tune
> of disparate wooden clogs
> carelessly clacking over
> a grease-stained filling station floor.

Bishop adds in brackets the observation that the clogs are imperfectly made:

> (In another country the clogs would all be tested.
> Each pair there would have identical pitch.)

Is this in praise of Brazil? She prefers the disparate music of these clogs to the perfectly made, perfectly pitched clogs of a more precise and efficient country. Such an observation and such a response is typical of Elizabeth Bishop. She can focus on the ordinary and the inconsequential and find them interesting and engaging. She is a poet who tells of things as they are.

In this third section, Bishop continues to give reasons to justify travel. She presents us with other enjoyed aspects of her journey: the music of the fat brown bird, the ornate, church-like, wooden songbird's cage, the pounding rain and the subsequent 'sudden golden silence'.

> – A pity not to have heard
> the other, less primitive music of the fat brown bird
> who sings above the broken gasoline pump
> in a bamboo church of Jesuit baroque:
> three towers, five silver crosses.

These are the details which Bishop notes and remembers, details which most tourists wouldn't notice, let alone remember, and it isn't a mere list. In this section we are shown how Bishop ponders the connection, if any, between the making of wooden clogs and the making of wooden cages. Why do these people put their efforts into ornate impractical objects, and not bother about perfecting the practical ones? It doesn't matter that the connection between clogs and cages is pondered 'blurr'dly and inconclusively' (she playfully blurs the very word blurr'dly). The form of the cage, with its 'weak calligraphy', encapsulates the colonized history of Latin American. The traveller who views the cage is seeing history.

She reveals herself to be good-humoured, curious, open-minded and tolerant when she writes:

> – Yes a pity not to have pondered,
> blurr'dly and inconclusively,
> on what connection can exist for centuries
> between the crudest wooden footwear
> and, careful and finicky,
> the whittled fantasies of wooden cages.
> – Never to have studied history in
> the weak calligraphy of songbirds' cages.
> – And never to have had to listen to rain
> so much like politicians' speeches:
> two hours of unrelenting oratory
> and then a sudden golden silence...'

Section 3 began with Bishop saying that 'it would have been a pity' not to have witnessed or experienced what she then describes, and each time a new aspect of her travels is added to the list, the phrase 'a pity' is repeated or implied: It would have been a pity 'Not to have had to stop for gas ...' (line 34); 'A pity not to have heard' (line 42); '– Yes, a pity not to have pondered' (line 47); 'Never to have studied ...' (line 53); '– And never to have had to listen to rain ...' (line 55).

The uncertainty of line 14, 'Should we have stayed at home and thought of here?', is now answered. And it is answered also in the final eight lines of the poem when Bishop imagines 'the traveller' (all travellers?) writing in a notebook, during 'a sudden golden silence', a philosophical musing on the nature of travel. There is no 'I' in this poem. Bishop has used 'we' five times already, and she also uses 'we' in the traveller's notebook, suggesting that the questions she has asked and the conclusions she has reached are shared with all travellers.

There is still some unease and some uncertainty in the traveller's notebook entry, despite the many convincing reasons given in section three in support and in praise of travel. The reference to the seventeenth-century French philosopher Blaise Pascal is a dramatic touch. Pascal was famous for staying at home. Elizabeth Bishop, his opposite, spent her life travelling, and 'Questions of Travel', dated 1965, when Bishop was in her mid fifties, asks questions which Bishop asked her entire life. She wonders whether the impulse or the need to travel is due to a lack of imagination:

> 'Is it lack of imagination that makes us come
> to imagined places, not just stay at home?'

The imagined places, however, once visited, as we have seen from the poem, do not disappoint. This is what allows her to suggest (Bishop is never dogmatic):

> *'Or could Pascal have been not entirely right*
> *about just sitting quietly in one's room?'*

The italicised final lines, like section 2, consists of questions, and the poem 'Questions of Travel' appropriately ends with a question mark. There are eleven known drafts or versions of this poem and the statement in line 65:

> *the choice is never wide and never free*

originally read as 'the choice perhaps is not great . . . but fairly free', proving that Bishop changed her mind during the writing of this poem (like many Bishop poems it was written over a period of time). For the traveller the world seems varied and huge. Does one choose 'continent, city, country, society'? (line 63). Does one choose 'here, or there'? Is one still restricted?

> *Continent, city, country, society:*
> *the choice is never wide and never free.*
> *And here, or there... No. Should we have stayed at home,*
> *wherever that may be?*

The placing of the word 'No' is important here, and the poem suggests that the restrictions need not invalidate the experience. The question 'Should we have stayed at home?' has already been answered.

Throughout this poem, there is the implied sense of a place called home, the place from which the traveller set out and to which the traveller returns. 'The Prodigal' also explores this idea. In Bishop's case, she lost home after home (an idea she writes about in her poem 'One Art'), and her final question in 'Questions of Travel' is shadowed by her own sense of homelessness. The speaker in the poem is a traveller. Beyond the questions of travel is the ultimate question of belonging:

> *'Should we have stayed at home,*
> *wherever that may be?'*

In Bishop's case, the question suggests that she has never felt at home.

The Armadillo

On the page, the structure and shape of 'The Armadillo' are ordered: ten four-lined stanzas. The rhyming scheme in the first stanza – abab – is not strictly observed throughout, but the second and fourth lines in each stanza rhyme.

The armadillo itself does not appear until line 30, and for most of the poem Bishop describes the balloon offerings associated with the religious festival. The balloons are 'frail, illegal', dangerous, fascinating and beautiful. Their delicacy is captured in a phrase such as 'paper chambers', and the simile 'like hearts' suggests that they are an expression of love.

From her house, Bishop watches the fire balloons rising towards 'a saint / still honored in these parts'. Bishop, though living in Brazil, is the observer, not the participant. The poem traces their movement as they move skywards, 'climbing the mountain height'. The balloons are offerings, forms of prayer, and they drift heavenwards. Bishop does not dwell on their religious source and symbolism, but their beauty is captured in stanza 3:

> Once up against the sky it's hard
> to tell them from the stars –
> planets, that is – the tinted ones:
> Venus going down, or Mars,
> or the pale green one.

They have become part of the night sky, the constellations where there is even a star group known as the Southern Cross. When she uses the phrase 'steadily forsaking us' in line 18, Bishop gives us a sense of our earth bound selves. The people who released these balloons watch them drift upwards and away. If we are forsaken, we are being abandoned or left behind. We cannot go with them. But they are also dangerous if caught in a downwind and line 21 introduces this other aspect:

> Last night another big one fell.
> It splattered like an egg of fire
> against the cliff behind the house.

The human world is threatened, as is the natural world. The house and its inhabitants, the owls, the armadillo and the rabbit are all threatened, and Bishop has seen the birds and animals suffer. 'Whirling', 'stained bright pink' and 'shrieked' all suggest confusion, pain and suffering. Fire that was once contained and distant has become destructive.

The armadillo makes its brief appearance in line 30: it is frightened and alone and can protect itself from almost everything, except fire. 'Glistening' and 'rose-flecked, head down, tail down' give the reader a vivid sense of the animal's presence. It has been suggested that the armadillo, a threatened creature on the edge of the human and the natural world, resembles the artist who has to discover a means of survival.

The owls, and the rabbit which appears suddenly in line 33, are even more vulnerable creatures. The birds flee their burning nest; the 'baby' rabbit, 'so soft!', is also frightened. Bishop's use of the dash in line 35 suggests that the rabbit is or will become 'a handful of intangible ash'; its eyes are 'fixed, ignited', yet she notices with surprise that the rabbit is 'short-eared'. The balloons have now become sources of threat and violence.

The last stanza is italicised, not only for emphasis and force:

> *Too pretty, dreamlike mimicry!*
> *O falling fire and piercing cry*
> *and panic, and a weak mailed fist*
> *clenched ignorant against the sky!*

These last four lines dismiss the earlier stanzas in a way, in that Bishop says that her descriptions of the fleeing animals are 'too pretty'. What the poem has presented to the reader so far is a 'dreamlike mimicry!'

Those closing lines emphasise the horrible reality:

> *O falling fire and piercing cry*
> *and panic*

Here, it is as if Bishop is questioning language and poetry itself; is poetry capable of conveying ugly, frightening reality? The italics and the exclamation marks in the final stanza add an urgency to the moment of suffering which has already been described in stanzas 7, 8 and 9. The final idea in the poem, which is that of

> *a weak mailed fist*
> *clenched ignorant against the sky!*

suggests both defiance and helplessness. The '*mailed fist*' could be taken to refer to the armadillo's coat of mail, its defensive armour. Here Bishop does not offer just the accurate, objective description of the armadillo. She has done that in lines 30 to 32. The last two lines of the poem describe the armadillo, but now from a different and sympathetic perspective – that of the armadillo itself. The animal is spoken of as clenching its weak mailed fist, but clenching it nonetheless. And it is 'clenched ignorant against the sky!' The word 'ignorant' in line 40 reminds us that the armadillo does not understand the origins of this threatening fire and, since fire is the one thing from which the armadillo's outer coat cannot protect him, we are asked perhaps to consider the objects of supposedly religious worship in another light.

The owls, the armadillo and the rabbit are all victims, but the armadillo is the most striking presence among the creatures mentioned. It is the armadillo that gives the poem its title and it is to the armadillo that Bishop, clearly moved, returns in that final stanza. These closing lines of the poem have also been interpreted as symbolic of an ignorant and victimised working class, society's underdog, and the attempt by the working classes to strike for and assert their rights.

Sestina

The first lines of the poem establish a mood. It is as if the world itself is in mourning: the September rain and the failing light suggest sorrow and dying; it is the dying of the year and the dying of the day, but what is at the heart of the stanza is the human sorrow of the grandmother holding back her tears. In Bishop's story 'In the Village', the grandmother is crying openly; in the poem, those tears are stifled.

The last word in the first line is the word 'house'. This being a sestina, the word will occur in every stanza and occur seven times in all; it is the word with which the poem ends. This house has a grandmother and child and, as Seamus Heaney points out, 'the repetition of grandmother and child and house alerts us to the significant absence from this house of a father and a mother'.

The scene in stanza 1 is part cosy and comfortable, part dark and painful. There is the grandmother sitting in the kitchen with the child. It is warm; they sit 'beside the Little Marvel Stove' and the grandmother is reading jokes from the almanac. However, the grandmother's laughter and talking hide her tears.

The speaker in 'Sestina' is the adult Bishop, but she records her own experience as if she were an observer at a play. Bishop also interprets what is going on. In stanza 2, for example, Bishop allows us to glimpse the workings of the child's mind.

There is a significant difference between the grandmother and the young girl: the grandmother thinks that her autumn tears and the rain beating on the roof were known about and recorded in the almanac. Sorrow and the autumn rain seem inevitable. This is experience. The grandmother

> thinks that her equinoctial tears
> and the rain that beats on the roof of the house
> were both foretold by the almanac...

Normality keeps returning to the poem. Lines 11, 12 and 13 are pictures of domestic ordinariness and harmony:

> The iron kettle sings on the stove.
> She cuts some bread and says to the child,
>
> *It's time for tea now...*

But then the child transfers the unwept tears of the grandmother to the drops, falling from the kettle on to the stove. As in 'First Death in Nova Scotia', the child's mind is attempting to connect and make sense of the world. In the Nova Scotia poem, the first person is used; here Bishop stands outside or apart from the experience by writing about herself and her childhood in the third person. The two people in the poem are never given personal names.

She knows that the grandmother has held back her tears and now the child

> is watching the teakettle's small hard tears
> dance like mad on the hot black stove,
> the way the rain must dance on the house.

To the child, it now seems as if the tears are everywhere and they are 'hard' tears; they 'dance like mad', and she imagines them dancing on the house. In these lines Bishop returns us again to the child's thinking, the child's inner world.

Line 17 switches back to the everyday and ordinary:

> Tidying up, the old grandmother
> hangs up the clever almanac
> on its string.

This domestic busyness and organisation indicates that life must go on, even if a life is overshadowed by great sadness. The almanac was said to have foretold this sorrow, in lines 7–10. In lines 19 and 20, the almanac is seen as a sinister presence, but this time it is not the child or the grandmother who thinks it, but Bishop, the adult poet.

> Birdlike, the almanac
> hovers half open above the child,
> hovers above the old grandmother
> and her teacup full of dark brown tears.

The future that the almanac represents hovers above child and grandmother. The tea in the teacup, like the water from the kettle, is described in terms of tears. Stanzas 2, 3 and 4 associate the ordinary things of the household with tears, but end with the business of the house. The 'tidying up' in stanza 3 and the building of the fire in stanza 4:

> She shivers and says she thinks the house
> feels chilly, and puts more wood in the stove.

Stanza 5 begins with a sense of inevitability and even the stove seems to have become a part of that inevitability:

> *It was to be,* says the Marvel Stove.
> *I know what I know,* says the almanac.

The italicised phrases are highly charged. The ordinary, familiar domestic world is no longer ordinary and familiar. The child withdraws by drawing an imaginary house, but that house is 'rigid' or tension filled and can only be reached by a 'winding pathway'.

> With crayons the child draws a rigid house
> and a winding pathway. Then the child
> puts in a man with buttons like tears
> and shows it proudly to the grandmother.

It is hardly straining the interpretation to see the presence of the man as a father figure; Elizabeth Bishop never knew her father. She, the child, does not shed any tears in the poem, but there are tears everywhere, even in the drawing.

The child is proud of her representation of a house, but the adult, in this instance the grandmother, the grown-up Elizabeth Bishop, and the reader, sees the drawing with a different understanding.

The grandmother is busy again while the little girl looks at the sun, moon and stars on the open pages of the almanac. She imagines 'little moons' fall secretly, and the description of these as tears reveals yet again the enquiring, puzzled, yet perceptive mind of the child. Reality and fantasy merge. Those same tears fall into the child's world of the flower beds.

The closing three lines tighten up: the six words focused on in the previous stanzas were each given a line of their own. Here, in the final stanza, the ideas which those same six words represent must be brought even closer:

> *Time to plant tears,* says the almanac.
> The grandmother sings to the marvellous stove
> and the child draws another inscrutable house.

What is past is past was how the literary critic David Kalstone interpreted those italicised words. The almanac, more often associated with future events, seems to declare the time of tears is over. The grandmother pretends to be cheerful in the same spirit in which she hid her tears in stanza 1. The child draws another house. The actual house in which the child lives with her grandparents is the only home she has really known. A child instinctively draws a house; it should be a familiar, comfortable and comforting place. But this house she draws is 'another inscrutable house'.

First Death in Nova Scotia

The poem 'First Death in Nova Scotia' is told from a child's point of view. The very title suggests this. It is as if no one had ever died in Nova Scotia before now. This is the child's first experience of death, and in the poem the child attempts to understand reality and, in doing so, makes confused, extraordinary, and sometimes almost fairytale connections. The fairytale element is most clearly seen, for example, when the child-speaker in the poem imagines that the royal presences in stanza 1 invite little Arthur in the final stanza to become 'the smallest page at court'. American academic Helen Vendler says that the poem 'goes steadily, but crazily, from little Arthur in his coffin to the royal pictures to the loon to Arthur to the child-speaker to the loon to Arthur to the royal pictures. This structure, which follows the bewildered eye of the gazing child trying to put together all her information (sense data, stories of an afterlife, and the rituals of mourning) is a picture of the mind at work.'

An elegy does not usually begin in such a stark manner, but in this poem it is the young uncomprehending child who speaks. It is as if Bishop can present us immediately with a grim picture. The repetition is chilling:

> In the cold, cold parlor
> my mother laid out Arthur

Bishop's mother is seldom mentioned in her poems, and she is mentioned here in a matter-of-fact way. The little body is spoken of in line 2, but the rest of the stanza describes the furnishings in the room. The royal presences lend the moment importance and dignity.

In line 7, the attention shifts to the stuffed bird on the table beneath the pictures. The stuffed loon, like Arthur, is dead. It has been

> shot and stuffed by Uncle
> Arthur, Arthur's father.

The room is 'cold, cold', and to the child observer it is as if everything has been frozen in time: the lifeless corpse, the still photographs, the stuffed loon. The use of repetition throughout the poem reflects the mind of a child attempting to make sense of the world it is describing.

In stanza 2 the child is wholly preoccupied with the bird, the violence of its death its silence, its cold stance and, contradicting everything else, its attractiveness ('caressable' and 'much to be desired' red glass eyes). Little Arthur is forgotten. Attention has shifted to the object:

> on his white, frozen lake,
> the marble-topped table.

The bird hasn't said a word since it was shot (nor of course has little Arthur since his death, but this is implied, never stated), and there is a sense of mystery, power and separateness in Bishop's phrase 'He kept his own counsel' in line 14. The child's mind works by association: an idea in stanza 1 recurs later; a phrase, 'deep and white', used once to describe the loon's breast, is later echoed in Bishop's description of the snow; and the red of the loon's eye recurs in the red of the Maple Leaf, little Arthur's red hair and the red royal clothes.

The child's gaze is broken by her mother's words:

> 'Come,' said my mother,
> 'Come and say good-bye
> to your little cousin Arthur.'

She is lifted up to place a lily of the valley in Arthur's hand. The poem's setting is the familiar, domestic world of the parlour, but death and the coffin turn the familiar into the strange. The mother asks the child to look on death and to put 'one lily of the valley' in her dead little cousin's hand. The coffin becomes in the child's mind 'a little frosted cake' and the loon is now seen almost as predator, as something alive:

> Arthur's coffin was
> a little frosted cake,
> and the red-eyed loon eyed it
> from his white, frozen lake.

Stanza 4 focuses on little Arthur. The language also marks the simplicity of childhood grappling with a first death:

> Arthur was very small.
> He was all white, like a doll
> that hadn't been painted yet.
> Jack Frost had started to paint him
> the way he always painted
> the Maple Leaf (Forever).

She imagines first that the body is like an unpainted doll, then that Jack Frost had 'started to paint him'. The child-speaker knows how Jack Frost always 'paints' the leaves red in autumn, specifically the maple leaf, and this thought is immediately connected with her being in Canada and the maple leaf as it is mentioned in the Canadian national anthem: 'the Maple Leaf (Forever).' The reference to the hair as red strokes/brush strokes is another indication of how the child's mind can process and transfer ideas: she imagines that hair on the white body has been painted red.

The 'Forever' associated with the Maple Leaf is the forever of Canadian patriotism.

The 'forever' in the last line of the stanza is the same word but with a different meaning; this time it signifies the finality of death:

> Jack Frost had dropped the brush
> and left him white, forever.

The poem ends with an imagined royal court, but there is no trace of a Christian or religious consolation. And the child invents this world, more fairytale than paradise; the mother does not offer one.

The cold is felt throughout the poem. Words such as 'cold, cold', 'white, frozen', 'marble-topped', 'white, cold', 'lily of the valley', 'frosted cake', 'white, frozen lake', 'all white', Jack Frost', 'white, forever' and the effect of repetition turn the parlour white and cold. But the last stanza brings warmth, pomp and ceremony:

> The gracious royal couples
> were warm in red and ermine;
> their feet were well wrapped up
> in the ladies' ermine trains.

Even the white of the ermine seems warm. The gracious presences of the two couples in the two pictures are warm, comfortable, welcoming. They invite little Arthur to join them; it is they who make possible his future.

> They invited Arthur to be
> the smallest page at court.

This, in the eyes of the observing child, is how and where little Arthur will live now that he has died.

In the closing lines, however, the speaker's fears return: Arthur is in his coffin. It is winter. How can Arthur escape from his coffin in the 'cold, cold parlor' and join the faraway royal court?

> But how could Arthur go,
> clutching his tiny lily,
> with his eyes shut up so tight
> and the roads deep in snow?

The details here ('clutching', 'tiny', 'tight', 'deep') suggest vulnerability, terror and fear. The final image in the poem is of Arthur, a child all alone in the world, incapable of reaching safety and a place he could call home.

Instead of heaven as Arthur's destination or Christian consolation, it is Bishop's imagination that makes possible and gives new life to the dead little boy; she imagines him, frightened, and wonders how he will travel 'roads deep in snow'.

Death is a powerful displacer. Of course there is a danger that biographical details will colour our reading of a poem too much, but the reader, realising that this poem was written by a woman whose father had died when she was eight months old and whose mother disappeared from her life when she was five, may see how fully 'First Death in Nova Scotia' reflects Bishop's uncomprehending childhood and her attempts to come to terms with absence and death.

In the Waiting Room

The poem begins with a place, a location, in this instance Elizabeth Bishop's own birthplace; it focuses on her place in the world and the distances between the personal world and the wider world beyond. There are references to 'in' and 'outside' throughout the poem.

In February 1918, Elizabeth Bishop was but a few days from her seventh birthday and the poem is spoken in the innocent, naive, unaffected voice of a seven year old. There is a matter-of-factness about it:

> In Worcester, Massachusetts,
> I went with Aunt Consuelo
> to keep her dentist's appointment
> and sat and waited for her
> in the dentist's waiting room.

The setting consists of unglamorous places: a waiting room suggests a form of displacement. In the waiting room one is neither here nor there. The ordinary world has been left behind: it is outside the door and can only be re-entered through that same door. The fact that it is a dentist's waiting room adds another dimension: waiting often involves tension, uneasiness and it often anticipates pain, but Bishop is not attending the dentist, merely accompanying her aunt. Later in the poem, a painful cry is heard from the dentist's room. The poem also explores how childhood can sometimes view adulthood harshly.

The scene is built up gradually. Bishop begins with town, state, waiting room, then the time of year.

Elizabeth Bishop sees herself as the odd-one-out. Everyone else in the waiting room is an adult:

> The waiting room
> was full of grown-up people,
> arctics and overcoats,
> lamps and magazines.

The adults in the room are never given personalities or individuality and are described in terms of what they wear. She is so shy of them that in line 64 she says 'I scarcely dared to look'.

The child-speaker in the poem retreats into the world of the *National Geographic* and carefully studies photographs of places and people very far away. Everything she sees in the magazine is different. The volcanic landscape with its black ashes and 'rivulets of fire' is different and in sharp contrast with a New England town in winter. The people she sees are also different: first the two explorers Osa and Martin Johnson in their travellers' attire and then 'the dead man slung on the pole', black women, black babies. The women have mutilated themselves in order to be sexually attractive. That this is a form of enslavement is not fully grasped by the seven-year-old child: it is certainly not articulated in the poem, but the reader recognises Bishop's genuine revulsion on seeing what they have done. 'In the Waiting Room' records Bishop's early and growing awareness of herself and the choices that await her, especially as a woman.

The language is simple and clear. The reader is presented with no difficulty in understanding what the child describes, but what is more important and interesting is Bishop's response.

> A dead man slung on a pole
> – 'Long Pig,' the caption said.
> Babies with pointed heads
> wound round and round with string;
> black, naked women with necks
> wound round and round with wire
> like the necks of light bulbs.

The dead man or 'Long Pig' will be eaten by the Polynesian cannibals; the babies have had their heads reshaped and the women's necks have been elongated, 'their breasts were horrifying.' This is inflicted and self-inflicted violence, and the child in the waiting room finds it repulsive and yet:

> I read it right straight through.
> I was too shy to stop.

Her emotions on reading the magazine are not shared or discussed with anyone in the room, and, having read and having been horrified, she attempts to objectify the experience by closing the magazine and observing mundane details:

> And then I looked at the cover:
> the yellow margins, the date.

The child has entered into an experience and, though not unmoved, she has retreated from it.

The child's gaze is abruptly broken at line 36. There is the cry of pain from the dentist's room. The dentist is unintentionally causing Aunt Consuelo to suffer:

> Suddenly from inside,
> came an *oh!* of pain
> – Aunt Consuelo's voice –
> not very loud or long.

The attitude to the pain in the next room is not Bishop's attitude to the pain of head shaping and neck lengthening she saw a moment before in the *National Geographic*. Instead, she sees her aunt as foolish and timid; she is neither surprised nor embarrassed:

> I wasn't at all surprised;
> even then I knew she was
> a foolish, timid woman.
> I might have been embarrassed,
> but wasn't.

However, the poem takes an interesting and unexpected direction when Bishop, the seven-year-old girl sees herself as a grown woman and as foolish as her aunt.

> What took me
> completely by surprise
> was that it was me:
> my voice, in my mouth.

Her aunt's cry becomes the speaker's own cry. The woman and the girl are one. It is as if the girl has no option but to grow up to become the kind of woman she does not want to be.

The child-speaker imagines, 'without thinking at all', that 'I was my foolish aunt', and, in a surreal leap of the imagination, both the aunt 'from inside' and the girl 'in' the waiting room are falling:

> I – we – were falling, falling,
> our eyes glued to the cover
> of the *National Geographic*,
> February, 1918.

The eyes are 'glued' to reality, to the magazine, the month and year, and then the aunt is forgotten about for 21 lines. The 'I' takes over and the defining 'I' is used nine times. Like Alice, she is falling but there is no Wonderland as such. It is, however, she says at lines 72–73, the strangest thing that could ever happen.

She hangs on to hard facts: her imminent birthday in three days.

> I was saying it to stop
> the sensation of falling off
> the round, turning world
> into cold, blue-black space.

The date of the experience recorded in the poem and given in the poem itself, in the closing lines, is 5 February and the facts give way to intense feeling:

> But I felt: you are an *I*,
> You are an *Elizabeth*

What she discovers with a sharp perceptiveness is that there is only one Elizabeth Bishop, separate, unique, but that that unique individual self is also one of womankind and destined perhaps to become like the women she has been thinking about – the trapped black women, the foolish Aunt Consuelo:

> you are one of *them*.
> *Why* should you be one, too?

Here the child-speaker wants to hang on, to stay on earth, and not to tumble into space or unknown territory.

Line 64 brings a lull. The language is no longer so insistent (the 'you are', 'you are' of the previous lines) and Bishop attempts to take her bearings:

> I scarcely dared to look
> to see what it was I was.
> I gave a sidelong glance
> – I couldn't look any higher –
> at shadowy gray knees,
> trousers and skirts and boots
> and different pairs of hands
> lying under the lamps.

This return to the familiar is comforting, and yet she is still shy, uneasy, and deeply aware that this moment has somehow altered and clarified her understanding of herself, that it is a moment of such insight and understanding that it will affect the rest of her life:

> I knew that nothing stranger
> had ever happened, that nothing
> stranger could ever happen.

And this sends her back to the earlier question (line 63 – '*Why* should you be one, too?') which Bishop now repeats with a different emphasis. The question at line 63 implies that Bishop resisted becoming a certain kind of woman. Now the question opens out into a question that explores the mystery of existence, the very strangeness of being alive:

> Why should I be my aunt,
> or me, or anyone?

It then opens out further to include the questions whether and how there are connections between people so obviously different:

> What similarities –
> boots, hands, the family voice
> I felt in my throat, or even
> the *National Geographic*
> and those awful hanging breasts –
> held us all together
> or made us all just one?

The child, almost seven, has been unnerved by the black women and their 'horrifying' breasts, their 'awful hanging breasts'. This is the outside world. She is also unnerved by the aunt's cry 'from inside',

> a cry of pain that could have
> got loud and worse but hadn't?

The poem ends with Bishop feeling faint and her sense of the waiting room

> sliding
> beneath a big black wave,
> another, and another.

The fainting spell is a loss of consciousness and then she is back in the waiting room. In the short closing section of the poem, there is an intense awareness again of place, outside and inside, and the specifics of time. In the first section of the poem, outside meant winter (line 6); later outside includes Polynesian culture and, in the final reference to a world beyond the waiting room, we are told that a war is being fought.

The young Elizabeth Bishop has waited in the waiting room. The place could be read as a symbol of childhood, a time spent waiting for adulthood, but everything that is spoken of in relation to the world beyond the immediate one is frightening, strange, confusing (what the academic Brett Millier calls 'the awful otherness of the inevitable world'). Elizabeth Bishop's relationship with that world and her feeling of not belonging to it recurs in many of her poems.

Emily Dickinson
(1830–1886)

Contents	Page

Emily Dickinson's house, Amherst, Massachusetts.

The Overview

Every true poet is unique and Dickinson's uniqueness is visually and verbally striking. She is the most instantly recognisable of poets. Her idiosyncratic genius is clearly seen in the imaginatively intense short lyrics without titles; the eccentric, unconventional punctuation; the capitalisations; the irregularities; the cryptic, puzzling images; the dash; the rhymes and half-rhymes; the hymn metre; the vigorous rhythm. Many of the lines in a Dickinson poem reach an abrupt and definite end; when she uses the run-on line, as she does in the closing stanzas of 'A narrow Fellow in the Grass', she does so effectively. It is said that, in Emily Dickinson's poetry, 'language remains itself and becomes at the same time brand new.'

These ten poems capture Dickinson's different moods, her extreme psychological states: there are moments of sudden intoxication ('I taste a liquor never brewed'), hopefulness, pain and suffering ('The Soul has Bandaged moments—'); there is a detailed exploration of the meaning of death; a delight in the world of nature ('A Bird came down the Walk') and its danger and mystery ('A narrow Fellow in the Grass').

Though Dickinson lived in Amherst for most of her life and lived in her father's house all of that time, it is characteristic that she only mentions Amherst by name in two of her 1,775 poems. Other personal details are never explicitly revealed in her poetry. It is not always possible to say if the poet is addressing another or if she is speaking to herself. In Adrienne Rich's words, Dickinson writes of 'the intense inner event, the personal and psychological'.

Many of her themes are abstract – she frequently writes about life, time, death and eternity – but her abstractions are often rendered vividly and imaginatively in her work. In 'I taste a liquor never brewed', she sees 'Seraphs swing their snowy Hats'; describing a numbed sensation, she says 'The Nerves sit ceremonious, like Tombs—'; and the poem 'I felt a Funeral, in my Brain' is typical of Emily Dickinson in its description of an interior state in such distinct, memorable, physical terms. Though short, the poems are intense. Compression is trademark. Her poems have been described as 'the drama of process'.

She is also a brilliant observer of nature. She watches a bird eat a raw worm or she sees the snake, 'a spotted shaft', and feels 'a tighter breathing'. On winter afternoons she notices 'a certain Slant of light' and finds it oppressive.

There is in her poetry an intense awareness of the private, inner self. 'Vesuvius at Home' was how she once described her domestic world, suggesting as it does an image of great emotional force and power. The poems often strike the reader as self-contained, riddling, elusive. Her tone is often confident, strong-willed and knowledgeable, as in 'I could bring You Jewels — had I a mind to'. She wrote for herself primarily; there was no audience for her work during her lifetime. In a letter she said 'Pardon my sanity in a world insane'.

Dickinson's poems on mortality ('I felt a Funeral, in my Brain' and 'I heard a Fly buzz — when I died') sometimes lead to uncertainty or despair ('And hit a World, at every plunge,/ And Finished knowing—then—' or 'And then the Windows failed—and then/ I could not see to see—'). The chilling mood is in stark contrast to a playful, delightful or happily confident note which is found in such poems as 'I taste a liquor never brewed' or 'I could bring You Jewels—had I a mind to'.

In one of these ten poems she adopts a persona: in 'A narrow Fellow in the Grass' she is remembering a time 'when as a Boy, and Barefoot' she saw a snake. 'I' is frequently used, but 'There's a certain Slant of light', 'After great pain, a formal feeling comes—' and 'The Soul has Bandaged moments—', where 'I' never occurs, achieve a different effect.

Dickinson believed that 'to shut our eyes is travel'. For her, the inner world of mind and imagination and heart were sufficient and these she explored brilliantly and honestly. 'My business,' she said in a letter, 'is circumference'. By circumference, one of her favourite words, she meant the 'comprehension of essentials'.

The interior of Emily Dickinson's home.

Biographical Notes

Emily Elizabeth Dickinson was born on 10 December 1830 in a house which her grandfather had built on Main Street, Amherst, Massachusetts. She was the second of three children born into a conventional Protestant family. Her grandfather was a lawyer, a pillar of the church and a founder of Amherst College; her father was also a lawyer. Amherst, at that time, was a small farming community of less than three thousand people.

Little is known of her childhood. When she was two and a half she stayed with her twenty-one-year-old aunt in Monson, twenty miles away, while Mrs Dickinson was recovering after the birth of her third child, Lavinia. Such details must seem trivial until one realises how little, outwardly, seems to have happened to Dickinson. In adult life, Dickinson rarely left home and her aunt, in a letter to her sister, tells of how, on that same journey, Dickinson's first, there was thunder and lightning which the little girl called 'the fire'. These are Emily Dickinson's first recorded words.

Emily Dickinson grew up in Puritan, small-town, New England and later she was to say that she viewed the world 'New Englandly' (Poem 285). Many books have argued that her childhood was bleak, but in a letter written when she was fourteen she says 'I am growing handsome very fast indeed! I expect I shall be the belle of Amherst when I reach my 17th year'. When she was sixteen she won second prize in the Bread Division at the local cattle show, and in 1858 was one of the judges. That same year she wrote 'Amherst is alive with fun this winter' and yet, when Dickinson was twenty-two, she wrote to her brother Austin, 'I wish we were children now. I wish we were *always* children, how to grow up I don't know'.

After primary school, Emily Dickinson attended Amherst Academy from 1840 to 1847, which she enjoyed very much. The Principal of the Academy remembered Emily Dickinson as 'a very bright, but rather delicate and frail looking girl; an excellent scholar, of exemplary deportment, faithful in all school duties; but somewhat shy and nervous. Her compositions were strikingly original; and in both thought and style seemed beyond her years, and always attracted much attention in the school and, I am afraid, excited not a little envy.' Another source described Emily Dickinson as one of 'the wits of the school' and named her as one of the liveliest contributors to *Forest Leaves*, the school paper, no copy of which survives.

At Amherst Academy, Dickinson's subjects included Latin, history, botany, geology and mental philosophy. A study of her poetry has revealed that the largest group of words in Dickinson's vocabulary drawn from special sources is drawn from contemporary technology or science; 328 words are technical terms generally found only in scientific or academic discourse.

In September 1847 Emily Dickinson attended Mount Holyoke Female Seminary at South Hadley, ten miles south of Amherst, but left after ten months or two terms.

The reasons for her not continuing there have been given as poor health, homesickness, her father wanting her at home, her dislike of the place and so on, but nothing definite is known. Subjects studied at Mount Holyoke included chemistry, physiology, algebra and ancient history.

Mount Holyoke was known for its missionary spirit and the young women were encouraged to become Christian and to commit themselves to Christianity in an open and public manner. Mary Lyon, who had founded the Seminary in 1837, divided the girls into three groups: 'No-hopers', 'Hopers' and 'Christians'. Emily Dickinson was classed among the 'No-hopers' and, in a letter written during her final term there, she said that she regretted the 'golden opportunity' of becoming a Christian but 'it is hard for me to give up the world'.

Back in Amherst, Dickinson dissociated herself from revivalist, religious fervour. An excerpt from a letter dated January 1850 gives us an idea of nineteen-year-old Dickinson's stance: 'Sewing Society has commenced again – and held its first meeting last week – now all the poor will be helped – the cold warmed – the warm cooled – the hungry fed – the thirsty attended to – the ragged clothed – and this suffering – tumbled down world will be helped to its feet again – which will be quite pleasant to all. I don't attend – notwithstanding my high approbation – which must puzzle the public exceedingly . . . – and my hardheartedness gets me many prayers'. Her closest friends and her sister Lavinia were answering Christ's call but Dickinson in that same letter says: 'I am standing alone in rebellion . . . I can't tell you what they have found, but they think it is something precious. I wonder if it is?'

It is at this time also that Emily Dickinson began to write poems. The very first poem in *The Complete Poems* is a poem dated 'Valentine week, 1850' when she was twenty, but it was not until her late twenties that Dickinson began to write what became her prolific output. From the beginning she was an original and her earliest work has all the characteristics of her idiomatic style and originality.

Though she rejected conventional religion, Dickinson never openly rebelled. Her biographer Richard B Sewell says that 'she was not geared to rebellion. She had been a model child, a good girl in school, a dutiful daughter. She had to find another way'. And one of those ways was undoubtedly the 1,775 poems which she wrote. In one poem (569) Dickinson writes about how much poetry and poets meant to her, more than Nature itself or God in Heaven. It begins:

> I reckon — when I count at all —
> First — Poets — Then the Sun —
> Then Summer — Then the Heaven of God —
> And then — the List is done —
>
> But, looking back — the First so seems
> To Comprehend the Whole —
> The Others look a needless Show —
> So I write — Poets — All —

Though Emily Dickinson was not part of the Revival Movement, she was deeply spiritual. When a friend died in Worcester, Massachusetts, she wrote to the minister there to enquire if 'he was willing to die, and if you think him at Home, I should love so much to know certainly, that he was today in Heaven'. The friend was Benjamin Franklin Newton, a law student in her father's office from 1847 to 1849. He was nine years older than her, an important influence who believed she would be a poet, but he died in 1853.

On 15 April 1862 Emily Dickinson, at thirty-one, wrote to Thomas Wentworth Higginson, enclosing four poems and asking 'if my Verse is alive? . . .' and 'Should you think it breathed'. Higginson was a man of letters and former Minister of the Free Church. He was a liberal thinker interested in promoting women writers. He had written an article in the *Atlantic Monthly* advising aspiring writers, and Dickinson, who by now had written three hundred poems, felt a need for criticism. Higginson, not fully understanding her work, advised her to tidy the 'irregularity' of her poems and her first printed poems have been 'tidied' up by him – he altered Dickinson's original punctuation, rhymes and vocabulary. It was not until 1955, with the publication of Thomas H Johnson's edition, that Emily Dickinson's work was restored to its original form. In that same letter to Higginson, written nine years after Newton had died, she wrote 'for several years, my lexicon – was my only companion –'.

The Dickinson family had to leave their home, known as 'The Mansion', for a clapboard house on North Pleasant Street, Amherst, where they lived from 1840–1855. By 1856 the Dickinsons, having overcome some financial difficulties, had returned to the Dickinson Homestead on Main Street, where Emily Dickinson had been born. We also know that by this time Dickinson had stopped going to church, though she remained deeply religious in her own way. A poem dated c.1862 contains the lines:

> Some keep the Sabbath going to Church —
> I keep it, staying at Home —

and in a letter written around 1884 Dickinson reveals her religious views: 'When Jesus tells us about his father, we distrust him. When he shows us his Home, we turn away, but when he confides to us that he is "acquainted with grief," we listen, for that is an Acquaintance of our own.'

When young, she took lessons in voice and piano, and music became a very important part of Emily Dickinson's life. She played the piano, especially late at night when the rest of the house was asleep, and the hymns which she had heard in church, hymns such as 'Our God, our help in ages past', were to become the metrical pattern for her poems.

So little is known of Emily Dickinson's adult life that the few details we do know have assumed an almost mythic quality, but it has been argued that something cataclysmic and decisive happened when she was thirty or thereabouts. On 25 April 1862 she wrote to Higginson: 'I had a terror – since September – I could tell to none – and so I sing, as the Boy does by the Burying Ground – because I am afraid . . .'

An unhappy love affair has been suggested. Benjamin Franklin Newton, Reverend Charles Wadsworth, Samuel Bowles and Thomas Wentworth Higginson were certainly important in her life, but Newton died in the early 1850s and she only met Higginson face to face twice. Here is an extract from Higginson's diary in which he describes his first meeting with Dickinson:

> a step like a pattering child's in entry . . . a little plain woman with two smooth bands of reddish hair and a face with no good feature . . . She came to me with two day-lilies, which she put in a sort of childlike way into my hand and said 'These are my introduction', in a soft, frightened, breathless childlike voice – and added under her breath, 'Forgive me if I am frightened; I never see strangers, and hardly know what to say'.

Ted Hughes writes that 'the central themes of the poems have suggested to many readers that the key event was a great and final disappointment in her love for some particular man, about this time' [early 1860s]. Three draft letters addressed to one whom she called 'Master' were found among her papers when she died. These are intense and passionate letters, but the identity of Master has never been known. The secret remains just that. What is significant is that in 1862, Dickinson wrote 366 poems; in 1863, 141 poems; and in 1864, 174 poems: more than one-third of her 1,775 poems were written during these three years when she was in her early thirties.

Philip Larkin put it like this: 'If Emily Dickinson could write 700 pages of poems and three volumes of letters without making clear the nature of her preoccupations, then we can be sure that she was determined to keep it hidden, and that her inspiration derived in part from keeping it hidden.' He concludes: 'The price she paid was that of appearing to posterity as perpetually unfinished and wilfully eccentric.'

And Dickinson herself wrote in poem number 1129:

> Tell all the Truth but tell it slant —
> Success in Circuit lies
> Too bright for our infirm Delight
> The Truth's superb surprise
> As Lightning to the Children eased
> With explanation kind
> The Truth must dazzle gradually
> Or every man be blind —

Dickinson rarely left her home in Amherst. In a letter dated 1853, when she was twenty-three, she wrote 'I do not go from home'. She read Shakespeare, the Brownings, George Eliot, the Brontes, Keats, Emerson, Ruskin, Sir Thomas Browne, the Bible, especially the Book of Revelations; she read the newspaper daily and wrote over a thousand letters. She even used letters to communicate with her brother Austin and sister-in-law, Susan Gilbert, who lived next door. Dickinson wrote more letters to Susan Gilbert Dickinson than to any other individual. Frequently her letters contained poems and her letters and poems share many stylistic similarities.

Dickinson spent ten months away from home in a boarding seminary when she was seventeen and in all she made seven trips from home during her lifetime, to Boston (for eye treatment), Washington D.C. and Philadelphia, but her life was very much lived indoors in Amherst, Massachusetts. Yet Dickinson chose to stay at home. Her niece, Martha Dickinson Bianchi, tells us that she once 'repeated to Aunt Emily what a neighbour had said – that time must pass very slowly for her, who never went anywhere – and she flashed back with Browning's line: "Time, why, Time was all I wanted!"' Once, when her niece visited her in her corner bedroom which overlooked the main street of Amherst in front and the path to her brother Austin's house to the side, Emily Dickinson pretended to lock the door with an imaginary key and said 'here's freedom'.

She always lived in her father's house. 'Probably no poet ever lived so much and so purposefully in one house; even, in one room,' says Adrienne Rich. But intellectually Dickinson was well-travelled. There are other well-known personal details: she wore white (one of her white dresses is displayed at her home in Amherst); she would lower little treats for the local children from her bedroom in a basket; when her nephew died from typhoid, aged eight, Emily Dickinson went next door for the first time in fifteen years.

Mabel Todd, who came to live in Amherst in August 1881, when she was twenty-six, wrote to her parents on 6 November 1881 and described 'a lady whom the people call the *Myth*':

> 'She is a sister of Mr Dickinson, & seems to be the climax of all the family oddity. She has not been outside of her own house in fifteen years, except once to see a new church, when she crept out at night, & viewed it by moonlight. No one who calls upon her mother & sister ever see her, but she allows little children once in a great while, & one at a time, to come in, when she gives them cake or candy, or some nicety, for she is very fond of little ones. But more often she lets down the sweetmeat by a string, out of a window, to them. She dresses wholly in white, & her mind is said to be perfectly wonderful. She writes finely, but no one ever sees her . . . No one knows the cause of her isolation, but of course there are dozens of reasons assigned.'

[Mabel Todd was the wife of a professor at Amherst College and she and Dickinson's brother Austin became lovers in 1882, a relationship which lasted until Austin's death in 1895. Austin Dickinson was fifty-two, while Mabel Loomis Todd was twenty-five. The two spouses knew of the relationship and the affair was widely known in Amherst. Dickinson, though she led a hidden life, was aware of these domestic difficulties and tensions. She was also aware of difficulties at a national level: the American Civil War was being fought, and many young men from Amherst went to war and never came home.]

After their mother's death in 1882 and towards the end of her own life, Dickinson and her sister Lavinia were living alone in their Amherst home. They were cared for by a servant and it was there that Emily Dickinson died, on 15 May 1886 of Bright's disease. The day before she died, Dickinson wrote to her cousins, the Norcross sisters, her final, short note: 'Little Cousins, – Called back. – Emily.'

Emily Dickinson had left directions for her funeral: her body was to be prepared for burial in one of her own white dresses, with a sprig of violets and a single pink orchid pinned at the throat. The coffin was also to be white and it was to be carried out the back door, around through the garden, through the open barn from front to back, and then through the grassy fields, 'three fields away', to the family plot in Amherst's West Cemetery, always in sight of the house. She was borne to her grave by six Irishmen, all of whom had worked at one time on her father's grounds.

At her funeral service which was held at the Dickinson home, Thomas Wentworth Higginson, whom she had written to twenty-four years earlier seeking advice, read Emily Bronte's poem 'Last Lines'. According to Higginson it was 'a favorite with our friend, who has put on that Immortality which she seemed never to have laid off':

> No coward soul is mine,
> No trembler in the world's storm-troubled sphere!
> I see Heaven's glories shine,
> And Faith shines equal, arming me from Fear . . .

And on her gravestone in West Cemetery, Amherst, are the words 'Called Back'.

During her lifetime, only eleven (some studies say seven, others ten) of her poems were published, anonymously, and after her death Dickinson's poems were published gradually. On going through her sister's belongings, Lavinia discovered a small box containing about 900 poems, arranged and sewn together in sixty little bundles or fascicles which make up two-thirds of Dickinson's poetry. Though it was known that Dickinson wrote poetry, no-one knew until after her death the range or the extent.

Lavinia asked Mabel Loomis Todd to prepare a selection of Dickinson's poems for publication. Todd asked Higginson to help and in 1890 they published 115 of Dickinson's poems in edited form. The book, *Poems by Emily Dickinson*, was a success. There were six printings of the book in six months. The following year, Todd and Higginson published *Poems, Second Series*, containing 166 poems. *Poems, Third Series*, edited by Todd, was published in 1896.

The first selection of 115 poems, with titles added, had certain words and punctuation altered to suit the prevailing tastes of the time. It was not until 1955, sixty-nine years after Dickinson's death, that an accurate and faithful edition of her poems was published. For example in the 1890 edition we read the following:

> There's a certain slant of light,
> On winter afternoons,
> That oppresses, like the weight
> Of cathedral tunes.

This is what Dickinson wrote:

> There's a certain Slant of light,
> Winter Afternoons —
> That oppresses, like the Heft
> Of Cathedral Tunes —

In the original, Dickinson's use of dashes, her capitalisation of certain words, her omission of the word 'on' in line two, gives the poem far greater force and focus. When printed as Dickinson intended, the poems, in Adrienne Rich's words, became 'jagged, personal, uncontrollable'. Ted Hughes has said of those Emily Dickinson dashes that they are 'an integral part of her method and style, and cannot be translated to commas, semicolons and the rest without deadening the wonderfully naked voltage of the poems'.

Ted Hughes also says of Emily Dickinson that 'There is the slow, small metre, a device for bringing each syllable into close-up, as under a microscope; there is the deep, steady focus, where all the words lie in precise and yet somehow fine relationships, so that the individual syllables are on the point of slipping into utterly new meanings, all pressing to be uncovered . . .'

Higginson, to whom Dickinson had sent four of her poems and who was one of the first to read her work, speaks of Dickinson's 'curious indifference to all conventional rules of verse' but wisely adds that 'when a thought takes one's breath away, a lesson on grammar seems an impertinence'.

●

Dickinson herself 'found ecstasy in living': the seasons, birdsong, sunset became the subject matter for her poems. And the darker aspects of life – a storm, 'a certain slant of light', our final moments, death itself – all were of interest to her. Though she wrote in a small way the big themes are all there: Life, Time, Nature and Eternity. And she uses language in a fresh and original way: 'Friday I tasted life. It was a vast morsel. A circus passed the house – still I feel the red in my mind'. She described herself as 'small, like the Wren, and my hair is bold, like the chestnut burr– and my eyes, like the Sherry in the Glass, that the Guest leaves.' Or she can capture a marvellously atmospheric image in a single line: 'The Day undressed – Herself –'

Sean Dunne described her poems as 'concise fragments from a diary, a logbook of the mind's voyages, and where Melville wrote of the sea and Whitman of the plains, she wrote of a space equally vast: her own mind.' Like Henry David Thoreau, she believed that self exploration is the only worthy kind of travel. Emily Dickinson understood the vast imaginative, intellectual world when she wrote:

The Brain — is wider than the Sky —

The Brain is deeper than the sea —

And it is worth remembering that Sewell concludes his detailed and wide-ranging biography of Dickinson with a reminder: 'The whole truth about Emily Dickinson will elude us always; she seems wilfully to have seen to that . . . There is a feeling of incompleteness, of areas still to be explored, of mysteries that still beckon.'

●

Of all poets in English, Emily Dickinson is one of the most strikingly original and eccentric. This is immediately seen in the unconventional capitalisations and the use of the dash. Although capitalisation was used earlier in English poetry, in Elizabethan printing houses capitalisation was up to the compositor and personified abstractions, the names of animals, plants, rocks, or minerals were capitalised. Later, Pope and Johnson, for example, in the eighteenth century, used capitals especially for abstractions, such as in this line from Johnson's 'A Short Song of Congratulation': 'Pomp and Pleasure, Pride and Plenty'. However, Dickinson gave the capital letter a new energy. Words which might have been considered commonplace (hats, sea, drum, walls, chill, bandaged, comb and so on) were given fresh attention and a more important role once capitalised.

The metre most often used by Dickinson was a conventional one, yet the poems sound anything but conventional because of the dash. Even if the poems were listened to and not read from the page, the dashes are felt and heard, and hearing the poem is every bit as important as seeing it on the page. Dashes are not only a striking feature of Emily Dickinson's poetry; her letters used a similar style and she often included poems in her letters. Here is part of a letter she wrote to console Mary Bowles, whose husband Samuel, whom, it has been argued, Emily Dickinson herself loved, had gone to Europe:

> Dear Mary –
> When the Best is gone – I know that other things are not of consequence – The Heart wants what it wants – or else it does not care –
> You wonder why I write – so – Because I cannot help – I like to have you know some care – so when your life gets faint for its other life – you can lean on us – We won't break, Mary. We look very small – but the Reed can carry weight . . .

Dashes were used much more frequently in the nineteenth century than they are today as Keats's or Queen Victoria's letters prove. Dashes, in Dickinson's hand, may be stately, dignified, measured; dashes can also be used for emphasis; they can suggest hesitation, the unknown.

POEMS

(The numbers given after each poem are the numbers given in *The Complete Poems of Emily Dickinson*; the first date is the conjectured date of composition; the second is the date of publication. Emily Dickinson gave none of her poems titles.)

I taste a liquor never brewed

I taste a liquor never brewed —
From Tankards scooped in Pearl —
Not all the Vats upon the Rhine
Yield such an Alcohol!

Inebriate of Air — am I —   5
And Debauchee of Dew —
Reeling - thro endless summer days —
From inns of Molten Blue —

When 'Landlords' turn the drunken Bee
Out of the Foxglove's door —   10
When Butterflies — renounce their 'drams' —
I shall but drink the more!

Till Seraphs swing their snowy Hats —
And saints — to windows run —
To see the little Tippler   15
Leaning against the — Sun —

Glossary

Line 2 Tankards: large open tub-like vessels, usually of wood, hooped with iron; a drinking vessel, formerly made of wooden staves and hooped; now, especially, a tall one-handled mug or jug, usually of pewter.

Line 2 scooped: hollowed out.

Line 3 Vats: large vessels used for the fermentation of alcohol.

Line 3 Not all the Vats upon the Rhine: a variant reading for line 3 is 'Not all the Frankfort Berries'.

Line 5 Inebriate: made drunk, exhilarated.

Line 6 Debauchee: one who has been seduced, one who over-indulges and neglects duty and allegiance.

Line 8 Molten: melted.

Line 11 renounce: reject.

Line 11 drams: a small drink of alcoholic liquor.

Line 13 Seraphs: angels of the highest of the nine orders.

Line 13 snowy Hats: haloes?

Line 15 Tippler: one who drinks often, but without getting drunk.

Line 16 Leaning against the – Sun –: a variant reading of this line is 'From Manzanilla come!', Manzanilla being in Cuba and famous for its rum.

> This is one of the very few poems published during Dickinson's lifetime. The *Springfield Daily Republican* printed it on 4 May 1861, when Dickinson was thirty. It was published anonymously as 'The May-Wine'.

Questions

1. The moment captured here is special. How does Dickinson convey that it is? How would you describe Dickinson's relationship with nature?

2. How would you describe the poet's mood in the second stanza?

3. List everything you find unusual about Emily Dickinson's poetry as revealed to us in this poem. Give reasons for your answer.

4. Would you agree that the final stanza is particularly imaginative? What details suggest this?

5. How does the poem achieve its momentum of increased happiness?

6. Consider the final dash. Of the ten poems by Dickinson on your course, seven end with a dash, one with a question mark and two with a full-stop. How significant is the punctuation here?

'Hope' is the thing with feathers

'Hope' is the thing with feathers —
That perches in the soul —
And sings the tune without the words —
And never stops — at all —

And sweetest — in the Gale — is heard —   5
And sore must be the storm —
That could abash the little Bird
That kept so many warm —

I've heard it in the chillest land —
And on the strangest Sea —   10
Yet, never, in Extremity,
It asked a crumb — of Me.

Glossary

Line 7 abash: astound, defeat.

In any anthology of quotations, the entries under Hope are many and varied. Among the best known are 'Hope deferred maketh the heart sick' from the Book of Proverbs in the Bible and Alexander Pope's couplet from his Essay on Man:

> 'Hope springs eternal in the human breast:
> Man never is, but always to be, blest.'

Dickinson in a poem written c. 1877 (poem number 1392) says:

> Hope is a strange invention –
> A Patent of the Heart –
> In unremitting action
> Yet never wearing out –
>
> Of this electric Adjunct
> Not anything is known
> But its unique momentum
> Embellish all we own –

This is Dickinson in her late forties. '"Hope" is the thing with feathers –' is dated about sixteen years earlier when Dickinson was thirty-one.

Questions

1. How does Emily Dickinson give something abstract a vivid presence? Do you think the 'little Bird' metaphor and associated images are effective? Why is the metaphor of the bird appropriate? Give reasons for your answers.

2. What qualities does the poet attribute to Hope? How do the words and rhythm capture these qualities? Examine, for example, the poet's use of 'And', its place in the line and the use of the dash.

3. What is Dickinson's attitude towards Hope? Is she grateful, perplexed?

4. What is the significance of 'chillest land' and 'strangest Sea'? What do such references tell us about the nature of Hope?

5. What do you think Dickinson reveals of herself in the last two lines?

There's a certain Slant of light

There's a certain Slant of light,
Winter Afternoons —
That oppresses, like the Heft
Of Cathedral Tunes —

Heavenly Hurt, it gives us —   5
We can find no scar,
But internal difference,
Where the Meanings, are —

None may teach it — Any —
'Tis the Seal Despair —   10
An imperial affliction
Sent us of the Air —

When it comes, the Landscape listens —
Shadows — hold their breath —
When it goes, 'tis like the Distance   15
On the look of Death —

Glossary

Line 1 Slant: an oblique reflection; in American English it can also mean a gibe, a sly hit, or sarcasm. Harold Bloom interprets the phrase 'Slant of light' to mean a way of looking at the world; he sees the 'slant of light' as an image for a particular slant in Dickinson's own consciousness.

Line 3 oppresses: overwhelms with a sense of heaviness in mind or body.

Line 3 Heft: weight (American English) also means vigorously strong.

Line 9 Any: here 'Any' means anything. Shortening the word in this way is part of Dickinson's personal idiom or form of expression.

Line 10 Seal: something that authenticates or confirms, a sign or symbol.

Line 11 imperial affliction: a state of acute pain or distress caused by a supreme authority.

Line 15/16 the Distance / On the look of Death —: In Richard Ellmann's and Robert O'Clair's edition of this poem, they supply the following observation in relation to the poem's last lines: In a letter dated 1878 Dickinson wrote 'I suppose there are depths in every Consciousness, from which we cannot rescue ourselves – to which none can go with us Mortally – the Adventure of Death –'.

> Light and its effect was something that interested Dickinson. For instance, in one letter she wrote that 'November always seemed to me the Norway of the year' and she told Higginson that the 'sudden light on Orchards' was one of the things that moved her to write. Winter, it seems, was her least favourite season, and in *Emily Dickinson: An Interpretative Biography*, Thomas H Johnson says she 'devoted the fewest poems to winter'. Dickinson, however, refers to summer in at least two hundred poems.

Questions

1. A certain mood is created in the opening lines of the poem. Identify this mood and say which details convey it best. What connection does Emily Dickinson make between 'a certain Slant of light' and 'Cathedral Tunes'?

2. Why, in your opinion, does Dickinson speak of 'Heavenly Hurt'? What causes such pain and suffering? What is the distinguishing characteristic of such hurt according to Dickinson in stanza two?

3. Would you agree that there is an oppressive air and a feeling of despair expressed here? What words or phrases suggest a feeling of helplessness?

4. The poet responds to the 'certain Slant of light'; so too does the 'Landscape'. Is their response similar? How?

5. Would you consider this an optimistic or a pessimistic poem?

6. What is the effect of the final line? Is the reader prepared for this ending by what has gone before?

I felt a Funeral, in my Brain

I felt a Funeral, in my Brain,
And Mourners to and fro
Kept treading — treading — till it seemed
That Sense was breaking through —

And when they all were seated,   5
A Service, like a Drum —
Kept beating — beating — till I thought
My Mind was going numb —

And then I heard them lift a Box
And creak across my Soul   10
With those same Boots of Lead, again,
Then Space — began to toll,

As all the Heavens were a Bell,
And Being, but an Ear,
And I, and Silence, some strange Race   15
Wrecked, solitary, here —

And then a Plank in Reason, broke,
And I dropped down, and down —
And hit a World, at every plunge,
And Finished knowing — then —   20

Glossary

Line 12 toll: to give out the slowly measured sounds of a bell when struck at uniform intervals, as at funerals.

Line 13 As all: as if all – another example of Dickinson's idiomatic style.

> Dickinson has been called the greatest realist of the interior that America has produced. 'I felt a funeral, in my Brain' is a poem of the interior. Here Emily Dickinson is imagining, anticipating, her own breakdown or her own funeral and death. It has also been suggested that the poem describes a fainting spell. Sewell, in his biography of Dickinson, says:
>
> *'I felt a Funeral, in my Brain' where Reason 'breaks' may be a tortured requiem on her hopes for Bowles [Samuel Bowles] both to love her and to accept her poetry; or it may commemorate a period of stagnation as a poet, when her mind, as she looked back, almost gave way under the weight of her despair; or it may refer to a mental or spiritual crisis of the sort she predicted . . . She seems as close to touching bottom here as she ever got. But there was nothing wrong with her mind when she wrote the poem.*

Questions

1. Identify how each stanza focuses on particular aspects of funeral rituals. What is unusual about this particular funeral?

2. Consider the effect of repetition in stanzas one, two and five. What do these repetitions suggest?

3. How would you describe the poet's mood throughout the poem? Which words and phrases, in your opinion, best convey this mood?

4. Is the poet's tone uncertain or fatalistic or both?

5. What is the effect of the thirteen 'ands' in the poem? What is the significance of 'And' at the beginning of each line in the final stanza?

6. Do you sense a change in the poem at the beginning of stanza four? How is this change achieved?

7. Comment on the significance of the imagery of 'Bell' and 'Ear' and 'strange Race' in stanza four.

8. What is the impact of the final stanza?

A Bird came down the Walk

A Bird came down the Walk —
He did not know I saw —
He bit an Angleworm in halves
And ate the fellow, raw,

And then he drank a Dew   5
From a convenient Grass —
And then hopped sidewise to the Wall
To let a Beetle pass —

He glanced with rapid eyes
That hurried all around —   10
They looked like frightened Beads, I thought —
He stirred his Velvet Head

Like one in danger, Cautious,
I offered him a Crumb
And he unrolled his feathers   15
And rowed him softer home —

Than Oars divide the Ocean,
Too silver for a seam —
Or Butterflies, off Banks of Noon
Leap, plashless as they swim.   20

Glossary

Line 3 Angleworm: any worm used as bait by anglers.

Line 20 plashless: splashless, without causing a splash.

Questions

1. Is this poem different in any way from the poems by Dickinson which have gone before? Is it a difference in subject matter or in style?

2. How does Dickinson respond to the bird? Which details indicate her powers of accurate observation? Which details indicate her attitude towards the bird? What do we learn about Dickinson from this poem?

3. What does this poem suggest about the world of nature and the relationship between man/woman and nature?

4. Can you suggest why this poem ends with a full stop?

5. What is the significance of the image of the butterflies in the final stanza? What is the connection between bird and butterfly?

6. How would you describe Dickinson's mood in this poem? Does the word 'Cautious' in line 13 refer to the bird or Dickinson or could it refer to both?

After great pain, a formal feeling comes

After great pain, a formal feeling comes —
The Nerves sit ceremonious, like Tombs —
The stiff Heart questions was it He, that bore,
And Yesterday, or Centuries before?

The Feet, mechanical, go round —   5
Of Ground, or Air, or Ought —
A Wooden way
Regardless grown,
A Quartz contentment, like a stone —

This is the Hour of Lead —   10
Remembered, if outlived,
As Freezing persons, recollect the Snow —
First — Chill — then Stupor — then the letting go —

Glossary

Line 1 formal: precise, ceremonious.

Line 3 He: Christ.

Line 6 Ought: what they are obliged to do (the feet move as they are obliged to move, mechanically); Helen Vendler suggests that *ought* here means nothing/void; it has also been suggested that Dickinson was thinking of 'aught' here, meaning 'in any respect at all'. In Shakespeare, Milton and Pope, *ought* and *aught* occur indiscriminately.

Line 9 Quartz: the commonest rock-forming mineral.

Line 13 Stupor: a state in which one feels deadened or dazed.

> 'After great pain, a formal feeling comes —' is dated circa 1862; Dickinson was thirty-two or so when she wrote it. It was first published in 1929.

Questions

1. What, according to Dickinson, occurs when one has experienced great pain? Is it a physical reaction only?

2. Why does Dickinson refer to Christ here? Why is there confusion in line 4?

3. Consider the shape and structure of the poem on the page. Can you suggest why stanza two is different from the others?

4. Which details capture best a state of numbness? Is 'Quartz contentment' similar to 'Wooden way' and 'Hour of Lead'? What is the significance of 'Remembered, if outlived'?

5. How would you describe the rhythm and how is it achieved?

6. Would you consider the final two lines hopeful in any way? Give reasons for your answer. Do you think this poem expresses an unusual view of human suffering?

I heard a Fly buzz — when I died

I heard a Fly buzz — when I died —
The Stillness in the Room
Was like the Stillness in the Air —
Between the Heaves of Storm —

The Eyes around — had wrung them dry —   5
And Breaths were gathering firm
For that last Onset — when the King
Be witnessed — in the Room —

I willed my Keepsakes — Signed away
What portion of me be   10
Assignable — and then it was
There interposed a Fly —

With Blue — uncertain stumbling Buzz —
Between the light — and me —
And then the Windows failed — and then   15
I could not see to see —

Glossary

Line 4 Heaves: force, great efforts.

Line 7 Onset: commencement, the action or act of beginning something; onset also means attack, assault.

Line 9 Keepsakes: things given to be kept for the sake of the giver.

Line 12 interposed: to put oneself forward or interfere in a matter.

> This poem says the impossible. *No one can speak the words 'I died'. Yet Dickinson writes of the moment of death as a moment inevitable and fascinating.*

Questions

1. Why is this poem written in the past tense? Once you have registered the unusual perspective from which this poem is written, trace through each stanza how the poet builds up the details of the story being told. Consider sensory details in your response.

2. How do you interpret the fly? Is it symbolic and, if so, what could it symbolise?

3. What is the poet's sense of the other persons in the room? How does she speak of witnessing the King (line 7)? Are her perceptions different from the others in the room? Is this a conventional nineteenth-century death-bed scene?

4. Consider the capitalised words. Do they form a short-hand narrative of their own?

5. The fly is mentioned in the opening line and again in line 12 which leads into the final stanza. What is the effect of beginning and ending with the fly?

6. It has been said that in this poem Emily Dickinson 'sees only disappointment' and that the poem tells of 'the terrible attempts of a soul to prolong life.' Would you agree with this view?

7. Is the light spoken of here the same as the light in 'There's a certain Slant of light'?

8. Which other poems by Emily Dickinson on your course would you compare with this one? Give reasons for your answer.

The Soul has Bandaged moments

The Soul has Bandaged moments —
When too appalled to stir —
She feels some ghastly Fright come up
And stop to look at her —

Salute her — with long fingers —   5
Caress her freezing hair —
Sip, Goblin, from the very lips
The Lover — hovered — o'er —
Unworthy, that a thought so mean
Accost a Theme — so — fair —   10

The soul has moments of Escape —
When bursting all the doors —
She dances like a Bomb, abroad,
And swings upon the Hours,

As do the Bee — delirious borne —   15
Long Dungeoned from his Rose —
Touch Liberty — then know no more,
But Noon, and Paradise —

The Soul's retaken moments —
When, Felon led along,   20
With shackles on the plumed feet,
And staples, in the Song,

The Horror welcomes her, again,
These, are not brayed of Tongue —

Glossary

Line 2 appalled: dismayed, made pale, made flat or stale, bereft of courage, etc. by sudden terror.

Line 7 Goblin: an evil or mischievous spirit; here it may mean 'goblin-like'.

Line 10 Accost: to approach or address.

Line 13 Bomb: in Dickinson's own lexicon, *Webster's American Dictionary*, 'bomb' has the alternative definition – 'the stroke upon the bell'.

Line 20 Felon: a wicked person; one guilty of a serious crime, a criminal.

Line 21 shackles: fastenings which confine the limbs and prevent free motion.

Line 21 plumed: feathered.

Line 22 staples: obstructions – the song is being held down.

Line 24 brayed: sounded harshly.

This is one of Dickinson's longer poems. It is irregular in shape with four four-line stanzas, one six-line stanza and a final two-line stanza.

Usually it is the body that is bandaged. Here, Dickinson imagines the soul as a physical and wounded entity.

Questions

1. What does the word 'bandaged' suggest?

2. How does Dickinson in this poem convey a feeling of helplessness? Is helplessness the only feeling associated with the soul in this instance? If not, how would you characterise the soul as revealed to us in the poem?

3. Who might Fright (line 3) stand for in the context of the poem? Lines 7–10 are particularly difficult. Who might the Goblin and the Lover be?

4. What change takes place at line 11? Is there anything to suggest what makes such change possible? What is the effect of such words as 'dances', 'Bomb', 'abroad', 'swings'? How does the third stanza contrast with what has gone before?

5. What is the significance of the bee simile? Do you think it an appropriate image? Why?

6. There is a shift of mood again in the final two stanzas. How is this achieved? Why does Horror welcome the Soul? Comment on the word 'welcomes'. Is it similar in any way to 'Caress' in line 6?

I could bring You Jewels — had I a mind to

I could bring You Jewels — had I a mind to —
But You have enough — of those —
I could bring You Odors from St Domingo —
Colors — from Vera Cruz —

Berries of the Bahamas — have I —   5
But this little Blaze
Flickering to itself — in the Meadow —
Suits Me — more than those —

Never a Fellow matched this Topaz —
And his Emerald Swing —   10
Dower itself — for Bobadilo —
Better — Could I bring?

📖 Glossary

Line 3 Odors: scents, fragrances.

Line 3 St Domingo: Santo Domingo in the Caribbean.

Line 4 Vera Cruz: city on the east coast of Mexico.

Line 5 Bahamas: a group of islands south-east of Florida.

Line 6 Blaze: a brilliant, splendid, clear light.

Line 11 Dower: dowry, the property which a woman brings to her husband in marriage.

Line 11 Bobadilo: braggart(?); in Ben Jonson's *Everyman in his Humour,* the character Bobadil is a swaggering boaster.

> The chapter containing the description of Jerusalem as a jewel in the biblical Book of Revelations was Dickinson's favourite chapter in the Bible. She called it the 'Gem Chapter'. Here jewels are rejected for something more precious.

❓ Questions

1. Who might the poet be speaking to here? Is it clear from the context? How would you describe her tone? Which words and phrases capture that tone?

2. Why does the speaker reject jewels, scents and other possible gifts? Are the exotic places – St Domingo, Vera Cruz, the Bahamas – significant? How do they compare with 'the Meadow' of line 7? What does she choose instead? What does the choice tell us about the poet?

3. What does Dickinson find attractive in 'this little Blaze'?

4. Compare this poem with 'I taste a liquor never brewed' as expressions of happiness and in terms of imagery drawn from nature.

5. What is the effect of the question mark with which the poem ends?

A narrow Fellow in the Grass

A narrow Fellow in the Grass
Occasionally rides —
You may have met Him — did you not
His notice sudden is —

The Grass divides as with a Comb —   5
A spotted shaft is seen —
And then it closes at your feet
And opens further on —

He likes a Boggy Acre
A Floor too cool for Corn —   10
Yet when a Boy, and Barefoot —
I more than once at Noon
Have passed, I thought, a Whip lash
Unbraiding in the Sun
When stooping to secure it   15
It wrinkled, and was gone —

Several of Nature's People
I know, and they know me —
I feel for them a transport
Of cordiality —   20

But never met this Fellow
Attended, or alone
Without a tighter breathing
And Zero at the Bone —

Glossary

Line 13 Whip lash: the lash or striking end of a whip.

Line 14 Unbraiding: unwinding, unravelling.

Line 20 cordiality: kindness, warm affection.

Line 24 Zero: a freezing sensation.

> 'A narrow Fellow in the Grass' was published as 'The Snake' during Dickinson's lifetime – in *Springfield Daily Republican*, 14 February 1866.
>
> In her poetry Dickinson sometimes adopts the voice of a persona. In 'A narrow Fellow in the Grass' the speaker is male and remembers boyhood. Dickinson has chosen to frame an eight-line stanza with two four-line stanzas.

Questions

1. Who is speaking here? What detail suggests a persona? What is revealed to us of the speaker? Consider, for example, the significance of the phrase 'Nature's People' (line 17).

2. There is a fascination with the 'narrow Fellow' for much of the poem but what feeling is expressed in the final stanza?

3. Which details do you think capture the snake best?

4. In the first three stanzas each line is self-contained and separate; in the final two stanzas Dickinson uses a run-on line. What is the effect of this?

General Questions

A. 'The poetry of Emily Dickinson is both startling and eccentric.' Discuss this view in the light of your reading the poems by Emily Dickinson on your course.

B. What would you identify as the principal preoccupations of Emily Dickinson as revealed to us in her poetry? In your answer, you should quote from or refer to the poems by Dickinson on your course.

C. Philip Larkin says of Emily Dickinson: Her epitaph might have been her own words: 'Nothing has happened but loneliness'. Discuss this view quoting from or referring to the Emily Dickinson poems on your course.

D. 'My business is circumference', says Emily Dickinson, and she defined circumference as 'the comprehension of essentials'. Discuss how she explores what is essential. In your answer you should quote from or refer to poems by Emily Dickinson on your course.

E. 'Dickinson's poetry is striking in its individual expression of happiness and suffering or death.' Discuss this statement, supporting your answer by quotation from or reference to the poems by Emily Dickinson on your course.

Critical Commentary

I taste a liquor never brewed

This poem begins with an intensely imagined moment. Here Dickinson speaks of a drink, unlike any ordinary drink, which she says she can taste:

> I taste a liquor never brewed —
> From Tankards scooped in Pearl —
> Not all the Vats upon the Rhine
> Yield such an Alcohol!

The moment is rare and special; the moment is hers. How special this particular drink is can be seen in line 1: liquor involves fermentation or distillation but this is a liquor which has not needed brewing. 'Tankards scooped in Pearl', line 2, is one of those lines which can be interpreted in different ways, yet labouring over this line is counterproductive. 'Tankards' can mean both large containers or drinking vessels. What is important here is the otherness or strangeness of the drink ('never brewed') and the unusual nature of the tankard. The tankard is made of pearl, or is so decorated that its surface looks as if it is hollowed out in pearl. The lustrous, beautiful pearl image makes the experience of drinking all the more special.

In line 3 Dickinson uses a negative to emphasise a positive. What she tastes is superior to what one of the world's finest, best-known wine regions can produce.

> Not all the Vats upon the Rhine
> Yield such an Alcohol!

This first stanza ends, as does stanza three, with an exclamation mark, signalling Dickinson's sustained delight.

The first stanza does not follow an exact rhyme, but Dickinson uses a regular end-rhyme in the following three stanzas: Dew / Blue; door / more; run / Sun.

[In an article published in *The Atlantic Monthly* in 1892, Thomas Bailey Aldrich set about 'correcting' the poem. His revised version of stanza one read:

> I taste a liquor never brewed
> In vats upon the Rhine:
> No tankards scooped in pearl could yield
> An alcohol like mine.

and 'in Miss Dickinson's book', he complained, 'for the most part the ideas totter and toddle, not having learned to walk'.]

The true nature of this liquor is revealed in lines 5–8:

> Inebriate of Air — am I —
> And Debauchee of Dew —
> Reeling — thro endless summer days —
> From inns of Molten Blue —

She is drunk on summer, its 'endless summer days', and that sense of a never-ending summer is captured even in her use of the dash. Stanza two is the only one to have a dash at the end of each line, suggesting the reeling, on-going sense of delight which Dickinson is celebrating.

The use of 'am I' and not the more usual 'I am' along with its place in the line give a mood of total happiness; 'am I' here is a phrase with flourish. And to describe herself as 'Debauchee' suggests a reckless sense of pleasure. She is drunk on summer air, morning dew; she is 'reeling', dizzy with excitement.

Line 8, 'From inns of Molten Blue —' suggests summer nights. When the night sky is melted or molten blue, the time is one of rest. The night-time is an inn, but once the summer days begin again Dickinson is reeling through them:

> Reeling — thro endless summer days —
> From inns of Molten Blue —

Like so many single lines from Dickinson, this yields a striking, memorable and original image.

The image of the inn is taken up in stanza three, when Dickinson speaks of nature:

> When 'Landlords' turn the drunken Bee
> Out of the Foxglove's door —

Here the bee is shown as having had enough; it is drunk and Dickinson imagines it is being told to leave the foxglove where it has been drinking its fill of nectar. Who or what the landlords are is difficult to say; it could well refer to the closing flower when the sun goes down. The inverted commas add a playful interpretation to the word. Perhaps she is referring to the stamens in the foxglove and how they prevent an already 'drunken Bee' from entering the flower. Dickinson then speaks of butterflies who, unlike the bee, realise that they have had enough to drink.

> When Butterflies — renounce their 'drams' —
> I shall but drink the more!

The bee, the butterflies and Dickinson herself have all been drinking in the experience of summer. The use of 'When' in lines 9 and 11 indicates a certain time when nature itself is satisfied. The drunken bee is told that it has had enough; the butterflies realise that they do not need more and 'renounce their "drams" –'; but Dickinson at such a moment is all the more inspired to drink on, and to experience summer to excess. 'I shall but drink the more!', with its exclamation mark, is joyfully determined in tone.

The final stanza pictures this ecstatically happy state, a state of drunken bliss. It is heavenly:

> Till Seraphs swing their snowy Hats —
> And saints — to windows run —
> To see the little Tippler
> Leaning against the — Sun —

Here is a self-portrait of Dickinson in a state of total happiness. The 'endless summer days' allow her to imagine that she is in heaven. 'When' and 'When' give way to 'Till' at the beginning of line 13. The 'Seraphs swing their snowy Hats —'. The highest order of the angels shares in Dickinson's delight. The verb 'swing' brings a music to the image, as does the alliteration on 'Seraphs', 'swing' and 'snowy'. The use of 'snowy' here also suggests hats or haloes the colours of bright clouds high in the heavens, and the excitement is shared by the saints who run to windows to see Dickinson. She is the centre of attention, the 'little Tippler', and she has achieved a heavenly state without ever mentioning death.

By stanza four, Dickinson has transported herself to a place close to heaven itself. She drinks often, is 'Inebriate of Air', has been 'Reeling – thro endless summer days –' but now in the final line of the poem she is leaning against the sun. The critic Charles R. Anderson speaks of stanza four and the 'unorthodox scene of hurrahing in heaven, with its bold metaphor converting the sun into a celestial lamp-post' and thinks that it may well be 'a comic version of spiritual intoxication as set forth in the Book of Revelation'.

The sun is the source of those 'endless summer days' and Dickinson has imagined herself growing closer to it, so close that she can lean against it. This final unique and striking image suggests ease and comfort.

The poem is exploring a heightened state. It is celebrating Dickinson's love of summer but it is also about inspiration: the inspiration of summer and the inspiration which makes possible the poem. Here Dickinson is a poet of euphoria ('I taste a liquor never brewed'); she is also a poet of great pain and suffering ('I felt a Funeral, in my Brain').

'Hope' is the thing with feathers

In the dictionary 'Hope' is defined: to entertain expectation of something desired. Dickinson offers her own understanding and definition. In '"Hope" is the thing with feathers—', Hope is a little song bird yet Dickinson refers to it throughout the poem as 'thing' and 'it'. Stanza one establishes the comparison. Hope, an abstraction, is given a strong physical presence in the bird metaphor:

> 'Hope' is the thing with feathers —
> That perches in the soul —
> And sings the tune without the words —
> And never stops — at all —

Hope is small; it 'perches in the soul', yet it is feathered and therefore capable of flying. The detail 'perches' suggests that hope has alighted or settled in the soul, its presence there permanent. Dickinson speaks of the song it sings as 'a tune without the words'. It cannot be understood on the level of language; it is beyond the verbal. The poem is made of words but tells of the song within the soul which transcends language.

Line 4 is very confident in tone. There is no end to hope; its song 'never stops':

> And never stops — at all —

Stanza one speaks of hope within, hope as something which inhabits the soul. In the second stanza, Dickinson speaks of 'the Gale', a storm that could be heard within or without. It is during such turmoil that the song of the bird is sweetest. The storm, Dickinson says, must be severe if it astounds and attempts to destroy the little bird of hope which has helped so many during other difficult times:

> And sweetest — in the Gale — is heard —
> And sore must be the storm —
> That could abash the little Bird
> That kept so many warm —

Hope, in this stanza, is portrayed as courageous. The bird will sing in the gale and its tune will be sweetest then. Sympathy for the bird is clearly felt in the line 'abash the little Bird'.

The phrase 'so many' in line 8 allows the poem to move from the individual to the many. Hope is experienced by others; many can be kept warm and can experience a warmth within, though the landscape be chill.

The final stanza turns to Dickinson and her own personal experience. Up to now she has spoken of hope in general terms. Stanza three has I and 'Me':

I've heard it in the chillest land —
And on the strangest Sea —
Yet, never, in Extremity,
It asked a crumb — of Me.

Hope is heard in times of difficulty and Dickinson represents such times in terms of landscape and seascape: 'the chillest land'; 'the strangest Sea'. Hope makes no demands. The 'never' in line 11 is absolute; Dickinson gives it extra power by placing it between two commas. In times of 'Extremity' the bird of hope never asked for so much as a crumb.

The poem is a celebration. All difficulties are overcome because of hope and Dickinson's confident belief in hope is the way she has structured her poem. The first two lines are a statement of belief and then follow four lines, each beginning with 'And', which gather momentum and emphasis through repetition and imagery. 'Gale', 'storm', 'abash' are all loud-sounding and destructive, but hope's 'sweetest' sound cannot be drowned out. The final stanza achieves a quieter sound but its tone is one of absolute conviction and gratitude.

The poem begins with an abstraction, 'Hope', and ends with the definite, unique self, 'Me'. The abstraction has been interiorised; the speaker here has learned through experience that hope is essential and that hope has proved to be a constant. [Elsewhere in her poetry, Dickinson also offers her own, unique definitions. In poem number 76, for example, she writes:

Exultation is the going
Of an inland soul to sea

In poem 709, she defines publication: 'Publication — is the Auction/ Of the Mind of Man —'; and in poem 910, experience: 'Experience is the Angled Road'.]

There's a certain Slant of light

This is both a mood poem and a meditative poem; it is also a poem in which Dickinson's meditation leads to an insight which she feels is shared by all. 'There's a certain Slant of light' explores, among other things, the relationship between man and God.

Though the poem focuses in line 1 on a slant of light, something that can often be beautiful in itself, there is a mood of heaviness and melancholy throughout the first stanza. 'Winter' and 'Afternoons' suggest the dying of the year and the dying of the day. The words 'oppresses' and 'Heft' add to this feeling of being weighed down. 'Cathedral Tunes' suggest solemnity, seriousness. Denis Donoghue thinks that 'The cathedral tunes oppress because of the sullen weight of faith which they ask the listener to receive and to lift'.

> There's a certain Slant of light,
> Winter Afternoons —
> That oppresses, like the Heft
> Of Cathedral Tunes —

The images conjured up here are neither light-hearted nor celebratory. The mood can be more fully grasped if these opening lines are read next to a poem such as 'I taste a liquor never brewed', where the words and sounds create a totally different mood. The mood here is sombre; the other is ecstatic.

In this first stanza, Dickinson uses the senses to convey the moment of perception. We see the beam or ray of winter light; it is compared to 'Cathedral Tunes' which we can imagine ourselves hearing. Light waves have become sound waves and 'oppresses' and 'Heft' are sensuous words, suggesting a heaviness which we can feel. A 'Slant of light' is not usually associated with heaviness, yet here in the context of a New England winter afternoon Dickinson has associated light with oppressiveness and dying. If it a heavenly light, it is also a light that brings about a darkened understanding of heaven and our life on earth.

The certain light of winter afternoons can cause hurt:

> Heavenly Hurt, it gives us —

and the word 'us' is interesting here. Dickinson does not use 'I' in this poem; 'us' and 'we' are the personal pronouns used. 'Us' is used twice, and by doing so Dickinson is involving and including the reader in a very direct way in the experience she is writing about. She is confident that her experience is also ours.

The hurt felt is a 'Heavenly Hurt', one whose source is heaven. This suggests that Dickinson sees heaven as a place which can cause humans pain. God is distant and this 'Heavenly Hurt' is the source of earthly pain. In Dickinson's dictionary 'slant' was also defined as a gibe which, if intended, suggests a merciless heaven. Its light mocks us. The scarless wound is a reminder to us of our mortality.

Ralph Waldo Emerson, the nineteenth-century American poet and essayist, influenced Dickinson's thinking and she heard him lecture in Amherst. Emerson believed that Nature was God's benign deputy; Dickinson differed from Emerson, in that for her God's deputy could be hostile.

The phrase 'Heavenly Hurt' is paradoxical yet, just as the Cathedral Tune can weigh upon us, it would seem that a slant of light can give us hurt. Light comes from the heavens; 'Hurt' causes pain and sadness, and 'Heavenly Hurt' perhaps suggests an intense awareness of mortality, dying. It is the hurt of knowing that we must die. Such knowledge wounds us, yet

> We can find no scar,
> But internal difference,
> Where the Meanings, are —

Knowing that life must end, just as the day and the year must end, is a profound part of our being. There is no 'scar' but there are 'internal differences'. Deep inside, one is aware of life's reality and it is the deep knowledge within that matters. That's 'Where the Meanings, are —'.

Line 9, 'None may teach it — Any' seems to mean that no human may teach anything to someone in a state of such hurt; it is a situation beyond hope.

> None may teach it — Any —
> 'Tis the Seal Despair –
> An imperial affliction
> Sent us of the Air –

Just as the 'Slant of light' comes from afar, so too does this 'Heavenly Hurt'. This third stanza is pessimistic. It speaks of the Seal of Despair and Dickinson sees this 'Seal despair' as an 'imperial affliction / Sent us of the Air —'. The 'Seal' suggests the sign of authority. The individual experiences despair and is marked by the seal of despair. Despair is a very strong and powerful word. Nowhere in the poem is there a sense of hope.

'Imperial affliction' could be read as an image of a cruel, distant, all-powerful, impersonal force. As human beings, Dickinson is suggesting that we are given moments of hurt, but such moments are also moments of insight and understanding about the human condition. Knowing the reality allows us to live with reality.

The final stanza uses a longer line than is found in the previous three:

> When it comes, the Landscape listens —
> Shadows — hold their breath —
> When it goes, 'tis like the Distance
> On the look of Death —

This line, though longer only by a syllable, slows down the rhythm and adds to the already sombre mood. There is a chilling quality in line 13:

> When it comes, the Landscape listens —

Critical Commentary

Such moments will come but it is as if we know not the day nor the hour. Similarly, the phrase 'When it goes' in line 15, suggests that we have no way of knowing when such moments occur. They come and they go, and they have a profound effect on us.

In lines 13–16, Dickinson speaks of the moment and the aftermath. It refers back to the moment which she has described in the first three stanzas and its effect but now not only the individual but the landscape is affected. When such moments occur, the very landscape 'listens'. By personifying the earth, Dickinson unites the human and our earthly home. There is a sense of tension: even the 'Shadows — hold their breath —'. If the 'Shadows — hold their breath —' the suggestion is that the shadows are frightened or uneasy. Shadows are the opposite to the slant of light. Dickinson herself sees the slant of light and therefore she is not in the light but in shadow. The landscape, the shadows, and Dickinson are all aware and affected by the certain slant of light. For Dickinson what remains from such moments is a feeling that one has looked down the distance left before our death and this gives the poem a cold and realistic seriousness. The final dash opens up before us that road to death which we must all travel. Words such as 'oppresses', 'Heft', 'scar', 'Despair', 'affliction', 'the look of Death' maintain and intensify the gloomy mood.

When the moment is over and we are left with 'internal difference', then Dickinson tells us in lines 15 and 16 that it is as if we have looked on death itself, something which each one of us has to do alone. Such moments as the one described in 'There's a certain Slant of light' are moments which signal and prepare us for death.

That said, the last two lines could also be read to mean that once the moment of oppression is over, we forget death and it becomes distant again. We were made aware of our mortality during such a moment as the one described in the first stanza. But when such moments go, death seems far away once more.

The dying of the year is inevitable and natural. Yet the winter light oppresses. Our own dying is inevitable and natural also. In the poem Dickinson begins with an observation about the season and this leads to the recognition of a change within herself, a change which serves as a learning experience.

The poem has a regular end-rhyme throughout: Afternoons / Tunes; scar / are; Despair / Air; breath / Death. Giving scar, Despair and Death a rhyme emphasises their importance. Also, the placing of certain words in the line make for special emphasis and effect. For example, 'Heavenly Hurt, it gives us —' is a more powerful expression than 'it gives us Heavenly Hurt'; the 'us' is the word which stands out here and it is 'us' or 'we', not winter or heaven, that Dickinson is primarily concerned with in the poem.

Heaven is often thought of as a place of supreme happiness and redemption, but it is not spoken about as such in this poem. There is only the phrase 'Heavenly Hurt'. Dickinson does not dwell on an after life. Her focus here is on our earthly existence, our disappointments and suffering.

I felt a Funeral, in my Brain

This poem is remarkable for several reasons: its dramatic narrative, its use of repetition and its rhythmic pattern. It is written in the past tense and records a painful and strange experience. The action of the poem takes place inside Dickinson's head and the startlingly unusual opening line immediately establishes the location of the poem:

> I felt a Funeral, in my Brain,

Here, something final, sad and public, the funeral, is interiorised. If one were to say 'I felt a jungle, a circus, a desert, a waterfall, a traffic jam, an ocean in my brain', a sensation is immediately communicated and understood; the idea is simple, vivid, original.

In Dickinson's case the moment is one of nervous tension and vulnerability:

> I felt a Funeral, in my Brain,
> And Mourners to and fro
> Kept treading — treading — till it seemed
> That Sense was breaking through —

Here it seems that she is imagining her own death, the time when mourners will come to pay their last respects. The movement of 'to and fro' and the harshness of 'treading — treading' are images of restlessness, unease.

From the opening line, Dickinson places herself at the centre of the poem: 'I felt', 'I thought', 'I heard', 'And I, and Silence', 'I dropped'; 'my Brain', 'My Mind', 'my Soul'. To feel, to think, to hear, not to hear, to drop are strong sensations and at each stage in the poem Dickinson records these sensations as if they are inevitable. The use of 'And' gives the poem an increasing momentum. 'And' is used thirteen times altogether, ten times to begin a line.

In line 4 'Sense was breaking through —'. 'Breaking through' seems to mean here breaking down or giving way. The other meaning of 'breaking through', i.e. a moment of clarification or understanding, does not seem to be supported by the context here. This is the first indication of breaking in the poem, but Dickinson continues to develop the idea, and the poem ends with the climactic breaking of reason.

Whatever the form of crisis or breakdown being described, which may or may not be Dickinson's own imagined funeral, the dominant imagery is funereal. In stanza two, the 'Mourners' introduced in line 2 are 'seated'. Their 'treading — treading' is no longer felt, but the 'Service' itself is now a 'beating — beating' sensation in her mind:

> And when they all were seated,
> A Service, like a Drum —
> Kept beating — beating — till I thought
> My Mind was going numb —

The rhyming of 'Drum' and 'numb' is particularly appropriate here; one leads to the other. The rhyming throughout is regular within the first four stanzas — fro/through (slant rhyme), Drum/numb, Soul/toll, Ear/here, but the rhyme breaks down in the final stanza mirroring the final stage of breaking: down/then.

The experience which Dickinson writes about in this poem is not fully understood by her: 'it seemed', 'I thought'. In stanza three it is as if she cannot see what is happening. She can only hear.

> And then I heard them lift a Box
> And creak across my Soul
> With those same Boots of Lead, again,
> Then Space — began to toll,

The story being told parallels that of an actual funeral. In stanza one there was the sense of an ending; the people came to mourn. Stanza two tells of a Service, and in stanza three there is the journey from place of Service to the burial ground, a space in the ground.

The 'Box' in line 9 is the coffin. The mourners lift the box and then Dickinson tells us that the mourners creak across her soul. The corpse is in the box or coffin; the body has died but the mention of the soul suggests an afterlife. The manuscript shows that Dickinson wrote 'across my Brain' first and then changed it to 'across my Soul'; brain and soul were interchangeable in the nineteenth century. When she does speak of a life after death, she speaks of it in terms of 'knowing'.

Imagining oneself in a coffin at one's own funeral is a courageous and chilling thought. The mind is still aware of what is going on, the phrase 'creak across my Soul' suggesting that the soul is being hurt.

The sounds in 'I felt a Funeral, in my Brain' are harsh and severe. The references – to treading feet, the beating, drum-like service, the creaking sound, boots of lead, the silence of the bell, dropped down, hit – all create a sense of inescapable, increasing pain.

It is in stanza three that a new and different sense of space is introduced. Up until now, Dickinson has spoken of the space within her head, the place where the mourners tread and sit, the confined space of the coffin. However, in line 12 having heard the 'Boots of Lead, again'

> Then Space — began to toll

A funeral bell is a tolling bell; when Dickinson speaks of 'Space' beginning to toll, the image is one of a space opening up. By placing a dash after 'Space', the only dash used in this stanza, Dickinson is suggesting, perhaps, a great unknown space before her. 'Toll' also suggests a mournful mood.

Having spoken of where she is now in terms of a 'Space' which 'began to toll', Dickinson in stanza four continues the bell imagery when she speaks of 'the Heavens':

> As all the Heavens were a Bell,
> And Being, but an Ear,
> And I, and Silence, some strange Race
> Wrecked, solitary, here —

The treading feet, the beating drum, the creaking sounds are now no more. The sense of hearing is vital throughout the poem. In line 15 there is absolute silence and it is a silence associated with unease. Dickinson speaks of 'all the Heavens' in terms of the image of 'a Bell', the heavens suggesting a happy life beyond death. Her sense of her own entire self-awareness is now reduced to 'an Ear'; Dickinson's 'Being' is 'but an Ear' and in a chilling description of desolation and ruin she tells us that she 'and Silence, some strange Race' are wrecked and solitary. The bell of 'all the Heavens' is not heard. [It has been pointed out that in Odilon Redon's (1840–1916) surreal painting 'Silence', painted in 1890, silence is painted as a huge ear.]

Line 15 speaks of 'I, and Silence, some strange Race'. This may be read as 'I and Silence which is a strange race' or it can also be read to mean, 'I, and Silence, (and) some strange Race'. Dickinson who has, at this stage in the poem, entered into a state of strange and silent intensity is by herself; she can hear nothing and yet she is aware of the presence of others, 'some strange Race' who are also wrecked and solitary. They have reached this space before Dickinson but both Dickinson and they are estranged from 'all the Heavens'.

The reference to 'here' in line 16 is a reference to a kind of limbo land or temporary resting place, but 'Wrecked' and 'solitary' suggest destruction and being cut off. She has arrived at this place; she hears nothing here and there is increasing isolation. Where once she had 'Mourners', now there is no one but 'Silence'.

Stanza five marks another and final stage in the journey. It has a sense of finality about it. It not only ends the poem but it describes a final frightening movement in a poem which has had a great deal of movement. This stanza has the word 'Finished' in its final line. An end has been reached. Reason breaks in this stanza; intellectual power is at an end:

> And then a Plank in Reason, broke,
> And I dropped down, and down —
> And hit a World, at every plunge,
> And Finished knowing — then —

The image here of the 'Plank in Reason' is in keeping with the imagery of the funeral throughout the poem. Reason is an abstract, but Dickinson gives that faculty a vivid immediacy in the image of the plank. A plank is often placed across the open grave; the coffin rests upon the plank before being lowered into the ground. If that plank were to break, the falling coffin would be a horrifying sight. A plank is a precarious thing over a void. If the plank breaks, you enter the void. What Dickinson describes is 'a Plank in Reason' breaking, but the subsequent image is of the speaker in the poem falling uncontrollably 'down, and down':

> And I dropped down, and down —
> And hit a World, at every plunge

The verbs 'dropped' and 'hit', the repeated 'down', the idea which 'plunge' conjures up all suggest a terrible ordeal.

The sense of the poem as story or narrative is not only suggested in the various stages of a funeral service, but the adverbs also point to the development of the narrative quality of the poem. In line 5 'when' signals a particular moment; 'then' is used in lines 9, 12 and 17, marking different stages in the poem. The final word in the poem is also 'then', this time presented as '— then —'.

When reason breaks then the end is near. 'And Finished knowing' is characteristically ambiguous and may be interpreted in two ways. Is knowing a noun or a present participle? First it could refer to the end of knowing. A moment comes when the mind is no more because reason has broken down. Second, 'Finished knowing' could be interpreted as that final moment of awareness, of knowing, of understanding. At the end of this experience, there is knowledge and insight. One finally understands what is to be — a nothing, a hell or a heaven? If Dickinson intended the second reading, that 'knowing', her knowing, is never shared with the reader. Dickinson knows something in that final moment which she has depicted as a moment of rapid downward movement. Did Dickinson intend us to think that she has reached a hellish state, hell conventionally being understood to be beneath the ground, just as heaven has traditionally been understood to be high above.

The final '— then —' is different from the other thens in the text. There is no world beyond this final then. She has 'hit a World, at every plunge' and that is her end.

Dickinson speaks of 'the Heavens' but God is invisible, uninvolved. There is no suggestion of comfort at this journey's end. The poem is communicating to us a message, as it were, from beyond the grave.

A Bird came down the Walk

Dickinson in 'A Bird came down the Walk' is the keen observer. The bird enters the world of the human, it 'came down the Walk —' and the human secretly observes the world of the bird. It has a delighted, playful tone in its opening stanza:

> A Bird came down the Walk —
> He did not know I saw —
> He bit an Angleworm in halves
> And ate the fellow, raw,

Dickinson is clearly interested in observing the bird, is pleased that she is the unobserved observer. The phrase 'the fellow' captures the playfulness of the moment. By contrast, the mention of 'raw' reminds us of reality.

The size of the bird and the even smaller worm bring the poem into a concentrated focus. When Dickinson says in line 5 that 'he drank a Dew' the focus becomes almost microscopic. The unconventional use of the indefinite article here – she doesn't say the dew – makes for minute detail and is yet another aspect of Dickinson's originality. Everything in Nature seems ordered and right. The bird finds its food and drink with ease and is also courteous and caring:

> And then he drank a Dew
> From a convenient Grass —
> And then hopped sideways to the Wall
> To let a Beetle pass —

The bird does not hop sideways on seeing the worm (that would be unnatural) and Dickinson is not concerned for the worm bitten in half and eaten. It is part of the food-chain; Nature is taking its course in this poem. Dickinson is showing us how everything fits into place. Even the grass is 'convenient'.

The poem is full of busyness. The bird eats, drinks, and in stanza three appears frightened and in danger:

> He glanced with rapid eyes
> That hurried all around —
> They looked like frightened Beads, I thought —
> He stirred his Velvet Head
>
> Like one in danger,

This is brilliantly accurate and effective: 'frightened Beads' and 'Velvet Head' are superbly precise images. It is at this point in the poem, when the bird is frightened, that Dickinson makes herself known to it. The word 'Cautious' could refer to the bird or Dickinson or both.

> Cautious,
> I offered him a Crumb

The human presence and the proffered crumb cause the bird to fly away. The bird is not described as flying away suddenly. Words such as 'unrolled' and 'rowed' and 'plashless' suggest a graceful departure, but what is interesting is that the bird does not accept Dickinson's kindness. The crumb is not an angleworm; the bird belongs to the natural world and it will return to it.

> I offered him a Crumb
> And he unrolled his feathers
> And rowed him softer home —
>
> Than Oars divide the Ocean,
> Too silver for a seam —
> Or Butterflies, off Banks of Noon
> Leap, plashless as they swim.

These closing stanzas capture the smooth, silent disappearance of the bird. Dickinson thinks of the bird as having rowed himself 'softer home' and home is significant. The 'walk' where Dickinson sees the bird is not his home but elsewhere, some other place; home for the bird is also nest and sky. The use of 'And' at the beginning of line 15, not but, suggests that the bird's going is totally natural.

Two elaborate images close the poem. A rowed boat will part the water and the water will be silver in its wake, 'Too silver for a seam —'; and butterflies swim silently above banks of flowers at noon. Dickinson uses these images to convey the silent, mysterious movement of the bird. The bird moves more softly than the rowing boat, more softly than the silent, swimming butterflies.

Nature is its own world. It has its own rhythms, its own beauty. In the first stanza of 'A Bird came down the Walk' the bird is very much present; in the final stanza the bird is absent and its absence is felt by Dickinson. That she finds images to match its departure suggests her lingering sense of the bird's absence. Dickinson belongs to one world, the bird to its world. Unlike Keats, who observed the sparrow outside his window and became that bird, Dickinson observes, is captivated and kind enough to offer the bird a crumb but also realises that he is separate. He refused to take her crumb.

If Dickinson is disappointed, she does not say so. The poem is one of celebration, delight, wonder.

After great pain, a formal feeling comes

Here Dickinson speaks of having known 'great pain' and the feelings which follow such an experience. She speaks with such confidence, knowledge and insight that one does not doubt that this is a felt experience.

Great pain is spoken of as something which does not last; the last words in the poem are 'the letting go —' but what interests Dickinson here is the numbed and gradual stages which the individual experiences in the process.

There is no 'I' in the poem; it is as if Dickinson is speaking for us all.

> After great pain, a formal feeling comes —
> The Nerves sit ceremonious, like Tombs —
> The stiff Heart questions was it He, that bore,
> And Yesterday, or Centuries before?

The word 'formal' suggests precision, excessive stiffness, ceremony, and the idea is followed through in lines 2 and 3. Human aspects are personified: the 'Nerves sit ceremonious' and the 'stiff Heart questions'. The word 'sit' in this context evokes an image of rigid, pained figures (reminiscent, perhaps, of the mourners who come and are seated in 'I felt a Funeral, in my Brain'); the image contained in 'like Tombs' is precise. After great pain, the body's strength and vigour, the Nerves, feel numb and cold. The dominant imagery throughout the poem is lifelessness and the reference to 'The Nerves', 'The stiff Heart', 'The Feet' emphasises this sense of lifelessness throughout the body. The poem moves from a mind that is numb to a numbed heart to numbed feet.

The heart is pained and tense. It asks in line 3 if it was Jesus Christ who carried the cross, the implication being that this heart is so pained that it is carrying a cross itself, is suffering just as Christ did.

The moment of pain is so intense that the heart has lost track of the everyday world and has lost all sense of time. Christ's suffering is suddenly brought very close. The heart wonders if Christ suffered his great pain yesterday or hundreds of years ago:

> The stiff Heart questions was it He, that bore,
> And Yesterday, or Centuries before?

In these lines Dickinson is also suggesting that a human being can know such great pain that it is as if that individual knows a suffering similar to Christ's.

The cause or the occasion of this great pain is never explicitly revealed to us in the poem. The reference to Christ's suffering and death suggests rejection, but what is more important than the circumstances is the fact that suffering great pain is part of the human condition.

The second stanza describes the feet, but the feet are so expressive of emotion here that we are given a sense of the body and how it copes with this great pain:

> The Feet, mechanical, go round —
> Of Ground, or Air, or Ought —
> A Wooden way
> Regardless grown,
> A Quartz contentment, like a stone —

There is movement but it is 'mechanical' and 'Wooden'. The feet touch the ground, lift again through the air and again 'go round'. The circular motion here suggests an endless, futile movement. The phrase 'A Wooden way' refers to the expressionless, spiritless, dull and inert feeling; it may also be used as an echo of Christ's wooden way, the way of the cross and his journey to Calvary. The pain and suffering of Christ was certainly linked to human pain and suffering in stanza one.

The four-line, pentameter stanza form used in the first stanza is broken down in stanza two. Dickinson shortens the line and breaks what could be line 7 into two:

> A Wooden way Regardless grown

becomes

> A Wooden way
> Regardless grown

These shorter lines create a slowing-down effect and the shortest lines in the poem are at the centre of the poem.

It is as if the 'great pain' and its subsequent feelings cause us to look inwards; our focus becomes narrow and our bodies, our sensations, almost close down. The final two lines of the poem return to the formal pentameter lines of stanza one. Pattern here becomes meaning; the stages in feeling are expressed in the very lines.

Dickinson speaks of the mechanical feet as 'Regardless grown'. They do not care anymore; they are indifferent, careless, without regard of anything, and the image of 'A Quartz contentment' in line 9 sums up the 'formal feeling'. The human being is like a stone. Quartz is not chosen at random. Dickinson said in a letter dated 1883: 'I hesitate which word to take, as I can take but few and each must be the chiefest'. So too in her poetry. Perhaps Dickinson chose Quartz because it is a common mineral and as a mineral it has been transformed by process into its present state. Similarly, human suffering, 'great pain', is known to many people and their 'Quartz' like state is as a result of having been transformed by the process of pain. The sound of the word quartz is severe and harsh, another reason, perhaps, for choosing it. The use of 'contentment' seems out of place here. The pain and the questioning heart of stanza one have given way to a cold contentment.

The first line in the third stanza is slow and monosyllabic. It has a dreadful knowing quality:

> This is the Hour of Lead —

The phrase 'Hour of Lead' is a definition of depression. It is an hour of such oppression and pain that not all survive it. Those who do survive the 'Hour of Lead' remember it as a slow and painful process:

> This is the Hour of Lead —
> Remembered, if outlived,
> As Freezing persons, recollect the Snow —
> First — Chill — then Stupor — then the letting go —

The freezing person will remember the reason for feeling frozen, just as the numbed person will remember the source or cause of the 'great pain'. Dickinson in the final line identifies three distinct yet connected stages, one leading to the other:

> First — Chill — then Stupor — then the letting go —

Chill is often the first stage or symptom of illness and the dictionary also describes it as a depressing influence upon the feelings. The second stage is a deadened, dazed state but the 'letting go', the third stage, is that ability to survive, to outlive the 'great pain' which Dickinson speaks of in the opening line. 'Letting go' of course may also be read as something negative, as losing a sense of everything, of going into a deeper state of depression.

'After great pain, a formal feeling comes —' describes mental anguish step by step. It is in many ways an impersonal poem. Dickinson never uses 'I' or 'my'. The nerves, the heart, the feet belong to no specific individual, but by the use of 'the' they belong to everyone.

I heard a Fly buzz — when I died

This poem is in the first person and, though it tells of the crucial moment of death, that moment, in stanza one, is not associated with knowledge, understanding or revelation, but with a sound:

> I heard a Fly buzz — when I died —
> The Stillness in the Room
> Was like the Stillness in the Air —
> Between the Heaves of Storm —

There are two sounds here or rather a sound and the absence of sound: the still, silent sound of the room and the buzz of the fly which is heard by the speaker at the moment of death. The buzzing fly is a distraction; it trivialises a serious and unique moment and the silence in the room is even more pronounced. That stillness is ominous. The storm will return. The fly has also been interpreted, not as a distraction, but as what John Ciardi calls 'a last dear sound from the world as the light of consciousness sank from her'. Caroline Hogue disagrees with this view; she associates the fly with decay.

Another reading of this poem argues that the fly represents death itself and that Dickinson, perhaps, is thinking of Beëlzebub, the devil, the lord of the flies?

The mood in stanza one is one of calmness and control. This is another of Dickinson's poems where the lines are written in the form of hymn metre:

> Our God, our help in ages past

> I heard a Fly buzz — when I died —

and that tight, formal control is maintained throughout.

The speaker is at the centre of the poem and she is, it seems, in the centre of the room. What the poem suggests is a death bed setting with family gathered round:

> The Eyes around — had wrung them dry —
> And Breaths were gathering firm

The weeping is done; the eyes of those around the speaker have wrung themselves dry and the next stage is anticipated with solemnity. Their 'Breaths were gathering firm' as they await Christ's presence in the room. This is

> that last Onset — when the King
> Be witnessed — in the Room —

'Onset' here marks the moment. Dickinson does not say if the one who has died will witness 'the King' or if His presence is witnessed only by the mourners. 'I died' in line 1 suggests, as does 'Breaths were gathering firm', that Christ the King will be witnessed by those at the bedside who believe in Him and not by the speaker. 'Onset' is ambiguous. It means both a commencement and an assault. Do the speaker and the mourners view 'the King' differently?

Having considered the King to be Christ, we owe it to the poem and to ourselves as readers to ask if 'the King' here could mean Death, our physical end, and not eternal salvation.

At a nineteenth century death-bed scene, it was usual for the family to gather round the dying person. There would be last-minute bequests and hymns sung and the person who was dying was expected to repent and thereby give witness to Christ's presence in the room. It was also believed that the last words of the dying person or a sign or gesture would indicate the destiny of the soul.

Line 9 refers to the practice of bequeathing one's precious possessions. The others in the room are spoken of impersonally, as 'Eyes' and 'Breaths', but the dying person is personal and intimate in willing her keepsakes. As Dickinson describes the moment she speaks once again of the fly, this time marking her awareness of its presence precisely:

> I willed my Keepsakes — Signed away
> What portion of me be
> Assignable — and then it was
> There interposed a Fly —

All seems ordered, lucid, calm, even wry ('What portion of me be/ Assignable'), until the fly interposes.

The fly has come between the dying person and the light. The words 'Blue – uncertain stumbling Buzz' suggest a blowfly or bluebottle (Musca vomitoria) with its large bluish body, a fly which deposits its eggs or larvae in dead flesh.

The final lines chart the dead person's final thoughts:

> There interposed a Fly —
>
> With Blue — uncertain stumbling Buzz —
> Between the light — and me —
> And then the Windows failed – and then
> I could not see to see —

The light is the light from the window, though the light of Christ or the light of Paradise may be hinted at. At any rate the fly has come

Between the light — and me —

The fly is 'uncertain' and 'stumbling', words which introduce a sense of the chaotic and directionless into a poem which is focusing on a natural and quiet death.

A fly is tiny and can hardly be said to block out the light, but for Dickinson the fly is the first stage in the dying of the light. First the fly comes between the 'light — and me —'. The next stage is signalled clearly:

And then the Windows failed — and then
I could not see to see —

The poem ends in darkness; it offers no vision of immortality. The light from the windows 'failed' and the speaker's own vision has failed; 'I could not see to see —'. The repetition of 'and then' in line 15 gives the line finality, tension, drama. The dash with which the poem ends invites the reader to consider the moment and beyond the moment of death and to ask if Dickinson intended to convey a sense of things beyond death.

The poem is built around the sensory details of hearing ('I heard'), seeing ('The Eyes around'), touching ('Signed away') and ends with silence, isolation, blindness.

The Soul has Bandaged moments

The opening line is arresting. It strikes the reader immediately:

The Soul has Bandaged moments —

and its meaning is clearly understood. At times the private, inner self (the soul suggests a spiritual self) is pained and bandaged or bound. Bandaged could imply that the soul is in a state of healing. Bandaged could also mean simply to bind or cover up.

The soul here is spoken of as female and Fright is personified:

The Soul has Bandaged moments —
When too appalled to stir —
She feels some ghastly Fright come up
And stop to look at her —

In this opening stanza the soul is at its lowest. It feels intimidated. It is frightened; Fright itself is a threatening presence. If the soul is female, does Dickinson intend us to read Fright as a male presence? Fright, however, is never referred to as 'he'.

The soul cannot move; it is 'too appalled to stir'. Dickinson never reveals to us the cause of this state of dismay, this rigidity, but in this state the soul is vulnerable, looked at; the phrase 'come up' suggests that the soul itself seems and feels small. Fright chooses to look; it stops to look at her, thereby making the soul even less powerful. Bandaged may imply that the soul cannot see, yet Fright can 'look at her'. Fright is the more powerful.

Moments is plural. Such bandaged moments occur again. The phrase 'Bandaged moments' begs the question who bandages or binds the wounded soul? Is it a sense of self-preservation?

The mood in stanza one is one of acute self-consciousness and this is intensified in the second stanza. A salutation is usually associated with a happy greeting, good wishes, respect. Here Fright's salute and Fright's 'long fingers' are eerie. Fright comes up and stops to look at the bandaged soul. Fright will:

> Salute her — with long fingers —
> Caress her freezing hair —

Even 'Caress' – to fondle or touch endearingly – becomes sinister in this context and 'freezing hair' is powerfully effective personification.

Fright stops to look, to salute, to caress, to sip. Lines 7–10 reveal, it seems, the nature and the reason for the soul's hurt:

> Sip, Goblin, from the very lips
> The Lover — hovered — o'er —
> Unworthy, that a thought so mean
> Accost a Theme — so — fair —

Goblin may be read as goblin-like, an adverb modifying 'Sip'. Fright will sip from lips the Lover did not kiss or sip.

Another way of reading 'Sip, Goblin,' is to interpret it as the soul's voice addressing Goblin, presumably Fright, and it is told to sip from the very lips which a lover had hovered over. This reading is less satisfactory in that soul is portrayed in stanza one and two as victim. It would hardly address Fright; it is 'too appalled to stir'.

Who the Lover is (line 8), we are not told. It could be a person; it could be God. The Lover hovered, was hesitant and indecisive. The Lover, it seems, is no longer loving and the soul is dismayed that Fright now sips from the lips of the bandaged soul.

> Sip, Goblin, from the very lips
> The Lover — hovered — o'er —

It seems that Dickinson is writing about unrequited love of some kind and perhaps it is this which has caused the Soul to be wounded and in need of bandaging.

Dickinson has dramatised the feeling of dismay and fear. There is the still presence of the Soul, 'too appalled to stir', and the 'ghastly' Fright whose presence is described as almost inevitable. The soul when bandaged feels 'Fright come up'. The soul has to accept Fright, a Goblin-like presence.

'Unworthy', line 9, refers to what or whom? Is Fright unworthy or does it refer to the Lover? Could it refer to 'the very lips'? A case can be made for each interpretation. At this point, one is truly aware of the difficulties of reading Emily Dickinson's poetry, so much so that some readers become exasperated, impatient, dismissive.

Richard B. Sewell suggests that 'No one of her poems . . . should be regarded as a signed and sealed position paper. It's the poetry, as Emerson put it, of portfolio . . . She'd never gone through the discipline of publication. They're the portfolio poetry of a poet who had written for herself, to herself, thinking out her life, investigating what was happening, especially inside, and coming out with an extraordinary, true, certainly realistic sense of the human psyche.'

If 'Unworthy' in line 9 refers to Fright, then lines 9 and 10 clearly express the Soul's preference for the Lover over Fright or Goblin. But 'Unworthy' can also refer to the Lover who, feeling unworthy in the soul's presence, 'hovered — o'er' and did not sip. Thinking itself unworthy, the thought of kissing the very lips becomes 'a thought so mean' could accost or address 'a Theme — so — fair —'. The theme here may be the soul or the union between the Soul and Lover.

Unworthy and fair are opposites. Fair is what is beautiful or desirable and a mean thought, a feeling of unworthiness, prevents the Lover from attaining its desire.

There is a complete mood swing in stanzas three and four. The first two stanzas presented us with the Soul in dismay; now we are given the very opposite, the Soul in bliss. No mention now of Fright, nor is there any mention of Lover.

> The soul has moments of Escape —
> When bursting all the doors —
> She dances like a Bomb, abroad,
> And swings upon the Hours,
>
> As do the Bee — delirious borne —
> Long Dungeoned from his Rose —
> Touch Liberty — then know no more,
> But Noon, and Paradise —

In contrast to what has gone before, there is extraordinary energy here: 'bursting', 'dances', 'swings', 'delirious borne' express freedom, release, frenzied excitement. The soul has escaped its confines; it is 'abroad' and flying with excitement. The soul

> dances like a Bomb, abroad,
> And swings upon the Hours

'Bomb' suggests an explosion of happiness in this context. It may also be meant as an anarchic and destructive force. The alternative definition of bomb as the sounding of a bell (cf. *glossary*) is not only appropriate but in keeping with the reference to the swinging upon the hours in the following line.

These are the 'moments of Escape', the opposite of 'Bandaged moments' of line 1, but whether in pain or joyful it is significant that Dickinson speaks of both states as existing as moments. The soul will know neither pain nor joy as a constant. The word 'moments' occurs three times in the poem (lines 1, 11, 19) but, once freed, the soul 'swings upon the Hours'. Time is viewed differently. But the poem is framed by Fright and Horror, which suggests that ultimately the moments of escape are short-lived, that a form of imprisonment, or 'Bandaged moments', is the norm.

Stanza four is a sustained image. The freed soul is likened to a bee who was 'Long Dungeoned' in the hive, then 'delirious borne' on air and seeking out 'his Rose'. The sensation is one of intense happiness:

> As do the Bee — delirious borne —
> Long Dungeoned from his Rose —
> Touch Liberty — then know no more,
> But Noon, and Paradise —

Stanzas three and four are a vivid contrast to the first two stanzas. The 'bursting all the doors', dancing, swinging soul, the image of the Rose, the brightness of noon are summery and free images and the very opposite of 'Bandaged' and 'freezing'.

Stanzas one and two are about constraint, unease and fear, stanzas three and four about release and delirium. The soul, once victim, is now shown as active, not passive. Dickinson does not say what makes possible such happiness. Just as the bee knows no more 'But Noon, and Paradise –', the soul delights in its 'Escape'; it does not dwell on how it has been set free.

Line 19, at the beginning of stanza five, signals the end of the moment of escape. 'The Soul has Bandaged moments'; 'The soul has moments of Escape'; and 'The Soul's retaken moments' (lines 1, 11, 19) mark the three separate stages of the poem. The structure is such that Dickinson ends as she began with the soul once again imprisoned:

> The Soul's retaken moments —
> When, Felon led along,
> With shackles on the plumed feet,
> And staples, in the Song,

There is no reason given as to why the soul should be retaken or recaptured and imprisoned. It is led along, as if it were a felon or criminal, and the imagery in lines 21 and 22 evokes a sympathetic response from the reader. The soul's plumed or feathered feet are bound, the soul's song hindered, prevented.

The most chilling moment of all perhaps is line 23:

> The Horror welcomes her, again,

The soul has been here before. We are given no indication why the soul is being led back to this place of horror, a place where the soul knows bandaged moments. The comma in line 23 and the word 'again' create a sense of inevitability. Soul, here, has no control, unlike those moments when she burst 'all the doors'. The word 'welcomes' is sinister and unnerving. Just as it is difficult to imagine Fright caressing the Soul, it seems totally inappropriate that Horror could welcome her.

The poem's final line reminds us that the 'Bandaged moments' of the soul are not loudly boasted about:

> These, are not brayed of Tongue —

No tongue speaks of them, loudly or quietly, but by using 'brayed' Dickinson is suggesting how impossible it is to speak of such moments. However, this is just what Dickinson herself has done in the poem.

There is a marked contrast in the poem between suffering and joy, between a feeling of imprisonment and freedom, between moments of misery and moments of ecstasy. Dickinson, in choosing not to identify the cause for these emotional states, allows for a more open interpretation. The poem may refer to depression and the release from depression, the lack of inspiration and the creative imagination, the state of fear, release from fear and the return of fear.

I could bring You Jewels — had I a mind to

There is a very definite sense of the self, the speaker in this poem. 'I' is used five times in twelve lines. The speaker is confident, self-assured. The tone throughout is knowing and controlled:

> I could bring You Jewels — had I a mind to —

The 'You' is never identified but the poem is clearly expressing praise and admiration for the 'You' whom it addresses. The speaker wishes to find something suitable to honour 'You':

> I could bring You Jewels — had I a mind to —
> But You have enough — of those —
> I could bring You Odors from St Domingo —
> Colors — from Vera Cruz —

There is poise here. Though the tone is confident, it is also relaxed. The extravagance of jewels, scents, colours, the exotic locations mentioned — St Domingo, Vera Cruz, the Bahamas — all create a world of plenty and sufficiency. 'I could bring You Jewels', 'I could bring You Odors', suggest wealth and privilege.

In stanza one, Dickinson speaks of bringing this 'You' a gift of jewels. She adds 'had I a mind to —' and then immediately qualifies the idea:

> But You have enough — of those —

What she seeks is something even more special. She mentions 'Jewels', 'Odors', 'Colors' only to dismiss them.

The listing continues into the second stanza but the tense changes. The 'I could' becomes 'have I —' but the 'Berries of the Bahamas' are also rejected. What could be got (jewels, odours, colours) and what already is to hand (berries) are not as good as what Dickinson calls 'this little Blaze':

> Berries of the Bahamas — have I —
> But this little Blaze
> Flickering to itself — in the Meadow —
> Suits Me — more than those —

In the first stanza Dickinson is contemplating possibilities and the ideas flow as freely as the lines. Slant end-rhymes, 'to, those, Domingo, Cruz', suggest a mind at leisure. In stanza two there is greater focus. Dickinson, having rejected certain options, now focuses on her preference and the lines become shorter, more concentrated, to match her thinking. What 'this little Blaze' is exactly is never revealed. It is a personal choice, more unusual than the colourful and the exotic listed earlier. It is spoken of as light, as 'Blaze' and 'Flickering'.

The choice is revealing and Dickinson intends it to be so: she states clearly that 'this little Blaze . . . Suits Me – more than those –'. Though little, it is precious and treasured and the phrase 'in the Meadow' suggests a little flower.

Once chosen, 'this little Blaze' outshines everything else. The tone in the final stanza is one of conviction, the 'Never' is absolute:

> Never a Fellow matched this Topaz –
> And his Emerald Swing –
> Dower itself – for Bobadilo –
> Better – Could I bring?

Topaz suggests a yellow, white, pale blue or pale green colour and Emerald is a brilliant bright green. These natural colours again suggest meadow flowers.

The exact rhymes of 'Swing' and 'bring' make for a flourishing confidence at the end. If her choice of gift is suitable as a dower, it enhances its value; it is a worthy gift for a woman to bring to her prospective husband. The reference to 'Bobadilo' suggests that even a swaggerer and a braggart could not be given a better gift. The poem's final question is rhetorical.

We can only imagine this perfect gift, but we are given indications of its qualities. It glows with colour; it seems to be natural and it is not difficult or inaccessible or expensive. The real wealth is in the spirit in which it is given.

Of the ten poems by Dickinson on the course, this is a poem without shadows. Like 'I taste a liquor never brewed' it is celebratory and happy, but, unlike the poem celebrating 'endless summer days', this poem focuses more on a relationship rather than the individual self.

A narrow Fellow in the Grass

Though first printed under the title of 'The Snake', Dickinson never refers to the strange creature of the poem as snake. The physical details, however, certainly suggest that it describes a snake. Line 1 refers to a 'Fellow', suggesting familiarity or friendliness, and his appearance in the grass is both occasional and sudden:

> A narrow Fellow in the Grass
> Occasionally rides —
> You may have met Him — did you not
> His notice sudden is —

Here, Dickinson is obviously addressing and involving the reader: 'You may have met Him – did you not'; and she adds her own observation as to how suddenly the 'Fellow' appears. The snake 'rides' according to Dickinson, not crawls, suggesting self-possession and confidence.

In this first stanza, there is no attempt at end-rhyme ('Grass'/'rides'/'not'/'is') and few internal rhymes ('His'/'is', line 4); whereas in the final two stanzas 'me'/'cordiality' and 'alone'/'Bone' are clear rhymes.

The elusive nature of the snake is captured in stanza two: its ability to move quietly, secretly and unpredictably. Its glimpsed, variegated body is compared to a shaft which suggests an arrow:

> The Grass divides as with a Comb —
> A spotted shaft is seen —
> And then it closes at your feet
> And opens further on —

In the poem's central stanza, Dickinson goes beyond the immediate presence of a snake in the grass by her feet to describe the general nature of the snake, its preferred habitat, its characteristics. Memory is also introduced here; the poem moves from present to past tense:

> He likes a Boggy Acre
> A Floor too cool for Corn —
> Yet when a Boy, and Barefoot —
> I more than once at Noon
> Have passed, I thought, a Whip lash
> Unbraiding in the Sun
> When stooping to secure it
> It wrinkled, and was gone —

The barefoot boy suggests innocence and simplicity and clearly the boy is fascinated by the snake. Dickinson describes the boy as he attempts to catch the unwinding, wrinkled, whip-like snake. The boy has met the snake 'more than once' but, it seems, has never managed to capture one.

The language here is effective. 'A Floor too cool for Corn' captures the coolness itself through the assonance of 'Floor' and 'Corn'. Line 8 runs on into lines 9 and 10. Dickinson uses no dash or other punctuating device to create a pause at the end of line 9. The lines seem to flow, sinewy fashion, like the snake itself.

In the fifth stanza, Dickinson speaks of the boy's/her relationship with animals and birds, or 'Nature's People' as she refers to them. It is a warm and affectionate relationship:

> Several of Nature's People
> I know, and they know me —
> I feel for them a transport
> Of cordiality —

There is a shared, a reciprocated friendship here. Just as the speaker recognises 'Nature's People', they recognise her. The phrase 'transport/ Of cordiality' emphasises the warmth of feeling. Transport suggests that the speaker feels a rapture or ecstasy.

The use of 'But' and 'never' in line 21 make a very separate distinction between 'Several of Nature's People' and this 'narrow Fellow in the Grass'. It makes no difference as to whether the speaker has met with the snake alone or with others, the sensation is always frightening and chilling:

> But never met this Fellow
> Attended, or alone
> Without a tighter breathing
> And Zero at the Bone —

Dickinson makes no reference in the poem to the serpent or snake in the Book of Genesis in the Bible, nor does she explain why she feels this way about the snake. The boy in stanza three approached the snake in order to 'secure it', yet the snake has a physical effect on the speaker, the 'tighter breathing', a cold feeling in the bones. There is both a fascination with the snake and a fear and the two feelings are brought together within the poem.

John Donne
(1572–1631)

Contents	Page

The Overview

Seven of these poems by John Donne address his lover and the other three are addressed to God but all ten, whether lyric or sonnet, share a distinctive, direct voice. The dates (1572–1631) suggest a poet remote and distant from us and yet reading Donne's poetry one is often struck by what seems a fresh and contemporary quality. The language may be old-fashioned but his way of viewing the world is striking: he wants the sun to go away so that he can stay in bed longer with his lover ('The Sun Rising'); he jokingly says a faithful woman is impossible to find ('Go, and catch a falling star'); he thinks that he and his love are at the centre of the world and more important than the King and that their spiritual love will outlive their physical relationship ('The Anniversary'); he bids his love a temporary farewell, knowing that one day death will separate them ('Sweetest love, I do not go'); he asks his love not to mourn his absence on his setting out on a journey, for their true union is spiritual and their souls will never be separated ('A Valediction: forbidding Mourning'); he asks his love to make his dream of their being together come true ('The Dream'); he pleads with his love to become intimate with him, just as the flea has been with her ('The Flea'); he asks God to help and guide him ('Thou hast made me'); he asks God to help him repent his sins ('At the round earth's imagined corners'); he asks God to batter him into shape, to ravish him so that he may become chaste ('Batter my heart three-personed God').

His tone is confident, assured and, even when he admits weakness, as in the confessional sonnets, God's help is confidently sought. John Donne is a love poet and a religious poet, but the term metaphysical poet is difficult to avoid when discussing Donne's work. Donne is numbered among a group of seventeenth-century poets known as Metaphysical Poets, though the term metaphysical poets was coined a century later by the poet and critic Samuel Johnson (1709–1784). Johnson spoke of these particular poets disparagingly when he said that 'about the beginning of the seventeenth century appeared a race of writers that may be termed the metaphysical poets' but the term 'metaphysical' had also been used by the poet Dryden, who said in 1693 that Donne 'affects the metaphysics'.

Meta-physical literally means beyond the physical and, though Herbert Grierson argues that 'Great poetry is always metaphysical, born of man's passionate thinking about life and love and death', the seventeenth-century Metaphysical Poets, of whom Donne is one, share a number of specific characteristics. These have been identified as follows: the complex relationships between lover and beloved, between time and eternity, between God and man.

Metaphysical Poetry: the following commentary, from the *Introduction to Poets of the English Language* by W.H. Auden and Norman Holmes Pearson, is useful:

'Metaphysical' is a somewhat misleading term, for it suggests that the poets to whom it is applied had a unique interest in the science of Being, in contrast, say, to 'Nature' poets. This is not the case: the subject matter of Donne and his followers is not essentially different from that of most poets. What characterises them is, first, certain habits of metaphor: instead of drawing their images from mythology, imaginative literature of the past, or direct observation of nature, they take their analogies from technical and scientific fields of knowledge, from, for example, cartography:

> My face in thine eye, thine in mine appears,
> And true plain hearts do in the faces rest,
> Where can we find two better hemispheres
> Without sharp North, without declining west?

> – Donne's 'The Good Morrow'

or mathematics:

> As Lines, so Loves oblique may well
> Themselves in every Angle greet:
> But ours so truly Paralel,
> Though infinite can never meet.

> – Marvell's 'The Definition of Love'

Secondly they are particularly intrigued by paradoxes, both of logic and emotion:

> For I
> Except you enthrall me, never shall be free,
> Nor ever chaste, except you ravish me.

> – Donne's 'Batter my heart'

Both the technical term and the paradox had appeared in poetry before Donne ... but elsewhere they are peripheral, not central to the style.

It seems possible – it is not provable – that the disruption of traditional values, cosmological and political, which was occurring at the beginning of the seventeenth century, encouraged this cast of mind and that metaphysical poetry is the reflection of a peculiar tension between faith and scepticism.'

●

One critic, Gosse, says that 'When Donne speaks of his personal experience, there is something so convincing in his accent, poignant and rude at once, that it is impossible not to believe it is the accurate record of a genuine emotional event.' This is certainly true of the poems here. His biographer, Bald, points out that 'Donne had a gift for creating a situation and presenting it vividly ... It is so skilfully done that one accepts without any questioning the illusion of a man speaking out of authentic and literal experience.' The poems, in several instances, are miniature dramas. A setting such as the intimate world of the bedroom, the step-by-step enactment of the exploits of a flea, the image of a heart being battered all heighten a situation and create and capture essential aspects of drama: mood, pacing, conflict.

Though viewed as one of the greatest love poets in English, Donne's love poetry does not dwell on physical description of his loved one nor does he ever name or identify his lover. In fact Donne himself said:

> Who ever guesses, thinks, or dreames he knowes
> Who is my mistris, wither by this curse

and that 'I did best when I had least truth for my subjects'. In other words, his poetry is not always based on actual experience.

In 1616, Thomas Campion, a contemporary of John Donne's, praised a woman as follows: 'There is a Garden in her face,/ Where Roses and white Lillies grow;/ A heav'nly paradice is that place,/ Wherein all pleasant fruits doe flow...' Donne does not indulge in such extravagance but there is, however, an extraordinarily convincing emotional and intellectual quality in his love poetry. A technique often used by Donne is the conceit, where dissimilar images are brought together, as in 'The Flea' or 'A Valediction: forbidding Mourning'.

It is said of Donne that he had the soul of a lover, the tongue of a wit and the mind of a lawyer-preacher accustomed to analysing complex problems and A. Alvarez says that 'Donne was the first Englishman to write verse in a way that reflected the whole complex activity of intelligence.' Donne repeatedly insists that the private world of lovers is superior to the wider public world but, following his wife's death in 1617, his poetry, which had celebrated sexuality and love, now focused on his relationship with God and his own life as a preacher became more public.

Samuel Taylor Coleridge (1772–1834) recognised the complexity of the work when he wrote 'On Donne's Poetry':

> With Donne, whose muse on dromedary trots,
> Wreathe iron pokers into true-love knots;
> Rhyme's sturdy cripple, fancy's maze and clue,
> Wit's forge and fire-blast, meaning's press and screw.

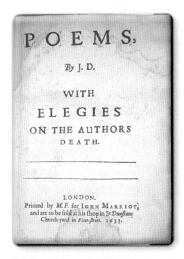

• Title page of John Donne's 1633 collection of poems.

Biographical Notes

John Donne, the third of six children, was born in Bread Street, London in 1572; the exact date is unknown but it is thought that he was born between January and June. His earliest biographer, Izaak Walton, gives the year of his birth as 1573. Shakespeare was then eight years old and Donne outlived his great contemporary by fifteen years. Donne's father, also called John, was a prosperous, Catholic, London merchant. His mother, Elizabeth, also a Catholic, belonged to a distinguished and celebrated family: she was the grand-niece of Sir Thomas More, who was beheaded by Henry VIII in 1535 because of his allegiance to Rome, and two of her brothers were Jesuit priests. [In 1534 Henry VIII had severed connections with Rome.] The family background was one of fidelity to the old religion; many members of the family had gone into exile and John Donne was brought up a Catholic. The importance of Donne's Catholicism and conversion to the Church of England have been much debated. John Carey begins his study of Donne by declaring that 'The first thing to remember about Donne is that he was a Catholic; the second, that he betrayed his Faith'. Two of Donne's contemporaries, the poets Robert Southwell (?1561–1595) and Chidiock Tichborne (?1558–1586), maintained their Catholic allegiance and were put to death for it.

When Donne was four his father died and his mother, within six months, married John Syminges, a distinguished medical doctor. Donne was educated at home in his stepfather's house by a private tutor and entered Oxford University in 1584 with a good command of French and Latin. By then three of Donne's sisters had died, leaving three children in all: Anne, John and Henry. The two boys matriculated from Hart Hall, Oxford in October 1584; John was twelve and Henry was eleven.

Having spent three years in Oxford, Donne then studied at Cambridge for approximately two years. He was an avid and voracious reader. At university, rhetoric and logic were the main subjects; a degree was awarded based on the undergraduate's skill in disputation. Such skill is evident in Donne's poetry and especially in his sermons.

Little is known of John Donne immediately after his time in Cambridge. Most likely he travelled to Italy and he may have had a military career, but records show that, in 1591, a nineteen-year-old Donne was studying law and that he entered Lincoln's Inn in 1592. He never practised law and was never called to the bar, but his time there was hugely important; it was during this time that much of Donne's early poetry was written. He was also now moving in distinguished circles and presented himself at court. The earliest known portrait of Donne dates from this time and shows a young man in fashionable clothes, long hair, light moustache and ear-ring.

Later, one of his contemporaries remembers 'Mr John Donne, who leaving Oxford, lives at the Innes of Court . . . very neat, a great visiter of Ladies, a great frequenter of Playes, a great writer of conceited Verses.' When he was twenty-one he inherited his dead father's bequest, a sum of £750.

His earliest poems were verse-letters addressed to friends, described by one critic, R. C. Bald, as 'little more than elaborate exchanges of compliment; they suggest a coterie of ingenious young men assiduously cultivating the Muse and warmly applauding each other's efforts.'

A legal education at that time was at least seven years of study. During Donne's time at Lincoln's Inn, London was plague-stricken and in a verse-letter Donne says of London that the theatres are filled with emptiness and 'in every street/Infections follow, overtake, and meet.' In 1593, Henry, Donne's only brother, died of plague in Newgate prison, where he was being held for harbouring a young priest.

As a Catholic, Donne knew that the road to success was barred to him, that his religion meant persecution and exile, and his intellectual curiosity prompted him to question his received creed.

The dating of Donne's poetry is conjectural but it is thought that the first two Satires, nearly all the Elegies and a number of the *Songs and Sonnets* date from the Lincoln's Inn days. Though he had studied law, Donne and many of his fellow students did not look on it as a career. Donne, in fact, wrote disparagingly of 'men who chuse/Law practise for meere gaine.'

In 1596, when he was twenty-four, Donne joined an expedition against Spain under the Earl of Essex. A patriotic gesture, and, in joining an English, Protestant expedition against Catholic Spain, John Donne was perhaps indicating another strong expression of his feelings. It was during the 1590s that Donne converted from Roman Catholicism to the English Church. He sailed from Plymouth and his poem 'A Burnt Ship', from this period, most probably describes how the English cannons targeted the largest Spanish Galleon, *San Felipe*: 'So all were lost, which in the ship were found,/They in the sea being burnt, they in the burnt ship drowned'. The following year, Donne, again under the Earl of Essex, set sail to the Azores. Many of the one hundred ships were battered by storms and had to return to Plymouth and Donne commemorated the delay in 'The Storme'. Donne's poem 'The Calme' dates from the same expedition some months later. Overall, the expedition was not a success. When Donne returned home to England in October 1597 he settled down; his military service was at an end.

In London, Donne found employment with the Lord Keeper of England, Sir Thomas Egerton, and acted as a Secretary. His legal background brought legal business his way and in one of his Satires he condemns corruption and lawyers' fees. Through his job, Donne tells us, he begins 'To know and weed out this enormous sinne.' The years spent in Egerton's service were important for many reasons. He became familiar with the ways of the Court of Elizabeth I, realised how careers were made and, most significantly, it was through the Egerton family that Donne met his future wife Ann More, who was the daughter of Thomas Egerton's brother-in-law. When he fell in love with her in 1600, she was sixteen, he was twenty-seven and, because Donne was ill-matched financially, they kept their affair secret. Ann More lived with her family in the country but she came up to London in October 1601 for the opening of Parliament. Her father was looking for a suitably wealthy and distinguished husband for his daughter. The two lovers married in secret three weeks before Christmas. Donne was marrying a girl, still a minor, from a wealthy family, without her father's knowledge or consent. Five were present at the wedding ceremony and, when Parliament was dissolved just before Christmas, it is thought that Ann, now Mistress (Mrs) Donne, returned to her father's house, Losely Park, near Guildford.

Donne did not tell his father-in-law of his marriage for two months, by which time he was in a state of anxiety. He became ill and eventually wrote to Sir George More with the news. More was furious, he had Donne and the witnesses to the marriage ceremony imprisoned and insisted that Donne be dismissed from the Lord Keeper's service. It was a brief imprisonment. Donne succeeded in opening up communications with Sir George but failed to be reinstated in Egerton's service. He was, however, allowed to write to his wife and the first letter supposedly ends punningly with 'John Donne, Anne Donne, Un-done'.

In April a suit lodged by Donne to test the validity of the marriage resulted in a judgement declaring them lawfully married. Sir George More unwillingly surrendered his daughter to Donne and refused to give her a penny.

Donne was thirty; he had no money, no job and a young wife to look after. Friends helped them out and they spent the early years of their married life, as guests, in Ann's cousin's house in Surrey. There, Donne helped in the running of the house and studied civil and canon law. There too, the first of their twelve children was born: Constance, born 1603; John, born 1604; George, born 1605; Francis, born 1606/7; Lucy, born 1608; Bridget, born 1609; Mary, born 1611; baby, still-born 1612; Nicholas, born 1613; [1614 – Mary dies; Nicholas dies]; Margaret, born 1615; Elizabeth, born 1616; baby, still-born 1617, and that same year Donne's thirty-three-year-old wife died. She and the still-born baby were buried together.

It is almost certain that Donne's love poem 'The Sunne Rising' dates from the early years of their marriage, when they were living at Pyrford. Elizabeth I died in 1603 and her successor James I is referred to in the poem. Donne's references to 'Court-huntsmen' and 'that the King will ride' are to James I's love of hunting.

Donne's third child was born in London, which suggests that the Donne family had left Pyrford by 1605, by which time Sir George had been reconciled with his daughter and granted her an allowance. Donne as a result took a house for himself and his family at Mitcham, near London, and he travelled to the continent that same year in search of work. He visited France and Italy and, on returning, although his Mitcham house became his home for the next five years, he took lodgings in the Strand in the city. Dividing his time in this way he followed the Court and sought patronage. He studied divinity, law, wrote poems to great ladies and theological pamphlets to the King.

Donne, however, failed to secure a position at Court. He had very close friends, and, while living a social life, he also lived a life of study and meditation, writing many of the 'Divine Poems' and taking a keen interest in the differences between Catholics and Protestants. Donne published *Pseudo-Martyr* in 1610, a book which pleased the King and earned him an M.A. from Oxford. Though Donne had hoped for a position within the Court, the King recommended that Donne take orders. His letters from this period reveal a disappointed and despondent Donne. He resisted the invitation to enter the Church, but he also wrote about this time that 'two of the most precious things which God hath afforded us here . . . are a thirst and inhiation [the act of gaping] after the next life, and a frequency of prayer and meditation in this' and that God had given him the 'comfort of sadder meditations.' Many of the 'Holy Sonnets' were written during the 'Mitcham' years in which he expressed doubts about his salvation, experienced a spiritual crisis and knew despair and suffering. It was once thought that these sonnets were written by Donne, having taken holy orders; it is now known that they were written by a man in his thirties, before he was ordained.

The next episode of note in Donne's life was his journey abroad with Sir Robert Drury, a wealthy man whose name was later given to Drury Lane. Donne wrote 'A Funerall Elegie' on the death of Sir Robert and Lady Drury's fifteen-year-old daughter Elizabeth. Sir Robert became one of Donne's patrons and invited him to accompany him and his family on an extended journey on the continent. Ann, his wife, was pregnant with her eight child and did not want Donne to go; Sir Robert, however, urged him and Donne, having been treated so well by his patron, agreed to travel (to France, Germany, Belgium), leaving his wife and children with her relations on the Isle of Wight. It is thought by some scholars that his Song 'Sweetest love, I do not go' and 'A Valediction: forbidding Mourning' date from this period, 1612. While Donne was away his wife gave birth to a still-born child in January and, on his return, in September, he and his family moved to a house on the Drury Estate, Drury Lane, London. The house was comfortable and their being in London meant that his elder boys would have access to a good education.

Donne's future was still uncertain. He travelled to visit friends in the country and, during his time there, resolved yet again to find state employment, and, with it, financial security, but again this proved unsuccessful. In May 1614, his three-year-old daughter Mary died and his seven-year-old son Francis died that November. The family were in need of money and, though Donne kept a French manservant, he had to sell his horse.

These sorrows and difficulties may have confirmed John Donne's decision to enter the church; the following year, at forty-two, he was ordained deacon and priest at St Paul's Cathedral. From this distance it is difficult to say how committed John Donne was to his new position. His writings from this time reveal a disappointed man who was aware of the low social prestige attached to this new profession, but the critic Helen Gardner thinks that Donne is to be honoured because, having received his vocation thus indirectly, he tried to fulfil it worthily and set himself an exacting standard of duty'. He presented himself to King James, who was head of Donne's Church, and was appointed a royal Chaplain to the King, thus providing Donne with access to the Court and an assured income.

Donne accompanied the King to Cambridge and was made a Doctor of Divinity by the University of Cambridge in late March 1615. Thus began Donne's distinguished career as a priest and preacher. He preached to monarchs, members of the Court, lawyers, merchants, magistrates, and his sermons, of which about 160 survive, indicate a brilliant, original mind. He drew on legal and courtly imagery whenever appropriate and he gave a series of anti-Catholic sermons, none of which survives. His most famous sermon gives us the well-known lines: 'No man is an island, entire of itself; every man is a piece of the continent, a part of the main[land]. If a clod be washed away by the sea, Europe is the less . . . Any man's death diminishes me, because I am involved in mankind; and therefore never send to know for whom the bell tolls; it tolls for thee'.

A great change happened when his wife Ann gave birth to a still-born child, their twelfth, on 10 August and died on 15 August 1617. We do not know much about Ann Donne but there can be little doubt that John Donne was devoted to his wife. His earliest biographer speaks of Donne's grief and of how he locked himself away from the world in sorrow; when he did enter public life again, in November, it was to preach in the church where his wife and baby were buried. This was a turning point in Donne's life. Until then Donne's deepest emotions were linked to his wife; now they were transferred to God and focused on the relationship between God and human beings, even though many of his finest religious poems pre-date Donne's ordination.

Eventually, Donne did resume a public life; he travelled to Germany, preached widely and was elected and installed as Dean of St Paul's on 22 November 1621. A chronology of Donne's later years is one of his busy involvement in church life. In March 1625 he wrote his last poem. King James died that same month and Donne preached the first sermon to his successor, Charles I, on 3 April. In his personal life there were private sorrows: his daughter Constance's marriage broke down; his daughter Lucy, aged 19, died; his mother, who lived into her eighties, died. Donne became ill in 1630 and in December he made his will. In keeping with the seventeenth-century realistic attitude towards death, early in 1631 he had a portrait made of him in his shroud which he contemplated during his final days. Donne had witnessed plague and reminders of death were seen as an everyday and essential part of life.

Izaac Walton, Donne's first biographer, tells of how Donne, very close to death, had a wooden urn carved and a plank, the length of his body, brought to his study. He then took off his clothes, put on his shroud and had knots tied at head and foot. With shroud turned back to reveal his face, Donne then faced the east, associated with the resurrection, stood on the urn, closed his eyes and had an artist sketch his life-size figure on the wooden plank. The body thus depicted was shown rising from the funeral urn. Donne kept this drawing by his bedside to remind him of what he would soon be. Then, having attended to final business and having summoned friends to his bedside to say goodbye, he was, in Walton's words, 'so happy as to have nothing to do but dye' and Walton adds that 'as his soul ascended, and his last breath departed from him, he closed his own eyes; and then disposed his hands and body into such a posture as required not the least alteration by those that came to shroud him.'

He died on 31 March 1631 and was buried in St Paul's. In his will, Donne asked that he be buried 'in the moste private manner that maye be'; his wishes were not followed and he was given a public funeral of wide acclaim. An unknown person wrote on the wall above his grave: 'Reader! I am to let thee know,/Donne's Body only, lyes below:/For, could the grave his Soul comprize,/Earth would be richer than the skies'. The year following his death a memorial statue, depicting John Donne in his shroud, was erected in St Paul's. On the monument a Latin epigraph, most likely written by Donne himself, appears. It reads: 'John Donne, Doctor of Divinity, after various studies, pursued by him from his earliest years with assiduity and not without success, entered into Holy Orders, under the influence and impulse of the Divine Spirit and by the advice and exhortation of King James, in the year of his Saviour 1614, and of his own age 42. Having been invested with the Deanery of this Church, November 27, 1621, he was stripped of it by Death on the last day of March 1631: and here, though set in dust, he beholdeth Him Whose name is the Rising'.

During his lifetime his poetry was circulated in manuscript, but Donne published only two poems – funeral elegies on the young daughter of his patron Sir Robert Drury. Some sermons had been published during his lifetime and he left his sermons carefully written out for his son to publish after his death, but it is thought that he did not want the poems which are known as *Songs and Sonnets* published. In 1633 the first collected edition of John Donne's poetry appeared. This was republished in 1635 as *Songs and Sonnets*.

Michael Schmidt says that Donne in his poetry intended to speak to a few: 'He allowed his poems to circulate in manuscript among special friends. One of them might copy out a piece for private pleasure, another make a secret record, but the public that knew Donne at court or later heard his sermons in St Paul's was generally ignorant of his poetry'.

The home where John and Ann Donne lived in the village of Pyrford, Surrey, England.

The dating of Donne's work is difficult as his printed poems were based on transcripts of his work. Very few of Donne's poems were published in his lifetime and only one copy of a poem written in Donne's own hand has survived. The first edition of his poetry was published in 1633, two years after his death. In the versions printed here, the spellings have been modernised, e.g. 'Sunne', 'Goe', 'Busie', 'windowes', 'halfe' have become 'Sun', 'go', 'busy', 'windows', 'half' ...

The Sun Rising

    Busy old fool, unruly sun,
    Why dost thou thus,
Through windows, and through curtains call on us?
Must to thy motions lovers' seasons run?
    Saucy pedantic wretch, go chide   5
    Late school-boys, and sour prentices,
  Go tell court-huntsmen, that the King will ride,
  Call country ants to harvest offices;
Love, all alike, no season knows, nor clime,
Nor hours, days, months, which are the rags of time.   10

    Thy beams, so reverend, and strong
    Why shouldst thou think?
I could eclipse and cloud them with a wink,
But that I would not lose her sight so long:
    If her eyes have not blinded thine,   15
    Look, and tomorrow late, tell me,
  Whether both th'Indias of spice and mine
  Be where thou left'st them, or lie here with me.
Ask for those kings whom thou saw'st yesterday,
And thou shalt hear, All here in one bed lay.   20

    She is all states, and all princes, I,
    Nothing else is.
Princes do but play us; compared to this,
All honour's mimic; all wealth alchemy.
    Thou sun art half as happy as we,   25
    In that the world's contracted thus;
  Thine age asks ease, and since thy duties be
  To warm the world, that's done in warming us.
Shine here to us, and thou art everywhere;
This bed thy centre is, these walls, thy sphere.   30

Glossary

Line 1 Busy: meddling, prying, interfering; never still.

Line 1 unruly: unmannerly.

Line 4 Must to thy motions lovers' seasons run?: must lovers live their lives according to your [the sun's] movements?; must lovers follow the sun's course as the earth does with the different, changing seasons?

Line 5 saucy: cheeky / impertinent.

Line 5 pedantic: strictly observing rules.

Line 5 chide: scold, rebuke.

Line 6 prentices: apprentices / juniors learning a trade.

Line 7 court-huntsmen: persons of the court who hunt; hangers-on. Donne is mocking those courtiers who sought promotion by ingratiating themselves with King James who was passionate about sport. This reference to King James I, who in 1603 succeeded Elizabeth I, allows us to date this poem with some accuracy.

Line 8 country ants: farmers, but the words suggest a kind of repetitive work or drudgery

Line 8 harvest offices: the routines of the countryside; autumn work. If 'harvest' is taken as a verb the line could mean call country workers to their autumn work.

Line 9 Love, all alike: Love, never changing; the same always.

Line 9 clime: climate.

Line 10 rags: man-made, clock-controlled divisions of time.

Line 11 reverend: deserving reverence / respect (**Line 11**: 'Why should you, Sun, think your beams so reverend and strong?')

Line 14 But that: Except that.

Line 17 both th'Indias: East Indies and West Indies, one famous for spice, the other for gold (gold is mined in the West Indies). These islands in the western Atlantic and in the south-western Pacific were mistakenly called Indias or Indies by explorers who thought they had reached India.

Line 21 She is all states, and all princes, I: she is, to me, all the states/nations there are, and I am all the princes there are of these states.

Line 23 play: imitate.

Line 24 All honour's mimic: everything considered honourable is but a mimic or an imitation [of us].

Line 24 alchemy: a flashy pretence. Alchemy was the name for chemical research up until circa 1600, which tried to turn base metal into gold. Donne is here saying that compared to his wealth in love all other wealth is inferior or false.

Line 25 Thou sun art half as happy as we: you are on your own, sun, you are single; we lovers have each other.

Line 26 the world's contracted thus: she and I have formed this unique world; the world has been reduced to the size of our bed.

Line 27 Thine age asks ease: you, sun, are old and therefore you deserve not to be asked to do too much.

Line 30 This bed thy centre is, these walls thy sphere: Donne here is telling the sun that the bed containing the lovers is the centre of the sun's orbit and the bedroom walls are the extent of the sun's orbit. Donne is drawing on imagery from Ptolemy. According to Ptolemy (c. 90–168 AD), the Egyptian mathematician, astronomer and geographer, the earth was the stationary centre of the universe and the heavenly bodies revolved round it. Ptolemy's earth-centred view dominated cosmological thought until the Polish astronomer Copernicus, (1473–1543) swept Ptolemy's theory aside and correctly stated that the universe was sun-centred.

John Donne's love poems were written over a period of twenty years, beginning circa 1595. They were not published during Donne's lifetime but were circulated widely in manuscript. The love poems were first published in 1633 and, when reprinted in 1635, they were given the title *Songs and Sonnets*.

'The Sun Rising', written circa 1605 and first published in 1633, two years after Donne's death, is an aubade with a difference. The aubade is a poem which either celebrates the dawn or laments that two lovers must part. One of the most famous aubades in literature is the poetry spoken by Romeo and Juliet on the morning after their wedding night, the last time they talk to each other. Here, Donne turns the aubade convention on its head. He does not greet the sun, nor welcome it – he reprimands it for waking up his love and him. He debunks the sun at dawn, telling the sun to go and bother others and get their lives going, but Donne and his love should be left alone. Donne believes that the love this man and woman now share makes them kings and princes of their own in the realm of love.

The poem, in three ten-line stanzas, has an abbacdcdee rhyming scheme. The metre used is varied: tetrameter, dimeter, pentameter, pentameter, tetrameter, tetrameter, pentameter, pentameter, pentameter, pentameter.

? Questions

1. The poet and his lover are together in bed in the early morning. How would you describe Donne's tone in the opening lines? How is that tone established?

2. What descriptions does Donne give of the world beyond the lovers' bedroom? What is the effect of the references to 'schoolboys', 'prentices', 'ants'? How would you describe that other world? Is it an attractive one? Give reasons for your answer.

3. Why does Donne consider himself superior to the sun? Which phrases in particular express that confidence best?

4. How can we tell that he truly loves this woman? Which details suggest this? Look at where the pronouns 'we', 'I' and 'us' are used.

5. Exploration and discovery of new lands were very exciting during the early seventeenth century, when Donne was alive.

What is Donne's view of such activities in line 17?

6. Stanzas one and two begin with references to the sun. Why do you think stanza three begins differently?

7. Consider Donne's reference to the King at line 7. How does Donne view the King and kingship by line 19, 20?

8. The poem begins with a complaint and it ends with an invitation. Why did he complain? Why did he change his mind? How has this change come about?

9. How would you describe the mood with which the poem ends? Is it a fitting mood with which to end the poem?

10. Is 'The Sunne Rising' a typical or atypical love poem? In your answer you should discuss what you regard as a typical and atypical love poem.

Song (Go, and catch a falling star)

Go, and catch a falling star,
   Get with child a mandrake root,
Tell me, where all past years are,
   Or who cleft the Devil's foot,
Teach me to hear mermaids singing,   5
   Or to keep off envy's stinging,
        And find
        What wind
Serves to advance an honest mind.

If thou be'est born to strange sights,   10
   Things invisible to see,
Ride ten thousand days and nights,
   Till age snow white hairs on thee,
Thou, when thou return'st, wilt tell me
All strange wonders that befell thee,   15
        And swear
        No where
Lives a woman true, and fair.

If thou find'st one, let me know,
   Such a pilgrimage were sweet,   20
Yet do not, I would not go,
   Though at next door we might meet,
Though she were true, when you met her,
And last, till you write your letter,
        Yet she   25
        Will be
False, ere I come, to two, or three.

Glossary

Line 2 Get with child a mandrake root: create a child with the help of a fork-rooted plant. The mandrake – *mandragora officinarum* – is a narcotic and a poisonous plant of the potato family and associated with many strange imaginings (for example, it was thought that the root shrieked when pulled from the ground and killed those who heard it.) The forked root of the plant resembles the lower half of the human body. It was also thought that if used as a medicine it would promote conception.

Line 4 Cleft: split; the devil supposedly has cloven hooves.

Line 5 mermaids singing: it was thought that to hear the song of the mermaids meant disaster and death.

Line 6 to keep off envy's stinging: to protect myself from jealous people attacking me.

Line 10 If thou be'est born to strange sights: If you really wish/are fated to see strange sights.

Line 15 befell thee: happened to you.

Line 18 true, and fair: faithful and beautiful – Donne is suggesting that it is impossible to find both qualities in the one woman.

'Song' was first published in 1633. Professor William Harmon, commenting on this poem, says that Donne is here indulging in a light-hearted joke about women's behaviour: 'the speaker advances a set of impossible conditions, and then remarks that, when these conditions are met, a woman will be fair in appearance and faithful in conduct. The first five lines contain flatly impossible challenges. From lines six to nine, however, the focus shifts to include matters of conduct: how to avoid envy and how to be honest without suffering for your honesty.'

The idea of the impossible is found both in classical and medieval poetry. The poet lists impossible tasks as a rhetorical device. Another instance would be the Simon and Garfunkel song – 'Are You Going to Scarborough Fair?'.

? Questions

1. What is the effect of the words 'Go', 'Get', 'Tell', 'Teach' 'find' in the opening stanza? What mood would you say the poet is in here?

2. Why does the poet deliberately ask for the impossible? What does the long list of impossibilities lead to? What, in your opinion, prompted the poet to write this particular poem?

3. How can line 19, 'If thou find'st one, let me know', be interpreted? By the end of the poem what has the poet concluded regarding woman 'true and fair'?

4. How would you describe the rhythm of the poem and do you think the rhythm appropriate to the poem's purpose?

5. Comment on the change of rhythm in the seventh and eighth lines in each of the three stanzas. What is the effect of this?

6. Is this a 'tongue-in-cheek' piece of writing? Is the poet being playful or deadly serious? Is there a bitterness here? Is it possible to say?

7. Donne studied law, rhetoric, logic. Consider words such as 'If' (lines 10, 19) 'Yet '(line 21) and 'Though' (lines 22, 23) and how they further his argument.

8. What feeling is the reader left with on reading the final three lines of the poem?

The Anniversary

All kings, and all their favourites,
   All glory of honours, beauties, wits,
The sun itself, which makes times, as they pass,
Is elder by a year, now, than it was
When thou and I first one another saw: 5
All other things, to their destruction draw,
   Only our love hath no decay;
This, no tomorrow hath, nor yesterday,
Running it never runs from us away,
But truly keeps his first, last, everlasting day.   10

   Two graves must hide thine and my corse,
   If one might, death were no divorce,
Alas, as well as other princes, we,
— Who prince enough in one another be —
Must leave at last in death, these eyes, and ears,   15
Oft fed with true oaths, and with sweet salt tears;
   But souls where nothing dwells but love
— All other thoughts being inmates — then shall prove
This, or a love increased there above,
When bodies to their graves, souls from their graves remove.   20

   And then we shall be throughly blessed,
   But we no more than all the rest.
Here upon earth, we are kings, and none but we
Can be such kings, nor of such subjects be;
Who is so safe as we? where none can do   25
Treason to us, except one of us two.
   True and false fears let us refrain,
Let us love nobly, and live, and add again
Years and years unto years, till we attain
To write threescore, this is the second of our reign.   30

📖 Glossary

Line 2 honours: people of importance and rank.

Line 3 makes times: makes the seconds, minutes, hours, days, etc.

Line 3 they: 'they' can be interpreted as referring to the people mentioned in lines 1 and 2, or more probably, the times – the seconds, minutes, hours, etc.

Line 4 Is: this refers only to the sun but the implication is that the Kings, favourites, honours, beauties, wits are also 'elder by a year'.

Line 9 Running it never runs from us away: love is on-going and it is always with us.

Line 10 his: its.

Line 11 corse: corpse. Here the poet speaks of the man and woman being buried separately. This has been interpreted to mean that their love was secret and a public union in the grave would not be possible. When Donne fell in love with Ann More and married her it was done in secret.

Line 12 If one might, death were no divorce: if they could be buried together then death would not separate them.

Line 16 sweet salt tears: the inclusion here of opposites - sweet and salt - suggests that love has its sorrows as well as happiness.

Line 17 nothing dwells but love: the soul is love's home.

Line 18 inmates: short-term/ temporary lodgers.

Line 18 prove: experience.

Line 19 or a love increased there above: beyond this earthly life, in heaven, there is a love greater than the love found in souls.

Line 20 souls from their graves: the souls leave their bodies.

Line 21 throughly: thoroughly.

Line 22 But we no more than all the rest: in heaven every soul will experience equal love – their happiness in heaven will be no greater than anyone else's. In some versions this line reads 'But now no more . . .'.

Line 24 nor of such subjects be: [none but we] can be subjects of such kings. This line has also been interpreted to mean [none but we] can be Kings of such subjects.

Line 26 Treason: disloyalty, treachery, betrayal.

Line 27 True and false fears let us refrain: let us curb, check, restrain our fears, whether they be real or not. Love will flourish if uncertainties and suspicions are put aside.

Line 30 threescore: sixty – the poet looks forward to their sixtieth (diamond) anniversary.

> Here, the poet looks back on the time when he first saw the woman he loves. The Italian poet, Petrarch, has written of the day he first saw his love, Laura, but she does not return that love, and he hopes to find love with her in the next world. Donne, by contrast, finds true love on earth and looks forward not only to sixty years of loving but to heavenly and eternal happiness also.

? Questions

1. This love poem begins and ends with images of kings and kingship. What has happened to the idea of kingship between line 1 and line 30? Why has one interpretation of kingship replaced the other?

2. The opening stanza is preoccupied with time. How does the poet view the passing of time in relation to the wider world and in relation to his own private world?

3. Why do you think the poet uses 'All' so often in the opening stanza? – 'All kings . . .', 'All glory . . .', 'All other things . . .'. Comment on the effect of 'Only' in line 7. Do you think the lines in stanza one should be read at the same pace? If not, which lines should be read slowly? Why?

4. Love poetry is traditionally a poetry of praise and celebration. Donne certainly praises and celebrates, but he also looks at grimness of reality – the passing of time, the reality of death, the destiny of the grave. Why do you think he includes such references in this love poem. Do you think it adds to or subtracts from the poem? Give reasons for your answer.

5. 'Here upon earth we are kings'; in heaven 'we shall be throughly blest'. Does the poet prefer life on earth or life in heaven? Why?

6. Is the poet realistic about the nature of love? What is the significance of 'sweet salt tears' and 'True and false fears'?

7. How would you describe the poet's mood or feeling throughout the poem? Does it change? Where?

8. Stanza one referred to kings and their subjects. In line 24 the poet sees himself and his lover as both king and subject. They rule each other and at the same time are subject to each other. What does this image reveal to us of their relationship?

9. Donne, referring to his own poetry, spoke of it as the expression of his 'naked, thinking heart'. Is this quality of directness, intellectual and emotional, evident here?

10. Both 'The Sun Rising' and 'The Anniversary' are love poems. Which one do you prefer and why? Which one do you consider the more passionate? Which one do you consider the more persuasive?

Song (Sweetest love I do not go)

Sweetest love, I do not go,
   For weariness of thee,
Nor in hope the world can show
   A fitter love for me;
     But since that I   5
Must die at last, 'tis best,
To use myself in jest
   Thus by feigned deaths to die.

Yesternight the sun went hence,
   And yet is here today,   10
He hath no desire nor sense,
   Nor half so short a way:
     Then fear not me,
But believe that I shall make
Speedier journeys, since I take   15
   More wings and spurs than he.

O how feeble is man's power
   That if good fortune fall,
Cannot add another hour,
   Nor a lost hour recall!   20
     But come bad chance,
And we join to it our strength,
And we teach it art and length,
   Itself o'er us to advance.

When thou sigh'st, thou sigh'st not wind,   25
   But sigh'st my soul away,
When thou weep'st, unkindly kind,
   My life's blood doth decay.
     It cannot be
That thou lov'st me, as thou say'st   30
If in thine my life thou waste;
   Thou art the best of me.

Let not thy divining heart
  Forethink me any ill,
Destiny may take thy part,   35
  And may thy fears fulfil;
    But think that we
Are but turned aside to sleep;
They who one another keep
  Alive, ne'er parted be.   40

 ## Glossary

Line 4 fitter: more suitable.

Lines 6–8 'tis best . . . to die: it is best to pretend to die in a joking way so that I can become accustomed to it.

Line 8 feigned deaths: pretended deaths (which in this instance are temporary separations, absences).

Line 16 wings and spurs: a reference to Donne's desire to travel swiftly so as to speed his return.

Line 21–24 But come bad chance,/And we join it to our strength,/And we teach it art and length,/Itself o'er us to advance: if we meet with misfortune we allow it to become part of us; our misery adds to it and we teach this bad luck how to get the better of us.

Line 25 wind: breath.

Lines 29–32 It cannot be/That thou lov'st me, as thou say'st,/If in thine my life thou waste;/Thou are the best of me: If you sigh and weep you are wasting my life away, for my life and yours are so intertwined that I am part of you.

Line 33 divining: prophetic, foreseeing.

> It is thought that Donne wrote this poem for his wife while travelling to the continent in 1611. Donne was 39, his wife Ann was 27.

? Questions

1. This poem has been set to music. What song-like qualities do you find in this poem? What is here to suggest that it ought to be sung?

2. In 'The Sun Rising' and 'The Anniversary' that the lovers were together was of paramount importance – together in bed and together for eternity. Here, the poet is parting from his lover for a while. List the reasons the poet gives by way of justifying his going. Do you think that they are convincing?

3. Is the poet being serious or playful or is he being both? Give reasons for your answer.

4. Comment on the poet's use of rhyme and repetition. How do these contribute to the poem's effect?

5. The poem is directly addressed to his beloved. Examine how the poet refers to 'I', 'thee', 'me' and 'we'.

6. Discuss the contrast between the journey, his going, her weeping, on the one hand, and the image with which the poem ends on the other – 'turned aside to sleep'.

7. If you did not know who wrote 'Sweetest love, I do not go', do you think that you could say whether it was written by a man or a woman? Why?

8. Is the central idea in this poem a suitable idea for a love poem? How do you think the person addressed in the poem would react to the poet?

[handwritten top margin:] Metaphysical intellect and tone of confidence. Tone of authority.

A Valediction: forbidding Mourning

[handwritten: sibilance]   *[handwritten: death]*   *[handwritten: tranquil e peaceful death]*

As virtuous men pass mildly away,   *[handwritten: Keenly aware of death]*
   And whisper to their souls, to go,
Whilst some of their sad friends do say,   *[handwritten: delicate, light]*
   The breath goes now, and some say, no: *[handwritten: Sound effects]*

[handwritten: Rhetoric, arguing his point]   *[handwritten: adressing a presumed listener]*   *[handwritten: secrecy]*   *[handwritten: understated departure]*

So let us melt, and make no noise,   *[handwritten: imperceptible moment of death]* 5
   No tear-floods, nor sigh-tempests move,

[handwritten: hyperbole]

'Twere profanation of our joys   *[handwritten: exciting references to the natural world (natural disasters)]*
   To tell the laity our love.

[handwritten: their love is extraordinary and exclusive]

[handwritten: earthquake] Moving of th'earth brings harms and fears,   *[handwritten: Rich terms of reference and variety of allusions makes the theme of love universal]*
   Men reckon what it did and meant,   10
But trepidation of the spheres
   Though greater far, is innocent.

[handwritten: arrogant condescending]   *[handwritten: below the moon]*
[handwritten: physical love]

Dull sublunary lovers' love   *[handwritten: their love is elevated to the heavens]*
   (Whose soul is sense) cannot admit   *[handwritten: their love is multifacited]*
Absence, because it doth remove   15
   Those things which elemented it.   *[handwritten: scientific]*

But we by a love, so much refined,
   That our selves know not what it is,   *[handwritten: mysterious and undefinable love]*
Inter-assured of the mind,   *[handwritten: intellectual]*
   Care less, eyes, lips and hands to miss.   *[handwritten: They do not depend on physical love as the "ordinary" lovers do.]* 20

[handwritten: convincing]   *[handwritten: rhetoric argument]*   *[handwritten: Paradox]*

Our two souls therefore, which are one,
   Though I must go, endure not yet
A breach, but an expansion,   *[handwritten: paradox]*
   Like gold to airy thinness beat.   *[handwritten: durability of their love]*

If they be two, they are two so   25
   As stiff twin compasses are two,   *[handwritten: conceit → love as a compass]*
Thy soul the fixed foot, makes no show   *[handwritten: compass: world of exploration adds excitement and passion. connection to maths and science]*
   To move, but doth, if th'other do.

[handwritten left margin: the lady is solid and loyal]

And though it <u>in the centre</u> sit, *centrality of their love*
    Yet when the other far doth roam,   30
It leans, and hearkens after it,
    And grows erect, as that comes home.

Such wilt thou be to me, who must,
    Like th' other foot, obliquely run; *circle of their love:*
Thy firmness makes my circle just,   *multiple meanings.*   35
    And makes me end where I begun. *→ she is the centre of*
                                            his world
                                    → he will return to her

Glossary

Title Valediction: to say farewell (a formal term; *vale* in Latin means farewell and *dicere* means to say) – a farewell poem.

Line 1 virtuous: holy.

Line 1 pass mildly: die calmly.

Lines 1–4: Donne here is saying 'Let us be as calm in our separating as holy men are in dying'.

Line 5 melt: blend; it has been suggested that Donne here is reminding us that love is not only physical. Love is capable of going through a change in state from physical to spiritual, just as the soul does in death, just as solid ice becomes fluid water. John Carey says of the word 'melt': 'What is happening is that the lovers' bodies are separating, leaving their souls behind, and Donne asks that the bodies should disappear from the scene (a quite normal seventeenth-century meaning of 'melt') as quietly as if they were dissolving'.

Line 6 tear-floods . . . sigh-tempests: this deliberate exaggeration/hyperbole is a familiar poetic convention, but Donne rejects this.

Line 7 profanation: desecration, insulting.

Line 8 laity: ordinary people who do not understand such love [both 'profanation' and 'laity' imply that Donne is thinking of his love as something holy and mysterious, suggesting that he sees their love as holy and spiritual, like a secret religious ceremony].

Line 9 Moving of th'earth: an earthquake.

Line 9 brings: causes.

Line 10 reckon what it did and meant: calculate the damage and try to measure its significance.

Line 11 trepidation of the spheres: according to Ptolemy the spheres sometimes moved violently and could cause a much greater and violent motion than an earthquake, but their motion is not even noticed.

Line 12 innocent: harmless.

Line 13 Dull: ordinary.

Line 13 sublunary: changeable, earthly, sensual (literally beneath the moon – sub luna). The line 'Dull sublunary lovers' love' refers to the love of the ordinary lovers who need to be by eachother's side and who are inconstant like the moon.

Line 14 Whose soul is sense: whose soul relies on sensation? Whose essence is sensuality?

Line 16 elemented: constituted.

Line 19 Inter-assured of the mind: each sure in mind that the other is faithful.

Line 23 breach: break.

Line 24 airy thinness: gold is capable of being beaten to an extraordinary thinness (an ounce of gold if beaten to the thinness of gold leaf – 1/250,000 of one inch – would cover 250 square feet). The word 'airy' also suggests that their love is so pure that it becomes a more special quality – that of air or spirit.

Line 26 stiff: firm.

Line 26 twin compasses: instrument for measuring and forming circles, with two legs connected at one end by a movable joint. Donne's simile is an example of conceit. Compasses were used as a symbol of constancy in change: the man is centred upon his lover even though he is apart from her. The image of the compass is particularly appropriate here: Donne is going on a journey ('Though I must go').

Line 32 that: the moving/roaming foot of the compass.

Line 34 obliquely: not straight – the foot of the compass which describes the circle follows a curved path.

Line 35 circle: a perfect circle can be drawn using a compass – one leg/foot of the compass is stable/constant, the other foot moves, and both create the symbol of perfection – the circle.

Line 35 just: perfect, complete.

In some manuscript versions of 'A Valediction: forbidding Mourning' the titles 'Upon the parting from his Mistress' and 'To his Love upon his departure from her' were given.

In his *Life of Dr John Donne* (1640), Isaak Walton says that Donne gave this poem to his wife when he set off for France in 1611 as part of Sir Robert Drury's retinue. But whether this is true or not is impossible to say. Walton knew Donne, he was his first biographer, and 'A Valediction: forbidding Mourning' was quoted in the 1675 edition of the biography.

Donne wrote five valedictions or farewell poems in which being apart is seen as something which tests the strength of love. Professor William Harmon has paraphrased 'A Valediction: forbidding Mourning' as follows:

'Dear, nothing I can say will adequately express either my love for you or my sadness at having to be away from you, and that's really all there is to it. However, I do want you to know that my feelings here are extremely powerful – so much so, indeed, that my imagination is driven to discover some means of telling you what's in my heart: Rather than resorting to one more meaningless cliché, I shall send my agitated spirit in search of a new figure of speech, and its outlandishness – although obviously inadequate – will at least show the strength of my love'.

Questions

1. The poem begins with a general statement and moves to the particular. Where does this occur? The poem begins with a variety of images; the closing lines focus on a single image. Identify these images through the poem.

2. Parting and absence are familiar topics in love poetry. Donne has written of these in 'Sweetest love I do not go'. How is this poem similar to and different from this other poem by Donne on a similar theme?

3. The poem is based on a carefully made argument: Parting causes sorrow/mourning. True lovers are never parted. True lovers have no need for mourning. What gives the poem this ordered and logical quality?

4. Poets draw their images from many different sources. Initially, the poet draws his images from the natural world. Examine the imagery used throughout the poem. Why are the final three stanzas so different from the preceding ones in terms of imagery? Do you think the imagery appropriate? Successful?

5. Where in the poem is Donne at his most confident? How is this confidence achieved?

6. In stanza six the poet sees the separation from his lover not as a 'breach' but as something positive and enhancing. How does he achieve this?

7. Donne in one of his Sermons wrote: 'In all Metrical compositions . . . the force of the whole piece is for the most part left to the shutting; the whole frame of the Poem is a beating out of a piece of gold, but the last clause is as the impression of the stamp, and that is it that makes it current.' Choose two or three poems by Donne which illustrate, in your opinion, Donne's viewpoint here and comment on Donne's choice of endings.

8. This poem begins with an image of dying; it ends with a perfect circle and the word 'begun'. Comment on the structure of the poem. Do you think this a convincing love poem? A realistic one? Why? Give reasons for your answer.

The Dream

Dear love, for nothing less than thee
Would I have broke this happy dream,
   It was a theme
For reason, much too strong for phantasy,
Therefore thou waked'st me wisely; yet   5
My dream thou brok'st not, but continued'st it;
Thou art so true, that thoughts of thee suffice,
To make dreams truths, and fables histories;
Enter these arms, for since thou thought'st it best,
Not to dream all my dream, let's do the rest.   10

As lightning, or a taper's light,
Thine eyes, and not thy noise waked me;
   Yet I thought thee
(For thou lov'st truth) an angel, at first sight,
But when I saw thou saw'st my heart,   15
And knew'st my thoughts, beyond an angel's art,
When thou knew'st what I dreamed, when thou knew'st when
Excess of joy would wake me, and cam'st then,
I must confess, it could not choose but be
Profane, to think thee anything but thee.   20

Coming and staying showed thee, thee,
But rising makes me doubt, that now,
   Thou art not thou.
That love is weak, where fear's as strong as he;
'Tis not all spirit, pure and brave,   25
If mixture it of fear, shame, honour, have.
Perchance as torches which must ready be,
Men light and put out, so thou deal'st with me,
Thou cam'st to kindle, goest to come; then I
Will dream that hope again, but else would die.   30

Glossary

Lines 3–4 It was a theme/ For reason, much too strong for phantasy: the dream was so convincing that it seemed true and not something merely imagined, a fantasy.

Line 6 brok'st: broke.

Line 6 continued'st: continued.

Line 7 Thou art so true: you are so real.

Line 8 fables histories: made-up stories are made real.

Line 10 do: the word 'do' appears in most manuscript versions of the poem, but some versions contain the word 'act'.

Line 11 taper's: slender candle's.

Line 14 (For thou lov'st truth): this is followed in some versions of the text by 'but an Angel'.

Line 16 beyond an angel's art: an angel does not know the thoughts of the heart, only God does.

Line 19 I must confess: 'I do confess' is a variant reading.

Line 19 It could not choose but be: I could only be. Some versions give 'it' for I'.

Line 20 Profane: irreverent.

Line 20 'to think thee anything but thee': Helen Gardner glosses this line as follows: 'only of God can it be said that "He is Himself only and divinely like Himself"'.

Line 21 showed thee, thee: showed you as yourself.

Line 22 doubt: suspect.

Line 25 pure: unalloyed, unadulterated.

Line 25 brave: sure, confident.

Line 27–29 Perchance as torches which must ready be,/ Men light and put out, so thou deal'st with me,/ Thou cam'st to kindle, goest to come': Theodore Redpath, in his edition of the poem, offers the following paraphrase: 'Perhaps in the same way as when torches have to be dry enough to light at once when required, people light them beforehand, and then put them out, so you came to set me alight, and are now only going away for a short while before you return to light me again'. A. J. Smith suggests: 'a used torch flares up more quickly than a new one'.

Line 30 but: several manuscript versions have 'or' instead of 'but'.

Line 30 die: 'to die' in Renaissance times carried with it, in certain contexts, a sexual meaning: to die meant to experience sexual climax.

> In 'The Dream' the dream is not broken but continued. He was sleeping and dreaming and on waking the dream becomes reality. John Carey says that here 'waking and sleeping life are not distinguished but superimposed: girl blends into dream, dream into girl'.

Questions

1. The poem begins with an immediate address, 'Dear love'; how does the poet feel towards his beloved in the opening two lines?

2. What is the particular situation being described here? Dream and reality are intermingled in the poet's mind. Examine how the poet explains that this is so. What is the poet's tone in line 5? Is there a different tone in lines 11-12?

3. The poem speaks to the beloved throughout. How would you describe her, and him, and their relationship as revealed to us in the poem?

4. Though Donne's poetry is four hundred years old, it is considered extraordinarily immediate and fresh and closer to modern times than his. Would you agree with this view? Which one of the poems by Donne on your course would you think best fits this description?

5. Is this yet another example of a poem by Donne which combines the serious with the playful? Where is the poet at his most serious? Where is the poet at his most playful?

6. What is the effect of 'I' and 'thee'/'thou' in the poem? In his love poetry Donne sometimes refers to the world beyond the world of the lovers. Does he do so here? What is the effect of this?

7. What causes the poet to doubt his lover in the final stanza? How does he interpret her going?

8. 'The Dream' has been praised for its rhythms, its sense of actuality, its wit (cleverness). Do you think this praise justified?

9. Donne's love poetry has been called unusual, anti-conventional, sensuous, erotic. Consider the love poems by Donne in this selection under some or all of these headings. What other words would you choose to describe Donne's love poetry?

The Flea

Mark but this flea, and mark in this,
How little that which thou deny'st me is;
Me it sucked first, and now sucks thee,
And in this flea, our two bloods mingled be;
Confess it, this cannot be said   5
A sin, or shame, or loss of maidenhead,
   Yet this enjoys before it woo,
    And pampered swells with one blood made of two,
    And this, alas, is more than we would do.

Oh stay, three lives in one flea spare,   10
Where we almost, nay more than married are.
This flea is you and I, and this
Our marriage bed, and marriage temple is;
Though parents grudge, and you, we'are met,
And cloistered in these living walls of jet.   15
   Though use make you apt to kill me,
   Let not to this, self murder added be,
   And sacrilege, three sins in killing three.

Cruel and sudden, hast thou since
Purpled thy nail, in blood of innocence?   20
In what could this flea guilty be,
Except in that drop which it sucked from thee?
Yet thou triumph'st, and say'st that thou
Find'st not thyself, nor me the weaker now;
'Tis true, then learn how false, fears be;   25
   Just so much honour, when thou yield'st to me,
   Will waste, as this flea's death took life from thee.

 **Glossary**

Line 1 mark: consider.

Line 2 How little that which thou deny'st me is: what you are denying me is a little thing – I wish to mingle my blood with yours in sexual intercourse and you have already allowed this flea to do just that.

Line 3 Me it sucked first: some scholars print this as 'It sucked me first' and have pointed out that in Donne's day, in printing typography, 's' (the long 's') and 'f' were interchangeable. Thus, in Herbert Grierson's 1912 edition of this poem, 'Edited from the Old Editions and Numerous Manuscripts', he prints this line as 'It fuck'd me firft'. However, many of the early manuscripts of the poem use the modern form of the 's'. It is impossible to say which form Donne chose or whether he intended to play on double meanings. According to the Oxford English Dictionary the earliest appearance of the most famous f-word in the language is 1503.

Line 4 our two bloods mingled be: the flea contains his and her blood. It was once commonly thought (an idea derived from the Greek philosopher Aristotle, 384–322 BC) that sexual intercourse between man and woman meant a mingling of bloods.

Line 5 said: called.

Line 6 maidenhead: virginity.

Line 8 pampered: here it means 'fed to the full'.

Line 9 alas: because his beloved will not yield to him.

Line 11 more than married are: within the flea their blood is mingled, man and woman are united.

Line 12 you: it is worth noting that Donne switches here from the more intimate thou/thee form of the second person pronoun to the more formal you; at this point in the poem Donne is expressing a feeling of distance between him and his love.

Line 14 parents grudge: Donne loved Ann More in secret and married her without her parents' knowledge or permission. Ann's father did not approve of their union and had Donne imprisoned, briefly, when their marriage was discovered (*cf.* Biographical Note on page 164).

Line 14 and you: you are also now grudging in that you are not allowing me what I desire.

Line 15 cloistered: a word suggesting a monastery/enclosed space.

Line 15 jet: black. John Carey commenting on line 15 of 'The Flea' – 'And cloistered in these living walls of jet' says that the 'delicate intentness' of the line 'treats a flea as no flea had been treated in English before'.

Line 16 use: habit, custom.

Line 16 apt: inclined.

Line 16 Though use make you apt to kill me: this line has been interpreted by one scholar as: 'Though you are used to killing me with your coldness, and so are well fitted to kill me again now'.

Line 16 kill me: an allusion to sexual intercourse may be intended here.

Line 18 sacrilege: violation of the sacred – because if she kills the flea she is in effect destroying the marriage-temple.

Lines 17–19: Donne is suggesting that, though she may be inclined to kill him, she should not kill herself in the flea for then she would be committing a triple sin – murder of him and of herself and sacrilege.

Line 24 not thyself, nor me the weaker now: the flea, which has fed on them both, has been killed but they have not been weakened.

Line 25 learn how false, fears be: this looks back to his urgings in line 2, where he suggested to his lover that what he was asking was little.

Lines 26–27: you will not lose your honour when you yield to me, just as the flea, when it died, did not take life from you.

The idea of the poet envying something on his lover's body is found in many sixteenth-century texts. In *Romeo and Juliet*, Romeo longs to be a glove upon Juliet's hand: 'See how she leans her cheek upon her hand;/O! that I might touch that cheek' but Donne, in 'The Flea', has written an even more startling poem. It is thought by some scholars that 'The Flea' was one of Donne's most popular poems in the poet's own day.

Questions

1. This poem, 'The Flea,' is, according to Sir Arthur Quiller-Couch (1863–1944), one-time Professor of English Literature at Cambridge, 'about the most merely [absolutely] disgusting in our language.' What does that tell us about Quiller-Couch? about John Donne? What do you think of Quiller-Couch's comment? How would you describe the poem?

2. Outline in your own words the poet's argument. Why is this such a clever poem? Do you think it has more to offer than cleverness?

3. The poet woos his lover in a series of arguments. Which lines do you find most persuasive and effective? Why?

4. How would you describe the poet's tone in stanza one? Is there a different tone in stanzas two and three? Which lines best express those tones?

5. Did you enjoy reading this poem? Give reasons for your answer.

6. This poem, it has been said, contains examples of 'preposterous boldness' and 'incredible originality'. Consider this statement, particularly in relation to lines 10-15.

7. What similarities and differences do you find between 'The Flea' and the other love poems by Donne on your course?

8. Pick out those words and phrases in the poem which strengthen and further the poet's argument.

9. 'The use of detail, almost microscopic detail, in the poem is particularly effective.' Would you agree with this view? Choose three such images to support your point of view.

10 Donne was praised for his eloquence. Do you think 'The Flea' an example of Donne's command of fluent and expressive language?

11. Titles sometimes give no hint of what follows. Comment on this statement in relation to Donne's 'The Flea'. Include your first impressions of the poem.

Shakespearean
Sonnet

themes: Sin and mortality

broken, sinful, undesirable
Dramatic opening

Thou hast made me, and shall thy work decay?

control → line control + tight structure — intellectual, intelligence

Thou hast made me, and shall thy work decay?

God as a craftsman
sonnet → love and devotion

Repair me now, for now mine end doth haste, logic to God

embraces death
personification

I run to death, and death meets me as fast, commanding, urgent tone

And all my pleasures are like yesterday, consonance → "d"

imagery/metaphor

I dare not move my dim eyes any way, alliteration "d" sounds 5

Despair behind, and death before doth cast are dark and heavy and portray death

negative imagery

Self-repugnance
Such terror, and my feeble flesh doth waste
climax

By sin in it, which it towards hell doth weigh; imagery of heaviness

volta
levels   humble
Only thou art above, and when towards thee humility

admiration & praise for God
dependence on God   spiritual rebirth

By thy leave I can look, I rise again; renewal - power of God 10
assonance   elevation/
But our old subtle foe so tempteth me, ascension

quiet and humble

That not one hour I can myself sustain;

capital letter awe
Thy Grace may wing me to prevent his art, surging climax rhyming couplet

And thou like adamant draw mine iron heart.

scientific allusion (magnetic force)   universalises the experience of sinning   visceral
Satan (not capitalised)

volta = the change or turn in a sonnet between octave and sestet

Glossary

Line 2 Repair: restore.

Line 5 dim: not seeing clearly.

Line 8 weigh: press hard.

Line 11 subtle: sly, artful, cunning.

Line 12 sustain: support.

Line 13 wing: lend me speed.

Line 13 prevent: frustrate.

Line 14 adamant: here it means the lodestone; in other words Donne is hoping that God will act as a guiding principle. The lodestone is the magnet or stone that guides, the magnetic oxide of iron. In the Middle Ages pilots were called lodesmen.

This sonnet is one of a group of sonnets known as Divine Meditations. It cannot be said with any certainty when these poems were written. Some argue that they must belong to Donne's time as a priest but others thinks that they date from before his ordination.

Questions

1. How would you describe the relationship between the poet and his maker? What tone of voice does the poet use to address God? Does the tone remain the same throughout? Explain.

2. There are several references in the poem to decay and despair, sin and hell. Trace these through the text. What marks the turning point in the poem?

3. The sonnet is written in iambic pentameter. The voice is measured, reasoned, at times pleading. What is the dominant mood or feeling in the poem?

4. What is the effect of 'our' in line 11?

5. The poem begins with a question in line 1 and the lines that follow provide the answer. Do you think Donne gives us a convincing answer to his own question? Why?

6. Compare this divine meditation with the other two sonnets included here. What characteristics are common to all three? Which one do you prefer and why?

→ scientific allusion at the end is a fresh and modern (at the time) view of faith/religion

→

At the round earth's imagined corners

At the round earth's imagined corners, blow
Your trumpets, angels and arise, arise
From death, you numberless infinities
Of souls, and to your scattered bodies go,
All whom the flood did, and fire shall o'erthrow,   5
All whom war, dearth, age, agues, tyrannies,
Despair, law, chance, hath slain, and you whose eyes,
Shall behold God, and never taste death's woe.
But let them sleep, Lord, and me mourn a space,
For, if above all these, my sins abound,   10
'Tis late to ask abundance of thy grace,
When we are there; here on this lowly ground,
Teach me how to repent; for that's as good
As if thou hadst sealed my pardon, with thy blood.

 Glossary

Line 1 the round earth's imagined corners: In the *Book of Revelation*, the final book of the *New Testament*, Chapter vii, verse 1 reads: 'And after these things I saw four angels standing on the four corners of the earth, holding the four winds of the earth' [all quotations from Authorised King James version, 1611].

Line 4 scattered bodies: the dust and bones of bodies of the dead, dispersed over time, will be reunited with their souls.

Line 5 flood did: flood did (o'erthrow).

Line 5 fire: signalling the end of the world; the flood at the beginning of the *Old Testament*, the fire at the end of the *New Testament*.

Line 6 dearth: famine/ scarcity (this reads as 'death' in several manuscript versions).

Line 6 agues: acute fevers.

Line 6 tyrannies: oppressive powers; cruel regimes.

Line 7 hath slain: has killed.

Line 8 and never taste death's woe: references to tasting death are found in the *New Testament*. In John Chapter viii, verse 52 ('If a man keep my saying, he shall never taste of death); in Hebrews Chapter ii, verse 9 ('But we see Jesus, who was made a little lower than the angels for the suffering of death, crowned with glory and honour; that he by the grace of God should taste death for every man'); and Christ's promise to his disciples in Luke Chapter ix, verse 27 ('But I tell you of a truth, there be some standing here, which shall not taste of death, till they see the kingdom of God').

Line 9 a space: for a short time.

Line 10 my sins abound: my sins are even more plentiful.

Line 11 abundance of thy grace: generous, plentiful blessing/forgiveness.

Line 12 this lowly ground: the speaker is kneeling; earth before the final disaster or Apocalypse as described in the *Revelation of St John* in the final book of the *New Testament*.

Line 13 repent: feel sorry, regret.

Line 14 sealed my pardon: confirmed my being forgiven/guaranteed my salvation.

> Donne wrote this sonnet circa 1609; it was first published in 1633. Like 'Batter my heart', it is known as one of the 'Holy Sonnets'.

Questions

1. Why is the sonnet's first sentence so effective? What is the effect of 'imagined corners'? What sounds are captured in the opening lines? Consider the verbs and the placing of the verbs 'blow', 'arise, arise'. Why does the poet use a list? What does this octet promise? What is conveyed by the word 'never' in line 8?

2. Identify the key words of the octet and justify your choice.

3. What mood is created in the octet? How does the repetition of the words 'All whom' contribute to this mood?

4. How would you describe the poet's mood when he addresses the angels, then the numberless infinities of souls?

5. A reading of the poem, in silence or aloud, reveals a change in line 9. How would you describe this change and how was it brought about? Consider, for example, the sounds in the octet and the sestet, the persons referred to in both.

6. Examine the sentence structure in the sestet. What is the effect, for example, of the pause in line 12? How does 'lowly ground' compare or contrast with the imagery of the earth in the octet?

7. What is the poet focusing on in lines 9–14? How would you describe the poet's understanding of God as revealed in this sonnet? How would you describe the poet's relationship with God? Is a similar relationship revealed in the other two sonnets, 'Thou hast made me' and 'Batter my heart'?

Batter my heart, three-personed God

Batter my heart, three-personed God; for, you
As yet but knock, breathe, shine, and seek to mend;
That I may rise, and stand, o'erthrow me and bend
Your force, to break, blow, burn, and make me new.
I, like an usurped town, to another due,   5
Labour to admit you, but oh, to no end,
Reason, your viceroy in me, me should defend,
But is captived, and proves weak or untrue,
Yet dearly I love you and would be loved fain,
But am betrothed unto your enemy,   10
Divorce me, untie, or break that knot again,
Take me to you, imprison me, for I
Except you enthral me, never shall be free,
Nor ever chaste, except you ravish me.

Glossary

Line 1 Batter: strike repeatedly, bruise, break.

Line 1 three-personed: the Trinity of Christian theology – God the Father, Son and Holy Spirit.

Line 3 bend: apply/direct.

Line 5 usurped: wrongfully seized/occupied/taken.

Line 5 to another due: owing loyalty/duty to someone other than the usurper; belonging to someone else.

Line 6 Labour: strive.

Line 6 to no end: without success.

Line 7 viceroy: ruler exercising authority on behalf of sovereign; king's substitute.

Line 8 captived: put in captivity.

Line 9 fain: willingly, gladly.

Line 10 betrothed: promised in marriage/engaged.

Line 13 enthral: make a slave of; enslave; capture.

Line 14 chaste: pure, virginal.

Line 14 ravish: take me by force/rape; enrapture; carry off.

This sonnet was composed circa 1609 and published in 1633. The sonnet form was very popular in the sixteenth century and was used mostly for love poetry of a secular nature. Exaggeration and paradox were frequently used. In 'Batter my heart' Donne is here using a form most often associated with worldly love to speak directly to his God. Donne uses paradox with dramatic effect; he also transfers the erotic feeling and images from love poetry to the religious poem.

This is a Petrarchan sonnet, which means that between the octet and the sestet there is a change in the rhyming scheme, signalling a new idea, a development with a new emphasis and energy. This psychological break is known as the turn. The rhyming scheme follows the Italian sonnet form: abbaabba cdcdee.

Questions

1. In this sonnet the poet sees himself as victim. What images convey this? What is he asking of God?

2. Consider the violence in the poem. How is this created? Make a list of those words which are particularly effective, in your opinion, in capturing that violence.

3. What is the poet's tone in the opening four lines? How does the poet achieve that tone?

4. What self-portrait emerges here? How would you describe the poet's relationship with God and with God's enemy?

5. 'This poem is both passionate and daring'. Would you agree with this view? Give reasons for your answer.

6. Dominant images include that of God as tinsmith, a captured town, a woman betrothed. How do these images compare with imagery used elsewhere by John Donne in his poetry?

7. What significant change occurs in the sestet? What is the effect of 'Yet' and 'But'? Is the change thematic or technical?

8. What makes this both a typical and atypical religious poem?

9. What are the paradoxes presented in the poem? What do these contribute to the overall effect of the poem?

10. Of the three sonnets from Donne's sonnet sequence, Divine Meditations, which one did you prefer and why?

General Questions

A. 'The poetry of John Donne, whether addressing his lover or his God, is intimate and immediate.' Discuss this view in the light of your reading of the poems by Donne on your course. You should refer to or quote from a number of poems in your answer.

B. 'Donne could write, with equal facility and depth, passionate poems of secular love and passionate poems of sacred love, both sorts informed by large-minded wit.' From the reading of the poems on your course, would you agree with this view? Support your answer by quotation from or reference to the poems.

C. 'Donne's poetry is intelligent, immediate and engaging.' Would you agree with this estimation of the poems by John Donne on your course? Support your view by relevant quotation or reference.

D. Write a short essay on the aspects of John Donne's poems - their content and/or style – that you found most interesting. Support your discussion by reference to or quotation from the poems by Donne on your course.

E. Would you agree that John Donne's ideas and attitudes and his use of the English language make his poetry unusual, memorable and timeless? Support your answer by reference to or quotation from the poetry by Donne on your course.

F. 'Donne, though a seventeenth-century poet, is well-worth reading in the twenty-first century.' Do you agree with this statement? Support your points of view by reference to or quotation from the poems by John Donne on your course.

G. 'The love poetry is energetic, original and highly persuasive.' Discuss this view, supporting the points you make by reference to or quotation from the poems by Donne on your course.

H. Donne in his poetry speaks of himself as a 'naked, thinking heart'. Discuss whether you think Donne achieves an honest, direct, thoughtful and emotional quality in his work. In your answer you should quote from or refer to the poems by Donne on your course.

I. Outline your personal response to the poems by John Donne on your course that you enjoyed most. Give reasons for your choice and in your answer you should quote from or refer to the poems chosen.

J. 'Donne, whether addressing his lover or his God, uses a similar tone and technique.' Discuss this view, supporting your answer by reference to and quotation from the poems by John Donne on your course.

The Sun Rising

This poem is a variation on the aubade or dawn song. Traditionally the aubade expressed lovers' regret that the day has come so soon to separate them. The most famous aubade is probably in Shakespeare's *Romeo and Juliet*, where the young lovers realise that they must part now as it is dawn. Donne's poem focuses not on the lovers parting, but on their being together and staying together; here the poet does not allow the sun to determine his life.

John Donne in his poetry often speaks in a very direct, immediate, conversational voice. One of John Donne's poems ('The Canonisation') begins 'For God's sake hold your tongue, and let me love'; 'He is stark mad, who ever says,/ That he hath been in love an hour' is how 'The Broken Heart' begins, and the opening line of 'The Sun Rising' is another example of such immediacy. The poet is addressing the sun but, in true aubade fashion, the sun is neither celebrated nor welcomed; it is dismissed as a nuisance. It is a 'Busy old fool'; it is unruly; it disturbs the lovers too early in the morning. The sun is vital for life; it begins each day and sets that day in motion, but Donne belittles the great sun by suggesting that he and his lover are outside of time; they belong to a world of their own.

This poem is four hundred years old and some words are archaic or sound old-fashioned to us; yet the idea here is fresh and striking, the tone is perky. In the poem's opening line every word used to describe the sun is an insult:

> Busy old fool, unruly sun

and Donne expresses surprise and incredulity that the sun 'through windows, and through curtains' should call on the lovers. The bright broad sunbeams are reduced here to a slant of light. He questions the intrusion and, in a dismissive tone, wonders why the sun should presume that it can rule over the lovers' lives:

> Must to thy motion lovers' seasons run?

The sun sets in motion the busy world of school and court and, according to the speaker, that is the sun's function:

> go chide
> Late school-boys, and sour prentices,
> Go tell court-huntsman, that the King will ride

The activity described here is everyday and workaday. Schoolboys who are late for school are reminded by the sun that they are late; grumpy apprentices are late for their task of learning a trade; the court is busy pleasing the King; the farmers, here referred to as 'country ants', are all condemned to live a life according to the clock.

Everyone else, apart from the lovers it would seem, is conscious of the hour, the day, the month. Donne lists each unit of time for effect for, in belittling them by calling them 'the rags of time', he is emphasising the timelessness of his own world, the world of true love. The tone throughout the first stanza is dismissive. The harsh sounds of 'pedantic,' 'wretch,' 'sour' confirm that tone. Donne never wavers in his condemnation. Instead the stanza gains more and more momentum as the poet describes the wide world beyond the room where the lovers are. City and countryside are captured in 'court' and 'harvest' but the line that sings with confidence

> Love, all alike, no season known, nor clime

is immediately striking for its positive mood. The poem's first two sentences were questions; the other sentences order the sun to shine its light elsewhere. 'Go chide,' 'Go tell,' and 'Call country ants' form a series of abrupt, crisp directives and they give way to the expansive, softer-sounding 'Love, all alike, no season knows, nor clime'. The rhyming scheme also changes from abba, cdcd to ee. The couplet achieves a closer music (clime/time), and one line following the other in an end-rhyme at the end of the stanza allows Donne to express his confident belief in how love alters everything, how love is not governed by time.

Thomas Docherty points out that 'The Sun Rising' looks at 'the rise of the sun, its triumphant ascent to centrality'. In stanza two Donne begins with words of high praise. Instead of the 'busy old fool' on line 1, line 11 speaks of the sun's 'reverend' and 'strong' beams, only to dismiss them immediately in the following line when Donne says that he 'could eclipse and cloud' such beams with a wink. This is a more playful tone than the poet's tone in stanza one and it is the first instance of the poet's use of 'I':

> I could eclipse and cloud them with a wink

In Donne's poetry there is a remarkably clear-sighted and logical argument and this second stanza illustrates one such argument. He does not close his eyes to the sun, for in doing so he would lose sight of his loved one. He also suggests that her bright, beautiful eyes might blind the sun itself. In asking the sun to look on the world 'If her eyes have not blinded thine' it is only to discover that every place wonderful and precious, and everything important are contained within the one bed. His confidence is such that the tells the sun to:

> Look, and tomorrow late, tell me,
> Whether both th'Indias of spice and mine
> Be where thou left'st them, or lie here with me.
> Ask for those kings whom thou saw'st yesterday,
> And thou shalt hear, All here in one bed lay.

Here the larger world is dismissed; the intimate world of the lovers is preferred. The lovers, in Thomas Docherty's words, 'become the world and occupy the same position of centrality as the sun. They become, in short, the still point around which all else is supposed to revolve, and around whom all time passes, while they remain in some kind of supposed transcendence of history itself.' The far-away islands famed for spice and gold have been magically re-located; the poet's imagination has gathered the Kings together, Kings which the sun saw yesterday are now within one bed – it is a clever and confident idea or conceit. The wide and important world has been shrunk; the smaller world of the bedroom contains everything; the macrocosmic has become the microcosmic. Every word in line 20 is a strong-sounding monosyllable that clinches Donne's argument:

> And thou shalt hear, All here in one bed lay.

The final stanza begins with renewed confidence and introduces the idea of man and woman forming a kingdom of love.

> She is all states, and all princes, I,
> Nothing else is.

The use and repetition of the words 'all' and 'Nothing' is how Donne views everything and this signals absolute happiness. It could be argued from this image of the woman, being 'all states,' is the one who is governed and that he, being 'all princes' is the one who governs but Donne's use of 'us' and 'we' and his tone throughout suggest that he sees their relationship as equal. The world of the lovers has expanded while the sun has been reduced. The apparently powerful, important, honoured – kings and princes – are but imitations of the lovers. Everything that is honoured, every form of wealth, is inferior by comparison:

> Princes do but play us; compared to this,
> All honour's mimic; all wealth alchemy.

And Donne turns once again to the sun this time to say that

> Thou sun art half as happy as we

and with playful logic informs the sun that since he and his lover are the world, and since it is the sun's duty to warm the world, and since the sun is old and should not be asked to do too much, then the sun need only shine on their room, their bed:

> Thine age asks ease, and since thy duties be
> To warm the world, that's done in warming us.
> Shine here to us, and thou art everywhere;
> This bed thy centre is, these walls, thy sphere.

The poem does a complete turn around in that it begins with a complaint and ends with an invitation and, though it focuses on two different places, a bedroom and the wider world, the bedroom becomes the world. There is confidence and assurance in the final two lines. The rhythm is stately, the tone warm and inviting.

As we read through the poem we realise that Donne has changed his mind. He speaks abruptly to the sun in the opening line, telling it to 'Go'; he adopts a gentler tone in the final stanza, admitting that the sun deserves to be treated with respect ('Thine age asks ease') and, instead of telling the sun to go, he now asks it to stay: 'Shine here to us'.

There is both argument and persuasion and a growing confidence throughout the poem. Words such as 'Why' (line 2); 'go chide' (line 5); 'Go tell' (line 7); 'Call' (line 8); 'But that' (line 14); 'If' (line 15); 'Look . . . tell me' (line 16); 'Whether' (line 17); 'since' (line 27) signal Donne's careful and playful argument. By the third stanza, Michael Schmidt points out that 'the poet's mind returns to bed, and his relationship, a microcosm, swells to the proportions of a macrocosm. Donne's attitude to the sun changes from rancour to charitable pity.'

John Donne's 'The Sun Rising' is a fine example of love poetry, it is unusual in that it does not dwell on the physical beauty of the woman, but proposes an argument which elaborates and confirms their great love. However, this has led some readers to suggest that not much is known about the relationship – the woman is never named, for example – and Schmidt adds that 'Donne's poem has wit, but one is undecided whether it has an actual subject or is a pretext for developing poetic conceit.'

Song (Go, and catch a falling star)

John Carey says that we don't go to Donne's poetry for 'flowers, pastoral, myth, warm humour or serene joy'. In this 'Song' there are no pretty pictures; the humour is wry and the poet's tone rigorous. 'Go', 'Get', 'Tell', 'Teach' are sharp directives or imperatives and the short lines and regular rhymes create an immediate and brisk voice. If the poem addresses a specific individual that person is not named, but Donne could just as well be speaking to his reader or every reader of the poem. The poem is a general statement rather than an intimate one. He begins by demanding the impossible and justifies his demands with an overall argument that

> No where
> Lives a woman true, and fair.

Several impossibilities are mentioned. The poem begins with these, five in all, and the reader immediately knows that what he asks for cannot be: the falling star cannot be caught; a child cannot be conceived with the help of a mandrake plant; no one knows where the past has gone or who split the devil's hooves; and no one can be taught to hear the singing of mermaids. Then, at line 6, the request takes a different turn when Donne focuses on a more probable situation, a situation involving human behaviour, and he asks to be taught how to avoid envy and how to be honest. The regular line length changes and this suggests a greater seriousness; what was impossible has been replaced by Donne's wishing for something possible. Teach me, Donne says,

> to keep off envy's stinging,
>> And find
>> What wind
> Serves to advance an honest mind.

Stanza two returns to an imagined moment where Donne urges his reader to go to the ends of the earth if strange sights are being sought: 'Ride ten thousand days and nights,/ Till age snow white hairs on thee'. The reader will have to travel a great distance over a long time and no matter how strange the sights they experience, Donne is convinced that:

> No where
> Lives a woman true, and fair.

In the third stanza he offers a final reason why no faithful woman can exist. He allows that whoever has gone to seek one out may succeed but even then she would have proved unfaithful by the time Donne got there. Even if one were found he would not go even if she were close by. The detail 'next door' is in stark contrast with the distance suggested by a journey of a thousand days and nights in stanza two, but it highlights Donne's strong disbelief that a faithful woman is to be found.

The word 'If' is used at the beginning of the second and third stanzas and this, together with 'Yet do not' and 'Yet she' in the final stanza, suggests a disillusioned, almost bitter utterance. The poem may be seen as a playful piece, but hardly by both sexes. Shakespeare in *Much Ado About Nothing* includes a song which says

> Men were deceivers ever,
> One foot in sea, and one on shore,
> To one thing constant never

Donne is saying the exact opposite here: in this poem it is women who are inconstant and unfaithful.

The Anniversary

Unlike 'Go, and catch a falling star', this is a poem which celebrates love's growth and continuity. It resembles 'The Sun Rising' in that it speaks confidently of the poet and his lover and in both poems the male poet is praising his love and is confident of her fidelity. 'The Sun Rising' and 'The Anniversary' are rooted in a particular place (a bedroom) and time (an anniversary) and as a result are much more convincing than 'Go, and catch a falling star', which is closer to a throwaway, simplistic, general argument founded on no particular experience or evidence.

In the opening stanza of 'The Anniversary' Donne makes a magnificent list, including the world of the court, those who have distinguished themselves, the beautiful and the clever and the sun itself, but the list is given in order to belittle it:

> All kings, and all their favourites,
> All glory of honours, beauties, wits
> The sun itself

are all subject to the passing of time. Their greatness is diminished by each passing day. 'All' is used three times in the first two lines and the impression is one of grandeur, importance. It could be a poem in praise of these until line 4 introduces a negative quality:

> The sun itself, which makes times, as they pass,
> Is elder by a year now than it was
> When thou and I first one another saw.

John Carey says these opening lines 'blending kings and glory with the sun, sound like a fanfare to majesty. But they are a dirge. The gorgeous blaze darkens, and the poet's individual claim springs clear of the dying splendours massed at the start. It is over the wreck of empires and solar systems that the first stanza strides forward. The lover of "The Anniversary" pits himself against the approaching dark.'

At the centre of this first stanza, at line 5, Donne speaks of what is most important: 'thou and I'. He and his lover are the centre of the universe and, unlike everything else, their love will increase, will not die:

> All other things, to their destruction draw
> Only our love hath no decay

Donne's love is timeless and its timelessness dates from that moment when 'thou and I first one another saw'. The 'Only' at the beginning of line 7 strengthens the poet's expression of belief in his love and that it is the shortest line in the stanza also highlights its importance. Once this love became a reality, Donne recognises how it will never die, 'This no tomorrow hath, nor yesterday', and his use of paradox here is both clever and effective. What appears to be a contradiction makes sense once it is teased out: 'Running it never runs from us away' turns time on its head. His love is not affected by the passing of time in any negative sense. Their first anniversary marks a year's love but their love is so special that

> This, no tomorrow hath, nor yesterday,
> Running it never runs from us away,
> But truly keeps his first, last, everlasting day.

Having spoken of this eternal day and having spoken of how their love is greater than kingship and even the sun, Donne in the second stanza brings his lover and his reader down to earth when he speaks of their graves.

> Two graves must hide thine and my corse,
> If one might, death were no divorce

In speaking of their graves he also speaks of how death will separate them. Man and wife are usually buried in the one grave but Donne, here, seems to refer to his actual circumstances, one year into his relationship with Ann More. Their love was secret and therefore on this first anniversary he speaks of how, it seems, when they die that they will be separated in death. Words such as 'graves', 'corse', 'death' are not often found in love poetry, but one of Donne's hallmarks as a love poet is his ability to confront reality and argue a case for love which transcends that reality. He mentions their deaths in order to highlight their eternal life their happiness beyond their graves.

The poet Dryden said of Donne that he 'perplexes the minds of the fair sex with nice speculations of philosophy, when he should engage their hearts' but Donne's logical and philosophical love poems are powerful expressions of his love. He does not dwell on the conventional material of the love poem; he does not describe the woman's physical beauty, nor does he draw on imagery from the natural world. Instead Donne proposes a realistic detail such as transience or death and defeats both with his interpretation of love and time.

'All kings' were dismissed in stanza one. In stanza two Donne admits to the reality of death and, just as royal princes must die, so too must he and she whom he has proclaimed princes in their own kingdom, the kingdom of love.

> Alas, as well as other princes, we,
> — Who prince enough in one another be —
> Must leave at last in death, these eyes, and ears,
> Oft fed with true oaths, and with sweet salt tears;

'Alas' introduces a note of regret. Actual princes and the prince-like lovers must all die but 'prince enough' suggests that Donne has found in love a quality to match royalty. With death their profession of love, their tears will end; their emotional, sensuous lives will draw to a close, but there is a further stage of heightened happiness awaiting them. The use of 'But' at the beginning of line 17 signals this spiritual manifestation of their love.

> But souls where nothing dwells but love
> — All other thoughts being inmates — then shall prove
> This, or a love increased there above,
> When bodies to their graves, souls from their graves remove.

The moment of their burial is not presented as grim or final. The movement implied in the phrase 'bodies to their graves' is a downward movement but the second half of that line, 'souls from their graves remove', effectively banishes any negative associations in the reader's mind. The final idea in stanza two is a movement heavenward, a journey towards heavenly and eternal happiness. The idea of love in heaven as an 'increased' love 'there above' also lends the poem at this point a forward-looking mood. The stanza began with burial; the stanza ends with release.

The final stanza imagines the life of these two lovers in heaven. The two simple words 'And then', with which Donne begins this third stanza, capture his confidence:

> And then we shall be throughly blessed

This sense of being thoroughly ('throughly') blessed, however, gives way to Donne's realisation that in heaven everyone is equally blessed. Whereas on earth Donne and his lover are superior, in heaven they will be 'no more than all the rest'. The use of 'But . . . but' in lines 22 and 23 is another indication of how Donne is making his argument, how he is carefully examining the reality of their love here on earth and in the afterlife.

> Here upon earth, we are kings, and none but we
> Can be such kings, nor of such subjects be;

Their status 'here on earth' is now kingly. 'All kings' were dismissed in stanza one; in stanza two he likened himself and his lover to princes, an idea similar to the final stanza of 'The Sun Rising' ('She is all states, and all princes, I') and the royal metaphor is extended in the closing stanza: they are no longer princes, they have become kings. The imagery is drawn from the world of the court and political intrigue, but it highlights the shortcomings and failings of that world and celebrates and praises their own world of love which does not know treason, nor will they ever know it. The poet's confidence is total:

> Who is so safe as we? where none can do
> Treason to us, except one of us two.

He is realistic enough to admit that they may know real and imagined fears, but he urges his lover to put uncertainties and suspicions aside. 'Let us love nobly' announces his wish for himself and his lover and the line grows in strength as he ends the poem on a gloriously upbeat note:

> Let us love, nobly, and live, and add again
> Years and years unto years, till we attain
> To write threescore, this is the second of our reign.

The lover and his beloved are central to 'The Anniversary'. In line 5 Donne speaks of 'thou and I', in line 7 of 'our love', in line 9, 'us'. But the key idea is the union of the lovers and the key word is 'we'. In stanza two 'we' is used once but, as the poem moves towards a complete understanding of how he and she become one, 'we' is used more often. In the third and final stanza, the word 'we' occurs six times and 'us' is used four times and 'our' once. The repetition of 'and' lends the closing lines a sense of continuity

> Let us love nobly, and live, and add again
> Years and years unto years . . .

The strong rhythmic pattern and the closing words, 'our reign', triumphantly replace the world of reigning monarchs with which the poem began.

There is something both moving and human in Donne's emphasis in the closing lines of the poem. He does not speak of heaven; instead he focuses on the here and now, and his wish that he and his lover will enjoy many years together, that they will live to see their sixtieth anniversary. Robert Frost, in his poem 'Birches', says 'Earth's the right place for love: I don't know where it's likely to go better'; Donne in 'The Anniversary' prefers their love on earth which allows them to be special.

Song (Sweetest love, I do not go)

This poem trips off the tongue. Even if it were not called 'Song', its musical qualities would be immediately evident. The regular rhyming scheme is one of the poem's most striking features – go/thee/show/me/I/best/jest/die and this rhyme scheme, ababcddc, is used in all five stanzas. 'The Sun Rising' and 'The Anniversary' are love poems which focus on the lovers being together. 'Song' tells of their having to part, but the poet argues that this temporary separation is but a preparation for their inevitable parting at death. It concludes, however, by suggesting that in the case of true love there is no such thing as parting: 'They who one another keep/ Alive, ne'er parted be.'

The free-flowing rhythmic pattern is established in the opening lines. A seven syllable line is followed by lines of six, seven and six syllables:

> Sweetest love, I do not go,
>   For weariness of thee,
> Nor in hope the world can show
>   A fitter love for me

but line five in each stanza stops the rhythm short:

> But since that I

and frequently the first word at the beginning of this shorter, four-syllable line (But, Then, But . . .) signals the poet's more serious tone. The opening words, 'Sweetest love', are tender and intimate and the speaker assures his lover that he is not parting because he has grown tired of her or he is not going in search of a new lover. As in 'The Anniversary', this love poem speaks of the reality of death but the mood is more playful than sombre:

> But since that I
> Must die at last, 'tis best,
> To use myself in jest
>   Thus by feigned deaths to die.

John Carey, in his commentary on the poem, says that Donne's 'departure is a joke, though a practical one. They will have to part when they die, so it is "best" to get used to it. His partings are miniature suicides, and, as the poem goes on, he urges her to take them in a calm, noble manner that befits a suicide. Her blubbering, he warns her, merely compounds ill fortune. By a haughty composure, she would defeat fate.'

At first the emphasis is on the speaker. 'I' occurs twice in stanzas one and two but the central stanza in the poem has 'we' twice, 'our' and 'we' reflecting the movement of the poem towards a sense of the union of the two lovers. In the opening lines the tone is realistic, but he also speaks about his journey and separation in a light-hearted and jokey tone. These journeys are but "little deaths" or 'feigned deaths' and it is all for the best that the lovers know a little sorrow now; it will prepare them for the sorrow of their ultimate parting, death.

Stanza two speaks of how the sun goes and returns. Donne too will return and even more eagerly than the sun, for the speaker has a stronger desire to be with his lover than the sun has. The sun has been spoken of and referred to also in 'The Sun Rising' and 'The Anniversary' and the effect is similar here. First he praises the sun for its constancy:

> Yesternight the sun went hence,
>   And yet is here today

but Donne sees himself as more interesting and more important than the sun. He will make an even speedier journey since he has an even greater reason for returning.

The middle stanza is a general philosophical meditation on how humankind allows setbacks and obstacles to get the better of us.

> O how feeble is man's power
> That if good fortune fall,
> Cannot add another hour,
> Nor a lost hour recall!

We allow ourselves to be undermined by misfortune and bad luck and we actively play a part in letting bad chance bring us down:

> But come bad chance,
> And we join it to our strength,
> And we teach it art and length,
> Itself o'er us to advance.

This observation is clearly addressed to his lover; it is Donne's attempt to encourage her not to give way to sorrow, to make the most of a bad situation. The poem adopts a much more personal tone in stanza four. If she gives way to sighing and weeping then her sighing and weeping will affect him also and both their sorrows will increase. Playfully, he also points out that sighing and weeping are wasteful ways to spend your life and, seeing that my life is yours and your life is mine, then I too am being wasted away by your behaviour. This is Donne at his most clever, a quality which is frequently found in his work. He is persuading his lover not to mourn his going and he is also viewing his own going in the best possible light. He repeats the word 'sigh'st' three times within two lines, which suggests that the woman is sighing excessively:

> When thou sigh'st, thou sigh'st not wind,
> But sigh'st my soul away

and when she weeps, though it is kind, it is unkind of her. He reprimands her arguing:

> It cannot be
> That thou lov'st me, as thou say'st
> If in thine my life thou waste

but the gentle scolding gives way at the end of the stanza to a line directly praising her

> Thou art the best of me.

The use of 'thou' in this fourth stanza, seven times in all, focuses attention on the poet's lover. There's an increasing urgency in the repetition of 'thou', especially in a line such as 'If thou lov'st me, as thou say'st' and the use of 'we' in the final stanza (line 37) is significant; it indicates that the poet's argument has worked its way towards this quietly confident conclusion.

In the first four stanzas the poet has explained and justified how he feels. The final stanza gently pleads with her to see things his way, not to imagine any dangers and to think of this temporary separation as two lovers back to back in bed together. The poem ends with this comfortingly warm and intimate image:

> think that we
> Are but turned aside to sleep;
> They who one another keep
> Alive, ne'er parted be.

There's some intellectual juggling going on in this 'Song' of Donne's and his voice is energetic and persuasive. 'Sweetest Love' has also been called one of Donne's tenderest love poems, dwelling as it does on a secure and stable relationship, one which has experienced 'turning aside to sleep'.

A Valediction: forbidding Mourning

This, like 'Sweetest love, I do not go,' is a poem in which the poet attempts to persuade his loved one not to grieve at his departure on, in this instance, a fairly long absence from her. The gist of Donne's argument in 'A Valediction: forbidding Mourning' is that true love is not just physical; it goes beyond the physical and becomes spiritual, just as the soul does when the body dies. It is a poem which shows how true love transcends the reality of separation and is enriched in the process.

The first stanza tells of a death-bed scene in which holy men calmly accept their deaths, quietly telling their souls to leave the body, and they slip away, though the use of the word 'forbidding' in the poem's title is forceful. Donne admires such men and wishes that he and his lover could part with a similar quiet, understanding dignity. In the opening stanza there is a whispering, silent quality. In 'Sweetest love' the tone was direct and strong; here the mood is the hushed mood surrounding the dying. The 's' sounds create this effect:

> As virtuous men pass mildly away,
> And whisper to their souls, to go,
> Whilst some of their sad friends do say,
> The breath goes now, and some say, no

Even the simile with which the poem begins ('As virtuous men . . .') is a gentle introduction of an image and the rhyme abab contributes to this quiet sense.

After the explanatory image at line 5, Donne draws the comparison. He admires these men; he wishes that he and his beloved might part now in a manner similar to the way the virtuous men depart this life. As in many of Donne's love poems, we find, yet again, references to death but Donne can speak of love and death in the one poem and in so doing his love gains greater credibility and strength.

Donne assures his beloved in this poem that his departure is not threatening or dangerous because the love they share is a purified love and their souls are united. What Donne stresses here, according to John Carey, 'is that they should part voluntarily: that they should exert power over their own fate, and be their own executioners. Instead of leaving it to circumstances to tear them noisily apart, they should cancel their happiness with dignity, like Christ, or a virtuous man, dispatching his soul.' This is why Donne, at line 5, begins the second stanza in an assured and confident voice:

> So let us melt, and make no noise,
>   No tear-floods, nor sigh-tempests move,
> 'Twere profanation of our joys
>   To tell the laity our love.

Paradoxically their separation allows them to become one. The lovers 'melt' into one and Donne asks that there should be no histrionics, no showy display. Their love is a holy thing and to tell the world of their love is only to demean or belittle it. It would render a sacred, holy love, less holy. It would profane or desecrate that love to let ordinary people, who could not understand such love, know of it.

The poet is about to embark on a long journey. He will travel many miles but what the poem achieves is an increasing sense of presence, despite absence. The deliberate exaggeration in the reference to 'tear-floods' and 'sigh-tempests' (line 6) pokes fun at the type of lover the poet does not admire. Floods and tempests are echoed in the third stanza, which speaks of physical catastrophe. An earthquake is dangerous and frightening:

> Moving of th'earth brings harms and fears

and Donne says that

> Men reckon what it did and meant

meaning that people try to measure the damage caused and try to understand why it happened. But the earthquake is mentioned to highlight an even greater event, namely the movement of the planets which can move violently and yet are not even noticed by people. It would seem that Donne is here comparing his parting from his lover to the abrupt movements and vibrations of the heavenly spheres. Both, essentially, are 'innocent', meaning harmless.

> But trepidation of the spheres
> Though greater far, is innocent.

Already the reader can sense that this is a complex and unconventional love poem. In the first twelve lines of the poem Donne has created an image of a death-bed scene, an earthquake and movement among the heavenly spheres and all to explain, understand and praise the nature of the love between him and his beloved.

Stanza five speaks of ordinary love between ordinary lovers. These are the couples who cannot be separated or cannot stand absence:

> Dull sublunary lovers' love
> (Whose soul is sense) cannot admit
> Absence . . .

and in calling such lovers 'sublunary', or literally 'under/beneath the moon', he is suggesting that these lovers are changeable, just like the inconstant moon. They cannot endure or survive absence

> because it doth remove
> Those things which elemented it.

In other words, the only bond between such lovers is the physical. Separate one body from another and the relationship ends; their love is dependent on the senses.

From line 17 onwards, through the remaining five stanzas of the poem, Donne focuses on the superior nature of his love, a love that is also intellectual, spiritual and mysterious, a love that cannot be explained away or fully understood by the lovers themselves:

> But we by a love, so much refined,
>   That our selves know not what it is,
> Inter-assured of the mind,
>   Care less, eyes, lips and hands to miss.

The use of 'But' here signals Donne's rhetorical structure, his persuasive technique. (It was also used for similar effect in line 37 of 'Sweetest love I do not go'.) The love they know is great and strong and so confident that each knows the other can be trusted. They therefore do not worry about missing the physical – 'eyes, lips and hands' – their two selves are two souls:

> Our two souls therefore, which are one,
>   Though I must go, endure not yet
> A breach, but an expansion,
>   Like gold to airy thinness beat.

Because their love is essentially a spiritual love, their parting will not suffer a breach or break. Instead Donne speaks of an expansion of their love; the image he uses is that of gold leaf. But Donne's simile, in A. J. Smith's words, suggests that 'their love will be so refined by absence as to pass beyond the highest condition of material to the still more exalted quality of air or spirit'. Absence, therefore, will make their love stronger and will allow it to achieve its purest form, that of 'airy thinness.'

Gold leaf is precious and provides a memorable image for the love between the poet and his lover. And there follows another image which is also drawn from the world of science and mathematics. The image of the compasses in stanza seven is one of the best-known images in English Literature. Donne found many of his images in the world around him. Some poets look to the *Bible* or Greek mythology or the world of nature for imagery; Donne found many of his images in the new discoveries being made at the time and in cartography and science, and one of these, of course, is the image of the compass:

> If they be two, they are two so
>   As stiff twin compasses are two,
> Thy soul the fixed foot, makes no show
>   To move, but doth, if th'other do.

The 'stiff twin compasses' are a symbol of their love. Donne sees the woman who will await his return as the 'fixed foot' and 'stiff' here means firm or stable. Therefore the steady and constant lover who remains at home is linked to him who travels away from her. He speaks of her in terms of the soul, emphasising yet again the connecting spiritual nature of their love. The woman who stays at home is one foot of the compass but leans towards and listens for her partner:

> And though it in the centre sit,
>   Yet when the other far doth roam,
> It leans, and hearkens after it,
>   And grows erect, as that comes home.

and the image with which the poem ends is the image of a circle, which is also an image of perfection. With the compass it is possible to draw a circle; on his returning to his lover the circle is complete and all the while there has been the unbroken and unbreakable connection between man and woman. He is away but she is ever in tune with him:

> Such wilt thou be to me, who must,
>   Like the other foot, obliquely run:
> Thy firmness makes my circle just,
>   And makes me end where I begun.

It has been pointed out that Donne has no real argument, that the poem uses rhetoric, not reason. There is no step-by-step proof; instead Donne presents his reader with a series of images which capture his intense feelings and which also engage the reader's intellect. But the images are so striking and effective and the feelings which they convey are so convincing that they add up to an unusual and successful love poem.

The Dream

Every poem we read can be summarised and this is a useful and necessary exercise. It highlights how well we have grasped the meaning of a poem, but it also shows up how well the poet has used language. Most poets are not remarkable for what they have to say but rather for the way they say it. Laurence Lerner sums up 'The Dream' as follows: 'The poet has been asleep, dreaming of his mistress: waking he finds her there. The poem consists of what he then says to her, his delight at her presence, his reflections on the relation of dreaming to reality, his praise of her for coming, his regret when she leaves.'

When we turn to the poem itself we see Donne's interesting and intellectual argument at work. The opening lines are yet another example of Donne's immediate and engaging voice. He is addressing his lover or mistress [mistress in Donne's day meant a woman beloved and courted] and his tone is easy and playful:

> Dear love, for nothing less than thee
> Would I have broke this happy dream

He does not mind being woken from a happy dream which featured his lover, for it is she who wakes him and therefore dream becomes reality.

> It was a theme
> For reason, much too strong for phantasy,
> Therefore thou waked'st me wisely

The dream itself was so convincingly true, so realistic, that it was not like a fantasy or something imagined. In other words, the subject matter of the dream was more suited to daylight reason than the sleeping imagination. But the poet then suggests that, though awake, he is still in the world of dream, for her appearance before him confirmed what he saw in his dream.

> yet
> My dream thou brok'st not, but continued'st it

Donne tells us that she is so real - 'Thou art so true' - that even thinking about her turns a dream into reality and fables or imagined stories are made real:

> Thou art so true, that thoughts of thee suffice,
> To make dreams truths, and fables histories

His argument is an intricate and challenging one and implies that he sees his lover as an equal. Donne does not simplify the train of thought nor does he treat her as an inferior. She embodies truth and her presence in the poet's dream is so real that he was virtually in the real world already. This is why her waking him is no disruption; it allows for continuity, and the poet acknowledges this when he invites her to

> Enter these arms, for since thou thought'st it best
> Not to dream all my dream, let's do the rest.

Though the mood in this opening stanza is relaxed, words such as 'Therefore' and 'since' indicate Donne's ability to pursue a line of argument, and 'Enter these arms' and 'let's do the rest' suggest a quickening of interest. The dream seems to have been an erotic one. The sexual invitation in the closing lines of the first stanza would suggest this and by line 10 the poet's dream is enacted. This poem is four hundred years old but such lines do not strike the reader at the beginning of the twenty-first century as archaic or old-fashioned.

In the second stanza, the speaker suggests that it was his lover's bright eyes that woke him and not any sound she made:

> As lightning, or a taper's light,
> Thine eyes, and not thy noise waked me

The exaggeration here in the simile emphasises her beauty. Her eyes are like lightning or a candle flame, and then he admits that he thought her an angel when he first saw her upon waking from his dream:

> Yet I thought thee
> (For thou lov'st truth) an angel, at first sight

Their relationship is open and honest. The bracketed phrase is a reminder that his lover loves the truth and he therefore admits his error. Having thought of her as an angel, he then suggests that she is more like God in that she can read the poet's thoughts. Angels cannot do this:

> But when I saw thou saw'st my heart,
> And knew'st my thoughts, beyond an angel's art

he realises that she knew that he was dreaming of her:

> When thou knew'st what I dreamed, when thou knew'st when
> Excess of joy would wake me

At this point the poet offers a different reason as to why he woke. It was the dream itself, not her bright eyes as he suggested in line 10, that woke him and she knew exactly at what point in the dream that 'excess of joy would wake him'. This last detail conveys a deep intimacy between the poet and his lover, a sensuous and sexual relationship. Stanza two ends with the poet's remembering why he woke but also admits that

>   thou knew'st when
> Excess of joy would wake me, and cam'st then,
> I must confess, it could not choose but be
> Profane, to think thee anything but thee.

She is not an angel therefore, and it would be irreverent to think of her as anything but herself. The stanza focuses in the closing lines on the physical presence of the woman, just as the closing lines of the first stanza did.

The first stanza speaks of the woman coming, the final one speaks of her going. She came and they enjoyed eachother's company but now she must go.

> Coming and staying showed thee, thee

suggests that when she was with him, when she entered his arms, she was most like herself. But by line 26 it seems that she is feeling 'fear, shame, honour'. Some critics claim that this must mean that the lovers are not married. At any rate the mood of the poem has changed significantly. Her going has resulted in the poet wondering if he was right about her, if he saw her true self when she stepped into his arms:

> Coming and staying showed thee, thee,
> But rising makes me doubt, that now,
>   Thou art not thou.

Every word in these lines is a simple, everyday one, but the structure of the thinking behind such lines is detailed and complex. Indeed many commentators have pointed out that John Donne's poetry contains few adjectives. Verbs and nouns dominate and these are almost always ordinary. John Carey lists verbs such as 'come', 'go', 'think', 'know', 'see', 'tell', 'love', 'give', 'get', 'live', 'die', 'kill', 'send', 'find' and the verb 'to be' in its many forms. Ordinary nouns include 'love', 'lover', 'eye', 'heart', 'thought', 'word', 'tears', 'name', 'thing', 'hour', 'year', 'day', 'life', 'death', 'part', 'man', 'woman', 'mind', 'soul', 'truth', 'world', 'hope', 'fear', 'pain', 'shame', 'fire', 'heat', 'cold', 'sun' and 'moon'.

The poet thinks that love should be 'all spirit, pure, and brave' but his lover is weak because her love is mingled with fear. He argues:

> That love is weak, where fear's as strong as he;
> 'Tis not all spirit, pure and brave,
> If mixture it of fear, shame, honour, have.

Such lines demand concentration if their meaning is to be teased out. There's a rigorous, challenging mind at work and the speaker challenges his lover (and his reader) to follow his line of thought.

The poem ends with a simile. Overall the poem is not rich in imagery; the image of lightning and the taper's light at line 11 and the angel metaphor at line 14 are other images in the poem, but both their presence highlights how few there are. The closing image reveals a somewhat disgruntled or unhappy poet. He wonders if he is like a torch, ready to be lit. When the woman comes, she, to borrow a more recent expression, lights his fire and then she goes only to return some other time to light his fire again:

> Perchance as torches, which must ready be,
> Men light and put out, so thou deal'st with me,
> Thou cam'st to kindle, goest to come; then I
> Will dream that hope again, but else would die.

The poem begins with the poet waking from a dream and ends with the poet dreaming of his lover returning to him. She was with him and they were together and were intimate; she has gone but he hopes that she will return. If his expectations are not fulfilled then he 'would die'. Donne, in one of his sermons, mentions how 'a torch that hath been lighted and used before is easier lighted than a new torch'. This is common knowledge but the imagery here also has a sexual implication. Laurence Lerner says that 'he is the torch, and she has aroused and put out his desire so that he is more easily aroused when they will be together next. That thought reassures him that she intends to come back, so he will dream of her again — "but else would die". If we accept that "die" in Elizabethan times had the slang meaning of having sexual intercourse, those four last words may hold a kind of threat.'

The voice throughout 'The Dream' is direct and achieves an immediacy in its use of active verbs such as 'waked'st', 'brok'st not', 'continued'st it'. 'Enter these arms' and 'let's do the rest' are in the present tense and are fine examples of the living, speaking voice of poetry. Other aspects of language which convey a sense of the actual are the poet's use of 'when', 'but', 'so', 'then'. The poem moves from a mood of pleasure and praise towards doubt, disappointment and expectation.

The Flea

Some of Donne's poems are immediately striking, fresh and unforgettable, and 'The Flea' belongs to such a category and, as in 'The Dream', reveals a highly original attitude towards sexual love. It illustrates one of Donne's more noticeable techniques in his love poetry, which is his tendency to presume that the woman he is speaking to will respond to clever and carefully made arguments. This poem was first published in 1635 and there were many coarse and smutty love poems about fleas in the sixteenth century. But Donne does not follow a tradition which had the flea roam while the poet comments on the woman's various body parts. Here, the poet, in John Carey's words, 'offers a toughly argued monologue on sexual union', does not mention the woman's body, but 'concentrates attention on the body of the flea, which has sucked, and so mingled in itself' the blood of the man and the woman.

The poem begins with emphasis: 'mark . . . mark'. Medieval preachers frequently asked their hearers to 'mark' (look at) something which illustrated a moral or philosophical lesson they wished to emphasise. 'Mark', as it is used here, is spoken in a more playful tone. Look at this flea, he says to his lover, and look at how you are denying me a simple thing. The flea has been intimate with you, and look, you are denying me intimacy:

> Mark but this flea, and mark in this,
> How little that which thou deny'st me is

The first word is immediate and particular and focused. It is in the present tense and the repetition adds emphasis. The flea has united the two lovers within itself. The tiny creature sucked him and her and so contains both of them:

> Me it sucked first, and now sucks thee,
> And in this flea, our two bloods mingled be

The poet is longing for an intimate and sexual relationship and, to strengthen his case, he asks his beloved to admit that what the flea has done cannot be thought wrong. By implication, if they were to mingle they would not be doing wrong either:

> Confess it, this cannot be said
> A sin, or shame, or loss of maidenhead

This mingling of blood is a reference to a medical theory of Donne's time, which held that in sexual intercourse blood was literally mingled and that this led to procreation.

His persuasive skills here are urgent and emotional. Line 5 ('Confess it, that cannot be said') illustrates his eagerness, but logic seems to have been abandoned. The flea has enjoyed sucking both; the mingling of their blood cannot be called sinful or shameful and the flea hasn't lost its virginity. However, should he and she become intimate, should they engage in sexual intercourse, it would involve 'a loss of maidenhead' but the speaker does not dwell on that.

The poet envies the little flea's pleasure, for the flea found enjoyment without wooing, whereas the poet is attempting to woo but without success:

> Yet this enjoys before it woo,
> And pampered swells with one blood made of two,
> And this, alas, is more than what we would do.

'Yet' captures the poet's mood, a mixture of feeling hurt and impatient. The tiny flea, 'as it sucks on speaker and lover in the poem', Thomas Docherty points out, 'changes in size and stature' and swells in response. The tone in the final line of the first stanza is regretful, impatient, almost petulant.

There is a dramatic development in stanza two and this is signalled in its sudden beginning. In lines 1-9 the poet has been contemplating and meditating on the flea. Now the flea's life is threatened. Between stanzas 1 and 2 the woman attempts to kill the flea. The woman is about to kill it and the speaker attempts to spare it with an abrupt utterance:

> Oh stay

And then there follows another elaborate interpretation and explanation as to why this flea should be spared:

> Oh stay, three lives in one flea spare,
> Where we almost, nay more than married are.
> This flea is you and I, and this
> Our marriage bed, and marriage temple is;

Though this is a poem focusing on lovers, the idea of the flea occurs throughout. In other words, the entire poem is a fine example of conceit, one of the characteristics of metaphysical poetry. The conceit has been defined as an extended image, often ingenious or extravagant, sometimes continuing throughout an entire poem. In 'The Flea' Donne uses the insect to reveal his views on his love relationship and, more importantly, to express his desire.

The flea in the second stanza has become a sacred symbol of their union – 'This flea is you and I' and that is why it must not be killed. It can be seen that here and elsewhere in Donne's poetry his treatment of love is unconventional. He uses vivid and dramatic expression and direct colloquial speech and he urges the woman to think of them as already married - they are almost married and then he qualified that almost, 'nay more than married are':

> Oh stay, three lives in one flea spare,
> Where we almost, nay more than married are.
> This flea is you and I, and this
> Our marriage bed, and marriage temple is

The 'three lives in one flea' becomes a daring "three-persons-in-one" image, suggesting that the flea's body is now sacred. This parasitic insect, feeding on human blood, is given sacred status. The flea has become 'a marriage bed' and 'marriage temple'. Line 14 would suggest that their actual marriage or union has yet to take place because of 'parents grudge' and the woman's reluctance to consummate the relationship. Biographical details remind us that Donne loved Ann More in secret, and her parents did not know of their relationship until they were married. Ann More's father did not approve of their union and had Donne imprisoned, briefly, when their marriage was discovered. The only union possible at the moment, however, is their union within the flea:

> Though parents grudge, and you, we'are met,
> And cloistered in these living walls of jet.

The last line here with its 'delicate intentness . . . treats a flea as no flea has been treated in English before', thinks John Carey. The idea of flea as 'cloister' echoes the religious image of 'temple' two lines earlier and the black shell of its body is 'living'.

This detailed focus on process, on what the flea now symbolises, is the speaker's attempt to save the flea's life. The closing lines of this stanza tend towards self-pity on the poet's part. Habit ('use'), it would seem, might prompt the woman to kill him, but he asks that she not kill the flea, for it would be 'self murder'; she would be killing a little bit of herself:

> Though use make you apt to kill me,
> Let not to this, self murder added be,
> And sacrilege, three sins in killing three.

Line 16 offers us a glimpse of how the speaker views their relationship. Donne playfully suggests that, while she might want to kill him ('familiarity breeds contempt'), by killing him in the flea she would also, in the process, kill herself and violate something sacred (the flea is now a marriage temple) and therefore commit three murders.

This poem has three different aspects of time. First, it considers the flea; then it recognises its impending death and the third stanza marks another movement in time. The flea is now dead. Between stanza 2 and 3 the woman has squashed and killed the flea with her fingernail. His elaborate and clever argument in stanza two has failed to convince. Stanza three begins dramatically. 'Cruel' and 'sudden' describe the woman's gesture. The living jet walls have been crushed by her fingernail and it did nor deserve to die:

> Cruel and sudden, hast thou since
> Purpled thy nail, in blood of innocence?

His questioning tone here is repeated in the next sentence:

> In what could this flea guilty be,
> Except in that drop which it sucked from thee?

Placing the only two sentences in the poem ending with a question mark side by side adds to the growing sense of pleading by the speaker. Her answer is implied in lines 23–24:

> Yet thou triumph'st, and say'st that thou
> Find'st not thyself, nor me the weaker now

She is untroubled, guiltfree, and refutes the poet's argument: she has killed a little part of them both but neither feels weaker.

The final sentence in stanzas one and two began with the terms of argument: 'Yet' and 'Though' signalled the poet's determination to prove a point. The closing sentence in the final stanza does a turnaround. It is a brilliantly clever move. He now agrees with her that he was wrong. The death of the flea did not diminish him or her and so he argues that if she yields to him she will not lose her honour:

> 'Tis true, then learn how false, fears be;
> Just so much honour, when thou yield'st to me,
> Will waste, as this flea's death took life from thee.

The tone is gently pleading and confident. Much of the poem is written in the present tense but the future is imagined in such a phrase as 'when thou yield'st to me'. The flea has been interpreted in every instance as a means of the poet winning his heart's desire. It ends in happy expectation of the union.

Thou hast made me, and shall thy work decay?

The seven poems by Donne that are on your course so far are termed love poems. Some celebrate with great confidence the joy and immortality of love ('The Anniversary'; 'Sweetest love, I do not go'); others tell of frustrations and difficulties ('The Flea'; 'The Dream') and all poems display an extraordinary skill. John Donne is inventive, persuasive, he creates interesting images and argues cleverly. We often remember a Donne poem for his way of viewing a particular topic. The three poems that follow belong to a different category in terms of subject matter. In 'Thou hast made me, and shall thy work decay?', 'At the round earth's imagined corners' and 'Batter my heart three-personed God' – all sonnets – Donne addresses God. What is remarkable and striking is that his technique here is often similar to the technique he uses in his love poetry.

'Thou hast made me, and shall thy work decay?', 'At the round earth's imagined corners' and 'Batter my heart three-personed God' belong to a group of poems, a sequence of nineteen sonnets, known as Divine Meditations.

'Thou hast made me' begins with a reflective mood. The first line suggests the poet's deep awareness of God and the question mark suggests, not doubt, but Donne's belief in the immortality of the soul. The poem is a direct address and the poet openly declares that he needs God's help now that his life is drawing to a close:

> Thou hast made me, and shall thy work decay?
> Repair me now, for now mine end doth haste

He admits his faults and failings and the pleading tone in 'Repair me now' indicates Donne's need. His description of how he sees his life now, close to death, is vivid and simple:

> I run to death, and death meets me as fast

The dramatic verb 'run', the personification of death as a figure rushing towards him, the use of 'fast' and the monosyllables quicken the line. Life's pleasures are no more and the speaker expresses a fear of what is before him:

> And all my pleasures are like yesterday,
> I dare not move my dim eyes any way,
> Despair behind, and death before doth cast
> Such terror

There's an increasing sense of hopelessness here; death is near and it is terrifying. He freely admits to sinfulness and how his sinful life has resulted in his feeling now that he is heading towards hell:

> and my feeble flesh doth waste
> By sin in it, which it towards hell doth weigh

'Weigh' in this context means to 'press hard'; that he is doomed, it would seem, is inevitable.

The octet therefore focuses on the end. Words such as 'decay', 'dim', 'despair', 'terror', 'feeble', 'hell' all suggest decline. The sestet brings with it a different rhyming scheme and announces a different mood. The first eight lines rhymed abba, abba, but 'Only', at line 9, signals a significant change. The sestet has a cdcd rhyme, concluding with ee in the couplet. The downward journey towards hell is replaced by a movement towards God above:

> Only thou art above, and when towards thee
> By thy leave I can look, I rise again

but, though willing, he is weak. Donne admits that 'our subtle foe' (Satan) tempts him and that temptation is so great that Donne himself will never be saved unless God helps him:

> But our old subtle foe so tempteth me,
> That not one hour I can myself sustain

This is very effective. The use of 'our' brings him closer to God and the honest, up-front admission that he cannot survive even an hour without God's help reveals Donne's helplessness and commitment. The poem began with a question; the final couplet suggests the answer – God's grace will help the speaker resist temptation and journey heavenward:

> Thy Grace may wing me to prevent his art,
> And thou like adamant draw mine iron heart

The verbs 'wing' and 'draw' create this effect and the idea of God as a kind of magnet or stone that guides Donne is drawn from science and is a powerful image.

It's an intensely personal poem – 'I', 'me' and 'my' are key words and the following list from the fourteen-line poem highlights Donne's preoccupation with himself: 'me', 'me', 'mine', 'I', 'me', 'my', 'I', 'my', 'my', 'I', 'I', 'me', 'I', 'myself', 'me', 'mine'. But of equal importance are the pronouns: 'Thou', 'thy', 'thou', 'thee', 'thy', 'Thy' and 'thou', which pinpoint Donne directly addressing his God.

At the round earth's imagined corners

This sonnet summons up a very dramatic and visual image in its opening line:

> At the round earth's imagined corners, blow

An urgent tone is established with the emphasis on the verb 'blow' at the end of the line; and the line flows into the second line and into the third, achieving a momentum and power in sound, repetition and imagery. The original image from the *Book of Revelations* is thrilling. The image of 'four angels standing on the four corners of the earth' is an impossible one; yet it fires the imagination and creates the image in our minds. The moment pictured here is the end of earthly life as human beings have known it; it is a powerful and involving moment for all mankind:

> At the round earth's imagined corners, blow
> Your trumpets, angels and arise, arise
> From death, you numberless infinities
> Of souls, and to your scattered bodies go

The moment is a grand and violent one; it is apocalyptic. These opening lines speak of the dead, everyone who has ever lived and died. The American novelist Saul Bellow says that 'Death does not keep a census'; there is no knowing how many people have died, but here Donne asks us to imagine such a number. The poem looks to the future, to the end of time as we know it and to the Last Judgement. Then the dead will rise up and they will be united with their bodies. And though the poem focuses on the dead, there is an extraordinary energy and force in the lines which describe the numberless who have died. The 'trumpets' suggest a loud, urgent music and the verb arise and its repetition add force. Three of the four lines in the first section end with a verb – 'blow', 'arise', 'go'; Donne is addressing God's angels, but he is also speaking to the souls who join their former bodies.

There is a great sense of sound and movement in this imagined scene and the poet elaborates further in line five when he thinks of how the numberless infinities died. The technique here is both familiar and effective. The poet lists all those circumstances, events and catastrophes which caused people to die. That the list begins with 'the flood' suggests a huge temporal perspective. The phrase 'numberless infinities' is unnecessary repetition, it could be argued: 'numberless' is the same as 'infinities', and yet the repetition is justified. All those who died since the beginning of the world is such an unimaginable concept that both numberless and infinities could hardly be said to capture the enormousness of it.

There is nothing to suggest that the flood is Noah's flood, but it could be. The Day of Judgement belongs to the closing book of the *Bible*; the flood is recounted in the opening of the *Old Testament*. The flood goes back a very long time and, by asking the reader to think of different and other causes, the effect is such that, even though one is reading only three lines, the sweep and scope is that of thousands of years:

> All whom the flood did, and fire shall o'erthrow,
> All whom war, dearth, age, agues, tyrannies,
> Despair, law, chance, hath slain . . .

What is interesting here, apart from the solemn list, is the time frame. Donne speaks of the future at the beginning of the sonnet, then of the past, but he also includes all the years that are to be from the time he is writing to the time when the earth shall be no more. The repetition of 'All whom' presents the reader with the enormity of man's destruction.

Though the catalogue of disasters is grim, the first eight lines end on a hopeful note. The angels are announcing the end and are summoning the dead, but the summons is to meet their maker. Donne's confidence is total and he achieves a striking intimacy in the direct personal address, 'you':

> . . . and you whose eyes,
> Shall behold God, and never taste death's woe.

Suffering and sorrow are no more; you shall behold God. The use of 'never' is powerful in that it counteracts death and it follows on from a detailed list outlining so many forms of death: natural catastrophes, man-made causes, natural causes, illnesses, deaths brought about by hopelessness, rules, random happenings.

There is a noticeable contrast between the octet and the sestet. Everything in the octet is loud and big – the world's corners, the idea of the scattered bodies, the flood; eight lines form one increasingly powerful sentence. In the final six lines there is a quietness and an intimacy. This is achieved with the focus on one individual, the poet himself. He asks that the future be suspended for a moment. He asks God to let the sleeping dead lie on, for he himself has a special request to ask and the Day of Judgement will be too busy and too late:

> But let them sleep, Lord, and me mourn a space;
> For if above all these my sins abound,
> 'Tis late to ask abundance of thy grace,
> When we are there

This is a direct, honest and humble plea. The speaker admits his sinfulness and wonders if his sins exceed those who have already died. He now asks for God's grace, for when the world ends it may be too late, and the image of Donne being on 'lowly ground' adds to his humility. The poem began with a request to the angels; it ends with Donne requesting God to teach him how to regret his sins:

> here on this lowly ground,
> Teach me how to repent

Donne emerges here as a man dependent on his God and believing in his might. If God will help Donne to repent then he is guaranteed salvation:

> for that's as good
> As if thou had'st sealed my pardon, with thy blood.

'Thou hast made me' ends with a strong awareness of the presence of God, as does this sonnet 'At the round earth's imagined corners'. In both the relation between Donne and his maker is an essential one. The image of the adamant or lodestone and the image of putting a seal on a pardon are vivid and memorable. The reference to Christ's blood is dramatic. It is God as a human not a distant figure, the God who became man and suffered to save the sins of the world.

Batter my heart, three-personed God

This is the most forceful and most daring of these three Divine Meditations. From the opening words, 'Batter my heart', with their violent, demanding tone, the poem is unconventional. The poet is demanding that his heart be struck, beaten into shape:

> Batter my heart, three-personed God

(A battering-ram was a swinging beam, once used for breaking through a wall, and perhaps Donne is suggesting that God must break through and reach him.) There is almost an accusatory tone when Donne reprimands his God for not making a sufficiently strong effort as yet:

> for, you
> As yet but knock, breathe, shine, and seek to mend

These verbs, less powerful than 'Batter', are nonetheless dramatic in their depiction of God. The image is a daring, original one: God is seen as tinsmith or tinker – a mender of kettles and pans and the opening quatrain is a series of pleas, requests, demands. The number of verbs per line is remarkable and each verb has an energy of its own:

> That I may rise, and stand, o'erthrow me and bend
> Your force, to break, blow, burn, and make me new.

In these two lines eight verbs capture Donne's urgent desire for God's help and his use of paradox creates memorable ways of viewing himself and God. The first of these paradoxes occurs in line three. In order for Donne to find himself he needs to be knocked down. A second paradox follows immediately: he will only be made whole and new if he is first broken. His tone is direct; he is clear in knowing what God must do. He seems hopeless without God's help.

The second quatrain is dominated by a single image, that of a town held captive. Donne compares himself to an occupied town. He is unhappy and helpless:

> I, like a usurped town, to another due,
> Labour to admit you, but oh, to no end

He struggles to allow God enter but confesses that he now belongs to someone else. God's enemy has taken him captive; the speaker admits that he has given in to sin.

He also realises that his reason has not been strong enough to help. Reason is seen as God's representative or viceroy, but reason too has failed him:

> Reason, your viceroy in me, me should defend,
> But is captived, and proves weak or untrue

The sonnet thus far argues his case and asks for God's help. The imagery is unusual, but the most unusual image of all is found in the sestet. Here, Donne compares himself to a woman and God is portrayed as her lover. Line nine prepares the reader for this image. It is an emotional and intense utterance:

> Yet dearly I love you and would be loved fain

He would willingly ('fain') allow himself to be loved just as he loves

> But am betrothed unto your enemy

The speaker is admitting to an intimate relationship with God's enemy; he is promised in marriage.

The final lines of the sonnet gather great momentum. Donne here proposes a solution. His engagement with the devil can be broken if God takes some drastic action and this is spelt out in a paradox that some may consider shocking:

> Divorce me, untie, or break that knot again,
> Take me to you, imprison me, for I
> Except you enthral me never shall be free,
> Nor ever chaste, unless you ravish me.

In these four lines 'me' occurs five times and each one is preceded by a verb. A pattern is established. The verbs in the octet were violent and forceful; each verb here is a strong, insistent plea: 'Divorce me . . . Take me . . . imprison me . . . enthral me . . . ravish me.' Donne is unashamedly thinking of no one but himself.

The three-personed God which Donne speaks of in line one is Father, Son and Holy Spirit, but Donne also rewrites that Trinity in this sonnet when he suggests that God is king (line 7), conqueror (line 12) and lover (line 14).

In these Divine Meditations God is not viewed as a distant presence. He speaks to God in a very personal, intimate, direct way. This direct speaking voice is found in all of Donne's poetry, whether he is addressing his lover or his God.

Patrick Kavanagh

(1904–1967)

Contents	Page

The Overview

In Chapter 3 of his novel *Tarry Flynn*, Kavanagh describes a summer sunset and, though sunsets have often been written about, when Kavanagh does it, like all true artists, he makes it his own:

> 'The summer sun was going down in a most wonderful yellow ball behind the hills of Drumnay. It turned the dirty upstairs windows of Cassidy's house into stained glass.'

Here the beauty of the evening sun is captured with all the simplicity of a child's painting: the sun is 'a most wonderful yellow ball'; the local place and people are named and the ordinariness of dirty windows is before us. But Kavanagh's way of seeing the world has transformed those windows into beautiful objects of praise.

These ten poems are often prompted and inspired by particular places: Inniskeen Road; Shancoduff; his small family farm in 'A Christmas Childhood'; Donaghmoyne ('The Great Hunger' *Part I*); his local place ('Advent'); Raglan Road; Ballyrush and Gortin ('Epic'); the Rialto Hospital; the Grand Canal Dublin. In Michael Schmidt's words, in Kavanagh's poetry, 'Naming of places and things is of almost magical significance.' He writes in praise and celebration, for the most part, but in the extract from 'The Great Hunger' a darker relationship with place is explored. In Sean O'Brien's words, 'The Great Hunger' depicts farming as 'hard labour and the bachelor male condition as sexually frustrated.' By contrast, in 'Epic' and 'Advent' the countryside is written about with affection and the rural images in his city poem, 'Canal Bank Walk', are happy, summery images of grass, trees, breeze and bird. Harry Clifton thinks that 'In Kavanagh's finest work, it is almost always high summer' – for example 'Inniskeen Road: July Evening' and the canal bank sonnets of mid-July.

In many of Kavanagh's poems, he is the outsider, and the speaker in the poem is aware that this has advantages and disadvantages. He himself felt that: 'A poet is never one of the people. He is detached, remote, and the life of small-time dances and talk about football would not be for him. He might take part but could not belong.' 'Inniskeen Road' and 'Epic' are poems which highlight the position of the poet; he feels cut off, at a remove from his neighbours, and yet the poems hint at how he is also content with his lot. In 'Raglan Road', the painful memories of unrequited love give way to the poet's own belief in himself and yet, in 'Lines Written on a Seat on the Grand Canal, Dublin', he chooses what has been described by Antoinette Quinn as 'an unegotistical tomb, a monument to his poetics rather than to his person' where 'Future visitors are asked to sit with their backs to the memorial description, reading instead the scene before them.'

Kavanagh's own experience of life is at the heart of a Kavanagh poem. He writes directly out of his own experience – rural life, farming, childhood memories, unrequited love, illness and convalescence, his love of nature, his gratitude to God. When he writes 'I', he is almost always writing in his own voice and, even when he writes in the third person, as when he writes about Patrick Maguire and what Kavanagh called 'the prison of a farmer's life' in 'The Great Hunger', he also includes the voice of a concerned, involved narrator which creates a closer link between the harsh, bleak world of the poem and the reader.

But the world of Kavanagh's poetry is also life-enhancing and celebratory. Poems such as 'Advent', 'The Hospital' and the Canal Bank sonnets are love poems to places that Kavanagh is familiar with. Here when Kavanagh looks, he sees 'the newness that was in every stale thing' and he delights in the ordinary, the natural, the physical world of 'bog-holes, cart-tracks, old stables', 'dreeping hedges', 'square cubicles in a row', 'The main gate that was bent by a heavy lorry,/ The seat at the back of a shed that was a suntrap', the trapped stick, the grass, Canal water 'stilly/ Greeny at the heart of summer.' In a lecture entitled 'Man and Poet', Kavanagh said: 'We are in too great a hurry. We want a person or thing to yield their pleasures and their secrets to us quickly for we have other commitments. But it is the days when we are idle, when nothing appears to be happening, which provide us when no one is looking with all that is memorable.' The Canal Bank sonnets are unhurried poems in which Kavanagh's idleness yields precious, unforgettable experiences.

Anthony Cronin has described Patrick Kavanagh as an intensely private man who lived his life in public places, a man who thought mediocrity the enemy of genius, the enemy of life. He did live a public life as journalist and man about town, but Kavanagh also claimed that 'the only subject that is of any real importance – Man-in-this-World-and-why.' He also believed that 'Parochialism is universal; it deals with the fundamentals' and that great beauty and profound truths can be discovered in apparently ordinary places.

John McGahern tells of how the forty-one-year-old Patrick Kavanagh once pointed out a particular grass and said: 'I love that grass. I've known it since I was a child. I've often wondered if I'd be different if I had been brought up to love better things.' In the end, though, he did believe in Ballyrush and Gortin, in ordinary things, for it was in the ordinary that not only meaning could be found but that Kavanagh discovered the extraordinary, because he knew that 'The material itself has no special value; it is what our imagination and our love does to it.'

There is a 'gravid powerful rough-cast' quality, says Seamus Heaney, in lines such as 'Clay is the word and clay is the flesh/ Where potato gatherers like mechanized scarecrows move/ Along the side-fall of a hill, Maguire and his men.' But that is only one aspect of the Kavanagh music. There is also a lyrical, gentle but impassioned quality in lines such as 'O unworn world enrapture me' or 'Feed the gaping need of my senses' and a sense of being totally at ease. Kavanagh's language can be what Patrick Crotty calls 'grittily realistic' (especially in 'The Great Hunger') but there is also a colloquial rhythm in such lines as 'There's a dance in Billy Brennan's barn tonight' or 'That was the year of the Munich bother' and what Antoinette Quinn calls 'a powerful lyrical impulse' in the unusually long, very luxuriant lines of 'Canal Bank Walk', for example, where 'pouring' and 'overflowing' seem to describe the poem's rhythm and mood: 'For this soul needs to be honoured with a new dress woven/ From green and blue things and arguments that cannot be proven.'

Kavanagh has an extraordinary ability to create fresh, surprising images – 'the wink-and-elbow language of delight'; 'a footfall tapping secrecies of stone'; 'I am king/ Of banks and stones and every blooming thing'; 'The sleety winds fondle the rushy beards of Shancoduff'; 'Mass-going feet/ Crunched the wafer-ice on the pot-holes'; 'The wind leans from Brady's, and the coltsfoot leaves are holed with rust'; 'And Christ comes with a January flower'; 'we tripped lightly along the ledge/ Of the deep ravine'; 'Homer's ghost came whispering to my mind'; 'the inexhaustible adventure of a gravelled yard'; 'a bird gathering materials for the nest for the Word' and 'A swan goes by head low with many apologies.'

Kavanagh's poetry is a record of a journey that brought him from Monaghan to the banks of the Grand Canal, a journey of discovery and exploration in which he reveals himself as one who found the ordinary, extraordinary, and that 'the things that really matter are casual, insignificant little things.' He offers us a version of himself in his poem 'If Ever You Go To Dublin Town.' 'If ever you go to Dublin town/ In a hundred years or so' he says, 'Inquire for me in Baggot Street/ and what I was like to know' and he goes on to tell us that he was 'a queer one', 'dangerous', 'a nice man', 'eccentric', 'a proud one', 'a vain one', 'slothful' and it ends:

> He knew that posterity had no use
> For anything but the soul,
> The lines that speak the passionate heart,
> The spirit that lives alone.
> O he was a lone one
> Fol dol the di do,
> Yet he lived happily
> I tell you.

Biographical Notes

Patrick Joseph Kavanagh, one of ten children and eldest son of a cobbler and small farmer, was born on 21 October 1904 in the Inniskeen townland of Mucker, County Monaghan, fifty miles from Dublin. His childhood was, in Antoinette Quinn's words, 'a safe and comfortable one' and Kavanagh 'grew to manhood in a secure and stable home in which both parents were almost permanently present.' The small kitchen also served as his father's workshop where he manufactured and repaired boots and shoes.

There were seven girls and three boys but one boy died as a baby and Peter, Kavanagh's younger brother, was born when Kavanagh was twelve which ensured that Patrick Kavanagh, son and heir, was given special treatment within the home. All the children had nicknames, Kavanagh's being "Gam" or "Long Nose". Both parents worked hard and the children were also expected to work within the home, drawing water, feeding animals and working on local farms. When Kavanagh was six his father bought nine acres locally – six were arable (suitable for growing crops) and three acres of bogland. The Kavanagh children attended the local National School at Kednaminsha where their grandfather had once taught. Patrick Kavanagh began his education at the age of four and experienced a harsh regime where physical punishment was commonplace. He had a very good memory and in a school essay, when the young Kavanagh wrote that 'the lover of nature . . . can see beauty in everything. He can see the finger of God even in a nettle', we can glimpse the future poet. He was increasingly bored by school and, having been made take fifth class twice, never reached sixth class. He was punished at home for idleness and grew up lacking self-confidence, but he was a bright child who enjoyed poetry but could not admit it for fear of being mocked.

When Kavanagh left school on 18 June 1918, four months before his fourteenth birthday, his formal education came to an end and he became a shoe-maker and part-time farmer like his father. He was an impatient shoe-maker, a clumsy, unsuccessful farmer, liked sport and the very first book he bought was a boxing manual when he was twelve. Books were also borrowed from neighbours and the poetry anthology, *Palgrave's Golden Treasury*, was particularly important to Kavanagh. Years later, Kavanagh also acknowledged the importance of school textbooks, claiming that 'If roots I had they were in the schoolbooks.' By the time he had left school he had learned many poems by heart and it was something he continued to do after school. While working in the fields or walking the roads, Kavanagh would say these poems aloud and, years later, a forty-eight year-old Kavanagh remembered how lines from a poem would bring him back to an October evening to 'a field called Lurgankeel away down a shady corner.'

He joined the Inniskeen pipers' band, became interested in Sinn Féin, joined in republican activities and once raided the post office in Inniskeen. When his father found out, he beat his son and made him return the stolen goods. At eighteen Kavanagh became ill with typhoid fever and was hospitalised in Carrickmacross Fever Hospital in County Monaghan for three months; it left him very weak and exhausted. Convalescence, however, allowed him even more time for reading and this played an important part in his growth as a poet, novelist and journalist. He had begun "poeming", as he called it, when he was twelve and was so at ease with verse that at twenty, on returning from a four-day stay in Monaghan County Infirmary, where he had a collar bone set, he wrote verse letters to his fellow-patients in the ward.

His father then became ill and Kavanagh had to take over the running of the farm. All this time shoe-making and shoe-repairing was dying out, as factory replaced cobbler, and the Kavanaghs set about buying another piece of land. This time it was a small farm at Shancoduff, three-quarters of a mile from their home in Mucker. It was poor land consisting of seven hilly fields covered in rushes, bought just before Kavanagh's twenty-first birthday, and in 1938 it was transferred to his name. Kavanagh in his twenties was publishing poems in newspapers – the *Dundalk Democrat* and *Irish Weekly Independent*. He also discovered the *Irish Statesman*, a literary journal, and, in the words of Antoinette Quinn, it 'was his university.' Edited by George Russell (AE), it was Russell who first recognised Kavanagh's talent and published three of his poems in the *Irish Statesman*. One of these is 'Ploughman' and it signalled the emergence of Patrick Kavanagh, poet. It begins:

> I turn the lea-green down
> Gaily now,
> And paint the meadow brown
> With my plough . . . .

and it was included in the London-published *Best Poems of 1930*. In May 1931, the literary magazine *John O'London's* printed one of his poems; *The Spectator* included two poems that May and June and towards the end of the year he began to be published in the *Dublin Magazine*. Kavanagh also visited Dublin for the first time in December 1931, having walked the sixty-mile journey. It took him three days.

Kavanagh's father had died in August 1929. By then the twenty-five year-old Kavanagh was man of the house and, for the next eight years or thereabouts, he lived the life of a small-time farmer and occasional cobbler but in the evening he would spend an hour or two reading and writing. He played football and, although he was considered an unreliable goalkeeper for Inniskeen, Kavanagh in 1932 was secretary, treasurer and captain of the Inniskeen team. But his footballing days ended when he was discovered to have stolen the team's funds in his care. As spectator, his interest in football continued for the rest of his life. He also went to local dances, knowing, as Antoinette Quinn points out in her biography, that the Archbishops and Bishops of Ireland condemned imported dances and their views were to be read out in every Catholic church four times a year. 'Inniskeen Road: July Evening', which speaks of a local dance, dates from this period.

When Kavanagh walked to Dublin to visit AE, he was welcomed and given over half a dozen books; he stayed in the Iveagh Hostel that night, before setting out for home. Dublin was visited as often as possible and 17 Rathgar Avenue, where AE lived, became for Kavanagh a centre of literary and cultural life. AE believed in Kavanagh, describing him in a letter, written April 1932 to W.B. Yeats, as 'a young shoemaker in Monaghan who has genius but no education' and later AE spoke of Kavanagh's poems as having 'a wild and original fire in them.' During this time Kavanagh got to know Frank O'Connor, Sean O'Faolain and F.R. Higgins and, though based in Inniskeen, would visit Dublin and discuss literary matters. He was reading Edward Thomas, Ezra Pound, Yeats, Hopkins and continued to write. 'When an idea or a phrase for a poem struck him out in the fields, he scribbled it on the inside of his cigarette packet' says Antoinette Quinn, linking farming and poetry.

Kavanagh was always interested in women, and regularly fell in love but usually from a distance. In 1934 he fell in love – he was thirty; she was eighteen. He wrote her poems and quoted her love poems by others, but poetry didn't interest her and their romance was short-lived. Others had poems dedicated to them and when Kavanagh was in his late twenties he had his first sexual relationship with a local girl.

In 1936, Kavanagh made his first broadcast on national radio, and, having had some difficulty finding a publisher for his first collection, was taken on by Macmillan. *Ploughman and Other Poems*, containing 'Inniskeen Road: July Evening', was published in London in September 1936, when Kavanagh was almost thirty-two, though in interviews he pretended that he was in his twenties.

Kavanagh left home in 1937 to try his luck in London. Leaving behind his mother, his sister Josie and brother Peter (who was by then teaching in Dundalk), Kavanagh said goodbye to Inniskeen. The thirty-three year-old Kavanagh met George Bernard Shaw, Sean O'Casey, Helen Waddell and John Gawsworth. It was Waddell who, as a reader for the publishing house Constable, commissioned him to write an autobiography and an advance allowed Kavanagh to live in London and write. Gawsworth was instrumental in introducing Kavanagh to literary life. For the first time in his life he worked without interruption and produced *The Green Fool* (1938), a work which was reviewed favourably but later dismissed by Kavanagh himself as 'a dreadful stage-Irish, so-called autobiography.' He also said that 'the common people of this country gobbled up this stage-Irish lie.' He also wrote many poems and had a second collection ready by late 1937, by which time he was back in Inniskeen. His brother had moved to Dublin, the only sister at home was getting married and Patrick Kavanagh was expected to return to farming. He spent much of 1938 in Inniskeen and, though the second farm was transferred to his name, writing was his first interest now.

In 1939, Oliver St. John Gogarty, medical doctor and poet, brought a libel case against the publisher and printer of *The Green Fool*, accusing Kavanagh of defamation. Gogarty won his case, being awarded £100 plus costs, and Kavanagh found the whole business so stressful that his hair turned grey. The book was withdrawn and Kavanagh's literary career experienced a major setback. Then came an invitation from two fans of *The Green Fool* – the Misses Blois of Gerrards

Cross outside London. They offered Kavanagh free accommodation so that he could write and May 1939 found him once more in England, availing of Blois hospitality. His patrons also bought him a typewriter and he set about writing a novel. The Blois sisters owned a cafe and, when Kavanagh made a pass at a waitress, the Misses Blois threw him out. Attempts at finding work in publishing failed and he returned to Ireland, determined to finish his book even though the book would be used to help his publisher defray libel costs.

Writing in *Self-Portrait*, Kavanagh says of his move to Dublin: 'Round about the late 1930s a certain prosperity came through and foolishly enough that was the time I chose to leave my native fields. I had no messianic impulse to leave. I was happy. I went against my will. A lot of our actions are like that . . . I came to Dublin in 1939. It was the worst mistake of my life. The Hitler war had started. I had my comfortable little holding of watery hills beside the Border.'

In Dublin he was now given free board and lodging by his brother Peter who was teaching at the Christian Brothers' school at Westland Row. They shared a flat at 51 Upper Drumcondra Road. Back in Dublin, Kavanagh fell in love with Maeve Mulcahy from Sligo. He was more interested than she but, when War was declared in September, she returned to Sligo and the romance ended. The Kavanagh brothers moved to cheaper accommodation at 35 Haddington Road, where Kavanagh would spend the mornings writing, the afternoons in town. Sometimes Peter Kavanagh invited his brother to talk to his class and a then pupil told Antoinette Quinn, almost fifty years later, that Patrick Kavanagh read to them from Herman Melville's *Moby-Dick* (one of his favourite books) and from Hopkins's poetry, holding the class spellbound.

He returned to Inniskeen occasionally to help his mother and she left the house and first farm to him in her will, dated April 1940, provided he lived there. But he stayed in Dublin, writing and looking for a job. His appearance was against him: he was unhygienic; his clothes were shabby and dirty; his manner was considered coarse; his language was considered very offensive by many. Afternoons were spent walking the streets and he was well-known on Nassau Street and Grafton Street. He chatted with street traders and children, visited bookshops and looked for someone in coffee shops who might buy him a coffee or he would read for free in the National Library on Kildare Street. Evenings were spent in the Palace Bar, which Kavanagh called the Malice Bar, where the editor of the *Irish Times* held court each evening from 6 p.m. to 9.30 p.m. and where artists, writers and journalists met. Some work followed; for example, he wrote a series of articles for the *Irish Times*, mainly on rural topics. He tired of the Palace Bar crowd, however, because, according to Antoinette Quinn, for him the gathering symbolised Dublin's 'smug' and 'self-congratulatory' who were 'talking about art rather than achieving it.'

Dublin also offered art exhibitions, literary evenings, classical music concerts. When T.S. Eliot gave a lecture on Yeats in the Abbey Theatre on 30 June 1939, Kavanagh was in the audience and met Eliot at the party afterwards. He continued writing his novel and finished it by November 1939, sending it to his publisher. *The Land Remains*, 75,000 words long, was never published and nothing of it remains. But it freed Kavanagh from his London publisher and he then wrote to Harold Macmillan who had admired *The Green Fool*, asking him for an advance on a new novel and a sequel he intended to write. In fact that novel became his long poem 'The Great Hunger'; the sequel was *Tarry Flynn*, which Kavanagh, in 1964, said he was 'humble enough to claim is not only the best but the only authentic account of life as it was lived in Ireland this century.' He asked Macmillan for an advance, claiming that 'the articles I am doing hardly keep me in cigarettes and I am just existing on the fringes of starvation.'

The AE Memorial Award of £100 was presented to Kavanagh in January 1940, a sum which his teacher brother would take seven months to earn, but he spent it quickly and by March was penniless again. Whenever he found a sympathetic ear he asked for money; journalism brought in a small income but a poetry reading he gave in Blackrock College in November 1940 brought him good luck. John Charles McQuaid was then President of Blackrock College; the following January he was inaugurated as Archbishop of Dublin and McQuaid, a Cavan man and formerly a teacher of English, was to become an important patron for Kavanagh.

In the autumn of 1939, Kavanagh fell in love with Peggy Gough, but not she with him. Their relationship was intellectual and sexual, but Peggy Gough had no interest in marrying the poet. Kavanagh and Peggy Gough spoke openly about sexual matters and Peggy Gough spoke of Kavanagh's sexual frustration as 'starving.' Kavanagh used the same image in 'The Great Hunger', which he completed in October 1941. Antoinette Quinn says that in 'The Great Hunger' Kavanagh 'preaches the gospel of the importance of human sexual fulfilment with all the zeal of the recently converted.' In 1941, their relationship came to an end but they remained friends. Remembering Kavanagh many years later, Peggy Gough said of Kavanagh that 'he was all for life.'

Kavanagh knew both Frank O'Connor and Sean O'Faolain, who were living and working in Dublin in the 1940s. Both O'Connor and O'Faolain believed that you should write about what you know in a realistic manner. The well-known literary and cultural journal *The Bell* was founded by O'Faolain late in 1940 and the Christmas issue contained what is now Part II of 'A Christmas Childhood.' Kavanagh was now also working on another novel, *Stony Grey Soil*, which also became the title of a poem and the novel, though rejected at first, when published was *Tarry Flynn*.

The Kavanagh brothers moved to a bedsitter at 122 Morehampton Road in 1940 and here, in October 1941, Kavanagh wrote 'The Great Hunger'. It was published in a limited edition of two hundred and fifty copies the following year but did not sell well. Poverty was a constant in Kavanagh's life. From Morehampton Road, Peter and Patrick moved to 55a Percy Place, then Kavanagh moved on his own to 9 Lower O'Connell Street, where he lived for a year. Here, in a fourth-floor bedsitter, Kavanagh wrote the long poem 'Lough Derg' and the novel *Stony Grey Soil (Tarry Flynn)* was on-going. He also wrote a series of articles on different pilgrimages – Lough Derg, Knock, Croagh Patrick and others. In September 1942, Kavanagh got his first regular job when he wrote a twice-weekly column, 'City Commentary', for *The Irish Press* under the pen-name Piers Plowman. The column, which ran for a year and a half, allowed Kavanagh to write an informal and friendly account of all aspects of Dublin life and his press card allowed him access to cultural, social and sporting events – art exhibitions, fashion shows, boxing matches, the opera, a garden party at Áras an Uachtaráin, racing fixtures and the theatre. Sometimes he would write light verse/doggerel for the columns, a birthday poem or a sonnet on a boxing tournament. He also reviewed books for *The Standard* in 1943 and it was here that Kavanagh was critical of the Anglo-Irish writers, including Yeats, Lady Gregory and Synge, seeing them as somehow not being part of the Irish consciousness.

In 1943, Kavanagh fell in love with Finola O'Driscoll, a beautiful, educated, middle-class woman. Kavanagh was thirty-nine; "Nola" was in her early twenties. Though they had only known each other for a few days, they holidayed together in Killarney and Dingle. He proposed, she accepted and an engagement ring was bought in Cork. The O'Driscoll family objected to his background, his lack of income and his uncertain future and the couple decided to keep the engagement secret, postponing wedding plans. Kavanagh, meanwhile, rented a large flat at 62 Pembroke Road for them to share and this was to be his Dublin address for almost fifteen years. The engagement was leaked and was broken off in March 1944. His 'City Commentary' column came to an end and Kavanagh was desperate for a job. He sublet the flat and spent the summer of 1944 in Inniskeen. Back in Dublin in the autumn, he stayed at a boarding house at 19 Raglan Road and was given financial assistance by Archbishop John Charles McQuaid, who also attempted and failed to find Kavanagh a secure job.

In the autumn of 1944, while living in the Raglan Road boarding house, Kavanagh fell in love again, this time with Hilda Moriarty, a twenty-two year-old UCD medical student from Dingle. So great was his fascination that he followed her to Dingle that Christmas, his first Christmas away from Inniskeen. He stayed at Kruger Kavanagh's well-known guesthouse and pub and covered his expenses by writing 'My Christmas in Kerry' for *The Irish Press*. Through 1945, having returned to 62 Pembroke Road, Kavanagh, in an attempt to win Hilda, spruced himself up. She, in turn, tried to find him work but failed. His second collection, *A Soul for Sale*, was accepted by Macmillan (published 1947) but he was offered his first regular job in August 1945 when he joined the Catholic weekly newspaper *The Standard* as sub-editor, reporter and later as film critic.

Kavanagh wrote three poems called 'Hilda' in honour of Hilda Moriarty and 'On Raglan Road' (first published in *The Irish Press* on 3 October 1946) was written in celebration of his meeting and losing her. Hilda had been trying to end the relationship but his mother's unexpected death on 10 November 1945 delayed the separation and on 7 December *The Standard* published one of his best-known poems 'In Memory of My Mother.' By the time Kavanagh's poem of unrequited love, 'On Raglan Road', was published, Hilda was in a new relationship and she married the following year, leaving the forty-three year old Kavanagh heartbroken and embittered. He kept a painting of Hilda in his Pembroke Road flat and when he died she sent an 'H' shaped wreath of red roses.

When *A Soul for Sale* was published in February 1947, it was the first time that 'The Great Hunger' was widely available and it as hailed as a major poem and masterpiece. Kavanagh returned to his novel, revised it, and it became *Tarry Flynn*. He had left *The Standard* but continued his cinema-review column and spent the summer of 1947 rewriting *Tarry Flynn*; it appeared in November 1948. 'After these small critical successes, however,' Shawn Holliday points out that 'the author's career ran into more trouble: he failed to find journalistic work in London, the Irish Cultural Committee refused to sponsor his proposed lecture tour of America, and Macmillan would no longer publish his work.' *Tarry Flynn* was banned by the Censorship Board because it was considered 'indecent and obscene' but the publisher's appeal resulted in the ban being lifted and sales of the novel were very good. It was also published in America. Kavanagh was so well-known and notorious by now that he was photographed for an advertisement selling an Odearest mattress.

Kavanagh drafted two more novels but they came to nothing. There was also trouble on the family front when the family home and first farm, which his sister and her family had taken over on a three-year lease, was disputed by Kavanagh. In the end he forced them to move, changed the lock and let the farm, having sold the second farm which he inherited on the death of his father. But he rarely visited the empty house; Dublin had become his home. To many people in Dublin, Patrick Kavanagh was a kind of tramp. His appearance was unkempt; he was a frequent spitter and his language was crude. He redecorated his flat with money from the sale of the farm and he was intent on finding a wife. He didn't succeed and the money ran out. A new interest, that of betting on horses, also drained his resources and in 1949 he sold some of his manuscripts to the National Library. The Director was disappointed that there was no manuscript of *The Green Fool,* but Kavanagh explained that there wasn't one because he had written it 'on the backs of envelopes and scraps of paper, including lavatory paper.' Instead Kavanagh agreed to supply a fair copy of the poem, sitting down and copying it out in the Library.

Envoy, a new arts journal, was founded and edited by John Ryan in 1949 and Kavanagh was asked to contribute a 'Diary' on a regular basis. Ryan was from a very wealthy family and Kavanagh enjoyed the generous patronage. The 'Diary' was iconoclastic and controversial, a talking point, and his association with the journal introduced him to a wide circle of writers, artists and intellectuals. The 1950s was a time of what Kavanagh termed 'poetic rebirth'; 'Epic', 'The Hospital' and 'Canal Bank Walk' belong to this period, but 1950 itself was another hard year for Kavanagh. He sublet the Dublin flat and headed for London where he picked up some broadcasting work with the BBC, some reviewing work and stayed with various friends. Back in Dublin, Kavanagh hoped to travel to America on a trip that was to be sponsored by the Cultural Relations Committee but plans were vetoed by the Fianna Fáil government of the day and Kavanagh, in a letter to his brother in New York, denounced the party as the 'dirtiest, lowest crowd we ever had.'

In July 1951, *Envoy* folded and Patrick and Peter Kavanagh set about founding their own journal, *Kavanagh's Weekly*, a literary and political publication which appeared in April 1952. It created a stir when published and continued to do so but publication ceased with issue thirteen in July. Kavanagh said of *Kavanagh's Weekly*: 'I wrote almost the whole paper including the poems, letters to the editor, etc. Why do people engage in such madness?'

Peter returned to America and Kavanagh went to London, where he survived on some journalism and hand-outs from friends. When *The Leader* back home printed an anonymous Profile of Kavanagh which he considered offensive, he sued for libel and hoped for a large out-of-court settlement. Meanwhile he returned to London, but again did not find success and came back to Pembroke Road in November 1952. The libel case, however, did go to the courts and was considered one of the most sensational and newsworthy court cases of the 1950s. The case, which involved thirteen hours of being cross-examined, exhausted Kavanagh and, when the jury returned a verdict of not libelled, he appealed the decision. The appeal was expensive but a fund was set up and contributions flowed in, including money from John Betjeman and T.S. Eliot. Kavanagh himself, as ever, had little or no money, could not pay his bills and he even had to pawn a raincoat. Many friends helped him out and Peter Kavanagh paid rent and bills. Kavanagh began to drink more, was often drunk and was, without knowing it, ill with cancer.

Kavanagh then turned to the Taoiseach of the day, John A. Costello, for help and eventually Costello arranged for UCD to hire Kavanagh as a part-time lecturer and for the Arts Council to commission a series of booklets on the arts in Ireland. This was in 1954-1955 and in the spring of 1955 lung cancer was diagnosed. He was admitted to the Rialto Hospital at the beginning of March and on 31 March his left lung and a rib were removed. Recuperation took another few weeks but Kavanagh later declared that the time in Rialto was the happiest in his life. He enjoyed many visitors, including the Archbishop of Dublin, the Taoiseach and the President of UCD; he remembered that special time in Ward 4 of the Rialto Hospital in his sonnet 'The Hospital.' John Ryan arranged for a nursing home for Kavanagh on his leaving hospital but Kavanagh asked that he be put up in the Royal Hibernian Hotel for a week instead and Ryan generously agreed. Kavanagh asked Ryan to extend his stay in the Hibernian but Ryan refused and Kavanagh was annoyed. He then stayed with a friend and later moved to be with his sister in Longford, where he stayed as an ungrateful guest for a month. Stories of Kavanagh's cantankerousness, vulgarity, insensitivity and crude nature abound. Antoinette Quinn observes: 'The difficulty of reconciling Kavanagh's person and his poetry, his often loutish behaviour and the lyrical poise of his printed lines, was remarked on by many of his contemporaries.' He was also fascinating, entertaining, humorous and unique. Larry Morrow, a journalist, writing of Kavanagh, says: 'Where Mr Kavanagh is concerned, indifference is impossible. He shares with Mr Frank Sinatra, Mr Dylan Thomas, Picasso and the Marx Brothers the capacity for rousing the emotions to screaming-point. You either scream for him or against him. Even Mr Kavanagh himself is in a state of almost chronic hoarseness, screaming at himself – be it said both for and against.'

While in hospital, the libel action appeal had been allowed and was subsequently settled but no details were disclosed. Kavanagh's lawyers were paid and he himself received a lump sum in May 1955. He spent the summer of 1955 convalescing in St. Stephen's Green but especially on the banks of the Grand Canal by Baggot Street Bridge. He saw this grassy spot as a little piece of his native Monaghan and the place inspired his two celebratory sonnets 'Canal Bank Walk' and 'Lines Written on a Seat on the Grand Canal, Dublin.' He visited his brother Peter in London that summer and Longford in November. That same month a hospital check-up gave Kavanagh the all-clear and Archbishop McQuaid on a Christmas visit promised Kavanagh a free private room in the Mater Hospital if it were ever needed.

In November 1955, Kavanagh also gathered together his next collection of poems but Macmillan rejected the book in January 1956. Meanwhile he gave a series of public lectures in UCD, the first of which drew a packed crowd, but as the series continued Kavanagh made less of an effort and numbers dwindled. During the summer of 1956 wealthy New York friends, the Farrellys, flew Kavanagh to a castle which they had rented in France where he stayed three weeks, visiting Paris en route. He became restless and returned to Dublin and then longed for France and the Farrellys paid for him to return for another two weeks. In September, before returning to the States, Mrs Farrelly paid for a thorough refurbishing of Kavanagh's filthy flat. She also gave him a present of a first-class return sailing to New York for Christmas 1956 and booked him into the Algonquin Hotel. He later moved into an apartment on 86th St and during his stay in New York Kavanagh met many poets, including Richard Eberhart, Conrad Aiken and Allen Ginsberg. He also visited Florida, Wisconsin, Boston and Washington, where he visited Ezra Pound. His US trip involved almost daily bouts of heavy drinking but very little writing and his wayward behaviour offended many. He sailed home in mid-April 1957, having traded his first-class ticket for one in steerage and cash back. He stopped off in London and was back in 62 Pembroke Road in early May. In June, Kavanagh attended a reading by Robert Frost, who was being conferred with an honorary degree by UCD, but he was excluded from lunches and dinners for the American poet, including a reception at Áras an Uachtaráin.

More journalism brought in an income but, when marriage was proposed by a well-off, unidentified woman during the summer of 1957, he turned her down, claiming that, though thirteen years younger, she was too old for him. During the autumn he returned to writing poetry and these were now added to the third collection, which had been rejected by Macmillan, and were published by Longmans under Kavanagh's title *Come Dance with Kitty Stobling*. The Arts Society in Kilkenny invited Kavanagh to lecture in February 1958 but his behaviour was insulting and anti-social. In July 1958, Kavanagh went to Barcelona with an American friend, staying in an expensive hotel, but complained that it was touristy and was glad to return to Dublin. That October, unable to continue the upkeep, he left 62 Pembroke Road. On leaving he lay prostrate on the floor of each room and wept. He returned to the boarding house at 19 Raglan Road and visited Inniskeen more often, where his two sisters were now living in a much-improved house.

He spent the summer of 1959 in Inniskeen, his first prolonged visit in over fifteen years, but kept aloof from the locals and even took his meals in the room his sisters had turned into a bedroom-cum-study for him. Back in Dublin in September he was, once again, soon penniless. One evening while returning home from the pub he fell into the Grand Canal and almost drowned, later claiming that he had been pushed. The episode distressed him greatly.

He visited London and thought of making it his home. He had been staying with Leland Bardwell and, through Anthony and Therese Cronin, had met thirty-one year-old Katherine Moloney. He fell in love and they lived together, marrying seven years later, just months before he died. Katherine Maloney was niece of the Irish patriot Kevin Barry and she worked in London as a bookkeeper. Kavanagh now travelled between Dublin and London but alcoholism had now taken such hold that he was sometimes ill and had to be hospitalised as a result. Katherine and he began living together in her flat in 1960; though he had had sexual relationships before now, it was Kavanagh's first time living with a woman and domesticity meant a tidier, cleaner Kavanagh. The early sixties, however, were restlessly spent in London, Dublin and Monaghan.

He recorded 'The Great Hunger' for BBC radio in May 1960 and *Come Dance with Kitty Stobling* was published in June. It was the Poetry Society's summer choice, which boosted sales, and the reviews were good. Two thousand copies sold by Christmas. In 1961, Kavanagh returned to Dublin to give the UCD lecture series and spent the spring and early summer in flats along Haddington Road and then a rented room at 37 Upper Mount Street. This was his Dublin base for the next four years, though he also stayed with Leland Bardwell and family in a flat at 33 Lower Leeson Street. Kavanagh was hospitalised in late December 1961, suffering from gastritis brought about by alcoholic poisoning and malnutrition, and saw in the New Year in Baggot Street Hospital. He was back in hospital in February and convalesced in Inniskeen. *Tarry Flynn* was paperbacked in 1962 and sold over 13,000 copies by the end of the year. He also wrote and recorded for Irish television *Self-Portrait*.

Ill-health and hospitalisation followed Kavanagh into 1963, though he also began a weekly column for the *RTV Guide* (now *RTE Guide*) which brought complaints from readers for his dismissal of the Beatles and for being out of touch. He spent the winter with Katherine in London and worked on revising earlier drafts of his two unfinished novels. When Professor Alan Warner proposed writing a book on his poetry, Kavanagh was flattered but, when he thought that Warner was thinking of a biographical work, Kavanagh himself said that he nearly went up a lamp-post. The critical study went ahead but ended up as an essay and Kavanagh opposed any biography.

Kavanagh was sixty in 1964 but as he had been secretive about his age, publishing his poem 'Song At Fifty' when he was fifty-four, his sixtieth birthday passed unnoticed. That same year he applied for a driving licence and gave his age as 'over 21.'

A Collected Poems was gathered by John Montague for publication in July 1964 but it was never promoted as a birthday tribute. Christmas 1964 was spent in Inniskeen and in January 1965 he was admitted to the Meath Hospital suffering bladder problems, was operated on successfully and refused to pay his medical bills. In April, Kavanagh travelled to Chicago to attend and contribute to a Yeats symposium, 1965 being Yeats's centenary. Kavanagh resented Yeats's privileged background and his hostile contribution, deliberately denouncing Yeats, caused uproar. He spent eight weeks in America, visiting New York and Wisconsin as well as Chicago, and returned to London in June. That autumn he visited an international writers' conference in Rome and met Jean Paul Sartre and Simone de Beauvoir.

By now Kavanagh was no longer writing poetry as illness and alcoholism prevented it, but he was becoming more and more famous. There was no sense of stability in his life; his books and papers were in Katherine's London flat or Inniskeen or in various friends' houses where he stayed in Dublin. He held court in Dublin pubs, especially McDaids or the Bailey, and poets such as Eavan Boland, Paul Durcan and Brendan Kennelly admired him. He continued to flirt and to propose to attractive young women. He wrote in one of his *RTV Guide* columns: 'in my view it is marvellous to be young and to realise the truth of Shakespeare's beautiful song: "Then come and kiss me sweet and twenty/ Youth's a stuff will not endure."' In late November, Kavanagh had a small room in a flat at 136 Upper Leeson Street while Katherine remained in London. Story after story portrays Kavanagh as rough, unpredictable and entertaining; he became a tourist attraction, first in McDaid's (until he fell out with the owner over bounced cheques) and then in the Bailey or Sheehan's pub on Chatham Street.

He was still looking for a way to earn more money. *The RTV Guide* weekly column was his only regular income and he was now staying with old friends in Dublin or visiting Inniskeen. Kavanagh had been spending very little time in Katherine's company and had not been to London for six months, but he stayed with her in June and July. During this London trip, a barman, seeing Kavanagh take bread soda to ease stomach pains and thinking it was cocaine, called the police.

On returning to Dublin, he agreed to a television profile featuring Inniskeen and his Dublin haunts; this was screened in October 1966 and a dramatised version of *Tarry Flynn* was produced at the Abbey in November. Kavanagh had returned to the Meath Hospital for three weeks but, accompanied by a nurse, was allowed out for an hour each evening in Sheehan's pub. Kavanagh attended the opening night of *Tarry Flynn*. Katherine had flown over for the event but his two sisters in Inniskeen received no tickets. Kavanagh was delighted with the production and told the audience after the bows that 'I wouldn't bring any of my friends to this vulgar play.' Kavanagh had been drinking before the play and continued after the performance. He became very drunk and passed out while being driven home to a new flat he had rented at 77 Palmerston Road.

Obviously, he needed looking after and Joan Ryan urged him to marry Katherine. *Tarry Flynn* meant he had money once more but he was drinking most of it and didn't pay the rent. Christmas 1966 was spent in London with Katherine. He gave up whiskey in January and confined himself to Guinness. Back in Dublin in February, he resumed his *RTV Guide* column and having proposed, it is said, to Katherine over the phone, made wedding plans. The Church of the Three Patrons on Rathgar Road was chosen, but Kavanagh, preferring privacy, rejected the Shelbourne Hotel reception which Katherine's father offered to pay for and his old friends Eoin and Joan Ryan held a reception for the wedding party in their own home. In March, he was once again in London for the publication of his *Collected Pruse*.

Returning to Dublin, he stayed with a friend at 41 Fitzwilliam Place and marriage plans were kept secret, Kavanagh insisting, against Katherine's wishes, that no one from his family be told or invited. His sisters in Inniskeen did not know of Katherine's existence, let alone her seven-year relationship with their brother. Katherine arrived for a weekend but Kavanagh went missing and she was unsure if the wedding was on or off. He made up, begged forgiveness and Patrick

Kavanagh and Katherine Moloney were married on 19 April 1967. They lived in a flat on Winton Road, Rathgar, and later at 67 Waterloo Road. In July Kavanagh read at a Poetry International Festival in London, the only Irish poet to read with Allen Ginsberg, W.H. Auden, Stephen Spender, Anne Sexton, Robert Graves, Pablo Neruda, Octavio Paz and others.

That same summer Kavanagh's health was in serious decline. To earn some money, Katherine had found a job as bookkeeper and in September his London publisher appealed to the Arts Council to provide financial support for Kavanagh. Plans to help were set in motion but he was dead before anything could be done. He died on 30 November 1967 in the Merrion Nursing Home, 21 Herbert Street, and mourners at his funeral mass included Paul Durcan, Eiléan Ní Chuilleanáin, Seamus Heaney, Brendan Kennelly and John Montague. The funeral procession moved through Pembroke Road, Raglan Road and Waterloo Road, before travelling to Inniskeen where he was buried. At his graveside poems were read including 'In Memory of My Mother' (read by John Montague) and 'A Christmas Childhood' (which Seamus Heaney read).

On his grave were placed flat stones gathered in the locality and a plain wooden cross bears the name, dates, 'Patrick Kavanagh 21 Oct. 1904 – 30 Nov. 1967; and the lines

> 'And pray for him
> Who walked apart
> On the hills
> Loving Life's miracles.'

Shancoduff

POEMS

Poems

[Handwritten annotations:]

Kavanagh

→ colloquial language/ conversation tone

→ aesthetic beauty of his language

→ transfiguration of the ordinary

→ verbal music

→ strong sense of place

→ community & isolation/identity parochial/introspective

→ Rich biblical symbolism

The poems printed here are in the order in which they were first published. In the case of 'A Christmas Childhood', Part II was first published in 1940 with Part I in 1943.

Inniskeen Road: July Evening

Swinging rythem (annotation)

The bicycles go by in twos and threes— *alliteration*
There's a dance in Billy Brennan's barn tonight, *familiarity*
And there's the half-talk code of mysteries *romantic, exciting*
And the wink-and-elbow language of delight.
Half-past eight and there is not a spot — *mood changes* / *hollow, empty*   5
Upon a mile of road, no shadow thrown *aware of Kavanagh's isolation*
That might turn out a man or woman, not
A footfall tapping secrecies of stone. *Sibilance conveys the whispering of secrets*

Volta: turning point

I have what every poet hates in spite
Of all the solemn talk of contemplation. *more internal and reflective than Stanza 1*   10
Oh, Alexander Selkirk knew the plight
Of being king and government and nation. *metaphor – figurative language*
A road, a mile of kingdom, I am king
Of banks and stones and every blooming thing. *pun*

Annotations left margin: sonnet / stanza 1 external / objective / strong sense of setting / Stanza 2 internal subjective / more internal & reflective

literary reference shows how different he is

📖 Glossary

Line 2 dance: During the 1930s the Irish Catholic Church disapproved of dances, especially foreign dances, which were considered dangerous and immoral. In her biography, *Patrick Kavanagh*, Antoinette Quinn says that 'during the 1930s, the Church's condemnation coloured his own views to the extent that the dance hall became a symbol of sensuality in his poetry, to be avoided or regarded as a temptation, not because it was sinful, but because it was at odds with the cultivation of the mind and the imagination.'

Line 8 footfall: footstep.

Line 11 Alexander Selkirk: Scottish sailor (1676–1721) and the inspiration for Daniel Defoe's *Robinson Crusoe*. Selkirk ran away to sea when he was nineteen. He quarrelled with his captain and, at his own request, was put ashore on one of the uninhabited islands of Juan Fernández (off the coast of Chile) in 1704 where he lived alone for four years and four months. William Cowper (1731–1800) wrote a poem in which he imagined Alexander Selkirk speaking about his time on the island. It begins:

> I am monarch of all I survey
> My right there is none to dispute
> From the centre all round to the sea
> I am lord of the fowl and the brute.
> O solitude! where are the charms
> That sages have seen in thy face?
> Better dwell in the midst of alarms,
> Than reign in this horrible place.

Line 14 blooming: the mildest of swear words; flowers; and Seamus Heaney suggests a third interpretation – the creative or poetic imagination. Heaney adds: 'The poet's stance becomes Wordsworth's over '*Tintern Abbey*', attached by present feelings but conscious that the real value of the moment lies in its potential flowering, its blooming, in the imagination.'

When this poem was first published in book form in 1936, poet and critic Donagh MacDonagh praised 'Inniskeen Road' but thought the last line spoiled the poem.

? Questions

1. Time and place; place and time: – Sahara Desert: Dawn; Croke Park: September afternoon; Eiffel Tower: May morning; Trafalgar Square: New Year's Eve; Golden Gate Bridge: August afternoon; the Taj Mahal in moonlight. What do these times and places suggest to you? Now consider the following: Inniskeen Road: July Evening?

2. The first two lines state facts. How would you describe the speaker's tone in the poem's opening lines? In the sestet Kavanagh tells us directly how he feels. Has he told us indirectly in part one? Which words or phrases suggest this?

3. What atmosphere is suggested by the references to 'mysteries' and 'delight' in lines 3 and 4?

4. How does the speaker feel about being an outsider? How would you describe Kavanagh's relationship with his native place as revealed in the octet? Consider particularly the phrase 'secrecies of stone.' What does this poem reveal to us about the nature of poetic life?

5. The poem is a personal one. Why do you think Kavanagh chooses to use the pronoun 'I' only in the sestet?

6. Do you think the comparison the poet makes between himself and Alexander Selkirk is effective? or absurd? or humorous? Give reasons for your answer. Is the poet being half-playful or half-serious?

7. 'We are satisfied with being ourselves, however small', wrote Kavanagh in *Self-Portrait*. Is there evidence of this in 'Inniskeen Road: July Evening'?

8. How would you describe the tone and mood of the poem's closing sentence?

9. What does this poem say about the writing of poetry? Has the poet chosen loneliness or has it been imposed?

Shancoduff

[handwritten annotations: ambivalence – love/hate relationship]

[handwritten: pride / ownership / distance]
[handwritten: transfiguration → the black hills into a beautiful place / strong sense of setting]

My black hills have never seen the sun rising,
Eternally they look north towards Armagh.
Lot's wife would not be salt if she had been *[handwritten: biblical references – sacred place to Kavanagh]*
Incurious as my black hills that are happy
When dawn whitens Glassdrummond chapel. *[handwritten: content]* 5

[handwritten: visual qualities]
My hills hoard the bright shillings of March
While the sun searches in every pocket. *[handwritten: imagery of light]*
They are my Alps and I have climbed the Matterhorn, *[handwritten: hyperbole / pride]*
With a sheaf of hay for three perishing calves
In the field under the Big Forth of Rocksavage. 10

[handwritten: synaesthesia] [handwritten: oxymoron] [handwritten: Personification, playful, lighthearted]
The sleety winds fondle the rushy beards of Shancoduff
While the cattle-drovers sheltering in the Featherna Bush
Look up and say: 'Who owns them hungry hills *[handwritten: colloquial grammar mistakes adds integrity]*
That the water-hen and snipe must have forsaken?
[handwritten: Struggling with his identity] A poet? Then by heavens he must be poor.' *[handwritten: the land is rich in poetic inspiration]* 15
I hear and is my heart not badly shaken? *[handwritten: ending left to reader's interpretation]*
[handwritten: inner conflict]

📖 Glossary

Title: Shancoduff – Shanco is linked to the Irish words 'sean', meaning 'old', and 'dubh' (duff), black. The poet's brother, Peter Kavanagh, gives *Sean cuach dubh*, meaning Old Black Hollow, in his essay 'Kavanagh Country.'
Shancoduff or Reynolds' Farm was a small farm half a mile from the Kavanagh home. It was bought by the Kavanagh family in the 1920s and later Patrick Kavanagh inherited it. It consisted of seven watery hills facing north.

Kavanagh himself said that 'those hills were sharp, crooked and triangular, the triangularity providing the most efficient system for drainage. Shancoduff is the name of a townland and whenever you get the duff (or *dubh*) in a townland's name it means that the land faces north. It was sour land, lime deficient. . . .'.

Line 3 Lot's wife: in the *Book of Genesis*, Chapter xviii, verse 19, God destroys the towns of Sodom and Gomorrah because they were centres of exceptional vice and immorality. God spared Lot, his wife and two daughters 'But his wife (while fleeing) looked back from behind him, and she became a pillar of salt.'

Line 6 shillings: small silver coins from an earlier currency. James J. Carey and Augustine Martin, in their edition of the poem, gloss the phrase 'hoard the bright shillings of March' as follows: 'facing north, Kavanagh's hillside fields retain the snow and hail long after the sun has melted them in south-facing fields.'

Line 8 Matterhorn: one of the highest and most dangerous peaks in the Alps.

Line 10 Forth: local pronunciation of Fort.

Line 11 sleety: an example of Kavanagh's ability to make an adjective from a noun (sleet); another example is 'greeny' in his sonnet 'Lines Written on a Seat on the Grand Canal, Dublin.'

Line 14 snipe: long-billed marshbird.

Line 16 heart: Kavanagh, in an earlier draft, had written 'my faith not badly shaken.' Originally the poem also had the following stanza, which was placed before the final one:

> My hills have never seen the sun rising,
> With the faith of an illiterate peasant they await
> The Final Resurrection when all hills
> Will face the East.

In her book *Patrick Kavanagh A Biography*, Antoinette Quinn says that 'Shancoduff' was nominated by Kavanagh as his favourite poem.

? Questions

1. How would you describe Kavanagh's relationship with Shancoduff? How might this poem be seen as 'a love poem to a place'?

2. Comment on the words 'never' and 'eternally' in the poem's opening lines. What is their effect? Kavanagh wrote 'My black hills … My hills' not 'The black hills … The hills.' What does this tell us about Kavanagh's relationship with Shancoduff?

3. Write a note on the colours and weather. What atmosphere do they help create? How does Kavanagh's attitude towards 'them hungry hills' differ from the cattle-drovers' attitude?

4. Kavanagh frequently uses placenames in his poetry, in this instance – Armagh, Glassdrummond, Matterhorn, Big Forth, Rocksavage, Shancoduff and Featherna. What is the effect of this?

5. In the closing lines the speaker asks 'is my heart not badly shaken?' What is, in your opinion, the answer to that question? Examine how Kavanagh views his native Monaghan and the role of the poet in 'Inniskeen Road: July Evening' and 'Shancoduff.'

6. What does Kavanagh suggest in the contradictory phrase 'The sleety winds fondle the rushy beards of Shancoduff'?

7. Choose any three images from the poem which you find effective and give reasons for your choice.

8. 'Then by heavens he must be poor.' Do you think that this poet is 'poor'? In your answer consider material poverty, emotional poverty and imaginative poverty.

9. 'Shancoduff was more than a farm for Patrick – it was a wonderland', says Peter Kavanagh, the poet's brother. Do you think Kavanagh conveys that sense of wonderland in this poem?

A Christmas Childhood

Biblical imagery & musical quality

I

One side of the potato-pits was white with frost—
How wonderful that was, how wonderful!
And when we put our ears to the paling-post
The music that came out was magical.

The light between the ricks of hay and straw   5
Was a hole in Heaven's gable. An apple tree
With its December-glinting fruit we saw—   *biblical allusions*
O you, Eve, were the world that tempted me

To eat the knowledge that grew in clay
And death the germ within it! Now and then   10
I can remember something of the gay *garden of eden → biblical*
Garden that was childhood's. Again

The tracks of cattle to a drinking-place,
A green stone lying sideways in a ditch,
Or any common sight, the transfigured face   15
Of a beauty that the world did not touch.

II

My father played the melodion
Outside at our gate;
There were stars in the morning east
And they danced to his music.   20

Across the wild bogs his melodion called
To Lennons and Callans.
As I pulled on my trousers in a hurry
I knew some strange thing had happened.

Outside in the cow-house my mother   25
Made the music of milking;   *aural music*
The light of her stable-lamp was a star
And the frost of Bethlehem made it twinkle.

                strong musical quality in this stanza
A water-hen screeched in the bog,   *rural, primitive*
Mass-going feet *aural imagery* *loneliness of the Irish*
Crunched the wafer-ice on the pot-holes,   *countryside*   30
Somebody wistfully twisted the bellows wheel.

My child poet picked out the letters
On the grey stone,
In silver the wonder of a Christmas townland,   35
The winking glitter of a frosty dawn.

Cassiopeia was over
Cassidy's hanging hill,
I looked and three whin bushes rode across
The horizon—the Three Wise Kings.   40

An old man passing said:
'Can't he make it talk'—
The melodion. I hid in the doorway
And tightened the belt of my box-pleated coat.

I nicked six nicks on the door-post 45
With my penknife's big blade—
There was a little one for cutting tobacco.
And I was six Christmases of age.

My father played the melodion,
My mother milked the cows, 50
And I had a prayer like a white rose pinned
On the Virgin Mary's blouse.

Glossary

Line 3 paling-post: wooden stakes connected by wire and forming a fence (a pale is a stake of wood driven into the ground for fencing).

Line 5 ricks: stacks.

Line 6 gable: the end-wall of a building; here Kavanagh is imagining that the light between the ricks of hay and straw is like a brightly lit window in a gable-end where the gable is Heaven's gable.

Line 11 gay: bright, lively ('gay', 'abandon' and 'explosive' were Kavanagh's favourite words, according to Paul Durcan).

Line 15 transfigured: changed. (Also a religious term, as in the transfiguration of Christ).

Line 17 my father played the melodion: Antoinette Quinn in her *Biography* says that Kavanagh's father's 'principal recreations were reading the local newspapers or journals such as *Tit Bits* and *Answers* and playing the melodion or small accordion, and his musical skills ensured that he was much in demand at dances and weddings.'

Line 32 wistfully: with sadness, regret, disappointed hope.

Line 32 bellows wheel: a mechanical device for pumping a current of air to help light a fire.

Line 33 My child poet: my younger self – a poet in the making.

Line 37 Cassiopeia: northern constellation (in Greek mythology an Egyptian Queen was sent to the heavens as a constellation because she boasted of her beauty; the Cassiopeia stars form the outline of a woman sitting in a chair and holding up both arms in a pleading gesture).

Line 39 whin: also called furze, gorse.

Line 44 box-pleated coat: a coat with a double fold of cloth in front turned opposite ways.

? Questions

1. Is this, in your opinion, a quaint, old-fashioned poem or do you identify with it? How does Kavanagh's memory of his six-year-old self compare and contrast with your memories of Christmas? Identify the differences and similarities.

2. In Part I, Kavanagh describes a 'wonderful' and 'magical' world. Which details in the childhood vision best capture those qualities, in your opinion? Which phrases capture a child's way of viewing the world?

3. Why should the speaker connect Christmas with the Garden of Eden and the Fall of Man? What does the reference to 'death the germ' (line 10) contribute to the overall effect of Part I?

4. The line-length and rhyming scheme (abab, cdcd, efef, ghgh) in Part I are regular. How would you describe line-lengths and the rhyming scheme in Part II? Why do you think Kavanagh uses a different music, a different technique in lines 17–52?

5. 'A Christmas Childhood' combines the ordinary and the extraordinary, the everyday or conversational and the poetic. Discuss this view under headings such as (i) language, (ii) place and (iii) people. Identify those words associated with religion and comment on their significance.

6. Consider the way in which silence and sounds are used in the poem. Which sound is heard most often? How would you describe that sound?

7. Since there is a marvellous sense of childhood excitement and happiness in 'A Christmas Childhood', why do you think the poet mentions that 'Somebody wistfully twisted the bellows wheel' (line 32)?

8. Patrick Kavanagh was one of several children. Why do you think he does not mention his siblings in this memory poem? Is it selfishness or has it something to do with the self-absorbed world of childhood?

9. How does Kavanagh structure the poem in Part II? If you were to draw each scene – gate, wild bogs, cow-house, Mass-going feet, Cassiopeia, Cassidy's hanging hill – what would you notice about place in the poem? Why so you think the final stanza contains an image of family: father, mother and child?

from *The Great Hunger*

I

Clay is the word and clay is the flesh
Where the potato-gatherers like mechanized scare-crows move
Along the side-fall of the hill—Maguire and his men.
If we watch them an hour is there anything we can prove
Of life as it is broken-backed over the Book   5
Of Death? Here crows gabble over worms and frogs
And the gulls like old newspapers are blown clear of the
    hedges, luckily.
Is there some light of imagination in these wet clods?
Or why do we stand here shivering?
                    Which of these men   10
Loved the light and the queen
Too long virgin? Yesterday was summer. Who was it
    promised marriage to himself
Before apples were hung from the ceilings for Hallowe'en?
We will wait and watch the tragedy to the last curtain
Till the last soul passively like a bag of wet clay   15
Rolls down the side of the hill, diverted by the angles
Where the plough missed or a spade stands, straitening
    the way.

A dog lying on a torn jacket under a heeled-up cart,
A horse nosing along the posied headland, trailing
A rusty plough. Three heads hanging between wide-apart   20
Legs. October playing a symphony on a slack wire paling.
Maguire watches the drills flattened out
And the flints that lit a candle for him on a June altar
Flameless. The drills slipped by and the days slipped by
And he trembled his head away and ran free from the
    world's halter,   25
And thought himself wiser than any man in the townland

When he laughed over pints of porter
Of how he came free from every net spread
In the gaps of experience. He shook a knowing head
And pretended to his soul   30
That children are tedious in hurrying fields of April
Where men are spanging across wide furrows,
Lost in the passion that never needs a wife—
The pricks that pricked were the pointed pins of harrows.
Children scream so loud that the crows could bring   35
The seed of an acre away with crow-rude jeers.
Patrick Maguire, he called his dog and he flung a stone in
    the air
And hallooed the birds away that were the birds of the years.
Turn over the weedy clods and tease out the tangled skeins.
What is he looking for there?   40
He thinks it is a potato, but we know better
Than his mud-gloved fingers probe in this insensitive hair.

'Move forward the basket and balance it steady
In this hollow. Pull down the shafts of that cart, Joe,
And straddle the horse,' Maguire calls.   45
'The wind's over Brannagan's, now that means rain.
Graip up some withered stalks and see that no potato falls
Over the tail-board going down the ruckety pass—
And *that's* a job we'll have to do in December,
Gravel it and build a kerb on the bog-side. Is that
    Cassidy's ass   50
Out in my clover? Curse o' God—
Where is that dog?
Never where he's wanted.' Maguire grunts and spits
Through a clay-wattled moustache and stares about him
    from the height.
His dream changes again like the cloud-swung wind   55
And he is not so sure now if his mother was right
When she praised the man who made a field his bride.

Watch him, watch him, that man on a hill whose spirit
Is a wet sack flapping about the knees of time.
He lives that his little fields may stay fertile when his
    own body   60
Is spread in the bottom of a ditch under two coulters
    crossed in Christ's Name.

He was suspicious in his youth as a rat near strange bread
When girls laughed; when they screamed he knew that
    meant
The cry of fillies in season. He could not walk
The easy road to his destiny. He dreamt   65
The innocence of young brambles to hooked treachery.
O the grip. O the grip of irregular fields! No man escapes.
It could not be that back of the hills love was free
And ditches straight.
No monster hand lifted up children and put down apes   70
As here.
              'O God if I had been wiser!'
That was his sigh like the brown breeze in the thistles.
He looks towards his house and haggard. 'O God if I
    had been wiser!'
But now a crumpled leaf from the whitethorn bushes   75
Darts like a frightened robin, and the fence
Shows the green of after-grass through a little window,
And he knows that his own heart is calling his mother a liar.
God's truth is life—even the grotesque shapes of its
    foulest fire.

The horse lifts its head and cranes   80
Through the whins and stones
To lip late passion in the crawling clover.
In the gap there's a bush weighted with boulders like
    morality,
The fools of life bleed if they climb over.

The wind leans from Brady's, and the coltsfoot leaves
    are holed with rust,   85
Rain fills the cart-tracks and the sole-plate grooves;
A yellow sun reflects in Donaghmoyne
The poignant light in puddles shaped by hooves.

Come with me, Imagination, into this iron house
And we will watch from the doorway the years run
    back,   90
And we will know what a peasant's left hand wrote on
    the page.
Be easy, October. No cackle hen, horse neigh, tree sough,
    duck quack.

Glossary

Title: *The Great Hunger* – a phrase also used to describe the Irish Famine (1845–1848). The poem was first entitled 'The Old Peasant'.

Line 1 *Clay is the word*: the opening line echoes the opening of St John's Gospel: 'In the beginning was the Word, and the Word was with God, and the Word was God.' Also The Angelus, a Catholic prayer familiar to Kavanagh, referring to the coming of Christ, contains the line 'And the Word was made flesh and dwelt among us.' Clay also refers to the human body.

Lines 5/6 *Book/ Of Death*: the opposite to the *Book of Life* which, according to the *Bible* (Revelations Chapter xx, verse 12 – 'another book opened, which is the *Book of Life*'), registers the names of those who will inherit eternal life.

Lines 11/12 *the queen/Too long virgin?*: the Virgin Mary also known as Queen of Heaven.

Line 18 *heeled-up cart*: a cart not harnessed to a horse and its tail-board on the ground.

Line 19 *posied*: flowery.

Line 25 *halter*: a device made of rope or straps fitted around a horse's head to guide, restrain it.

Line 32 *spanging*: walking with long, quick steps; bounding.

Line 34 *harrows*: heavy frames set with spikes or discs used to break clods and level soil.

Line 42 *probe in this insensitive hair*: according to Antoinette Quinn, 'the narrator and Patrick Maguire invest most of the daily sights and happenings on the farm with sexual significance' – 'picking potatoes', Quinn says, 'is groping in pubic hair.'

Line 47 *Graip*: a pronged fork used for digging potatoes (Scottish dialect word) – used here as a verb.

Line 48 ruckety: uneven.

Line 54 clay-wattled moustache: a moustache caked with mud in a way similar to how wattles (flexible rods) are coated with mud as building material.

Line 61 coulters: sharp iron cutter/blades in front of the plough.

Line 64 fillies: young female ponies or horses.

Lines 65/66 He dreamt/ The innocence of young brambles to hooked treachery: an image of young girls and how he has been made think of them as snares.

Line 74 haggard: a yard near a farmhouse where hay is kept.

Line 85 coltsfoot: a plant with shaggy stalk and large soft leaves.

Line 86 sole-plate: horse-shoe.

Line 87 Donaghmoyne: parish next to Inniskeen.

Line 88 poignant: touching, painful, pathetic.

Line 91 what a peasant's left hand wrote on the page: Antoinette Quinn suggests that this line implies that "The Great Hunger' presents an unorthodox, anti-official view of the Irish subsistence farmer.'

Line 92 sough: a sighing or murmuring sound.

'The Great Hunger' (originally called 'The Old Peasant') is a poem in fourteen sections (I-XIV) and is over seven hundred lines long. It was written in October 1941 in a bedsitter, which Kavanagh shared with his brother, at 122 Morehampton Road in Dublin. Part I is printed here. The poem tells the story of 'Poor Paddy Maguire', a forty-seven-year-old bachelor and potato farmer who works a fourteen-hour day, lives with his sister and mother and 'stayed with his mother till she died/ At the age of ninety-one.' It tells of his loneliness, frustration and wasted potential, and Terence Brown says of 'The Great Hunger' that 'This bleak, uncompromising report from the heart of rural Ireland uncovers no hint of the idyllic: rather, it reveals how emotional and sexual poverty are the inevitable concomitants of grinding economic deprivation. Paddy Maguire is seen in this starkly analytic work as the victim of economic, religious and familial forces, mercilessly crushing the life instinct.'

According to Shawn Holliday, Kavanagh's 'main purpose in writing this long poem was to depict the harsh realities of rural life by showing how one man's will is suffocated by unending labour and religious confinement.'

In 1960, in an Introduction to a radio broadcast of the poem, Kavanagh said: 'It was in 1942 (October 1941 is given in Antoinette Quinn's *Biography*) in darkest Dublin ... that I wrote 'The Great Hunger' – and if I say now that I do not like it, this will not mean as some of you might think, a sensational repudiation of my own work ... I'm afraid I'm too involved in 'The Great Hunger'; the poem remains a tragedy because it is not completely born. Tragedy is underdeveloped comedy: tragedy fully explored becomes comedy ... But I am not debunking the unfortunate poem entirely; I will grant that there are some remarkable things in it, but free it hardly is, for there's no laughter in it.'

? Questions

1. Having read the complete poem, how do you interpret the title? Is there more than one form of hunger being explored here?

2. Patrick Kavanagh once described the life of the poor rural Irish as 'sad, grey, twisted, blind, just awful.' Is this an accurate description of the life depicted in Part I of 'The Great Hunger'? Give reasons for your answer.

3. 'In the beginning was the word...' is how St John begins his gospel. What is the effect of Kavanagh's opening words, which echo that Biblical phrase?

4. If you filmed this extract from 'The Great Hunger', what images would predominate? Choose any three images which you find interesting and comment on each one, justifying your choice in each case.

5. How would you describe the narrator's attitude towards 'Maguire and his men', whom he describes in lines 1–17? Which details, in your opinion, best convey his tone? Comment on the speaker's use of 'we' in line 4. Who is he referring to? Look at lines 89/90.

6. What do you think the poet means when he writes 'Yesterday was summer' (line 12)? Since this section of the poem is set in autumn (October), why do you think there are references to summer and June? Comment on the significance of these.

7. In lines 18–38 how does Patrick Maguire feel about himself?

Why did he pretend that 'children are tedious'? Explain lines 38/39: 'he flung a stone in the air/ And hallooed the birds away that were the birds of the years.' How would you describe the overall mood of lines 18–38?

8. What is the speaker/narrator's attitude towards Patrick Maguire in lines 39–42?

9. In lines 43–57, first we hear Maguire speaking and then we glimpse his private thoughts. What kind of a portrait emerges from this section? Does Maguire regret having made 'a field his bride'? Why?

10. 'Watch him, watch him...' (line 58 and following) once again belongs to the narrator. What do we learn of Maguire in this section? Comment on the images 'a wet sack flapping about the knees of time' and the 'innocence of young brambles.'

11. How does the poet create a sense of despair in lines 62–79? What does Patrick Maguire see as his mistake? Why now does he think his mother is a liar?

12. Sections of the poem concentrate on Maguire in close-up. The closing lines, 80–88, focus on the bigger picture. Do you think this an effective ending to this section? Why? Give reasons for your answer. In the final four lines the poet imagines that 'the years run back' and he asks 'Be easy, October...' Why? What does it reveal of the speaker and his attitude towards Maguire and his world?

13. 'The Great Hunger' has been viewed as the story of Ireland in the 1930s and 1940s. Is Paddy Maguire your idea of a typical Irishman? Why? Why not? Give reasons for your answer.

14. Patrick Maguire 'grunts and spits' (line 53). He has been described as 'lonely, puzzled, pathetic.' Is this the full picture? Is Patrick Maguire, as portrayed here, impulsive or inhibited or is he a mixture of both? Give reasons for your answer and refer to the text to support the points you make.

15. In 'The Great Hunger', Terence Brown says that 'Flesh becomes clay, spirit becomes matter in this tour de force of disillusionment.' What do you think he means by this? Is it true of Part I of the poem?

16. Poetry should be a celebration and affirmation of life. This extract from 'The Great Hunger' is neither and should be ignored.' Would you agree or disagree with this view? Support the points you make by reference to the text.

17. Do you think a Great Hunger poem could be written about the Ireland you live in today? If so, how similar, how different would it be from Patrick Kavanagh's version?

18. It has been said that Patrick Kavanagh adopted cinematic techniques in the narrative in 'The Great Hunger', 'close-ups, long-shots, and skilful editing.' Would you agree with this view?

19. This is but an extract. Would you like to read on? Why? Why not?

Advent

We have tested and tasted too much, lover—
Through a chink too wide there comes in no wonder.
But here in this Advent-darkened room
Where the dry black bread and the sugarless tea
Of penance will charm back the luxury   5
Of a child's soul, we'll return to Doom
The knowledge we stole but could not use.

And the newness that was in every stale thing
When we looked at it as children: the spirit-shocking
Wonder in a black slanting Ulster hill   10
Or the prophetic astonishment in the tedious talking
Of an old fool, will awake for us and bring
You and me to the yard gate to watch the whins
And the bog-holes, cart-tracks, old stables where Time
    begins.

O after Christmas we'll have no need to go searching   15
For the difference that sets an old phrase burning—
We'll hear it in the whispered argument of a churning
Or in the streets where the village boys are lurching.
And we'll hear it among simple, decent men, too,
Who barrow dung in gardens under trees,   20
Wherever life pours ordinary plenty.
Won't we be rich, my love and I, and please
God we shall not ask for reason's payment,
The why of heart-breaking strangeness in dreeping
    hedges
Nor analyse God's breath in common statement.   25
We have thrown into the dust-bin the clay-minted
    wages
Of pleasure, knowledge and the conscious hour—
And Christ comes with a January flower.

263

📖 Glossary

Title: Advent – a four-week period in the Church calendar, to include four Sundays, of spiritual preparation before Christmas (from the Latin: *ad*, 'to', *venire*, 'to come'). In Kavanagh's lifetime it was a period of penance and strict fasting.

Line 1 We . . . lover: is the poet speaking to his soul? His inner-self? Antoinette Quinn says 'the apostrophised 'lover' here is either an unsexed muse or an amenable alter-ego.'

Line 6 we'll return to Doom: we will reject as useless.

Line 14 Time begins: a reference to Christ's birth, when B.C. became A.D.

Line 17 churning: the making of butter where cream is turned in a large metal can until butter is produced.

Lines 22/23 and please/ God we shall not ask for reason's payment: please God we will experience/accept the world's mystery without looking for a rational explanation.

Line 24 dreeping: a word invented by Kavanagh to capture a dripping, weeping quality.

> 'Advent' was originally called 'Renewal' and there was a space between lines 21 and 22 which divided the poem into four stanzas, each containing seven lines, one, as it were, for each week of Advent. The poem is composed of two sonnets and it was first published in *The Irish Times* on 24 December 1942.

? Questions

1. How would you describe the speaker's mood in the opening line? Which sounds contribute to that mood?

2. Why is a child's soul seen as something special? What is the difference between the adult's soul and the child's? Explain the apparent contradiction/paradox of line 5: 'penance will charm back the luxury.'

3. How is the world of childhood innocence and wonder evoked in the second stanza? Which phrases are particularly effective in capturing a sense of newness?

4. In 'A Christmas Childhood' and 'Advent' a special time in the Church calendar makes possible a way of viewing the world. Compare and contrast both poems.

5. 'Kavanagh fuses the ordinary and the extraordinary in his poetry.' Where is this evident in 'Advent'?

6. Are wealth and riches redefined in this poem? Do you find Kavanagh's argument a convincing one? Why? Give reasons for your answer. Antoinette Quinn sees 'Advent' as 'a manifesto poem.' What do you think she means by this?

7. The poem focuses on the four weeks leading up to Christmas. How does the poem's structure reflect that? Comment particularly on the movement from 'darkened-room' to the village streets, 'gardens under trees', 'dreeping hedges' and the 'January flower.'

8. Trace the religious imagery through the poem. Which image is your favourite? Give reasons for your answer.

9. Write a short note on the flower imagery with which both 'A Christmas Childhood' ('a white rose pinned/ On the Virgin Mary's blouse') and 'Advent' ('And Christ comes with a January flower') end.

On Raglan Road

On Raglan Road on an autumn day I met her first and
    knew
That her dark hair would weave a snare that I might
    one day rue;
I saw the danger, yet I walked along the enchanted way,
And I said, let grief be a fallen leaf at the dawning of
    the day.

On Grafton Street in November we tripped lightly along
    the ledge   5
Of the deep ravine where can be seen the worth of
    passion's pledge,
The Queen of Hearts still making tarts and I not making hay—
O I loved too much and by such by such is happiness
    thrown away.

I gave her gifts of the mind, I gave her the secret sign
    that's known
To the artists who have known the true gods of sound
    and stone   10
And word and tint. I did not stint for I gave her poems
    to say
With her own name there and her own dark hair like
    clouds over fields of May.

On a quiet street where old ghosts meet I see her walking
    now
Away from me so hurriedly my reason must allow
That I had wooed not as I should a creature made of
    clay—   15
When the angel woos the clay he'd lose his wings at the
    dawn of day.

Glossary

Title: *Raglan Road* – a spacious, tree-lined road in Dublin 4. Kavanagh lived at nearby Pembroke Road from 1946 to 1958; he lived on Raglan Road from 1958 to 1959. 'On Raglan Road' has been sung by thousands and has been recorded by, among others, Luke Kelly, Van Morrison and Sinéad O'Connor.

Air *'The Dawning of the Day'*: when Kavanagh was a teenager he joined the Inniskeen pipers' band, a band of sixty that met three nights a week and eventually they learned three tunes – 'The Barren Rock of Aden', 'The Little House on the Hill' and 'The Dawning of the Day.'

Line 2 snare: trap.

Line 2 rue: regret.

Line 6 ravine: deep, narrow gorge.

Line 6 pledge: sign, token.

Line 7 The Queen of Hearts still making tarts and I not making hay—: echoing a nursery rhyme ('The Queen of Hearts/ She made some tarts,/ All on a summer's day…) and a proverbial saying (to make hay while the sun shines) – here a reference to the woman's success in affairs of the heart and the speaker, though trying to take advantage of opportunity, only meets with failure. When the poem was first published this line read: 'Synthetic sighs and fish-dim eyes and all death's loud display.'

Lines 10/11 sound and stone/ And word and tint: a succinct reference to different art forms – music, sculpture, literature and painting.

Line 11 stint: hold back.

Line 14 my reason must allow: my mind must admit.

> 'On Raglan Road' was first published in the *Irish Press* on 3 October 1946 under the title 'Dark Haired Miriam Ran Away.' Peter Kavanagh, Kavanagh's brother, says that 'It was written about Patrick's girlfriend Hilda but to avoid embarrassment he used the name of my girl-friend in the title.' The poem was inspired by Hilda Moriarty.

? Questions

1. Why is there something both beautiful and heart-breaking in this story of unrequited love? How important is (i) the setting and (ii) the season?

2. Kavanagh intended that this poem be sung. What song-like qualities do you find in this poem?

3. What evidence do you find in the poem that the poet 'loved too much'? Do you believe him? Give reasons for your answer.

4. Though this is a love poem set in a city, is the urban description a typical one? Pick out some atmospheric words and phrases and comment on them.

5. The poet uses 'I' fourteen times, 'we' once. Comment.

6. How would you describe the music which Kavanagh achieves here? Discuss how he uses end-rhyme and internal rhyme.

7. Is 'On Raglan Road' a poem of many moods? Trace the feeling from stanza to stanza. What, in your opinion, in the dominant mood in the poem?

8. The speaker here, as in 'Inniskeen Road: July Evening', is conscious of being a poet. How does this affect the relationship and his understanding of the relationship? Compare and contrast the two poems.

9. In the closing stanza the speaker sees the woman whom he loves as 'a creature made of clay' and he sees himself as an angel. What does this tell us of the speaker? How did he come to see himself in this way?

Epic

I have lived in important places, times
When great events were decided: who owned
That half a rood of rock, a no-man's land
Surrounded by our pitchfork-armed claims.
I heard the Duffys shouting 'Damn your soul'   5
And old McCabe stripped to the waist, seen
Step the plot defying blue cast-steel—
'Here is the march along these iron stones.'
That was the year of the Munich bother. Which
Was most important? I inclined   10
To lose my faith in Ballyrush and Gortin
Till Homer's ghost came whispering to my mind.
He said: I made the *Iliad* from such
A local row. Gods make their own importance.

Glossary

Title: **Epic** – a very long work of literature that records and celebrates great events and heroic exploits; the adjective epic means 'impressive, large scale.'

Line 7 Step the plot defying blue-cast steel: walk the land in spite of the threats from neighbours carrying pitchforks.

Line 8 march: boundary.

Line 8 iron: the poem focuses on a dispute over a field – or parish-boundary but Paul Muldoon, in his book *To Ireland I*, adds that the 'iron' in 'these iron stones' is 'a near version of "Erin", so we're dealing with a national dispute as well. Then there's the international aspect of "That was the year of the Munich bother".' Do you find Muldoon's reading of 'iron' interesting, far-fetched, infuriating or valid?

Line 9 Munich bother: here Kavanagh plays down the 1938 Munich crisis. A world war was imminent due to Hitler's taking of Czechoslovakia, but the Munich conference helped delay it. The Munich 'bother' was also about boundaries.

Line 10 most important?: this reads as 'more important?' in *Collected Poems* (1964) and *Complete Poems* (1972).

Line 11 Ballyrush and Gortin: townlands in Inniskeen parish.

Line 12 Homer: Greek epic poet from circa 8th Century B.C. author of the *Odyssey* and the *Iliad*. The *Iliad* tells of a "row" between the Greeks and Trojans and the war fought by the Greeks against Troy in an attempt to win back Helen, wife of Menelaus, whom Paris, a Trojan Prince, had carried off.

'Epic' was inspired by a row over half-a-rood of rocky land in 1938. It was first published in *The Bell* in November 1951. Seamus Heaney, commenting on the poem, says: 'even though the poem gives the stage over to two Monaghan farmers and successfully sets Ballyrush and Gortin in balance against Munich, it is not saying that the farmers and the Monaghan region are important in themselves. They are made important only by the light of the mind which is now playing upon them. It is a poem more in praise of Kavanagh's idea of Homer than in praise of Kavanagh's home.'

In *Lifelines New and Collected* (2006), Graham Norton chose 'Epic' as his favourite poem. He wrote: 'I've chosen a poem that I come back to again and again. 'Epic' by Patrick Kavanagh is one of the wisest poems I know. Whatever one is going through or experiencing in life, it always helps to try and see it in perspective. Everything matters and doesn't matter in equal measure depending on where one stands. It seems to me that remembering this will keep you sane and help your happiness.'

? Questions

1. 'Epic' suggests something on a grand scale. Why does Kavanagh give his sonnet that title? Is there anything grand or heroic here?

2. 'I have lived in important places.' What is important about the places where he has lived?

3. How would you describe the language used here? Is it the language usually associated with poetry? Why? Why not? Give reasons for your answer. What is the significance of the poet's naming local surnames and Monaghan townlands?

4. How do we respond to the events described in lines 2–8? How do we view those same events when we read lines 12–14? Do you find the poet's argument a convincing one?

5. Kavanagh frequently speaks of the doubts and uncertainty of the poet within the poem itself – in 'Inniskeen Road: July Evening', 'Shancoduff' and 'Epic.' How does he resolve these uncertainties? Consider this idea in the light of your reading of the sonnets that he wrote late in life –'The Hospital' and the Canal Bank poems.

6. 'Gods make their own importance.' What do you understand by the poem's closing sentence? What is its tone?

PATRICK KAVANAGH

[handwritten annotations: brush with mortality awakens his love of life · love poem · sonnet · spiritual rebirth · transition from local → universal · transforming the banal into the spectacular]

The Hospital

A year ago I fell in love with the functional ward
Of a chest hospital: square cubicles in a row
Plain concrete, wash basins—an art lover's woe,
Not counting how the fellow in the next bed snored.
But nothing whatever is by love debarred,   5
The common and banal her heat can know.
The corridor led to a stairway and below
Was the inexhaustible adventure of a gravelled yard.

This is what love does to things: the Rialto Bridge,
The main gate that was bent by a heavy lorry,   10
The seat at the back of a shed that was a suntrap.
Naming these things is the love-act and its pledge;
For we must record love's mystery without claptrap,
Snatch out of time the passionate transitory.

[handwritten annotations: extended epiphany · love is associated with heat · [volta] · sestet is more reflective · fragile, flawed, imperfect · imperfect, vulnerable, normal things · litany (lists) · love must be recorded in the word · the word 'love' is repeated frequently · condensed line · inviting the readers to partake · so it is without claptrap · these 2 words capture the theme of the whole poem · transience of time]

Glossary

Title: The Hospital – the Rialto Hospital in Dublin (now closed) where Kavanagh was treated for lung cancer and had a lung removed in March 1955. The sonnet was originally called 'April 1956' and first published in the winter of 1956.

Line 1 functional: practical.

Line 3 an art lover's woe: the place would make an aesthete miserable.

Line 5 debarred: excluded. Line 5 originally read: 'From opening windows on a creative show.'

Line 6 banal: commonplace.

Line 8 the inexhaustible adventure of a gravelled yard: Kavanagh, famously, once said something similar – that 'it would take a lifetime to describe the corner of a field.'

Line 12 pledge: solemn promise.

Line 13 claptrap: flashy display, empty words.

Line 14 the passionate transitory: the deeply-felt passing/fleeting moment/experience. When first published line 14 read: 'Experience so light-hearted appears transitory.'

? Questions

1. 'I fell in love with …' Does this love poem surprise you? Why? Give reasons for your answer.

2. The subject matter of the poem and the details (hospital – cubicles, concrete, wash basins, snoring …) are usually considered anti-poetic. How does Kavanagh succeed in turning such subject matter into poetry?

3. What does the phrase 'inexhaustible adventure of a gravelled yard' tell us about the speaker?

4. How would you describe the tone of the sonnet? Does the tone change as you read the poem through? Comment on how the speaker uses 'I' in the octet, 'we' in the sestet.

5. Comment on the feelings of gratitude and confidence in the poem. How would you describe the mood in (i) the octet and (ii) the sestet?

6. 'We must record love's mystery without claptrap.' Which poems by Kavanagh 'record love's mystery without claptrap?' In your opinion, does he succeed?

7. 'Advent' was originally called 'Renewal.' This poem is also about renewal. Compare and contrast the two poems.

PATRICK KAVANAGH

Canal Bank Walk

Leafy-with-love banks and the green waters of the canal
Pouring redemption for me, that I do
The will of God, wallow in the habitual, the banal,
Grow with nature again as before I grew.
The bright stick trapped, the breeze adding a third   5
Party to the couple kissing on an old seat,
And a bird gathering materials for the nest for the Word
Eloquently new and abandoned to its delirious beat.
O unworn world enrapture me, encapture me in a web
Of fabulous grass and eternal voices by a beech,   10
Feed the gaping need of my senses, give me ad lib
To pray unselfconsciously with overflowing speech,
For this soul needs to be honoured with a new dress woven
From green and blue things and arguments that cannot be
     proven.

Handwritten annotations:

each aspect is connected — eg the will of God

Sonnet — mix of shakespearean & petrarchan

Prayer-like

Kavanagh has found where he belongs — worshipping nature — celebration of nature — love poem to nature

musical, sensuous, heightened

faith

mundane is elevated

water = cleansing

"l" sounds

rebirth — return to simplicity — aware of aging

the cycle of love

personification of the breeze

sensuous

turn

drama — poem intensifies

gentle, lyrical language

extreme joy

love of life — climactic

energy of childhood — passion — passing of time

sustained desire

dramatic urgency — piecing — tempo propelled by nature

urgency, passion

flow of water

metaphor — clothing — rebirth

very few pauses

proven. does God exist? — childlike

living in the moment, accepting mystery

* and write poetry unselfconsciously?

theme: finding wonder in the ordinary

📖 Glossary

Line 2 redemption: deliverance from sin, freedom.

Line 3 habitual: usual.

Line 3 banal: ordinary, commonplace, flat.

Line 7 Word: the capitalisation echoes 'The Word' in St John Chapter I, verse i:
'In the beginning was the Word. . .'

Line 10 fabulous: Kavanagh gives the word renewed energy, force, by placing 'fabulous'
and 'grass' side by side. In addition to 'amazing', 'wonderful', fabulous also means 'as
related in fable', 'celebrated in story.'

Line 11 gaping: hungry; literally 'open mouthed' (from Old Norse *gapa*, to open the mouth).

Line 11 ad lib: shortened version of Latin phrase *ad libitum* literally meaning 'at pleasure';
to speak '*ad lib*' is to speak freely, easily.

'Canal Bank Walk' was first published in May 1958 and, in an essay entitled 'From
Monaghan to the Grand Canal', Kavanagh wrote: 'I have been thinking of making
my grove on the banks of the Grand Canal near Baggot Street Bridge where in
recent days I rediscovered my roots. My hegira was to the Grand Canal Bank where
again I saw the beauty of water and green grass and the magic of light. It was the
same emotion I had known when I stood on a sharp slope in Monaghan, where I
imaginatively stand now, looking across to Slieve Gullion and South Armagh...'

In *Self-Portrait* Kavanagh says that 'There are two kinds of simplicity, the simplicity of
going away and the simplicity of return. In the final simplicity we don't care whether
we feel foolish or not. We talk of things that earlier would embarrass. We are satisfied
with being ourselves, however small. So it was that on the banks of the Grand Canal
between Baggot and Leeson Street bridges in the warm summer of 1955, I lay and
watched the green waters of the canal. I had just come out of hospital. I wrote:

> Leafy-with-love banks and the green waters of the canal
> Pouring redemption for me, that I do
> The will of God wallow in the habitual, the banal
> Grow with nature again as before I grew.

. . . That a poet is born, not made, is well known. But this does not mean that he was
a poet the day he was physically born. For many a good-looking year I wrought hard
at versing but I could say that, as a poet, I was born in or about nineteen-fifty-five, the
place of my birth being the banks of the Grand Canal. Thirty years earlier Shancoduff's
watery hills could have done the trick, but I was too thick to take the hint.'

? Questions

1. How does the imagery in the opening lines suggest baptism? Trace the religious imagery through the poem?

2. In 'The Hospital' Kavanagh speaks of 'the common and banal' and here he speaks of 'the habitual, the banal.' Why is he drawn to the ordinary and the everyday?

3. Kavanagh, in 'Advent', 'Canal Bank Walk' and elsewhere, expresses his belief that this world reflects a heavenly, divine one. Which details best capture that belief in your opinion?

4. How would you describe the poem's rhythm? Consider especially the one-sentence sestet, the run-on lines and the few commas.

5. Kavanagh prays: 'give me ad lib/ To pray unselfconsciously with overflowing speech.' Do you think that the poet has been granted his wish?

6. Comment on 'pouring', 'wallow', 'Eloquently new', 'delirious beat', 'enrapture', 'encapture', 'fabulous', 'overflowing' . . . . What mood is being created through such words? How would you describe the overall mood of the poem.

7. In the closing lines the poet speaks of his soul being dressed anew in a 'dress woven/ From green and blue things and arguments that cannot be proven.' What does such a garment symbolise? Why 'green and blue', why 'arguments that cannot be proven'?

8. Seamus Heaney says that 'Kavanagh belongs all over the place, high and low, far and wide.' Would you agree? Give reasons for your answer.

[handwritten: 'ly' sounds]
[handwritten: Petrarchan Sonnet but with loose rules → freedom]
[handwritten: enthusiastic his past feeling of displacement is rectified/gone]

Lines Written on a Seat on the Grand Canal, Dublin

'Erected to the memory of Mrs Dermod O'Brien'

[handwritten: baptismal /cleansing/ spiritual water]
[handwritten: playful extravagance.]
[handwritten: sense of belonging (contrast with Inniskeen Road)]

[handwritten: passion →] O commemorate me where there is water,
[handwritten: conversational tone prosaic language] Canal water preferably, so stilly *[handwritten: slant rhyme]* *[handwritten: coined his own words]*
Greeny at the heart of summer. Brother *[handwritten: at once with others community/home]*
Commemorate me thus beautifully *[handwritten: coined word]* *[handwritten: hyperbole]*
[handwritten: juxtaposes the ordinary and extraordinary] Where by a lock niagarously roars *[handwritten: exaggerating shows his love for the place]* 5
The falls for those who sit in the tremendous silence
Of mid-July. No one will speak in prose *[handwritten: Poetic inspiration]*
Who finds his way to these Parnassian islands. *[handwritten: understated, tranquil personification]*
[handwritten: turn in the poem (sestet)] A swan goes by head low with many apologies, *[handwritten: pauses in unusual places —]*
[handwritten: hyperbole] Fantastic light looks through the eyes of bridges— 10
[handwritten: excitement] And look! a barge comes bringing from Athy *[handwritten: flows (like water)]*
And other far-flung towns mythologies. *[handwritten: series]* *[handwritten: motif of enchantment]*
[handwritten: the reader is invited in to the poem] O commemorate me with no hero-courageous *[handwritten: Sestet]*
Tomb—just a canal-bank seat for the passer-by. *[handwritten: the sense of isolation from early poems is gone]*

[handwritten: humility → doesn't need a big tomb, just a 'humble' canal bank seat]

Glossary

Line 3 Brother: Peter Kavanagh? His fellow man? Or, perhaps, it could mean nature?

Line 5 niagarously: a word invented by Kavanagh. Niagara Falls is on the Niagara river in the US; the Falls stand on the border of United States and Canada and water from most of the Great Lakes flows through the Niagara river – each minute about 450,000 tonnes of water plunge about 50 metres from a cliff into a gorge.

Line 8 Parnassian: Mount Parnassus, near Delphi in Greece, with two summits, is associated with poetry and music. One summit is consecrated to Apollo and the Muses, the other to Bacchus and is seen as the source of poetry and music.

Line 12 mythologies: tales of extraordinary, fabulous people and events.

Line 13 O commemorate me: Kavanagh later changed this to 'O memorial me.'

Questions

1. Why is the sub-title important to Kavanagh? Why do you think he includes it here? What does it reveal of the poet? Does it matter that he tells us nothing of Mrs Dermod O'Brien?

2. The Pyramids. A poem. Newgrange. Climbing Mount Everest. Music. A portrait. Discuss the various ways in which people have chosen to be remembered. Which one would you prefer?

3. Look at lines 1, 4 and 13. What tone do you register here? How would you describe the main tone? How would you describe the mood?

4. Who, in your opinion, is the 'Brother' he speaks to in line 3?

5. Kavanagh exaggerates for effect. Discuss why he does so and whether you think the technique successful.

6. What is the speaker's idea of beauty? Identify the different beautiful things in the sonnet and comment on each one.

7. Listen to the sounds in the poem. What does Kavanagh invite (i) to hear, (ii) to see and (iii) to imagine? Comment on the sensuous quality in Kavanagh's writing in this poem and others on your course.

8. Kavanagh said that the sonnet was like an envelope for a love letter – the perfect way of wrapping up your love poem. Consider how the sonnet form suits Kavanagh's purpose here and elsewhere.

9. Of the poems by Kavanagh on your course which one do you like best? Why? Give reasons for your answer. Which one did you find least interesting? Justify your choice.

10. Peter Kavanagh described his brother as a 'Christian mystic.' What do you understand by this? Is it evident in Patrick Kavanagh's poetry?

General Questions

A. What does Patrick Kavanagh's poetry mean to you? In your answer you may, if you wish, refer to the poems on your course under one or more of the following headings: (a) the world evoked, (b) the poet's way of viewing the world, (c) the poet's use of language.

B. 'Kavanagh's poetry combines the ordinary and the extraordinary.' Would you agree with this view? Support the points you make with reference to or quotation from the poems by Kavanagh on your course.

C. 'Kavanagh poetry is the poetry of rediscovery and celebration.' How true is this of the poems by Kavanagh that you have studied? Support your discussion by reference to or quotation from the poems on your course.

D. According to Kavanagh, the vocation of the true poet was to 'name and name the obscure places, people, or events.' Discuss this view in the light of your reading the poems by Kavanagh on your course.

E. What impact did the poetry of Patrick Kavanagh make on you as a reader? In shaping your answer you might consider some of the following:
- Your overall sense of the personality or outlook of the poet,
- The poet's use of language and imagery,
- Your favourite poem or poems.

F. 'The relationship between person and place is central to the poetry of Patrick Kavanagh.' Discuss this view of the poems by Kavanagh on your course. Support your discussion by quotation from or reference to the poems you have studied.

G. 'Kavanagh's poems are eloquent revelations of the ordinary.' Discuss this view, supporting your answer by quotation from or reference to the poems by Kavanagh on your course.

H. Identify and discuss what, in your opinion, are the distinctive qualities of Patrick Kavanagh's poetry. In your answer you should support the points you make by reference to the poems by Kavanagh on your course.

I. 'The things that really matter are casual, insignificant little things', says Kavanagh. Do you think that this is this evident in his poetry? Support the points you make by quotation from or reference to the poems by Kavanagh on your course.

J. Kavanagh's poetry has been described as 'new and wonderful.' Would you agree with this view? Support your answer by quotation from or reference to the poems you have studied.

Critical Commentary

In 2000, the *Irish Times* published *Book of Favourite Irish Poems* which 3,500 readers of the *Irish Times* had nominated. Of the one hundred poems chosen, Patrick Kavanagh appeared twelve times, second only to Yeats, who was represented by twenty-five poems. Nine of Kavanagh's poems prescribed here for Leaving Certificate were included ('The Hospital' was excluded) and 'On Raglan Road', was placed fifth after Yeats' 'The Lake Isle of Innisfree' and 'He Wishes for the Cloths of Heaven', Heaney's 'Mid-Term Break', and Yeats' 'The Song of Wandering Aengus'.

Inniskeen Road: July Evening

Both place and time are named in the title, placenames being of particular significance in Kavanagh's work. The opening lines are casual, colloquial and closer to the rhythms of ordinary, everyday speech than to poetry. 'There's a dance in Billy Brennan's barn tonight' is language at its simplest and most ordinary, and naming a real person roots the poem in the ordinary. The opening lines flow easily, with the help of alliteration, end-rhyme and repetition:

> The **b**icycles go **b**y in **t**wos and **t**hrees—
> There's a dance in **B**illy **B**rennan's **b**arn tonight,
> *And* there's the half-talk code of mysteries
> *And* the wink-and-elbow language of delight

Kavanagh belongs to the place but he also feels like an outsider. He is aware of the sense of companionship and togetherness among those going to the dance; they are going by 'in twos and threes' but he also feels cut off, not part of the 'half-talk code of mysteries/ And the wink-and-elbow language of delight.' The poet's sense of being separate, even dispirited, is expressed in the way Kavanagh uses 'And' and a repeated 'And' to describe what he's missing:

> And there's the half-talk code of mysteries
> And the wink-and-elbow language of delight.

The sounds flow less freely from here on as Kavanagh comes to terms with his sense of alienation. In the first four lines of the sonnet there is activity, movement and anticipated excitement. Then the poem becomes quieter. In lines 5–8 the poet is alone and silent and the place itself is still:

> Half-past eight and there is not a spot
> Upon a mile of road, no shadow thrown
> That might turn out a man or woman, not
> A footfall tapping secrecies of stone.

The poet is not going to the dance. Kavanagh himself has said, in *Self-Portrait*, that 'A poet is never one of the people. He is detached, remote, and the life of small-time dances and talk about football would not be for him. He might take part but could not belong' and, in his Introduction to his *Collected Poems*, Kavanagh says that 'poetry made me a sort of outcast.' Seamus Heaney points out that 'There are two solitudes, the solitude of the road and the solitude of the poet,' and he adds that the road's solitude mirrors that of the poet's.

And yet, though Kavanagh is alone, he is connected with the place in a profound and mysterious way. He shows us how his understanding of the place is different and special when he speaks of the 'secrecies of stone.' It is as if the very stones on the ground contain and could tell secrets. What these secrets are, we are not told but they may be connected to the lovers' delight and excitement in the opening lines. Antoinette Quinn says that Kavanagh 'contrasts the lonely solitude of the poet with the carefree companionship of dance-goers.'

This sonnet is divided into an eight-line stanza and a six-line one. The second section of the poem begins with 'I' and signals a more direct tone. There is no 'I' used in lines 1–8 but in lines 9–14 the poet is centre-stage and yet he seems unhappy with his lot. The poet is, in Seamus Heaney's words, 'at once marooned and in possession.' He knows what he's missing and pokes fun at and gently mocks the familiar, clichéd idea of the contemplative poet. If poetry demands contemplation, it also demands solitude and Kavanagh has a hate-relationship, it would seem, with his art. He calls himself 'king' only to send himself up and then to put himself down. He is king:

> Of banks and stones and every blooming thing

This last phrase, however, can be interpreted both negatively and positively. Blooming has dismissive and celebratory connotations; it can mean a slang term or it could refer to the flowering landscape and the creative imagination. If it means both then the complexity of the poet's position is captured. He is both insider and outsider.

Shancoduff

This poem, divided into two five-line stanzas and a concluding six-line stanza, finds something to love in something that might seem unlovable. The opening line suggests a place in permanent shadow. The 'never' and 'Eternally' are final but 'my' in the phrase 'my black hills' and 'happy' (line 4) reveal the poet's deep affection for his locality:

> My black hills have never seen the sun rising,
> Eternally they look north towards Armagh.

The Biblical reference suggests that these hills are steadfast, purposeful, of sound moral standing:

> Lot's wife would not be salt if she had been
> Incurious as my black hills that are happy
> When dawn whitens Glassdrummond chapel.

Kavanagh's protective tone is found in the repeated 'My' with which the second stanza begins: 'My black hills . . . ' (line 1), 'my black hills . . . ' (line 4), 'My hills . . .' (line 6). He also attributes a precious and mysterious quality to his hills. Though these hills look north towards Armagh, though they have turned their backs on the sun, the sun seeks out the bright shillings of March which the hills hoard on their north-facing slopes:

> My hills hoard the bright shillings of March
> While the sun searches in every pocket.

These 'bright shillings' have been interpreted as pockets of snow and hail on north-facing slopes and such an interpretation suggests that, though these hills are bleak, they have their own beauty.

He praises the hills further when Kavanagh says, in deliberate and wonderful exaggeration, that

> They are my Alps and I have climbed the Matterhorn

but reality intervenes again in the following lines:

> With a sheaf of hay for three perishing calves
> In a field under the Big Forth of Rocksavage.

Kavanagh realises that his view of Shancoduff is different and unusual. The place is cold and harsh and punishing ('perishing calves' (line 9), 'Rocksavage' (line 10), 'rushy' (line 11)) and in the closing lines he admits that the cattle-drovers only see its bad side. But the poet, in one word, shows how he can see a beauty and tenderness in the bitterly cold and impoverished land when he writes:

> The sleety winds fondle the rushy beards of Shancoduff

Details here suggest a grim picture but 'fondle', in sound and meaning, brings a surprising softness and beauty to the picture. Throughout the poem Kavanagh has spoken of Shancoduff in terms of his involvement with place. They are 'my' hills but the cattle-drovers see them as 'them hungry hills.' These are hills:

> That the water-hen and snipe must have forsaken

Kavanagh declares himself a poet and is known as such and, though it is a dismissive term to cattle-drovers, the speaker manages to express both unease and pride in his being a poet. In the final line, perhaps, the opposite is meant, Kavanagh is being ironic, and his heart is not badly shaken. Kavanagh imagines that the cattle-drovers think him impoverished like the place itself:

> 'Who owns them hungry hills
> That the water-hen and snipe must have forsaken?
> A poet? Then by heavens he must be poor.'
> I hear and is my heart not badly shaken?

The poem itself is evidence enough that Kavanagh, though impoverished perhaps in terms of material wealth, is rich in thought, feeling and imagination. The cattle-drovers are measuring him by what they see before them but they do not know, unless they read this poem, that Kavanagh can look on the very same world and see it differently.

A Christmas Childhood

In this memory poem Kavanagh is remembering a magical and mysterious time from his childhood. 'A Christmas Childhood' tells of the extraordinary in the ordinary and this is clearly seen in the opening two lines:

> One side of the potato-pits was white with frost–
> How wonderful that was, how wonderful!

Line one is a factual, accurate description; line two is powered with emotion in tone, repetition and an exclamation mark.

The experience was Kavanagh's and, it would seem, everyone's, for in Part I Kavanagh speaks for all, when he says 'we put our ears to the paling-post ...' and 'An apple tree/With its December-glinting fruit we saw–.' But the poem mainly focuses on Christmas as seen and an experienced through one person's, a six-year-old's, imagination.

This first section, four stanzas, has a regular rhyme and regular line-length. The wonderful and the magical dominate in that everything Kavanagh mentions is transformed in the boy's imagination. Una Agnew says that 'There is something familiar yet idyllic in his earliest memories of Christmas morning in the Kavanagh home. Work and leisure, mothering and fathering, the earthy and the spiritual: all intermingle.' Hay and straw are ordinary sights on a farm, but for Kavanagh

> The light between the ricks of hay and straw
> Was a hole in Heaven's gable.

Earth gives way to heaven, everything seems possible, and, as usual in Kavanagh's poetry, the ordinary is never forgotten. Heaven is spoken of in terms of a building whose 'gable-end' has a lit window. The frosted apple tree in winter introduces a different atmosphere. When Kavanagh remembers 'An apple tree/ With its December-glinting fruit we saw', the adult Kavanagh associates the tree with the Tree of Knowledge in the *Book of Genesis* and how the eating of the fruit led to man's Fall and sinful state.

Adulthood had blinded Kavanagh to the beauty, freshness and innocence of childhood, but occasionally he can relive and recapture the wonder of an earlier time:

> Now and then
> I can remember something of the gay
> Garden that was childhood's.

The Garden of Eden is no more but Christmas is a time when an Eden-like world becomes possible. Kavanagh makes this very clear in stanza four when he says

> Again

> The tracks of cattle to a drinking-place,
> A green stone lying sideways in a ditch
> Or any common sight the transfigured face
> Of a beauty that the world did not touch.

Part I describes place – potato-pits, ricks of hay and straw, apple tree, cattle-tracks, a green stone … In Part II the poem has a cast of characters, including his father and mother and neighbours, the Lennons and Callans, and, in Antoinette Quinn's words, 'Through a series of crisp, lucid images it conjures up the child's sense of being part of a family and of a closely knit Catholic community.' Quinn has also pointed out how Part II 'radiates outwards from a domestic interior to gate, cowshed, road, bogland, neighbourhood, townland; a world awakening to music.' In the opening stanza of Part II a new note is sounded:

> My father played the melodion
> Outside at our gate;
> There were stars in the morning east
> And they danced to his music.

Here rhyme is dropped, line length is varied and the stanza has a music to it that is close to the modulating music of a melodion. The only stanza in this second part that has a second line rhyming with a final line is the closing one. Music unites one place with another and neighbour with neighbour.

> Across the wild bogs his melodion called
> To Lennons and Callans.

Kavanagh includes a very ordinary, almost comical, detail. He speaks of how 'I pulled on my trousers in a hurry' but the gesture is contrasted with the emotion he is feeling:

> I knew some strange thing had happened.

The strangeness is in how the ordinary becomes special. This little country place in out-of-the-way Ireland becomes the Bethlehem where Jesus was born. The mundane and the magical are side by side:

> Outside the cow-house my mother
> Made the music of milking;
> The light of her stable-lamp was a star
> And the frost of Bethlehem made it twinkle.

His parents both make music, through melodion and milking, and their everyday place in 1910 (when Kavanagh was six) is imagined to be Bethlehem in the year of Christ's birth.

Other sounds are also captured; the contrasting onomatopoeic 'screeched' and 'crushed' paint an atmospheric landscape and the word 'wistfully' conveys some unnamed person's emotion on Christmas morning:

> A water-hen screeched in the bog,
> Mass-going feet
> Crunched the wafer-ice on the pot-holes,
> Somebody wistfully twisted the bellows wheel.

The poem tells of the young Kavanagh waking up to the world, its music and beauty, and it is appropriate that the 'child poet' is drawn towards writing. He makes his mark:

> My child poet picked out the letters .
> On the grey stone,
> In silver the wonder of a Christmas townland,
> The winking glitter of a frosty dawn.

Here, Kavanagh is doing what a painter does when an artist paints a picture of themself painting a picture. Kavanagh writes a poem in which he describes himself responding to the poetic impulse; he writes a poem in which the child poet writes about 'the wonder of a Christmas townland,/ The winking glitter of a frosty dawn.'

The rhythm has not followed the same pattern throughout. Kavanagh introduced a different sound pattern in Part II and this is clearly seen and heard, for example, in:

> Cassiopeia was over
> Cassidy's hanging hill,
> I looked and three whin bushes rode across
> The horizon—the Three Wise Kings.

Kavanagh here creates what Seamus Heaney calls a stanza with a 'nice lift' and an 'inspired wobble.' Here the very regular end-rhyme used in Part I of the poem (abab) has been abandoned and a different music emerges. This can also be heard in lines such as:

> An old man passing said:
> 'Can't he make it talk'—
> The melodion.

where Kavanagh has included the ordinary speech of the people in his poetry. The young poet is a shy observer:

> I hid in the doorway
> And tightened the belt of my box-pleated coat.

He is clearly pleased at his sense of growing up. His penknife, presumably a Christmas present, is a grown-up's one:

> I nicked six nicks on the door-post
> With my penknife's big blade—
> There was a little one for cutting tobacco.
> And I was six Christmases of age.

The line 'I nicked six nicks on the door-post' is particularly effective. Each short word and sound imitates the very gesture being described.

The poem's final stanza returns to the opening line of Part II – 'My father played the melodion' – and the poem's final image, that of father, mother and child, and the domestic scene, says Una Agnew, 'evokes something of the aura surrounding the Holy Family of Nazareth.' The final image of the flower, unlike many images in this poem, is an imagined one. He is filled with a prayerful feeling but he does not spell out in words what his feelings are; instead he captures those feelings in the picture of this rare and special white rose:

> My father played the melodion,
> My mother milked the cows,
> And I had a prayer like a white rose pinned
> On the Virgin Mary's blouse.

from *The Great Hunger*

This poem differs from the others poems by Kavanagh on the course in that the grim note of the opening words finds no release or leads to no sense of joy or celebration. Kavanagh is writing of the world he knew best as a man in his thirties living in rural Ireland in the 1930s.

Part I of 'The Great Hunger' is in nine sections. They could be described as follows:

Section 1.	lines 1-17	The landscape where Maguire and his men live doomed lives.
Section 2.	lines 18-38	The sense of loss Maguire experiences with the passing of the years.
Section 3.	lines 39-42	The narrator interprets Maguire's longing.
Section 4.	lines 43-57	Maguire's involvement in his work and his doubts about his way of life.
Section 5.	lines 58-61	The narrator's concern for Maguire and his awareness of Maguire's lack of spirit and his commitment to the land.
Section 6.	lines 62-79	Maguire's youth and how his personality determined his future.
Section 7.	lines 80-84	A description of the horse searching for food becomes an image of the search for pleasure and how this may lead to hurt.
Section 8.	lines 85-88	A description of the October landscape in Donaghmoyne.
Section 9.	lines 89-92	The narrator's overview of the place and the life lived there.

Patrick Maguire, the poem's central character, is, in Antoinette Quinn's words, 'an overworked slave, brutalised, vegetised even, by a life of unremitting drudgery, culturally deprived, compelled to be chaste . . . . a victim of a religiously enforced rural economy which values property and propriety at the expense of love and self-fulfilment.' Una Agnew sees it as poem where 'Physical, mental, emotional and spiritual famine stalk the land, bringing not death but half-life to these rural people.'

Kavanagh does not speak in the first person, nor does he allow Patrick Maguire to speak directly to the reader. Kavanagh's technique here is to create a sympathetic, involved narrator who knows the world and the people depicted in the poem. In ninety-two lines, Part I of 'The Great Hunger', the speaker describes the landscape and Maguire, and the opening lines reveal a sense of a deadening and dehumanised existence:

> Clay is the word and clay is the flesh
> Where the potato-gatherers like mechanized scare-crows move
> Along the side-fall of the hill—Maguire and his men.

Clay, the first word in the poem, suggests an earth that is wet and heavy. If 'Clay is the word' and 'the flesh,' it would seem that Kavanagh is rewriting a prayer well-known to him which says that 'the Word was made flesh and dwelt among us.' Instead of the life-enhancing moment of Christ's birth, which the Angelus prayer refers to, Kavanagh's version suggests that Maguire and his men only know a life that is base or earth-bound and hopeless.

These men, according to the speaker of the poem, who observes them, belong to the *Book of Death*, a phrase which echoes the *Book of Life* in the *Bible*. Kavanagh's tone is a questioning one but the answer is implied:

> If we watch them an hour is there anything we can
> prove
> Of life as it is broken-backed over the Book
> Of Death?

The work that Maguire and his men do is mechanical, repetitive, harsh, in bad weather. The phrase 'broken-backed' refers to their physical posture but it also becomes an image of their lives. They are living but it would seem that *The Book of Life* is closed to them. Even nature is unattractive, noisy, cold:

> Here crows gabble over worms and frogs
> And the gulls like old-newspapers are blown clear of the
> hedges...

and though the poet's question ('Is there some light of imagination in these wet clods?') suggests a hope that there might be some release, hope, beauty, a 'light of imagination' in the grim lives they live, the reality seems to be otherwise. The speaker, having presented us with description, then imagines

> Which of these men
> Loved the light and the queen
> Too long virgin?

Such a question focuses on the part religion played in these men's lives. They never loved a real woman but they loved the Virgin Mary. And then, in a short, simple but powerful sentence, the poet captures the passing of time and how youth gives way to old age, just as summer leads to autumn:

> Yesterday was summer.

Marriage was once hoped for but now all that awaits these figures on the hillside is decline and death, which Kavanagh conveys in the image of the 'last soul' passively rolling down the side of the hill.

The section beginning 'A dog lying on a torn jacket ...' places Patrick Maguire centre-stage. The world he belongs to is shabby, tired and listless:

> A dog lying on a **torn** jacket under a **heeled-up** cart,
> A horse **nosing** along the posied headland, **trailing**
> A **rusty** plough. Three heads **hanging** between wide-apart
> Legs. October playing a symphony on a **slack** wire paling

and, though the image of the posied or flowery headland is beautiful and the image of the symphony harmonious, the mood is one of disappointment. The image of hope recurs in the reference to the lit candle on a June altar, but the candle in Maguire's mind is now without flame:

> Maguire watches the drills flattened out
> And the flints that lit a candle for him on a June altar
> Flameless.

This passage emphasises the passing of time, transience. Ploughing the land is never ending:

> The drills slipped by and the days slipped by
> And he trembled his head away and ran free from the
> world's halter

Just as the horse is haltered, so too Maguire is kept in harness by social codes, but he likes to think that he escapes them, that he knows freedom. Maguire has an image of himself as happy, wise and sociable, lucky, as one who escaped the nets. We are told that he

> thought himself wiser than any man in the townland
> When he laughed over pints of porter,
> Of how he came free from every net spread
> In the gaps of experience.

and that he finds children annoying and a hindrance in the fields

> He shook a knowing head
> And pretended to his soul
> That children are tedious in hurrying fields of April
> Where men are spanging across wide furrows.
> Lost in the passion that never needs a wife—
> The pricks that pricked were the pointed pins of harrows.
> Children scream so loud that the crows could bring
> The seed of an acre away with crow-rude jeers.

Even in the language there is a recognition of the sexual intimacy on which he has missed out ('prick' is a term for sex as far back as medieval literature, but farming, 'the pointed pins of harrows', has replaced sex in Maguire's life), but Maguire does not allow himself to think about it:

> Patrick Maguire, he called his dog and he flung a stone in
>   the air
> And hallooed the birds away that were the birds of the years.

In the third short section (lines 39–42), the speaker's tone draws us closer. In cinematic terms it is a close-up. He addresses Maguire directly and now the reader is close to the earth:

> Turn over the weedy clods and tease out the tangled skeins

and with the question he asks we are drawn into Maguire's mind. The narrator, however, tells the reader that Maguire's fingering the muddy ground is in effect searching for something he hardly understands. It has been suggested that Maguire's fingering the tangled skeins could be interpreted as a man's sexual longing. Augustine Martin, commenting on these lines, says that 'the pulsations of their live flesh' is 'numbed with groping in the October clay.'

The mood then shifts, in section four (lines 43–57), to a brisk, colloquial, immediate one. Maguire speaks to his helper Joe about the work, gives directions – 'Pull down the shafts of that cart, Joe/ And straddle the horse', comments on the weather, plans a December job, notices Cassidy's ass eating his clover, curses the dog. The writing here resembles a dramatic monologue and the tone is convincing. The passage ends on a sombre note:

> His dream changes like the cloud-swung wind
> And he is not so sure now if his mother was right
> When she praised the man who made a field his bride.

Section four began with the external world, seen through Maguire's eyes. Maguire is involved in his work, anxious, planning. By the end of section four the poet has entered into Maguire's private thoughts and feelings.

Lines 58–61 (section five) is both tender and sad. The speaker asks that we watch Maguire, a man who gave his life to the land:

> Watch him, watch him, that man on a hill whose spirit
> is a wet sack flapping about the knees of time.
> He lives that his little fields may stay fertile when his
>   own body
> Is spread in the bottom of a ditch under two coulters
>   crossed in Christ's Name.

Maguire in death has returned to the earth (clay to clay?) Kavanagh's use of the verb 'spread' suggests farming rather than burial and the cross made from coulters (the iron cutters, part of the ploughshare) suggests Maguire's close contact with the land. These four lines paint a disillusioned man – his spirit is 'a wet sack flapping about the knees' – and the image of the sack that Maguire would have wrapped about his waist becomes an image of his life. The wet sack doesn't just flap about Maguire's knees; Kavanagh tells us that it flaps 'about the knees of time.' Time is referred to frequently in the poem – the passing of time and the harshness of time.

In the sixth section the poem offers a glimpse of Maguire's youth. He was 'suspicious', aware of girls' sexual awakening, uneasy; and he could not allow himself give into his natural impulses. The image that follows ('young brambles to hooked treachery') shows how brainwashed he has been by the culture in which he lives and by its images of women as dangerous and treacherous. Maguire himself tries to reassure himself that there is no better life, that no-one escapes his plight:

> It could not be that back of the hills love was free
> And ditches straight.

The following sentence seems to continue this thought, with Maguire again telling himself that everywhere children become 'apes', a savage, grim condemnation of himself and his workers:

> No monster hand lifted up children and put down apes
> As here.

'Monster hand' suggests power, control and the powerlessness of those affected. Maguire's cry is an impassioned one:

> 'O God if I had been wiser!'
> That was his sigh like the brown breeze in the thistles.
> He looks towards his house and haggard. 'O God if I
>   had been wiser!'

Wisdom, it seems, would have brought happiness and fulfilment but the nature of that happy, fulfilled life is never described explicitly and the image of a crumpled leaf with which the passage ends becomes an image of Maguire's life. He has 'made a field his bride', on his mother's advice, but he now knows

> that his own heart is calling his mother a liar

Here we see how the poem, in Augustine Martin's words, explores 'the human tragedy suffered by the sensitive individual caught upon the treadmill of those relentless rituals, law, custom and religion.'

Part I of 'The Great Hunger' ends with three short stanzas. Lines 80–84 (section seven) describe a horse craning through a harsh, stony landscape in search of clover:

> The horse lifts its head and cranes
> Through the whins and stones
> To lip late passion in the crawling clover.
> In the gap there's a bush weighted with boulders like
>   morality,
> The fools of life bleed if they climb over

The horse wanting to 'lip late passion in the crawling clover' is following its desires and its subsequent bleeding is due to risk-taking. This reference to the horse could be interpreted as a symbol of longing and hurt. Kavanagh offers no judgement, no interpretation, but he leaves it up to the reader to make whatever connection he or she will.

Lines 85–88 (section eight) focus on the bleak October landscape of Donaghmore but, though the coltsfoot leaves are blighted and the cart-tracks are filled with rain, the speaker finds a beauty and a sadness in the yellow sun reflected in the horse-shoed puddles:

> The wind leans from Brady's, and the coltsfoot leaves
>   are holed with rust,
> Rain fills the cart-tracks and the sole-plate grooves;
> A yellow sun reflects in Donaghmoyne
> The poignant light in puddles shaped by hooves.

In the closing lines, the speaker invites 'Imagination' to join him in 'this iron house.' An iron house is hard-sounding, the opposite of soft or comfortable. The world that Patrick Maguire inhabits could be seen as an iron house. As readers we have been within this world. The speaker's tone is welcoming when he says

> Come with me, Imagination, into this iron house

and Imagination will allow him to review the past:

> And we will watch from the doorway the years run
> back

Looking back will allow the speaker an understanding of the past and the present:

> And we will know what a peasant's left hand wrote on the page

The reference to 'what a peasant's left hand wrote on the page' suggests that Patrick Maguire's account of his life will be a different, unsettling account of the life of an Irish peasant. The poem was originally called 'The Old Peasant', which suggests one individual but in re-naming it 'The Great Hunger', the poem becomes a poem about a people. The closing line is a plea for a momentary calm and quietness. October, as described in the poem is a grim, harsh month but the speaker asks that it offer not the harshness of cackling hen, neighing horse, sighing tree or quacking duck:

> Be easy, October. No cackle hen, horse neigh, tree sough,
> duck quack.

Advent

Originally called 'Renewal', this poem looks closely at the four weeks in the church calendar during which time the devout prepare for Christmas. In Kavanagh's day, religious practices were more strictly observed than they are now and Advent was a time of penance and deprivation. The poem, appropriately, is divided into four sections and originally had four separate stanzas.

Una Agnew sees 'Advent' as a poem in which the poet 'sets about remaking his soul, opting for simplicity over superfluity.' It begins with a feeling of excess and a feeling of being jaded. The 't' and 'st' sounds in the opening line contribute to this feeling of distaste:

> We have tested and tasted too much, lover

'Lover' has been interpreted in different ways (cf. Glossary of poem) but, whichever interpretation one prefers, what is important is that 'lover' is a close and intimate presence in the speaker's life. The poet's present state is dull and lacking in wonder. The 'chink' is precious because it allows us a glimpse of the mysterious and wonderful and

> Through a chink too wide there comes in no wonder

The chink, in Una Agnew's words, is seen as 'the cleanser, the purifier and renewer of vision' and so 'he surrenders again to the purification of darkness, fasting and penance.' These voluntary penitential exercises (dark rooms, dry black bread, sugarless tea) will allow him to experience again a childlike freshness and a childlike way of seeing the world.

The speaker in adulthood has knowledge and sophistication and yet he feels the need to

> return to Doom
> The knowledge we stole but could not use.

This may refer to the eating of the fruit of the Tree of Knowledge in the Garden of Eden, as told in the Book of Genesis. With that knowledge came man's Fall and sinful state. If such knowledge could be undone, returned, then an innocence would be possible and the second stanza offers examples of how the child's imagination sees 'the newness that was in every stale thing.' The ordinary landscape, the old man are 'spirit-shocking' and astonishing. So much so that in wishing to journey back to childhood one is also returning to the wonder associated with Christ's birth. Kavanagh does not make this link in an explicit way but when he writes of

> bog-holes, cart-tracks, old stables where Time begins

Bethlehem and Christ's birth are being alluded to.

The poem's second section looks to the future. This sonnet contains more end-rhymes than the first and the first four lines all have the same end-rhyme:

> O after Christmas we'll have no need to go searching
> For the difference that sets an old phrase burning—
> We'll hear it in the whispered argument of a churning
> Or in the streets where the village boys are lurching.

The 'O' registers the tone of happy expectation. When Advent is over the world will be seen anew. The November and December darkness will end, even the 'whispered argument' of a churning will sound special, the phrase 'whispered argument of a churning' itself capturing the sounds of making butter. And as Antoinette Quinn points out, 'Once the indoors rites of purification have been completed the poem moves outdoors.'

The riches of life are evident everywhere, 'my love and I' are renewed and restored, life's 'ordinary plenty' surrounds the poet. Ordinary plenty is a key idea here. Kavanagh is not looking for the exotic or the extravagant, as they might ordinarily be understood. Instead he finds the extraordinary and the abundant about him in the ordinary, rural world. After Christmas the world is now experienced intuitively, instinctively. A reasoned, rational explanation is not appropriate or relevant. The speaker says

> Won't we be rich, my love and I, and please
> God we shall not ask for reason's payment

His belief in God is such that he senses God's breath in the colloquial, common speech of the people but he will experience and enjoy God's presence rather than analyse it.

In the closing lines the poet speaks of throwing off 'the clay-minted wages/ Of pleasure'; 'clay-minted' reminds us that we are but dust and suggests that adult, conscious, mortal knowledge should be abandoned and thrown into the dust-bin.

The poem ends with a new beginning. The year begins, the earth is beginning to produce growth and the striking, wonderful, rare image with which the poem ends points to the future with a 'January flower' (snowdrop?). The use of the present tense in the final line stands out. Lines 15–28 began with the future ('we'll have...', 'We'll hear...', 'we'll hear...', 'Won't we be rich...', 'we shall not ask...') then the poem moves to the past perfect ('We have thrown) and ends with the immediate joyful present:

> And Christ comes with a January flower.

In this two-sonnet poem, the first sonnet ended with a reference to Christ's birth in Bethlehem and the second sonnet also ends with Christ's coming, each year, at Christmas time.

On Raglan Road

'On Raglan Road' has been described, by Antoinette Quinn, as 'one of those sweetest songs that tell of saddest thoughts.' The long line, the rhyming scheme (aabb, ccdd, eeff, ggbb), assonance, alliteration, and the autumnal setting unite to create a memorable and haunting poem. That it was written with a slow, sad tune in mind adds to the overall effect.

From the outset the speaker of this love song links his falling in love in autumn with an inevitable sorrow. He 'saw the danger' but was nevertheless enchanted. The mood in the opening stanza is a mixture of happiness and doom, the tone is one of inevitability:

> And I said let grief be a fallen leaf at the dawning of
> the day.

Love's dangers are captured in the image of the deep ravine in stanza two and the failure of the poet to win her love is expressed in a well-known saying, with an image that would have been very much a part of Patrick Kavanagh's background: 'and I not making hay.' The poem is written in retrospect and line eight:

> O I loved too much and by such by such is happiness
> thrown away

sums up the poet's love for the unnamed woman. The poem focuses on his feelings rather than hers (the word 'I' occurs fourteen times) and, in telling us how his love for her was so great, there is a feeling of self-indulgence.

The poem is rooted in real places – Raglan Road, Grafton Street – but, side by side with these placenames, are imagined places, abstract ideas. Grafton Street in November becomes 'a ledge of the deep ravine' and even an emotion is expressed in terms of an object: 'let grief be a fallen leaf.'

In the third stanza the speaker paints a self-portrait in which he tells of all that he has given her. He is very much aware of his being an artist/poet and the gifts he has given were intellectual, imaginative, emotional – gifts of the mind, the secrets of creativity, poems. His secrets as a writer or wordsmith are similar to the secrets known to musicians ('sound'), sculptors ('stone') and artists ('tint').

The closing stanza has moved forward to a time when any hope of a love relationship has faded:

> On a quiet street where old ghosts meet I see her walking
> now
> Away from me so hurriedly

but any feeling of sorrow and loss is replaced by arrogance. He admits to having made a mistake in thinking that he could have ever wooed her:

> my reason must allow
> That I had wooed not as I should a creature made of
> clay—
> When the angel woos the clay he'd lose his wings at the
> dawn of day.

Here we have what Antoinette Quinn calls the poet's 'defensively arrogant posturing as an angel who has wooed an unworthy creature made of clay.'

Though drawn to this dark-haired, beautiful woman, he consoles himself in the end with the image of himself as a superior being. He is an artist, an outsider, and, in this instance, one who is aloof and apart.

Epic

Five of the prescribed ten Kavanagh poems for Leaving Certificate are sonnets and it is significant that this particular sonnet is called 'Epic', which is not only defined as momentous deeds and the heroic but also as a poetic form. That Kavanagh calls his fourteen-line poem 'Epic' is visually playful. An epic poem is usually hundreds, if not thousands of lines long, and tells of great exploits, covering large geographical areas and long periods of time. Kavanagh's poem tells of an argument between neighbours in a townland in rural Ireland.

This poem illustrates Robert Frost's belief that 'locality is art.' The personal, the particular, the parochial become universal. An ordinary event is given Homeric grandeur. The opening lines refer to 'important places' and 'great events.' The reader supplies his/her own examples but our expectations are mocked when Kavanagh gives his own example of an important place and great event.

The incident described is on a small scale and would seem worthless:

> who owned
> That half a rood of rock, a no-man's land

The use of real names for people and place (the Duffys, old McCabe, Ballyrush, Gortin) gives the poem immediacy, as does the use of quoted outburst ('Damn your soul') and speech ('Here is the march along these iron stones').

Reference to Munich opens up the poem and introduces a new perspective. The imagination shifts from Monaghan to Munich and there is a momentary waver in the poet's belief in his native place:

> Which
>
> Was most important?

and he is inclined to lose his faith 'in Ballyrush and Gortin.' The big political picture is presented for a moment but only to be dismissed. It is altogether appropriate for a poet that a fellow-writer (Homer's ghost) reassures him that great, epic literature can be made from local events. The artist can tell of universal truths in a literature rooted in a particular place.

The poet therefore is seen as the one who will decide what is important. Seamus Heaney says that 'even though the poem gives the stage over to two Monaghan farmers and successfully sets Ballyrush and Gortin in balance against Munich, it is not saying that the farmers and the Monaghan region are important in themselves. They are made important only in the light of the mind that is now playing upon them.'

The poem ends confidently: what he himself says is important is important. The poem's final sentence 'Gods make their own importance' suggests that what Gods consider important is their concern; the poet has discovered what is important to him and both are valid. The key sentences ('Which/ Was most important?' and 'Gods make their own importance.') in this sonnet are effective not only because they are short but because they capture his hesitation and resolution.

The Hospital

The title itself would not usually suggest that this is a love poem. Hospitals are frequently associated with illness, pain, suffering and death but Kavanagh is focusing not on his illness but on the transformation that took place as a result of his being in hospital.

'I fell in love' are familiar words, but these casual-sounding opening lines are unexpected and arresting:

> A year ago I fell in love with the functional ward
> Of a chest hospital:

The details belong to a practical, harsh, ugly world – 'square cubicles', 'concrete' floors, 'wash-basins.' Nothing here is aesthetically pleasing ('an art lover's woe') and yet Kavanagh in this poem is creating a new aesthetic.

Even the snoring from 'the fellow in the next bed' becomes, in Antoinette Quinn's words, 'a lyrical sound.' The place, the sounds, the people are all attractive to the speaker. Hospital has taught him that life is fragile and precious and he has come to cherish things that usually passed over. There is a tone of conviction in the lines:

> But nothing whatever is by love debarred,
> The common and banal her heat can know

Kavanagh has learned how to see afresh and anew. The rhymes suggest a mood of calm and happy acceptance. Between 'ward' and 'yard', the end-rhymes that frame the first stanza, are close if not identical end-rhymes ('roe', 'woe', 'snored', 'debarred', 'know', 'below'). It is as if everything is contained within the world of hospital and yard, that everything can be found there:

> The corridor led to a stairway and below
> Was the inexhaustible adventure of a gravelled yard.

The octet offered description and the sestet offers interpretation, explanation:

> This is what love does to things: the Rialto Bridge
> The main gate that was bent by a heavy lorry,
> The seat at the back of a shed that was a suntrap

again listing the most ordinary things. If 'the Rialto Bridge', 'a heavy lorry', a 'seat at the back of a shed' were taken out of context they would be considered un-poetic, banal. But here they are transformed by Kavanagh's emotional and imaginative response and he is unapologetic. The poet believes that to name such things is a love gesture and love can be found in the most ordinary of places and things:

> Naming these things is the love-act and its pledge;
> For we must record love's mystery without claptrap,
> Snatch out of time the passionate transitory.

The 'I' in line one offers a personal experience; the use of 'we' in the closing lines is a warm invitation to see the world as Kavanagh sees it. The final words capture not only the pleasures of life but its reality. We seek love, but we also know that what we love is governed by the passing of time. This sonnet has snatched out of Kavanagh's life a period of time that was precious and significant.

Francis Stuart, commenting on this poem, says that love and humility are the inspiration. And he adds 'Clumsy, unworkable grammar, no literary graces, not "about" anything, not illustrating a previously conceived idea, but to those to whom it speaks, new and wonderful.'

Canal Bank Walk

The part of Dublin that Patrick Kavanagh loved best was that area around the canal at Baggot Street Bridge. It was the closest one could get to the countryside in the heart of Dublin with its grass and trees and water and pathways. And when Kavanagh wrote the poem it was also a much quieter place than it is now. In the Canal Bank sonnets this part of Dublin is associated with convalescence and renewal.

In 'Canal Bank Walk' a feeling of gratitude is prevalent and, unusually, illness is seen as something positive. Kerry Hardie also speaks of the transforming power of illness in a positive light in her poem 'She Replies to Carmel's Letter' when she writes that:

> . . . . sometimes even sickness is generous
> and takes you by the hand and sits you
> beside things you would otherwise have passed over.

Kavanagh's sonnet begins with a marvellous adjective – 'Leafy-with-love.' Its sounds are soft and lyrical and it conjures up an image of the beauty and generosity of nature:

> Leafy-with-love banks and the green waters of the canal
> Pouring redemption for me

The sense of self is strong in this poem through the use of 'me', 'I' and 'my' and yet the speaker does not appear self-important. His tone and mood, his love of the natural world and his gratitude welcome the reader in and, though he writes of his own experience, he shares this experience with us.

The imagery of baptism, re-birth, is found in the image of water and the words 'Pouring redemption' suggests a generous flowing and a sense of freedom, delivery and release. He sees his recovery as God's will and he is profoundly happy to 'wallow in the habitual, the banal' and

> Grow with nature again, as before I grew.

Nature, here, is seen as a healing power, a reminder of renewal and continuity, and there is a harmonious relationship between the human and the natural world. This is not only seen in the speaker's own relationship with the canal bank walk but it is also evident when the speaker tells of how the breeze adds 'a third/ Party to the couple kissing on an old seat.'

The poet's eye for detail gives the sonnet an immediacy and freshness. The ordinary is made extraordinary in pictures such as the 'bright stick trapped' and the contrast between the kissing couple on the old seat brings together in a single image young love and age. The poet, though alone, is feeling at one with the world, not lonely and separate.

The poem speaks of a special time in the poet's life but there is also a sense of timelessness in lines seven and eight:

> And a bird gathering materials for the nest for the Word
> Eloquently new and abandoned to its delirious beat

The 'And' suggests a never-ending process and the 'nest for the Word' conveys a feeling of "in the beginning" and God's creation.

The poem's final sentence, the sestet, becomes a prayer. Six lines long, it gathers momentum with each line. The tone is felt in the 'O' at the outset and the verbs 'enrapture', 'encapture', 'Feed', 'give' and the run-on lines (enjambment) all create a powerful feeling of longing and hope of fulfilment. Kavanagh takes the word 'fabulous' and, in using it in relation to grass, gives ordinary, everyday grass a newness; 'fabulous' itself can be seen for its true meaning.

This sestet also focuses on the nature of language. Earlier the poet experienced 'Pouring redemption'; he now desires the ability to 'pray unselfconsciously with overflowing speech.' In 'Advent' the poet wanted to return to a childlike state. Here there is a similar wish to rid himself of self-consciousness. The sensuous delight is everywhere throughout the sonnet and the closing couplet, containing the longest, most leisurely lines of the poem, highlights the poet's spiritual self, the soul.

> For this soul needs to be honoured with a new dress woven
> From green and blue things and arguments that cannot be proven.

The colours of sky (blue) and trees, grass, canal water (green) are fitting colours with which to dress this soul that has returned to this place and has been restored. The rational is not needed. The speaker finds contentment in the natural world and in the soul's awareness.

Lines Written on a Seat on the Grand Canal, Dublin

This sonnet not only has a title, it has a sub-title and one is as important as the other. 'Erected to the memory of Mrs Dermod O'Brien' is a symbol of love, affection and commemoration. Mrs Dermod O'Brien is not well-known but this seat remembers her; it is her memorial. A seat on the banks of the Grand Canal is inviting, welcoming and involving. If we sit on that seat we are finding some moments of ease and relaxation and, even if we are unaware of the inscription on the seat and the name of the person being remembered, we are part of the continuity of life.

'Canal Bank Walk', a companion poem, focused on Kavanagh's re-birth after a serious illness. Here in 'Lines Written on a Seat on the Grand Canal, Dublin' he dwells not only on the here and now but on the future, when he will no longer be here to enjoy the scene before him.

Mrs Dermod O'Brien must have loved this very spot, she and many others. Kavanagh is perpetuating that love of place in this sonnet. The poem's first words express a tone of longing, a mood of adoration, and the opening lines

> O commemorate me where there is water,
> Canal water preferably, so stilly
> Greeny at the heart of summer

present the reader with sounds and pictures of stillness, tranquillity. The pace and mood are, according to Antoinette Quinn, 'poised, assured, serene' and the speaker emerges as a humble, life-loving individual, without a hint of self-importance.

He addresses a presence whom he calls 'Brother' and, like the 'lover' in 'Advent', it is never stated explicitly who the poet is referring to. 'Brother' could be his actual brother Peter Kavanagh, his fellow man or, in this instance, nature. The words 'commemorate me' are used three times in the sonnet and they express his deep desire to be associated forever with this little "rural" part of urban Dublin.

In the deliberate exaggeration or hyperbole which Kavanagh creates in the Niagara metaphor there is a humour but there is also a confidence. The canal lock falls are more interesting and spectacular to this viewer than the real Niagara Falls. The poet creates a special space: the water falling through the lock can be heard but, paradoxically, there is also a 'tremendous silence.' It is 'mid July' and these very words are placed in line seven, the middle of the poem.

The experience captured here is such a transforming one that any one who experiences it would be affected. The poem speaks of how it becomes, appropriately, a poetic experience:

> No one will speak in prose
> Who finds his way to these Parnassian Islands.

Parnassus, sacred to the gods in ancient Greece, has been transported to the banks of the Grand Canal, Dublin.

This oasis of peace and beauty is highlighted further by the description of the swan and light. The senses were vividly evoked earlier (sight and sound) and now Kavanagh paints a mysterious and bright picture:

> A swan goes by head low with many apologies,
> Fantastic light looks through the eyes of bridges—
> And look! a barge comes bringing from Athy
> And other far-flung towns mythologies.

In five words — 'head low with many apologies' — Kavanagh has memorably given us a swan's movement and there's a quickening energy and excitement ('And look!') felt by the speaker on seeing the bridges and the barge. The reader is not told anything as banal as what the barge is carrying by way of cargo. Instead, we are told that this barge from towns in Kildare and beyond is carrying 'mythologies' and the ordinary world of commerce is transformed into something exotic and strange. And the poem, though intensely personal, opens up and opens outwards. The reader is invited to look at the swan, the barge, the surroundings; the canal bank seat and this particular place allows us to become involved in life.

The sonnet's ending echoes the opening line and the poet rejects the formality and importance of a hero-courageous tomb. His preference is for something involving, on-going, giving: – 'a canal-bank seat for the passer-by.' He qualifies his choice with the word 'just', a word that usually belittles, but here it has the opposite effect. When he says 'just a canal-bank seat for the passer-by' he is praising a canal-bank seat above all other forms of memorials.

Derek Mahon
(1941–2020)

The Overview

'There must be three things in combination, I suggest, before the poetry can happen: soul, song and formal necessity' writes Mahon, and his own work meets his own requirements. Mahon's poetry has the sensibility of a thinking, feeling self, a music and a mastery of construction; 'Grandfather' is a sonnet, 'Antarctica' a villanelle (a nineteen-line poetic form consisting of a tercet (five three lines of poetry) followed by a quatrain) and, in general, his organisation of the stanza, his line length and rhyme are impressive accomplishments. He is a formalist, believes in pattern and structure and has said: 'Look at rap – that's the best poetry being written in America at the moment; at least it rhymes.' Derek Mahon writes about landscape, seascape; he writes of what Edna Longley calls the 'conflict between poetry and the ethos of Protestant Ulster' (evident in 'Ecclesiastes'). A poet of place (Donegal, Co. Wexford, Portrush, Rathlin, Antarctica, Kinsale), he is also a philosophical poet, a poet of ideas and a poet with a broad literary background. The literary, philosophical aspect of his work can be seen in his poem 'Heraclitus on Rivers', when he writes:

> The very language in which the poem
> Was written, and the idea of language,
> All these will pass away in time.

'For Mahon, the past is significantly present' says Thomas Kinsella and this can be seen particularly in 'Rathlin' and 'A Disused Shed in Co. Wexford.' His sympathetic nature is evident in 'After the Titanic', 'The Chinese Restaurant in Portrush', 'Antarctica.' In these three poems Mahon demonstrates his ability to enter into the lives of others. In one he speaks in the voice of the persona (Bruce Ismay); in another he imagines what the owner of the restaurant is thinking, feeling, dreaming; and in 'Antarctica' he recreates a scene from an Antarctic expedition where an individual makes an extraordinary decision for the benefit of others. He is drawn to solitary, forgotten figures and in his poetry Mahon often reveals himself to be a solitary, observing figure.

Sean O'Brien points out that 'For the most part, Mahon's world exists outdoors' and the 'wide-open spaces are, naturally enough, rather thinly populated, but even when Mahon writes about the city ... it is somewhere whose population is hardly to be seen. Belfast, for example, in 'Ecclesiastes', is 'the/dank churches, the empty streets,/ the shipyard silence, the tied-up swings.' There is also, however, a sense of beauty and celebration in Mahon's response to the physical world, as in his description of Donegal ('the nearby hills were a deeper green/ Than anywhere in the world') or Kinsale ('sky-blue slates are steaming in the sun').

He is a very visual poet, as captured in such details as 'the grave/ Grey of the sea', 'the empty streets,/ the shipyard silence, the tied-up swings', 'a pandemonium of/ Prams, pianos, sideboards, winches,/ Boilers bursting', 'Between ten sleeping lorries/ And an electricity generator', 'a flutter/ Of wild flowers in the lift-shaft', 'one/ By one the gulls go window-shopping', 'The whole island a sanctuary where amazed/ Oneiric species whistle and chatter', 'The tent recedes beneath its crust of rime', 'yachts tinkling and dancing in the bay.'

'The strongest impression made on me when I read any poem by Derek Mahon' says Eamon Grennan, 'is the sense that I have been spoken to: that the poem has established its presence in the world as a kind of speech ... What I hear in these poems is a firm commitment to speech itself, to the act of civil communication enlivened, in this case, by poetic craft.' These Mahon poems speak to us in a voice that is calm, reflective, self-aware and never self-important. The speaker sometimes uses 'I', sometimes 'we', and all the time the reader is invited into the poem. Mahon's poems ask us to reflect on a range of themes, from an individual's mystery and elusiveness ('Grandfather'), uncertainty and failure ('Day Trip to Donegal'), guilt and suffering ('After the Titanic'), cultural inheritance and community ('Ecclesiastes'), threat and violence ('As It Should Be'), the dispossessed and neglected ('A Disused Shed in Co. Wexford'), loneliness and longing ('The Chinese Restaurant in Portrush'), history's legacy ('Rathlin'), the solitary, selflessness ('Antarctica'), changing times viewed optimistically ('Kinsale').

His best known poem, and the poem which many regard as his greatest, is 'A Disused Shed in Co. Wexford.' There the mushrooms become a symbol of lost voices struggling to be saved and the poem's references to Peru, India, Treblinka and Pompeii allow the poem a huge historical and cultural framework and create what Hugh Haughton calls 'a wonderful long perspective of historical time.' When Declan Kiberd says that Mahon 'has the mind of a conscience-stricken anthropologist', we can see what he means when we read this particular poem.

●

In his recent poetry, especially *The Yellow Book*, Mahon casts a cold eye on our consumerist, image-obsessed world. He writes of how nowadays 'Everywhere aspires to the condition of pop music,/ the white noise of late-century consumerism –' and of how our lives are affected by 'road rage/ spy cameras, radio heads, McDonalds, rowdytum,/ laser louts and bouncers, chat shows, paparazzi,/ stand up comedians and thug journalist.' But the same poet can also write a poem called 'Everything Is Going To Be All Right' where he offers the following heartening lines:

> The sun rises in spite of everything
> and the far cities are beautiful and bright.

In the 1991 *Field Day Anthology of Irish Writing*, Declan Kiberd describes Derek Mahon as 'the most underrated Irish poet of the century' and Michael Schmidt, in his *Lives of the Poets*, says that Mahon's work has been 'consistently undervalued for fifty years, not that neglect has seemed to bother or inhibit him.' Derek Mahon is more interested in his poetry than in his reputation. He knows that

> The lines flow from the hand unbidden
> and the hidden source is the watchful heart.

Biographical Notes

Derek Mahon, an only child, was born in Belfast on 23 November 1941 during World War II, and grew up in the city's Glengormley region. In his poem 'Courtyards in Delft', he describes himself as a 'strange child with a taste for verse.' Talking about his childhood in a *Paris Review* interview, Mahon speaks of the objects he remembers: a 1940s radio set, a Japanese lacquered cigarette case, an aunt's white shoes; and these, for Mahon, are 'the little things that you saw with a child's eye when you were a child and that will never go away.' He adds: 'That's what consciousness is all about.' Being an only child was significant he thinks: 'I think it was important that I was an only child, an only child whose best friends were the objects I've been talking about.'

He has described the house he grew up in as 'a quiet house.' 'Usually my mother was doing this or that, practical things around the house; while my father was usually out at work, away a forty- or forty-eight-hour week perhaps. He worked in the shipyard. A quiet man. Due to the absence of siblings, 'I had time for the eye to dwell on things, for the brain to dream about things. I could spend an afternoon happily staring.'

His background was Protestant but his parents 'weren't really serious church people ... It was all appearances. I tagged along, scrubbed and kempt.' His going to church was significant, however: the Church of Ireland Minister asked the young Derek Mahon to join the choir. This meant two services on Sunday and a choir practice on Wednesdays. 'The hymnology invaded my mind: "Ransomed, healed, restored, forgiven."'

He was educated at Skegoneil Primary School, and 'all I see is sunlight, classrooms full of light, or windows streaked with rain as everyone does.' He then attended the Royal Belfast Academical Institution and admits that he didn't feel at home in secondary school: 'I started moping, brooding; I didn't go in for sport' but he published what Michael Longley called 'amazingly accomplished verses' in *School News*. Mahon viewed Trinity College, Dublin, where he studied Modern Languages, as a place apart: 'Physically the surroundings were extremely attractive. Beautiful college, beautiful trees, beautiful girls ... golden days, golden moments.' He left Trinity in 1965 and went to the United States via Canada, living for a while in Cambridge, Massachusetts, and coming into contact with the literary scene around Harvard Square. Having worked at odd jobs in Canada and the States for two years, Mahon returned to Ireland and worked as a teacher in Belfast and Dublin. He published his first collection of poems, *Night-Crossing*, in 1968. 'Grandfather' is from this collection.

The Northern Troubles in the late 1960s took Mahon by surprise; 'I felt very far from home in those years. (In fact, for a large part of my life I've been *terrified* of home.) ... I couldn't deal with it. I could only develop a kind of contempt for what I felt was the barbarism, on both sides. But I *knew* the Protestant side; I knew them inside out. I was one of them, and perhaps I couldn't bear to look at my own face among them. So I adopted a "plague on both your houses" attitude.'

In the late 1960s Mahon taught for a year in Belfast and two in Dublin, but in 1970 he moved to London and in 1972 he published his second collection, *Lives*. He also married Doreen Douglas in 1972 and they had two children, Rory and Katie. There followed *The Snow Party* in 1975, which contains one of Mahon's most celebrated poems, 'A Disused Shed in Co. Wexford.' He was appointed poet-in-residence at the New University of Ulster between 1977 and 1979 but he came depressed, was ill and resolved 'never to live in Northern Ireland again.'

In 1982, *The Hunt By Night* appeared, followed by *Antarctica* in 1985. A *Selected Poems* was published in 1991, *The Hudson Letter* in 1995 and *The Yellow Book* in 1997. His collection, *Harbour Lights*, was published in 2005. He lived in London for fifteen years, working as a freelance journalist, and was writer-in-residence in British, Irish and American universities. His marriage ended and Mahon lived in New York for several years in the early 1990s, writing a series of articles, 'Letter from New York', for the *Irish Times*.

He has had various jobs, including warehouseman, Xerox operator, barman, teacher and lecturer. When it comes to poetry, Mahon has described himself as 'an out-and-out traditionalist.' For Mahon there are three principles essential to poetry: Soul, Song and Formal Necessity, and writing a poem is 'a visual experience as well as an aural one.' He adds: 'It's important to me what a poem looks like on the page. I'm interested in organisation. I'm interested in at least the appearance of control, orchestration, forceful activity; something intense happening, something being intended and achieved – purposefulness instead of randomness.'

Derek Mahon agrees with Eamon Grennan when asked if composing a poem is an attempt to link the human condition and the song. Mahon feels that every poem, in attempting that link, achieves something relating to the notion of art as consolation, the belief that "everything will be all right", but he also believes that his poems are 'products of a broken world.'

He lived an essentially solitary life in Dublin, moved to Kinsale in 2003, and admitted that to live in this way, at a slight distance from community, is 'practically my subject, my theme: solitude and community; the weirdness and terrors of solitude; the stifling and the consolations of solitude.' What interests him is a poetry 'written by solitaires in the cold, written by solitaires in the open, which is where the human soul really is. That for me is where poetry really is.' A *Collected Poems* was published in 1999, but Mahon asked his publisher not to send the book out to be reviewed and there was no book launch, something unheard of in an age of media hype and publicity. *Harbour Lights* (2005), received the *Irish Times* Poetry Now award, as did *Adaptations* (2006), *Life on Earth* (2008). A *New Collected Poems* was published in 2011. Derek Mahon's final collection, *Washing Up* was published posthumously in October 2020.

Writing in the year 2000, Mahon said that 'Whether we mean to or not, we offer ourselves and our works, such as they are, as illustrative symptoms of a period – the later 20th Century, say – and in that sense, everything has value, however slight. No doubt poetry, good or bad, is a waste of time; but waste, drift, contingency are the better part of wisdom. If it serves any useful purpose, it might be to retrieve the lost stuff: lost experience, lost ideas. Whatever proves uncanonical is at least documentary, evidential. We are all contributors. What was once true is true forever. What seemed like a good idea at the time retains the cautionary or diversionary function; and "failure", much under-rated, is where all the ladders start.'

Derek Mahon died on 2 October 2020. In his obituary, published in The Guardian, Sean O'Brien spoke of Mahon's poetry as 'lyrical, witty, ironic, succinct, cosmopolitan, rich in phrase and image' and mentioned how his short lyric poem, 'Everything is Going to Be All Right', from 1979, with its 'encouraging calm', found 'fresh prominence' and many new readers during the coronavirus pandemic. It was read on the RTÉ main evening news on 27 March, 2020, the day the Irish Government announced the country's first lockdown.

POEMS

[Handwritten mind map annotations:]

includes the reader (inclusive language used in Disused shed, Kinsale, Rathlin) and addresses the reader directly in Disused Shed & After the Titanic

the sea/nature (ominous)

transience of time

tragic vision of the world

form

Derek Mahon

isolation

huge historical and cultural framework

central male character → solitary figure

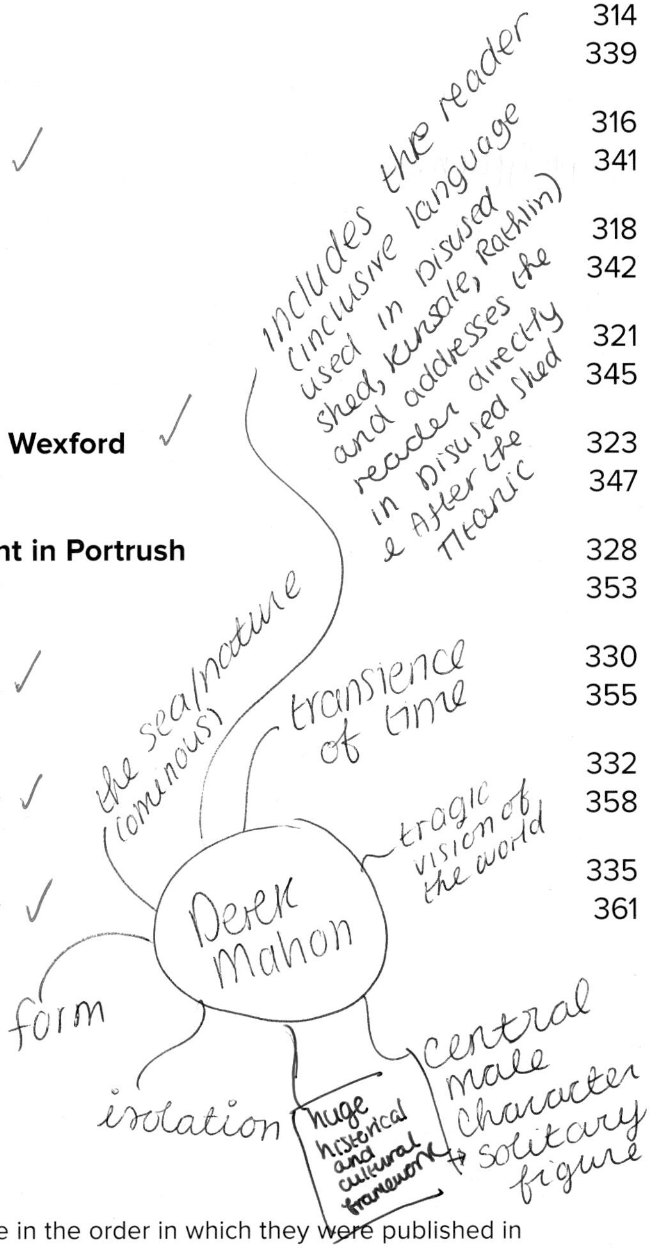

The poems printed here are in the order in which they were published in *Collected Poems*, Gallery Press, May 1999.

[handwritten: Petrarchan sonnet]

[handwritten: unsentimental, absence of possessive pronoun "my"]

Grandfather

*[handwritten annotations surrounding poem: auto biographical; impersonal; wonder, innocence; * Mahon awards; sense of mystery surrounds the grandfather; perfect rhyme; caesura suggests the shock of the injury; time passing; multiple meanings; playfulness; draws a comparison between the Grandfather and a naughty child; (the grandfather is elusive) defiant doesn't want to be infantilised; darkens the mood; rule breaking; loving fondness also patronizing → ambivalent do the childish terms imply dementia; fear - afraid of death? ageing? illness?]*

They brought him in on a stretcher from the world,
Wounded but humorous; and he soon recovered.
Boiler-rooms, row upon row of gantries rolled
Away to reveal the landscape of a childhood
Only he can recapture. Even on cold   5
Mornings he is up at six with a block of wood
Or a box of nails, discreetly up to no good
Or banging round the house like a four-year-old—

Never there when you call. But after dark
You hear his great boots thumping in the hall   10
And in he comes, as cute as they come. Each night
His shrewd eyes bolt the door and set the clock
Against the future, then his light goes out.
Nothing escapes him; he escapes us all.

📖 Glossary

Title Grandfather– Mahon's grandfather worked in the Harland and Wolff shipyard in Belfast.

Line 3 gantries: platforms for travelling-cranes.

Line 7 discreetly: unobtrusively; separately.

Line 12 shrewd: sharp, sensible.

? Questions

1. How was the grandfather affected by his injury? Do the details 'wounded' and 'humorous' suggest the usual or the unusual?

2. Do you think that the past is important to the grandfather, according to the poet? What does he mean by 'the landscape of a childhood'?

3. What do the details in lines 5–9 suggest? Are they contradictory, do you think?

4. Would you think the poet's grandfather a secretive man? A sly man? A cautious man? A liberated man? Give reasons for your answer. In what way is he like a four-year-old?

5. Does the final line of the poem – 'Nothing escapes him; he escapes us all.' – sum up the man as he is portrayed in the poem, in your opinion?

6. Comment on lines 12 and 13. What do these lines reveal of the grandfather?

7. Why do you think Mahon chose the compact, well-made sonnet form for this poem about his grandfather?

Day Trip to Donegal

We reached the sea in early afternoon,
Climbed stiffly out; there were things to be done,
Clothes to be picked up, friends to be seen.
As ever, the nearby hills were a deeper green
Than anywhere in the world, and the grave   5
Grey of the sea the grimmer in that enclave.

Down at the pier the boats gave up their catch,
A writhing glimmer of fish; they fetch
Ten times as much in the city as here,
And still the fish come in year after year —   10
Herring and mackerel, flopping about the deck
In attitudes of agony and heartbreak.

We left at eight, drove back the way we came,
The sea receding down each muddy lane.
Around midnight we changed-down into suburbs   15
Sunk in a sleep no gale-force wind disturbs.
The time of year had left its mark
On frosty pavements glistening in the dark.

Give me a ring, goodnight, and so to bed . . .
That night the slow sea washed against my head,   20
Performing its immeasurable erosions —
Spilling into the skull, marbling the stones
That spine the very harbour wall,
Muttering its threat to villages of landfall.

At dawn I was alone far out at sea   25
Without skill or reassurance — nobody
To show me how, no promise of rescue —
Cursing my constant failure to take due
Forethought for this; contriving vain
Overtures to the vindictive wind and rain.   30

Glossary

Line 5 grave: slow-moving, threatening.

Line 6 enclave: a place surrounded by another; in this instance the hills surrounding the sea.

Line 8 writhing: rolling, twisting.

Line 19 and so to bed: possibly the most famous words from the *Diary of Samuel Pepys* (1633–1703). Pepys wrote 'And so to bed' on 20 April 1660.

Line 22 marbling: staining, colouring.

Line 24 villages of landfall: villages on land approached on sea.

Line 29 Forethought: preparation.

Line 29 contriving: devising.

Line 29 vain: futile.

Line 30 Overtures: proposals.

Line 30 vindictive: revengeful; in an earlier version Mahon wrote 'mindless' but changed it to 'vindictive' in the *Collected Poems*.

Questions

1. How would you describe the speaker's mood in the opening stanza? Did the poem's title prepare you for something else? Explain, using quotations from the text to support the points you make.

2. Pick out those words which convey a sense of beauty and a sense of something unattractive and disturbing in the first two stanzas. Which one would you say predominates?

3. In stanza three, the speaker is returning to the city. How is the city described? How different is it from the rural world of Donegal? What is the relationship between man and nature for the city dweller?

4. The rhyming scheme is very regular throughout. Is this a noticeable feature of the poem? Comment on the effect of the run-on line.

5. Do you think the poet conveys well how 'the slow sea washed against my head.' Which details are particularly effective? How would you describe what the speaker experiences in the closing two stanzas? What does he conclude about himself in lines 28–30?

6. Would you say that the speaker enjoyed the day trip to Donegal? Give reasons for your answer. Comment on the significance of the closing words 'vindictive wind and rain.'

[handwritten: theme of exile]

[handwritten: narrative poem from the perspective of Bruce Ismay]

After the Titanic

[handwritten left margin: deviate, "others", exclusion, sense of lamentation]

They said I got away in a boat
And humbled me at the inquiry. I tell you
   I sank as far that night as any
Hero. As I sat shivering on the dark water
   I turned to ice to hear my costly   5
Life go thundering down in a pandemonium of
   Prams, pianos, sideboards, winches,
Boilers bursting and shredded ragtime. Now I hide
   In a lonely house behind the sea
Where the tide leaves broken toys and hatboxes   10
   Silently at my door. The showers of
April, flowers of May mean nothing to me, nor the
   Late light of June, when my gardener
Describes to strangers how the old man stays in bed
   On seaward mornings after nights of   15
Wind, takes his cocaine and will see no one. Then it is
   I drown again with all those dim
Lost faces I never understood, my poor soul
   Screams out in the starlight, heart
Breaks loose and rolls down like a stone.   20
   Include me in your lamentations.

[handwritten right margin: form - waves short line followed by a long line no structure / no stanzas - conveys Ismay's sense of disorder, lost.]

[handwritten left margin: personify the tide - the tide knows his guilt]

[handwritten: passage of time]

📖 ## Glossary

Title After the Titanic– an earlier version of this poem was called 'Bruce Ismay's Soliloquy.' Bruce Ismay was manager of the White Star Line shipping company. The Titanic, which was built in Belfast and operated by the White Star Line, sank on its maiden voyage from Southampton to New York on the night of 14 April 1912 at 11:40 p.m. The British White Star liner Titanic, measuring 882 feet 9 inches and 100 feet high to the bridge level, was the largest ship afloat. It cost £1,500,000. The Titanic collided with an iceberg in the North Atlantic and sank in less than three hours; c.1550 of c.2206 passengers died. J. Bruce Ismay was 49 at the time of the disaster. Robert Ballard, in *The Discovery of the Titanic*, writes that 'Bruce Ismay, the wealthy president and managing director of International Mercantile Marine, which owned the White Star Line, had hopped into the partly filled collapsible C (lifeboat) as it was about to be lowered away, and lived to regret his instinct for survival. After his public vilification as J. "Brute" Ismay, he became a recluse and eventually died a broken man.'

Line 2 inquiry: from 2 May to 3 July 1912 the British Board of Trade Inquiry was conducted; 25,622 questions were asked of 96 witnesses. There were only three passenger witnesses – Sir Cosmo and Lady Duff Gordon and J. Bruce Ismay.

Line 6 pandemonium: uproar, utter confusion; literally all (pan) demons, the home of demons.

Line 7 winches: hoisting machines.

Line 8 ragtime: music of American Negro origin; during the sinking of the Titanic the band began to play lively ragtime tunes.

Line 16 cocaine: drug from coca, a Latin American shrub, used as anaesthetic or stimulant.

Line 21 lamentations: expressions of grief, mourning.

? Questions

1. Why do you think Derek Mahon wrote 'After the Titanic'? Do you think it a more effective title than the original one, 'Bruce Ismay's Soliloquy'? Give reasons for your answer.

2. How would you describe Bruce Ismay's life after the Titanic? How does the poem convey loneliness and misery?

3. Does this poem succeed in making you view the Titanic disaster differently? Why?

4. How does the speaker here view the other passengers on the Titanic? Quote from the poem to support your answer.

5. Comment on the line 'I turned to ice.' Why is it particularly effective in this instance?

6. How is nature portrayed in this poem? Look at phrases such as 'the tide leaves broken toys,' 'flowers of May,' 'Late light of June.'

7. Eamon Grennan, commenting on this poem, says that Bruce Ismay delivers a 'distraught yet dignified' confession to the world. Would you agree with this description. Give reasons for your answer.

8. Consider the shape of this poem on the page. Most of Mahon's poems use a straight, left-hand, vertical line. Only eight poems in his *Collected Poems* (including 'After the Titanic' and 'Ecclesiastes') follow an irregular left-hand pattern. Why do you think Mahon opts for it here?

Ecclesiastes

God, you could grow to love it, God-fearing, God-
   chosen purist little puritan that,
for all your wiles and smiles, you are (the
   dank churches, the empty streets,
the shipyard silence, the tied-up swings) and   5
   shelter your cold heart from the heat
of the world, from woman-inquisition, from the
   bright eyes of children. Yes, you could
wear black, drink water, nourish a fierce zeal
   with locusts and wild honey, and not   10
feel called upon to understand and forgive
   but only to speak with a bleak
afflatus, and love the January rains when they
   darken the dark doors and sink hard
into the Antrim hills, the bog meadows, the heaped   15
   graves of your fathers. Bury that red
bandana and stick, that banjo; this is your
   country, close one eye and be king.
Your people await you, their heavy washing
   flaps for you in the housing estates —   20
a credulous people. God, you could do it, God
   help you, stand on a corner stiff
with rhetoric, promising nothing under the sun.

Glossary

Title Ecclesiastes – *Old Testament* book also known as The Preacher which begins 'The words of the Preacher, the son of David, king in Jerusalem. Vanity of vanities, says the Preacher, vanity of vanities! All is vanity.' The main theme of the *Book of Ecclesiastes* is the worthlessness and vanity of human life. 'Ecclesiastes' is a version of the Hebrew 'Qoheleth' meaning 'The Preacher' or 'a speaker in an assembly.' The most famous passage in Ecclesiastes begins 'For everything there is a season, and a time for every matter under heaven: a time to be born and a time to die . . . '

The phrase 'under the sun', which is also the closing words of the poem, recurs numerous times throughout the book. In the *Field Day* anthology this title is glossed, 'The poem imagines God as a "black (extreme) Protestant" preacher.

Line 2 purist: one who insists on pureness, cleanness.

Line 2 puritan: one who practises extreme strictness in morals or religion.

Line 3 wiles: tricks, cunning ways.

Line 4 dank: unpleasantly cold and damp.

Line 5 tied-up swings: In Northern Ireland Protestant-controlled town councils refused to open children's playgrounds on Sundays; it was considered inappropriate for children to play on the Sabbath.

Line 7 woman-inquisition: the kinds of questions women ask.

Line 9 zeal: fervour, earnestness.

Line 10 locusts and wild honey: in the Gospel of Saint Matthew (3:4) we are told that John the Baptist had
a raiment of camel's hair and a leathern girdle about his loins; his meat was locusts and wild honey.

Line 13 afflatus: divine impulse, inspiration.

Line 17 bandana: coloured handkerchief/neckerchief; 'that red/bandana and stick, that banjo' represent a flamboyant, bohemian way of life.

Line 18 close one eye: echoing, perhaps, *'In regione caecorum rex est luscus*:
In the country of the blind the one-eyed man in king' – Erasmus, Dutch Christian humanist (?1469–1536).

Line 21 credulous: apt to believe without sufficient evidence, unsuspecting.

Line 23 rhetoric: persuasive, declamatory expression.

> This poem was published in July 1968 under the title 'Ecclesiastes Country' and in 1970, the year he left Northern Ireland to work in London, Mahon published a pamphlet, *Ecclesiastes*, which contained the poem called 'Ecclesiastes.'

? Questions

1. What could you 'grow to love', according to the speaker? Who is the 'God-chosen purist little puritan'? How would you describe the speaker's tone in the opening lines?

2. Pick out those details which you think best evoke the world of the poem. Are they attractive or unattractive?

3. Is this a grim poem, do you think? Do you think that the poet is exaggerating? Give reasons for your answer.

4. What do the 'red bandana and stick, that banjo' represent? Why are they rejected? Who is saying to 'bury' them?

5. Is this, in your opinion, a harsh or humorous portrait of the poet's native place? Do you think that the speaker is being ironic when he urges himself to become one of the tribe?

6. What do you understand by 'Your people await you' (line 19)? Is it welcoming or threatening? Give reasons for your answer.

7. Do you think that the poem reveals the strengths and weaknesses of the Protestant identity? Is it possible to say what the poet intended?

As It Should Be

We hunted the mad bastard
Through bog, moorland, rock, to the starlit west
And gunned him down in a blind yard
Between ten sleeping lorries
And an electricity generator.   5

Let us hear no idle talk
Of the moon in the Yellow River;
The air blows softer since his departure.

Since his tide-burial during school hours
Our children have known no bad dreams.   10
Their cries echo lightly along the coast.

This is as it should be.
They will thank us for it when they grow up
To a world with method in it.

Glossary

Line 3 blind: dead-end.

Line 7 Yellow River: the Hwang-Ho in China? – so called from the yellow earth that it carries in suspension. Denis Johnston's play *The Moon in the Yellow River* refers to Lo Pi, the Chinese poet, attempting to catch the yellow moon's reflection in the river. The image is an emotional, imaginative one. In that same play, set in Ireland in 1927, a character attempts to blow up an electricity generator and is shot dead. Perhaps Mahon is alluding to it here.

Line 14 method in it: an allusion, perhaps, to *Hamlet* Act 2, Scene ii 201 – 'Though this be madness, yet there is method in it.'

? Questions

1. Who do you think the 'We', 'They', 'us' are in this poem?

2. How would you describe the speaker's tone? Is there any sympathy for the murdered man? Does the speaker reveal a sensitive side at any stage? Is the absence of pity in the closing three lines chilling or reassuring?

3. What do the setting/landscape details contribute to the poem?

4. The poem does not reveal the reasons why the man was hunted and gunned down. Do you think the poem is more effective or less effective because of this?

5. Is this a poem promoting a certain mind-set? Give reasons for your answer. Why do you think the speaker uses the word 'method' in the final line?

6. Is this poem deliberately too extreme? Why might the poet have chosen such a viewpoint?

7. Is there any connection, in your opinion, between this poem and the other poems by Derek Mahon on your course?

8. Does this poem combine the public and the private? In what way can it be read as a political poem?

DEREK MAHON

A Disused Shed in Co. Wexford

Let them not forget us, the weak souls among the asphodels.
— Seferis, Mythistorema

(for J. G. Farrell)

Even now there are places where a thought might grow —
Peruvian mines, worked out and abandoned
To a slow clock of condensation,
An echo trapped for ever, and a flutter
Of wild flowers in the lift-shaft,   5
Indian compounds where the wind dances
And a door bangs with diminished confidence,
Lime crevices behind rippling rain-barrels,
Dog corners for bone burials;
And in a disused shed in Co. Wexford,   10

Deep in the grounds of a burnt-out hotel,
Among the bathtubs and the washbasins
A thousand mushrooms crowd to a keyhole.
This is the one star in their firmament
Or frames a star within a star.   15
What should they do there but desire?
So many days beyond the rhododendrons
With the world waltzing in its bowl of cloud,
They have learnt patience and silence
Listening to the rooks querulous in the high wood.   20

They have been waiting for us in a foetor
Of vegetable sweat since civil war days,
Since the gravel-crunching, interminable departure
Of the expropriated mycologist.
He never came back, and light since then   25
Is a keyhole rusting gently after rain.
Spiders have spun, flies dusted to mildew
And once a day, perhaps, they have heard something —
A trickle of masonry, a shout from the blue
Or a lorry changing gear at the end of the lane.   30

323

There have been deaths, the pale flesh flaking
Into the earth that nourished it;
And nightmares, born of these and the grim
Dominion of stale air and rank moisture.
Those nearest the door grow strong —   35
'Elbow room! Elbow room!'
The rest, dim in a twilight of crumbling
Utensils and broken pitchers, groaning
For their deliverance, have been so long
Expectant that there is left only the posture.   40

A half century, without visitors, in the dark
Poor preparation for the cracking lock
And creak of hinges; magi, moonmen,
Powdery prisoners of the old regime,
Web-throated, stalked like triffids, racked by drought   45
And insomnia, only the ghost of a scream
At the flash-bulb firing-squad we wake them with
Shows there is life yet in their feverish forms.
Grown beyond nature now, soft food for worms,
They lift frail heads in gravity and good faith.   50

They are begging us, you see, in their wordless way,
To do something, to speak on their behalf
Or at least not to close the door again.
Lost people of Treblinka and Pompeii!
'Save us, save us,' they seem to say,   55
'Let the god not abandon us
Who have come so far in darkness and in pain.
We too had our lives to live.
You with your light meter and relaxed itinerary,
Let not our naive labours have been in vain!'   60

Handwritten annotations:

- "these stanzas are more obviously referencing pain and suffering"
- "humanises the mushrooms"
- "assonance & alliteration / verbal music"
- "deaths" (circled)
- "survival of the fittest / ruthless"
- "entrapment, claustrophobic"
- "beautiful imagery"
- "reminds us of the setting → shed"
- "deliverance" (circled)
- "biblical salvation/redemption / more than just freedom"
- "N.B punctuation slows down"
- "french revolution?"
- "frozen in time"
- "'strange' 'other' 'alien'"
- "onomatopoeia"
- "shift in perspective: POV of the people entering the shed"
- "copious references to other times/history"
- "simple gesture / optimistic"
- "tone of supplication (sympathy)"
- "weakness / suffering"
- "begging us" (underlined)
- "silent understanding"
- "simple language — easy to understand"
- "caesura"
- "unequivocal references (definite - named places)"
- "all the different strands of the poem come together"
- "we don't actually hear them speak"
- "indirectly writing about the Troubles"
- "tone of urgency"
- "very simple, monosyllabic language"
- "meter" (circled) "relaxed itinerary" (circled)
- "tourists / our inability to pause and reflect"
- "elicits a deep emotive response -dignity, nobility / formal / lack of anger despite their suffering - they have kept their faith - humanity at its best"
- "criticism of his own work - poets use metres. Do his words do the past justice or is it superficial"

Glossary

Epigraph: 'Let them not forget us, the weak souls among the asphodels' is taken from the closing lines of the Greek poet George Seferis's poem 'Mythistorema', which was published in 1935. The asphodel is a type of lily and is particularly associated with death and the underworld in Greek legend. Asphodels were planted on graves.

Dedication: English novelist J. G. Farrell (1935–1979), whose novels include *The Lung* (1965), *Troubles* (1970), *The Siege of Krishnapur* (1973) and *The Singapore Grip* (1978), was a friend of Mahon's and this poem was partly inspired by an image from his work. In the closing pages of *Troubles* a body is found in a potting-shed in the grounds of the Majestic Hotel – 'the shed was a damp and draughty place, smelling of vegetation'; Lavinia Greacen, in her *Biography of J.G. Farrell*. says that the poem was inspired by *The Lung* not *Troubles*. Farrell moved to West Cork and drowned in Bantry Bay while fishing off rocks in 1979.

Line 6 compounds: – a word probably from Malayalam '*kampong*' meaning enclosures, system of housing in India and China where workers live.

Line 11 the grounds of a burnt-out hotel: in J.G. Farrell's novel *Troubles* the Majestic Hotel burns down in the closing pages.

Line 13 crowd to a keyhole: a marvellous image and an example of poetic license; the image is inaccurate in that mushrooms grow in the dark and do not respond to light.

Line 20 querulous: complaining.

Line 21 foetor: strong, stinking smell.

Line 22 civil war days: the war fought in Ireland in the 1920s between those who were pro- and anti-Treaty.

Line 23 interminable: endless.

Line 24 expropriated: dispossessed.

Line 24 mycologist: one who studies fungi.

Line 38 pitchers: vessels, usually of earthenware (in an earlier version Mahon wrote 'flower-pots').

Line 43 magi: wise men. Perhaps the poet speaks of mushrooms as magi here because the three wise men in the *Bible* followed the light of the star just as the mushrooms view the light in the keyhole.

Line 43 moonmen: the astronaut wears white and its globed headgear is shaped like a mushroom? Both magi and moonmen are associated with visitations.

Line 45 triffids: in John Wyndham's (1903–1969) novel *The Day of the Triffids* (1951), triffids are a race of menacing plants, possessed of locomotor ability and a poisonous sting, which threaten to overrun the world. As an image 'triffids' implies anything invasive or rapid in development.

Line 54 Treblinka: a concentration camp in Poland where the Jews of the Warsaw ghetto were exterminated by the Nazis. In *The Paris Review Interview* (1994) Mahon speaks of the difficulty of writing about conditions in the North of Ireland: 'You couldn't take sides. In a kind of way, I still can't'; but Mahon adds, 'It's possible for me to write about the dead of Treblinka and Pompeii: included in that are the dead of Dungiven and Magherafelt. But I've never been able to write directly about it.'

Line 54 Pompeii: in A.D. 79 Pompeii, a small Roman city, was destroyed when the nearby volcano, Vesuvius, erupted and showered the city with ash and cinder. One citizen in ten was poisoned by fumes or burned to death. The city was buried and in the 1700s archaeologists uncovered it, finding hollows in the hardened ash caused by the decayed bodies of people and animals killed in the eruption.

Line 59 itinerary: a planned journey usually with tourists in mind.

Line 60 naive: innocent, simple.

'A Disused Shed in Co. Wexford' was published in *The Listener* in 1973 and was first published in book form in *The Snow Party*, Mahon's third collection, in 1975.

In *The Oxford Companion to Twentieth-Century Poetry*, Neil Corcoran writes of how in 'A Disused Shed in Co. Wexford' the plight of the North of Ireland is seen in a context of wider contemporary breakdown and comments on how Mahon discovers in the image of the shed 'an unforgettable emblem for Irish historical suffering in what begins as the almost humorous fantasy of a "thousand mushrooms" crowding to the keyhole of a shed as the poet-photographer opens its door.' For Terence Brown it is a poem that explores 'the crisis and the catastrophe of an age.'

Seamus Deane, writing in 1992, says that 'A Disused Shed in Co. Wexford' is a poem that 'heartbreakingly dwells on and gives voice to all those peoples and civilisations that have been lost and/or destroyed. Since it is set in Ireland, with all the characteristic features of an Irish "Big House" ruin, it speaks with a special sharpness to the present moment and the fear, rampant in Northern Ireland, of communities that fear they too might perish and be lost with none to speak for them.'

Seamus Heaney thinks this poem 'is now simply part of our culture's dialogue with itself, and that "our" extends well beyond those who live in Ireland to include every individual conscious of the need to live something like an examined life in a dark time. The poem's intellectual furor means that it cannot quite yield in its belief that "our naive labours have been in vain," and yet, as in all poetic achievements, there is a residually transcendent trust implicit in the very radiance and consonance and integrity of the poem itself.'

? Questions

1. The poem describes the plight of a 'thousand mushrooms' in a disused shed in Co. Wexford. What does the title suggest? Why do you think Mahon chose that title? When and how does the reader sense that it is a poem about so much more?

2. How would you describe the atmosphere of the opening stanza? Which words in particular best convey that atmosphere? The speaker mentions places as far apart and as different as Peru and Wexford in this stanza. What, in your opinion, is the effect of this?

3. Why do you think the speaker begins with the words 'Even now'? What do those words reveal to us of the speaker? What do you understand by the phrase 'a thought might grow'?

4. Comment on 'worked out and abandoned', 'burnt-out.' How might these details be significant? How do the images in the poem further the poet's theme?

5. What feeling does the speaker most associate with the mushrooms? Why do you think mushrooms are an appropriate image in this context?

6. 'Time plays an important part in this poem.' Would you agree with this view? Support the points you make by referring to or quoting from the text.

7. The speaker refers to 'us' in line 21 and to the 'expropriated mycologist' in line 24. Who is being spoken of here, do you think?

8. Consider 'A Disused Shed in Co. Wexford' as a political poem. How effective is it? How would you describe the speaker's stance? What is his view of historical suffering?

9. Is this an optimistic or a pessimistic poem or is it a mixture of both? Give reasons for your answer.

10. Stanzas 4–6 focus on struggle and longing. Which particular details evoke these best, do you think? How is a sense of oppression conveyed in this section?

11. Why are 'wordless', 'Treblinka' and 'Pompeii' key ideas in the closing stanza? What moral obligation is being conveyed here? Do you think the poet succeeds in convincing the reader of something important? Explain.

12. For Eamon Grennan this poem 'inscribes a journey from silence to speech.' Listen to the silences and sounds in the poem and comment on their significance.

13. This poem is considered one of the major Irish poems of the twentieth century. Can you suggest reasons why?

The Chinese Restaurant in Portrush

Before the first visitor comes the spring
Softening the sharp air of the coast
In time for the first seasonal 'invasion.'
Today the place is as it might have been,
Gentle and almost hospitable. A girl   5
Strides past the Northern Counties Hotel,
Light-footed, swinging a book-bag,
And the doors that were shut all winter
Against the north wind and the sea-mist
Lie open to the street, where one   10
By one the gulls go window-shopping
And an old wolfhound dozes in the sun.

While I sit with my paper and prawn chow mein
Under a framed photograph of Hong Kong
The proprietor of the Chinese restaurant   15
Stands at the door as if the world were young,
Watching the first yacht hoist a sail
— An ideogram on sea-cloud — and the light
Of heaven upon the hills of Donegal;
And whistles a little tune, dreaming of home.   20

Glossary

Title Portrush – a seaside resort on the north Antrim coast.

Line 13 prawn chow mein: fried noodles with prawn.

Line 18 ideogram: in Chinese writing a character symbolising an idea – a symbol that stands not for a word or sound but for the thing itself directly; Mahon imagines that for the Chinese man the yacht in the distance is like an ideogram.

> This is a revised version. Mahon made some slight changes in this poem for his *Collected Poems*: e.g. 'visitor' was 'holidaymakers'; 'mountains' became 'hills.'

? Questions

1. How would you describe the atmosphere in this poem? Which details in the poem capture that atmosphere? Is it significant that the owner of the Chinese Restaurant is a long way from home?

2. How does the poet capture a sense of beginning? Pick out the words and phrases which convey freshness and beginnings.

3. What does this poem reveal to us about the speaker?

4. In the second stanza, the poet focuses on the proprietor of the restaurant and imagines his mood. What does the speaker see which allows him do this?

5. What do you like best about this poem?

6. Place is important here and in many of Derek Mahon's poems. Pick three poems by Mahon and comment on how the poet evokes a sense of place.

7. The Chinese Restaurant in Portrush' focuses on ordinary lives of ordinary people in the North of Ireland at a time of civil unrest and sectarian violence. Why do you think Mahon chose to write a poem which make no mention of the Northern Troubles?

written during the troubles

form : 3 10-line stanzas

theme of history (past & present)

lack of communication

Rathlin

reflective, pensive, honest

tight consonants — dash conveys

A long time since the last scream cut short – the life cut short

every silence suggested by sibilance

Then an unnatural silence; and then — caesura comma conveys the silence

A natural silence, slowly broken

By the shearwater, by the sporadic   Meditative

we cannot forget

Conversation of crickets, the bleak   the world of nature goes on despite the loss of human life – nature is restorative

Reminder of a metaphysical wind.

fatigue

Ages of this, till the report

Of an outboard motor at the pier   past mahon is sensitised to the past – suffering and vulnerability

spiritual peace

Shatters the dream-time and we land

As if we were the first visitors here.   sanctuary   mahon envisages peace

northern Ireland → Ireland is a fractured island

The whole island a sanctuary where amazed

by using latin & greek words, mahon shows his respect for the past

Oneiric species whistle and chatter,   conversation = lack of communication during the troubles

Evacuating rock-face and cliff-top.

Cerulean distance, an oceanic haze –   mesmeric and enchanting

Nothing but sea-smoke to the ice-cap

And the odd somnolent freighter.

present

many references to sleep dreams → calm sanctuary

Bombs doze in the housing estates

But here they are through with history –

sleep
oneiric
haze
somnolent
doze
dream-time

Custodians of a lone light which repeats

One simple statement to the turbulent sea.   the sea is always conveyed as an uneasy place in mahon's poetry

communication

naming him makes it personal

A long time since the unspeakable violence –   future

Since Somhairle Buí, powerless on the mainland,

Heard the screams of the Rathlin women   this poem has a slow, meditative, mesmeric rhythm.

Borne to him, seconds later, upon the wind.

Only the cry of the shearwater   brings us back to the present

And the roar of the outboard motor

Disturb the singular peace. Spray-blind,   blind, anxiety lack of direction

We leave here the infancy of the race,

Unsure among the pitching surfaces   sense of uncertainty

Whether the future lies before us or behind.   will history repeat itself?

Line numbers: 5, 10, 15, 20, 25, 30

Mahon's poetry is full of reflection

Glossary

Title Rathlin – Rathlin Island, Antrim. In Queen Elizabeth I's reign, when the people of North Antrim were fighting the forces of the English crown, they sent all their old people, women and children to Rathlin for protection. But in 1575 the English fleet, three frigates commanded by Captain Francis Drake, and troops under Captain John Norris, under orders from Walter Devereux, Earl of Essex, sailed to Rathlin and killed everyone there, leaving the place uninhabited for many years. Roy Foster, in *Modern Ireland 1600–1972,* says that Essex's massacre on Rathlin was carried out with a 'grisly sportiveness.'

Line 1 cut short: was silenced.

Line 4 shearwater: long-winged sea-bird.

Line 4 sporadic: occurring here and there, now and then; scattered.

Line 6 metaphysical: supernatural, fanciful?

Line 9 dream-time: a time of peace, no trouble (an Australian term, dream-time or alcheringa, meaning 'Golden Age' in the mythology of some Australian Aboriginals).

Line 11 sanctuary: a nature reserve, (a place of refuge; a holy place); Rathlin Island is home to multitudes of sea birds – guillemots, razorbills, puffins, kittiwakes, gulls.

Line 12 Oneiric: belonging to dreams.

Line 14 Cerulean: sky-blue.

Line 16 somnolent: sleepy.

Line 16 freighter: cargo-carrying boat.

Line 19 Custodians: guardians.

Line 20 turbulent: stormy.

Line 22 Somhairle Buí: also spelt Somhairle Buidh(e) – fair-haired Charles – the famous Sorley Boy MacDonald , a member of the powerful MacDonald clan who ruled over what is now County Antrim.. Originally from Scotland, Sorley Boy, 'fierce in war and wily in council', made Ireland his home. Cyril Falls, in his book *Elizabethan Irish Wars*, says that, following the Rathlin massacre, Sorley Boy, 'stung to passion, advanced to Carrickfergus and burnt the wretched town .˙. . Sorley Boy, who had gone almost crazy over the tragedy of Rathlin.' Rathlin was the scene of more than one massacre in the 16th century. The one relating to Somhairle Buí took place in 1557 and Somhairle Buí, it is said, heard the cries in his castle on the mainland.

Questions

1. How does Mahon convey a sense of past and present in the opening stanza? Look particularly at 'last scream', 'unnatural', 'natural', 'first visitors.' What do you think the poet means by 'dream-time' (line 9)? Whose dream-time is he referring to?

2. Why might the word 'sanctuary' be ironic in this instance? Which detail in stanza two connects past atrocities on Rathlin with contemporary violence in the North of Ireland?

3. Which details in the poem create a sense of timelessness and natural beauty? Is it possible to say from this poem how the speaker views history?

4. 'A long time' is repeated. What is the effect of this? How would you describe the poet's mood in the closing lines of the poem? What do you think is meant by 'the infancy of the race' (line 28)?

5. Identify and list the different sounds in the poem and write a note on their significance.

6. 'Mahon writes on big themes in an effective and indirect way.' Would you agree with this statement? Support the points you make with reference to the text.

7. 'Day Trip to Donegal' and 'Rathlin' both describe journeys and their effect. Examine the similarities and the differences between the two poems. Which, in your opinion, in the more interesting of the two?

[handwritten: key element of Mahon's poetry = solitary male figures]

Antarctica

[handwritten: Villanelle = strict form]

(for Richard Ryan)

[handwritten: Gives Oates a voice — his real words makes him human]

'I am just going outside and may be some time.' *a*
The others nod, pretending not to know. *b*
At the heart of the ridiculous, the sublime. *a*

[handwritten: tight rhyming scheme]

[handwritten: confining, remorseless rhyming makes us feel trapped]

He leaves them reading and begins to climb, *a*
Goading his ghost into the howling snow; *b*
He is just going outside and may be some time. *a* 5

The tent recedes beneath its crust of rime *a*
And frostbite is replaced by vertigo: *b*
At the heart of the ridiculous, the sublime. *a*

[handwritten: callous space reflection]
[handwritten: perturbing = unsettling]
[handwritten: is suicide for the sake of others noble or ignoble?]

[handwritten: slight unravelling in the tight structure as Oates approaches his death]

[handwritten: existential questions]
[handwritten: reflection]

Need we consider it some sort of crime, *a* 10
This numb self-sacrifice of the weakest? No, *b*
He is just going outside and may be some time— *a*

[handwritten: N.B pause emphasises that he may be some time]

[handwritten: enjambment]
[handwritten: Oats's death affects others]
[handwritten: is he the weakest or the strongest?]

In fact, for ever. Solitary enzyme, *a*
Though the night yield no glimmer there will glow, *b*
At the heart of the ridiculous, the sublime. *a*

[handwritten: use of the superlative]
[handwritten: drags out the moment of his death] 15

[handwritten: cesura not in the middle of the line, unsettling]
[handwritten: restrained / dignified]
[handwritten: ridiculous — people see a light before death]

He takes leave of the earthly pantomime *a*
Quietly, knowing it is time to go. *b*
'I am just going outside and may be some time.' *a*

[handwritten: rhythmic/hollow]
[handwritten: tragi-comic man is both noble and absurd]

At the heart of the ridiculous, the sublime. *a*

[handwritten: Pantomime Quietly = contradiction]
[handwritten: Repetition go where? afterlife!]

Glossary

Title Antarctica – the Antarctic is the south polar region; arktos in Greek means 'bear', which gives us 'arctic'; 'anti' or 'opposite' and arktos gives 'antarctic.' The great South Pole expedition at the beginning of the twentieth century was captained by Robert Scott who, together with Edward Wilson, Lawrence Oates, H. R. Bowers and Edgar Evans, reached the South Pole on 17 January 1912, only to discover that a Norwegian expedition under Roald Amundsen had beaten them by a month. None of the five ever made it home. Evans and Oates died first and the other members of the team perished in late March 1912. Their bodies and diaries were found by a search party eight months later.

Line 1 'I am just going outside and may be some time': last words recorded by Robert Scott in his Diary and attributed to Lawrence Oates (1880–1912), who was one of the party of five to reach the South Pole in 1912. On the return journey illness and blizzards caused severe delay. Oates was lamed by frostbite and, convinced that his condition would delay his fellow-explorers' success, walked out into the storm. He deliberately sacrificed his life to help his comrades' chance of survival. On a cairn erected in the Antarctic in November 1912 is the epigraph: 'Hereabouts died a very gallant gentleman, Captain L.E. G. Oates of the Inniskilling Dragoons. In March 1912, returning from the Pole, he walked willingly to his death in a blizzard to try and save his comrades, beset by hardships.' Rory Brennan comments that 'Captain Oates's stiff-upper-lippery in the face of Antarctic starvation is perhaps the best known quote from the first decade of the twentieth century.'

Line 3 sublime: elevated in thought or tone, lofty. 'From the sublime to the ridiculous' is a well-known phrase and is used to describe a movement from one state to an opposite one, where sublime refers to a heightened state, ridiculous to a banal one. Tom Paine in his *Age of Reason* wrote: 'The sublime and the ridiculous are often so nearly related that it is difficult to class them separately. One step above the sublime makes the ridiculous, and one step above the ridiculous makes the sublime again.'

In 'Antarctica', Mahon shows how Lawrence Oates's apparently ridiculous words and actions achieve a heightened, courageous quality.

Line 5 Goading: urging.

Line 7 rime: ice.

Line 8 vertigo: dizziness.   *Enzymes affects others*

Line 13 enzyme: the dictionary defines enzyme as 'any one of a large class of protein substances produced by living cells'; here, Mahon uses 'solitary enzyme' as a metaphor for Oates.

Line 16 the earthly pantomime: life as a showy spectacle with clowns.

The poem is written in the form of a villanelle – a poem of five three-line stanzas and a concluding quatrain. It has the following rhyming scheme: aba aba aba aba aba abaa. 'Antarctica,' according to Derek Mahon, is a feminist poem. Nuala Ní Dhomhnaill says that 'it chronicles the moment when the more-than-faintly-ridiculous heroic male ego snuffs it. The rigidity of the metre and the constant repetitions are a very symptom of the state of the soul. The psyche is an ice-box, a house in mid-winter with the heat turned off. In this state you wander about, metaphorically, in furs and highboots, in a frozen stupor, stamping your feet and repeating yourself constantly. The pipes, the conduits of emotion, are frozen solid, rigid like the lines of the poem. Thus for me 'Antarctica' is the supreme example of a formal poem that is not merely emptily so, but where the metre and strict rhyming scheme play an essential part in building up the reality enacted.'

? Questions

1. The glossary offers the background to the poem. What would you consider the poem's central theme?

2. The poem tells of bitter hardship. Examine how this is described. Which words, in your opinion, best capture the Antarctic landscape and the men's mood? How is death viewed in this poem?

3. Why do you think the speaker here thinks that there is 'At the heart of the ridiculous, the sublime'? What is ridiculous? What is sublime?

4. What is the effect of the very regular rhyme scheme and the repetition?

5. Is this a dramatic poem, do you think, or has the poet played down the dramatic qualities?

6. In 'After the Titanic' Derek Mahon portrays Bruce Ismay. Compare and contrast his portrait of Ismay with his portrait of Lawrence Oates in 'Antarctica.' Why are such figures interesting, do you think?

7. This poem has been described as an evocation of 'the cold, impenetrable regions of the psyche.' What do you understand by that? Would you agree with this interpretation.

Handwritten annotations: septec – 7 line poem – unusual · dramatic monologue quality · secrets · communal/inclusive · caesura · conversational quality · pause/reflection · theme of the past – all Mahon poems · inclusion/by communities · relationships · pathetic fallacy · powerful alliteration (and sibilance) · presence of the sea · Irish life: church and farming · n.b reflection · celebratory/kinetic energy · light/soft · he has shed the weight of the past · affluence · wealth · musical · full stop in the middle → contemplate

Kinsale

The kind of rain we knew is a thing of the past –
deep-delving, dark, deliberate you would say,
browsing on spire and bogland; but today
our sky-blue slates are steaming in the sun,
our yachts tinkling and dancing in the bay   5
like racehorses. We contemplate at last
shining windows, a future forbidden to no one.

Glossary

Title Kinsale: Cionn tSáile; Head of the Sea; fishing town in Co. Cork; Mahon lived in Kinsale for a time in the 1980s. The town has an interesting historical past, notably its occupation by the Spanish in 1601 under Don Juan d'Aguila. The Lord Deputy Mountjoy, with 12,000 men, then besieged the town and, though the Irish from the North under O'Donnell, Tyrone and O'Neill came to the aid of the Spaniards, Mountjoy won. Mahon makes no mention of Kinsale's historic past in this short lyric poem but past, present and future are key ideas here.

The rhyme scheme is abbcbac

Questions

1. What makes this a wonderful, musical and optimistic poem?

2. The speaker here uses 'we' and 'our.' What is the effect of this?

3. Pick out your favourite image from the poem and justify your choice.

4. Examine how the poet uses contrast between, say, images of dark rain on spire and bogland and yachts tinkling and dancing in the bay like racehorses.

5. Is this a poem about Ireland's past and present?

6. Where in the poem is a change of tone evident? What is the effect of the final sentence?

7. Look at the end rhymes. What do the rhymes 'the past' and 'at last' invite the reader to focus on?

8. If you were to paint this poem which colours would you need? Which colours would dominate?

Rathlin Island

General Questions

A. 'In Derek Mahon's poetry past and present play a very important part.' Discuss this view of the poems of Derek Mahon on your course. Support your discussion by quotation from or reference to the poems you have studied.

B. 'Mahon in his poetry has a very observant eye and a sympathetic nature.' Would you agree with this estimation of the poems by Derek Mahon on your course? Support your view by relevant quotation or reference.

C. What would you see as the principal preoccupations of Derek Mahon, as revealed to us in his poetry? Support your discussion by quotation from or reference to the poems you have studied.

D. 'Derek Mahon's poems focus on themes large and small but always from an individual perspective.' Discuss this view and support the points you make with relevant quotation or reference.

E. 'Mahon's poetry is remarkable for its striking and unforgettable imagery.' Would you agree with this statement? Support your point of view by relevant quotation or reference.

F. Write a short essay in which you outline the reasons why reading Derek Mahon's poetry is a rewarding and worthwhile experience. Support your discussion by reference to or quotation from the poems you have studied.

G. Discuss the importance and significance of place in the poetry of Derek Mahon. In your answer you should quote from or refer to the poems by Mahon on your course.

H. 'Derek Mahon in his poetry is extraordinarily visual but, above all else, he is a poet of ideas.' Would you agree with this view? In your answer you should support the points you make with relevant quotation or reference.

Critical Commentary

Grandfather

Mahon is a poet who values traditional poetic forms and techniques such as structure and rhyme. 'Grandfather' is a sonnet, a nostalgic lyric, with a regular rhyming scheme in the octave (abba abba) and a less regular pattern of rhyme and slant-rhyme in the sestet (cd cc cd). The speaker is remembering how his grandfather survived an accident and injury but no specific details are given. He was brought home on a stretcher but the image of being brought in 'on a stretcher from the world' suggests a vast world beyond the house where the grandfather will now recover. His personality is captured in the two contradictory words 'Wounded but humorous' and these suggest a man who is capable of making the most of a bad situation; 'and he soon recovered' suggests his determination.

The 'Boiler-rooms, row upon row of gantries' in line three belong to the grandfather's world of work at Harland and Wolff, where he was a foreman. But the speaker imagines that the world of the shipyard fades away and his grandfather returns to his own private world of memory and childhood:

> Boiler-rooms, row upon row of gantries rolled
> Away to reveal the landscape of a childhood
> Only he can recapture.

Here the present is contrasted with the past. It is as if the 'Boiler-rooms' and 'row upon row of gantries' represent a harsh, confining world, whereas the words 'rolled/ Away' suggest the magical, expansive world of childhood. His early years are referred to as 'landscape', thus highlighting a difference between the enclosed, mechanised world of work and the broad expanse and ease of boyhood, a private, unique world known only to the poet's grandfather.

For the remainder of the poem, Mahon describes his grandfather pottering around the house, his habits and his personality. The poet moves from dawn to dusk – he is up at six and busy, and at night he secures the house. He is happy to repair and mend and to make noise – 'banging round the house like a four-year-old' – and is cautious and careful after dark, ensuring that the door is bolted and the clock wound. And yet the speaker makes several references to his grandfather's elusive, "unget-at-able", mysterious self. He is 'Never there when you call'; he is 'as cute as they come' and that

> Nothing escapes him; he escapes us all.

Though very much a definite and noisy presence ('banging', 'thumping'), he is nonetheless difficult to pin down. When he goes to sleep 'his light goes out', but there's an energy within him that seems to shine.

The poem celebrates the mystery of the individual and the fact that the individual, in this instance, is an ordinary man in an ordinary place. This reminds us that everyone is an individual and mysterious in one's own way.

Day Trip to Donegal

This poem tells of a four-hour trip from Belfast to Donegal and back again in the same day. The speaker does not describe the morning journey and the poem begins with their arrival in early afternoon. Two of the poem's five stanzas focus on Donegal, the remaining three on the journey home and Donegal's haunting effect. The opening is matter-of-fact. There is a sense of contrast between the expanse of sea and coastline and the cramped, stiff bodies after the car journey:

> We reached the sea in early afternoon,
> Climbed stiffly out; there were things to be done,
> Clothes to be picked up, friends to be seen.

The journey seems functional, necessary, but then there comes the realisation that this place is special, beautiful, different and striking:

> As ever, the nearby hills were a deeper green
> Than anywhere in the world, and the grave
> Grey of the sea the grimmer in that enclave.

The initial impression is one of light and colour but, though beautiful ('deeper green'), there is also something unattractive and grim ('grave/ Grey of the sea') about the place. The special green highlights the greyness of the sea.

Stanza two moves from the general towards the particular, from the landscape and seascape to the fishing boats and, more particularly still, to the 'writhing' and 'flopping' fish:

> Down at the pier the boats gave up their catch,
> A writhing glimmer of fish

but the Belfast-born Mahon not only has a fine eye for detail but he thinks practical thoughts – 'they fetch/ Ten times as much in the city as here.' Though the poet marvels that there are plenty of fish in the sea ('And still the fish come in year after year'), he thinks of the netted fish that have been caught as suffering:

> Herring and mackerel, flopping about the deck
> In attitudes of agony and heartbreak.

This is important for it shows us Mahon's intense awareness of the many, the afflicted, the sufferers. (Originally 'Day Trip to Donegal' contained the following stanza but it was later omitted: 'How could we hope to make them understand?/ Theirs is a sea-mind, mindless upon land/ And dead. Their systematic genocide/ (Nothing remarkable that millions died)/ To us is a necessity/ For ours are land-minds, mindless in the sea.' In his later poem, 'A Disused Shed in Co. Wexford', the poet feels for the mushrooms and they in turn symbolise the oppressed.) The speaker's sympathy is evident here and he not only thinks of physical suffering ('agony') but he also imagines that the fish are suffering emotionally, that they are heartbroken.

The middle stanza announces the return journey. The sea is behind them as they drive east and the world of city and suburb is described as low-lying, sunken, sleeping and undisturbed by gale-force winds. The man-made pavements are touched by the natural world in the detail that the poet records:

> The time of year had left its mark
> On frosty pavements glistening in the dark.

In the final two stanzas the speaker tells of how he feels the sea still, but first he speaks a line that is part everyday, ordinary, and in part a deliberate literary echo:

> Give me a ring, goodnight, and so to bed . . .

The poem then becomes a different order of experience. The poet looks towards himself. The Donegal landscape and seascape, which he has seen earlier that day, seem to have stayed with him and his mood is explained in terms of sea imagery:

> That night the slow sea washed against my head,
> Performing its immeasurable erosions —
> Spilling into the skull, marbling the stones
> That spine the very harbour wall,
> Muttering its threat to villages of landfall.

Here the poet combines the real and the imagined. The sea does erode the Donegal coast but it also washes against his head. Both the land and the poet are experiencing something similar. It is through very few words ('my head', 'the skull') that Mahon turns the image of the sea washing against the land into an image of his own unease and unrest.

The experience has been an unsettling one, so much so that

> At dawn I was alone far out at sea

and the image of being "at sea" has replaced the image of 'the slow sea' washing 'against my head.' He got to bed late; he wakes early and feels helpless, lacks confidence and feels isolated. This feeling is a familiar one and yet he curses that he seems unable to prevent such moods. He does not explain why it has come about, but it would seem that it was prompted by the day trip to Donegal. The 'wind and rain' are 'vindictive' and they become symbols of life's bitter, opposing forces. At a time like this the speaker says that, though he has experienced such moments before, he constantly seems to fail to prepare for such onslaughts and to ward them off. The situation seems bleak – 'no promise of rescue' – and the poem, which began with a sense of the ordinary, ends on a dark note.

The iambic pentameter and the rhyming scheme indicate yet again Mahon's interest in the making of a poem.

After the Titanic

This poem illustrates what Eamon Grennan calls 'Mahon's belief in speech as value and as an epitome of identity.' In 'After the Titanic', Mahon does not speak in his own voice; he invents another speaker and so the story of the Titanic is told from Bruce Ismay's point of view.

The speaker begins with how he himself has been viewed and treated:

> They said I got away in a boat
> And humbled me at the inquiry

and phrases such as 'got away' and 'humbled' suggest accusation and hurt. The story is well-known but Mahon has Bruce Ismay, with great economy, summon up again the terror and commotion of that night. The cold night, Ismay's cold fear, the list of objects and the incongruous sounds of bursting boilers and jazz all create in five lines a sense of the disaster:

> I sank as far that night as any
> Hero. As I sat shivering on the dark water
> I turned to ice to hear my costly
> Life go thundering down in a pandemonium of
> Prams, pianos, sideboards, winches,
> Boilers bursting and shredded ragtime.

The 'I tell you' which introduces this confession is emphatic and pleading. Over one and a half thousand people died; Bruce Ismay was not one of these and yet he says that his life since the tragedy is a living death. The poem then focuses on the present – 'Now I hide/ In a lonely house behind the sea.' Even though he hides 'behind the sea' there is no escaping his past. The sea itself keeps reminding him; the tide leaves

> broken toys and hatboxes
> Silently at my door.

Earlier 'Prams' reminded the reader of the children aboard the Titanic; here 'broken toys' achieve a similar effect, broken reminding us further of loss.

The speaker is unable to escape the past. The beauty of the natural world, spring becoming summer, makes no difference to him and he sees himself as others see him when he says:

> my gardener
> Describes to strangers how the old man stays in bed
> On seaward mornings after nights of
> Wind, takes his cocaine and will see no one.

The speaker, Ismay, does not contradict this bleak, drugged, isolated portrait of himself and he ends the poem with an image of reliving the torment of 14 April 1912. He suffers again and again and admits that he never 'understood' 'those dim/ Lost faces' of those who drowned. The verbs are particularly effective at capturing his anguish – his soul 'screams', his heart 'breaks' and 'rolls like a stone.' The drowned that night cried out in their sorrow and lamentations. The poem's final line is the poem's shortest sentence and here Bruce Ismay asks that he be included in the lamentation of those who perished. He feels that he is part of this great expression of grief, that he wants to be part of it too.

Ecclesiastes

Derek Mahon has described himself as 'a recovering Ulster Protestant from County Down.' In this poem the speaker addresses himself and the tradition he belongs to and says that, though the serious, dour, earnest world of Northern Protestantism might not seem attractive at first, you could grow to love it. The poet, the poem suggests, could become an extreme Protestant like the people which the poem describes. Mahon depicts his fellow Northern Protestants as a God-fearing, dedicated, strict people who turn Sunday into a day of no work and no play. They praise their God in unpleasantly cold, damp churches.

The colloquial opening phrase 'God, you could grow to love it' is an abrupt, immediate expression and catches the poet's ambivalent, uneasy relationship with his religious background. It is also blasphemous according to strict religious practice: he is taking the Lord's name in vain. Here the speaker expresses surprise and astonishment in tones that border on harshness and exasperation.

Mahon admits that he is a:

> God-fearing, God-
> chosen purist little puritan

even though his 'wiles and smiles' might suggest otherwise, he also admits that he could become an extreme, fanatical, religious zealot. 'You' is used seven times, 'your' is used three times and this lends the voice greater focus and emphasis: 'you could grow to love it . . . you could wear black . . . you could do it . . . '

In line six, he speaks of how the strict life of the Northern Protestant is one which, if followed, would for him involve being cut off from and giving up 'the heat of the world.' He admits to having a cold heart and that heart could be sheltered within such a regulated and strict world.

As a poet, Mahon is aware of the imaginative, emotional life and, if he were to embrace his cultural inheritance, he would turn away from

> the heat
> of the world, from woman-inquisition, from the
> bright eyes of children.

These austere, fun-rejecting people worship and adore God; the world they inhabit is controlled and hard-working. The poet ponders how he himself could become more and more like them and the consequences of this.

He tells himself that he

> could
> wear black, drink water, nourish a fierce zeal
> with locusts and wild honey, and not
> feel called upon to understand and forgive

Here, the tone is mocking the extreme fervour of these Protestants, and the image of locusts and wild honey suggests a primitive form of penance. The speaker thinks he should adopt a John the Baptist like existence when he fasted and prayed in the desert.

In such an extreme world there would be no need to worry about understanding and forgiveness. In this God-fearing religion all that is called for is divine impulse or inspiration ('afflatus') but even this is portrayed negatively when the 'afflatus' mentioned is spoken of as 'bleak.' The image he paints of himself is one where he need not feel the need to be compassionate. All he would be called upon to do would be 'to speak with a bleak/ Afflatus.' The life proposed is black, grim and bleak. There is nothing celebratory in this religion, but the poet says that he could

> love the January rains when they
> darken the dark doors and sink hard
> into the Antrim hills, the bog meadows, the heaped
> graves of your fathers.

The sense of continuity is conveyed in the reference to the 'heaped graves of your fathers', which also introduces a sense of tradition. It is as if the speaker could and should abandon the more colourful life of 'bandana' and 'banjo.'

The mention of 'red bandana', 'stick' and 'banjo' bring life and colour and music, a sense of the unusual and unconventional, to the otherwise cold, dreary world of the poem. Such objects, perhaps, could be said to symbolise the poet, the adventurer, the wanderer, but they are mentioned only to be rejected. Such objects are neither suitable nor appropriate here:

> Bury that red
> bandana and stick, that banjo

The speaker thinks that this is his country and if he closes one eye he will be king. This reference to the well-known saying that 'in the country of the blind the one-eyed man is king' implies that the people themselves are blind. And yet from the outset and throughout the poem Mahon suggests that he does belong to such a world. His fellow Northern Protestants await him:

> Your people await you, their heavy washing
> flaps for you in the housing estates –
> a credulous people.

The ordinary is once again summoned up in the unattractive detail of 'heavy washing' and 'housing estates' suggests uniformity; it is there, the speaker ironically suggests, he will find his true home. His people are ready to believe ('credulous') and his people await him; Mahon, as poet, is an outsider but he finds a reason to love their way of life. He began with the admission that

> God, you could grow to love it . . . .

and ends with a similar idea:

> God, you could do it, God
> help you, stand on a corner stiff
> with rhetoric, promising nothing under the sun.

The landscape of the poem is bleak and the weather that Mahon has chosen to describe it in, with its January rains, is also bleak. There is a suggestion of an other world to this Northern Protestant background, a world warm and colourful, and yet the closing lines imply that if he were to become one of them, his poetry would be replaced with a different kind of language – the language of religious fervour and zeal where he could end up standing on a corner spreading the word of God.

The final image of the poem highlights a stern religious life where he imagines himself 'promising nothing under the sun.' The preacher in Ecclesiastes in the *Old Testament* preaches that all is vanity. Perhaps Mahon's preacher is reminding people that human life is worthless and vain.

The tone is vital here and Eamon Grennan thinks that the 'vigorously ironic cadences' of the poem 'actively disengages him from his native place.' Mahon is writing about a world he grew up in and knows well but it is a world he has left behind. But he does not condemn it outright. Much of the detail used to describe this world is unattractive and negative ('dank', 'empty', 'tied-up', 'cold'), but he does not dwell on the attractions of an opposite or other world; instead he spends most of the poem examining how he could become involved with a world that seems at first to be unattractive.

As It Should Be

The voice here is the voice of the fanatic, and the poem describes a ruthless, brutal killing which is justified by the speaker. The voice is plural, not singular, 'we' not 'I', multiplying the fanaticism. The victim is described as a 'mad bastard' and his crime is hinted at in the reference to the children's nightmares.

The poem achieves force and energy from the outset, especially in the verbs 'hunted' and 'gunned', and the tone is unapologetic. The landscape of 'bog, moorland, rock' also suggests determination:

> We hunted the mad bastard
> Through bog, moorland, rock, to the starlit west
> And gunned him down

Even where the shooting took place is harsh and inhuman:

> in a blind yard
> Between ten sleeping lorries
> And an electricity generator.

The words 'starlit west', on their own, are magical and beautiful but in context they do not blind us from the harshness of the murder.

The remaining stanzas explain why this man had to be killed. The speaker is prepared for any objections:

> Let us hear no idle talk
> Of the moon in the Yellow River

What this image means it is difficult to say, but 'idle talk' is everything the speaker does not want. He has taken the law into his own hands and a rigorous, methodical, ordered world is what he prefers. A moon reflected in a river is a soft, attractive, romantic image and, if offered somehow by those who disapprove of what the speaker has done, it is rejected. And there is proof, according to the speaker, that he is right:

> The air blows softer since his departure.

Departure is a euphemism for his savage death and it seems as if the victim's body was buried by the sea-shore – he was given a 'tidal-burial during school-hours.' The reference to 'school-hours' links the 'mad bastard' once again to children and his being buried when the children are safe in school is yet another clue as to the crimes perpetrated. The speaker thinks it right that children should not see him being buried; their nightmares, we are told, have disappeared and the children's cries echoing lightly along the coast seems to suggest that children are once again playing freely. They are out of danger.

Line twelve echoes the poem's title and sums up the self-righteous mind of the speaker:

> This is as it should be.
> They will thank us for it when they grow up
> To a world with method in it.

The world proposed here is a world in black and white where there is a very definite sense of right and wrong. The short, confident sentences which the poem gives way to after the long, descriptive description of the hunt and killing is a movement from description to opinion and prescription. The voice of the persona which Mahon features here is a headstrong, determined, unwavering, brutal voice. Ironically, the brutality is justified out of love and concern for the children who will grow up to 'a world with method in it.' This line, perhaps, alludes to the line in *Hamlet*: 'Though this be madness, yet there is method in it.'

A Disused Shed in Co. Wexford

From the title one might not guess that this is a poem which achieves great scope and power, nor might one guess that what follows is a sympathetic and lyrical meditation on people and politics. A disused shed suggests abandonment but shed itself suggests something unimportant; the epigraph 'Let them not forget us, the weak souls among the asphodels' also suggests abandonment, this time a fear of being abandoned. The poem, according to Hugh Haughton, is based on an anecdote about a forgotten shed in the grounds of a 'burnt-out' hotel somewhere in Wexford. The fact that it is dedicated to J.G. Farrell, author of *Troubles*, reminds us, says Haughton, that it is 'a retrospective meditation on a time of civil war.'

The opening line reveals a mind deep in contemplation:

> Even now there are places where a thought might grow —

'Even now' suggests that the speaker views the past as a time more suited to thought. The late twentieth century is a time of speed and noise and busyness, but even now there are places where a thought could grow, where insight and understanding might be reached, where there are occasions and places which might prompt contemplation and deep thought. The word 'might', however, suggests that the speaker is not certain that 'a thought will grow'; all he can say is that it might.

In the following lines the speaker gives examples of such places where the individual might experience a thought as it grows. The image of a thought growing is an image of gaining a depth and understanding. The places mentioned by Mahon are abandoned, deserted places – places as far away as Peru and India, abandoned mines and empty compounds. In the case of Peru, the description is one of silence and emptiness and the fact that this place was once busy and noisy adds to the silent, empty atmosphere:

> Even now there are places where a thought might grow —
> Peruvian mines, worked out and abandoned
> To a slow clock of condensation,
> An echo trapped for ever, and a flutter
> Of wild flowers in the lift-shaft,

and then a landscape in India empty of people:

> Indian compounds where the wind dances
> And a door bangs with diminished confidence,
> Lime crevices behind rippling rain-barrels,
> Dog corners for bone burials

These lines are extraordinary examples of atmospheric language. The sense of time passing, the absence of sound, the sense of abandonment and emptiness, the unseen wild flowers in the lift shaft, the wind dancing, the banging door, the rippling surfaces of the rain-barrels is a gathering together of haunting images. If they were filmed it would be a sequence of visually effective and fascinating pictures.

The Peruvian mines and the Indian compound are offered by the poet as instances of where a thought might grow. He does not express the nature of those thoughts but a worked out mine was once a place of difficult work, perhaps exploitation, and the empty Indian compounds might prompt thoughts on the very idea of enclosures for people to live in. Both places involve the world of work, work for the many, ordinary people living ordinary lives in places where no people live anymore.

The poet T. S. Eliot felt that poetry can communicate without being understood and in *The Use of Poetry and the Use of Criticism* Eliot writes of the powerful effect of symbol when he asks: 'Why, for all of us, out of all that we have heard, seen, felt, in a lifetime, do certain images recur, charged with emotion, rather than others? The song of one bird, the leap of one fish, at a particular place and time, the scent of one flower, an old woman on a German mountain path, six ruffians seen through an open window playing cards at night at a small railway junction where there was a water-mill: such memories may have symbolic value, but of what we cannot tell, for they come to represent the depths of feeling into which we cannot peer.'

Such lines as these by Mahon operate on the level of symbol; they effectively communicate a mood, a feeling, an idea, though the reader may never fully grasp every meaning. The opening lines of 'A Disused Shed' inhabit the reader's mind and imagination and take hold and, as Mahon suggests, 'a thought might grow.'

The poem is in six stanzas, each ten lines long. Stanza one flows into stanza two, the only instance of a run-on line between one stanza and the next, but it allows the speaker to offer another example of where a thought might grow. Having presented the reader with two examples of isolation from far away, the speaker moves closer to home and gives as his third example 'a disused shed in Co. Wexford.' An emptiness surrounds all three.

The remaining five stanzas of the poem not only describe a shed but illustrate how this is a place where a thought does indeed grow. There is description to begin with. We are told that this shed can be found

> Deep in the grounds of a burnt-out hotel,
> Among the bathtubs and the washbasin

and then the arresting image of a thousand, trapped mushrooms all looking towards a keyhole:

> A thousand mushrooms crowd to a keyhole.

The use of the word 'thousand' here serves as a image of crowds, multitudes, and the keyhole becomes a sign of hope, expectation:

> This is the one star in their firmament
> Or frames a star within a star.

The speaker, in Kathleen Shields's words, 'zooms in on the mushrooms while they focus on a keyhole, looking out.' The mushrooms are introduced, says Shields, 'after the evocation of other places and objects united by an endless falling away from happiness.'

Shields says of these opening lines that 'Even now, in what is for the narrator a fallen world, there are places where other fallings can be imagined. If he is alienated from some kind of happiness so too are the objects. In the Indian compound the wind dances, no Indians do, and even the door's confidence is diminished.' And there is a loneliness associated with the disused shed in that the mushrooms are filled with longing and expectation:

> What should they do there but desire?
> So many days beyond the rhododendrons
> With the world waltzing in its bowl of cloud,
> They have learnt patience and silence
> Listening to the rooks querulous in the high woods.

The mushrooms have lived in darkness and isolation and the world has continued without them. The 'world waltzing in its bowl of cloud' is a carefree contrasting image to the crowded mushrooms. The phrase 'querulous rooks' suggests discontent but these complaining sounds have taught patience to the silent mushrooms. In this emptiness and loneliness the scene echoes the opening stanza with its Peruvian mines and Indian compound.

There is a sense of a world beyond the disused shed but it is a world that the inhabitants, the mushrooms, can only aspire towards, to which they cannot belong. Why is the shed no longer used? In this instance it is because the hotel has been burnt down and this hotel was burnt down because of the civil war. It may not be straining interpretation, therefore, to read this as an image of a weaker power or people being forgotten about in a time of conflict.

That these mushrooms have been waiting for release for some time and their uncomfortable, long wait are what the speaker focuses on at the beginning of the third stanza. There is a stench or smell and the smell which has been there since 'civil war days' links this shed to Irish history:

> They have been waiting for us in a foetor
> Of vegetable sweat since civil war days

Speaking of himself as 'us' suggests that he sees himself and others as pivotal. He and others are somehow obliged and capable of helping. The mushrooms were abandoned by the mycologist all those years ago and it was 'an expropriated (dispossessed) mycologist' (one who studies fungi) – someone knowledgeable but someone who was forced to move away. Kathleen Shields sees the 'expropriated mycologist' in terms of a landlord who left Ireland after the civil war in the 1920s and comments: 'The memory of the man who took an interest in them lingers on (his departure is "interminable") and yet they know it is useless to hope ("he never came back").

> He never came back, and light since then
> Is a keyhole rusting gently after rain.

The sense of the mushrooms having been cut off and the sense of time passing are evoked in the details:

> Spiders have spun, flies dusted to mildew
> And once a day, perhaps, they have heard something —
> A trickle of masonry, a shout from the blue
> Or a lorry changing gear at the end of the lane.

During that long stretch of time the poet gives a realistic picture of death and suffering. In this instance the speaker is referring to mushrooms, but the reader registers a human dimension, a political dimension, in words such as 'deaths', 'nightmares', 'grim/ Dominion' and 'groaning/ For their deliverance', 'so long expectant':

> There have been deaths, the pale flesh flaking
> Into the earth that nourished it;
> And nightmares, born of these and the grim
> Dominion of stale air and rank moisture.

Their struggle is emphasised in their cry of desperation and longing:

> Those nearest the door grow strong —
> 'Elbow room! Elbow room!'
> The rest, dim in a twilight of crumbling
> Utensils and broken pitchers, groaning
> For their deliverance, have been so long
> Expectant that there is left only the posture.

an observation on the effects of being abandoned? i.e how leads to infighting in a community (i.e the Troubles) Lord of the flies style

These are sensuous, atmospheric lines. They are immediately understood at face value but memorable in themselves and in their symbolism. Some of the mushrooms 'grow strong'; 'The rest' groan in empty expectation. They could be interpreted to mean a people abandoned and forgotten. Mahon's own Unionist and Protestant background was most clearly realised and determined when the Treaty was signed in 1921 and the Six Counties were formed. John Goodby, in *Irish Poetry Since 1950*, writes that one way of interpreting this fourth stanza 'is that the shed, as the self-isolated ("dim" and locked) statelet of Northern Ireland, contains two kinds of "mushrooms", the Protestants who assertively monopolise most of what little light there is ("Elbow room! Elbow room!") and the Catholics defined by their supplicant, abject posture' but he thinks that '(t)his possible allegory of sectarianism, however, is countered by the poet's presentation of their common plight, and by the far broader vistas of human suffering.' The Northern Protestants were, in many minds, seen to be abandoned by Britain but to read the poem in terms of that one interpretation would be too limiting and does not do the poem justice. Peter McDonald points out that 'Mahon does not anatomise a given community when he encounters its plight; rather he sets that plight deep in a context of change and human isolation.'

Fifty years of neglect, of being in the dark, of waiting for the door to open are ideas all contained in the opening lines of the fifth stanza:

> A half century, without visitors, in the dark —
> Poor preparation for the cracking lock
> And creak of hinges

and then there follows an image of these powdery prisoners who knew the old system of government ('regime') in their affliction. The speaker refers to them as 'magi' and 'moonmen' and

> Powdery prisoners of the old regime,
> Web-throated, stalked like triffids, racked by drought
> And insomnia

biblical

The thousand mushrooms are seen as wise men (drawn towards the light?) and physically resemble astronauts who walked on the moon, but the more vivid image is the triffids and the description of the mushrooms as tortured, crowded, sleepless, troubled victims. When the speaker, as photographer, opens the door and photographs them they are weak, feverish and distorted. Christina Hunt Murphy sees the poet with his 'light meter and relaxed itinerary' as one leading 'a postmodern photographic safari in an endangered and exotic land.' She reads this as an expression of the poet's purpose to "shed" light, even if the light is dangerous, on the silent victims of history. There is

> only the ghost of a scream
> At the flash-bulb firing-squad we wake them with

but even that ghost of a scream

> Shows there is life yet in their feverish forms.
> Grown beyond nature now, soft wood for worms,
> They lift frail heads in gravity and good faith.

The speaker with his camera becomes a threatening presence; they long to be recognised and listened to but they are greeted with a 'flash-bulb firing squad', a phrase which represents, John Goodby suggests, 'the media discovering Northern Ireland.'

This is the moment of contact between past and present, between abandonment and rescue, and the speaker has a very clear understanding of their plight in the poem's final stanza:

> They are begging us, you see, in their wordless way,
> To do something, to speak on their behalf
> Or at least not to close the door again.

The 'us' involves and implicates the reader; it addresses himself and his reader directly and, as Eamon Grennan points out, the poem ends 'by transforming the speaker into a listener.'

In stanza one, the poem contained a wide panorama and a wide frame of reference. It then focused on the particular setting of a disused shed in Co. Wexford and in the closing lines the poem opens out again when it remembers placenames that have entered history and the human consciousness as places of great human suffering, one due to man's calculated evil, the other to natural disaster:

> Lost people of Treblinka and Pompeii!

Peter McDonald says this line from the final stanza 'makes explicit a parallel which has already been felt just beneath the surface. The discovery of fungi in a disused shed carries the symbolic weight of all the "lost lives" that make up history, and that "lift frail heads in gravity and good faith" into the present.'

The mushrooms, in Eamon Grennan's words, like 'other refugees and exiles from history have learned "patience and silence"' but in this final stanza they are given a voice. The speaker imagines their cry and the voice becomes the voices of all the lost and dispossessed and oppressed:

> 'Save us, save us,' they seem to say,
> 'Let the god not abandon us
> Who have come so far in darkness and in pain.
> We too had our lives to live.

You with your light meter and relaxed itinerary,
Let not our naive labours have been in vain!'

The speaker allows the mushrooms to view him with his 'light meter and relaxed itinerary' and this has been seen as an image of the relationship between Mahon and his fellow Protestants, an image of alienation and division, but it has also been pointed out that it is too narrowing and limiting to think of the mushrooms as Northern Irish Protestants and of the speaker as Derek Mahon. The poem is too open and too deliberately vague for that; the disused shed, in Hugh Haughton's words, represents 'global human violence.' Mahon is writing about victimisation, oppression, injustice and holocaust, but he does it indirectly. The mushrooms in their disused shed symbolise people everywhere and in every time who have been subjected to such abuse.

But their 'naive labours' have not been in vain. The poem recognises their presence and gives them a voice. The poem itself becomes a place where 'a thought might grow' in that the reader is invited to contemplate places and circumstances associated with emptiness, oppression and sorrow – Peruvian mines, Indian compounds, Treblinka, Pompeii and the significance which the poet has found in a disused shed in Co. Wexford.

Brian Donnelly sees this poem as an expansive meditative work that gets much of its effect from 'the blend of highly orchestrated, formal stanza structures and the apparent naturalness and freedom of colloquial speech.' This poem, published in *The Listener* in 1973, gives, according to Tom Paulin, 'a voice to the victims of political violence', and John Redmond speaks of how it begins 'with a characteristic panorama, a total vision, which rapidly shrinks through a gothic keyhole into a garden shed ... the mushrooms, having festered unseen for fifty years, are creepily animated by the prospect of a threshold being crossed.'

The Chinese Restaurant in Portrush

So many of Derek Mahon's poems contain placenames in their titles. In the ten poems selected here, for example, six do – Donegal, Co. Wexford, Portrush, Rathlin, Antarctica and Kinsale. 'The Chinese Restaurant in Portrush' not only names a town in Co. Antrim but it also brings China to mind; the one title connects the local and the distant. Portrush which the poet describes here is the off-season, almost-empty town and it is how the speaker prefers it – 'Gentle and almost hospitable':

Before the first visitor comes the spring
Softening the sharp air of the coast
In time for the first seasonal 'invasion.'
Today the place is as it might have been
Gentle and almost hospitable.

The poet does not view himself as a visitor, and the softening spring and the sense of quiet before the invasion are qualities which he cherishes. The first stanza looks out onto the world of the street. The light-footed girl, the window-shopping gulls and the dozing wolfhound are details chosen by the poet to suggest ease. The winter wind from the north has abated and spring is in the air. The poem contains very few similes or metaphors and yet each detail creates an atmospheric image; its clear language is direct and straightforward: – 'the doors that were shut all winter/ Against the north wind and the sea-mist/ Lie open to the street.'

In the second stanza the descriptive voice becomes more personal: the poet enters the poem as a customer in the Chinese restaurant

> While I sit with my paper and prawn chow mein
> Under a framed photograph of Hong Kong

and he also imagines what the proprietor must be thinking of. In stanza one the poet describes the girl striding by, 'Light-footed, swinging a book-bag', but does not go beyond external description; in the case of the Chinese proprietor he sees him as someone 'dreaming of home.' The description of the yacht as an 'ideogram on sea-cloud' indicates how sympathetically the speaker views the Chinese man. He thinks as he imagines how the Chinese man must think.

This second stanza is still and silent except for the hoisting of the sail in the distance and the whistling of the little tune. It is an indoor scene but, like stanza one, it looks out, and out beyond the streetscape of stanza one to include the yacht, 'the light/ Of heaven upon the hills of Donegal' and the proprietor's home.

This poem was published in the *New Statesman* in November 1978 and, according to Eamon Grennan, 'offers an image of peace in spite of the vulgar and violent actualities of the North.' The harsh reality of the Northern Troubles are not mentioned here. What Mahon picks up on is the sense of renewal that spring brings, a purposeful girl with a book-bag and a man dreaming of a distant land. The gulls and the dog suggest casualness. The tone is relaxed, the rhythm unhurried and Mahon's speech here, in Eamon Grennan's words, 'is one of celebration, of alertness to the actual, of honest elegy, and of the acceptance of all these as elements in a single consciousness of the world.'

There is a feeling of expectation and preparation in stanza one. In stanza two there is also a feeling of loss:

> The proprietor of the Chinese restaurant
> Stands at the door as if the world were young

We are given a glimpse of the world as young; the year is young and spring has come but the poet reminds us that it is as if it is but an echo of an even more beautiful time. There is also the feeling of loss and loneliness in the poet imagining that the man standing at the door is dreaming of home.

Rathlin

This poem, first published in 1980, remembers a deliberately vicious incident, in 1557, over four hundred years ago, on Rathlin Island off the coast of County Antrim. The poet visits Rathlin, sees an island bird-sanctuary and contemplates how little or nothing remains of that earlier bloodshed and violence, that pain and suffering. The past lives on, however, in memory and in the poem itself. Ironically, Rathlin was chosen as a sanctuary or safe-haven for the old, the woman and the children who were sent there in the late sixteenth century but, were massacred. The killings then were political killings and Mahon is living through a time that also knows civil unrest. The deaths on Rathlin have ended but he says in stanza two that 'Bombs doze in the housing estates', suggesting that violence is never-ending.

Stanza one connects past and present; the dramatic opening lines require a knowledge of history:

> A long time since the last scream cut short —
> Then an unnatural silence

Mahon is prompted to remember the terrible slaughter centuries ago on this very island that he is now approaching. (In another massacre in late July 1575 over two hundred people were killed. 'Some of the bodies were thrown into the sea and others piled into a huge common grave dug by the captives at the point of the sword' writes Wallace Clark in his book *Rathlin its Island Story*.) When the last person was killed, Mahon imagines that there was 'a last scream' and that the silence that followed then was unnatural. An ordinary silence was not possible because of what had gone before but that unnatural silence gave way, in time, to natural silence. Nature is seen as a form of healer:

> and then
> A natural silence, slowly broken
> By the shearwater, by the sporadic
> Conversations of crickets

The use of 'then', twice, in line two pinpoints the particular time of slaughter and its aftermath. The repetition of 'silence' in the opening lines also highlights this island's dramatic history.

The shearwater bird and the crickets have been on Rathlin for ages and they connect time past with time present. Over the past five hundred years the cry of the shearwater and the sporadic conversation of the crickets have broken the natural silence. These are the sounds of the island but the speaker is also aware of 'the bleak/ Reminder of a metaphysical wind', a wind that is beyond the physical, a supernatural or imagined wind. The natural silence could be interpreted as the bleak reminder of a metaphysical wind that once carried the unnatural silence.

Stanza one begins with a human sound, unnatural, distressed; that it is 'the last scream' reminds us that other screams went before. Others sounds, the shearwater, the crickets, follow and the final sound in the stanza is the sound announcing the presence of man. The sound of the outboard motor at the pier as the speaker lands on Rathlin. Here, as elsewhere in his poetry, Mahon uses 'we', not 'I.' He speaks not as an individual but uses a collective voice which suggests a shared experience. The life of the island before their noisy arrival is spoken of as 'dream-time', a golden time ('dream-time' is an Aboriginal concept; 'alcheringa' is the Golden Age in mythology of some Australian Aboriginals) a time of calm and natural silence ('Ages of this') which followed the violence. But this is shattered now:

> the report
> Of an outboard motor at the pier
> Shatters the dream-time and we land
> As if we were the first visitors here.

The first three lines in stanza two paint a picture of the 'dream-time' on Rathlin. The birds are seen as belonging to the world of dream ('oneiric') and are amazed by the visitors. The place is a safe-haven or sanctuary for the species that live here, just as it was once, supposedly, a sanctuary or place of refuge for those whose lives were in danger in the 1570s. What the poet sees is a happy scene and he hears happy sounds:

> The whole island a sanctuary where amazed
> Oneiric species whistle and chatter,
> Evacuating rock-face and cliff-top.

And beyond the island itself, as far as the eye, is described as beautiful, calm and restful. Even the freighter is sleeping and the speaker imagines that there is sea-smoke from Rathlin as far as the Arctic ice-caps:

> Cerulean distance, an oceanic haze —
> Nothing but sea-smoke to the ice-cap
> And the odd somnolent freighter.

The poem then takes an abrupt turn and in one line:

> Bombs doze in the housing estates

Mahon summons up an image of contemporary violence. It is not straining interpretation to see this as a housing estate in the North of Ireland; Rathlin, off the coast of north Antrim, once knew violence and Mahon was all too aware that when this poem was being written violence was a reality in the North of Ireland.

There is a contrast between Rathlin and elsewhere in that Rathlin has had its experience of violence; man's turbulent history no longer seems to affect it. The island has returned to being a home for natural life:

> But here they are through with history —
> Custodians of a lone light which repeats
> One simple statement to the turbulent sea.

The guardians of the island in this instance seem to be the keepers of the lighthouse who look out over the stormy sea and ensure that the lighthouse sends its single, rhythmic, repeating light. That the island is now the safe home of the 'oneiric species' and that its lighthouse protects those who sail by is a very different picture of Rathlin from the Rathlin of the 1570s, when so much blood was shed.

The final stanza returns to that earlier time. The repetition of the opening words of the poem, 'A long time', conveys a mood of reflection and sadness:

> A long time since the unspeakable violence —

and yet the poet has chosen to speak of it here. The only person named in the poem is now introduced:

> A long time since the unspeakable violence —
> Since Somhairle Buí, powerless on the mainland,
> Heard the screams of the Rathlin women
> Borne to him, seconds later, upon the wind.

The moment from the past is re-created dramatically, vividly and sympathetically. The great soldier is 'powerless'; the women's 'screams' are carried on the wind; they are heard 'seconds later.' That dreadful moment serves as a backdrop to this scenic island. Mahon says nothing of himself or his fellow 'visitors', nor does he mention the people who live on Rathlin island now. To do so would seem a distraction in a poem which prompts serious thoughts about inheritance as a people in a given place.

Having imagined Somhairle Buí he then cuts, cinematic-fashion, to the present and their leaving the island. The screaming sounds are no longer heard; they have been replaced by the shearwater, a sound we heard in stanza one. The poem is framed by the natural sounds of Rathlin now:

> Only the sound of the shearwater
> And the roar of the outboard motor
> Disturb the singular peace.

The final image is one of returning over the 'pitching surfaces' of the sea. The sea spray is blinding but the suggestion is that there is another form of blindness, being blind to understanding this part of the world and its history. The poet again uses 'we', not 'I.' He speaks on behalf of others and, though the poem does not end with a question mark, there is nonetheless a mood of uncertainty:

> Spray-blind,
> We leave here the infancy of the race,
> Unsure among the pitching surfaces
> Whether the future lies before us or behind.

He includes his fellow passengers on the boat; perhaps that 'we' also includes his fellow Ulster men and woman, the Irish people as a whole. The thought with which the poem ends is a complex one. The boat is heading towards the mainland, the province of Ulster, the island of Ireland. Is the violence behind us as we leave Rathlin or are we heading towards it? Is there a future or are possibility and hope things of the past? The phrase 'the infancy of the race' is a potent one. On Rathlin people, ancestors, including infants, were violently killed. Violence is on-going, hence the implied confusion of the poem's final line.

The poem at line seventeen – 'Bombs doze in the housing estates' – reminds us that there are places where violence is not a part of history, but very much a part of the present. The word 'doze' is innocent and gentle sounding in itself but, coupled with 'Bombs', 'Bombs doze', the image is one of hatred, the unexpected, the loss of innocent lives. 'Rathlin' therefore seems to suggest that the future is bleak and uncertain.

Antarctica

This poem begins in the voice of a persona, that of Lawrence Oates, and his one-line utterance is repeated in the final stanza; for the remainder of the poem Mahon re-creates an extraordinary moment in the lives of extraordinary men. In the poems in this selection we have seen how Mahon was drawn to the life of Bruce Ismay and here he is drawn to someone very different. Both poems share very dramatic settings and individuals responding to enormous pressure but Ismay was seen as a coward, Oates as a great hero; one was frightened and selfish, the other courageous and selfless.

The form chosen here, the villanelle, is interesting and, it could be argued, very appropriate. To tell the story of Oates's last moments Mahon has chosen a very ordered, disciplined poetic structure and the repeated rhymes suggest a kind of deliberate numbing quality.

The opening word of the poem are Lawrence Oates's last recorded words and are a striking example of good-manners, diffidence and understatement:

'I am just going outside and may be some time.'

Clearly, Oates felt that he had become a hindrance and had made a decision to head out into the snow and die. But the words convey nothing self-pitying, histrionic, attention-seeking. And the others on the expedition show the same remarkable restraint. They will honour their companion's decision and grant him the dignity he obviously wants:

> The others nod, pretending not to know

and the first stanza ends with a line which reoccurs in every second stanza until the final one:

> At the heart of the ridiculous, the sublime.

The first and third line of the opening stanza are woven through the poem and come together to form a concluding couplet. They are, therefore, central to the poem as a whole and sum up the poem's central theme: how heroic sacrifice can be found in what could be viewed as apparently ridiculous words and actions, that there is something magnificent in the 'numb self-sacrifice of the weakest.'

The phrase 'just going outside' does not immediately conjure up the frozen wastes of the Antarctic but that is exactly what the poet creates in stanza two. The tent, it would seem, is cosy, companionable and snug, but Oates is willing himself to die in harsh and bitter circumstances:

> He leaves them reading and begins to climb,
> Goading his ghost into the howling snow;
> He is just going outside and may be sometime.

'I am just going outside …' has been switched to 'He is just going . . .' and could represent the poet or the men who remain in the tent. There is no suggestion of panic or crisis. Derek Mahon deliberately does not name the men involved and this allows the poem to achieve a greater symbolic power and force. It becomes an image of enforced isolation, an image of breaking away from the group for the welfare of the group, a picture of extraordinary dignity.

The entire poem moves at a measured pace. The lines are slow-moving and suit the slow, determined movement of Oates as he trudges up and on. All hope is being left behind; he is deliberately walking away from it:

> The tent recedes beneath its crust of rime
> And frostbite is replaced by vertigo:
> At the heart of the ridiculous the sublime.

The poem began within the intimate world of the tent and by line five the scene has shifted to the harsh panorama of the white, bitterly cold landscape with its solitary figure.

The speaker's voice becomes more engaged at the beginning of stanza four. The tone is now questioning:

> Need we consider it some sort of crime,
> This numb self-sacrifice of the weakest?

Heroism is being re-defined here. The harsh terms 'crime' and 'weakest' suggest cowardice and shame but the question is answered confidently. The placing of the word 'No' at the end of the line gives the answer greater emphasis:

> No,
> He is just going outside and may be some time —

but then, in a run-on line, the only one from stanza to stanza in the poem, there is a grim qualification:

> No,
> He is just going outside and may be some time —
>
> In fact, for ever.

This admission increases our admiration for the solitary figure in the snow. He is determined never to return, never to be a burden. He is a solitary who will radiate light and heat, an image that is singular and all the more striking within the context of the world of the poem:

> Solitary enzyme
> Though the night yield no glimmer there will glow,
> At the heart of the ridiculous, the sublime.

The final stanza, the only four-line stanza in the villanelle, not only picks up on the two repeated lines but introduces them in a voice that is gentle and supportive. The phrase 'earthly pantomime' gently mocks humanity's endeavours. The speaker attributes to Oates an insight, acceptance and wisdom, and his death is seen as a release. The words 'He takes leave' suggests someone in total control and the familiar phrase, 'time to go', here creates a sense of something naturally drawing to a close:

> He takes leave of the earthly pantomime
> Quietly, knowing it is time to go.
> 'I am just going outside and may be some time.'
> At the heart of the ridiculous, the sublime.

The word 'sublime' occurs four times in the poem and so does 'ridiculous', but 'sublime' wins out not only in terms of meaning ('At the heart of the ridiculous the sublime') but sublime is rhymed each time it occurs ('time', 'rime', 'enzyme', 'pantomime'). Even if the speaker does recognise that life may be an 'earthly pantomime' and 'just going outside' is faintly ridiculous, the poem moves towards a strong awareness that Lawrence Oates's act was something noble, grand and majestic.

Kinsale

This, above all, is a celebratory, a musical poem. In seven lines Mahon casts aside a gloomy, wet, dark landscape and replaces it with a colourful, life-enhancing, lyrical image. The contrast is between the past and the present. There is a sense of yesterday, today and tomorrow but the poem, though short, opens up to become a poem about a mood within the poet and a mood within the country as a whole. Though titled 'Kinsale', it could be said to be about a shift of mood within Ireland. It was written at a time of significant economic and cultural change.

The first three lines speak of the 'kind of rain we knew', which suggests that it is something familiar and frequent. But the opening line is upbeat and confident in tone:

> The kind of rain we knew is a thing of the past —

a rain that was harsh and oppressive and therefore all the better that it is over:

> deep-delving, dark, deliberate you would say,
> browsing on spire and bogland;

The three alliterating adjectives emphasise the power of the rain and the 'you' addressed is invited to agree. The mind pictures heavy rainfall, downward motion, a sense of oppression. Whether 'spire and the bogland' are deliberately chosen as representative of Ireland's religious tradition and landscape is difficult to say, but the images they suggest contrast with the carefree pictures that follow.

Over half the poem, lines 4–7, focuses on brighter happier images and the pictures presented are not the usual clichéd images of Ireland. Kinsale has always been considered a very attractive and affluent town and home to a diverse and colourful range of people. The 'sky-blue slates' and the 'tinkling' yachts are bright and musical and, as in many of Mahon's poems, the use of the inclusive 'we' involves the reader more:

                                    but today
      our sky-blue slates are steaming in the sun,
      our yachts tinkling and dancing in the bay
      like racehorses. We contemplate at last
      shining windows, a future forbidden to no one.

The 'our' is not specific to actual owners of roofs or yachts, but somehow the
speaker is recognising a feeling of potential and hope. Looking at sunshine and
water, at slates and yachts at Kinsale, the poet feels part of this world of leisure
and affluence. Even the simile used, 'dancing in the bay/ like racehorses', is classy;
'tinkling' and 'dancing' are light-sounding and elegant, unlike the 'deep-delving'
rain or the heaviness of 'bogland.' We have put the past behind us, is what
the poem seems to say and the movement of this little lyric poem is towards a
heartening optimism.

Ten poems by Derek Mahon were chosen by committee but Mahon himself, on seeing
the list, wished to replace two of the poems nominated for Leaving Certificate by
poems of his own choosing. Therefore 'A Lighthouse in Maine' and 'Midsummer' were
replaced by 'Rathlin' and 'Kinsale'.

Paula Meehan
(Born 1955)

Contents	Page

The Overview

'Nothing is ever lost that makes its way into poetry.'

– Paula Meehan

Paula Meehan changed the map of Irish poetry. When she began to write, the places and the people that Meehan wrote about, and the themes she highlighted in her unique voice, were not familiar ones. This is no longer the case.

The ten poems by Paula Meehan on your Leaving Certificate course explore private and public themes. In 'Buying Winkles', 'The Pattern', 'Cora, Auntie' and 'Hearth Lesson', the setting is the family flat on Seán MacDermott Street in inner city Dublin, where Meehan grew up, and these poems recall childhood memories and family relationships, some happy, some sad. 'The Exact Moment I Became a Poet' recalls a pivotal moment from Meehan's childhood when, in her primary school, she, a young girl from a working-class background, was told that she faced what her teacher considered to be a grim future unless she worked hard at school. Education, her teacher said that day, would allow Paula Meehan to choose a better pathway through life.

In 'My Father Perceived as a Vision of St Francis' the setting is no longer the inner city but Finglas, a Dublin suburb. Here, her father is older and different from the father as portrayed in 'Hearth Lesson' and the mood is tender. Though the setting is ordinary, the moment captured is magical and celebratory.

Public themes, such as the shocking and dreadful death of fifteen-year-old Ann Lovett, the rezoning of land, an unusual take on a momentous event in Irish history, and inner city deprivation, are explored in 'The Statue of the Virgin at Granard Speaks', 'Death of a Field', 'Them Ducks Died for Ireland' and 'Prayer for the Children of Longing'.

Paula Meehan composes her poetry aloud and believes that it should be performed, either in a reader's mind or recited. The voice in a Paula Meehan poem is immediate, direct and compelling. Hearing her and seeing her read her own poetry is unforgettable. Meehan speaks of the tune of the poem, the dance of the poem, and she speaks her words in an almost chant-like way, rocking back and forth. She says that 'it's a kind of catatonic rock, and I suspect it goes back to the heartbeat we hear while we're in the womb.'

In *A Poet's Dublin* (2014) Meehan says: 'I have always sensed that poetry is public speech. A communal art . . . I experience poetry as public speech. It pre-dates literature. It's not the same thing as literature, though since moveable type was invented, it has had a long and fascinating relationship with the book.' But whether the poem is on the page or screen or whether it's being spoken, for Meehan the poem 'desires another human consciousness to resonate with or through.'

What should poets write about? In Galway, in 1980, a woman came up to Paula Meehan after a reading to ask why she didn't write about anything nice. The woman said that Meehan's poetry was brutal. Speaking of the subject matter of poetry in *A Poet's Dublin*, Meehan says: 'I remember a girl in my class in the Central Model Girls' School, a beautiful child called Clare, who died of diphtheria in the early sixties. Diphtheria! She lived in a two-room flat with her parents and twelve siblings in corporation buildings. That experience and many others like it haunted, and I believe formed my imagination. Why shouldn't I remember Clare in a poem?

'The seven tower blocks of Ballymun, named for the executed leaders of the 1916 Rising, became a byword for disastrous urban planning within one generation. Ill-conceived, ill-managed and eventually demolished. We played as young teenagers in the foundations, having walked across the backfields from Finglas. Am I not supposed to remember this?

'Then there were the inner city flat complexes named after Marian shrines and Catholic saints: Lourdes House, Fatima Mansions (where I lived for a few years in the eighties), St. Mary's Mansions: communities in crisis as traditional sources of work in the city disappeared. You'd need a miracle to get housed out of them was the joke. I remember attending funeral after funeral burying the brightest and the best of the kids as heroin swept like a juggernaut through the poor communities. Should I not speak of this? I had to believe that there was a home in poetry for the lives I saw about me. I had to believe I could find a language to honour the courage I saw everywhere.'

Meehan says her poems, though 'autobiographical in one way, are public speech. And the way they're made, what is crafty about them, is to give them battle dress to survive.' And in a 1990 interview, Meehan said that she was less concerned with literal truth than with imaginative truth, adding that in Estonian the word for 'poet' is *liar.*

In her introduction to *Three Irish Poets: An Anthology* (2003), Eavan Boland says Meehan is a superb poet of place. Boland sees Paula Meehan's Dublin streets as streets 'alive with incident and memory.' Meehan also celebrates people, their personalities, their resilience, their sorrows, what Boland calls Meehan's ability to write of 'thwarted love and confident visions', and she praises Meehan's ability to create 'both a new sound and reveal an old silence.'

In his poem 'It Takes Trees in Summer', dedicated to Meehan, Brendan Kennelly says of her:

It Takes Trees in Summer

Her city is streets and people
not out there
but in her heart.
Throughout the years
she has taken us for long walks
through places we'll never forget,
visions we have not seen yet

Meehan's poetry, says Peggy O'Brien in *Irish Women's Poetry* (2011), 'is free of all preening and self-importance.' She has given voice to what Katie Donovan calls an 'urban, working-class perspective', and Meehan as poet and as activist has been a passionate advocate for justice and equality. For Patrick Crotty, 'Meehan's poems are remarkable for their unaffected confidence and directness of address and for their sudden, intense bursts of lyricism.' According to Doireann Ní Ghríofa, 'Paula Meehan writes with the eye of a painter and there's something about her that picks me up at soul level.'

●

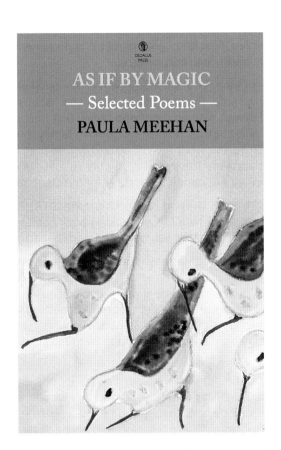

Biographical Notes

Born in Dublin's north inner city in 1955, Paula Meehan, the eldest of six children, five girls and one boy, grew up in the family flat at the corner of Seán MacDermott Street ('named' says Meehan, 'for one of the signatories to the Proclamation, as the streets of the poor so often were') and Gardiner Street. The door of their second-floor flat was on Seán MacDermott Street; 'its high windows looked out onto Gardiner Street, named after Luke Gardiner, First Viscount Mountjoy' (a prominent eighteenth-century Irish landowner and politician).

And that square mile of inner city Dublin, between the canal and the river, became for Meehan 'a huge resource, my own poetic heartland.' She remembers it as 'a very magic kind of place', with an extended family that included aunts and grannies and uncles and cousins. It wasn't a bookish family, but her grandfather taught her to read before she went to school, and her mother, says Meehan, 'extremely intelligent and very frustrated . . . by the role assigned her as mother and housewife . . . ranked education, especially for her daughters, as a priority.'

In a 1992 interview with Theo Dorgan (*Colby Quarterly*, 28.4), Meehan says: 'In retrospect you make sense of your life; so looking back I can see that poetry was the main patterning agent' and that 'all roads seemed to lead to it.'

In one of her lectures as Ireland Professor of Poetry, Meehan explains how her grandfather taught her to read and write: 'He would give me a page of his newspaper and a soft pencil that made a mark as black as jet, and he'd have me fill in the hole in every letter "O". That was the first letter I knew and I was entranced by the patterings I could find, especially where two "O"s came together, as in moon, swoon, spoon, drool, fool, platoon. All the pairs of owl eyes staring up at me . . .'

Meehan's paternal grandfather was a tic-tac man for a bookie (tic-tac is a kind of manual semaphore signalling or signaller used by racecourse bookmakers to exchange information), so he had 'that strange mute language, signs in the air made by white gloves. There were a few books in his bookcase – there was a book about horses which gave their forms and genealogies, there was a teach-yourself bookkeeping course that one of the uncles had been doing, a correspondence course in bookkeeping as well as *The Vicar of Wakefield* and the poems of Emily Dickinson.'

Already a self-confessed 'print junkie', Paula Meehan 'started going to school at about five', but she found school 'terrifying.' She told Theo Dorgan: 'We were beaten mercilessly, and it was also the first time where I was consciously made aware that we were girls from the tenements. And, as we were monotonously told, we would end up in the sewing factory. Now in my book there was nothing wrong with the sewing factory, many of my relatives and neighbours worked there, but I began to perceive that those words "end up" held the key to *what*? – something that was going on that had to do with class and power. We would have all sensed this, though obviously we'd have been unable to articulate it. The analysis came later. I liked poetry then; we had to learn a verse of English and Irish poetry every day off by heart. And I remember the sensation of trancing off on the rhythms. Even though we hadn't a clue what half the words meant, or what the poems "meant". But I found the rocking immensely comforting.'

Even though Paula Meehan wasn't surrounded by books growing up, '[she] was surrounded by poetry in a very, very vital and vivid way. Not only the songs, the poetry of songs, folk songs of the street, the games we played as children, the stories heard from the old people who would form an unbroken link in history back to the Famine. That folk memory has been a huge resource for all my work.'

And Meehan thinks of her maternal grandmother as a poet even though she never wrote. 'She would come down and tell us first thing every morning about her dreams.'

She still remembers her early love of language in nursery rhymes, street rhymes, Mass, prayer, patterns of sounds. Phrases such as 'on the warpath', 'I'll have your guts for garters' or 'swing for you.'

Meehan loved lists. Her grandfather, Walter (Wattie) Meehan, brought her to the races and the sounds made their way into her poem 'Evens Swannee River, 7/4 Navarone, 4/1 Rocky's Doll'. And Meehan remembers being struck by the look on the page of the Emily Dickinson poems given to an aunt by an American boyfriend: 'They were like jewels set, I can still see the space, the quatrains.'

In an interview with Michael Collier (*The Writing Life*, 2000), Meehan elaborates: 'One of my aunts had got from a boyfriend, who was at Trinity College on the GI Bill, the *Collected Poems of Emily Dickinson*. He had given it to her as a present when he was going back to the States. I found this book and I opened it up and I remember thinking this is so strange, the way on the page these look like jewels, these little quatrains, though I wouldn't have had the language for the effect it was having on me. I supply that now. But I remember the startling moment of looking at these beautiful-looking uses of language shapes and patterns on the page. And I remember, later, writing in school for a composition things in this shape and getting into trouble because the teacher thought I was trying to get out of writing a full-length composition.'

By fifteen she was reading Snyder, Roethke, Brooks, Ginsberg, Ferlinghetti, preferring American poets to British poets, and the Irish poet Michael Hartnett's *A Farewell to English* (1975) made a huge impression for its 'passion and rhetoric.'

She liked the Central Model Girls' School on Gardiner Street, but she remembers a moment in Miss Shannon's fifth class, as she explains in her lecture 'Imaginary Bonnets With Real Bees in Them' (published by UCD Press, 2016): 'I'm in trouble. Again. Usually I'm in trouble for something I've said. This time it's for something I've written. A poem, when I'd been told specifically to write a composition about Milk. I'm in deep mourning at the time for my dog Prince. Prince got run over by a bus the week before. I wrote an elegy. I didn't have that word then. *Elegy*. Poor dog. Poor dead dog. Miss Shannon thought I was up to something. "If I wanted a poem, I'd have asked for a poem." "But . . ." "But nothing. I'll hear no excuses. And I'll have those three pages.'"

Meehan's parents 'away in England, working' were 'back and forth to London, throughout the fifties, migrant workers. I was left with my grandparents a good deal, a great blessing.' For a while she joined her mother and father in London where 'I started school in Saint Elizabeth's in Richmond upon Thames. My memories from there: learning to sing "God Save Our Gracious Queen", and longing, longing to be back with grandfather bear and grandmother bear.'

Back in the Central Model Girls' School, Meehan read through 'the cast-off Victorian schoolbooks that Miss Shannon kept in the old wooden presses in the classrooms . . . In retrospect, hindsight being twenty-twenty vision, I can see that the girl children of the tenements and the inner city social housing were being given the vestiges of a Victorian value system . . . We were also being educated to be faithful Catholics, to make May altars, to worship Our Lady, the Virgin Mother. The version of Mary that I most loved showed her standing on the horned moon crowned with stars . . . We were also being prepared, in the run up to 1966, to commemorate the founding event of the Republic, The Easter Rising. Our little girl hearts were bursting with ideas of the heroic; we were ready to die for Ireland.'

The family moved from the inner city to the suburbs, where Meehan was expelled from St. Michael's Holy Faith Convent, referred to in a poem as 'a poxy convent in Finglas.' She had been threatened with expulsion when her notebook was confiscated and they found 'vile filth' – 'my innocent hormone-driven daydreams featuring swords and beast and wolves, beings of light and creatures of darkness.' Expulsion happened when Meehan and two friends organised a protest march against '. . . well? What? Nuns? The class system? The state of the world? The war with nuns and their henchgirls had been ongoing since my first day in the place.' But for Meehan, 'being thrown out of school was the best thing that could have happened to me', though at the time she didn't think so. 'Not after the ritual humiliation of being brought into every single classroom and made apologise for bringing the whole school into disrepute.'

That was 1968, a year after free secondary-school education was introduced, and 'there was a whole new social system. From being relatively exclusive, it was now kids from the estates. For once there was a chink of optimism that working-class children would get a chance but the chink closed.'

Meehan studied for the Intermediate Certificate on her own and then attended Whitehall House Senior Girls' [vocational] School, where she sat her Leaving Certificate in 1972. Despite having written from a very early age, she has spoken of the state educational system as a system 'that would not have encouraged me, or would not have challenged me, or necessarily gave me any aspirations. The culture I grew up in, in the '50s and '60s was very class-bound.'

Meehan has described her adolescent self as a 'rebel, a right handful' but she went to Trinity College, then one of the .04% of the student population from working-class backgrounds, where she studied English, history and classical civilisation. 'I think it was designed for the leisured classes, a polishing off before they returned to their country residences. But I was delighted to be back in the city. We had moved out from Seán MacDermott Street to a new corporation estate in Finglas and I had felt like an exile. At Trinity I was left to my own devices. I have great fondness for Brendan Kennelly, who had the human mark and dimension, but the less said about some of the others the better.'

She was writing 'on and off' in college, didn't publish, and 'didn't link into any of the literary societies.' But Meehan was involved in street theatre. 'In fact I made my living for the last few years in college from this, putting together plays for the streets, very experimental, lots of music, mime, colour, and it taught me a lesson that no amount of academic training could have given me.'

After her BA, she set off on her travels. First Crete, then the Shetland Islands, where she lived in 1978 on a small island, Papa Stour, in a small croft within yards of the sea. Meehan told Ann Owens Weekes (*Unveiling Treasures*, published by Attic Press, 1993) that she always wrote and considers writing a 'natural occupation' and that during her time in Scotland she began to shape her poetry with the idea of art rather than self-expression.

About her time in Scotland, Meehan, in her lecture 'Planet Water', says: 'in the calm of the solstice, the bay below the house was a saucer of blue milk but there were also nights when the waves battered at the door. Literally battered at the door. There was candlelight and a cranky range that I beachcombed to feed in order to heat water and to cook.

'I was fit and strong and slept in the song of the sea, rocked in dreams that made me write in a fluid, emotionally-free way as the moods and the humours washed through me. . . I nearly didn't write poetry at all, it seemed like such a puny act compared to the forces of nature shaping and energising this place. There could be no competition in craft terms. Could I harness some of this power? Was there a lesson in it for my poetry . . . I persisted with the notebooks. And then one morning, I wrote some lines that I read with sudden understanding – I scanned what I had written with a cold eye, the eye of another gaze as it were. I knew then that I would publish what I was writing. I was writing then for someone who was other than myself to read. Whoever that reader was, I was grateful she came at that moment. That flash of understanding was the intimation of the journey I would make again and again, the journey I still make, or aspire to making, again and again: the critical distance. The journey from a purely expressive mode to something I was beginning to understand as art.'

Then one night in 1977, reading *I Ching* by firelight, Meehan, aged twenty-two, asked herself should she go home to Dublin. 'I got the hexagram Fu-Return. One of the lines in the hexagram was a moving line with the interpretation: Noble-hearted return. No remorse. Which seven years later, I rendered into the title of my first collection of poems, *Return and No Blame*' (1984).'

Next to Washington State in 1981, where she was a teaching assistant in the Master of Fine Arts writing programme directed by the Dublin poet James J. McAuley and where she received a Master of Fine Arts. She didn't worry about or think about a career. 'The only constancy in my life has been my poetry', but, in a 1990 interview in *Stet* magazine, she adds: 'I must have had a very strong guardian angel.'

Back in Ireland, she worked on literacy programmes, taught in prisons, organised writers' workshops. 'The single greatest adventure of my lifetime', says Meehan, 'has been watching and participating in the reassertion of the female power on the planet. This is both fated and necessary if the species is to continue. I was a community activist in a large flats complex at the time and my mind was more occupied by meetings to get the heroin pushers out of the area and surviving on the dole.'

She lived and worked in Fatima Mansions, became involved in workers' co-operatives, and was fuelled by anger at the oppression and the ghettoised lives of the underprivileged. 'The sewage seeped up through the pavements of Fatima Mansions and nothing was being done about it. In the end we got organised and staged a sit-in at the Civic Offices on a Friday evening at 5:15 when the officials wanted to go home. This was the only way we could be heard. But it left me burnt out. I didn't have the cold professional distance I needed to sustain it.'

During the 1980s Paula Meehan married, and between 1985 and 1989 she lived on 'three wild, rushy acres' in Leitrim. 'I wanted to build a garden, watch something grow and harvest it. The idea of cycles interested me. I've written Leitrim poems but I had problems with the language at first. I had my *Collins Guide to Wild Flowers* but it was not my felt language. The rural Irish landscape has a language of its own and I didn't want my poems to be English and pastoral.' In Leitrim, 'deep in lake and river country', at the end of the eighties I wrote a short poem for each of the [elemental Tarot] cards . . . They were the last poems written in that house. And that winter was the last winter of my marriage.'

Speaking of her early poetry, Meehan says: 'I learned all my techniques, tricks if you like, from men – the "great" tradition. But a lot of the things I felt I had to say, when I looked for precedents there was silence.' And Theo Dorgan asked her about why she was looking for precedents. 'Because that's a totally natural thing for a poet to do. The apprenticeship is long, incredibly long, and involves an invigilation of language itself. There were very few women's voices. Sappho's poems, for instance, we only have fragments; some were burned by the Popes.' And 'though I became aware that the dead hand of the tradition was the hand that fed me, I knew it was a hand I would ultimately bite.'

Ferdia MacAnna thinks Paula Meehan belongs to 'the Dirty Dublin School of Poetic Realism', but Meehan rejects this, saying that she doesn't belong to any group. 'Groups only last for a while and there are different voices within a group. What you write about is less important than how you write about what.' Meehan is aware of the dangers of the lyric poem, of 'the impulse to mythologise the self. And it's too easy to romanticise and patronise the material from childhood.'

Asked if she owed a debt to her grandfather, mother, neighbours, Meehan told Theo Dorgan: 'Oh, a huge debt; the one to my grandfather is obvious because he equipped me to take on the world in a particular way. But I'd be conscious of the world of my mother, her sisters, my grandmother. The central fact about poetry is that it talks about one thing in terms of another thing, and the women in my family lived totally in a world of signs, symbols, portents – where nothing was ever what it seemed, people's dreams were as important as the news, and so talking about one thing in terms of another was a familiar way to operate in the world.'

In 1990, Paula Meehan met Theo Dorgan. At the time he was editing *The Great Book of Ireland*, a book on vellum of Irish art and poetry begun in 1989, completed in 1991, and acquired, through philanthropic donations, by University College, Cork in 2013 for $1 million dollars. When they met, Dorgan says he just thought 'Ah, there you are', and he and Meehan have been together ever since. 'Home', he says 'is wherever Paula is.'

For Paula Meehan a poem 'speaks into the mind but it is also a text for performance. I hate the build up to a reading, but the enactment I love.'

'The common iambic is slightly faster than the heartbeat and is good for you. Poetry, all art, attempts to heal some kind of wound and, if it communicates this, is also subversive.'

In 1984, when Meehan was twenty-nine, she published her first collection, *Return and No Blame*. This was followed by *Reading the Sky* (1986), *The Man Who Was Marked by Winter* (1991), *Pillow Talk* (1994), *Dharmakaya* (2000), *Painting Rain* (2009), *Mysteries of the Home* (1996, 2013), *Geomantic* (2016) and her plays *Mrs Sweeney* (1999), *Cell* (2000), *The Wolf of Winter* (2003) and *Music for Dogs: Work for Radio* (2008). Poet and playwright, Paula Meehan is also an artist and has exhibited her work. The cover of her *Mysteries of the Home* (2013) features one of her paintings, as do *Geomantic* (2016) and *As If By Magic: Selected Poems* (2020).

Winner of the Marten Toonder Prize, the Butler Award for Poetry, the Denis Devlin Award, the PPI Award for Radio Drama and the Lawrence O'Shaughnessy Award, Paula Meehan was honoured by the Hennessy Literary Hall of Fame, is a member of Aosdána and was Ireland Professor of Poetry 2013–2016. Her lectures were published as *Imaginary Bonnets With Real Bees in Them: Writings From the Ireland Chair of Poetry* (2016). In 2015, 'The Statue of the Virgin at Granard Speaks' was one of ten poems shortlisted for RTÉ's A Poem for Ireland: The Best-Loved Irish Poem of the Last 100 years.

Meehan's work has been translated into Estonian, French, Galician, German, Hungarian, Irish, Italian, Japanese and Spanish.

POEMS

The poems printed here are in the order in which they were published in Meehan's five published volumes: *The Man who was Marked by Winter* (1991), *Pillow Talk* (1994), *Dharmakaya* (2000), *Painting Rain* (2009), and *As If By Magic: Selected Poems* (2020).

female presence – gives 2 women voices in the poem

Buying Winkles

cinematic quality

money was tight

My mother would spare me sixpence and say,
'Hurry up now and don't be talking to strange
men on the way.' I'd dash from the ghosts   *energy, movement*
on the stairs where the bulb had blown

place names give familiarity out into Gardiner Street, all relief.   *unhappy home environment?*   5
A bonus if the moon was in the strip of sky
between the tall houses, or stars out,

beauty in mundane winkles but even in rain I was happy – the winkles   *lyrical, many aural effects make the poem flow – conveys the movement*
would be wet and glisten blue like little

adventure night skies themselves. I'd hold the tanner tight   10
and jump every crack in the pavement,   *childhood playfulness*
I'd wave up to women at sills or those

friendly to women lingering in doorways and weave a glad path through
men heading out for the night.   *Men head out, women are at sills – societal roles*

She'd be sitting outside the Rosebowl Bar   *Place names – familiarity*   15
on an orange-crate, a pram loaded
with pails of winkles before her.   *negative*
When the bar doors swung open they'd leak   *divide between men and women – men separate*
the smell of men together with drink
and I'd see light in golden mirrors.   20
I envied each soul in the hot interior.

I'd ask her again to show me the right way   *women as mentors wisdom of life experience*
to do it. She'd take a pin from her shawl –
'Open the eyelid. So. Stick it in
till you feel a grip, then slither him out.   25
Gently, mind.' The sweetest extra winkle   *the child has a sense of adventure wants to explore and discover new places*
that brought the sea to me.
'Tell yer Ma I picked them fresh this morning.'

I'd bear the newspaper twists
bulging fat with winkles   30
proudly home, like torches.   *imagination, pride, triumph childhood innocence*

represent the fire on energy and excitement that burns in the child

Glossary

Title Winkles: periwinkles or winkles – small edible sea snails.

Line 1 sixpence: old currency of Irish pounds, shillings and pence before decimalisation was introduced on 15 February 1971.

Line 5 Gardiner Street: in inner city Dublin.

Line 6 bonus: an extra and unexpected advantage.

Line 10 tanner: slang word for sixpence.

Line 16 orange-crate: a wooden box used to transport oranges.

Line 17 pails: buckets.

Line 20 I'd see light: in *As If By Magic: Selected Poems*, published in October 2020, Meehan changed 'I'd see light' to 'I saw light'.

Line 25 slither: slide.

In the *Lifelines* anthologies, where well-known people were invited to choose a favourite poem, Ferdia MacAnna (in *Lifelines*, 1992) and Robert Dunbar (in *Lifelines 3*, 1997) chose Paula Meehan's 'Buying Winkles'.

MacAnna wrote: 'My favourite poem of the moment is "Buying Winkles" from Paula Meehan's collection *The Man Who Was Marked by Winter*. I like it because it is direct, simple and beautiful and because it conjures up images of a child's experience of the adult world. Each time I read it, I find something new to savour. Most of all though, I like this poem because of its strong cinematic flavour. Reading it is a bit like being inside an imaginary Fellini film set in Dublin – there is colour, dash, charm, light and character as well as an ever-present tinge of danger.'

And of 'Buying Winkles', Robert Dunbar wrote: 'It is a poem about love, about warmth, about the intimacy of mother and daughter, abstractions all given wonderful concrete expression in the details of the setting, characterisation and dialogue. The note of pride in the closing line – 'like torches' – is a triumphant conclusion to this beautifully observed and brilliantly reported anecdote.'

Questions

1. How would you describe the speaker's childhood world as revealed to us in the poem? Which details, do you think, best capture that world?

2. In many ways the world of the poem is very different from the world today. How does it compare and contrast with the world you've grown up in, in the twenty-first century?

3. This poem has been described as a poem with 'a strong cinematic flavour'. What do you think that means and do you agree with that view?

4. Comment on the world of women and men in the poem. Which details best capture these worlds?

5. Do you agree that there is a hint of danger?

6. 'I'd see light in golden mirrors./ I envied each soul in the hot interior.' Comment on these lines. What do they tell us about the speaker?

7. There are many sensuous and dramatic images in the poem. Choose three and comment on their effect within the poem.

8. The mother and the woman selling winkles are given a voice. Comment on the poet's use of direct speech.

9. How would you describe the speaker's mood in the closing lines? Which details best capture that mood?

10. Eavan Boland admired this poem for its 'precise and genial details'. Identify such details.

authentic voice

PAULA MEEHAN

- theme of women (central in Meehan's poetry)
- history
- tradition
- society

The Pattern

narrative poem
- reflective
- reconciliation

• complexity of the relationship

• troubled, damaged

Little has come down to me of hers,
a sewing machine, a wedding band,
a clutch of photos, the sting of her hand
across my face in one of our wars

• enjambent lines: lack of closure

plosives *adds drama, emphasises the pain*

when we had grown bitter and apart.
Some say that's the fate of the eldest daughter.
I wish now she'd lasted till after
I'd grown up. We might have made a new start   5

• middle lines of the stanza rhymes

regret
loss
tragic

as women without tags like *mother, wife,*
sister, daughter, taken our chances from there.
At forty-two she headed for god knows where.
I've never gone back to visit her grave.   10

• yearning to know her mother as an individual

- dismissive, hiding behind nonchalance
unresolved, lack of closure

sensuous descriptive •

First she'd scrub the floor with Sunlight soap,
an armreach at a time. When her knees grew sore
she'd break for a cup of tea, then start again
at the door with lavender polish. The smell
would percolate back through the flat to us,
her brood banished to the bedroom.

absence of father figure

*- reflecting by going back on key memories   15
of their relationship*

- women in domestic roles
- women trapped by society

trapped *harsh*

And as she buffed the wax to a high shine
did she catch her own face coming clear?
Did she net a glimmer of her true self?
Did her mirror tell her what mine tells me?   20

(less certain than previous)
- inquisitive, uncertain
- attempting to understand her mom

I have her shrug and go on
knowing history has brought her to her knees.
She'd call us in and let us skate around
in our socks. We'd grow solemn as planets
in an intricate orbit about her.   25

- metaphor for role of women in 1950s

figurative, metaphorical language

- ritual, part of the "pattern" of the family's life

- the mother is central in their lives, she is the sun and they are the planets

379

She's bending over crimson cloth,
the younger kids are long in bed.
Late summer, cold enough for a fire,   30
she works by fading light
to remake an old dress for me.
It's first day back at school tomorrow.

•

'Pure lambswool. Plenty of wear in it yet.
You know I wore this when I went out with your Da.   35
I was supposed to be down in a friend's house,
your Granda caught us at the corner.
He dragged me in by the hair – it was long as yours then –
in front of the whole street.
He called your Da every name under the sun,   40
cornerboy, lout; I needn't tell you
what he called me. He shoved my whole head
under the kitchen tap, took a scrubbing brush
and carbolic soap and in ice-cold water he scrubbed
every spick of lipstick and mascara off my face.   45
Christ but he was a right tyrant, your Granda.
It'll be over my dead body anyone harms a hair
    of your head.'

•

She must have stayed up half the night
to finish the dress. I found it airing at the fire,
three new copybooks on the table and a bright   50
bronze nib, St Christopher strung on a silver wire,

as if I were embarking on a perilous journey
to uncharted realms. I wore that dress
with little grace. To me it spelt poverty,
the stigma of the second hand. I grew enough to pass   55

it on by Christmas to the next in line. I was sizing
up the world beyond our flat patch by patch
daily after school, and fitting each surprising
city street to city square to diamond. I'd watch

Handwritten annotations: more caring, maternal image; descriptive, vivid, feel the warmth of the fire; Practicality, poverty, skilfullness; dialogue adds drama to the poem; colloquial language; reminisance; generational trauma; theme of youth, childhood; Meehan's mother parents like her parents did; Meehan is discovering more about her mother (as an individual); cruel; strong woman; ironic; gradual epiphany that the mother truly cared and loved her; enjambment; adventure; imagination; Sibilance conveys the meaning - looking down on second hand; assonance; sibilance

the Liffey for hours pulsing to the sea   60

movement, life, energy

and the coming and going of ships,   *busy, exciting*

certain that one day it would carry me

to Zanzibar, Bombay, the land of the Ethiops.

ambition

sudden contrast between the exotic places and back home

There's a photo of her taken in the Phoenix Park

alone on a bench surrounded by roses   65

as if she had been born to formal gardens.   *sense of belonging*

She stares out as if unaware   *assonance*

that any human hand held the camera, wrapped

entirely in her own shadow, the world beyond her

already a dream, already lost. She's   *trapped /poignant/*   70

eight months pregnant. Her last child.   *lost possibility*

Her steel needles sparked and clacked,

the only other sound a settling coal

or her sporadic mutter

at a hard part in the pattern.   75

She favoured sensible shades:

Moss Green, Mustard, Beige.

conflict between dreams and reality ambition and duty

I dreamt a robe of colour

so pure it became a word.

Sometimes I'd have to kneel   80

an hour before her by the fire,

a skein around my outstretched hands,

while she rolled wool into balls.

If I swam like a kite too high

amongst the shadows on the ceiling   *adventure*   85

or flew like a fish in the pools

of pulsing light, she'd reel me firmly

home, she'd land me at her knees.

theme of belonging

Tongues of flame in her dark eyes,

she'd say, 'One of these days I must   *mother as a mentor*   90

teach you to follow a pattern.'

📖 Glossary

Title The Pattern: both actual and metaphorical. The mother's knitting pattern and a mother offering a daughter advice on how to live her life.

Line 9 tags: labels.

Line 12 I've never gone back to visit her grave: fifteen years after her mother died, Paula Meehan did go back to visit her mother's grave. 'One day I got up and knew I was ready for it. I had made my peace with her spirit. It took me that long to work out whatever her legacy was to me.'

Line 13 Sunlight soap: first manufactured in 1884, used for general household cleaning and for washing clothes.

Line 17 percolate: spread gradually.

Line 18 brood: young children.

Line 19 buffed: polished.

Line 21 net a glimmer: catch a faint sign or trace.

Line 41 lout: a rough man.

Line 44 carbolic soap: a disinfectant soap.

Line 51 St Christopher: Patron Saint of travellers and, since the twentieth century, motorists. In 1969, his name was dropped by the Roman Catholic Church from its list of Saints. (Legend has it that Christopher was a giant of a man who carried a child across a river. Midstream, the child became very heavy but Christopher persevered and placed the child on the opposite bank. The child then explained that he was Jesus and that Christopher carried the weight of the world on his shoulders.)

Line 63 Zanzibar, Bombay, the land of the Ethiops: far away, exotic places; Zanzibar is on an archipelago off Tanzania, East Africa, Bombay (now called Mumbai) on the west coast of India, and Ethiopia is also in East Africa.

Line 64 Phoenix Park: well-known public park in Dublin, since 1747. The largest, enclosed public park in any European capital city.

Line 74 sporadic: occasional.

Line 82 skein: length of wool loosely coiled or wound.

> In *The Writing Life* interview (2000), Paula Meehan said that she doesn't know 'if there's life after death, or what happens, or whatever, but I do think you are haunted in a very real way by your personal dead, that you carry them with you wherever you go. Your mind is populated with your own dead.'

❓ Questions

1. How would you describe the relationship between mother and daughter in the first three stanzas? How would you describe the speaker's tone of voice here? Sad? Regretful? Defiant?

2. The poem begins in the present and then revisits the past. Consider how the poet handles time here; how are the present and the past juxtaposed?

3. 'I've never gone back to visit her grave.' What is the effect of that line within the structure of the poem as a whole?

4. Meehan has described her mother as a woman of 'ferocious intelligence and ferocious energy.' Are these qualities, do you think, evident here?

5. This memory poem contains many different moments: her mother scrubbing the floor, remaking a dress, her mother in the Phoenix Park, her mother knitting. What do each of these moments tell us about the speaker's mother?

6. How do you interpret the line 'knowing history has brought her to her knees' (line 24)? Do you think it is a pun?

7. The poem is in seven sections. Consider section four, the middle section. How does it differ from the rest of the poem? Why is this memory important? What does it tell us about the past? About the relationship between fathers and daughters?

8. 'The Pattern' contains different styles of writing. Section one and section five, for example, use end rhymes and regular line lengths. We hear the mother's voice in section four. Comment on each section and its effect.

9. Do you think this poem more sad than happy? Why? Give reasons for your answer.

10 This poem is a portrait of family life and a portrait of a mother–daughter relationship. Is it, also, a portrait of a poet in the making? Are there details in the poem to suggest that the girl in the poem would grow up to become a poet? Look especially at sections five and seven.

11. There are many vivid images in this poem. Choose three that you think are particularly interesting and give reasons for your choice.

12 'the world beyond her/already a dream, already lost' (lines 69–70). Comment.

13 'The Pattern' is a very atmospheric poem. Explore how atmosphere is created through colour, movement and sensuous details.

14 Though the poem is rooted in a particular childhood, do you think it's a poem that can be read and appreciated by everyone, anywhere? Give reasons for your answer.

15 Meehan has said that 'writing is a way of saving yourself.' What do you think she meant by that? And do you think 'The Pattern' is an example of that?

16 In *Watching the River Flow: A Century in Irish Poetry* (1999), Nuala Ní Dhomhnaill says 'The Pattern' is a 'richly textured evocation of a childhood growing up in Dublin's inner city and the deeply ambiguous relationship between mother and daughter.' What do you think 'deeply ambiguous' means in this context?

17. In the poem's closing lines the mother has the last word. The poem ends with her voice. Comment on the significance of this.

tone of realism   *purity*

The Statue of the Virgin at Granard Speaks

plosive   *dynamic, energy*   *weather is central*

pathetic fallacy It can be bitter here at times like this,

November wind sweeping across the border. *troubles, fear, pain, suspicion*

sharp incisive language Its seeds of ice would cut you to the quick. *metaphor* *cacophony*

The whole town tucked up safe and dreaming,

even wild things gone to earth, and I *blissful ignorance – criticism of society*   5

trapped + isolated stuck up here in this grotto, without as much as

star or planet to ease my vigil. *we enter a dark, brutal world.*
darkness *non religious, scientific, pagan*

echoes of references to mth Levelt →indirect The howling won't let up. Trees *the natural world is in turmoil because of the tragedy ≠ unlike the town that don't care*

cavort in agony as if they would be free *all souls day*

and take off – ghost voyagers   10

on the wind that carries intimations *suffering*

of garrison towns, walled cities, ghetto lanes *ominous*

critiquing sectarian violence where men hunt each other and invoke

the various names of God as blessing

↑abuse of religion hypocrytical on their death tactics, their night manoeuvres.   15

Closer to home the wind sails over *in touch with nature*

dying lakes. I hear fish drowning. *death is a strong presence*

I taste the stagnant water mingled *sensuous*

with turf smoke from outlying farms.

society *Church is male* *male presence* *anti- cleric*

They call me Mary – Blessed, Holy, Virgin.   20

They fit me to a myth of a man crucified:

the scourging and the falling, and the falling again,

the thorny crown, the hammer blows of iron *visceral*

into wrist and ankle, the sacred bleeding heart.

alliteration "m" They name me Mother of all this grief   25

though mated to no mortal man. *sarcasm*

They kneel before me and their prayers *the statue's indifference*

fly up like sparks from a bonfire *– pagan*
anger

that blaze a moment, then wink out.

statue has a blasphemous voice. (ironic)

the mood lightens

intimit *languid, easy, free*

assonantal patterning 30

It can be lovely here at times. Springtime,
early summer. Girls in Communion frocks

lyrical language → beauty of nature

free impulsive pale rivals to the (riot) in the hedgerows,
of cow parsley and haw blossom, the perfume

sensuous

from every rushy acre that's left for hay

sibilance

when the light swings longer with the sun's (push) north. 35

nature is female *female presence* *childbirth*

Or the grace of a midsummer wedding
when the earth (herself) calls out for coupling
and I would break loose of my stony robes,

free, impulsive world of nature vs. punitive, judgemental church

pure blue, pure white, as if (they) had robbed
a child's sky for their colour. My being

brings us back to 40 earlier in the poem → "they call me"

cries out to be incarnate, incarnate,
maculate and tousled in a honeyed bed.

Everything the virgin Mary is not

Even an autumn burial can work its own pageantry.
The hedges heavy with the burden of fruiting

lyrical

crab, sloe, berry, hip; clouds scud east

cesura *Ann lovett* 45

pear scented, windfalls secret in long

heavily pregnant

orchard grasses, and some old soul is lowered
to his (kin.) Death is just another harvest

acknowledgement of death after portraying cyclical rhythm of life

scripted to the season's play.

metaphor of drama

familiarity

Tone - more serious

But on this All Souls' Night there is

back to stanza 1 50

lamenting no respite from the keening of the wind.

The virgin, as a statue, is not subject to the temporality of life but she celebrates it.

pagan I would not be amazed if every corpse came risen
from the graveyard to join in exaltation with the gale,
a cacophony of bone imploring sky for judgement

extreme joy OR fear

and release from being the conscience of the town. 55

Implication that the dead are the conscience of the town → criticism of the town.

'sky' instead of 'God'

On a night like this I remember the child
who came with fifteen summers to her name,
and she lay down alone at my feet
without midwife or doctor or friend to hold her hand
and she pushed her secret out into the night,
far from the town tucked up in little scandals,
bargains struck, words broken, prayers, promises,
and though she cried out to me in extremis
I did not move,
I didn't lift a finger to help her,
I didn't intercede with heaven,
nor whisper the charmed word in God's ear.

On a night like this I number the days to the solstice
and the turn back to the light.
O sun,
centre of our foolish dance,
burning heart of stone,
molten mother of us all,
hear me and have pity.

Handwritten annotations:
- simple language
- (the raw truth) bare language —effective
- poignant
- simplicity
- 60
- satirical, sharp tone / sarcasm, anger
- device of a list exposing the people of the town
- brings us back to stanza 1
- anaphora (repetition at the start of a line)
- Short line
- Meehan at her most savage - tone of condemnation
- latin, her most solemn note
- 65
- guilt, complicity / she is no better than the townspeople
- universal
- pagan
- O sun, sun/nature as a source of comfort instead of religion
- 70
- paradox
- matriarch - someone who could show pity

Glossary

Title Granard: a town in north-east County Longford. In January 1984, Ann Lovett, a fifteen-year-old girl, died giving birth in secret to her baby son at the hillside grotto on the outskirts of her home town of Granard. She was found by passers-by, but by then her baby boy was dead and she herself also died later that day, 31 January, in hospital. A whole generation still remembers that name and the awful sadness and heartbreak associated with it. Though Ann Lovett's name might not be recognised by future generations, this poem by Paula Meehan remembers the young woman, and in doing so gives voice to another young woman, the Virgin Mary, who also experienced a strange, troubled pregnancy.

Line 2 across the border: Granard, in north-east County Longford, is close to the border with Northern Ireland.

Line 6 grotto: a small cave, natural or artificial; in Ireland a grotto is associated with the statues of Mary and Saint Bernadette at Lourdes.

Line 7 vigil: time of staying awake to keep watch or pray.

Line 9 cavort: prance, move around excitedly or with exaggerated movements.

Line 11 intimations: hints.

Line 12 garrison towns, walled cities, ghetto lanes: a garrison town is a place which commonly has a military base, while a ghetto is a part of a city often occupied by minority groups. The places mentioned here are associated with power, perhaps violence and minorities.

Line 15 death tactics . . . night manoeuvres: phrases that suggest oppression and danger.

Line 18 stagnant: motionless and often unpleasant smelling.

Line 41 incarnate: embodied in human form.

Line 42 maculate: stained. According to Roman Catholic dogma, the Virgin Mary is immaculate, meaning in this context that she was conceived without sin. The feast of her Immaculate Conception is on 8 December.

Line 42 tousled: untidy.

Line 43 pageantry: elaborate ceremony.

Line 45 scud: move fast.

Line 50 All Souls' Night: the Feast of All Souls (in Irish Lá Fhéile na Marbh, the feast of the dead) is celebrated on 2 November, the day after the Feast of All Saints. It's a day when Catholics traditionally pray for the souls in Purgatory and visit graveyards. In Ireland, 1 November, Samhain, is the Celtic Feast of the Dead and it is said that at Samhain the doors between the natural and the supernatural worlds are ajar and the dead, especially the unhappy dead, are free again to walk on earth (cf. *Brewer's Dictionary of Irish Phrase & Fable*).

Line 51 respite: relief, rest.

Line 53 exaltation: extreme happiness.

Line 54 cacophony: harsh, disharmonious mixture of sounds.

Line 63 in extremis: (Latin) at the point of death.

Line 66 intercede: intervene, interpose, on behalf of another. One of the Virgin Mary's principal roles in Catholicism is to intercede with God on behalf of human beings.

Line 68 solstice: here the winter solstice, usually 21 December.

Line 73 molten: liquefied, turned into liquid, by heat.

In Meehan's poem, set on All Souls' night, there is a keening wind, and the statue of the Virgin remembers the biting cold of January, the May communions, a midsummer wedding, the autumn harvest, the year's cycle, but the overpowering feeling in the poem is one of grief, helplessness and longing. The poem's closing section speaks of the fifteen-year-old girl giving birth before her, and the Virgin admits to feeling powerless, helpless and of being disconnected from God. She didn't, she tells us, 'intercede with heaven', but now she turns to the approaching solstice and the sun for strength and comfort.

As a young girl, one of Paula Meehan's favourite images was that of the statue in the Pro-Cathedral in Dublin of Stella Maris/Star of the Sea. The Virgin Mother stands upon a crescent moon, her head surrounded by stars.

'The Statue of the Virgin at Granard Speaks' is from Meehan's 1991 collection *The Man who was Marked by Winter*.

? Questions

1. In this poem the speaker is the statue of the Virgin Mary, the Mother of God. The date is 2 November. The reason the statue speaks is tragic. What was your first response to the voice in the poem? What was your first impression of the poem as a whole?

2. How would you describe the speaker's mood in the opening stanza (lines 1–7)? What details create that mood or feeling?

3. Explore the poet's use of contrast in the opening stanza and the poet's choice of 'sweeping' and 'dreaming' in terms of place and time.

4. The second stanza describes not only the Longford winter landscape, but 'garrison towns, walled cities, ghetto lanes.' Why do you think these other places were included?

5. The men who 'hunt each other' and 'invoke/ the various names of God as blessing/ on their death tactics' (line 13–15) represent what, in your opinion? What kind of image do those words summon up? Sinister? Threatening? Frightening? Corrupt?

6. What does Mary's self-portrait in stanza three (lines 20–29) tell us about how she views herself? Comment on the word 'myth.' How does the statue view those who come and kneel before her and pray?

7. Winter, Spring, Summer, Autumn . . . The poem moves through the seasons and each season is associated with ritual: First Holy Communion; wedding; funeral. Explore how the poet describes each one, paying special attention to nature imagery.

8. In the stanza celebrating a midsummer wedding (lines 36–42) the statue speaks forcefully and personally. What prompted the statue to speak in this way? Were you surprised by what she had to say? Give reasons for your answer.

9. Both Ann Lovett and the Virgin Mary experienced troubled pregnancies. Compare and contrast the circumstances they found themselves in.

10. January, summer solstice, All Souls' Day and the winter solstice are significant here. Explore how the different times of the year are associated with very different moods.

11. Why is the description of an autumn burial (lines 43–49) particularly effective in the context of the poem as a whole?

12. 'Death is just another harvest/ scripted to the season's play.' How would you describe the tone here? Calm? Accepting? Indifferent?

13. The use of 'But' at line 50 focuses on a particular night, All Souls' Night. What does the speaker imagine? And why? Is it a frightening, surreal image? Consider the word 'judgement' and its significance. Comment on 'the conscience of the town.'

14. The poem ends with a bleak and stark description of a lonely fifteen-year-old girl giving birth outdoors in January. How would you describe the speaker's tone of voice here? Compassionate? Sympathetic? Uneasy? Guilty?

15. Mary is often seen as someone who intercedes on behalf of those in distress. The statue says 'I didn't intercede with heaven'. Why is this particularly significant in this instance?

16. The poem ends with a prayer to the sun. Why do you think the poet chose to end in this way? What does the sun symbolise here? Examine carefully the meanings of 'back to the light', 'our foolish dance' and 'burning heart of stone'.

17. The death of Ann Lovett and her baby boy is private and personal and very, very sad. When they died there was extensive media coverage in Ireland and throughout the world. And this poem remembers the tragedy. What are your thoughts regarding the poet's response to this tragedy?

18. Paula Meehan wrote this poem in response to the 1984 tragedy but did not publish it until 1991. Do you agree with the publishing of this poem? Give reasons for your answer.

19. Do you think poetry can make a difference? Is this such a poem? Explain.

[handwritten: Previous Meehan poems showed the fractious relationship Meehan had with her parents whereas this poem is positive]

My Father Perceived as a Vision of St Francis

– for Brendan Kennelly

[handwritten: understanding implies imagination] *[handwritten: loving, gentle, close with nature]*

[handwritten: nature]
It was the piebald horse in next door's garden

[handwritten: Sudden startling]
frightened me out of a dream

with her (dawn) whinny. I was back *[handwritten: onomatopoeia aural imagery]*

[handwritten: magical time of day]
in the boxroom of the house,

my brother's room now, *[handwritten: alliteration propels the memory]* 5

full of ties and sweaters and secrets. *[handwritten: sibilance]*

[handwritten: changes the atmosphere creates a more pensive tone slows down the poem]

Bottles (chinked) on the doorstep,

[handwritten: aural imagery]
the first bus pulled up to the stop.

The rest of the house slept

[handwritten: enjambment emphasises and isolates the father]

except for my father. I heard 10

him rake the ash from the grate, *[handwritten: assonance]* *[handwritten: NB. SENSE OF HEARING]*

plug in the kettle, hum a snatch of a tune.

Then he unlocked the back door

and stepped out into the garden.

[handwritten: ageing]
Autumn was nearly done, the first frost *[handwritten: beauty nature]* 15

whitened the slates of the estate. *[handwritten: soft consonants]*

[handwritten: father suddenly seen in a new light]
He was older than I had reckoned, *[handwritten: lyrical, calming, dream-like]*

his hair completely silver,

and for the first time I saw the stoop *[handwritten: maturity natural]*

of his shoulder, (saw that *[handwritten: vulnerability epiphany]*

his leg was (stiff. What's he at? *[handwritten: sibilance]* 20

[handwritten: unexpected questions adds drama]

(So early and (still (stars in the west? *[handwritten: nature awakening]*

[handwritten: as though the birds are coming from everywhere]
[handwritten: repetition]

They came then, birds *[handwritten: anticipation slows the rhythm down]* *[handwritten: the father seems central and powerful]*

of every size, shape, colour, they came *[handwritten: triadic form]* *[handwritten: → he has the power to summon all the birds]*

from the hedges and shrubs, *[handwritten: the father is transfigured from a fragile ageing man]* 25

from eaves and garden sheds,

from the industrial estate, outlying fields, *[handwritten: exciting sense of crescendo kinesis (movement)]*

[handwritten: repetition is climactic] from Dubber Cross they came

and the ditches of the North Road. *[handwritten: place names (proper nouns) – common in Meehan's work]*

[handwritten: 'from' → aware of the world beyond the house]

the whole poem is an extended epiphany

The garden was a pandemonium   *energetic verbs*   30
when my father threw up his hands
and tossed the crumbs to the air. The sun   *a fleeting, ephemeral moment*

cleared O'Reilly's chimney   *parochial, familiar, proper nouns*
and he was suddenly radiant,   *mythical, holy, epic*
a perfect vision of St Francis,   *biblical, idolised*   35
made whole, made young again,   *immortalised in this moment*
in a Finglas garden.   *juxtaposition = this miracle, extraordinary moment happens in a mundane setting*

📖 Glossary

Title St Francis: St Francis of Assisi (c.1181–1226) was the Italian founder of the Franciscan order. Born in Assisi to a wealthy family, he enjoyed the good life. In his twenties, c.1205, he joined a military expedition but a dream caused him to return to Assisi, where he abandoned his wealth, lived as a hermit and attended the sick and the poor. By 1210 he had formed a brotherhood of eleven, and in 1212 he assisted in the foundation of the Poor Clares, a Franciscan order for women. Canonised in 1228, he was named patron saint of ecology in 1980. Known for his love of nature, his preaching to the birds became a favourite subject for artists. His feast day is on 4 October.

Line 1 piebald: of two-colours irregularly arranged.

Line 3 whinny: gentle, high-pitched horse's neigh.

Line 4 boxroom: a very small room.

Line 7 Bottles chinked on the doorstep: the sound of milk bottles being delivered. Long before cartons, milk used to be delivered door-to-door every morning and empty bottles were collected for reuse.

Line 16 whitened: made white by frost, perhaps a reference to the line 'When dawn whitens Glassdrummond Chapel' in Patrick Kavanagh's poem 'Shancoduff'.

Line 30 pandemonium: an uproar, a noisy confusion (a word invented by John Milton. In his poem 'Paradise Lost' (1667), pandemonium is 'the place of all demons').

Line 34 radiant: shining, glowing brightly; displaying great joy, love.

Line 37 Finglas: a Dublin suburb (in Irish Fionnghlas, meaning clear, little stream).

In *The Writing Life* interview with Michael Collier (YouTube), Meehan introduced this poem as follows: 'Like most children of my generation who were brought up as Catholics in the Republic of Ireland, we had these little books on the lives of the Saints, simplified versions of their lives, and they were all quite a terrifying bunch. They all had spears in their sides and streaming blood coming out of their stigmata and they were frightening. I remember as a very young child being quite frightened by these images, except for St Francis, who was in the classic pose, speaking to the birds and surrounded by animals and creatures, and that image always stuck in my mind as an image of great comfort.

'My Father Perceived as a Vision of St Francis' is from Meehan's 1994 collection *Pillow Talk*.

? Questions

1. Meehan has described her father as 'an unsung hero.' Here she sings his praises. What qualities does she admire in her father?

2. The opening two stanzas (lines 1–14) paint a vivid picture of a place. Which details and sounds capture that place?

3. The speaker watches her father in the garden. What strikes her first about him?

4. At line 23, the words 'They came then' signal a change in the poem. How would you describe this change? Comment on the rhythm and the poet's use of repetition.

5. The setting is ordinary and it has been said of Meehan's poetry that 'the imagination charges ordinary occurrences with transcendental significance.' Is that true of this poem? Give reasons for your answer.

6. Paula Meehan is both poet and painter. Is this a painterly poem? Give reasons for your answer, quoting from the poem to support your answer.

The Exact Moment I Became a Poet
– for Kay Foran

society/convention
form: strict 3 line stanza form

was in 1963 when Miss Shannon *respect, formality for the teacher's position*
rapping the duster on the easel's peg
half obscured by a cloud of chalk *vivid description, sensuous language, aural imagery*

said *Attend to your books, girls,* *dialogue brings the teacher*
or mark my words, you'll end up *to life and adds* 5
in the sewing factory. *drama to the poem*

It wasn't just that some of the girls'
mothers worked in the sewing factory *societal norms, commentry*
or even that my own aunt did, *on society*

and many neighbours, but 10
that those words 'end up' robbed *reflective, pensive*
the labour of its dignity.

Not that I knew it then,
not in those words – labour, dignity. *childhood innocence*
That's all back construction, 15

making sense; allowing also
the teacher was right
and no one knows it like I do myself.

But I *saw* them: mothers, aunts and neighbours
trussed like chickens *humiliating, degrading image* 20
on a conveyor belt, *formulaic, strips the women of their individuality*

getting sewn up the way my granny
sewed the sage and onion stuffing
in the birds. *generational, traditional, sense of belonging + family*

harsh word, compares
Words could pluck you, *the people to the chickens* 25
leave you naked, *shame, humiliation*
your lovely shiny feathers all gone.
visual imagery

Glossary

Line 1 1963: Meehan was eight years old.

Line 2 easel's peg: the classroom blackboard was placed on an easel or wooden frame.

'The Exact Moment I Became a Poet' is from Meehan's 2000 collection *Dharmakaya*.

Questions

1. What happens in the classroom can change your life. Were you surprised or shocked by what the teacher said? The speaker says 'the teacher was right.' Why?

2. How did the speaker respond, at first, to Miss Shannon's advice?

3. What kind of a world will the schoolgirls 'end up/ in' if they do not attend to their books? Which image best captures that world in your opinion?

4. Could this poem be written about classrooms today? Give reasons for your answer.

5. How would you describe the tone in line 18: 'no one knows it like I do myself.'

6. The closing stanza reflects on the negative power of words. Explore this negativity and the impact on the speaker.

Death of a Field

The field itself is lost the morning it becomes a site
When the Notice goes up: Fingal County Council – 44 houses

The memory of the field is lost with the loss of its herbs

Though the woodpigeons in the willow
The finches in what's left of the hawthorn hedge   5
And the wagtail in the elder
Sing on their hungry summer song

The magpies sound like flying castanets

And the memory of the field disappears with its flora:
Who can know the yearning of yarrow   10
Or the plight of the scarlet pimpernel
Whose true colour is orange?

And the end of the field is the end of the hidey holes
Where first smokes, first tokes, first gropes
Were had to the scentless mayweed   15

The end of the field as we know it is the start of the estate
The site to be planted with houses each two- or three-bedroom
Nest of sorrow and chemical, cargo of joy

The end of dandelion is the start of Flash
The end of dock is the start of Pledge   20
The end of teasel is the start of Ariel
The end of primrose is the start of Brillo
The end of thistle is the start of Bounce
The end of sloe is the start of Oxyaction
The end of herb robert is the start of Brasso   25
The end of eyebright is the start of Persil

Who amongst us is able to number the end of grasses
To number the losses of each seeding head?

                    I'll walk out once
Barefoot under the moon to know the field   30
Through the soles of my feet to hear
The myriad leaf lives green and singing
The million million cycles of being in wing

That – before the field become map memory
In some archive on some architect's screen   35
I might possess it or it possess me
Through its night dew, its moon-white caul
Its slick and shine and its profligacy
In every wingbeat in every beat of time

Glossary

Title Death of a Field: The sacrifice of green space for housing. Ireland's rural population is decreasing. Urbanisation is on the increase and in 2018, 63.17% of Ireland's total population lived in urban areas and cities. Almost half of Ireland's urban population lives in Dublin.

Line 2 Fingal: one of three counties into which County Dublin was divided in 1994.

Line 2 houses: in *As If By Magic: Selected Poems*, published in October 2020, Meehan changed 'houses' to 'units'.

Line 8 castanets: single wooden instruments clicked by the fingers to provide a rhythmic accompaniment to Spanish dancing.

Line 13 hidey holes: hiding places.

Line 14 tokes: to 'toke' is to pull on a cigarette or pipe containing cannabis.

Line 18 chemical: a substance that has been artificially prepared, in this instance a reference to cleaning agents.

Line 18 cargo: transported goods.

Line 32 myriad: an indefinite, large number (from the Greek murioi, meaning 10,000).

Line 35 archive: a complete record of the data in a computer system.

Line 37 caul: here means covering (caul – the amniotic membrane enclosing a foetus, occasionally found on a child's head at birth and thought to bring good luck).

Line 38 profligacy: reckless extravagance, wastefulness.

Near her house in north County Dublin there was once 'a small coastal meadow with an abundance of wild flowers' and during the boom years this meadow became a site that was fought over by developers and resulted in what Meehan calls jerry-built houses. Though now home to a vital community of forty-four houses, the speaker laments the death of that field. For Meehan 'All of us lost a field during the boom' and she agrees with American poet Gary Snyder who, in his poem 'What You Should Know to Be a Poet', says what you should know are the names of trees and flowers and weeds.

For Jody Allen Randolph this poem 'set in a suburban building site becomes an elegy for communal losses during the boom years.' Mary O'Malley sees it as 'a witness poem of quiet insistence'.

In a 2009 Interview with Jody Allen Randolph (who says that 'Death of a Field' is an anti-pastoral poem and that the woman is walking into a future of environmental destruction), Meehan says: 'In this poem, I'm playing with the idea of Mother Ireland and the Four Green Fields and the serious environmental damage we're doing to the island. Certainly at the back of "Death of a Field" is the very strange poem of Christopher Smart (1722–1771), "Jubilato Agno" ("Rejoice in the Lamb") . . . it's a fantastic synthesis of listing of herbs, minerals, the great families of Britain . . . And because of the chant elements, what it does to your breath, it's a litany, pure litany, prayer of the highest order. If you actually read it aloud you will be transcendentally elevated.'

'Death of a Field' is from Meehan's 2009 collection *Painting Rain*.

? Questions

1. How would you describe the impact of the opening line? What is the speaker's tone of voice? What mood is captured in those eleven words?

2. Comment on the poet's use of the words 'lost', 'loss' and 'herbs' at the end of line 3.

3. From line 4 the poem achieves a different atmosphere, a different music. How is this achieved? Examine the images, the rhythm, the naming of birds and flora.

4. What change occurs at line 13? What does the speaker associate with this field as revealed in lines 13–15?

5. 'The end of' occurs eleven times in the poem. Every line in lines 19–26 begins with 'The end of' and each line moves from herb to a chemical cleaning agent. How does repetition contribute to the poem's theme?

6. Contrast is a powerful technique in the poem. Where, do you think, is it most effective?

7. The poem is a series of statements but a change takes place at lines 27–28. Comment on this and its effect.

8. What does the speaker wish for in lines 29–33? And how would you describe the picture painted in those lines?

9. Comment on 'That . . . I might possess it or it possess me.' What does this tell us about the speaker and the speaker's relationship with nature?

10. This poem was, according to Paula Meehan, 'impelled by Fingal County Council's dodgy development out the back of our house.' Do you think writing a poem such as this can make a difference?

11. Is 'Death of a Field', in your view, a lament or a celebration or a mixture of both?

12. This is a poem 'marked by what could be called a modern nostalgia'. Discuss.

13. 'Death of a Field' has no full stop at the end. Why do you think the poet omitted it?

Them Ducks Died for Ireland

*'6 of our waterfowl were killed or shot, 7 of the garden seats broken and
about 300 shrubs destroyed.'*
Park Superintendent in his report on the damage to
St Stephen's Green, during the Easter Rising 1916.

Time slides slowly down the sash window   5
puddling in light on oaken boards. The Green
is a great lung, exhaling like breath on the pane
the seasons' turn, sunset and moonset, the ebb and flow

of stars. And once made mirror to smoke and fire,
a Republic's destiny in a Countess' stride,   10
the bloodprice both summons and antidote to pride.
When we've licked the wounds of history, wounds of war,

we'll salute the stretcher-bearer, the nurse in white,
the ones who pick up the pieces, who endure,
who live at the edge, and die there and are known   15

by this archival footage read by fading light;
fragile as a breathmark on the windowpane or the gesture
of commemorating heroes in bronze and stone.

📖 Glossary

Title: Six ducks died and 485 people lost their lives during Easter week, 1916.

Line 10 Countess' stride: during the 1916 Rising, Commandant Michael Mallin and his
second in command, Countess Markievicz, were assigned to St. Stephen's Green. There is
a statue to her in Stephen's Green, erected in 1932 replaced in 1954; the earlier work was
damaged by vandals and removed.

Line 11 antidote: something that counteracts an unpleasant situation.

Line 16 archival: formally recorded.

In an interview with Jody Allen Randolph (*An Sionnach*, 2009), Meehan explains how the poem came about: 'The Office of Public Works . . . had a commission going . . . they were putting in a link between two Georgian houses on the east side of St. Stephen's Green – their national headquarters. Because I grew up in a Georgian house, albeit a tenement slum, I know how they work . . . I love those buildings; the intricacies of the craftwork, and the imagination, the ceilings, the stuccodoring work, [sic], and yet what they stand for: the ascendancy class, the class privilege of the whole colonial adventure, I have real problems with. That tension between something I love and something that oppressed me interested me, so I tendered for that commission.

I thought that the sonnet would be a good form to mirror something of the architectural complexity and ornamentation of the houses themselves and how they had been shells for many different kinds of lives, for office workers now, for tenement families, for the rich, for the original owners of the houses, for the merchant and professional classes. I think of the sonnet as a kind of a shell in the literary tradition. Both house and poem are received forms that can be re-inhabited and are re-inhabited, that can be played with and changed.'

'Them Ducks Died for Ireland' is a sonnet from a twelve-sequence poem named 'Six Sycamores', whose subtitle reads: The original leaseholders around St. Stephen's Green had to plant six sycamores and tend them for three years.

'Them Ducks Died for Ireland' is from Meehan's 2009 collection *Painting Rain*.

? Questions

1. What does the poem's subject matter reveal to us about the poet? Why do you think she chose to use 'Them' not 'Those' in the title?

2. Stanza one begins with the word 'Time' and the setting is an elegant room in a house overlooking St. Stephen's Green. Why is time significant here?

3. Explore the contrast between the flow of time and the time of 'smoke and fire.'

4. How would you describe the poem's mood? Is it the same throughout?

5. The speaker mentions 'a Republic's destiny', but what does the speaker focus on 'When we've licked the wounds of history, wounds of war'? Consider lines 11–13 and their significance.

6. What is the effect of 'are known' at the end of line 15? Were you surprised or disappointed by what followed?

7. How would you describe the speaker's attitude towards heroes who are commemorated 'in bronze and stone'?

8. How does the title relate to the poem itself? What does the title contribute to your overall understanding of the poem?

Cora, Auntie

Staring Death down
with a bottle of morphine in one hand,
a bottle of Jameson in the other:

laughing at Death –
love unconditional keeping her just this side   5
of the threshold

as her body withered
and her eyes grew darker and stranger
as her hair grew back after chemo

thick and curly as when she was a girl;   10
always a girl in her glance
teasing Death – humour a lance

she tilted at Death,
Scourge of Croydon tram drivers and High Street dossers
on her motorised invalid scooter   15

that last year:
bearing the pain,
not crucifixion but glory

in her voice.
Old skin, bag of bones,   20
grinning back at the rictus of Death:

always a girl in her name –
Cora, maiden, from the Greek KoÞñ,
promising blossom, summer, the scent of thyme.

                    ●

Sequin: she is standing on the kitchen table.   25
She is nearly twenty-one.
It is nineteen sixty-one.

They are sewing red sequins, the women,
to the hem of her white satin dress
as she moves slowly round and round.   30

Sequins red as berries,
red as the lips of maidens,
red as blood on the snow

in Child's old ballads,
as red as this pen   35
on this white paper

I've snatched from the chaos
to cast these lines
at my own kitchen table –

Cora, Marie, Jacinta, my aunties,   40
Helena, my mother, Mary, my grandmother –
the light of those stars

only reaching me now.
I orbit the table I can barely see over.
I am under it singing.   45

She was weeks from taking the boat to England.
Dust on the mantelpiece,
dust on the cards she left behind:

a black cat swinging in a silver horseshoe,
a giant key to the door,   50
emblems of luck, of access.

All that year I hunted sequins:
roaming the house I found them
in crack and crannies,

in the pillowcase,   55
under the stairs,
in a hole in the lino,

in a split in the sofa,
in a tear in the armchair
in the home of a shy mouse.   60

With odd beads and single earrings,
a broken charm bracelet, a glittering pin,
I gathered them into a tin box

which I open now in memory –
the coinage, the sudden glamour   65
of an emigrant soul.

Glossary

Line 2 morphine: a drug to relieve pain (from Morpheus, the Roman god of sleep).

Line 3 Jameson: brand of whiskey.

Line 9 chemo: chemotherapy, cancer-treatment therapy.

Line 12 lance: a long weapon with a wooden shaft and a pointed steel head.

Line 14 Croydon: a large town in south London.

Line 14 dossers: a person who sleeps rough.

Line 18 crucifixion: here, severe suffering.

Line 21 rictus: fixed grimace or grin.

Line 23 KoÞñ (Greek): means maiden; pronounced 'kooree'); maiden also means daughter, girl, lassie, damsel.

Line 25 Sequin: small, shiny disc sewn on clothing for decoration.

Line 31/33 red . . . red . . . red: the critic Anne Mulhall interprets the red sequins 'that the speaker's female relatives stitch on to her aunt's white satin dress' as symbolic of a girl's passage from childhood to puberty.

Line 34 Child's old ballads: Francis James Child compiled an anthology of 305 traditional English and Scottish ballads, first published in five volumes, 1882–1898.

Line 51 access: admission, opportunity.

Line 57 lino: linoleum, a hard, durable floor covering.

Line 65 coinage: a collection of coins; the invention of a new word or phrase.

'Cora, Auntie' is from Meehan's 2009 collection *Painting Rain*.

? Questions

1. In twenty-two three-line stanzas the reader is told many interesting and memorable things about Auntie Cora. List them. How would you describe the speaker's aunt?

2. The poem begins with a description of aunt Cora's final year and then returns to 1961 when Cora is nearly twenty-one. Why do you think the poet structured the poem in this way?

3. In the first section (lines 1–24) the word 'Death' occurs five times. How would you describe the attitude of an ill and dying Cora towards death?

4. What do you think the meaning of the name Cora (lines 23–24) contributes to the poem as a whole?

5. The second section revisits a time when Cora, aged twenty, is about to emigrate, her whole life before her. How does the poet portray the world of women in this section?

6. Two kitchen tables are mentioned in section two (lines 25–51). The poet remembers her six-year-old self being under a table, and the poet, years later, tells us she is writing this poem at her own kitchen table. Explore the way both girl and woman are portrayed and the connection between the two.

7. The final section also refers to the past and the present. What does the gathering and the keeping of sequins symbolise?

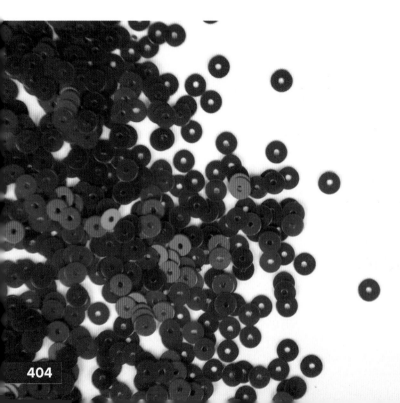

Prayer for the Children of Longing

*A poem commissioned by the community of Dublin's north inner city for
the lighting of the Christmas tree in Buckingham Street,
to remember their children who died from drug use.*

Great tree from the far northern forest
Still rich with the sap of the forest
Here at the heart of winter
Here at the heart of the city

Grant us the clarity of ice   5
The comfort of snow
The cool memory of trees
Grant us the forest's silence
The snow's breathless quiet

For one moment to freeze   10
The scream, the siren, the knock on the door
The needle in its track
The knife in the back

In that silence let us hear
The song of the children of longing   15
In that silence let us catch
The breath of the children of longing

The echo of their voices through the city streets
The streets that defeated them
That brought them to their knees   20
The streets that couldn't shelter them
That spellbound them in alleyways
The streets that blew their minds
That led them astray, out of reach of our saving
The streets that gave them visions and dreams   25
That promised them everything
That delivered nothing

The streets that broke their backs
The streets that we brought them home to

Let their names be the wind through the branches   30
Let their names be the song of the river
Let their names be the holiest prayers

Under the starlight, under the moonlight
In the light of this tree

Here at the heart of winter   35
Here at the heart of the city

Glossary

Epigraph: At the 16th annual Service of Commemoration and Hope on 1 February 2015, Paula Meehan recited this poem. At the same gathering it was announced that between 2004 and 2012, 5,289 deaths in Ireland were recorded by the National Family Support Network, 3,112 due to poisoning, 2,177 among drug users.

'Prayer for the Children of Longing' is from Meehan's 2009 collection *Painting Rain.*

Questions

1. The circumstances are heart-breaking. Who is being addressed in this prayer poem?

2. How would you describe the effect that the poem's opening image ('Great tree from the far northern forest/ Still rich with the sap of the forest') has on the reader/listener?

3. The first two stanzas describe the natural world, forest, ice, snow. How would you describe the speaker's attitude towards this world of ice and snow?

4. A dramatic change occurs at stanza three. What is the speaker wishing for here? What kind of picture is being painted of the city?

5. The speaker asks that we listen for and hear '(t)he song of the children of longing . . . (t)he breath of the children of longing.' How would you describe that song?

6. Stanza five paints a vivid picture of the lives these children lived. The word 'streets' occurs seven times. How would you describe the speaker's tone of voice here? Angry? Despairing? Helpless?

7. In Paula Meehan's poetry repetition is frequently a powerful aspect of the work. Explore the poet's use of repetition here. Which key words are repeated?

8. In the closing stanzas the imagery changes. Comment on this and discuss the images of branches, river, moonlight, starlight.

9. This is a poem with very little punctuation. Why do you think the poet chose to omit commas and full stops?

10. 'I believe that two lines of poetry can save a life' – Paula Meehan. Comment on this view in relation to 'Prayer for the Children of Longing'.

[handwritten: ironic ↓ warmth]
[handwritten: central female figure = the mother has the last word]

Hearth Lesson

[handwritten: memory | pause for reflection | idiomatic expressions → colloquial]

Either phrase will bring it back –
money to burn, burning a hole in your pocket.

[handwritten: present tense describing the past]
[handwritten: conveys the child as small, helpless]

I am crouched by the fire
[handwritten: mundane setting]
in the flat in Seán MacDermott Street,
[handwritten: place name – locality, familiarity]
while Zeus and Hera battle it out: 5

[handwritten: cinematic]
[handwritten: tension & drama | childhood imagination | mythical allusions elevate the parents]

[handwritten: elements of dialogue]
for his every thunderbolt
[handwritten: aggression, sudden]
she had the killing glance;
[handwritten: exciting, fantastical portrayal of her parents' fight]
she'll see his fancyman
[handwritten: retaliation – competitive, cruel game of hurt, back-and-forth]
and raise him the Cosmo Snooker Hall;
he'll see her 'the only way you get any
[handwritten: authentic voices of her parents]   10
attention around here is if you neigh';
[handwritten: add dramatic quality]

[handwritten: father gambles]
he'll raise her airs and graces
[handwritten: bitterness, acrimony]
or the mental state of her siblings,
[handwritten: lack of trust in the parents relationship]

[handwritten: analogy of poker, adds danger → poker can cost you everything]
every last one of them.
[handwritten: litany of insults]

[handwritten: simple language]
[handwritten: it's like a game for her]
I'm net, umpire, and court; most balls   15
are lobbed over my head.
[handwritten: the child seems invisible]
[handwritten: game – coping mechanism?]
Even then I can judge it's better
[handwritten: figurative language]
than brooding and silence and the particular hell of the unsaid,
of 'tell your mother . . .' 'ask your father . . .'.
[handwritten: breakdown of communication]

Even then I can tell it was money
[handwritten: theme of poverty]   20
the lack of it day after day,
[handwritten: emotional fatigue]
at the root of the bitter words
but nothing prepared us one teatime
when he handed up his wages.

She straightened each rumpled pound note, then   25
a weariness come suddenly over her,
[handwritten: present tense – the event is playing out in front of us]
she threw the lot in the fire.

[handwritten: child's innocence / wonder]
The flames were blue and pink and green,
[handwritten: rich descriptive language]
a marvellous sight, an alchemical scene.
[handwritten: changing a base metal (worthless) into a valuable metal]
[handwritten: incredulous]

suggestion that the father was keeping
more money for himself for gambling, drink, ect.

'It's not enough,' she stated simply. *language of prose* 30
And we all knew it wasn't.

Meehan's brilliant use of verbs
The flames sheered from cinder to chimney breast
like trapped exotic birds; *n.b - birds* *sibilance*
the shadows jumped floor to ceiling, and she'd
had the last, the astonishing, word. 35

Glossary

Title Hearth: fireplace and 'hearth' are sometimes used as symbols of home. (A pun, perhaps, on the Roman statesman and scholar Pliny the Elder's phrase 'Home is where the heart is'. In Irish, the proverb is 'Is é an baile an áit a bhfuil an croí.') Meehan says in an Ireland Chair of Poetry lecture: 'And in my grandmother Hannah's kitchen I was learning the hearth words, the common-or-garden nouns that spoke of food and home and fire. She called the kitchen the *scullery*. There was *crockery* and *cutlery*, she washed the *delph*.'

Line 2 money to burn: meaning you have so much money that you spend it on unnecessary things.

Line 2 burning a hole in your pocket: having money and feeling the need to spend it quickly.

Line 3 crouched: huddled, positioned so that the knees are bent and the upper body is brought forward and down.

Line 4 Seán MacDermott Street: in inner-city Dublin, where the Meehan family lived in a flat.

Line 5 Zeus and Hera: in Greek mythology Zeus is the god of sky and thunder and king of the gods; Hera is the goddess of woman, marriage, childbirth and family.

Line 8 she'll see his fancyman: a fancyman is a woman's lover.

Line 9 Cosmo Snooker Hall: a snooker club on Dublin's O'Connell Street, now closed.

Line 9/12 raise him . . . raise her: a term in poker to indicate that one player is trying to gain advantage over the other player.

Line 11 neigh: make a sound like a horse.

Line 15 net, umpire, and court: tennis terms; in this instance the speaker observes her parents arguing as though she is watching a tennis match, with her parents on either side of the net and herself in the middle, where the umpire is usually positioned.

Line 16 lobbed: hit in a high arc.

Line 29 alchemical: a seemingly magical process of transformation.

Line 32 sheered: swerved and changed course quickly.

'Hearth Lesson' is from Paula Meehan's 2009 collection *Painting Rain*.

several perspectives in this poem:
the child, adult Meehan reflecting back,
the child's fantasy ect.

? Questions

1. How would you describe the atmosphere in the speaker's childhood home? Which details best capture that atmosphere in your opinion?

2. This poem remembers a dramatic, unusual event. Were you surprised or shocked by it? Could you understand why it happened?

3. Stanza three describes the mother and father arguing. How would you describe their argument, their tone and the technique they use?

4. What do the Zeus and Hera references contribute to the poem? Do you think it a serious or a humorous touch?

5. What role does the speaker play during this domestic scene? How does she view her parents as they argue?

6. Explore the effect of stanza six and how particular words and the rhythm here adds to the drama.

7. Why are lines 30–31 so powerful?

8. Who won the argument in your opinion? Why do you think the poet ended the poem where she did?

9. Consider this poem in the light of other mother–daughter, father–daughter poems by Paula Meehan on your course. Which one do you like best and why?

10. Hearth Lesson. What lesson has been learned here? Think about the sound of these words when said aloud. What do they sound like?

Giovanni Lanfranco, 1624-25. *Council of Gods*. Galleria Borghese, Rome.

General Questions

A. 'Paula Meehan creates many dramatic and sensuous moments in both her private and public poetry.' Discuss the extent to which you agree or disagree with the above statement. Develop your response with reference to the poems by Meehan on your course.

B. 'Though Meehan's poetry offers a sharp and critical view of many aspects of Ireland and Irish life, there is a warmth and generosity in her work.' Discuss this statement, supporting your answer with reference to the poetry of Paula Meehan on your course.

C. 'Meehan's poetry tells memorable stories in a very engaging and powerful way.' Discuss this statement, supporting your answer with reference to the poetry of Paula Meehan on your course.

D. 'Meehan uses a range of images to develop her themes and to add drama to her poetry.' Develop how effectively she does this and, in your response, refer to the poems by Paula Meehan on your course.

E. From your study of the poetry of Paula Meehan on your course, select the poems that, in your opinion, best demonstrate the poet's ability to engage the reader through her effective use of poetic narrative and dramatic scenes. Justify your selection by demonstrating how Paula Meehan helps you to engage with her work through her effective use of poetic narrative and dramatic scenes.

F. 'Place and people are central to Paula Meehan's poetry and are remembered in evocative and vivid images and powerful symbols.' To what extent do you agree or disagree with this assessment of her poetry? Support your answer with suitable reference to the poetry of Paula Meehan on your course.

G. 'Meehan uses evocative language to create poetry that includes both personal reflection and public commentary.' Discuss this statement, supporting your answer with reference to both the themes and language found in the poetry of Paula Meehan on your course.

H. 'In her poetry, Meehan's voice can be both harsh and tender, but always compelling.' Would you agree with this view? Support your answer with suitable reference to the poetry of Paula Meehan on your course.

I. 'Meehan's poems are remarkable for their confidence and directness of address and for their sudden, intense bursts of lyricism.' Discuss this statement, supporting your answer with reference to the poetry of Paula Meehan on your course.

Critical Commentary

Buying Winkles

In this memory poem, a happy-childhood-memory poem, it's a woman's world – mother, daughter, the winkle-seller. The men mentioned, against whom the mother warns her daughter, are 'strange men' and the girl heading out into the night is both a little scared and excited.

The inner city world described is long gone, but the speaker remembers it vividly. It begins with an action, a speech act. There is no introduction:

> My mother would spare me sixpence and say,
> 'Hurry up now and don't be talking to strange
> men on the way.'

Details capture that sense of being scared and excited – 'dash', 'ghosts', the dark staircase 'where the bulb had blown', but from this enclosed world the speaker takes us out into the street and if the moon and stars were out it was a 'bonus'.

It's clear that the girl has been sent before to buy winkles and she always enjoyed it: 'even in rain I was happy'.

The use of direct speech in the opening lines gives the poem an immediacy and drama, but even here in those ordinary words there is a music:

> My mother would **s**pare me **s**ixpence and **s**ay

We follow the girl on her journey, the poem is filled with movement, and the present moment gives way to a future moment when the speaker pictures the winkles:

>   – the winkles
> would be wet and glisten blue like little
> night skies themselves.

Here the vast blue-black night skies are, in the poet's imagination, contained in the tiny glistening blue-black winkles.

The language is both special and ordinary. The simile 'like little/ night skies' contrasts with 'I'd hold the tanner tight/ and jump every crack in the pavement', but even here there's a keen awareness of how words work: 'I'd hold the tanner tight' has alliteration (**t**he, **t**anner, **t**ight) and conjures, in the image of a closed hand, excitement and expectation; by contrast, the image of jumping every crack in the pavement has an energy to it.

It's a poem filled with lively, happy details: waving to the women at windowsills or the women lingering in doorways, though the women in doorways could perhaps be prostitutes. The speaker would be unaware of this as she weaves 'a glad path through/ men heading out for the night'. Here, women are associated with the house, the home, with windowsills and doorways; the men 'heading out' suggests a freedom that only they can experience.

Yet the speaker is very much part of this world. The places and the people are familiar and that first section is filled with movement. It flows.

In the second section the winkle-seller is introduced.

> She'd be sitting outside the Rosebowl Bar
> on an orange-crate, a pram loaded
> with pails of winkles before her

A regular presence, the orange crate and the pram suggest that she's a practical woman, well-placed to catch the Rosebowl Bar customers. The pram also suggests that her childrearing is over but that she is still putting it to good use.

To the girl, the bar is another world; it's the world of men, 'men together', male camaraderie, a feeling of warmth and belonging. The details, 'the smell of men together with drink', 'light in golden mirrors', 'the hot interior' (smell, sight, feeling), create a sensuous atmosphere.

Section three enacts a little drama between the winkle-seller and the girl. It has speech and action and there's a gentleness in the exchange:

> I'd ask her again to show me the right way
> to do *it*. She'd take a pin from her shawl –
> 'Open the eyelid. So. Stick it in
> till you feel a grip, then slither him out.
> Gently, mind.' The sweetest extra winkle
> that brought the sea to me.
> 'Tell yer Ma I picked them fresh this morning.'

Details here are very effective: the pin in the woman's shawl, the verbs, 'Open', 'Stick', 'slither'; the pacing created by the short sentences, 'Open the eyelid. So.' The language is practical, but then a beautiful, musical sentence follows:

> The sweetest extra winkle
> that brought the sea to me.

The 'swee/sea/me' rhyme, the 't' sound in 'swee**t**est ex**t**ra', the alliterative 'sweetest . . . sea', the flow of the sentence make for a beautiful sentence. And it echoes the earlier image of the winkles being like 'little night skies' in that the little winkle is associated with the wide night sky and the wide, open sea.

The closing three lines are given their own space. The mood is triumphant. And though the poem speaks about something in the past, it is relived here as a vivid moment.

When the speaker set out to buy winkles, there was some unease and anxiety. Returning home is different:

> I'd bear the newspaper twists
> bulging fat with winkles
> proudly home, like torches.

The use of 'bear', 'bulging' and the simile 'like torches' lifts the experience and gives it a feeling of grandeur; it becomes a procession through ordinary Dublin streets. The speaker is proud and happy, we picture her walking tall.

The Pattern

This poem, in seven movements, has been described (by Peggy O'Brien) as 'a simple, clear unflinching portrait of her working-class mother and the guilty rebellion of a poet-daughter'. Eavan Boland sees it as a 'tough meditation on inheritance'.

An overview at the outset would look something like this:

I	The speaker reflects on her dead mother, their relationship, the speaker's regret.
II	A memory of her mother scrubbing and polishing the floor.
III	A memory of her mother remaking an old dress.
IV	Her mother remembers her girlhood and her protectiveness towards the speaker.
V	The speaker dreaming of a future beyond inner city Dublin.
VI	Her mother captured in a photograph, on her own, in the Phoenix Park in summer.
VII	Another memory: her mother knitting.

The mother remembered in this mother-and-daughter poem is a caring, selfless mother, almost always busy: cleaning, dress making, knitting. The daughter reflects on their relationship and how her mother's early death, at forty-two, means that the mother and daughter, who argued and fought, never had the chance to become friends and make up when the speaker had grown up.

Section I, in three quatrains with regular end-rhyme, is an ordered account, a summing-up of the speaker's relationship with her mother. The vivid images of tension, disagreements, even violence are contained in details such as 'the sting of her hand/ across my face', 'our wars', 'bitter and apart'.

Though the poem's first word, 'Little', suggests that the speaker, the eldest daughter, has inherited few actual possessions from her mother, by the poem's end we realise that she has inherited many precious memories.

The past and the present come together in this opening section. Her dead mother, the past, is remembered, but the focus is now on the speaker as she was making the poem:

> I wish now she'd lasted till after
> I'd grown up. We might have made a new start
>
> as women without tags like *mother*, *wife*,
> *sister*, *daughter*, taken our chances from there.

The longed-for relationship is one between two grown women, but it was not to be. The two lines, each an abrupt, complete sentence,

> At forty-two she headed for god knows where.
> I've never gone back to visit her grave.

are stark in tone and unsentimental. The words 'god knows where' do not allow for any religious comfort or consolation. 'I've never gone back to visit her grave' is a blunt, sharp, honest admission.

Section II, however, begins with 'what has come down to me', the many memories of a hard-working, working-class mother. The picture here, though written in the past tense, is brought alive through physical and sensuous details. The pride this mother took in her work and her determination to do her very best are evident. It's there in the energy in 'scrub' and 'armreach', her starting again, and the 's' and 'b' sounds, alliterating across the run-on lines (she'd scrub, Sunlight soap, sore, start, smell; brood banished, bedroom), create a fluent movement. The scent of lavender transforms the flat.

> First she'd scrub the floor with Sunlight soap,
> an armreach at a time. When her knees grew sore
> she'd break for a cup of tea, then start again
> at the door with lavender polish. The smell
> would percolate back through the flat to us,
> her brood banished to the bedroom.

This section also moves from physical description to reflection. The speaker wonders what her mother might have thought as she 'buffed the wax to a high shine'; the speaker questions 'did she catch her own face coming clear?/ Did she net a glimmer of her true self?/ Did her mirror tell her what mine tells me?'

These three questions bring daughter and mother closer together across time. They lead to the realisation that 'I have her shrug and go on/ knowing history has brought her to her knees'. Those words, 'brought her to her knees', not only refer, of course, to the mother actually on her knees as she cleans the floor but also become an image of a woman oppressed by the circumstances of her birth, and by the attitude towards women at the time.

Section II ends with a happy image of the work done, the floor waxed and getting the final polish. The metaphor of the planets in intricate orbit becomes a harmonious moment that brings mother and young children together:

> She'd call us in and let us skate around
> in our socks. We'd grow solemn as planets
> in an intricate orbit about her.

The ordinary living room in the flat is transformed by the mother's work and by the child's imagination. The world they know becomes other worldly. The mother, though bent down with work, creates a freedom for her children.

Section III, just six lines, is an atmospheric scene. The speaker observes her mother sewing and the fading light, the end of summer, the crimson cloth, the light from the fire makes for a quiet and shadowy scene. That the mother is 'bending' suggests she is intent on her task.

> She's bending over crimson cloth,
> the younger kids are long in bed.
> Late summer, cold enough for a fire,
> she works by fading light
> to remake an old dress for me.
> It's first day back at school tomorrow.

That she is preparing her eldest daughter for 'first day back at school tomorrow' reminds us of the importance the speaker's mother attaches to education.

Section IV This poem brings us back in time and **section IV** brings us farther back again. A dramatic mini-episode is played out when the mother remembers her teenage self, the memory prompt being the very dress she is remaking.

> 'Pure lambswool. Plenty of wear in it yet.
> You know I wore this when I went out with your Da.

The use of ordinary speech in a Paula Meehan poem roots the poem in a specific world. The mother's account of how her disapproving father 'dragged me in by the hair', 'in front of the whole street', is an ugly, frightening one. The added detail, that her hair 'was long as yours then', unites mother and daughter, whereas the male figure of the Granda is harsh, authoritarian, cruel. The young man that became the mother's husband and father of the speaker is called 'every name under the sun,/ cornerboy, lout'.

It's a scene locked in time in many ways. The mother sees her father as 'a right tyrant' and his treatment of his daughter is terrifying:

> He shoved my whole head
> under the kitchen tap, took a scrubbing brush
> and carbolic soap and in ice-cold water he scrubbed
> every spick of lipstick and mascara off my face.

Here, 'shoved my whole head', 'scrubbing brush', 'ice-cold water', emphasise his cruelty and contrast with the mother scrubbing the floor in section II, one kind, one cruel. The speaker's mother, using Sunlight soap, scrubbed to make things better; the speaker's Granda, using carbolic soap, scrubbed thinking he was making things better.

The scene ends with the mother's words: her swearing and telling her daughter, 'It'll be over my dead body anyone harms a hair/ of your head' are powerful and forceful. Her mother emerges as a very strong, loving, protective woman.

Section V, like section I, is in formal stanzas with regular end-rhyme. Here the speaker acknowledges her mother's generosity – 'She must have stayed up half the night/ to finish the dress' – and her own lack of gratitude: 'I wore that dress/ with little grace'. Speaking of those sections I and V, their formal pattern, the quatrains, the abba rhymes, Wes Davis says that in her mother's own story, the quatrain evaporates but '(it) later returns – as if Meehan is reasserting her own control – only to be overwhelmed again by the story. Remembering her mother, it seems, Meehan is losing track of her own pattern. But she does so in a way that recognises her mother's deeply rooted influence on her life's work.'

Section V speaks of the reality of poverty, second-hand clothes, the bright hope that school and education should symbolise – 'new copybooks on the table and a bright/ bronze nib' and it also contains one of the poem's most lyrical moments when the speaker dreams of sizing up

> the world beyond our flat patch by patch
> daily after school, and fitting each surprising
> city street to city square to diamond

and travelling far beyond Dublin and the Liffey. Her dream is a confident one. She watches 'the coming and going of ships,/ certain that one day it would carry me/ to Zanzibar, Bombay, the land of the Ethiops.'

The deliberate choosing and naming of these faraway, exotic places introduce a world very different from the confining world of a flat on Seán MacDermott Street in Dublin.

Section VII, unlike the closing lines of section VI which looked to the future, returns to her mother's past. The setting is elegant. She is both out of place and at home in such surroundings, and the speaker imagines that her mother in this photograph is dreaming too, just as she herself would dream of 'the world beyond our flat'. Both mother and daughter had their dreams, but for her mother 'the world beyond her/ already a dream, already lost'. That she is described as 'wrapped/ entirely in her own shadow' could suggest her early death. That 'She's eight months pregnant. Her last child.' adds to the sadness.

Section VII The final section, opens with bright activity, her mother knitting:

> Her steel needles sparked and clacked

We are back indoors, in the flat, in a mother–daughter scene. The assonance in 'steel needles' and the onomatopoeic 'sparked and clacked' bring the scene vividly before us. Hard-working as ever and sensible, the mother's practicality is revealed in her choice of colours, 'Moss Green, Mustard, Beige'.

Her mother, she imagines, had dreams; she, her daughter, dreams of colours other than those 'sensible shades'. In this final scene, mother and daughter are physically close, bound together by the task in hand. The daughter kneels before her mother to help her roll wool. But the imagery conveys longing, freedom, escape. The speaker, impatient at being tied down, yearns to be a kite, a fish, something filled with movement. The imagery is alive:

> If I swam like a kite too high
> amongst the shadows on the ceiling
> or flew like a fish in the pools
> of pulsing light

but, for now, she can escape only in her imagination; her mother brings her down to earth:

> she'd reel me firmly
> home, she'd land me at her knees.

It is in the poem's final section that the poem's title can be found. Her mother is knitting and is at 'a hard part in the pattern' and the poem's final word repeats 'pattern'. And the mother is given the last word in the poem. The image of 'Tongues of flame in her dark eyes' suggests depth and passion.

'By the end of the poem', says Wes Davis, 'the snatch of speech it seems created to remember becomes a joke about its own form':

> 'One of these days I must
> teach you to follow a pattern.'

The poem has its own pattern and that pattern has been shaped by the poet's relationship with, and memories of, her mother.

The Statue of the Virgin at Granard Speaks

The terribly sad and shocking events of the deaths of fifteen-year-old Ann Lovett and her baby, in January 1984, in Granard, County Longford, made headlines around the world. Paula Meehan was twenty-nine at the time and when she published this poem in 1991, seven years later, she chose to speak the poem in the voice of the Virgin Mary, another young woman who gave birth to a son, and whose statue was one of the last things Ann Lovett saw as she lay dying. Traditionally, the Virgin Mary is a silent presence. Here, Meehan gives her a voice.

The poem takes place on All Souls' Night, 2 November, a day when Catholics traditionally prayed for the souls in Purgatory and visited graveyards. The poem, in nine movements, could be summed up as follows:

Lines 1–7: the speaker, in her grotto, describes the bitter cold of a November night.

Lines 8–19: a wider world of towns, cities, lanes, where men hunt each other, a reference to what was happening in Northern Ireland at the time.

Lines 20–29: the speaker introduces herself, speaks of what she is associated with and how people kneel before her and pray to her.

Lines 30–35: the year's cycle – springtime, a time of promise and ease.

Lines 36–42: summer – a time of freedom – the speaker longs for a lover.

Lines 43–49: autumn – a time of abundance – and, like the dying of the year, death is natural.

Lines 50–55: All Souls' Night – the speaker imagines the dead rising up and demanding a judgement from above.

Lines 56–67: the speaker remembers the fifteen-year-old girl who died before her last January and how she did nothing to help.

Lines 68–74: the speaker looks to the winter solstice, the turn in the year when the days get longer, brighter, and calls on the sun to hear her and have pity.

The opening lines create a cold, lonely atmosphere. Outdoors, it is 'bitter'; indoors, 'The whole town tucked up safe and dreaming'. The sound of the howling wind is the only sound, 'even wild things gone to earth'.

From the title we know that it is the statue that speaks, and at line 5, with the word 'I', the impossible but arresting idea of a statue speaking is made clear. An inanimate object speaking a poem is both an unusual and powerful device. In the eighth-century Old English poem 'The Dream of the Rood', the cross on which Christ was crucified tells its story. Here in Meehan's poem it is the Mother of Christ who speaks. That she describes herself as:

> stuck up here in this grotto, without as much as
> star or planet to ease my vigil

suggests her discomfort, unease, loneliness. The use of 'stuck' is accurate – the statue is firmly situated in the grotto – but it also suggests a state of mind. Mention of 'star or planet' allows us to picture a vast night sky. Small-town Ireland is asleep, the statue in the small grotto is complaining, but the star-and-planet image opens up the setting and invites the reader/listener to think about the cosmos.

The statue longs for some 'ease' during her 'vigil', the word vigil implying that she is a watching, attentive, caring presence.

The second stanza speaks of the trees cavorting in agony and longing for escape. Here, the personification of the trees adds drama to the landscape, and the wind that might carry them away is also the wind that

> carries intimations
> of garrison towns, walled cities, ghetto lanes
> where men hunt each other and invoke
> the various names of God as blessing
> on their death tactics, their night manoeuvres.

Such details conjure up a cruel, perverse world of sectarian hatred, both sides claiming to be acting in the name of God, a world in which men commit dark deeds. These details are left vague but their effect is clear. The statue is speaking of underhand, violent acts carried out by men in places over the border in Northern Ireland.

In the stanza's closing lines the focus shifts back to the immediate world of the Marian grotto:

> Closer to home the wind sails over
> dying lakes. I hear fish drowning.
> I taste the stagnant water

Words such as 'dying lakes', the drowning fish and 'stagnant water' paint a negative image of the natural world, a world polluted, though the scent of 'turf smoke from outlying farms' suggests a homely, safe one.

The third stanza summarises the trauma and violent suffering of Christ's Crucifixion. But first she calls herself by those names given to her. 'Blessed, Holy, Virgin', and the statue then speaks of the Crucifixion as myth. Myth is an interesting choice of word (it can mean a traditional story that explains something about a society or religious belief, a widely held but false belief, an exaggerated tale) and it would not be the first word that would come to the mind of a devout Christian contemplating the Crucifixion of Christ.

The horror of Christ's death is undeniable:

> the scourging and the falling, and the falling again,
> the thorny crown, the hammer blows of iron
> into wrist and ankle, the sacred bleeding heart

and the details and the emphatic use of 'and' and 'the' here heighten the suffering. But the statue would seem to be uneasy that

> They name me Mother of all this grief

Though she is a mother, but 'mated to no mortal man', she conceived her son in a strange and mysterious way that results in people coming to the grotto to pray to the Virgin. Those who pray at the grotto are filled with faith, conviction; they implore, beseech, petition the statue to intercede and help them. The statue, however, speaks of those prayers as futile:

> They kneel before me and their prayers
> fly up like sparks from a bonfire
> that blaze a moment, then wink out.

In her private thoughts she offers them little comfort. Later in the poem the statue admits offering no help to the young girl who gave birth at that same grotto.

Stanzas four, five, six and seven speak of the seasons. The poem evokes spring, summer, autumn, winter and the first three are beautifully atmospheric. What characterises spring, summer and autumn are the rituals (Communion; wedding; funeral), the nature imagery ('riot in the hedgerows'; 'earth herself calls out for coupling'; 'hedges heavy with the burden of fruiting'), the feeling of joy and freedom and the natural and inevitable sorrow of dying.

The statue is happiest during those seasons and the poem's energy and sense of delight and celebration are evident: the delight in seeing cow parsley and haw blossom, the scent of hay, the long sun-filled evenings, 'crab, sloe, berry, hip'; 'clouds scud east/ pear scented', 'windfalls secret in long/ orchard grasses' are musical in their descriptions.

The speaker rejoices in this desire and urge to procreate, 'the earth herself calls out for coupling', so much so that she wishes she could

> break loose of my stony robes,
> pure blue, pure white, as if they had robbed
> a child's sky for their colour.

Everywhere about her at this time of year there is positive activity.

>   My being
>   cries out to be incarnate, incarnate,
>   maculate and tousled in a honeyed bed.

The Virgin here regrets her situation, that she conceived a child not in a natural, human way. The repetition and the rhyme are emphatic. The words 'tousled' and 'honeyed bed' convey physical freedom and pleasure.

Even death, 'an autumn burial', is seen as natural: 'Death is just another harvest/ scripted to the season's play' – the tone here one of quiet acceptance.

The mood darkens at the beginning of stanza seven when the poem returns to the present and a bitterly icy-cold All Souls' Night.

Even the wind is mourning and 'there is/ no respite from the keening of the wind.' There follows then a surreal scenario befitting All Souls' Night:

>   I would not be amazed if every corpse came risen
>   From the graveyard to join in exaltation with the gale,
>   a cacophony of bone imploring sky for judgement
>   and release from being the conscience of the town.

The statue imagines that this very time could be the Day of Judgement, when, in Christian thought, the dead will rise up to be judged. The phrase 'cacophony of bone' is a startling image, one of skeletons raising their hands and arms skywards. The speaker imagines the dead in the nearby graveyard pleading for 'release from being the conscience of the town'.

Paula Meehan never names the dead girl and her baby in the poem, but stanza eight returns to the winter day in January when they died. That the girl is described as a child 'with fifteen summers to her name' reminds us not only of how young she was but that her happiness was short-lived.

The details of the birth are stark, grim. The use of mainly monosyllabic words in the line

>   and she lay down alone at my feet

slows the rhythm and the speaker's use of 'my' points to the physical connection between the statue and the young girl. Why she came to this place to give birth (she was nine months' pregnant) is not clear, but such statues symbolise for many a maternal, caring presence.

That she is alone is spelt out:

> without midwife or doctor or friend to hold her hand
> and she pushed her secret out into the night

and the statue speaks disapprovingly of the town as a

> town tucked up in little scandals,
> bargains struck, words broken, prayers, promises

but she also faults herself in a recital of all that she did not do:

> and though she cried out to me *in extremis*
> I did not move,
> I didn't lift a finger to help her,
> I didn't intercede with heaven,
> nor whisper the charmed word in God's ear.

'I did not', 'I didn't', 'I didn't' is a stark admission.

Lucy Collins, commenting on these lines, says that '(the) relentless nature of this denial simultaneously marks the girl's estrangement from all the sources of support and comfort that should have been available to her, and the alienation of religion from humility and compassion.'

The Virgin Mary is often seen by Catholics as an intermediary between the individual and God. But the statue tells us that she was silent even though the girl called out to her. 'I did not move' could be interpreted as a touch of black humour. (Statues do not move, though in the summer of 1985, in Ballinspittle and elsewhere in Ireland, statues of the Virgin Mary were said to move. Psychologists in UCC said these 'visions' occurred when people stared at the statue at twilight and explained them as optical illusions.) In this instance, it is an image of the statue's failure to respond to the girl's cry for help.

The girl turned to the statue and there was no response. In the poem's closing lines the statue turns to the sun, not to God, for comfort. There is a deep tone of longing, a sense of life being a 'foolish dance', a pleading by the statue for light and for pity.

> On a night like this I number the days to the solstice
> and the turn back to the light.
> O sun,
> centre of our foolish dance,
> burning heart of stone,
> molten mother of us all,
> hear me and have pity.

The world in these closing lines becomes huge. The sun holds the solar system together and it is mother sun whom the statue addresses, not God the Father.

The statue of the Virgin is no longer the traditional Catholic Virgin Mary; she longs to be part of a bigger picture, part of the natural world, a nature goddess.

●

'The Statue of the Virgin at Granard Speaks' touches on many aspects of life: sexuality, men, women, religion, belief, nature, the seasons. The poem is giving voice to a woman and gives her a voice that is unexpected, uneasy, direct and honest. It questions accepted opinion. The Virgin Mary as revealed here is a flawed human being, a woman filled with regret and longing.

The poem brings together two women from across the centuries. Both gave birth to baby boys in difficult circumstances. The setting of this poem is Ireland in the 1980s, an Ireland very different from the Ireland of the twenty-first century. In an interview (*Stet*, Winter 1990), Paula Meehan, speaking of the Catholic Church, said 'You'd laugh at the church if you didn't know it is causing so much misery.'

In Meehan's poem 'Hannah, Grandmother', she remembers her grandmother telling her when she was twelve or thirteen: 'Tell them priests nothing . . . Keep your sins to yourself./ Don't be giving them a thrill/ Dirty oul feckers.' And in her poem 'The Ghost of My Mother Comforts Me', Meehan, in the voice of her mother, says 'Because I am your mother I will protect you/ as I promised you in childhood./ You will walk freely on the planet,/ my beloved daughter. Fear not/ the lightning bolts of a Catholic god, or any other,/ for I have placed my body and soul between you and all harm.'

'Within the Buddhist religion, there are many different strands of Buddhism: Zen, Tibetan Buddhism, Taoist thought. That's been a constant source. I wouldn't even like to describe myself as a Buddhist – I'm probably as bad a Buddhist as I was a Catholic – but it did give me a powerful support system at a time when I couldn't have had any kind of spiritual life within Catholicism. It was just so septic, the whole patriarchy, the priesthood, the role in our culture, the way I saw my mother's generation churning out children because they were denied access to contraceptives. There was no way I could go to the church after about fourteen or so even though I had great respect for the piety of my grandmother, her generation, how much they loved Our Lady, the May altars; I too loved all that ceremony, devotion. And that's the word, devotion; they were so devout and good and powerful models as women. But I just couldn't handle the whole patriarchal thing, the hierarchy of these men in skirts calling the shots; I was very disaffected from the church. In Buddhism you don't even have to believe in a god, it's a practice; well it can be as practical as building a table. It's part of my daily routine, trying to live a mindful and compassionate life and I like the holistic vision at the heart of it: the interpenetration of all species and all creatures on the planet. I've heard stuff that leads me to believe that the monastic systems in places like Thailand or Japan can be as corrupt as anywhere else, they're open to the same venal impulses and vices, but as a path it's been very useful to me.' (Extract from 'The Body Politic: A Conversation with Paula Meehan', by Jody Allen Randolph.)

My Father Perceived as a Vision of St Francis

Some poems explore public themes, some explore private worlds. Paula Meehan writes both. 'Death of a Field' and 'Prayer for the Children of Longing', for example, are public utterances; 'The Pattern' and 'My Father Perceived as a Vision of St Francis' are more private in nature, one a daughter–mother poem, this one a daughter–father poem.

The long title is stately and the use of 'perceived' adds a formality. This is a special moment; it deserves this ceremonial touch.

This poem speaks of something ordinary and something extraordinary and the ordinary and the extraordinary are one and the same.

The opening sentence establishes the scene. The setting is a house in Finglas. It begins with a sound outdoors and then the second sentence brings the reader to the confined space of a box bedroom. If this poem were a film it would begin, perhaps, with an aerial shot of frosty rooftops, gardens, the piebald horse and then an interior shot of a bedroom. Later it moves gradually beyond the room, beyond the house and becomes freeing and celebratory in its praise for the speaker's father and the natural world.

The sound of a whinnying piebald horse at dawn is not the most beautiful sound to wake up to. The speaker, we learn, is 'frightened . . . out of a dream' and the bedroom,

> my brother's room now,
> full of ties and sweaters and secrets

is economically and effectively described. The word 'secrets' is the unusual word here. Ties and sweaters are normal, but the choice of 'secrets' adds a private, interesting inner aspect to her brother's life.

The waking world beyond the bedroom is conveyed through sounds:

> Bottles chinked on the doorstep,
> the first bus pulled up to the stop.

And 'The rest of the house slept/ except for my father'.

That the father is introduced at line 10, following a stanza break, gives him more focus, importance. His early-morning activity reveals a caring and contented man.

It's a poem full of sounds — 'whinny', 'Bottles chinked', 'first bus pulled up to the stop', 'rake the ash from the grate', 'plug in the kettle', 'hum a snatch of a tune', 'unlocked the back door' — and these sounds in stanzas one and two contrast with the implied sounds of birdsong.

It's an ordinary morning. The speaker pictures her father in her mind's eye as he moves about the kitchen downstairs and then she sees her father below in the garden. The 'first frost' in late autumn 'whitened the slates of the estate' and just as the year is getting older, so too is her father and she notices this:

> He was older than I had reckoned,
> his hair completely silver,
> and for the first time I saw the stoop
> of his shoulder, saw that his leg was stiff

This sympathetic response marks a different mood. Stanzas one and two are more descriptive. Now a feeling of concern enters the poem and the questions

> What's he at?
> So early and still stars in the west?

suggest more engagement. The daughter is noticing things about her father that she hasn't noticed before: he is older, more frail. The time of year, late autumn, and her father's time of life are similar.

The mood in this third stanza and the images of whitened slates, silver hair, stooping shoulders convey sadness in the speaker. Alliteration ('first frost'; 'saw the stoop/ of his shoulder, saw that his leg was stiff'), rhyme ('slates of the estate'), repetition (his hair ... his shoulder ... his leg') and rhythm all create a quiet, reflective mood.

But then the poem takes a different turn and what makes this possible is her father's interaction with the birds. The rhythm is different. That the speaker asked 'What's he at?' suggests that this early-morning ritual is something special, private, not widely known.

Stanza four is a flurry of excitement. The birds are never named but they are

> of every size, shape, colour

and the back garden is suddenly the focus for birds from hedges and shrubs, eaves and garden sheds, the industrial estate, outlying fields, Dubber Cross, the ditches of the North Road. The list here expands the reader's/listener's sense of place. Four of the lines begin with 'from' and this gives a sense of many directions, endless arrivals.

The poem moves outwards towards those places, only to draw back again to focus on a man feeding a large number of birds in his back garden. Her father is the centre of the world.

The place is transformed. 'The garden was a pandemonium' captures the movements, sounds, excitement of the birds and the detail 'my father threw up his hands' is an open, generous, liberating one. The verbs 'threw' and 'tossed' convey this movement and the poem's final image is a bright and brilliant image of sunshine and saintliness and youth-like energy.

The closing lines reintroduce the St Francis metaphor, already announced in the poem's title. And the run-on line between stanzas five and six, as between stanzas one and two, gives the effect of one lyrical flowing final sentence matching the joy felt on witnessing the father transformed into 'a perfect vision of St Francis'.

The description of the sun is fresh and childlike; it's an image full of energy:

> The sun
> cleared O'Reilly's chimney

Here the inclusion of the neighbour's name adds a very ordinary, down-to-earth, realistic touch, but this is followed by 'suddenly' and 'radiant'.

> and he was suddenly radiant,
> a perfect vision of St Francis,
> made whole, made young again,
> in a Finglas garden.

Everything that was ordinary and familiar and everyday has been transformed. Her father is now made young again, washed in a golden glow of early-morning light. The speaker presents us with a new vision of a stooped, silver-haired, stiff-legged old man, a vision that is uplifting and beautiful.

The final detail, 'a Finglas garden', reminds us that miracles occur and in the most ordinary of places.

Writing about this poem, Eavan Boland says: 'The scene is unassuming, delicately drawn. An early morning in a Dublin suburb. Frost on the roof-slates. A father, seen by his daughter as older and more frail than she had quite realised, unlatching the back door and going into the garden. When the birds come from other neighbourhoods, flying in for the crumbs he will throw, we know at one level that this is an entirely private and local moment. But at another level, a wonderful series of inferences has been started and continues: of faith, of the iconography of Catholicism, of shifts of power between a daughter and a father, of the ordinary landscape of a suburb claimed as a visionary moment.'

Wes Davis notes how Meehan 'first perceives her father's presence in the rattling soundtrack of an ordinary day – "I heard/ him rake the ash from the grate,/ plug in the kettle, hum a snatch of a tune" – before witnessing his saintly metamorphosis . . . The sun, the breadcrumbs, the birds, the father's accidental posture: what turns the scattered details into poetry, and the moment into a housing-estate epiphany, is a triumph of the imagination that occurs when a chance thought flickers through the mind stitching them all together.'

The Exact Moment I Became a Poet

The title is precise and confident. And that the title flows into the poem's opening line gives the statement more power and momentum. Paula Meehan remembers her eight-year-old self and a pivotal, life-changing moment. The year is 1963, the setting a classroom and the details belong to world of duster and chalk, a blackboard on an easel, a world long gone.

> The Exact Moment I Became a Poet
>
> was in 1963 when Miss Shannon
> rapping the duster on the easel's peg
> half obscured by a cloud of chalk
>
> said . . .

The rapping sound suggests a brisk, pay-attention note, and Miss Shannon's message is clear, concise, abrupt: '*Attend to your books, girls,/ or mark my words, you'll end up/ in the sewing factory.*'

The poem's first two stanzas focus more on the outer world, but the remaining stanzas trace the interior thoughts and feelings of the speaker as she processes Miss Shannon's words and their implication.

The young girl, a poet in the making, questions words and their significance. She knows women, 'some of the girls'/ mothers', her aunt, neighbours who work in the sewing factory, but

> those words 'end up' robbed
> the labour of its dignity.

The speaker is uneasy. She senses in her teacher's words a dismissive attitude towards those women who work in the sewing factory. The phrase 'end up' diminishes their lives.

But the eight-year-old couldn't articulate how she felt then.

> Not that I knew it then,
> not in those words – labour, dignity.
> That's all back construction,
>
> making sense

She comes to realise and recognise, however, that the teacher's warning and advice to her young pupils were well-meaning. She admits that the teacher was right in a single line, with its nine words, eight of them monosyllables, that achieves a quiet force.

and no one knows it like I do myself.

The speaker did not '*end up/ in the sewing factory*' and there is a tone of gratitude, but at line 19 the word 'But' paints a picture of those women who did work there. She pictures them clearly: 'I *saw* them' we are told, and the image is one of women, 'mothers, aunts, neighbours' as 'trussed like chickens/ on a conveyor belt'.

This depersonalised image strips the factory workers of their individuality. 'Factory', 'labour', 'dignity' are keywords and are repeated in the poem.

The final stanza is a meditation on the power of words, the poet's medium.

> Words could pluck you,
> leave you naked,
> your lovely shiny feathers all gone.

That eight-year-old girl is now a grown woman and a poet. She remembers that exact moment in the classroom, a moment when words hurt. That words 'could pluck you,/ leave you naked'. Words can strip you of your dignity, but, being a poet, she also knows that words empower. And this very poem on the page empowers its maker. It also empowers the reader and everyone who sits in a classroom.

The poem's argument turns on 'It wasn't', 'Not that', 'But' at the beginning of lines 7, 13, 19. The nine three-line stanzas that make up the poem contain a clear tone of voice, a voice that quietly protests, understands, and a mood in the closing stanza that is both sad and protective.

Death of a Field

Even on a first reading of this poem, with its chant-like mood, it has, in Mary O'Malley's words, a 'calm certainty of tone'. It's the first poem in Meehan's 2009 collection *Painting Rain* and addresses a public event. A field is being turned into a site, a housing estate. (The Irish economy from the mid-1990s to 2007 is known as the Celtic Tiger. During that time property prices peaked and many mistakes were made. Meehan laments the death of this particular field.)

Meehan's poem focuses on one field near her home in Baldoyle, County Dublin, but that field and what happens to it are both real and symbolic. Lines 1–28 make statements, ask questions and tell of how this field in north County Dublin has been sacrificed for forty-four housing units. The remaining lines, lines 29–39, are the speaker's personal response. She uses 'I' for the first time and describes how she will walk this field, barefoot, in moonlight; she will remember it and possess it in her mind, her heart, her imagination. And by implication in her poem.

The opening line announces, in mainly impersonal, functional language, a dramatic change:

> The field itself is lost the morning it becomes a site
> When the notice goes up: Fingal County Council – 44 houses

Here, the words 'site', 'notice', 'Fingal County Council' are words not often associated with poetry. But the word 'lost' in this context brings a sadness and reveals the speaker's personal regret.

The structure of the poem and the use of repetition are effective here. One-line, two-line, three-line stanzas and longer sections create a rhythm that reinforces the poem's theme.

Line 3, for example, a single line, speaks of memory, an idea Meehan returns to in the closing lines. Memory is associated with herbs, fragrant plants used in cooking, with medicinal and spiritual associations, summing up positive images.

> The memory of the field is lost with the loss of its herbs

Then the birds 'woodpigeons', 'finches', 'wagtail', 'magpies' are listed, the details and the alliteration and simile used – woodpigeons in the willow, the hawthorn hedge, the wagtail in the elder, magpies sounding like flying castanets – create happy and musical images.

The poem's next focus is flora. Yarrow and scarlet pimpernel are not just named, they are given feelings: the yearning of yarrow, the plight of the scarlet pimpernel. Here too, just like with the loss of the herbs, the loss of its flora marks the disappearance of the field.

'Line by line', says Mary O'Malley, 'she names the birds, the vetches and worts and flowers and holds the field in the poem.'

Then Meehan speaks of the field as a place where young people experienced rites of passage:

> And the end of the field is the end of the hidey holes
> Where first smokes, first tokes, first gropes
> Were had to the scentless mayweed

The language is the informal language of teenagers and the stanza evokes a world that contrasts with the world of birds and flowers, a world where teenagers explored and experimented, and those three worlds will be no more when the field is replaced with forty-four houses.

Houses. They are never called homes

> The end of the field as we know it is the start of the estate
> The site to be planted with houses each two- or three-bedroom

The use of 'planted' is ironic and the image of the site as a 'Nest of sorrow and chemical, cargo of joy' captures the sadness of losing the field and the sorrow felt when a man-made world replaces a natural one, even if the phrase 'cargo of joy' is hopeful.

The stanza beginning 'The end of . . .', a phrase repeated seven times, is insistent. Both of the two previous stanzas began with 'The end of the field' and now, using a very simple and powerful technique, the reality is drummed home. The technical name for this repetition at the beginning of a line is anaphora. That and the repeated 'the start of' and the contrast between something natural (plants) and something synthetic (cleaning agents) in every line emphasises the poet's concern. The names Flash, Pledge, Ariel, Bounce have positive connotations, but dandelion, dock, teasel, primrose, thistle, sloe, herb robert, eyebright are placed first and win out.

The reader, every reader, 'us', is addressed in the lines

> Who amongst us is able to number the end of grasses
> To number the losses of each seeding head?

The infinite number of grasses, the countless number of grass seeds highlight the huge loss felt by the speaker in this rhetorical question.

Despite the subject matter, the death of a field, the poem's final image is a happy one. The line 'I'll walk out once' is given a special place and space on the page and the lines that follow become a pastoral dream:

> I'll walk out once
> Barefoot under the moon to know the field
> Through the soles of my feet to hear
> The myriad leaf lives green and singing
> The million million cycles of being in wing

It will be the poet's final moment with a field that will soon no longer be a field. The details – barefoot, the moon, the leaves, the birds, the insects – are simple and beautiful. The poet going barefoot, knowing the field 'through the soles of my feet', means closer contact with the earth and the use of 'myriad' and 'millions, millions' highlights the riches of that ecosystem.

The hopeful note in the closing lines captures Meehan's wish to preserve the field for herself, and even then she acknowledges its power when she says 'I might possess it or it possess me'.

There will come a time when the field will be no more than

> map memory
> In some archive on some architect's screen

but the very poem on the page remembers the field before it was concreted over.

The poem's final image contrasts with its harsh opening lines. She has possessed the field

> Through its night dew, its moon-white caul
> Its slick and shine and profligacy
> In every wingbeat in every beat of time

The final line echoes the wingbeat of birds, but it also reminds us that this field will be remembered by the poet through time. The image of moon-white is beautiful, calm, and 'caul' suggests a protective layer, even though nothing can protect the field now.

●

In *A Fine Statement*, John McDonagh says that in this poem Meehan 'alludes to all that is lost in the process of development and the irony that one of the consequences of the economic drive towards increased prosperity is the destruction of the very environment that supports it in the first place, a clear metaphor for the problems facing the environment in the future.'

Them Ducks Died for Ireland

The park superintendent's report which serves as the introduction to the poem focuses on the damage caused in St. Stephen's Green during the Easter Rising:

> '6 of our waterfowl were killed or shot, 7 of the garden seats broken and about 300 shrubs destroyed.'

It's unexpected information in one way. Regarding the Easter Rising, one might expect a report of the wounded and the dead and yet there is something endearing in the superintendent's use of 'our'. He cares for all aspects of Stephen's Green.

The poem's opening word, 'Time', signals both present and past. The setting is an elegant room overlooking Stephen's Green. Its sash windows and oaken boards suggest it's an old building, a building that witnessed the activity of The Rising. Time is seen as sliding slowly down the window and the image of a window puddling in light creates a very attractive, shimmering image.

In that same opening stanza, the sense of time expands beyond the moment. Beyond the window 'The Green/ is a great lung, exhaling like breath on the pane'. Here the outside world is reflected on the glass and now time contains 'the seasons' turn, sunset and moonset, the ebb and flow/ of stars'.

Two four-line stanzas and two three-line stanzas with regular end-rhyme suggest a neat, ordered poem. But that second stanza returns us to 1916 and the turmoil of revolution. That very window reflected the great lung of Stephen's Green, but at that time the place was alive with 'smoke and fire', and Countess Markievicz is portrayed as a determined figure. Her stride embodies 'a Republic's destiny' and the line

> the bloodprice both summons and antidote to pride

captures the complexity surrounding the blood sacrifice involved in The Rising. Countess Markievicz fought, but the speaker sees her gesture as one to be proud of and yet something that would also prevent a feeling of pride.

The line 'When we've licked the wounds of history, wounds of war' looks to a future when

> we'll salute the stretcher-bearer, the nurse in white,
> the ones who pick up the pieces, who endure,
> who live at the edge, and die there

Here the poem goes beyond the singular, striding Markievicz and includes others who played their part, the stretcher-bearer, the nurse, their names never known. They are the ones Meehan wishes to acknowledge and praise now, and by using 'we' as in 'we'll salute' she is recognising the need for the Irish people to recognise them. It should be a communal act.

The poem she is writing acknowledges them; those forgotten names will be remembered in 'this archival footage read by fading light'. In the opening lines there were puddles of light on the oaken floor; now the light is fading. The archival footnote she speaks of is fragile, and the simile 'fragile as a breathmark on the windowpane' echoes and returns us to the window in the opening line.

This poem commemorates 'them ducks' in its title and introduction, but they are not mentioned again. The poem does focus on and wishes to remember those men and women, such as stretcher-bearer and nurse, who might have been forgotten. Names lost to history. Meehan says that remembering them now in this poem is fragile, but the poem's final note is quietly confident. This archival footnote is as delicate as 'the gesture/ of commemorating heroes in bronze and stone'.

Cora, Auntie

This sixty-six-line (22 x 3-line stanzas) memory poem, a family poem, reads fluently, easily. Meehan remembers her aunt, Cora. And she begins towards the end of Auntie Cora's life:

She's

> Staring Death down
> with a bottle of morphine in one hand,
> a bottle of Jameson in the other

Death, given a capital letter, is the enemy, but Cora is portrayed as a fighter. Armed with a painkiller and whiskey, she laughs at Death and a positive note is struck when we read she is much loved: 'love unconditional keeping her just this side/ of the threshold'.

The opening lines describe Cora's strong personality and the poem then describes her physical self, a withered body, her eyes darker and stranger. The detail that 'her hair grew back after chemo// thick and curly as when she was a girl' brings together the young Cora and the older, ill Cora.

The poem, in three parts, speaks first of Cora when she is close to death; then of Cora, in her prime, aged twenty-one, about to emigrate; and finally, of Meehan, haunted by memories which she gathers in a tin box and in the very poem on the page.

Cora stares at Death, laughs at Death, teases Death, tilts at Death, grins at Death. In that first part Death is mentioned five times, but Cora's attitude towards it, as contained in those five vibrant verbs, captures her defiant attitude. Meehan does not glamorise Cora's final year; she was 'old skin, bag of bones', she is the

> Scourge of Croydon tram drivers and High Street dossers
> on her motorised invalid scooter

but her youthfulness, 'always a girl in her glance', her spirited personality, her ability to bear the pain 'that last year', comes through

> not crucifixion but glory// in her voice.

The harsh reality of her illness and her sense of humour are captured vividly, but this first part ends with a gentle, beautiful, lyrical three lines:

> always a girl in her name —
> Cora, maiden, from the Greek KoÞñ,
> promising blossom, summer, the scent of thyme.

That these positive images follow the chilling words 'the rictus of Death' somehow defeats death. Cora herself challenged and tried to defeat death. Focusing here on Cora's name and its meaning brings the reader to Greece and to a place full of promise, sunshine, fragrance.

In part one, Cora, on her 'motorised invalid scooter', is described outdoors on Croydon High Street. Part two is set indoors in a flat in inner city Dublin in 1961 and in the poet's own kitchen many years later. The domestic scene in the flat belongs to women: grandmother, mother, aunties, the young girl underneath the table.

The dominant image in this second (and in the third section) is Sequin, italicised at the beginning of line 25 and followed by a colon indicating its importance. Cora is the centre of attention: she is standing on the kitchen table, taller, therefore, than the other women in the room who attend to her. The details are clearly stated:

> She is nearly twenty-one.
> It is nineteen sixty-one.
>
> They are sewing red sequins, the women,
> to the hem of her white satin dress
> as she moves slowly round and round.

Here is a young woman, her whole life before her. That we know, from part one, that Cora, later, became ill, had chemo, used a motorised invalid scooter, makes this section a sadder one even though it contains so many happy details.

The list of similes, 'Sequins red as berries,/ red as the lips of maidens,/ red as blood on the snow// in Child's old ballads' is deliberately poetic. The 'red as this pen/ on this white paper' simile is a here-and-now more ordinary image and Meehan's description of the making of the poem is interesting.

> I've snatched from the chaos
> to cast these lines
> at my own kitchen table –

The poem is in praise of Cora, but in naming 'Marie, Jacinta, my aunties,/ Helena, my mother, Mary, my grandmother' and referring to them as 'the light of those stars', the poem becomes a celebration of those other women in her family.

In her mind's eye Meehan sees that moment from years ago (she was six years old) as if it is travelling towards her through space and

> only reaching me now.
> I orbit the table I can barely see over.
> I am under it singing.

It is a happy, harmonious, special moment, a moment that contrasts with the mood in the poem's first section, which was overshadowed by illness and Death.

The closing lines tell of change:

> She was weeks from taking the boat to England.

Of her life in England, we know of it only towards the end. But she left Dublin with the good wishes contained in her good-luck cards.

> Dust on the mantelpiece,
> dust on the cards she left behind:
>
> a black cat swinging in a silver horseshoe,
> a giant key to the door,
> emblems of luck, of access

Those good wishes covered in dust suggest, perhaps, that those good wishes and hopes did not all come true?

The poet enters the poem at line 37 ('I've snatched . . .') and, though the entire closing section is in the 'I' voice, it is all about Cora, Auntie. It is 1961 and the hunting of sequins by the young girl captures her wish to be part of Cora's world.

Sequins are shiny, glamorous, feminine. Cora has gone. But traces of that happy-together, dressmaking moment remain in the dropped, lost sequins.

> 'I found them/ in crack and crannies,// in the pillowcase,/ under the stairs/
>
> in a hole in the lino,// in a split in the sofa,/ in a tear in the armchair/ in the home of a shy mouse.'

The repeated use of 'in' here captures Meehan's persistence and determination.

That she still has them

> With odd beads and single earrings,
> a broken charm bracelet, a glittering pin

in a tin box allows Meehan to relive her memories and value the connection between her younger self and an aunt whom she loved. 'I gathered them' and she treasured them and the tin box

> which I open now in memory –

allowing her to remember vividly 'the sudden glamour/ of an emigrant soul'.

'Cora, Auntie' is a poem that dwells on the past but the use of the present tense 'I open' and 'now' in that closing stanza gives the poem an immediacy and brings the past into the present.

Prayer for the Children of Longing

The explanatory note gives the background to the poem:

> *A poem commissioned by the community of Dublin's north inner city for the lighting of the Christmas tree in Buckingham Street, to remember their children who died from drug use*

and in this poem Paula Meehan writes of a world she knows first hand. It proves Meehan's concern for and commitment to her community. As an activist in the inner city in the early 1980s, Meehan knew of the devastation caused by drug use and worked towards ridding that part of Dublin of its drug pushers.

Dublin City Council provides local communities with Christmas trees that are often sourced in far northern forests and the opening lines describe a place remote, a place natural and beautiful, a place far from Dublin, the place where this tree was sourced.

> Great tree from the far northern forest
> Still rich with the sap of the forest

is a striking image from nature. A tall tree still rich with sap is about to be lit, 'Here at the heart of winter/ Here at the heart of the city'.

The speaker's tone is prayerful. The title announces that. With 'Grant us' at line 5, repeated at line 8, the speaker asks for clarity, comfort, silence, a clarity, comfort, silence associated with ice, snow and trees in the forest.

'The snow's breathless quiet' is seen as something that would console, soothe, strengthen those who know terrible suffering. The speaker asks the tree

> For one moment to freeze
> The scream, the siren, the knock on the door
> The needle in its track
> The knife in the back

The rhythm in stanzas one and two carries a formal sound. Line by line, repetition gains a quiet momentum:

> Great tree from the far northern **forest**
> Still rich with the sap of the **forest**
> **Here at the heart of** winter
> **Here at the heart of** the city
>
> **Grant us the** clarity of ice
> **The** comfort of snow
> **The** cool memory of trees
> **Grant us the** forest's silence
> **The** snow's breathless quiet

and alliteration (from, far, forest; still, sap; clarity, comfort, cool; silence, snow) creates its own music.

Stanza three paints a picture of a very different world, the frightening, destructive, violent world of scream, siren, needle and knife. This stanza, unlike the earlier stanzas, is full of sound and danger. The contrast between the two worlds, one natural, one man-made, highlights how children's lives have been ruined.

The poem focuses on children. 'Every child begins the world again' says Henry David Thoreau, but not every child is given the opportunities they deserve. Meehan's poem speaks of how lives are cut short. The phrase 'children of longing' is contained in the title, used twice in stanza four. Longing – yearning, desiring – is a positive idea. These north-inner-city children died young; they never realised their dreams. What they longed for never happened. Their song was never sung.

The longed-for silence of the forest, symbolised in this 'Great tree', is a silence where 'The song of the children of longing' will be heard, where 'The breath of the children of longing' will be caught.

Stanza five (lines 18–29), the longest stanza, moves up a gear in terms of its tone of passionate concern. The twelve lines are given force and power: each line begins with 'The' and 'That' and Meehan tells of lives ruined, of children who were promised everything and were given nothing:

> The echo of their voices through the city streets
> The streets that defeated them
> That brought them to their knees
> The streets that couldn't shelter them
> That spellbound them in alleyways
> The streets that blew their minds
> That led them astray, out of reach of our saving
> The streets that gave them visions and dreams
> That promised them everything
> That delivered nothing
> The streets that broke their backs
> The streets that we brought them home to

These lines lament their absence and offer a grim, realistic account of children oppressed and destroyed by drugs. The words are harsh: 'defeated them', 'brought them to their knees', 'couldn't shelter them', 'led them astray', 'broke their backs'. Meehan prays for a silence where their song, their voices, might still be heard, but the brutal truth is that these children died. A phrase such as 'blew their minds' tells of the mind-altering effect of drugs. Words such as 'visions and dreams' often have positive, happy associations. In this context they could refer to the false promises of drugs and drug pushers. That there is nothing glamorous about drug use is clearly evident here.

Having presented us with image after image of destruction, the three short, closing stanzas are filled with prayerful hope. They dwell on the lost children, their being remembered. Again, repetition at the beginning of the line, a Meehan hallmark, heightens the tone of voice. These children grew up in the inner city but the streets let them down.

> Let their names be the wind through the branches
> Let their names be the song of the river
> Let their names be the holiest prayers

Now the trees in the forest and the river are preferred as places to remember them by, 'under the starlight, under the moonlight', and lines from the opening stanza conclude the poem. Meehan returns us to here and now, to the Christmas tree, the 'Great tree from the far northern forest' at the heart of winter, at the heart of the city.

The poem charts the healing power of nature, laments the dead children, prays that they will be remembered. That their names will become part of the prayers spoken

> Under the starlight, under the moonlight
> In the light of the tree
>
> Here at the heart of winter
> Here at the heart of the city

Hearth Lesson

The dramatic episode recounted in 'Hearth Lesson' is just unforgettable. Once read, the mother's gesture will stay with you. The family is poor and this makes it all the more strange. The speaker has not forgotten that episode from her childhood. Well-known sayings and proverbs about money 'will bring it back'. Back to 'the flat in Seán MacDermott Street', where Meehan remembers being 'crouched by the fire'. The words 'I am', in the present tense, give the moment immediacy: the past becomes the present.

Sitting by the fire is a cosy image, but 'crouched' suggests a feeling of unease, an image of the young girl protecting herself.

The flat is a battlefield. The speaker's mother and father are arguing about money, 'the lack of it day after day'. Her father and mother are Zeus and Hera as they battle it out.

The Zeus and Hera metaphor brings us beyond the impoverished setting on Seán MacDermott Street'. The comparison of an Irish couple in Dublin in the 1960s to a passionate and stormy relationship between husband and wife figures from Greek mythology suggests the seriousness of the argument, but the exaggeration also introduces a humorous touch.

In the exchanges between Meehan's parents, recorded in stanza three, there is a spirited exchange; each one is well able for the other. Many women were not financially independent in Ireland in the 1960s. The man going out to work, the woman staying at home to look after the house and bring up the children was the usual scenario. Words such as 'thunderbolt', 'killing glance' and the poker terms all suggest a harsh, competitive atmosphere.

Lines such as

> she'll see his fancyman

could mean that the wife accuses her husband of being some other woman's lover, of being unfaithful, and

> raise him the Cosmo Snooker Hall;
> he'll see her 'the only way you get any
> attention around here is if you neigh';
> he'll raise her airs and graces

and lines such as capture a dangerous game being played out between husband and wife. There is a playful cruel humour in this exchange, until the playfulness gives way to pure cruelty as when the man mocks his wife's siblings:

> the mental state of her siblings,
> every last one of them.

The tennis metaphor places the young girl between her parents and 'lobbed' that the poet didn't understand all that was being said — it went "over her head".

> I'm net, umpire, and court; most balls
> are lobbed over my head.

Much is being said by her father and mother, but

> Even then I can judge it's better
> than brooding and silence and the particular hell of the unsaid,
> of 'tell your mother . . . ' 'ask your father . . .'.

Here, the speaker is recognising how language works in different ways. The 'hell of the unsaid', where Meehan is a go-between and her parents communicate with each other through their child, is worse than the loud arguments, however, perhaps the 'hell of the unsaid' are two different things: (i) Things that are not said (brooding and silence) and (ii) Things that Meehan communicates on behalf of each parent, and these are not necessarily the same thing.

Something occurs at line 20: the rhythm changes. 'Even then', used three lines earlier, marks a feeling of awareness in the speaker; the second 'Even then', at the beginning of line 20, deepens that mood:

> Even then I can tell it was money
> the lack of it day after day,
> at the root of the bitter words

Poverty was a reality. Money, the lack of it, was a problem 'day after day'.

The bitter words recalled earlier in the poem were just that: bitter words. The dramatic gesture that now follows is astonishing. A gesture totally unexpected:

> but nothing prepared us one teatime
> when he handed up his wages.

That a husband gave his wife his wages on a Friday evening back then was not unusual. When Meehan's father handed his wife the money, the reader might expect a truce, a reconciliation, peace.

The moment is carefully described. The detail

> She straightened each rumpled pound note

could lead to happiness, gratitude, harmony.

But 'then' is pivotal. It comes at the end of the line and on the turn everything changes:

>   then
> a weariness come suddenly over her,
> she threw the lot in the fire.

441

Money was needed. And the interesting thing here is how to interpret Meehan's mother's gesture. The money, burning in the fire, makes for a brief, beautiful moment:

> The flames were blue and pink and green,
> a marvellous sight, an alchemical scene.

But the words spoken by the mother, 'It's not enough', are 'stated simply'. This could mean that the father is not earning enough or that he has not given her all of his wages or that he has to give more than money in this relationship.

What makes those words all the more powerful is the line that follows:

> And we all knew it wasn't.

Does that 'we' include Meehan's siblings, Meehan's father? It's clear her mother at that point in time felt money was 'not enough'. If money had been the source and cause of the arguments, then only the father could solve that problem. Their exchanges were cruel and bitter and although money would offer security, perhaps, the mother also wanted respect, kindness. Her husband had a life beyond the flat; she was confined to home.

The final stanza paints a beautiful, colourful picture.

> The flames sheered from cinder to chimney breast
> like trapped exotic birds;
> the shadows jumped floor to ceiling, and she'd
> had the last, the astonishing, word.

The lines are filled with energy ('sheered', 'jumped') and the simile ('like trapped exotic birds') suggest a freedom.

A change has occurred. Something has happened. That the mother is given the last word, 'the last, the astonishing, word' not only empowers her but allows the reader to imagine an outcome, a different world from the world of conflict depicted in the poem.

Adrienne Rich
(1929–2012)

Contents	Page

The Overview

Adrienne Rich, poet and political activist, has been a striking and important presence for several decades and Michael Schmidt in *Lives of the Poets* sees her in the context of the 1960s and Black Power, the rise of feminism and the gay movement and Vietnam. 'It is necessary to see her in these contexts,' he argues, 'because they provide occasions first for her formal strategies and tentativeness, then for the emerging assurance that has made her a figure central to the American women's movement and to the liberalisation of American poetry.' But she is important for more than her political activism. Her poetry is a powerful response to the time but it is also a poetry which is acutely aware of a poetic tradition.

The ten poems prescribed here focus on themes central to Rich's work: power, gender, sexuality, the private, the political. 'Storm Warnings' is a poem that looks at change and its implications; 'Aunt Jennifer's Tigers' explores male power and authority within a domestic setting; a similar theme is found in 'The Uncle Speaks in the Drawing Room'. The role of the female, expected and otherwise, is a central idea in 'Living in Sin' and 'The Roofwalker' with its powerful image becomes an image of the unfulfilled speaker's sense of a life that is dangerous and different and longed for. 'Our Whole Life' reviews a relationship and admits that the situation is dishonest and hopeless but this poem is, in Adrienne Rich's words, 'concerned with an entire society facing its self-delusions'.

The tension between a man and a woman is also found in 'Trying to Talk with a Man' and the speaker feels 'helpless'. A more assertive voice speaks in 'Diving Into the Wreck', in which the central image of a woman exploring wreckage and returning to the surface with a new understanding becomes an image of a woman surviving her past. 'From a Survivor', written in 1972, addresses her dead husband, 'wastefully dead', and acknowledges with tenderness and regret – 'Like everybody else, we thought of ourselves as special' – the mystery, complexities and strangeness of human relationships. And in 'Power' Rich celebrates an extraordinary, selfless woman, Marie Curie, who dedicated herself to scientific knowledge and discovery with courage and determination.

Change is central to Adrienne Rich's life and work. 'What does not change is the will to change' writes Charles Olson in his poem 'The Kingfishers' and, quoting Olson, *The Will to Change* became the title of Rich's 1971 collection. Her poetry is a record of private and public, of the personal and the political and at the heart of her work is the need for and the courage for change.

Her changing life is reflected in her poetry both thematically and stylistically: her poetry became more urgent and less formal, less conventional. In her Foreword to *Collected Early Poems 1950–1970*, Rich notes that 'The word "change" occurs in the titles of both the first and the last books in this collection and in the first and last poems'.

In January 1984, when Adrienne Rich wrote a Foreword to *The Fact of a Doorframe Poems Selected and New 1950–1984*, which included the ten poems here, she said that 'The poems in this book were written by a woman growing up and living in the fatherland of the United States of North America. One task for the nineteen- or twenty-year-old poet who wrote the earliest poems here was to learn that she was neither unique nor universal, but a person in history, a woman and not a man, a white and also Jewish inheritor of a particular Western consciousness, from the making of which most women have been excluded'.

●

In a 1991 interview with David Montenegro in which she discussed how the language of poetry contains a kind of code, Rich admits that for her, from the beginning, 'poems were a way of talking about what I couldn't talk about any other way' and that 'I learned while very young that you could be fairly encoded in poems, and get away with it. Then I began to want to do away with the encoding, or to break the given codes and maybe find another code. But it was a place of a certain degree of control, in which to explore things, in which to start testing the waters'.

In a Foreword to *Collected Early Poems 1950–1970,* Rich says: 'My generation of North Americans had learned, at sixteen, about the death camps and the possibility of total human self-extinction through nuclear war. Still, at twenty, I implicitly dissociated poetry from politics. At college in the late 1940s, I sat in classes with World War II vets on the G.I. Bill of Rights; I knew women who campaigned for Henry Wallace's Progressive party, picketed a local garment factory, founded a college NAACP chapter, were recent refugees from Nazism. I had no political ideas of my own, only the era's vague and hallucinatory anti-Communism and the encroaching privatism in the 1950s. Drenched in invisible assumptions of my class and race, unable to fathom the pervasive ideology of gender, I felt 'politics' as distant, vaguely sinister, the province of powerful older men or of people I saw as fanatics. It was in poetry that I sought a grasp on the world and the interior events, 'ideas of order', even power.

I was like someone walking through a fogged-in city, compelled on an errand she cannot describe, carrying maps she cannot use except in neighborhoods already familiar. But the errand lies outside those neighborhoods. I was someone holding one end of a powerful connector, useless without the other end'.

Reviewing *Diving into the Wreck* in the *New York Times* Book Review, 10 December 1973, Margaret Atwood said that 'When I first heard the author read from it, I felt as though the top of my head was being attacked, sometimes with an ice pick, sometimes with a blunter instrument: a hatchet or a hammer. The predominant emotions seemed to be anger and hatred, and these are certainly present; but when I read the poems later, they evoked a far more subtle reaction. *Diving into the Wreck* is one of those rare books that forces you to decide not just what you think about yourself. It is a book that takes risks, and it forces the reader to take them also.'

'I never had much belief in the idea of the poet as someone of special sensitivity or spiritual insight, who rightfully lives above and off from the ordinary general life,' says Adrienne Rich and her poetry is very much an including experience. Her passionate interest in her fellow human being and her belief in the power of the poem are both wonderfully captured in her poem 'In A Classroom' from 1986:

In A Classroom

Talking of poetry, hauling the books
arm-full to the table where the heads
talking of consonants, elision,
caught in the how, oblivious of why:
I look in your face, Jude,
neither frowning nor nodding,
opaque in the slant of dust-motes over the table:
a presence like a stone, if a stone were thinking
What I cannot say, is me. For that I came.

Here we are also reminded of the importance of the making of the poem, the 'how'; and that an awareness of the technical aspects of the work such as 'consonants, elision' are vital.

The Harper American Literature Anthology [Volume 2] says that Adrienne Rich resembles the Victorians in 'her earnestness, her direct gaze at social conditions, and her tone of public moral assertion' and that her poetry 'lacks suppleness, play, wit, and humour; she is always serious'.

These last descriptions are intended as negative and yet Adrienne Rich's poetry speaks to hundreds of thousands of readers. Why this is so is best understood when we read Rich's own account of her sense of relationship with her reader: 'In writing poetry I have known both the keen happiness and the worst fear – that the walls cannot be broken down, that these words will fail to enter another soul. Over the years it has seemed to me just that – the desire to be heard, to resound in another's soul – that is the impulse behind writing poems, for me. Increasingly this has meant hearing and listening to others, taking into myself the language of experience different from my own – whether in written words, or in the rush and ebb of broken but stubborn conversations. I have changed, my poems have changed, through this process, and it continues.'

Her poetry has charted change both private and public. It is no coincidence that Adrienne Rich is thought to have coined the term 're-visioning' – which recasts the past and reworks received opinion and received stories and in turn her poetry has changed the way people live and think about their lives.

As an American she has seen her country, the most powerful in the world, exert its power. And she is outspoken. Writing of the Persian Gulf War, in 'What Is Found There', she says that 'War comes at the end of the twentieth century as absolute failure of imagination, scientific and political. That a war can be represented as helping a people to "feel good" about themselves, their country, is a measure of that failure.' All the more reason then that poetry plays its part. In that same book she writes: 'Poetry becomes more necessary than ever: it keeps the underground aquifers flowing; it is the liquid voice that can break through stone'.

She was undoubtedly serious, determined and sane: 'I intend to go on making poetry. I intend to go on trying to be part of what I think of as an underground stream – of voices resisting the voices that tell us we are nothing, that we are worthless, or that we all hate each other, or should hate each other. I think that there is a real culture of resistance here [United States, 1995] – of artists' and of other kinds of voices – that will continue, however bad things get in this country. I want to make myself part of that and do my work as well as I can. I want to love those I love as well as I can, and I want to love life as well as I can'.

The poems deal with many issues and work best when, in Margaret Atwood's words, 'they resist the temptation to sloganize, when they don't preach at me'.

In her poem 'Delta' dated 1987, Adrienne Rich writes:

> If you think you can grasp me, think again:
> my story flows in more than one direction
> a delta springing from the riverbed
> with its five fingers spread

and the poem, flowing in many directions, needs its readers: 'I believe that a poem isn't completed until there's a reader at the other end of it. It just can't be produced, it also has to be received.'

Biographical Notes

Adrienne [pronounced AHdrienne] Rich was born 'white and middle-class' on 16 May 1929 in Baltimore, Maryland. Encouraged by her father, she began writing poetry as a child and she also read from her father's 'very Victorian, pre-Raphaelite' library. As a girl growing up, she read Keats, Tennyson, Arnold, Blake, Rossetti, Swinburne, Carlyle and Pater. Such was her father's encouragement to read and write that 'for twenty years I wrote for a particular man, who criticised me and praised me and made me feel "special" . . . I tried for a long time to please him, or rather, not to displease him'. Her grandmother and mother, Rich said, were 'frustrated artists and intellectuals, a lost writer and a lost composer between them'.

Speaking of her early years, Rich herself said in 1983: 'I was born at the brink of the Great Depression; I reached sixteen the year of Nagasaki and Hiroshima. The daughter of a Jewish father and a Protestant mother, I learned about the Holocaust first from the newsreels of the liberation of the death camps. I was a young white woman who had never known hunger or homelessness, growing up in the suburbs of a deeply segregated city in which neighbours were also dictated along religious lines: Christian and Jewish. I lived sixteen years of my life secure in the belief that though cities could be bombed and civilian populations killed, the earth stood in its old indestructible way. The process through which nuclear annihilation was to become a part of all human calculation had already begun, but we did not live with that knowledge during the first sixteen years of my life.'

In 1951, Rich graduated from Radcliffe College, part of Harvard University, in Cambridge, Massachusetts. As an undergraduate, Rich read male poets – Frost, Dylan Thomas, Donne, Auden, MacNeice, Stevens, Yeats and at first she saw those male poets as her models. That same year she published her first collection, *A Change of World*, which had been chosen by W. H. Auden for the Yale Younger Poets Award. In a Foreword to the book, Auden said that the twenty-one-year-old 'Miss Rich' displayed 'a modesty not so common at that age, which disclaims any extraordinary vision, and a love for her medium, a determination to ensure that whatever she writes shall, at least, not be shoddily made'. But most famously, Auden said that the poems in Rich's first collection 'are neatly and modestly dressed, speak quietly but do not mumble, respect their elders but are not cowed by them, and do not tell fibs'.

In 1952–1953 Adrienne Rich travelled to Continental Europe and England on a Guggenheim Fellowship and in 1953 she married Alfred H. Conrad, an economist at Harvard. Later, writing of this time, Rich said: 'My husband spoke eagerly of the children we would have; my parents-in-law awaited the birth of their grandchild. I had no idea of what I wanted, what I could or could not choose'.

They lived in Cambridge from 1953 to 1966 and in the 1950s had three children. In 1955, Rich published her second collection *The Diamond Cutters and Other Poems*, which won the Ridgely Torrence Memorial Award of the Poetry Society of America. In 1960 she was honoured with the National Institute of Arts and Letters Award and the Phi Beta Kappa poet at William and Mary College. In 1961–1962 she and her family spent a year in the Netherlands on a Guggenheim Fellowship.

Wife, mother, prize-winning poet, Adrienne Rich, in the words of Richard Ellmann and Robert O'Clair, 'seemed to have everything a woman was supposed to want in the American Fifties'. And in her 'When We Dead Awaken' (1971) essay, Rich said that to think otherwise about that 1950s life 'could only mean that I was ungrateful, insatiable, perhaps a monster'. Yet the 1950s and early 1960s were in Ellmann and O'Clair's words 'desperate years for her'. It was a time in Rich's life when 'I think I began at this point to feel that politics was not something "out there" but something "in here" and of the essence of my condition'.

In 1963, her breakthrough collection, *Snapshots of a Daughter-in-Law* was published, with its themes of rebellion and disaffection, and in 1966 the family moved to New York City. She and her husband became radically political, especially in relation to the Vietnam War. She was teaching inner-city minority young people in an Open Admissions programme at City College, New York and this brought her into contact with young writers from different social and ethnic backgrounds. Her next three poetry collections, *Necessities of Life* (1966), *Leaflets* (1969) and *The Will to Change* (1971), in their very titles signalled a strong political awareness.

Married for seventeen years, Rich left her husband in 1969 and the following year he took his own life. In 1973, *Diving Into the Wreck* was published and won the National Book Award the following year. Rich, however, rejected the award as an individual but accepted it 'in the name of all women'. Audre Lorde and Alice Walker, the two other nominees, together with Adrienne Rich wrote the following statement: 'We . . . together accept this award in the name of all the women whose voices have gone and still go unheard in a patriarchal world, and in the name of those who, like us, have been tolerated as token women in this culture, often at great cost and in great pain . . . We symbolically join here in refusing the terms of patriarchal competition and declaring that we will share this prize among us, to be used as best we can for women . . . We dedicate this occasion to the struggle for self-determination for all women, of every colour, identification or derived class . . . the women who will understand what we are doing here and those who will not understand yet; the silent women whose voices have been denied us, the articulate women who have given us strength to do our work.'

Over forty years, Adrienne Rich published more than sixteen volumes of poetry and four books of non-fiction prose. She writes of being white, Jewish, radical and lesbian in America; she writes 'in full knowledge that the majority of the world's illiterates are women, that I live in a technologically advanced country where 40 per cent of the people can barely read and 20 per cent are functionally illiterate'. As a writer, Rich sees her work 'as part of something larger than my own life or the history of literature' and 'I feel a responsibility to keep searching for teachers who can help me widen and deepen the sources and examine the ego that speaks in my poems – not for "political correctness", but for ignorance, solipsism, laziness, dishonesty, automatic writing.'

In 1986, Rich wrote 'I had been looking for the Women's Liberation Movement since the 1950s. I came into it in 1970 . . . I identified myself as a radical feminist, and soon after – not as a political act but out of powerful and unmistakable feelings – as a lesbian'.

In an Interview with Bill Moyers in *The Language of Life, A Festival of Poets*, Adrienne Rich says: 'I believe that poetry asks us to consider the quality of life. Poetry reflects on the quality of life, on us as we are in process on this earth, in our lives, in our relationships, in our communities. It embodies what makes it possible for us to continue as human under the barrage of brute violence, numbing indifference, trivialization, and shallowness that we endure, not to speak of what has come to seem in public life like a total loss on the part of politicians of any desire even to appear consistent, or to appear to adhere to principle.'

Her works have been translated into Dutch, French, German, Greek, Hebrew, Italian, Japanese, Spanish, Swedish and Ukrainian and her many honours and awards include the Brandeis Creative Arts Commission Medal for Poetry, the Elmer Holmes Bobst Award in Poetry from New York University and the Fund for Human Dignity Award from the National Gay Task Force. She was a member of New Jewish Agenda, a national organisation of progressive Jews which disbanded in the 1980s and was a founding editor of the Jewish feminist journal *Bridges*.

Her most recent books of poetry are *Telephone Ringing in the Labyrinth: Poems 2004–2006* and *The School Among the Ruins: 2000–2004*. A selection of her essays, *Arts of the Possible: Essays and Conversations*, appeared in 2001. She edited Muriel Rukeyser's *Selected Poems for the Library of America. A Human Eye: Essays on Art in Society* appeared in April 2009. She is a recipient of the National Book Foundation's 2006 Medal for Distinguished Contribution to American Letters, among other honours.

Adrienne Rich lived in California since 1984 where she taught English and feminist studies at Stanford University until 1992. She died on 27 March 2012.

POEMS

The poems, as they are printed here, are in the order in which they are printed in *Collected Early Poems 1950–1970* and *The Fact of a Doorframe Poems Selected and New Poems 1950–1984*. Rich began dating her poems in 1954, as if, in Richard Ellmann and Robert O'Clair's words, 'to underline their provisional or journal-entry nature'. Rich herself said that she began dating poems in 1954 because she 'felt embarked on a process that was precarious and exploratory; I needed to allow the poems to acknowledge their moment'.

Storm Warnings

The glass has been falling all the afternoon,
And knowing better than the instrument
What winds are walking overhead, what zone
Of gray unrest is moving across the land,
I leave the book upon a pillowed chair   5
And walk from window to closed window, watching
Boughs strain against the sky

And think again, as often when the air
Moves inward toward a silent core of waiting,
How with a single purpose time has traveled   10
By secret currents of the undiscerned
Into this polar realm. Weather abroad
And weather in the heart alike come on
Regardless of prediction.

Between foreseeing and averting change   15
Lies all the mastery of elements
Which clocks and weatherglasses cannot alter.
Time in the hand is not control of time,
Nor shattered fragments of an instrument
A proof against the wind; the wind will rise,   20
We can only close the shutters.

I draw the curtains as the sky goes black
And set a match to candles sheathed in glass
Against the keyhole draught, the insistent whine
Of weather through the unsealed aperture.   25
This is our sole defense against the season;
These are the things that we have learned to do
Who live in troubled regions.

ADRIENNE RICH

Glossary

Line 1 glass: weather glass or barometer – an instrument for measuring atmospheric pressure.

Line 9 core: centre/central region.

Line 11 undiscerned: unnoticed, not perceived by mind or body.

Line 12 polar realm: cold kingdom.

Line 15 averting: preventing.

Line 23 sheathed: protected by, enclosed.

Line 25 aperture: opening, gap.

'Storm Warnings' was written in 1949 when Adrienne Rich was twenty. Writing in the Foreword to *Collected Early Poems 1950–1970*, Rich says: 'Storm Warnings' is a poem about powerlessness — about a force so much greater than our human powers that while it can be measured and even predicted, it is beyond human control.' All 'we' can do is create an interior space against the storm, an enclave of self-protection, though the winds of change still penetrate keyholes and 'unsealed apertures'. Nothing in the scene of this poem suggests that it was written in the early days of the Cold War, within a twenty year old's earshot of World War II, at the end of the decade of the Warsaw Ghetto and Auschwitz, Hiroshima and Nagasaki, in a climate of public fatalism about World War III. The poet assumes that change is to be averted if it can be, defended against if it must come . . . 'Change' here means unpredictability, unrest, menace — not something 'we' might desire and even help bring to pass.

Questions

1. How would you describe the atmosphere in the opening lines? Which details, in your opinion, best capture that atmosphere?

2. The poet says that she knows better than the instrument that a storm is on the way. What does that tell us about the poet?

3. How do you interpret the words 'a silent core of waiting'?

4. The poet describes where she is at as 'this polar realm'. What does this tell us about the speaker?

5. What connection does the speaker in the poem make between 'Weather abroad/ And weather in the heart'?

6. Do you think that there is a feeling of helplessness in the third stanza? Give reasons for your answer.

7. The setting of the poem is that of a room with a woman in it and her awareness of a gathering storm. Could this be read as a metaphor? Explain.

8. How does the speaker react to the situation that she finds herself in? Is it a head or a heart response or a mixture of both do you think?

Poems

455

9. Comment on the image of the guarded candle flames 'sheathed in glass/ Against the keyhole draught'. What feeling does it create?

10. How would you describe the speaker's attitude towards the drawing of the curtains, the lighting of candles? Empowered? Threatened? Defenceless? Resigned?

11. Examine how this poem explores the tensions between the individual and the wider world. Who do you think the speaker is referring to when she says 'we' in line 27?

12. 'Storm Warnings' is both an atmospheric piece of writing and an interesting personal statement. Discuss this view. Which aspect of the poem appealed to you most?

13. Commenting on this poem, W.H. Auden said that the emotions that motivated 'Storm Warnings' were feelings of 'historical apprehension'. What do you think he meant by this? Would you agree that such emotions are found in the poem?

14. The word 'change' is in the title of the collection from which 'Storm Warnings' [A Change of World] is taken. It also occurs in 'Storm Warnings', the opening poem in the collection. Why is change an important idea here?

15. It has been said that Rich in her poetry has chosen to write about people 'Who live in troubled regions'. Discuss this in relation to the poems by Rich on your course.

16. Would you agree that this is a well-crafted poem? Identify aspects which make it so. How does the formal structure contribute to the poem's theme?

bourgeois = middle class   *theme of entrapment*

ADRIENNE RICH

Celebrating Aunt Jennifer's creativity
possesion - the aunt owns the tigers-
she doesn't share them
with her husband

Aunt Jennifer's Tigers

Quatrains   *energy, pride, movement, freedom*

Aunt Jennifer's tigers prance across a screen,   *rhyming couplets*

Bright topaz denizens of a world of green.   *↳ tightness + control*

They do not fear the men beneath the tree;   *what aunt Jennifer*

They pace in sleek chivalric certainty.   *[assonance] * topaz is precious*
wants for herself

Conflict between *(noble, confident* *- the tigers are*
men vs. tigers - *heroic* *precious to*
tigers will win *Aunt Jennifer*

weakness

Aunt Jennifer's fingers fluttering through her wool

Find even the ivory needle hard to pull.   *Adhering to Societal*
norms

hyperbole

The massive weight of Uncle's wedding band   *Aunt Jennifer's marriage*

Sits heavily upon Aunt Jennifer's hand.   *is unhappy, oppressive*
she is trapped
metaphor

When Aunt is dead, her terrified hands will lie

Still ringed with ordeals she was mastered by.   10

The tigers in the panel that she made

Will go on prancing, proud and unafraid.

Aunt Jennifer is the antithesis of the tigers

📖 Glossary

Line 1 prance: bound, spring forward from hind legs.

Line 1 screen: an ornamental panel placed before an empty firegrate or used to keep off the heat from a fire. Not very common nowadays.

Line 2 topaz: the golden, yellow colour of the precious stone.

Line 2 denizens: inhabitants.

Line 4 sleek: smooth, glossy.

Line 4 chivalric: brave, gallant, like knights.

Line 6 ivory: made of animal tusk.

Line 10 ordeals: difficult experiences, severe trials, endurances.

Rich, in her essay 'When We Dead Awaken' (1971), says: "Looking back at poems I wrote before I was twenty-one, I'm startled because beneath the conscious craft are glimpses of the split I even then experienced between the girl who wrote poems, who defined herself writing poems, and the girl who was to define herself by her relationships with men. 'Aunt Jennifer's Tigers' (1951), written while I was a student, looks with deliberate detachment at this split."

? Questions

1. Having read through the text, how would you act out this poem? How could a class group create an effective tableau of the situation within the poem?

2. Draw your version of the panel or screen that Aunt Jennifer is embroidering. What does the image tell us about the relationship between men and animals?

3. The poem is a series of descriptions, statements, imaginings. Which of these is the most powerful in your opinion?

4. Comment on 'fluttering' and 'massive'.

5. What does the regular rhyme contribute to the overall effect? Does the poem's formal structure match its theme? Explain.

6. What is the effect of the rhythm and rhyme here?

7. Is this, in your opinion, an out-of-date poem for today's teenage reader? Give reasons for your answer.

8. Why do you think Adrienne Rich ends her poem with a reference to the tigers 'prancing, proud and unafraid'?

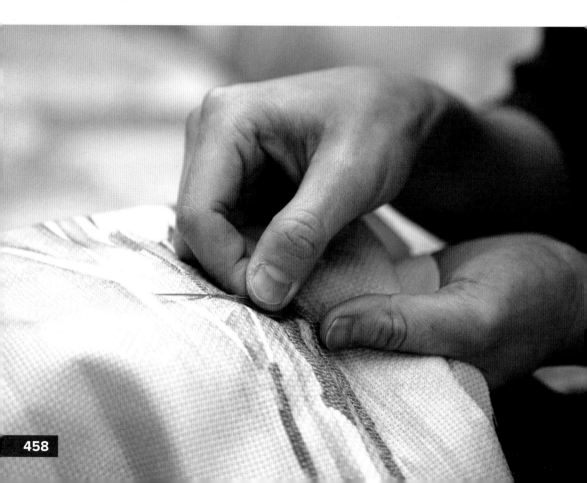

The Uncle Speaks in the Drawing Room

I have seen the mob of late
Standing sullen in the square,
Gazing with a sullen stare
At window, balcony, and gate.
Some have talked in bitter tones,   5
Some have held and fingered stones.

These are follies that subside.
Let us consider, none the less,
Certain frailties of glass
Which, it cannot be denied,   10
Lead in times like these to fear
For crystal vase and chandelier.

Not that missiles will be cast;
None as yet dare lift an arm.
But the scene recalls a storm   15
When our grandsire stood aghast
To see his antique ruby bowl
Shivered in a thunder-roll.

Let us only bear in mind
How these treasures handed down   20
From a calmer age passed on
Are in the keeping of our kind.
We stand between the dead glass-blowers
And murmurings of missile-throwers.

📖 Glossary

Title Drawing Room: an elegant and beautifully furnished room; originally 'withdrawing-room' – a room to which the company withdraws after dinner; also the room to which ladies withdraw from the dining-room after dinner.

Line 1 mob: the rabble, the vulgar, the common people; a disorderly crowd, a riotous assembly [from Latin mobile vulgus = excitable/mobile crowd].

Line 2 sullen: angry, silent.

Line 7 follies: foolish behaviour.

Line 13 missiles: weapons/objects that can be thrown or fired.

Line 16 grandsire: grandsire is an old-fashioned word for grandfather (sire means a senior or elder).

Line 16 aghast: terrified, frightened.

Line 22 in the keeping of our kind: in the custody and safe-keeping of people like us.

❓ Questions

1. What is the effect of 'The Uncle' as opposed to 'Uncle' or 'My Uncle' in the title? Comment on 'Speaks' as opposed to, say, 'shouts'. What do the words 'Drawing Room' suggest?

2. The poet here is speaking in the voice of The Uncle. Which words in stanza one best sum up the mob in the square? What image do the words 'window, balcony, and gate' summon up?

3. Consider the effect of the drumbeat rhyme and rhythm in the opening lines. How do they suit what is being said?

4. The Uncle is confident ('These are follies that subside' – line 7) that the mob is not a realistic or serious threat. Who is he addressing when he says 'Let us consider'? What, do you think, has created that confidence?

5. He fears for 'crystal vase and chandelier'. What do these precious objects symbolise?

6. How would you describe the Uncle's tone? Smug? Superior? How do you respond to line 22: 'the keeping of our kind'?

7. What does this poem say about the relationship between the privileged classes and the ordinary people?

8. Does this read like a poem from the 1950s? Why? Why not?

9. What does this poem say about the past, the present, the future? What does this poem say about women?

10. This poem was written by an American woman in the world's supposedly greatest democracy. Why do you think Adrienne Rich wrote such a poem? Does it make you angry? Does it sadden you? Do you think it is a political poem? Give reasons for your answers.

Living in Sin

She had thought the studio would keep itself;
no dust upon the furniture of love.
Half heresy, to wish the taps less vocal,
the panes relieved of grime. A plate of pears,
a piano with a Persian shawl, a cat   5
stalking the picturesque amusing mouse
had risen at his urging.
Not that at five each separate stair would writhe
under the milkman's tramp; that morning light
so coldly would delineate the scraps   10
of last night's cheese and three sepulchral bottles;
that on the kitchen shelf among the saucers
a pair of beetle-eyes would fix her own—
envoy from some village in the moldings . . .
Meanwhile, he, with a yawn,   15
sounded a dozen notes upon the keyboard,
declared it out of tune, shrugged at the mirror,
rubbed at his beard, went out for cigarettes;
while she, jeered by the minor demons,
pulled back the sheets and made the bed and found   20
a towel to dust the table-top,
and let the coffee-pot boil over on the stove.
By evening she was back in love again,
though not so wholly but throughout the night
she woke sometimes to feel the daylight coming   25
like a relentless milkman up the stairs.

📖 Glossary

Line 1 studio: an artist's workplace, here a studio (one-room) apartment – where he lives and works.

Line 3 heresy: opposite to accepted beliefs.

Line 6 picturesque: worthy of being a picture.

Line 8 writhe: twist or squirm in extreme pain.

Line 10 delineate: show, outline (an art term).

Line 11 sepulchral: gloomy, dismal.

Line 14 moldings: strip of wood or plaster used for decoration.

Line 19 demons: evil spirits, devils.

Line 26 relentless: never-ending, persistent, merciless.

> Unlike the previous three poems in this selection, 'Living in Sin' uses a different format. In her early work Rich chose a formal structure – stanza and rhyme. She began to abandon formalism but said that formalism was once necessary: 'Like asbestos gloves, it allowed me to handle materials I couldn't pick up barehanded'. Reading through the ten Rich poems here [from 1949 to 1974], there is a change in the way that the poem is arranged on the page.

❓ Questions

1. The phrase 'Living in sin' is rarely heard or used now. What does it refer to in the poem? What does it tell us about people's attitudes at the time the poem was written?

2. The poem opens with a realisation. How would you describe the speaker's understanding of the situation (lines 1–2) that she finds herself in?

3. Why are morning and evening associated with different thoughts and feelings in the speaker?

4. How is the man portrayed in the poem? List those details which give us a sense of his personality. Do you find him interesting? Why do you think the woman found him interesting? How would you describe the relationship between the He and She of the poem?

5. There is dust on the actual furniture and on 'the furniture of love'; the speaker imagines that the beetle on the kitchen shelf belongs to a 'village' of beetles. How relevant are the grubby, grotty surroundings in the poem?

6. The man is an artist. The woman is his lover. She is also the person who cleans and tidies. What might Rich be suggesting here about gender roles? What do you understand by the words 'minor demons' (line 19)?

7. What mood dominates the closing lines of the poem? Pick out the details that best help to create that mood.

8. Comment on art in relation to this poem: the painting which the man makes and the poem which Adrienne Rich writes.

9. The critic Margaret Dickie says that Rich has never been able to write 'love' without writing 'politics'. Would you agree with this view in relation to this poem?

10. Comment of the shape of the poem on the page. Why do you think Rich chose this form instead of separate stanzas, regular rhyme as in earlier poems such as 'Aunt Jennifer's Tigers' and 'The Uncle Speaks in the Drawing Room'?

The Roofwalker

– for Denise Levertov

Over the half-finished houses
night comes. The builders
stand on the roof. It is
quiet after the hammers,
the pulleys hang slack.   5
Giants, the roofwalkers,
on a listing deck, the wave
of darkness about to break
on their heads. The sky
is a torn sail where figures   10
pass magnified, shadows
on a burning deck.

I feel like them up there:
exposed, larger than life,
and due to break my neck.   15

Was it worth while to lay—
with infinite exertion—
a roof I can't live under?
—All those blueprints,
closings of gaps,   20
measurings, calculations?
A life I didn't choose
chose me: even
my tools are the wrong ones
for what I have to do.   25
I'm naked, ignorant,
a naked man fleeing
across the roofs
who could with a shade of difference

be sitting in the lamplight 30
against the cream wallpaper
reading—not with indifference—
about a naked man
fleeing across the roofs.

1961

Glossary

Dedicatee: Denise Levertov (1923–1997), poet and anti-war activist.

Line 5 pulleys: grooved wheel and rope devices used for hoisting material.

Line 7 listing: leaning.

Line 7 deck: echoing/remembering, perhaps, the once well-known opening lines from Felicia Hemans's (1793–1835) poem 'Casabianca' – The boy stood on the burning deck/ Whence all but he had fled . . . Her poetry was especially popular in America.

Line 17 infinite exertion: endless effort.

Line 19 blueprints: detailed plans of work to be done; white upon blue photographic prints representing the final stage of engineering or other plans.

Questions

1. Why is the speaker drawn to the roofwalker as an image for her own situation?

2. Comment on details such as 'half-finished', 'the wave of darkness', 'a burning deck'. How significant are they, in your opinion?

3. How would you describe the speaker's mood in lines 13–15?

4. The half-finished houses will one day become homes where families – Mom and Dad and children – will live. Relate this to the idea in lines 22–25: 'A life I didn't choose/ chose me: even/ my tools are the wrong ones/ for what I have to do.'

5. The poem ends with the idea of choice. Explore how and why this is a central idea in the poem.

6. Comment on the poem's final image.

7. How does this poem explore gender issues?

8. Examine how Rich makes and shapes this poem. Consider, for example, the run-on line and the absence of end-rhyme.

Our Whole Life

Our whole life a translation
the permissible fibs

and now a knot of lies
eating at itself to get undone

Words bitten thru words   5

meanings burnt-off like paint
under the blowtorch

All those dead letters
rendered into the oppressor's language

Trying to tell the doctor where it hurts   10
like the Algerian
who walked from his village, burning

his whole body a cloud of pain
and there are no words for this

except himself   15

1969

📖 Glossary

Line 1 translation: interpreted by another?

Line 2 permissible fibs: acceptable lies – Rich here is suggesting that she and others are living a lie?

Line 7 blowtorch: (blowlamp) – instrument that produces powerful, hot flame used to remove paint.

Lines 8/9 dead letters/rendered: letters which form words and which have been taken over and thereby murdered/killed by the oppressor? Or, letters which were written and sent but never delivered, read and responded to?

Line 9 oppressor's language: the words used/spoken by those who rule with cruelty/ tyranny.

Line 11 Algerian: a North African whose body has been set alight as a result of political unrest/protest? Many nations controlled Algeria. In 1830 France invaded Algeria and occupied the country until the Algerian rebellion of 1954. The country won its independence in 1962. [Adrienne Rich has said that 'My politics is in my body.']

❓ Questions

1. Why does the speaker feel excluded? Who is being referred to when she says 'Our whole life'?

2. What, according to the speaker, happens when 'a knot of lies' is the reality?

3. How does the poem create a sense of helplessness? Which words, images, feelings create this sense?

4. In some poems by Adrienne Rich there is a strong narrative or storyline. What technique is the poet using in 'Our Whole Life'? Do you think it is effective?

5. The image of a man 'burning his whole body' suggests desperation, courage, the extreme. Adrienne Rich herself said that 'My politics is in my body'. Discuss this idea in relation to the closing lines of the poem.

6. Is this a typical Adrienne Rich poem? Which other poems by Rich on your course does it resemble? Explain.

Trying to Talk with a Man

Out in this desert we are testing bombs,

that's why we came here.

Sometimes I feel an underground river
forcing its way between deformed cliffs
an acute angle of understanding   5
moving itself like a locus of the sun
into this condemned scenery.

What we've had to give up to get here—
whole LP collections, films we starred in
playing in the neighborhoods, bakery windows   10
full of dry, chocolate-filled Jewish cookies,
the language of love-letters, of suicide notes,
afternoons on the riverbank
pretending to be children

Coming out to this desert   15
we meant to change the face of
driving among dull green succulents
walking at noon in the ghost town
surrounded by a silence

that sounds like the silence of the place   20
except that it came with us
and is familiar
and everything we were saying until now
was an effort to blot it out—
coming out here we are up against it   25

Out here I feel more helpless
with you than without you

You mention the danger
and list the equipment
we talk of people caring for each other   30
in emergencies—laceration, thirst—
but you look at me like an emergency

Your dry heat feels like power
you eyes are stars of a different magnitude
they reflect lights that spell out: EXIT   35
when you get up and pace the floor

talking of the danger
as if it were not ourselves
as if we were testing anything else.

1971

 ## Glossary

Line 1 desert: Margaret Atwood, commenting on this poem, says the poem occurs in a desert, a desert which is not only deprivation and sterility, the place where everything except the essentials has been discarded, but also the place where bombs are tested. The "I" and the "You" have given up all the frivolities of their previous lives, "suicide notes" as well as "love-letters," in order to undertake the risk of changing the desert; but it becomes clear that the "scenery" is already "condemned," that the bombs are not external threats but internal ones. The poet realises that they are deceiving themselves, "talking of the danger/ as if it were not ourselves/ as if we were testing anything else."

Line 4 deformed: misshaped.

Line 5 acute: sharp.

Line 6 locus: in Adrienne Rich's *Poetry* [Norton Critical Edition (1975)] locus is glossed as follows. 'In geometry, the set or configuration of all points satisfying specified geometric conditions'.

Line 9 LP collections: long-playing vinyl music records – from a pre tape, CD and iPod era.

Line 17 succulents: thick, fleshy plants.

Line 31 laceration: torn, mangled flesh.

? Questions

1. What does the title, 'Trying to Talk with a Man', imply? If the title read 'Trying to Talk to a Man', how different would that have been? In your opinion, have relations between men and women changed since 1971, when this poem was written? Why?

2. Who, do you think, is the 'we' of the opening line? Why do you think the first two lines of the poem are on their own?

3. The speaker in lines 3–7 uses an image to convey her situation. What mood is created here through imagery? Which words best capture that mood?

4. There is a striking contrast between the 'condemned scenery' of the desert and the world which 'we've had to give up to get here'. How would you describe the world that they had to give up?

5. The man and woman in this poem came to the desert for a specific reason. What is meant by 'testing bombs'? Are these actual bombs or an image of their relationship? Discuss.

6. Comment on the silence – 'the silence of the place' and the silence that 'came with us'.

7. In lines 26/27 the speaker says 'Out here I feel more helpless/ with you than without you'. Why do you think the speaker feels this way? Were you surprised by the admission?

8. How does the man respond to the private and emotional situation? Why do you think he speaks of 'the danger' and lists 'the equipment'?

9. Why do you think Rich uses punctuation the way she does in this poem?

10. Does this poem offer a convincing portrait of a relationship in your opinion? How would you imagine the poem from the man's point of view?

11. In your opinion, does the title and the poem itself offer a negative, hopeless, pessimistic view?

Diving Into the Wreck

First having read the book of myths,
and loaded the camera
and checked the edge of the knife-blade,
I put on
the body-armor of black rubber   5
the absurd flippers
the grave and the awkward mask.
I am having to do this
not like Cousteau with his
assiduous team   10
aboard the sun-flooded schooner
but here alone.

There is a ladder.
The ladder is always there
hanging innocently   15
close to the side of the schooner.
We know what it is for,
we who have used it.
Otherwise
it's a piece of maritime floss   20
some sundry equipment.

I go down.
Rung after rung and still
the oxygen immerses me
the blue light   25
the clear atoms
of our human air.
I go down.
My flippers cripple me,
I crawl like an insect down the ladder   30
and there is no one
to tell me when the ocean
will begin.

First the air is blue and then
it is bluer and then green and then   35
black I am blacking out and yet
my mask is powerful
it pumps my blood with power
the sea is another story
the sea is not a question of power   40
I have to learn alone
to turn my body without force
in the deep element.

And now: it is easy to forget
what I came for   45
among so many who have always
lived here
swaying their crenellated fans
between the reefs
and besides   50
you breathe differently down here.

I came to explore the wreck.
The words are purposes.
The words are maps.
I came to see the damage that was done   55
and the treasures that prevail.
I stroke the beam of my lamp
slowly along the flank
of something more permanent
than fish or weed   60

the thing I came for:
the wreck and not the story of the wreck
the thing itself and not the myth
the drowned face always staring
toward the sun   65

the evidence of damage
worn by salt and sway into this threadbare beauty
the ribs of the disaster
curving their assertion
among the tentative haunters.   70

This is the place.
And I am here, the mermaid whose dark hair
streams black, the merman in his armored body
We circle silently
about the wreck   75
we dive into the hold.
I am she: I am he

whose drowned face sleeps with open eyes
whose breasts still bear the stress
whose silver, copper, vermeil cargo lies   80
obscurely inside barrels
half-wedged and left to rot
we are the half-destroyed instruments
that once held to a course
the water-eaten log   85
the fouled compass

We are, I am, you are
by cowardice or courage
the one who find our way
back to this scene   90
carrying a knife, a camera
a book of myths
in which
our names do not appear.

1972

Glossary

Title: The wreck she is diving into,' says Margaret Atwood, 'is the wreck of obsolete myths, particularly myths about men and women. She is journeying to something that is already in the past, in order to discover for herself the reality behind the myth, "the wreck and not the story of the wreck/ the thing itself and not the myth." What she finds is part treasure and part corpse, and she also finds that she herself is part of it, a "half-destroyed instrument." As explorer, she is detached; she carries a knife to cut her way in, cut structures apart; a camera to record; and the book of myths itself, a book which has hitherto had no place for explorers like herself.'

Line 1 the book of myths: in this instance the stories and legends about the relationships between men and women.

Line 9 Cousteau: Jacques Yves Cousteau (b. 1910), French naval officer and underwater explorer who, in 1950, made the first underwater film. Best known for *The Undersea World of Jacques Cousteau* (1968–1976).

Line 10 assiduous: diligent, hard-working, persevering.

Line 11 schooner: swift-sailing vessel, usually with two masts.

Line 20 maritime floss: floss can be a cottony fibre and maritime relates to the sea. Here Rich is speaking of the ladder as a means of going down into the depths. But for those who have not gone down, it is just a piece of unimportant, insignificant substance.

Line 21 sundry equipment: unimportant tool, apparatus.

Line 48 crenellated fans: a reference to the swaying, indented, irregularly shaped, fan-shaped sea plants which Rich imagines as fans in the hands of those who live in the wreck.

Line 56 prevail: triumph, dominate, succeed.

Line 58 flank: side.

Line 64 the drowned face: a reference to the ornamental/decorative female figurehead which once formed the prow of old sailing ships.

Line 67 threadbare: worn, faded.

Line 69 assertion: declaration, claim.

Line 70 tentative: uncertain.

Line 70 haunters: the word suggests that those who dive into the wreck are frequent divers.

Line 80 vermeil: metal, as silver or bronze, which has been gilded; bright red, scarlet.

Questions

1. What does the title of this poem suggest? Is this an actual or a metaphorical journey?

2. What do we learn about the speaker in the opening lines (1–12)?

3. She dives alone but speaks of others who have also dived into the wreck. What does this tell us about the speaker's understanding of herself and others in relation to the wreck on the ocean floor?

4. The word 'down' is repeated ['I go down . . . I go down . . . I crawl like an insect down the ladder'] and she uses the image of an insect. Comment on the effect of this.

5. Re-read the first four stanzas. Is the speaker well-prepared for this dive? Which details suggest this? How does she feel as she descends?

6. At line 44 [And now . . .] the poem shifts from journeying to being there. What does the speaker say about being in the wreck? Why do you think 'so many . . . have always lived here'?

7. The speaker says 'it is easy to forget/ what I came for'. How would you sum up what the speaker came for? Why do you think it was easy for her to forget why she came?

8. How would you describe the atmosphere of the underwater world? Is 'the evidence of damage' physical? Is there evidence of emotional, psychological damage?

9. 'This is the place./ And I am here' (lines 71/72). Who are the mermaid and the merman? What can you tell about them from how they are described?

10. 'I' is used in eight of the ten sections of the poem and is used sixteen times in all. Comment on the poet's use of 'I', 'we' and 'you'. Who is the speaker referring to when she says 'we' and 'you'?

11. How does the past play a significant part in the experience explored in the poem 'Diving into the Wreck'? Comment on the link between past and present.

12. Why did the speaker dive into the wreck? Did she find what she sought there? How did she respond to the experience?

13. In line 88 the speaker says that 'cowardice or courage' played an important part. Why the contradiction? Which do you think was the one that made the journey possible?

14. In the poem's closing lines, the poet speaks of 'half-destroyed instruments that once held to a course'. Who or what is she referring to here?

15. Ruth Whitman, reviewing Rich's *Poems Selected and New* in *Harvard Magazine* July–August 1975, said of 'Diving into the Wreck': it is 'one of the great poems of our time'. Would you agree or disagree with this view? What, in your opinion, makes a poem 'great'? Does this poem match your criteria? Give reasons for your answer.

From a Survivor

The pact that we made was the ordinary pact
of men & women in those days

I don't know who we thought we were
that our personalities
could resist the failures of the race   5

Lucky or unlucky, we didn't know
the race had failures of that order
and that we were going to share them

Like everybody else, we thought of ourselves as special

Your body is as vivid to me   10
as it ever was: even more

since my feeling for it is clearer:
I know what it could and could not do

it is no longer
the body of a god   15
or anything with power over my life

Next year it would have been 20 years
and you are wastefully dead
who might have made the leap
we talked, too late, of making   20

which I live now
not as a leap
but a succession of brief amazing movements

each one making possible the next

1972

Glossary

Line 1 pact: agreement.

Line 17 Next year it would have been 20 years: a reference to the nineteen years Adrienne Rich and Alfred Conrad spent together.

Line 18 wastefully dead: here wastefully expresses the woman's belief that her husband's death achieved nothing, that it was a waste. Her husband, whom she separated from in 1969, took his own life in 1970.

Questions

1. The poem focuses on and explores the speaker's marriage, its beginning, its ending. What does the word 'survivor' suggest in this context?

2. Looking back, what did marriage mean at the time of their wedding? Why was it viewed as an 'ordinary pact'?

3. Rich rarely uses the ampersand [&]. Why do you think she deliberately uses '&' between the words 'men' and 'women' in line 2? What does it suggest?

4. Why do you think the poet chose to arrange the poem on the page the way she did? Consider especially the two lines that are on their own.

5. Why did Rich not place a full stop at the end of the final line?

6. How would you describe the speaker's mood in this poem?

7. Is this a realistic poem, in your opinion? An optimistic poem? A pessimistic one? Give reasons for your answer.

8. Explore the significance of the speaker's reference to 'the race', 'the body of a god'.

9. How would you describe the speaker's understanding of her dead husband, her feelings for her dead husband? What does she wish for him?

10. The speaker describes her life now as 'a succession of brief amazing movements'. Comment on this.

Power

Living   in the earth-deposits   of our history

Today a backhoe divulged   out of a crumbling flank of earth
one bottle   amber   perfect   a hundred-year-old
cure for fever   or melancholy   a tonic
for living on this earth   in the winters of this climate   5

Today I was reading about Marie Curie:
she must have known she suffered   from radiation sickness
her body bombarded for years   by the element
she had purified
It seems she denied to the end   10
the source of the cataracts on her eyes
the cracked and suppurating skin   of her finger-ends
till she could no longer hold   a test-tube or a pencil

She died   a famous woman   denying
her wounds   15
denying
her wounds   came from the same source as her power

1974

📖 Glossary

Line 2 backhoe: a heavy mechanised digger – a JCB.

Line 2 flank: side.

Line 4 melancholy: sad, gloomy state.

Line 6 Marie Curie: Polish-born French physicist (1867–1934) who with her husband Pierre Curie worked on magnetism and radioactivity (a term she invented in 1898); they were jointly awarded the Nobel Prize for Physics in 1903 with Antoine Henri Becquerel. In 1911 Marie Curie received the Nobel Prize for Chemistry. She died of leukaemia, probably caused by her long exposure to radioactivity.

Line 7 radiation sickness: an illness caused by excessive absorption of radiation in the body. Symptoms include internal bleeding and a decrease in blood cells.

Line 8 bombarded: attacked.

Line 11 cataracts: an opaque condition of the lens of the eye which allows no light through.

Line 12 suppurating: oozing thick yellowish fluid, pus.

❓ Questions

1. The speaker refers to 'earth-deposits'. What does the speaker mean by this? How do you think the bottle, unopened, unused ended up in the earth?

2. How is the present portrayed by the speaker? How do you interpret 'the winters of this climate'?

3. Why do you think Adrienne Rich was drawn to Marie Curie?

4. Identify different kinds of power. What type of power is being explored here? Explain 'denying/ her wounds came from the same source as her power'. What caused Curie's illness? Why did Curie allow her illness to continue?

5. Compare and contrast Aunt Jennifer and Marie Curie.

6. Comment on the way Rich has deliberately spaced and paced certain lines. How does that affect your reading of the poem?

7. Is Marie Curie a victim of her success? How does the speaker feel about Curie? Which details in the poem best express the speaker's viewpoint?

8. Rich has said [in 1964] that 'In my earlier poems I told you, as precisely and eloquently as I knew how, about something; in the more recent poems something is happening, something has happened to me and, if I have been a good parent to the poem, something will happen to you who read it.' Discuss this statement in the light of your reading of the poems by Adrienne Rich on your course.

General Questions

A. Write an essay on the impact the poetry of Adrienne Rich has had on you. Support the points you make by reference to the poetry of Adrienne Rich on your course.

B. Write an article for a school magazine introducing the poetry of Adrienne Rich to Leaving Certificate students. Tell them what she wrote about and explain what you liked in her writing, suggesting some poems that you think they would enjoy reading. Support the points you make by reference to the poetry by Adrienne Rich on your course.

C. 'Adrienne Rich is both a personal and a political poet.' Discuss this view, supporting your answer by quotation from or reference to the poems by Rich on your course.

D. 'Rich, in her poetry, creates memorable and powerful images.' Would you agree with this view? You should support the points you make with relevant quotation from or reference to the poems by Adrienne Rich on your course.

E. 'The poetry of Adrienne Rich explores a woman's difficulty in maintaining an identity.' Discuss this view and in your response refer to the poetry of Adrienne Rich on your course.

F. 'I enjoy (or do not enjoy) the poetry of Adrienne Rich.' Respond to this statement referring to the poetry of Adrienne Rich on your course.

G. 'There are many reasons why the poetry of Adrienne Rich is worth reading.' In response to the above statement write an essay on the poetry of Adrienne Rich. Your essay should focus clearly on the reasons why you think Rich's poetry is worth reading and should refer to the poems by Rich on your course.

H. 'Though Adrienne Rich is a woman poet who writes about the world from a woman's point of view, she is a poet who deserves to be read by men and women.' Write a personal response to this statement and in your answer refer to the poems by Rich on your course.

Critical Commentary

Storm Warnings

This poem, with its dramatic title, was written when Rich was twenty years old.

The title is both actual and metaphorical. There is a storm coming but the speaker also senses change of another kind, change that the speaker is aware of.

Though the poem is about change and disorder, it is well-organised and shaped on the page. Four seven-line stanzas, many of the lines iambic pentameter, the final line in each stanza being shorter than the others, Rich's use of repetition and occasional rhyme all reveal the careful and skilful writing of the poem.

In stanza one the barometer is but one indicator of the approaching storm. The speaker knows 'better than the instrument/ What winds are walking overhead' and the image that emerges of the speaker is of someone who belongs to a comfortable, civilised, protected world. The 'book', the 'pillowed chair', the 'walk from window to closed window' suggest privilege, comfort, an elegant drawing room. The long opening sentence runs through twelve lines and from stanza one into stanza two, a technique which could suggest the impending, unstoppable energy of the oncoming storm.

The speaker reflects on the changing weather not only in terms of 'watching/ Boughs strain against the sky' but attributes to this change something even more interesting. For the speaker the storm connects one world and another. As it moves 'inward toward a silent core of waiting', the world of the speaker is portrayed as a world anticipating, even welcoming change. And yet the speaker's natural impulse is to guard against it. Albert Gelpi in his essay 'Adrienne Rich: The Poetics of Change' says that Rich 'seeks shelter as self-preservation' and in 'Storm Warnings' the speaker 'prepares against the threats within and without by sealing off a comfortable, weather-proof sanctuary. The only exposure is the keyhole that locks the door.'

The actual weather reflects an interior state: 'Weather abroad / And weather in the heart' are known to the speaker and both external and internal storms cannot be prevented or avoided, nor can they be easily ordered, predicted or controlled. 'I', though it is only used twice, is a strong presence in the poem: 'I leave the book . . .'; 'I draw the curtains'. The restlessness of walking 'from window to closed window' leads to the speaker's attempts to protect herself against the elements. The drawing of the curtains and the lighting of candles suggest an attempt at comfort. And yet the speaker concludes in stanza four that the storm creates an 'insistent whine/ Of weather' through a keyhole draught. There is no locking it out. The lighting of candles may seem an old-fashioned detail in a poem written in 1949 but the lighting of candles in this context becomes a powerful symbol of hope and their delicate flames must be protected – they are 'sheathed in glass'. It is a small but vital gesture and the candles within the room and the woman who lit them while the storm rages outside become images of resilience.

The mood of unease, the feeling of premonition in the opening stanza changes through the poem. In stanza one 'the winds are walking overhead' and by stanza four 'the sky goes black'. The use of the present tense gives the poem an immediacy and the disturbance, the darkness, once again, become images of the poet's inner world.

Rich herself has said [in the Foreword to *Collected Early Poems 1950–1970*] that 'Storm Warnings' is about powerlessness and the need 'to create an interior space against the storm, an enclave of self-protection'. The poem ends not with the storm abating but focuses on the speaker's strong awareness of how there is a need to summon up inner resources and a keen awareness that she lives 'in troubled regions'.

Rich has said [in that same Foreword] that change in this instance means 'unpredictability, unrest, menace' and yet the mood in those closing lines reveals a clear-sightedness, strength and determination. The storm may be inevitable and unavoidable but awareness is essential. The final lines use 'we', not 'I'. The poet includes others and in doing so includes the reader. The effect is empowering and reassuring.

W.H. Auden said that 'Storm Warnings' was motivated by feelings of 'historical apprehension' and the poem, if interpreted in this way, could be seen as a reference to political unrest. A poem which tells of a woman in a room and her awareness of a gathering storm can be read at many different, interesting levels.

Aunt Jennifer's Tigers

Rich was twenty-one when this poem was published in her first collection, *A Change of World*. On the page, this poem looks neat, formal and well-organised. There are three four-line stanzas, several of the lines are written in iambic pentameter and there is a regular end-rhyme (aabb, ccdd, eeff). The poem may seem conventional but there is a feminist quality to the poem which makes it powerful and memorable and prompts important questions about gender issues. 'Aunt Jennifer's Tigers' focuses on a familiar theme, that of marriage, in this instance the speaker's aunt and uncle, but the relationship at the heart of the poem is unequal. The woman, Aunt Jennifer, is oppressed by her dominating husband. Though the aunt and uncle are fictional, this does not diminish the power or the impact of the poem.

The title suggests something powerful, exotic, unusual. The tigers in this instance belong to an embroidered image which Aunt Jennifer is working on. Aunt Jennifer's choice of image, in this context, is interesting. She is creating strong, fearless, untamed creatures the very opposite of her own life.

The poem's opening lines are powerful and are filled with movement and colour. Everything would suggest confidence, energy. The verbs 'prance' and 'pace' with the alliterative echo; the colours 'topaz' and 'green' create an upbeat feeling. That these wild animals do not fear 'men' adds to their powerful presence. The use of 'Bright' brings the embroidered panel alive. Aunt Jennifer has created these creatures; it is a striking creative act.

In the second stanza the mood changes. The energy ebbs. The speaker tells us that Aunt Jennifer's fingers are 'fluttering through her wool' which suggests nervousness, unease. The making of the panel, vividly described in stanza one, is difficult and the poet speaks of the 'massive weight of Uncle's wedding band'. The wife is engaged in making a decorative, embroidered panel but her husband's presence, their marriage, 'Sits heavily' upon Aunt Jennifer. The never-ending circle of the wedding ring usually symbolises eternity, union but in this instance the speaker sees it as a massive, heavy presence. Aunt Jennifer is trapped in a marriage and it is as if the tapestry she weaves is her only means of speaking.

The poem begins in the present tense but in the final stanza the poet focuses on the future. Here the speaker imagines a time when Aunt Jennifer is dead. The words 'terrified', 'ordeals', 'mastered' capture the attitude of the niece as she contemplates her aunt's life. The image of the wedding ring recurs in the image of the aunt's life 'ringed with ordeals'. It's an unattractive portrait of a marriage – the husband is controlling. Even in death Aunt Jennifer is terrified. And yet the poem's final image is one of freedom, escape, fearlessness. The brave, gallant tigers 'Will go on prancing, proud and unafraid'. The final two lines, perfect iambic pentameters, are charged with energy and convey a feeling of defiance. Aunt Jennifer, though she was cowed into submission, succeeded in creating an image of assertion. The hands that fluttered and found 'even the ivory needle hard to pull' paradoxically made possible the very opposite: an image of certain power and pride.

The poem offers a glimpse of Aunt Jennifer's life. The speaker expresses an opinion but does not pass judgement. It could be argued that the male/female divide is depicted in a simplistic manner – the man is a bully; the woman is a victim – and yet it prompts important questions about the nature of relationships, marriage, self-assertion and creativity. 'Aunt Jennifer's Tigers' is also a very fine illustration of the power of symbol.

The Uncle Speaks in the Drawing Room

Rich here uses a male persona and like 'Storm Warnings' the poem speaks of unrest, threat. In this instance, however, the disturbance is explicitly political. It refers to people power and their disquiet. That the title refers to uncle as 'The Uncle', not 'My Uncle' or 'An Uncle' gives the poem a particular tone. The setting of 'the Drawing Room' also creates an atmosphere of order, elegance, privilege. There is an interior world and an outer world. The aunt and uncle in 'Aunt Jennifer's Tigers' were not real people; the same may be true of this particular uncle but he stands for a way of viewing the world that is strikingly memorable.

One of the most notable aspects of this poem is picked up by the ear on a first reading. The regular rhyme scheme [abbacc] and the seven-syllable line used throughout establishes an authoritative and confident tone of voice. The speaker is a commanding presence. He speaks from his drawing room in a house with 'balcony, and gate' which suggests an impressive, wealthy structure.

The people outside the gate are referred to by the Uncle as 'the mob'. They are a 'sullen' presence and their discontent and silent anger are associated with their 'gazing' at this house. We are never told much about the Uncle's life or profession. He is wealthy and he has inherited wealth but if he is political or not we are never told. But this is a poem that is preoccupied with politics. It looks at privilege, inheritance, inequality but all from the Uncle's perspective.

The opening stanza contains an atmosphere of menace. The reader hears in the Uncle's voice a tone of distaste. The word 'mob' and the repeated use of 'sullen' ['I have seen the mob of late/ Standing sullen in the square,/ Gazing with a sullen stare'] convey a superior attitude. The closing two lines in stanza one summon up an image of a disgruntled group. There is nothing to suggest that these people are not justified in their protest.

Stanza two refers to these people's actions as 'follies'. The Uncle is not too troubled by these people beyond the gate; he feels that their sullen presence will fade away. To refer to their behaviour as foolish ['follies'] is unsympathetic, patronising, condescending. Lines 8–12 ['Let us consider . . . chandelier'] are preoccupied with the speaker's concerns for his opulent possessions. The contrast between the world of the gated house and the public square is sharpened by such details as 'fingered stones' and 'crystal vase and chandelier'.

The third stanza begins with a smug tone. The Uncle is confident that no missiles will be thrown and yet he offers an historical perspective when an earlier 'storm' resulted in an ancestor's 'antique ruby bowl' being 'Shivered in a thunder-roll'. That upheaval is spoken of in terms of a storm but it could also perhaps refer to a political riot or upheaval?

The irony here is very effective. The Uncle speaks as if the reader will agree with his view of things. He presumes that he is speaking to like-minded people. The use of 'us' [line 19] and 'We' [line 23] would suggest this. The Uncle's main concern is his material wealth and possessions. The earlier age is viewed as 'calmer' but he feels that it is his duty to ensure that the divide between privileged and underprivileged be maintained. The poem's final line is an interesting image of the world since c. 1950 when this poem was written. The Uncle does not welcome change. It suits him to be conservative.

Living in Sin

This poem is from Rich's 1955 volume *The Diamond Cutters and Other Poems*. In it Rich uses a different technique. This poem is not arranged in regular stanzas; instead it is written in free verse, a type of poetry that does not use rhyme or regular line length but depends on rhythm and repetition for effect.

The freedom of free verse allows Rich to create on the page a different kind of poem from 'Storm Warnings', 'Aunt Jennifer's Tigers' and 'The Uncle Speaks in the Drawing Room'. Not only does it look different but a more intimate connection between the poet and reader is established. The fluid line, the flow of the poem invite the reader to share the woman's private world.

The title 'Living in Sin' is still a well-known phrase, though it is rarely heard today; it meant much more in the early 1950s when the poem was written than it does now. 'Living in sin' was how church and society viewed young lovers who lived together without being married. It was seen as a disgrace by those who thought themselves morally superior and it took great courage for a man and woman to go against this attitude. Rich's use of the title prompts the reader not only to question its meaning, but also to explore why such a term should exist and how such a moral climate affects young people.

The poet uses the third person to describe a woman's situation. Everything is told from her point of view and throughout there is an important connection between past and present: between what the woman thought would happen and what actually happened. There was a time when the speaker looked on her relationship in glowing terms. Practical matters such as housework did not occur to her. They would share their love for each other and live together in a small apartment: 'She had thought the studio would keep itself;/ no dust upon the furniture of love.'

The speaker realises that it is 'Half heresy' to view household chores as something she has no interest in. This woman is not comfortable with her assigned role as housekeeper. She was expected to play housewife by society at large but her partner also seems to take it for granted that the woman's role is primarily a domestic one. The use of the word 'heresy', with its religious connotations, is interesting here. It suggests that her experience of love should be almost religious and yet this speaker opposes an established doctrine.

The poem expresses her dissatisfaction with her situation. It begins with references to the place where she and her male partner live but gradually she explores her growing unhappiness with her lover. The place is small, confined. It would seem that he is an artist; she seems to have no occupation other than homemaker and partner and these are no longer enough. The sharp contrast between the 'dust' and 'grime' and the 'plate of pears,/ a piano with a Persian shawl' highlights the difference between his world and hers. He is painting still-life pictures; she sees herself now in terms of cleaning and providing.

The studio apartment is less than glamorous, especially in the early morning light. It looks cold, lifeless at five o'clock. Lovers at dawn is a familiar subject in literature and is often associated with parting and intense expressions of undying love as in *Romeo and Juliet*. Rich rewrites that scenario. In this instance the woman is awake and listening to the sound of the milkman's steps on 'each separate stair'; 'the scraps of last night's cheese' image sums up their life.

The speaker refers to 'a pair of beetle-eyes' returning her stare. It is an original detail with a touch of black humour and she imagines that beetle living in its own space, 'some village in the moldings'.

Line 14 peters out. The poet uses ' . . . ' to indicate, in this instance perhaps, a mood of resignation. The word 'Meanwhile' which begins line 15 shifts the focus of the poem to the man. In lines 15–18 he is portrayed as easy-going, relaxed, casual: he yawns, plays 'a dozen notes upon the keyboard', shrugs at his image in the mirror, rubs his beard and goes out to buy cigarettes.

The woman's plight is emphasised in the contrasting lines 19–22. She feels 'jeered'. She makes the bed, dusts and lets 'the coffee-pot boil over on the stove'.

The line 'By evening she was back in love again' captures the complexities of a love relationship and because of this 'Living in Sin' is a realistic, convincing, necessary love poem. It alerts the reader to the romantic and realistic view; the love she feels for her partner is waning. She is back in love again but 'not so wholly'. The poem's structure is that of dawn to dusk, a life-in-a-day poem and the final image returns to that of the unsettled sleep and an unattractive description of dawn leaving the reader with a bleak picture of a once-loving relationship grown cold. That it ends with a new beginning but a beginning that is unattractive suggests that love will not survive in this particular world.

The Roofwalker

The image of a roofwalker is interesting in many ways. A figure is walking 'on top of the world'; someone is building a house or home; an individual is taking risks. At one level, a roofwalker is a male construction worker on a building site but in this Rich poem it becomes so much more.

The poem's opening line is atmospheric. The houses are 'half-finished' and the day is ended. That beautiful word 'crepuscular' could be used to describe dusk, the coming on of night. The speaker captures an in-between moment: the day's work is done and the contrasting silence on the building site is striking. There is an easy feel to such lines as: 'The builders/ stand on the roof. It is/ quiet after the hammers,/ the pulleys hang slack.'

Poets have an original way of looking at the world. Here the poet's imagination sees the rooftops as a ship, the encroaching darkness is a 'wave of darkness' and the sky becomes a 'torn sail'. The men on the rooftops are 'magnified'; they are 'Giants' and the words 'burning deck' suggest danger, adventure, courage, echoing, as they do, an earlier poem by Felicia Heman (1793–1835) in which a boy stood on a burning deck alone, the others on board having fled.

Being a roofwalker is dangerous. In the poem's middle section the speaker identifies with the roofwalker. Lines 13–15 introduce the pronoun 'I' and the poem becomes more personal, confessional, intimate: 'I feel like them up there:/ exposed, larger than life,/ and due to break my neck.'

Beyond the obvious image of male workers and the speaker's identifying with them is the image of males in general and male writers in particular who have dominated for centuries. Man not woman has played the dominant role and the poet recognises the risks in joining them. 'The Roofwalker' has been described by Albert Gelpi as 'a redefinition of psychological and poetic perspective' and the speaker knows that she must take risks, she will face danger, she will expose herself. She may break her neck.

The poem's third section begins with a question. The image of the roof recurs but now the poet refers to living beneath the roof, not walking on it. In the poem's final section she admits that she cannot live beneath this roof. The roof becomes an image of the man-made, the work they have done, the poems they have written and Rich will find her own voice, will write her own poem. The writing life is difficult; it involves truth, it involves exposure. She knows of others who have written but she did not choose to be a writer, it chose her: 'A life I didn't choose/ chose me'. She feels 'naked, ignorant', inadequate.

The poet is young, is aware of the houses of literature built by men. They have had the tools but the speaker here says 'even/ my tools are the wrong ones/ for what I have to do.'

Though she feels ill-equipped, there is also an admirable sense of purpose. She could stay at home, as it were, and read about courage and commitment – 'a naked man fleeing/ across the roofs' or become that person who will take risks and express herself. The use of 'difference' and 'indifference' here highlights her understanding of male and female worlds.

The speaker in the poem is unfulfilled but is keenly aware of the need to find expression in a male-dominated world, whatever the risk. The poem is written in free verse which allows for a more direct and immediate voice. The question asked in lines 16–18 is not answered directly but in raising the issue the speaker and reader take on board the complex situation of woman as outsider, someone who has been excluded. That very fact prompts the necessary and obvious answer.

The poem contains a simple but powerful image, an image that remains with the reader capturing as it does the complex relationship between men and women, power and inequality. She quietly asserts the woman's role and explores how women are disadvantaged as possible roofwalkers. Different tools are needed. Rich herself discovered and used those tools.

Our Whole Life

The three familiar, monosyllabic words, our whole life, contain a huge idea. 'Our Whole Life' is both title and opening words of the poem, thus giving them even greater power. But any suggestion of a big, romantic idea is quashed in the opening lines. The speaker begins with a conclusion. She has reached an understanding of her whole life, its lies and pains and silences and with admirable honesty confesses that her life is empty.

The 'Our' could refer to the speaker's understanding of herself in relation to one other person – partner, lover perhaps who is never identified; the poem focuses on her acceptance of a situation, her disillusionment, her deep understanding of a complex, difficult situation. However, the poem, as its title implies, goes beyond the idea of a relationship.

At first, however, the poem seems to dwell on a personal relationship. That relationship is also seen within a wider context. Indeed the poem may be read not as a poem that focuses on one relationship but on a whole way of life. More than a relationship between two people is implied here. 'Our whole life a translation' suggests a whole society, a society where life is lived at a remove. It is a life that is not authentic, a life that is lost in translation: there has been a failure to communicate, to understand or to be understood. If a person or persons are living a life that is determined by 'permissible fibs', then that life is a lie and the poet addresses such a situation in this poem. The speaker uses a kind of short-hand, a summary of her situation. Line 1, 'Our whole life a translation', has dropped the verb and this gives the line an urgency. Line 2, 'the permissible fibs', highlights another aspect of her life and this direct, open expression of the speaker's realisation that life, as the speaker now knows it, is somehow false.

The image of 'a knot of lies' and the use of 'and now' create a greater sense of urgency. Language has become tangled, untruthful and details such as 'bitten', 'meanings burnt-off', heighten this image.

The poem shifts its focus from the personal to the political at lines 8 and 9. 'All those dead letters/ rendered into the oppressor's language' summon up a picture of an oppressor, someone who has abused, distorted or melted down language. A translation. The speaker is acutely aware of being overpowered, helpless and the closing lines of the poem present the reader with a searing image of an Algerian walking from his village, 'burning/ his whole body a cloud of pain'. That it is a North African man whose country has known invasion and a colonial presence, that he lives in a village, that 'his whole body is a cloud of pain' are significant details. But the most important detail is found in the poem's final two lines: 'and there are no words for this/ except himself' suggest that some situations go beyond and need to go beyond language, that the body can express something profound in its very being. This could be skin colour, sexual orientation, political conviction. Rich herself has said that 'My politics is in my body' and this belief is reflected in the poem.

The image of the burning man echoes an earlier image of burning. In one instance words need to be bitten and burnt through towards meaning; the burning body is another image of extremity.

Adrienne Rich says that this poem is 'concerned with an entire society facing its self-delusions'. It looks at a whole life and can be read as an indictment of enforced, allowed, accepted oppressions and dishonesties.

There is no punctuation, the language is succinct and 'Our Whole Life' does not end with a full stop. The poet has chosen to leave this poem open-ended. The situation as described here has not ended. The lay-out of the poem on the page also plays a part. Each idea is so potent that the poet uses spacing and single-line sections for emphasis.

Trying to Talk with a Man

The opening line of this poem is immediately arresting and the use of 'we' is intriguing: 'Out in this desert we are testing bombs'. 'We' here could refer to the American nation, its military. Line 1 refers to the speaker's country, the 'we' of line 2 could also refer on a more personal level to the speaker and her partner. That lines 1 and 2 are on their own and are the only lines in the poem on their own also creates a powerful impact. The use of the full-stop, ending line 2, is particularly effective especially when one considers the number of full-stops in the poem as a whole. Though highly dramatic in their subject matter, the tone in these opening lines is almost matter-of-fact.

The setting is a desert where controlled nuclear explosions are taking place and the poem's title suggests gender conflict. The 'we' of line 2 gives way to the 'I' voice and an image that conveys a stifled individual, a person labouring to express herself. This image of an underground river 'forcing its way between deformed cliffs' suggests rigid restrictions, oppression, imprisonment. A river in a desert landscape is naturally a vibrant, nourishing source but that river is 'underground'; her feelings therefore, the image suggests, are hidden, confined, trapped.

The fourth section [lines 8–14] looks to their life together as man and woman, the experiences they have shared. The speaker lists various aspects of their relationship: music, food, her Jewishness, the intensity and extremities of their feelings during that time. The details of 'love-letters' and 'suicide notes' suggest an intensely happy and at once troubled relationship. These lines in the poem are not transparent or easily grasped but then they refer to a very private and complex experience in the life of the speaker. The reader can sense in the short-hand style a strong confessional urgency and a feeling of lived experience.

Being in the desert for the speaker means silence. The silence, significantly 'came with us/ and is familiar'. Being in the desert allows them to confront the reality of their relationship. It is a desert where bombs are being tested and the poem has shifted its focus from public to private, from military to personal so that the main thrust of 'Trying to Talk with a Man' is the speaker's attempt to confront her own relationship. That the title reads 'a Man' could also suggest that the speaker is thinking of 'a man' in particular and every man in general.

The speaker's partner speaks of nuclear testing. He focuses on the general whereas she looks to the two of them and realises that 'Out here I feel more helpless/ with you than without you'. He turns to the dangers of testing weapons; he steers clear of testing their own one-to-one relationship.

The coming to this desert is a metaphor for a relationship that is perhaps about to explode. It is certainly being tested. The poem speaks of a collapsing relationship or marriage. A huge change is occurring in the lives of the speaker and her partner and the poem assesses and evaluates their relationship.

The poem's ending signals the end of their relationship. In his eyes she reads the word 'EXIT'. She has to leave this relationship. It has been tried, tested. It has failed. The mood in the closing lines is one of honest acceptance. He paces the floor but cannot confront what is really happening here. The speaker courageously admits that their relationship is over. The man seems unable to come to terms with this. Men are portrayed as inadequate, insensitive, ill-equipped to deal with emotions. His emotions are repressed. He looks at her 'like an emergency' and paces the floor. Talking might have solved the problem but the title suggests it is not possible to talk with a man and certainly not this man. The men in the military are the ones who make the bombs and the speaker's man is the one who fails to recognise or chooses to ignore the seriousness of their personal situation.

Diving Into the Wreck

In Adrienne Rich's work, titles are often so powerful that they become in themselves mini-poems. This is certainly true of one of Rich's best-known poems 'Diving into the Wreck'. The poem is dated 1972. Rich was then forty-three and was identifying strongly with the radical feminist movement. In this poem the speaker explores her own inheritance and past, but it also speaks for all women who have been disempowered, sidelined and written out of history. This poem is her story. 'Diving into the Wreck' could also be read as a journey into the subconscious.

The poem, in free verse and in nine sections of different lengths, describes a woman going down into the ocean depths. However, as with many Rich poems, an image becomes a potent symbol and the poem goes far beyond the narrative to explore essential concerns.

The first section portrays a woman preparing for a dark and difficult journey. That she is alone makes her both vulnerable and courageous. Her preparations are thorough. But before she mentions the practical aspects such as camera, knife, wetsuit, flippers, oxygen mask, she first speaks of a mental, emotional, imaginative preparation. One usually dives to explore or to plunder; in this instance it is to explore.

Line 1 tells us that the speaker has read 'the book of myths'. This was the most important of all: 'First having read the book of myths . . .' It was this reading experience that has prompted the speaker to undertake the dive and the book of myths, according to Margaret Atwood, is a book of 'obsolete myths, particularly myths about men and women'.

The poet has clearly reached a point in her life where she is questioning, challenging assumptions and situations that she is uncomfortable with. She is prepared to go deeper in search of the truth and the image of diving into the wreck already signals that what she will find there is something broken. That she is making this journey on her own is hugely significant: 'I am having to do this/ not like Cousteau with his/ assiduous team/ aboard the sun-flooded schooner/ but here alone'. Cousteau represents the male adventurer and he was part of a team. The woman's journey is undertaken alone and the journey is not so much an adventure, but rather something necessary and essential.

'I' is used sixteen times and phrases such as 'I go down', 'I go down', 'I crawl', 'I have to learn alone', 'I am she: I am he . . .' are crucial. Each one registers the speaker's position, her strong awareness of the nature of the journey and what it involves. Details can be read at a factual level but details also resonate with symbolic significance. For example the speaker tells us: 'There is a ladder./ The ladder is always there/ hanging innocently/ close to the side of the schooner./ We know what it is for,/ we who have used it./ Otherwise/ it's a piece of maritime floss/ some sundry equipment.' Here the ladder becomes something more than a climbing instrument. It is a means of entry, a way into the dark. There is also a strong sense of others having made this same journey. She is alone but she knows that others have gone down into the depths too.

The journey is a difficult and painful one – 'My flippers cripple me', 'I am blacking out' and though others have made this journey 'I have to learn alone/ to turn my body without force/ in the deep element'. The insect image at line 30 ['I crawl like an insect down the ladder'] suggests someone small, vulnerable, undignified. Changing colours – from blue, to green, to black – describe the speaker's sense of descending and this painterly technique offers strikingly visual pictures. The 'blacking out' suggests danger, terror but 'my mask is powerful/ it pumps my blood with power'. She is willing to face danger in her search for truth and understanding.

The ocean contains the wreck and the speaker has come to explore the wreck. A vast, dark, mysterious area such as an ocean can be read as a symbol of a place within, a place where the past and memories are stored, the unconscious.

In her essay 'This Woman's Movement', Nancy Milford says that in 'Diving into the Wreck' Rich 'enters more deeply than ever before into female fantasy; and these are primal waters, life-giving and secretive in the special sense of not being wholly revealed. The female element . . .' She came to explore the wreck. And what is the wreckage; is it of marriage, or of sex, or of the selfhood within each? Is it the female body, her own? The question is never answered explicitly and the poem is all the more effective because of that. It allows the reader to journey with the speaker and interpret the journey in her or his own way. Adrienne Rich has said that: 'We go to poetry because we believe it has something to do with us. We also go to poetry to receive the experience of the not me, enter a field of vision we could not otherwise comprehend.' Whether we identify or not with the speaker in 'Diving into the Wreck', the poem takes us on a powerful journey.

The pictures which the poet paints are haunting, private and beautiful. The use of the present tense creates an immediate link between speaker and reader. The poem though it tells of a difficult, confusing and painful experience is also, like many of Adrienne Rich's poems, empowering and liberating.

The key moment occurs at lines 55 and thereabouts, the poem's central section. The diver trains the beams of her lamp and they illuminate 'the thing itself', the actual wreck.

The poem's rhythm and the use of repetition in these lines [52–65] are very effective in creating a beautiful, quiet mood. The mind is calm as it observes the wreck. The description of the 'drowned face always staring/ toward the sun' is moving and evocative. It not only describes the figurehead on the ship's prow but captures the power and thrust of the ship as it sailed. Its energy is no more, the ship is now wrecked on the ocean floor and this is what is found there. 'Diving into the Wreck' is a wonderful example of what Eavan Boland has called Rich's ability to create 'a private kingdom of music and perception'.

The speaker is interested in discovering the truth, 'the wreck and not the story of the wreck/ the thing itself and not the myth'. A central image is that of the mermaid and merman, creatures from myth, circling silently 'about the wreck' and then the dramatic detail: 'we dive into the hold'. She becomes the mermaid, she encounters the merman and she and he merge; the female and male become one: 'we dive into the hold./ I am she: I am he'. This merging of the human speaker with the mythical merman and mermaid is not only an interesting surreal touch but it is the moment when truth meets myth. It also allows us to contemplate how each one of us embody male and female qualities. The deliberately grammatical awkwardness of 'one' in 'We are, I am, you are/ by cowardice or courage/ the one who find our way . . . ' [conventionally, it should read 'ones'] emphasises the need for us to make this journey alone.

In the second-last stanza, the speaker, now androgynous, identifies with the wreck itself. The 'she' and the 'he' have become 'we' and the speaker, now mermaid and merman 'are the half-destroyed instruments/ that once held to a course'. The diver identifies with, has become the wreck. There is no doubt that this is a mysterious and complex passage but it mirrors the complex and mysterious exploration of the unconscious. Claire Keyes argues [in her study *The Aesthetics of Power: The Poetry of Adrienne Rich*] that "A man who is 'half-destroyed' has denied the woman in him; a woman, just the opposite. Both 'once held to a course'; both, however, must become whole again so that they can function properly. We are, as in Rich's poem, 'instruments'. Referring at the close of the poem to the 'book of myths' which her diver consulted at the start of the venture, Rich's speaker notes that in it 'our names do not appear'. If our names do not appear in the myths, they have no reality for us. If we are male-female, female-male, then pure 'masculinity' is a myth; femininity likewise."

Here on the ocean floor the wreck is being explored. The speaker has returned to the source. Life on earth began as a unicellular organism in the sea and she is returning to the source, the primitive. The poem tells us that she 'came to see the damage that was done/ and the treasures that prevail'. Who inflicted that damage? Were the treasures that she discovered salvaged? These questions are not answered. The poem began with a solitary figure journeying towards the wreck and ends with an image of a figure and figures, the singular and plural, finding their way to this wreck and discovering there that the book of myths does not contain their names. Perhaps this would suggest that she and women like her have been excluded from the book of myths. The past is revisited, re-examined and rewritten.

In classical mythology the male hero frequently descended into the Underworld. In Rich's poem, a woman heroically enters into the darkness of her own being and discovers that the book of myths where men predominated and which was written by men do not contain the whole truth. This other truth which Rich is acknowledging here, the truth of her own being as a woman, is equally valid.

In lines 53/54 the speaker says 'The words are purposes./ The words are maps'. Such an interpretation of language alerts us to its power. The language that the book of myths is written in is male; Rich in this poem has forged her own understanding of her relationship with words and more importantly has forged her own language.

Neil Astley says of this poem that 'When Adrienne Rich goes beneath the surface . . . her underwater exploration is a metaphorical journey back through the mind which turns into a feminist argument with the poetic tradition she has emerged from.'

Rich herself has said [in a statement on the dust-jacket of *Diving Into the Wreck* (1973)] that she is 'coming-home to . . . sex, sexuality, sexual wounds, sexual politics.'

'Diving into the Wreck', a vivid, memorable, sensuous journey poem explores these issues and affirms woman's role, woman's courage, womanhood.

From a Survivor

This poem is dated 1972. In 1968 Rich's father died. In 1969 she and her husband separated and in 1970 he took his own life. Such difficult events inform this poem; the speaker charts the difficult stages of grief and survival.

It is an intensely personal poem. The speaker has survived the death of loved ones but as with so many of Rich's poems, the poem goes beyond the immediately personal and contains a universal emotional truth.

The word survivor has many meanings and reference points. What one individual survivor experiences emotionally, psychologically in a given situation can be compared to what another's experiences of survival are in a different situation.

The poem begins by looking back to the time when a man and a woman, in this instance the speaker and her husband, made a pact. The pact was a marriage and 'in those days' it was an 'ordinary pact'. A sorrow informs the opening lines. The passing of time has changed the speaker's life and her understanding of the marriage pact. She speaks of how he and she thought that they were different from other couples, that they might somehow not know 'the failures of the race'.

Twenty-four lines long, the poem is divided into ten parts which could be said to suggest fragmentation, loss, fragility, a feeling of tentativeness. The longest line, line 9, is tinged with youthfulness and sadness. There was a time when she viewed the world not in terms of disappointment or failure: 'we didn't know/ the race had failures of that order'.

The poem becomes increasingly personal. It begins with the legal, official word 'pact' but at line 10 the speaker addresses her dead husband, his physical self and the nature of their relationship. His body was once 'the body of a god'. Now the speaker, through experience, views life differently. The past, the present and the future are all referred to in the poem and the speaker thinks of an anniversary that will never be: 'Next year it would have been 20 years'. Rich had married in 1953 and 1973 would have represented a conventional anniversary but the marriage was not conventional. The speaker is acknowledging the distances between life as it might have been and life as it had to be.

Line 16 speaks of her husband who once had 'power over my life'. Such a detail gives us a glimpse into a strained marriage and also allows us to understand the subsequent course of events.

The image of the leap which the poet uses in line 19 conveys risk, adventure, imagination. Her husband 'might have made the leap' but instead is 'wastefully dead'. This is a clear-sighted comment on their complex relationship. It offers a glimpse of a happier future but he did not survive. She did. She changed and learned to cope with change and the poem ends with a quiet optimism. Though there is regret that her husband did not survive, there is also an awareness that the end of their marriage released her, made possible the new life she now lives.

They spoke of survival, of his making the leap but, when they talked of it, it was too late. She made the necessary leap but her life now is not lived 'as a leap' but as 'a succession of brief amazing movements'. This last description captures the speaker's grateful, calm state. The absence of the full stop here suggests survival and surviving, something that is on-going.

Power

This poem differs from the other Adrienne Rich poems on the Leaving Certificate course: the subject matter is a public, historical figure and it uses spaces between words in an interesting and effective way.

The opening line captures past and present:

>   Living   in the earth-deposits   of our history

and the word earth-deposits reminds us of another time. The placing of the word between 'Living' and 'history' highlights the links between now and then. Line 1, on its own, is a meditative line. With 'Today', at the beginning of line 2, the speaker focuses on the immediate present, the here and now, the finding of the medicine bottle and what has prompted her to think of the past. This then leads to Marie Curie's story which she had been reading about 'Today'.

Lines 2–5 reflect on the modern and the old, the way they lived then and the differences between that time and this. A mechanical digger connects with a one-hundred-year-old medicine bottle, a 'cure for fever or melancholy a tonic'. Such cures are still being sought and the phrase 'the winters of this climate' describes the speaker's world as a bleak time.

The bottle has been found 'Today' and 'Today' the speaker has been reading about this woman scientist. The poet admires Marie Curie, physicist and chemist, for her great scientific discovery, which helped save many lives, achieved power. Yet Curie could not face the deleterious effects of radium on her own body and those of her associates. Ironically, Curie's discovery caused her own decline [and Curie's assistant Blanche Wittman lost an arm and both of her legs to radiation].

At the heart of the poem is this sense of contradiction. Words such as 'bombarded', 'cataracts', 'the cracked and suppurating skin' convey pain. Marie Curie would not admit that her research led to her illness and death; she 'denied to the end'. Curie devoted herself to a cause, to what she believed in and she refused to believe that it was destroying her. She denied the truth. Yet Curie was determined and though a scientist she symbolises every woman's struggle.

The poem presents the reader with two contradictory realities. Curie's position embodies contradictions, and these contradictions challenge the reader.

The poem, using a stream of consciousness technique, goes beyond narrative. The speaker focuses on the nature of power: 'her wounds came from the same source as her power'. The poet admires the scientific achievement but was the sacrifice too great? She was world-famous: 'She died a famous woman'. But the price she paid was high. The closing lines are more downbeat than celebratory.

'Power' is a sequence of observations and insights. The use of the long lines and the pauses within them create an effective rhythm. One has to stop, focus and consider particular words in the line.

'Diving into the Wreck' and 'Power', according to Eavan Boland, 'speak to the injustices of a society' and one of those injustices involves women. The injustice here is not immediately obvious perhaps. A woman is successful in a man's world but as Rich implies the price has been too high.

The first word in the poem is the poem's title 'Power' and 'power' is also the final word. Power has traditionally been associated with men and this poem looks at one woman's experience of power, its challenges and its demands.

Monument to Marie Curie in Warsaw, Poland.

William Butler Yeats
(1865–1939)

Contents	Page

IF I WERE FOUR-AND-TWENTY
BY
WILLIAM BUTLER YEATS.

THE CUALA PRESS
DUBLIN, IRELAND.
MCMXL

The Overview

Two poets, one American, one Irish, dominate English Literature during the first half of the twentieth century: T.S. Eliot and W.B. Yeats. So powerful is Yeats's distinctive poetic voice that his poetry has been described as 'magisterial', 'authoritative', 'commanding', 'formidable', 'compelling', 'direct', 'exhilarating', 'overbearing'. Before he died, Yeats arranged for an epitaph to be cut in stone 'by his command' and by then, Seamus Heaney says, that '"command" had indeed characterised the Yeatsian style'. But there is also in Yeats the voice of the dreamer and idealist. We see it in 'The Lake Isle of Innisfree', which he began writing when he was twenty-three. The life imagined on Innisfree is simple, beautiful and unrealistic and the longing for the ideal is also found in the sixty-one year old Yeats when he sails, in his imagination, to Byzantium.

Yeats lived in a time of extraordinary change. A world war was fought and Ireland struggled for and attained its Independence and went through civil war; his poetry charts the political turmoil of those times. Yeats writes of his private and his public life and sometimes those two aspects overlap. He is a public poet in a poem such as 'September 1913', where he becomes a self-elected spokesman in his condemnation of small-mindedness and the absence of vision. He played a public role, was committed to Ireland (he refused a knighthood in 1915) and was made a senator in 1922; one of his early ambitions, says the writer Michael Schmidt, was 'to reconcile the courteous Protestant heritage with the martyred, unmannerly Roman Catholic tradition in Ireland towards a political end.' In 'In memory of Eva Gore-Booth and Con Markiewicz' he touches on these themes. 'All his life,' wrote the scholar Augustine Martin, 'Yeats sought for a harmonious way of life as well as a perfect form of art and he re-invents himself several times during the course of his life and work.'

Yeats in these thirteen poems writes of the beauty of the natural world ('The Lake Isle of Innisfree'), his disillusionment with contemporary Ireland ('September 1913'), his heartbreak and his ageing self ('The Wild Swans at Coole'), war and patriotism and modern heroism ('An Irish Airman Foresees his Death'), political commitment, fanaticism, a crucial time in Ireland's history ('Easter 1916'), anarchy and breakdown ('The Second Coming'), nature versus art and the transforming power of art ('Sailing to Byzantium'), the bitterness of civil war and the continuity of nature ('The Stare's nest by My Window'), friendship, cultural legacy, choice ('In Memory of Eva Gore-Booth and Con Markiewicz'), determined, justified individuality ('Swift's Epitaph'), the ageing body, the ageing mind ('An Acre of Grass'), longing ('Politics'), poetry, Irish identity (from 'Under Ben Bulben'). Though similar themes recur, Yeats rarely repeated himself. In *Irish Classics* Professor Declan Kiberd identifies this aspect of Yeats's poetry and comments: 'The greatness of Yeats lay in his constant capacity to adjust to ever-changing conditions...As the years passed, he grew simpler in expression, using shorter lines dominated by monosyllables, with more nouns and fewer adjectives. He said himself that a poet should think like a wise man, but express himself as one of the common people.'

Poets frequently write on similar themes. When Yeats writes on his love of the ideal, nationalism, his preoccupation with the passing of time and the reality of growing old, his belief in the extraordinary power of art, it could be argued that thematically his poetry is not startlingly unusual, but it is the way he writes on such topics that makes him unique.

In a letter to Herbert Edward Palmer, dated 9 August 1922, Yeats offered Palmer some advice regarding style when he wrote, 'Examine your style, word for word, study the dictionary, study the most concentrated masters till writing grows very arduous and you will attain to a greater general height of accomplishment, to a steadier light, and yet not lose your flashes of lightning.' And, when he was old, Yeats wrote 'A General Introduction to My Work' where he says: 'I tried to make the language of poetry coincide with passionate normal speech. I wanted to write in whatever language comes most naturally when we soliloquise, as I do, all day long upon the events of our own lives or of any life where we can see ourselves for the moment . . .' Yeats, in that same piece, says 'I need a passionate syntax for a passionate subject matter', and so he accepted 'those traditional metres that had developed with the language'.

His tone can be harsh ('What need you, being come to sense'); regretful ('The ceremony of innocence is drowned;/ The best lack all conviction, while the worst/ Are full of passionate intensity.'); didactic ('An aged man is but a paltry thing,/ A tattered coat upon a stick, unless/ Soul clap its hands and sing, and louder sing/ For every tatter in its mortal dress'); prayer-like ('Come build in the empty house of the stare'); tender ('Dear shadows, now you know it all,/ All the folly of a fight'); defiant ('Grant me an old man's frenzy'); filled with longing ('But O that I were young again/ And held her in my arms!'); and authoritative ('Sing whatever is well made,/ Scorn the sort now growing up/ All out of shape from toe to top').

Imagery, especially his use of symbols, is another striking aspect of Yeats's work. Powerful, memorable images remain with the reader, such as the 'purple glow' of noon; the fumbling in 'a greasy till'; 'the hangman's rope'; the nine-and-fifty swans 'Upon the brimming water' and the 'bell-beat of their wings'; 'the stone in the midst of 'the living stream'; a creature 'somewhere in sands of the desert/ A shape with lion body and the head of a man'; 'sages standing in God's holy fire'; 'The bees build in the crevices/ Of loosening masonry'; 'Two girls in silk kimonos'; 'Shake the dead in their shrouds'; and 'Porter-drinkers' randy laughter'.

In 'Under Ben Bulben', written five months before he died, he praised the well-made poem and scorned and condemned the shapeless, badly made one. All his life he valued form and his mastery of rhythm, rhyme and the stanza are testimony to this; form contained and ordered his emotional, intellectual and imaginative outpourings. Yeats is intensely personal: he names names and writes about events and happenings that are recorded in newspapers and history books, but he knew that 'all that is personal soon rots, it must be packed in ice and salt'. The 'salt' and 'ice', in this instance, are the structures and techniques of the art of writing. The poems speak to us with great immediacy and directness but they do so in elaborate and musical forms.

'My poetry is generally written out of despair', said Yeats. As he grew older, he searched for ways to overcome his weakening body. He raged against old age, wrote about it with great honesty and accepted the inevitability of death. His poetry reminds us of the immortality of art, that 'Man can embody truth but cannot know it' and that 'we begin to live when we have conceived life as a tragedy'.

Biographical Notes

Though W.B. Yeats spent two-thirds of his life out of Ireland, it is with Ireland that he is most associated, especially Sligo and Dublin. He was born in a house called 'George's Ville' on Sandymount Avenue in Dublin on 13 June 1865, the first born of the family. His father John Butler Yeats was a well-to-do landlord who was reading for the Bar but who, in reality, preferred drawing; his mother Susan (Pollexfen) Yeats was the daughter of a wealthy Sligo family, the Pollexfens. Yeats's grandfather, a clergyman, was also called William Butler Yeats and his father, Yeats's great grandfather, a Reverend John Butler Yeats, had been appointed to Drumcliff in County Sligo.

In August 1866 a second child, Susan Mary Butler Yeats (nicknamed Lily), was born and soon afterwards John Butler Yeats, now a barrister, decided to give up law and go to London to study art. He moved to London early in 1867. His family meanwhile went to live with his wife's family in Sligo until he had found a place for them all to live in. In July 1867 the Yeatses were re-united in London and there they lived for the next five and a half years. Susan Yeats hated London, where Elizabeth (known as Lollie), Robert (Bobby) and John (Jack) were born. Her husband was having little success as an artist. John B. Yeats was becoming increasingly interested in Irish politics and he began to view James Stephens, who founded the Irish Republican Brotherhood, and John O'Leary with sympathy and understanding. He also admired the poetry of Walt Whitman and William Blake for their celebration of individuality and at one stage prevented his wife from teaching their children Church of Ireland prayers. They returned to Sligo every year for holidays but, in 1872, the Yeatses left London and settled once more in Ireland. Willie was seven years old. Years later Yeats wrote: 'I remember little of childhood but its pain.'

They stayed in Sligo for over two years. The Pollexfens lived in Merville, a house on sixty acres, but Yeats described it as a place where 'all was serious and silent'. Though seven years old, Willie did not know the alphabet; he did attend a local primary school but his spelling throughout his life was inconsistent and inaccurate. When his father visited, the young Yeats loved to hear his father read to him and Lily. In Sligo, Yeats grew up hearing many stories of the supernatural; fairies, banshees and ghosts were part of ordinary, everyday life in Sligo and it coloured his imagination. In autumn 1874, when Yeats was nine and a half, the family returned to London, but John Butler Yeats continued to have little success as an artist. Willie was homesick for Sligo and he later admitted that as a boy in London he 'longed for a sod of earth from some field I knew, something of Sligo to hold in my hand.'

In 1875, amidst the family's continuing financial difficulties, a sixth child was born but she died within a year. John Butler Yeats changed from portraiture to landscape painting. Susan and the younger children returned to Sligo and Willie joined his father at Burnham Beeches where he was painting. There John B. Yeats took his son's education in hand but in 1877, when the family was once more together in London, Willie was sent to Godolphin School in Hammersmith. He was eleven and a half and school reminded him of how different he was from other English schoolboys. He was mocked for being Irish and anti-Irish feeling was prevalent among the English, who governed a quarter of the earth's land surface at that time. A school report in 1877 placed him twenty-first in his class of thirty-one; his performance was 'only fair'. And yet he had a belief in himself and knew from an early age that, like his father, he would dedicate himself to his work (poetry) and make it his life.

In 1881, Willie left Godolphin School, where he was now known for his interest in science. The family returned to Ireland and settled at Howth and Willie's mind began to show strong intellectual ambition: he planned to write a book on the yearly cycle of a rock pool and read Darwin and others seriously. It was also at this time, between fifteen and sixteen, that he began writing poetry. He used to travel into Dublin on the train every morning with his father to his studio at 44 York Street and later at 7 St Stephen's Green. There John Butler Yeats would read to Willie passages from favourite poets, especially Shakespeare, Keats, Shelley, Byron and Rossetti. Willie enrolled himself at the Erasmus Smith High School in Harcourt Street, having been told by his father to do so. He was sixteen, was known to the other pupils as the 'insect collector' and later confessed that 'I was worst of all at literature, for we read Shakespeare for his grammar exclusively.'

The studio conversations were to have an important influence on Willie. It was there that ideas and literature were discussed and, gradually, the poet W.B. Yeats was born. As a young man, Yeats was attracted to the poetry of Spenser, Keats, Byron and Rossetti; his trips to Sligo continued to feed his imagination. There he heard tales of the supernatural and once, when he was walking with his cousin Lucy Middleton late one evening, passing a graveyard and abandoned village, they both believed they saw a flaming, brilliant presence moving towards them and then it disappeared and began to climb a mountain slope seven miles away. Yeats's fascination with the supernatural was lifelong.

Yeats left school in 1883. He was eighteen and had already written a verse play and his family were by then used to the sound of Yeats composing. He would murmur and hum aloud his verses in his room and he was determined to devote his life to writing. In November 1883 Yeats went to hear Oscar Wilde give a lecture in Dublin and in May 1884, academically too weak to go to Trinity College, he enrolled at the Metropolitan School of Art in Kildare St but he stopped attending the following summer and enrolled at the Royal Hibernian Academy. But overall Yeats was disillusioned and bored (years later he said that his artistic training was 'destructive of enthusiasm'.) He continued to write and he preferred verse drama and narrative to lyric poetry at first; in March 1885 he published two lyrics in the *Dublin University Review*, 'Song of the Faeries' and 'Voices'.

That year too, Yeats attended the newly formed Contemporary Club with his father, a club founded to discuss the social, political and literary topics of the time; another important influence on the young W.B. Yeats was his reading of a book entitled *Esoteric Buddhism* which his aunt Isabella Pollexfen had given him, a book that explored Eastern and Western religions. A third influence was Yeats's joining the Young Ireland Society, urged by John O'Leary, the Fenian journalist who had returned from exile in Paris at the beginning of 1885.

John O'Leary was a very influential figure in Yeats's life and poetry. When a student, O'Leary had abandoned medicine and had become a Fenian leader. He held nationalistic, romantic views and had been arrested in 1865 for his part in the Fenian movement. Condemned to twenty years in prison, he served five and had to spend the remaining fifteen years in exile. O'Leary was highly respected and Yeats later wrote that the meetings he attended at the Contemporary Club and the books O'Leary lent or gave him determined all that he subsequently set his hand to. Something else very important happened at this time in terms of Yeats's poetry and, in his *Autobiographies,* he explains how he realised that: 'We should write out our own thoughts in as nearly as possible the language we thought them in, as though in a letter to an intimate friend. We should not disguise them in any way for our lives give them force as the lives of people in plays give force to their words. Personal utterance, which had almost ceased in English literature, could be as fine an escape from rhetoric (and abstraction) as drama itself. But my father would hear of nothing but drama; personal utterance was only egotism. I knew it was not... I tried from that on to write out of my emotions exactly as they came to me in life, not changing them to make them more beautiful.' The Irish poet Eavan Boland says that 'it would be hard to overestimate the importance of that particular passage.' Yeats had made up his mind that he was going to take his life and use it as the raw material for his art. Boland adds that 'there have been a lot of poets since Yeats who have written about their lives. But Yeats lived at a time when it was believed you couldn't do that, at least not in that way. So Yeats was moving against the current; Yeats made his art out of his life and he did so deliberately.'

Yeats was friends with the poet Katherine Tynan and they attended a seance together. It was a frightening experience for them both; Yeats felt that his body experienced the supernatural, felt there was something 'very evil' in the room and he did not attend a seance again for many years. In April 1886, Yeats left art school and in October 1886 – he was twenty-one – published his first volume, *Mosada*, which did not impress Gerard Manley Hopkins, the poet and Jesuit priest, who thought it 'strained'. But already Yeats was finding new subject matter and themes: Irish settings and themes now began to figure in his writing and his well-known poem 'Down By the Salley Gardens', which was inspired by an old Sligo woman's song, belongs to this time. But in April 1887 the Yeats family were back in London where Yeats worked as a reviewer, made contacts in the literary world and visited Madame Blavatsky the theosophist, who encouraged Yeats's interest in myth and folklore. In August 1887, Yeats returned to Sligo to finish his poem 'The Wanderings of Oisin', a work which drew on myth and politics. Also in 1887 Yeats edited an anthology of poetry, dedicated to John O'Leary, which was published in

Dublin under the title *Poems and Ballads of Young Ireland*. Yeats finished his long narrative Oisin poem in Sligo and it was published in 1889 in a volume entitled *The Wanderings of Oisin and Other Poems* and reprinted that same year under the title *Crossways*. There are sixteen poems in all; the first eight are preoccupied with Indian, exotic themes; the final eight are inspired by Ireland.

Though Yeats described London as 'hateful', he met and became friends with William Morris, G.B. Shaw, Oscar Wilde and others. He carefully researched and edited a book called *Fairy and Folk Tales of the Irish Peasantry* and worked as a freelance journalist, but the financial situation at home was so serious that the entire family suffered hardship. It was in London, in December 1888, that Yeats was inspired to write what would become his most famous poem, 'The Lake Isle of Innisfree'. It was published in 1890 and was an immediate success. Robert Louis Stevenson wrote from Samoa and praised Yeats for a work 'so quaint and airy, simple artful, and eloquent to the heart'.

On 30 January 1889, a tall, beautiful, twenty-two year-old ardent Irish nationalist named Maud Gonne visited the Yeatses at their home in Blenheim Road. Though English born and the daughter of a British army colonel serving in Dublin, she had recently become involved in radical politics and insisted that Ireland be freed of British rule. Yeats's father was shocked by her outspoken nature but Yeats himself defended her and he was smitten. Maud Gonne invited Yeats to dine with her that evening and they also dined together on the next nine evenings of Gonne's London stay. Yeats had fallen in love. He was twenty-three years old and, many years later, he spoke of how it was at this time that 'the troubling of my life began'.

In 1891, Yeats founded the Irish Literary Society in London. He also returned to Ireland on a visit and while there asked Maud Gonne to marry him. She refused but Yeats continued to be fascinated by her and proposed to her several times. She had gone to Donegal to be with and to help the impoverished Irish. There, Gonne witnessed evictions, violence, death. She campaigned for the release of political prisoners and, when she asked Yeats to write a play for her on an Irish theme; he created his play *The Countess Cathleen*, which tells of a beautiful woman who sells her soul to the Devil in a bid to save the Irish people.

In 1896, Yeats had his first sexual relationship when he had a year-long affair with Olivia Shakespear. Also in 1896, Yeats met Lady Augusta Gregory, forty-five and a widow, who lived at Coole Park in County Galway. She had an enormous influence on Yeats. It was in 1897 that Yeats, with Lady Gregory and Edward Martyn, spoke of creating a theatre for new Irish plays and the idea of the Abbey Theatre, which opened on 27 December 1904, was born. In their book *W.B. Yeats and His World,* Micheal MacLiammoir and Eavan Boland wrote of Lady Gregory that 'It is impossible to over-estimate her influence on Yeats. She was his friend and counsellor, an understanding eye in the tumultuous and haunted places of his mind. She was to help him more than he had ever been helped in his life, chiefly, and most significantly, by offering him access to her house at Coole. This became Yeats's most important home; for more than thirty years he spent all his summers there, and often his winters.'

Yeats was interested in Buddhism, magic, spiritualism, astrology, and the Cabbala – a secret, traditional lore which allowed Jewish Rabbis to read hidden meanings in the Bible. He studied William Blake's work and co-edited an edition of Blake's poetry in 1893. To please Maud Gonne, Yeats joined the Irish Republican Brotherhood but he and she resigned from the organisation in 1900. Yeats was making his living at this time from journalism and he was very involved with the founding of the Irish National Dramatic Society which later became the Abbey Theatre.

Yeats and Maud Gonne had entered into a non-physical, "spiritual union". She played the title role in Yeats's 1902 play *Cathleen Ní Houlihan* and she converted to Catholicism around then because 'every political movement on earth has its counterpart in the spirit world'; she travelled Ireland, America and France fund-raising for the nationalist cause and addressed political rallies. Maud Gonne's marriage to Major John MacBride in 1903 (she and MacBride separated a few years later) upset Yeats but he continued to write poetry about her throughout his life. In a poem published in 1912, Yeats says of Maud Gonne: 'She lived in storm and strife,/ Her soul had such desire' .

In 1907 Yeats travelled to Italy with Lady Gregory and her son Robert where he saw the great Byzantine mosaics at Ravenna, mosaics which feature in Yeats's poem 'Sailing to Byzantium' (1926). Italian artistic achievements convinced Yeats that patronage played a vital role in the making of great art. When Sir Hugh Lane, Lady Gregory's nephew, offered the city of Dublin his collection of thirty-nine, very valuable, French Impressionist paintings if Dublin Corporation would house them and the Corporation refused, Yeats was enraged and wrote angry, political poems, including 'September 1913', denouncing the decision.

John MacBride was executed after the Easter 1916 Rising and Yeats once again proposed to Maud Gonne. She refused and Yeats then proposed to her twenty-year-old daughter Iseult, whose father was a French journalist and politician. Iseult Gonne refused him in 1916. In 1917 Yeats, again, asked Iseult Gonne to marry him and, on being rejected, proposed to an English woman Georgie Hyde Lees (born 1892). He was 52, she was 24 and they had first met in 1911. W.B. Yeats and Georgie Hyde Lees, known as 'George', were married in London, at the Harrow Road Register Office, on 20 October 1917.

Both husband and wife had an interest in the occult. Stephen Coote points out in his biography of Yeats that their wedding date had been chosen because the revolving planets moved into a position promising stability, inspiration, children, philosophic friendship and public acclaim for creative endeavour. During their honeymoon, George Yeats attempted automatic writing and later developed a gift for mediumship and they experimented in many occult practices. During the next few years George Yeats, in response to Yeats's questions, filled thousands of pages with automatic writing.

They lived in Oxford and London during the early months of their marriage and in 1918 the Yeatses moved to Ireland, first to Dublin and later to a Norman Tower, with two cottages attached, in Ballylee, County Galway, which Yeats had bought in 1917 for £35. The tower, known as Tur Bail' i Liaigh, was Anglicised by Yeats to Thoor Ballylee (something he did with all Irish names) and, having restored the tower, in 1919 they moved in. It became their summer home from 1919 until 1929 and Thoor Ballylee, four miles from Gort, a few hours' walk from Coole Park, was dedicated to George. Carved on a stone at Thoor Ballylee are the words:

> I, the poet William Yeats,
> With old mill boards and sea-green slates,
> And smithy work from the Gort forge,
> Restored this tower for my wife George;
> And may these characters remain
> When all is ruin once again.

A daughter, Anne, had been born in Dublin on 24 February 1919. In October the family went to America where Yeats read and lectured. In 1919 Yeats also published his seventh collection, *The Wild Swans at Coole*, which opened with the title poem. They returned to live in Oxford and in August 1921 a son, Michael, was born. In 1922 Yeats bought a house at 82 Merrion Square, Dublin. Micheal MacLaimmoir and Eavan Boland sum up this particular time in the Yeatses' life as follows: 'Yeats and his wife found themselves in an Ireland which was at once rebellious, active, joyous, defiant, up in arms, inflamed with love and hate, and deeply orthodox in terms of religious observance. To most Irishmen at the time, the preoccupation with the occult of Yeats and his wife must have seemed uncanny, obscure, cranky and heretical.' And yet Yeats was appointed to the Irish Senate of the Free State Government in 1922, a position he took up in January 1923, when he was fifty-eight. Yeats was also awarded the Nobel Prize for Literature in 1923 and, in a letter to Edmund Gosse, dated 23 November 1923, he wrote that 'I know quite well that this honour is not given to me as an individual but as a representative of a literary movement and of a nation and I am glad to have it so.'

In *A Vision* (1925), a prose work, Yeats produced a work of mystical philosophy based on his wife's automatic writings; in 1926 he translated Sophocles's play *Oedipus the King* for the Abbey, in 1927 Sophocles's *Oedipus at Colonus*. Early in 1928 poor health dictated a complete rest and Yeats with his wife and two children moved to Rapallo in Italy. In 1928 also he published his collection *The Tower* which included 'Meditations in Time of Civil War' (a sequence which includes 'The Stare's Nest by My Window') and 'Sailing to Byzantium.' It was a book which, in Micheal MacLiammoir and Eavan Boland's words, 'set him indisputably among the greatest living poets of the English language. His genius is at its height in these thirty-six poems, with their superb imagery, their perfection of form, and their ominous hatred of age and death.' Yeats thought Rapallo 'an indescribably lovely place' and, in a letter to Lady Gregory, confessed that he had re-read *The Tower*, was astonished by 'its bitterness' and intended to write 'amiable verses.'

Yeats and his family returned to Ireland in the spring of 1929 and the summer of 1929 marked his last visit to Thoor Ballylee. Winter found the Yeats family once again in Rapallo but he spent the winters of 1930 and 1931 in Ireland. His play, *The Words Upon the Window Pane*, featuring a seance, was performed at the Abbey and was very successful and he was awarded an honorary Doctorate of Letters by Oxford University.

Yeats spent the summer of 1931 at Coole, where Lady Gregory was ill; she died in May 1932. Yeats had once written in his diary [1909] that she 'has been to me mother, friend, sister and brother' and 'I cannot realise the world without her.' Late in 1932, Yeats gave a lecture tour in America in order to raise money for an Irish Academy of Letters which Yeats, George Bernard Shaw and AE [George Russell] had founded that year. By 1932, Yeats had also moved from Merrion Square to 'Riversdale', an early nineteenth-century house in Rathfarnham, his last home in Ireland.

In 1933, his tenth collection, *The Winding Stair and Other Poems*, was published; it opened with 'In Memory of Eva Gore-Booth and Con Markiewicz', a poem written in October 1927.

In April 1934, when he was sixty-nine, Yeats underwent a Steinach rejuvenation operation, which supposedly restored sexual potency. Whether or not the operation was a success, it certainly liberated his imagination. Yeats believed that he produced new poems which were 'among his best work'. In his final years there was what has been termed an astonishing revolution in Yeats's style and yet, during all this time, he was having difficulty with his health and suffered from lung congestion In 1936 he published *The Oxford Book of Modern Verse* and in 1938 travelled to the south of France, where he died of heart failure in Roquebrune on 29 January 1939, at the age of seventy-three. He was buried there, but in 1948 his remains were exhumed and brought to Sligo, though evidence now suggests that the wrong bones were exhumed, where he was buried in Drumcliff churchyard, as had been foretold by Yeats in his poem 'Under Ben Bulben', dated 4 September 1938:

> Under bare Ben Bulben's head
> In Drumcliff churchyard Yeats is laid.
> An ancestor was rector there
> Long years ago, a church stands near,
> By the road an ancient cross.
> No marble, no conventional phrase;
> On limestone quarried near the spot
> By his command these words are cut:
>
> *Cast a cold eye*
> *On life, on death.*
> *Horseman, pass by!*

'W.B. Yeats' (1907) by Augustus John.

POEMS

Dates refer to the year in which these poems were first published in book form.

The Lake Isle of Innisfree

I will arise and go now, and go to Innisfree,
And a small cabin build there, of clay and wattles made:
Nine bean-rows will I have there, a hive for the honey-bee,
And live alone in the bee-loud glade.

And I shall have some peace there, for peace comes dropping
     slow,   5
Dropping from the veils of the morning to where the cricket
     sings;
There midnight's all a glimmer, and noon a purple glow,
And evening full of the linnet's wings.

I will arise and go now, for always night and day
I hear lake water lapping with low sounds by the shore;   10
While I stand on the roadway, or on the pavements grey,
I hear it in the deep heart's core.

📖 Glossary

Title: Innisfree means the island of heather (from 'Inis' meaning island and 'fraoch' meaning heather) – hence the 'purple glow' of line 7.

Line 2 clay and wattles: (also known as wattle and daub) wattles are flexible rods and intertwined wattles were plastered with mud/clay and used as a building material.

Line 7 midnight's all a glimmer: in his essay on weather in the poetry of W.B. Yeats, John Holloway says that 'in such an open and unlighted place . . . on a cloudless and moonless night the stars will appear in astonishing brilliance' and he points out that Yeats's description is 'an understatement by far'.

Line 8 linnet's wings: the linnet, a songbird, is the common finch.

Line 10 lapping: rippling/splashing; can also mean caressing.

This poem began in London's Fleet Street. Yeats was standing on the pavement and looking at a little toy fountain in a shop window. The sound of the water reminded him of Sligo, where he spent his summer holidays.

This is how Yeats himself described the poem's origin: 'I had still the ambition, formed in Sligo in my teens, of living in imitation of Thoreau on Innisfree, a little island in Lough Gill, and when walking through Fleet Street very home-sick I heard a little tinkle of water, and saw a fountain in a shop-window which balanced a little ball upon the jet, and began to remember lake water. From the sudden remembrance came my poem "Innisfree"'.

The three stanzas rhyme abab; the first three lines in each stanza are hexameters, the fourth a tetrameter. Robert Louis Stevenson, author of *Treasure Island* and *Kidnapped*, wrote to Yeats on 14 April 1894 to say that he had been deeply moved by 'The Lake Isle of Innisfree'. Stevenson said of the poem that 'It is so quaint and airy, simple, artful, and eloquent to the heart — but I seek words in vain. Enough that "always night and day I hear lake water lapping with low sounds on the shore," and am, yours gratefully, Robert Louis Stevenson.'

In 2000, the *Irish Times* published its *Book of Favourite Irish Poems* which 3,500 readers had nominated. Yeats's poetry made up twenty-five per cent of the one hundred poems chosen and 'The Lake Isle of Innisfree' was voted number one.

Yeats included the first draft of 'The Lake Isle of Innisfree' in a letter he wrote to Katharine Tynan on 21 December 1888 and he prefaced the poem as follows: 'Here are two verses I made the other day: 'There is a beautiful Island of Innisfree in Lough Gill, Sligo. A little rocky island with a legended past' and added that 'to go away and live alone on that island' was 'an old daydream of my own'. The draft was as follows:

I will arise and go now and go to the island of Innis free
And live in a dwelling of wattles – of woven wattles and wood work made,
Nine bean rows will I have there, a yellow hive for the honey bee
And this old care shall fade.

There from the dawn above me peace will come down dropping slow
Dropping from the veils of the morning to where the household cricket sings.
And noontide there be all a glimmer, midnight be a purple glow,
And evening full of the linnet's wings.

In a recording, Yeats introduced his reading of the poem: 'I have gone to a lot of trouble to get into verse the poems that I am going to read and that is why I will not read them as if they were prose. I am going to begin with a poem of mine called "The Lake Isle of Innisfree" because if you know anything about me you will expect me to begin with it. It is the only poem of mine that is very widely known. When I was a young lad in the town of Sligo I read Thoreau's *Essays* and wanted to live in a hut on an island in Lough Gill called Innisfree which means Heather Island. I wrote the poem in London when I was about twenty-three. One day in the Strand I heard a little tinkle of water and saw in a shop window a little jet of water balancing a ball on the top. It was an advertisement, I think, for cooling drinks but it set me thinking of Sligo and lake water. I think there is only one obscurity in the poem: I speak of noon as "a purple glow." I must have meant by that the reflection of heather in the water.'

? Questions

1. How would you describe the particular appeal of this 'escapist' poem?

2. What is the effect of the opening words 'I will arise and go now' and their repetition in line 9? Why do you think Yeats opted for such formal language here?

3. Yeats wrote this poem in 1888–89. Do many details in the poem suggest the times he lived in, the contemporary? List the details which you would consider timeless and comment on their effect.

4. Why do you think Yeats chose a long line for this particular poem? Why is the final line in each of the three stanzas a shorter line?

5. Comment on how Yeats uses the senses to evoke a place. Identify how assonance and alliteration are used for particular effect, especially in the final stanza.

6. Robert Louis Stevenson said that the poem was both 'simple and artful'. Explain what you think he meant by this. Identify what is simple about the poem and artful.

7. How would your own version of Utopia compare with Yeats's?

September 1913

What need you, being come to sense,
But fumble in a greasy till
And add the halfpence to the pence
And prayer to shivering prayer, until
You have dried the marrow from the bone?   5
For men were born to pray and save:
Romantic Ireland's dead and gone,
It's with O'Leary in the grave.

Yet they were of a different kind,
The names that stilled your childish play,   10
They have gone about the world like wind,
But little time had they to pray
For whom the hangman's rope was spun,
And what, God help us, could they save?
Romantic Ireland's dead and gone,   15
It's with O'Leary in the grave.

Was it for this the wild geese spread
The grey wing upon every tide;
For this that all that blood was shed,
For this Edward Fitzgerald died,   20
And Robert Emmet and Wolfe Tone,
All that delirium of the brave?
Romantic Ireland's dead and gone,
It's with O'Leary in the grave.

Yet could we turn the years again,   25
And call those exiles as they were
In all their loneliness and pain,
You'd cry, 'Some woman's yellow hair
Has maddened every mother's son':
They weighed so lightly what they gave.   30
But let them be, they're dead and gone,
They're with O'Leary in the grave.

Glossary

Title September 1913: This poem, dated 7 September 1913, first appeared in the *Irish Times* on 8 September 1913, under the title 'Romance in Ireland (On reading much of the correspondence against the Art Gallery)'. Like Yeats's poem 'To a Wealthy Man who promised a Second Subscription to the Dublin Municipal Gallery if it were proved the People wanted Pictures', it was prompted in part by the controversy surrounding the Hugh Lane pictures. Lane's important collection of French Impressionist paintings was offered to Dublin on condition that they would be properly housed. Yeats and his friends tried to raise money for an art gallery but there was a poor response from the wealthy Catholic middle class. The owner of the *Irish Independent*, William Martin Murphy, publicly disagreed with Yeats on the issue. In 1913 also there was a workers' strike and lock-out in Dublin, which was led by Jim Larkin. William Martin Murphy opposed the workers and had the support of the Catholic Church and Yeats, together with many Irish writers and intellectuals, took the workers' side in the dispute.

Line 1 you: the Irish people, especially the Catholic wealthy middle class.

Line 2 greasy till: A. Norman Jeffares notes in his *Commentary on the Collected Poems of W.B.Yeats* that the image came from a speech Yeats made in July 1913. He wrote to Lady Gregory that he had spoken with Lane as well as possible subscribers to the Gallery in his mind: 'I described Ireland, if the present intellectual movement failed, as a little greasy huxtering nation groping for halfpence in a greasy till but did not add except in thought, "by the light of a holy candle"'.

Line 5 You have dried the marrow from the bone: destroyed everything essential to life.

Line 7 Romantic Ireland: an Ireland with vision, idealism.

Line 8 O'Leary: John O'Leary (1830–1907) influenced the young W.B. Yeats, especially because of his role in the struggle for Irish independence. He studied medicine but soon devoted himself to the struggle for Irish freedom. Between 1863 and 1865, O'Leary edited the *Irish People*, the Irish Republican Brotherhood newspaper, which openly promoted the overthrow of British rule. He was arrested in 1865 and sentenced to twenty years of penal servitude in Britain. He was released in 1871, as part of a general amnesty, but was not permitted to return to Ireland until 1885. He lived mainly in Paris and, on returning to Dublin in 1885, he met the twenty-year-old Yeats, who was deeply impressed by him.

Line 10 names: the names of Irish patriots.

Line 17 the wild geese: In Declan Kiberd's words, the Wild Geese were 'those Irish Rebels who sought training in the armies of Catholic Europe after 1691 in hopes of returning to expel the occupier.' These Irishmen served in French, Spanish and Austrian armies. After the Treaty of Limerick was signed in 1691, Patrick Sarsfield and 11,000 men went to France and fought with the French. In all, it was thought that 120,000 Wild Geese left Ireland between 1690 and 1730.

Line 20 Edward Fitzgerald: Lord Edward Fitzgerald (1763–1798), Irish republican politician; joined the United Irishmen in 1796 and went to France to arrange for a French invasion of Ireland. The plot was exposed and a price of £1,000 was placed on Fitzgerald's head; he was seized and was fatally wounded in Dublin.

Line 21 Robert Emmet (1778–1803): Irish republican, a member of the United Irishmen; his plot to seize Dublin Castle failed. He was tried for high treason and was hanged in 1803.

Line 21 Wolfe Tone (1763–1798): in 1791, he published a pamphlet, *An Argument on Behalf of the Catholics of Ireland*, and helped to found the Society of United Irishmen. He enlisted French help and, in September 1798, led a French force to Ireland; he was captured in Lough Swilly. In Dublin he was tried and condemned to be hanged as a traitor. It is said that he cut his own throat in prison.

Line 22 delirium: fervour, selflessness.

Line 28/29 You'd cry, 'Some woman's yellow hair/ Has maddened every mother's son': 'the bloodless rabble, beholding the fervour of the old patriots, would find a banal explanation for it' is Daniel Albright's explanation of these two lines. Gus Martin says: 'Yeats suggests that people who were incapable of understanding the fervour of the patriotism of these men might be inclined to say that they were motivated by something, perhaps by love for a woman.'

Line 30 weighed: calculated.

> Micheál MacLiammóir and Eavan Boland in their book *W.B. Yeats and His World* comment: 'in "September 1913", Yeats looked about him at the country which he had served with such devotion and found nothing but disillusion. Seeing with sudden bitter clarity the littleness, the greyness, the meanness, the self-glorification, the prudish savagery and false piety gathering – as it seemed, incurably – over the face of the land and her people, he cried:
>
> *Romantic Ireland's dead and gone,*
> *It's with O'Leary in the grave.'*

? Questions

1. Who is Yeats addressing in this poem? How would you describe Yeats's tone in the opening stanza? Which words best describe that tone?

2. Examine how Yeats focuses on the present, the past, and the present again and comment on the significance of this.

3. Identify the sharp contrast between the men who 'were born to pray and save' (line 6) and those 'For whom the hangman's rope was spun,/And what, God help us, could they save?' (lines 13–14)

4. What is Yeats's idea of a Romantic Ireland? Why does the poet think 'Romantic Ireland's dead and gone'?

5. Is this a public or a private poem? Give reasons for your answer.

6. Comment on the use of rhyme, rhythm, repetition and questions throughout the poem.

7. Why do you think Yeats uses a question mark in every stanza except the final one? How would you describe the poet's tone in the line 'But let them be they're dead and gone'?

8. The didactic poem is a poem which instructs or teaches. Why is 'September 1913' considered a didactic poem and what does it teach?

9. Seamus Heaney says of W.B. Yeats that 'He never accepted the terms of another argument, but proposed his own.' Outline in your own words Yeats's argument in this poem.

The Wild Swans at Coole

The trees are in their autumn beauty,
The woodland paths are dry,
Under the October twilight the water
Mirrors a still sky;
Upon the brimming water among the stones   5
Are nine-and-fifty swans.

The nineteenth autumn has come upon me
Since I first made my count;
I saw, before I had well finished,
All suddenly mount   10
And scatter wheeling in great broken rings
Upon their clamorous wings.

I have looked upon those brilliant creatures,
And now my heart is sore.
All's changed since I, hearing at twilight,   15
The first time on this shore,
The bell-beat of their wings above my head,
Trod with a lighter tread.

Unwearied still, lover by lover,
They paddle in the cold   20
Companionable streams or climb the air;
Their hearts have not grown old;
Passion or conquest, wander where they will,
Attend upon them still.

But now they drift on the still water,   25
Mysterious, beautiful;
Among what rushes will they build,
By what lake's edge or pool
Delight men's eyes when I awake some day
To find they have flown away?   30

Glossary

Title Coole: Coole Park, Gort, Co. Galway, the home of Augusta Gregory, Yeats's friend and patron. The house was built circa 1770 and in 1927 the estate was sold to the Department of Lands, Lady Gregory being allowed to live there during her lifetime. In 1941, nine years after Lady Gregory's death, the house was demolished.

Line 5 brimming water: that autumn (October 1916), the water in Lough Corrib was particularly low; it had been one of the driest autumns on record. That did not prevent Yeats from altering the facts for poetic effect. Water, according to Curtis B. Bradford, is always a symbol of the sensual life in Yeats's poetry.

Line 12 clamorous: loud-sounding.

Line 15 All's changed: a reference perhaps to the political changes (World War I and the Easter Rising) and the personal (Yeats's own personal sorrow – his unrequited love for Maud Gonne, his growing old).

Line 19 lover by lover: swans mate for life and their being together highlights Yeats's solitariness.

Line 21 companionable: friendly.

Line 24 Attend upon them still: (Will) stay with them always.

The first draft of the opening lines reads as follows:

These/ The woods are in their autumn colours
But the Coole Water is low
And all the paths are dry under
And all paths dry under the foot
In the soft twilight I go...

In an earlier version of the poem, the final stanza was printed third. Yeats was fifty-one when he wrote 'The Wild Swans at Coole'. The rhyme scheme used here, abcbdd, is unusual for Yeats.

? Questions

1. What impresses Yeats about the swans? What do they stand for? What qualities of theirs does he admire? What differences does the speaker recognise between the swans and himself? Which details, in your opinion, express these best?

2. How do you think this poem achieves its slow and dignified rhythm? Look, for example, at the choice of words, the line length, the rhyme.

3. How might this poem be seen as a poem of regret and lament? How would you describe the speaker as he is portrayed in this poem?

4. Why do you think Yeats calls the cold streams 'companionable'? Explain what is meant by 'Passion or conquest, wander where they will,/ Attend upon them still.' What do these lines imply about Yeats?

5. Do you think Yeats has convinced the reader that the swans are 'Mysterious, beautiful'? What does this poem tell us about man's relation with nature?

6. How would you describe the mood in the closing stanza? Is it similar to or different from the mood elsewhere in the poem?

7. It has been said of this poem that Yeats expresses a universal state of mind and emotion and he does so in a diction and rhetoric that can rightly be called noble. Do you agree with this view? Give reasons for your answer.

An Irish Airman Foresees his Death

I know that I shall meet my fate
Somewhere among the clouds above;
Those that I fight I do not hate,
Those that I guard I do not love;
My country is Kiltartan Cross,   5
My countrymen Kiltartan's poor,
No likely end could bring them loss
Or leave them happier than before.
Nor law, nor duty bade me fight,
Nor public men, nor cheering crowds,   10
A lonely impulse of delight
Drove to this tumult in the clouds;
I balanced all, brought all to mind,
The years to come seemed waste of breath,
A waste of breath the years behind   15
In balance with this life, this death.

Glossary

Title Irish Airman: Robert Gregory (1881–1918), Lady Gregory's only son, who died in action on the Italian front on 23 January 1918. He had trained as an artist and Yeats saw him as a Renaissance man, in other words a man of great learning, talent and accomplishment. Yeats wrote several poems in honour of Robert Gregory and in 1918 paid him the following tribute: 'I have known no man accomplished in so many ways as Major Robert Gregory, who was killed in action a couple of weeks ago and buried by his fellow-airmen in the beautiful cemetery at Padua... He had so many sides: painter, classical scholar, scholar in painting and in modern literature, boxer, horseman, airman – he had the Military Cross and the Legion d'Honneur. . .'

Line 3 Those that I fight: the Germans, in Italy.

Line 4 Those that I guard: the English; Gregory fought with the English army.

Line 5 Kiltartan Cross: crossroads near Coole Park, the Gregory home, in Co. Galway.

Line 12 tumult: commotion, din.

Line 13 I balanced all: Daniel Albright points out that the poem is a series of balances: enemies and friends (lines 3–4); loss and gain (lines 7–8); the past and the future (lines 14–15).

Yeats wrote this poem in 1918, the year Robert Gregory was killed.

? Questions

1. This poem is written in the voice of thirty-seven year old Major Robert Gregory. How does Yeats create a sense of the inevitable in this poem? In your answer, consider the title, the tone and rhythm of the lines.

2. Robert Gregory fought with the British against the Germans in Italy. Why does he say 'Those that I fight I do not hate,/ Those that I guard I do not love'? What is the significance of line 5: 'My country is Kiltartan Cross'? Do you think that there is a sense of confusion and contradiction in the speaker's mind?

3. What reasons does the speaker give for choosing to fight? Are they the usual reasons? What do you understand by 'A lonely impulse of delight'? Is there a recklessness in the poem? A futility? Where?

4. In the closing lines the speaker says 'I balanced all'. How do the lines themselves create a sense of balance in their very structure?

5. Is this a well-made poem? In your answer, you should consider the rhyming scheme and the regular, four-beat, eight-syllable line.

Easter 1916

I have met them at close of day
Coming with vivid faces
From counter or desk among grey
Eighteenth-century houses.
I have passed with a nod of the head   5
Or polite meaningless words,
Or have lingered awhile and said
Polite meaningless words,
And thought before I had done
Of a mocking tale or a gibe   10
To please a companion
Around the fire at the club,
Being certain that they and I
But lived where motley is worn:
All changed, changed utterly: 15
A terrible beauty is born.

That woman's days were spent
In ignorant good-will,
Her nights in argument
Until her voice grew shrill.   20
What voice more sweet than hers
When, young and beautiful,
She rode to harriers?
This man had kept a school
And rode our wingèd horse;   25
This other his helper and friend
Was coming into his force;
He might have won fame in the end,
So sensitive his nature seemed,
So daring and sweet his thought.   30
This other man I had dreamed,
A drunken, vainglorious lout.

He had done most bitter wrong
To some who are near my heart,
Yet I number him in the song;   35
He, too, has resigned his part
In the casual comedy;
He, too, has been changed in his turn,
Transformed utterly:
A terrible beauty is born.   40

Hearts with one purpose alone
Through summer and winter seem
Enchanted to a stone
To trouble the living stream.
The horse that comes from the road,   45
The rider, the birds that range
From cloud to tumbling cloud,
Minute by minute they change;
A shadow of cloud on the stream
Changes minute by minute;   50
A horse-hoof slides on the brim,
And a horse plashes within it;
The long-legged moor-hens dive,
And hens to moor-cocks call;
Minute by minute they live: 55
The stone's in the midst of all.

Too long a sacrifice
Can make a stone of the heart.
O when may it suffice?
That is Heaven's part, our part   60
To murmur name upon name,
As a mother names her child
When sleep at last has come
On limbs that had run wild.
What is it but nightfall?   65

No, no, not night but death;
Was it needless death after all?
For England may keep faith
For all that is done and said.
We know their dream; enough   70
To know they dreamed and are dead;
And what if excess of love
Bewildered them till they died?
I write it out in a verse—
MacDonagh and MacBride   75
And Connolly and Pearse
Now and in time to be,
Wherever green is worn,
Are changed, changed utterly:
A terrible beauty is born.   80

 ## Glossary

Date: Though dated specifically 25 September 1916 in *The Collected Poems*, Yeats in fact began working on the poem on 11 May 1916 and completed it on 25 September 1916.

Title Easter 1916: the Easter Rebellion in Dublin on 24 April 1916. Seven hundred of the Irish Republican Brotherhood took to the streets of Dublin and proclaimed Ireland a republic and no longer under British rule. British troops moved in and the uprising collapsed after five days. Fifteen of the leaders were executed between 3 and 12 May. In all, there were 450 dead and 2,614 wounded. Yeats was deeply moved by the event.

Line 1 them: the rebels, revolutionaries.

Line 2 vivid: intense, animated Latin (*vividus*, full of life).

Line 10 gibe: jeer, put-down.

Line 12 the club: Yeats was a member of the Arts Club.

Line 14 motley: clothing associated with fools; motley was a jester's particoloured dress.

Line 17 That woman: Constance Gore-Booth (Countess Markiewicz) who commanded a garrison at the College of Surgeons, St Stephen's Green, during the Rising. She was sentenced to death but that was commuted to penal servitude for life; she was eventually granted amnesty and released in 1917.

Line 23 harriers: pack of hunting hounds.

Line 24 This man: Patrick Pearse (1879–1916) – he founded a school for boys, St Enda's in Rathfarnham, where Irish language, culture and patriotism were promoted. Pearse was the chief of the Easter Rebellion; he was executed on 3 May.

Line 25 rode our wingèd horse: Pegasus a winged horse is a traditional symbol of poetic inspiration; here, the phrase means that Pearse wrote poetry.

Line 26 This other: Thomas MacDonagh (1878–1916) – poet, dramatist, taught English at UCD; he was executed in 1916.

Line 31 This other man: John MacBride (1865–1916), whom Maud Gonne had married in 1903; they separated in 1905. Mac Bride had fought against the British in the Boer War, was second-in-command at Jacob's Factory during the Easter Rising and was executed on 5 May 1916.

Line 34 some: Maud Gonne and Iseult Gonne.

Line 35 I number him in the song: this line and line 74, 'I write it out in a verse—' are not only self-conscious references to the making of the poem but acknowledge, perhaps, what Helen Vendler calls the 'numerological artifact' that is the poem. The Easter Rising began on 24 April 1916: stanza 1 is 16 lines long, stanza 2 is 24, stanza 3 is 16 and stanza 4 is 24.

Line 43 stone: the Yeats scholar A. Norman Jeffares says: 'hearts enchanted to a stone were Yeats's symbol for those who had devoted themselves to a cause without thought of life or love. The stone was a symbol of how politics had affected, in particular, Maud Gonne. To be choked with hate was the chief of all evil chances'.

Line 58 a stone of the heart: a reference to Maud Gonne's commitment to revolutionary ideals. Yeats sent a copy of 'Easter 1916' to Maud Gonne; she told Yeats 'I don't like your poem, it isn't worthy of you & above all it isn't worthy of the subject'. Terence Brown comments that Gonne 'was in no mood for a poem that could imagine England keeping faith' and 'She resented the idea that sacrifice could turn any heart to stone'.

Line 67 needless death: Yeats asks if these revolutionaries died in vain.

Line 68 England may keep faith: the British parliament passed the Home Rule Bill which gave Ireland some independence in 1913; the Bill was suspended at the outbreak of World War I. It was thought that the suspension would one day be lifted.

Line 76 Connolly: James Connolly (1870–1916) was Commandant in the General Post Office during the Rising. A trade union leader and author of *Labour in Irish History*. Severely wounded, he was arrested and executed on 12 May 1916, tied to a chair because he was unable to stand.

In 1938, the year before he died, Yeats wrote to Maud Gonne, who was writing her autobiography, *A Servant of the Queen*, to say that 'you can say what you like about me.' But he added: 'I do not however think that I would have said "hopeless struggle". I never felt the Irish struggle "hopeless." Let it be "exhausting struggle" or "tragic struggle" or some such phrase. I wanted the struggle to go on but in a different way.' (16 June 1938)

Commenting on this poem, Micheál MacLiammóir and Eavan Boland in their book *W.B. Yeats and His World*, write: 'It would seem to the single-minded imagination, unhampered by any legion of detailed facts, that the rising of the Irish Republican volunteers in Easter Week, 1916, was a direct answer to the melancholy challenge of Yeats's September poem ["September 1913"]. It is strange that his nostrils, usually sensitive to the approach of a storm as the nostrils of cat or horse, or of some nervous woman, seemed unaware of the gathering of the hosts of battle. But it was so: he sensed nothing at all. Nevertheless, the Easter Week Rising – from any point of view the most considerable of all Irish demonstrations of the ancient feud – certainly did take place, and when he heard of it the poet was deeply moved. His poem "Easter 1916", composed within a few weeks of the executions of the leaders of the rising, remains one of his finest. Its recurring couplet, with its insistent, irregular, beaten-out rhythm, like that of mournful bells, has become to Irish ears as familiar as a nightly prayer: 'All changed, changed utterly: A terrible beauty is born.'

? Questions

1. What atmosphere is created in the opening lines of the poem? Why do you think Yeats mentioned 'Eighteenth-century houses'? How did Yeats view the revolutionaries before the Easter Rising? Why did he speak 'polite meaningless words'?

2. What do you understand by the lines: 'All changed, changed utterly:/ A terrible beauty is born'?

3. Yeats initially thought the sacrifice of the leaders wasteful. In the second section, Yeats names those who fought and died for Irish freedom. Why has his tone of 'a mocking tale or a gibe' changed? How would you describe Yeats's tone in section 2? Do you admire Yeats's honesty here?

4. What do the words 'casual comedy' mean and what do they tell us about Yeats?

5. The third stanza marks a significant change in the poem. Descriptive detail of place and people is replaced by symbols – stone, stream, rider and horse, cloud, shadow, moor-hens, moor-cocks. What might each represent? Which ones are permanent? Which ones symbolise change? What is the effect of Yeats's use of symbols in the poem?

6. Stanza 3 begins and ends with the image of a stone. Yeats views those who fought as seeming to have hearts which changed to stone. What does such an image suggest? Is this related to the phrase 'terrible beauty'?

7. In the closing stanza, how does Yeats feel about the patriots? Why do you think he uses the word 'bewildered' (line 73)?

8. What is the significance of the image of a mother soothing and comforting her exhausted child? Do you think it is an effective image in the context of the poem as a whole?

9. What is Yeats's role as revealed in this poem? Look particularly at the final seven lines.

10. 'September 1913' and 'Easter 1916' are similar in some ways, different in others. Consider this and give your own view.

The Second Coming

Turning and turning in the widening gyre
The falcon cannot hear the falconer;
Things fall apart; the centre cannot hold;
Mere anarchy is loosed upon the world,
The blood-dimmed tide is loosed, and everywhere   5
The ceremony of innocence is drowned;
The best lack all conviction, while the worst
Are full of passionate intensity.

Surely some revelation is at hand;
Surely the Second Coming is at hand.   10
The Second Coming! Hardly are those words out
When a vast image out of *Spiritus Mundi*
Troubles my sight: somewhere in sands of the desert
A shape with lion body and the head of a man,
A gaze blank and pitiless as the sun,   15
Is moving its slow thighs, while all about it
Reel shadows of the indignant desert birds.
The darkness drops again; but now I know
That twenty centuries of stony sleep
Were vexed to nightmare by a rocking cradle,   20
And what rough beast, its hour come round at last,
Slouches towards Bethlehem to be born?

Glossary

Title The Second Coming: Matthew, Chapter 24, verses 29–44, speaks of Christ's return to earth, a second coming, to reward the righteous and to establish the Millennium of Heaven on earth. Yeats, in this poem, saw the times he lived in as the end of the Christian era.

Line 1 gyre: for Yeats, a gyre was a cycle of history. Gyre is a spiral; a falcon is trained to fly in a spiralling motion, following the falconer's directions unless it flies so far away that it can no longer be controlled.

Seamus Heaney's comments on 'gyre' are detailed and interesting: 'A word of great potency in Yeats's vocabulary, suggestive of unstoppable process, of turbulent action that is part of a larger pattern. Yeats used the geometrical figure of two cones or vortices interpenetrating to represent the simultaneous processes of waxing and waning, rise and fall, which are necessarily at work at any moment in the life of an individual or a society. The extreme moment of risen, waxing life (the far-flung base of one cone) is also the moment when there arrives the original movement of new counter-swirling growth (the apex of the other cone, sharp-set at the centre of the wide base). So, when the 'widening gyre' reaches its fullest unwinding circumference, we are to expect a 'Second Coming', a new life which initiates an opposite motion. (Following upon this symmetrical pattern of antithesis, the 'rough beast' will replace the gentle Christ child at the same spot, in Bethlehem.)'

Line 2 The Falconer cannot hear the falconer: in Dante the falcon represents man and the falconer is Christ. Yeats, perhaps, is suggesting here that man has lost touch with Christianity.

Line 4 mere: nothing more than; 'mere' also used to mean absolute.

Line 4 anarchy: the absence of government; this frequently occurred after the First World War. In his book *A Vision*, Yeats wrote that anarchy and the adoration of violence are characteristic of the end of an historical era.

Line 5 blood-dimmed: war is seen as a flood of destruction.

Line 12 Spiritus Mundi: Spirit or Soul of the World; Yeats saw the spirit of the world as a universal consciousness or memory – something from which poets drew their images and symbols; the Swiss psychiatrist Jung called it the collective unconscious.

Line 14 lion body and the head of a man: the (Egyptian) sphinx.

Line 17 desert birds: birds of prey.

Line 19 twenty centuries: the time since Christ was born.

Line 20 vexed: harassed, distressed.

Line 22 Bethlehem: Christ's birthplace; the critic A. Norman Jeffares comments that the poem prophesies the arrival of a new god and adds: 'The location of the birthplace in Bethlehem, traditionally associated with the idea of the gentle innocence of infancy and maternal love, adds horror to the thought of the rough beast.'

Line 22 born: Yeats later wrote – 'Our civilisation was about to reverse itself, or some new civilisation about to be born from all that our age had rejected… because we had worshipped a single god it would worship many'.

> The poem, in unrhymed iambic pentameter or blank verse, was written in January 1919, immediately after World War I ended. There are several references in the Bible to the end of the world: Daniel Ch 9 ('the end thereof shall be with a flood'); Matthew Ch 24 ('there shall be famines, and pestilences, and earthquakes, in divers places…'); and the Book of Revelation (the Apocalypse).

Yeats saw history as dependent on cycles of about 2000 years. The Graeco-Roman civilisation ended with the birth of Christ; now, it seems to Yeats that the Christian cycle is coming to an end. The next cycle, as predicted by Yeats, is not viewed with optimism.

In his edition of Yeats's Poems, Daniel Albright writes: 'According to orthodox Christianity, the faithful live in expectation that, after a Second Coming, Christ will establish on earth a kingdom of sanctity and bliss. The purpose of "The Second Coming" is to subvert that happy hope: the poet predicts that, at the end of the millennium, there will arise not Christ but Christ's opposite, a savage god whose reign will establish a system of behaviour antithetical to that recommended by Christ.'

The editor Maurice Wollman says that 'Yeats has a vision, a moment of insight into the future. It arises from a mood of doubt and despair, inspired by the anarchy of the world, the increase of bloodshed, and the growth of disbelief. He sees the present era as dying; the first two thousand years of Christianity have brought discord and strife because man has forgotten Christ. The new era that is about to be born is symbolised by the "rough beast," which is the antithesis of the gentle Bethlehem. It is not sought for or created: it comes uninvited, unwanted almost, upon the consciousness... It is Yeats's theory that a period of anarchy and violence follows a period of innocence and beauty.'

? Questions

1. Which details, do you think, best convey a sense of anarchy in the opening lines? What do you think Yeats meant by the phrase the 'ceremony of innocence'?

2. How would you describe Yeats's mood in the first stanza? Why does he praise 'conviction' and condemn 'passionate intensity'?

3. Does Yeats welcome the Second Coming? Is it possible to say? Look at lines 9–11. How would you describe Yeats's theme and overall mood in the poem?

4. How does Yeats view two thousand years of Christianity? What does 'nightmare' (line 20) suggest?

5. Is this a visual poem or a poem of ideas? Or does it combine both? If you were to paint this poem which images would predominate?

6. What evidence do you find in the poem to support the view that this poem 'foresees a future that, for all the horror of its approach, will offer a civilisation superior to that in which the poet lives'?

Sailing to Byzantium

I

That is no country for old men. The young
In one another's arms, birds in the trees
—Those dying generations—at their song,
The salmon-falls, the mackerel-crowded seas,
Fish, flesh, or fowl, commend all summer long   5
Whatever is begotten, born, and dies.
Caught in that sensual music all neglect
Monuments of unageing intellect.

II

An aged man is but a paltry thing,
A tattered coat upon a stick, unless   10
Soul clap its hands and sing, and louder sing
For every tatter in its mortal dress,
Nor is there singing school but studying
Monuments of its own magnificence;
And therefore I have sailed the seas and come   15
To the holy city of Byzantium.

III

O sages standing in God's holy fire
As in the gold mosaic of a wall,
Come from the holy fire, perne in a gyre,
And be the singing-masters of my soul.   20
Consume my heart away; sick with desire
And fastened to a dying animal
It knows not what it is; and gather me
Into the artifice of eternity.

IV

Once out of nature I shall never take   25
My bodily form from any natural thing,
But such a form as Grecian goldsmiths make
Of hammered gold and gold enamelling
To keep a drowsy Emperor awake;
Or set upon a golden bough to sing   30
To lords and ladies of Byzantium
Of what is past, or passing, or to come.

📖 Glossary

Title Byzantium: city founded in 660 B.C. It was known as Byzantium until A.D. 330, when it was re-named Constantinople; in 1930 it became Istanbul. Byzantium was the capital and holy city of Eastern Christendom from the late fourth century until 1453. Yeats never visited the city. The mosaics described in the poem are probably inspired by mosaics in the church of S. Apollinare Nuovo in Ravenna, which Yeats had visited in 1907. Yeats also saw Byzantine mosaics in the cathedrals at Monreale and Cefalu in Sicily in 1925.

Yeats in *A Vision* wrote: 'I think if I could be given a month of Antiquity and leave to spend it where I chose, I would spend it in Byzantium, a little before Justinian opened St Sophia and closed the Academy of Plato... I think that in early Byzantium, maybe never before or since in recorded history, religious, aesthetic and practical life were one, that architect and artificers... spoke to the multitude and the few alike.'

Line 1 That: Ireland – rejected by Yeats because it represents the temporal and natural world.

Line 3 dying generations: an effective rhetorical device known as an oxymoron.

Line 5 commend: praise, celebrate; 'Fish, flesh, or fowl' commend their life-cycle and death.

Line 7 sensual: worldly; not intellectual or spiritual.

Line 9 paltry: worthless, unimportant.

Line 10 tattered coat: an old man is like a scarecrow; in his poem 'Among School Children', Yeats says that old men are 'Old clothes upon old sticks to scare a bird'.

Line 10/11 unless/ Soul clap its hands and sing: poet William Blake (1757–1827) claims to have seen his brother's soul flying Heavenwards and clapping its hands for joy.

Line 13 Nor is there singing school but studying: the only singing school is studying.

Line 17 sages: wise men.

Line 19 perne in a gyre: spinning/whirling in a spiral, coiling motion, so that his soul may merge with the spiralling motion and thus enter a timeless world and leave behind the natural and historical world. Yeats made the word 'perne' from the Scots word 'pirn', meaning a reel, bobbin, spool. Augustine Martin, commenting on this line, wrote that Yeats 'asks the figures in the mosaic to come back to him through time and teach him the perfection of Byzantium and finally gather his soul into the eternity of art.'

Line 29 Emperor: 'I have,' wrote Yeats, 'read somewhere that in the Emperor's palace at Byzantium was a tree made of gold and silver, and artificial birds that sang.'

Line 32 past, or passing, or to come: Yeats, intensely aware of transience and mortality, longed for eternity; the golden bird, in eternity, sings of the passing of time.

'Sailing to Byzantium' is the first poem in Yeats's 1928 collection *The Tower*, a collection which, Yeats admitted, astonished him by its bitterness when he re-read it. MacLiammóir and Boland argue that what Yeats saw as 'mere bitterness was viewed by certain critics as an immortal fury against the tragedy of decay, the inevitability of death. And it is this emotion that evokes in his mind a bizarre, strangely assured speculation on life after death in 'Sailing to Byzantium'. There he celebrates what man can create, and rejects the way in which man himself has been created, the ill-starred slave of his inevitable passing into dust.'

Yeats has said of this poem that he was 'trying to write about the state of [his] soul, for it is right for an old man to make his soul'.

? Questions

1. Why do you think Yeats chose the word 'sailing' to describe the journey? Read the note on Byzantium and sum up in your own words why you think Yeats wants to go there.

2. If you were to edit out certain lines from the opening stanza, so that it read 'The young/ In one another's arms, birds in the trees... The salmon-falls, the mackerel-crowded seas ... all summer long... ', what impression would the reader be presented with? Now read the stanza as Yeats wrote it. What has happened to those beautiful, sensual images? Why does Yeats reject them?

3. Why does Yeats value 'monuments of unageing intellect' so highly? What is Yeats's view of Ireland and its destiny in relation to art?

4. Is it clear from the poem that the journey is a metaphorical or imagined one rather than an actual one? Give reasons for your answer.

5. Which details do you think emphasise Yeats's old age?

6. Music and singing are referred to in each of the four stanzas. Comment on this and its significance.

7. The poem has a very regular, patterned rhyme scheme. Is this obvious? What is the effect of the run-on line?

8. Yeats, in line 2, speaks of 'birds in the trees'; in the final stanza he speaks of a golden bird upon a golden bough. Compare and contrast these birds and say why one has replaced the other. Why should the golden bird, out of nature, out of time, sing of the passing of time? Are there similarities between the wild swans and the golden bird? Why has a city replaced the natural world?

9. The poet John Montague has praised 'Sailing to Byzantium' for its defiance and clangour. Discuss these qualities in the poem.

10. In 'The Lake Isle of Innisfree' and 'Sailing to Byzantium', Yeats imagines being in an ideal world. What are the essential differences between the two? Which one would you prefer and why?

from *Meditations in Time of Civil War*

VI

The Stare's Nest by My Window

The bees build in the crevices
Of loosening masonry, and there
The mother birds bring grubs and flies.
My wall is loosening; honey-bees,
Come build in the empty house of the stare.   5

We are closed in, and the key is turned
On our uncertainty; somewhere
A man is killed, or a house burned,
Yet no clear fact to be discerned:
Come build in the empty house of the stare.   10

A barricade of stone or of wood;
Some fourteen days of civil war;
Last night they trundled down the road
That dead young soldier in his blood:
Come build in the empty house of the stare.   15

We had fed the heart on fantasies,
The heart's grown brutal from the fare;
More substance in our enmities
Than in our love; O honey-bees,
Come build in the empty house of the stare.   20

📖 Glossary

Title Stare: starling, bird with blackish-brown feathers.

Line 3 grubs: larvae of insect, caterpillar, maggot.

Line 12 civil war: the Irish Civil War (1922–3) was fought between those who supported and rejected the Anglo-Irish Treaty (1922); the treaty stated that six counties would remain within the United Kingdom.

Line 13 trundled: wheeled, rolled.

Line 17 the fare: being fed (on fantasies).

Line 18 enmities: hatreds, hostilities, ill-will.

Meditations in Time of Civil War is a sequence of seven poems, each with a separate title: I Ancestral Houses; II My House; III My Table; IV My Descendants; V The Road at my Door; VI The Stare's Nest by My Window; VII I see Phantoms of Hatred and of the Heart's Fullness and of the Coming Emptiness. Poems II to VII were written at Thoor Ballylee during the Irish Civil War of 1922 and were first published in *The Dial* in January 1923.

Yeats, in a note to the poem 'The Stare's Nest by my Window', wrote: 'I was in my Galway house [Thoor Ballylee] during the first months of civil war, the railway bridges blown up and the roads blocked with stones and trees. For the first week there were no newspapers, no reliable news, we did not know who had won nor who had lost, and even after newspapers came, one never knew what was happening on the other side of the hill or of the line of trees. Ford cars passed the house from time to time with coffins standing upon end between the seats, and sometimes at night we heard an explosion, and once by day saw the smoke made by the burning of a great neighbouring house. Men must have lived so through many tumultuous centuries.

One felt an overmastering desire not to grow unhappy or embittered, not to lose all sense of the beauty of nature. A stare (our West of Ireland name for a starling) had built in a hole beside my window and I made these verses out of the feeling of the moment... Presently a strange thing happened. I began to smell honey in places where honey could not be, at the end of a stone passage or at some windy turn of the road...'

? Questions

1. Pick out those words in the opening stanza which you would consider negative and positive. Does a positive or negative feeling predominate?

2. What is Yeats's mood in line 5? The line is repeated three times. What is the effect of this?

3. In stanza 1, the poet looks at little details – crevices, grubs and flies, an empty nest. What happens in the second and third stanzas?

4. How does Yeats suggest a sense of fear, uncertainty, violence in lines 6–15? What is Yeats's reaction? Can it be summed up in the final line of each stanza?

5. In 'The Lake Isle of Innisfree', Yeats speaks of 'a hive for the honey-bee'. What do both poems say about the natural world? Is nature viewed thesame or differently in both poems?

6. The final stanza focuses on fantasies and hatred. Why has the heart grown brutal, according to Yeats? Is he referring to something similar in 'Easter 1916' when he speaks in that poem of how hearts can turn to stone?

7. 'Come build… Come build… Come build.' What is the effect of 'O' in the final stanza, when Yeats writes 'O honey-bees,/ Come build in the empty house of the stare'?

8. 'There must be many millions all over the world who make the same prayer for honey-bees to come to the empty house', says the novelist Penelope Fitzgerald. What do you think she means by this?

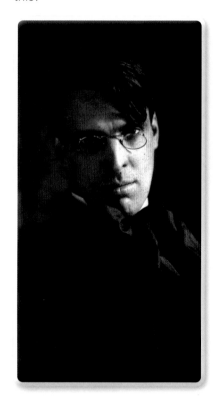

In Memory of Eva Gore-Booth and Con Markiewicz

The light of evening, Lissadell,
Great windows open to the south,
Two girls in silk kimonos, both
Beautiful, one a gazelle.
But a raving autumn shears   5
Blossom from the summer's wreath;
The older is condemned to death,
Pardoned, drags out lonely years
Conspiring among the ignorant.
I know not what the younger dreams—   10
Some vague Utopia—and she seems,
When withered old and skeleton-gaunt,
An image of such politics.
Many a time I think to seek
One or the other out and speak   15
Of that old Georgian mansion, mix
Pictures of the mind, recall
That table and the talk of youth,
Two girls in silk kimonos, both
Beautiful, one a gazelle.   20

Dear shadows, now you know it all,
All the folly of a fight
With a common wrong or right.
The innocent and the beautiful
Have no enemy but time;   25
Arise and bid me strike a match
And strike another till time catch;
Should the conflagration climb,
Run till all the sages know.
We the great gazebo built,   30
They convicted us of guilt;
Bid me strike a match and blow.

October 1927

Glossary

Title Eva Gore-Booth and Con Markiewicz: Eva and Constance Gore-Booth, sisters, were born into a world of privilege. Eva (1870–1926) became a political activist, an ardent socialist and poet. She moved to Manchester in 1922 and devoted herself to the women's trade union movement, feminism, socialism and pacifism. She died of cancer.

Countess Markiewicz: Constance Gore-Booth of Lissadell, County Sligo, Irish nationalist and first British woman MP, was born in 1868 in London. The family home was Lissadell in County Sligo and, though she was privileged and wealthy, she was unconventional. Stephen Coote, in *W.B. Yeats: A Life*, writes that Constance Gore-Booth 'was to play a wholly remarkable part in the struggle for Irish independence and, from her earliest days, when she invited the bare-footed peasant children home for tea, she had shown her instinctive defiance of convention and sympathy for the poor.'

A beautiful woman, she studied art in London and Paris, where she met and married the Polish count Casimir Markiewicz in 1900. They moved to Dublin in 1903 and in 1908 she joined Sinn Fein and became a friend of Maud Gonne. In 1916 Countess Markiewicz fought in the Easter Rising and was sentenced to death; the death sentence was reprieved in the 1917 amnesty. In 1918 she was elected Sinn Fein MP for the St Patrick's division of Dublin – thus becoming the first British woman MP – but she refused to take her seat, in line with Sinn Fein policy. In 1919 she was elected to the first Dáil and was appointed Minister for Labour. She was imprisoned twice. Following the Civil War she was a member of Dáil Éireann from 1923. She died in 1927. Yeats also writes about Countess Markiewicz in his poem 'On a Political Prisoner'.

Line 1 Lissadell: Lissadell House, a large Grecian-Revival house on the northern shore of Sligo Bay, was built 1830–1835 for Sir Robert Gore-Booth MP. During the Famine, Robert Gore-Booth mortgaged his estate so as to be able to feed everyone for miles around. Yeats first visited this ascendancy house in November 1894. Yeats was impressed by the aristocratic way of life, its grace and ease, but Constance and Eva were to leave that world behind when they became politically active as suffragettes and socialists.

Line 4 one a gazelle: Eva (a gazelle is a small, graceful, soft-eyed antelope).

Line 5 raving: howling, roaring.

Line 5 shears: cuts.

Line 7 The older: Constance was two years older than Eva.

Line 9 conspiring: plotting something unlawful; Constance was a political activist who trained the Fianna Scouts, worked with Fianna Fail Clubs and joined the Citizen Army in 1914.

Line 10 the younger dreams: Eva Gore-Booth studied philosophy and mystical literature.

Line 11 Utopia: an ideal world, an imaginary state (from ou, not, topos, a place).

Line 28 conflagration: great and destructive fire.

Line 30 gazebo: Seamus Heaney says: 'A summer house in the grounds of Lissadell; but equally important is the gazebo's association with a point of view that is spacious, contemplative and unconstrained.' Augustine Martin thinks 'gazebo' may refer to the decorative, non-utilitarian contribution of the Anglo-Irish to Irish life, for which some of them – not the Gore-Booths – were punished in the burning of their mansions by 'incendiary or bigot'.

Line 31 They convicted us of guilt: they, meaning the Catholics, felt the Protestant Ascendancy class should feel guilty for being Protestant.

This poem, the first in Yeats's 1933 collection *The Winding Stair and Other Poems*, has been described as 'a poignant recall of a passing time, its later ravages, the withering of dreams and the arrested pictures of young beauty' by Niall McCarthy in *Lifelines*. The Cork-based poet Thomas McCarthy also chose this poem by Yeats as his favourite in the same anthology. McCarthy praises the poem for 'its spectacularly beautiful opening images, the kimonos, the south-facing windows – but also for its maturity of insight and its underlying sadness'.

In a letter, dated 23 July 1916, to Eva Gore-Booth, Yeats wrote that 'Your sister and yourself, two beautiful figures among the great trees of Lissadell, are among the dear memories of my youth'. Eva Gore-Booth died in 1926 and Con Markiewicz died in August 1927. This poem is dated 21 September 1927 in manuscript but the date October 1927 is given in the *Collected Poems*.

Eva and Constance Gore-Booth when they lived at Lissadell.

? Questions

1. How does Yeats conjure up a magical and beautiful series of pictures in the opening four lines of this poem? Pick out those words which, in your opinion, are particularly effective. How is the feeling of leisure and ease conveyed? How different would it be if it were the light of morning?

2. What effect does Yeats achieve by the abrupt change at line 5?

3. A harsh reality is conveyed through sound and imagery in lines 7–13. Pick out those details which, in your opinion, best capture such harshness.

4. Is it possible to say how Yeats feels about what happened to these two beautiful women? Why does the image of the skeleton serve as an image of both Eva and her politics? Why does he want to seek out one or the other and speak of the past? Why should he prefer 'pictures of the mind' and to recall the past rather than the present?

5. If you were to paint pictures of the first twenty lines, what colours would you need? What movements? What settings?

6. 'Dear shadows, now you know it all' (line 21). What does this line tell us? How would you describe his tone towards the sisters here?

7. How would you describe this second stanza? How does it differ from the first? Look at the images. Why are lines 24–25 so important within the poem as a whole?

8. Yeats never took up arms. The Gore-Booth sisters did. How does Yeats view these women and what they dedicated their lives to? What does he ask their ghosts to do in the second stanza? What do you understand by his wish to burn time? Who is Yeats referring to when he says 'they' in line 31?

9. Yeats begins with the distancing phrase 'Two girls'; in line 21 he speaks to them as 'you'; in the closing lines Yeats switches to 'We'. What is the significance of this in your opinion?

10. Both 'Easter 1916' and 'In Memory of Eva Gore-Booth and Con Markiewicz' are elegies, one a public one, the other private, but in both Yeats speaks of politics and public involvement. Are his attitudes similar in both poems?

Constance Gore-Booth
(Countess Markievicz)
shortly before the 1916 rising.

Swift's Epitaph

Swift has sailed into his rest;
Savage indignation there
Cannot lacerate his breast.
Imitate him if you dare,
World-besotted traveller; he   5
Served human liberty.

📖 Glossary

Line Title Swift: Dean Jonathan Swift (1667–1745), satirist and clergyman, author of
Gulliver's Travels. Born in Dublin of English parents, educated at Kilkenny Grammar School
and Trinity College

Line Title Epitaph: an inscription for a stone or tomb (literally 'over a tomb'). Yeats
considered Swift's epitaph the finest he knew.

Line 3 lacerate: tear, mangle, wound (Swift's Latin epigraph says that his body lies where
'saeva Indignatio/ Ulterius/ Cor lacerare nequit' – where savage indignation can no longer
lacerate his heart').

This poem is a translation/version of the epitaph Swift wrote for himself, though Yeats
added line 1 and the word 'World-besotted' (line 5) instead of 'Go Traveller', a literal
translation of 'Abi Viator'. It can be seen in St Patrick's Cathedral Dublin, where Swift is
buried:

Hic depositum est Corpus

IONATHAN SWIFT S.T.D.*

Hujus Ecclesiae Cathedralis

Decani,

Ubi saeva Indignatio

Ulterius

Cor lacerare nequit.

Abi Viator

Et imitare, si porteris,

Strenuum pro virili

Libertatis Vindicatorem

Obiit 19 Die Mensis Octobris

A.D. 1745 Anno Aetatis 78

* S[acrae] T[heologiae] D[octoris] – Doctor of Scared Theology

A literal translation of the above, by Elspeth Haren, reads as follows:

Here is laid the body

of JONATHAN SWIFT, Doctor of Theology,

of this cathedral church

Dean,

where furious disdain*

further

cannot rend the heart.

Go forth, traveller,

and imitate, should you be able,

one vigorous to his utmost

as a champion of freedom.

He died on the 19th day of the month of October

A.D. 1745 in the 78th year of his age.

* saeva Indignatio has been translated as 'savage indignation' by Yeats

? Questions

1. What qualities are being identified here by Swift in his own epitaph? Why do you think Yeats chose to translate it?

2. How would you describe the tone of this poem? Who is being addressed?

3. The first line is not a translation but Yeats's own. Why do you think Yeats added this line and chose to use the verb 'sailed'?

4. Yeats wrote this poem when he was sixty-five. Compare this epigraph by Swift with the one Yeats wrote himself for his own tombstone:

Cast a cold Eye.
On Life, on Death.
Horseman, pass by!

Which one do you find the more personal? And the more interesting? Which one tells us more about the individual?

Jonathan Swift (1710)
by Charles Jervas

An Acre of Grass

Picture and book remain,
An acre of green grass
For air and exercise,
Now strength of body goes;
Midnight, an old house   5
Where nothing stirs but a mouse.

My temptation is quiet.
Here at life's end
Neither loose imagination,
Nor the mill of the mind   10
Consuming its rag and bone,
Can make the truth known.

Grant me an old man's frenzy,
Myself must I remake
Till I am Timon and Lear   15
Or that William Blake
Who beat upon the wall
Till Truth obeyed his call;

A mind Michael Angelo knew
That can pierce the clouds,   20
Or inspired by frenzy
Shake the dead in their shrouds;
Forgotten else by mankind,
An old man's eagle mind.

📖 Glossary

Title An Acre of Grass: this is a reference to Yeats's house in Riversdale in Rathfarnham, County Dublin. The acre in this instance is a garden containing tennis and croquet lawns and a bowling green. In letters written to Olivia Shakespear during the summer of 1932, Yeats described his new home as follows: 'apple trees, cheery trees, roses, smooth lawns'. … 'I shall have a big old fruit garden all to myself – the study opens into it and it is shut off from the flower garden and the croquet and tennis lawns and from the bowling-green.' The poem was written in November 1936 and was first published in April 1938 in *Atlantic Monthly and London Mercury.*

5 an old house: Riversdale, Rathfarnham, County Dublin.

13 frenzy: wild excitement; paroxysm of madness.

15 Timon and Lear: in Shakespeare's tragedies *Timon of Athens* and *King Lear,* the tragic heroes Timon and Lear ask questions about existence with a great raging anger. Augustine Martin, commenting on these lines, says that 'Timon and Lear question their place in the world with a ferocity and insistence akin to the "demonic rage" of such heroic artists as Blake and Michael Angelo.'

16 William Blake: English poet, painter, engraver and visionary (1757–1827).

19 Michael Angelo: Michelangelo di Lodovico Buonarroti Simoni (1475–1564), Italian sculptor, painter and poet.

22 shrouds: burial clothes.

❓ Questions

1. What kind of life does Yeats describe in the first stanza? What mood is created in these opening lines?

2. How would you describe what Yeats discovers at his 'life's end'? Comment on Yeats's descriptions 'loose imagination' and 'the mill of the mind'.

3. Why do you think Yeats, in the third stanza, asks for a form of wild excitement or frenzy in his old age? Why does he find inspiration in the characters he names?

4. Explain in your own words what Yeats is saying in the closing two lines.

5. The poem begins quietly. Identify the words that give the poem a gathering sense of energy and momentum. Why is this appropriate to the poem's meaning?

6. Yeats believed that 'Man can embody truth but he cannot know it'. Is this reflected in this poem?

Politics

*'In our time the destiny of man presents its meaning
in political terms.'* — Thomas Mann

How can I, that girl standing there,
My attention fix
On Roman or on Russian
Or on Spanish politics?
Yet here's a travelled man that knows   5
What he talks about,
And there's a politician
That has read and thought,
And maybe what they say is true
Of war and war's alarms,   10
But O that I were young again
And held her in my arms!

Glossary

epigraph: Thomas Mann (1875–1955), German novelist.

Line 10 alarms: sounds of danger.

Towards the end of his life, Yeats, in a letter to Dorothy Wellesley, dated 24 May 1938, wrote: 'There has been an article upon my work in the *Yale Review* which is the only article on the subject which has not bored me for years. It commends me above other modern poets because my language is "public". That word, which I had not thought of myself, is a word I want. Your language in "Fire" is "public", so is that of every good ballad . . . It goes on to say that, owing to my age and my relation to Ireland, I was unable to use this "public" language on what is evidently considered the right public material, politics. The enclosed little poem is my reply. It is not a real incident, but a moment of meditation.'

The version that Yeats included in that letter is as follows; a revised version appeared in *Last Poems*, published in 1939.

Politics

'In our time the destiny of man presents its meaning in political terms.'
(Thomas Mann)

Beside that window stands a girl;
I cannot fix my mind
On the analysis of things
That benumb mankind.

Yet one has travelled and may know
What he talks about;
And one's a politician

That has read and thought.
Maybe what they say is true
Of war and war's alarms;
But O that I were young again
And held her in my arms.

'Politics' was written on 23 May 1938 and was first published in January 1939 in the *Atlantic Monthly and London Mercury*. The day after he wrote it, Yeats explained the poem's origin in a letter to Olivia Shakespear. In Spring 1938, Archibald MacLeish, the American poet, had quoted Thomas Mann's words in his article 'Public Speech and Private Speech in Poetry'. Yeats was highly praised by MacLeish because his language was 'public' and Yeats, in his letter, says of the word 'public' – 'That word which I had not thought of myself is a word I want'. Then Yeats explains how the MacLeish article went on to say that 'owing to my age and my relation to Ireland, I was unable to use this "public" language on what it evidently considered the right public material, politics.'

In that same letter, dated 24 May 1938, Yeats says: 'The enclosed little poem is my reply. It is not a real incident, but a moment of meditation.' In a postscript, Yeats added 'No artesian well of the intellect can find the poetic theme', which shows, according to Daniel Albright, that 'Politics' is a meditation on the propriety of themes for poems. Yeats placed 'Politics' as the final poem in *Last Poems*, his 1939 collection; Albright adds that 'its placement at the end of Yeats's last volume of poems makes it a kind of valediction: and it fulfils this role, first by dismissing every topical theme in favour of the most universal, and second by its deliberate appeal to one of the oldest and most famous lyrics, the anonymous 'Westron Wind':

Westron Wind
Westron winde, when wilt thou blow,
The small raine downe can raine?
Christ if my love were in my armes,
And I in my bed againe.

Questions

1. Why does Yeats dismiss politics and what does he choose to value instead?

2. In this poem, Yeats wishes for love and youth to return. Does he convince you that love and youth are all that matter?

3. Yeats was seventy-three when he wrote this poem, a year before he died. Does our knowing this cast a different light on the poem?

4. Why do you think Yeats quoted Thomas Mann's words? How do they influence your reading of the poem?

from Under Ben Bulben V, VI

V

Irish poets, learn your trade,
Sing whatever is well made,
Scorn the sort now growing up
All out of shape from toe to top,
Their unremembering hearts and heads   5
Base-born products of base beds.
Sing the peasantry, and then
Hard-riding country gentlemen,
The holiness of monks, and after
Porter-drinkers' randy laughter;   10
Sing the lords and ladies gay
That were beaten into the clay
Through seven heroic centuries;
Cast your mind on other days
That we in coming days may be   15
Still the indomitable Irishry.

VI

Under bare Ben Bulben's head
In Drumcliff churchyard Yeats is laid.
An ancestor was rector there
Long years ago, a church stands near,   20
By the road an ancient cross.
No marble, no conventional phrase;
On limestone quarried near the spot
By his command these words are cut:

> *Cast a cold eye*
> *On life, on death.*
> *Horseman, pass by!*

4 September 1938

📖 Glossary

Line 7/8 Sing the peasantry, and then/ Hard-riding country gentlemen: elsewhere in his poetry ('At Galway Races' and 'The Fisherman'), Yeats praises and addresses the horsemen and fisherman.

Line 16 indomitable: not to be overcome, stubbornly persistent.

Line 17 Under bare Ben Bulben's head: Yeats, in a letter dated 22 August 1938, wrote: 'I am arranging my burial place. It will be in a little remote country churchyard in Sligo where my great grandfather was the clergyman a hundred years ago. Just my name and dates and these lines: Cast a cold eye/ On life on death;/ Horseman pass by'.

Line 19 ancestor: Reverend John Yeats (1774–1846), Yeats's great-grandfather, was rector of Drumcliff, County Sligo, from 1805 until his death; he was a friend of Robert Emmet (1778–1803) who was hanged in 1803 for his involvement in the fight for Irish freedom.

Line 27 Horseman: in the first section of 'Under Ben Bulben', Yeats speaks of visionary horsemen; an old family servant, Mary Battle, claimed to have seen these figures and described them to Yeats. Daniel Albright says that 'It is significant that a poem that begins with supernatural horsemen should end with this address – almost a challenge. Yeats seems to have attained such a comprehensive view of life and death that he is on equal terms with the unearthly riders of Part I.' Albright also points out that much of 'Under Ben Bulben' is written in catalectic trochaic tetrameter, a metre proper to charms and incantations ('Eye of newt and toe of frog' – *Macbeth* [the witches' spell]).

These two sections, V and VI, are the final sections from a longer poem dated 4 September 1938 and which was first published on 3 February 1939 in the *Irish Times*, *Irish Independent* and *Irish Press*.

Stephen Coote in his biography of Yeats tells of how 'The night before Yeats left Ireland for the last time he read "Under Ben Bulben" aloud to F. R. Higgins. The evening came to an end and "we parted", Higgins recalled, "on the drive from his house. The head of the retiring figure, erect and challenging, gleamed through the darkness as I turned back; while on the road before me my thoughts were still ringing out with the slow powerful accents of his chanting".'

? Questions

1. In this poem, why does Yeats speak directly to Irish poets and why does he refer to contemporary poetry? Does the poem itself illustrate his ideas?

2. How would you describe Yeats's tone here? How does he view his Irishness?

3. What sense of time is created in these lines? What is the significance of 'seven heroic centuries' (line 13)?

4. This poem is written in a rhythm used for charms and incantations. Why do you think Yeats chose such a rhythmic pattern here?

5. What do we learn about Yeats the man and Yeats the poet in this poem? Do you think this poem a suitable and appropriate late poem?

6. Looking back over these poems by Yeats on your course, do you think that Yeats himself 'cast a cold eye on life, on death'?

'W.B. Yeats' by his father John Butler Yeats

General Questions

A. 'In his poetry, Yeats explores public and private themes through powerful imagery.' Discuss this view in the light of your reading of the poems by Yeats on your course. Support the points you make with the aid of suitable quotation or reference.

B. 'Yeats is remarkable both for what he has to say and for the way he says it.' Would you agree with this view? In your answer, you should support the points you make with relevant quotation from or reference to the poems by Yeats on your course.

C. What would you consider the principal preoccupations of W.B. Yeats, as revealed to us in his poetry? Support your discussion by quotation from or reference to the poems you have studied.

D. In Yeats's poetry, 'the defiant self is pitted against hostile or disabling conditions'. Discuss this statement, supporting your answer by quotation from or reference to the poems by Yeats on your course.

E. 'Symbolism in Yeats's poetry is strong and memorable.' Discuss this view, supporting the points you make by relevant quotation from or reference to the poems by Yeats on your course.

F. According to Seamus Heaney, 'Command' has characterised the Yeatsian style. Examine how Yeats creates and achieves this tone of command in the poems on your course.

G. Write a short essay on those aspects of the poems by Yeats on your course that you found most interesting.

H. 'Though Yeats's poetry is rooted in the particular, it also achieves a universality.' Would you agree with this view? In your answer, you should support the points you make with quotation from or reference to the poems by Yeats on your course.

I. 'W.B. Yeats is both a personal and political poet.' Discuss this view, supporting your answer by quotation from or reference to the poems by Yeats on your course.

W.B. Yeats in old age.

Critical Commentary

The Lake Isle of Innisfree

Human nature is such that we have all known the desire to escape to a quieter, more beautiful world. For Yeats it is an island on a lake in Co. Sligo, but what is even more important than place is the feeling which the poem contains. Innisfree, as described by Yeats, is beautiful and tranquil but equally significant is the desire to be elsewhere.

The poem adopts a deliberately quaint, old-fashioned style. Yeats does not simply say 'I'll go to Innisfree'; he lends the occasion a ceremony and seriousness with the expression 'I will arise and go now, and go to Innisfree'. It has been pointed out that 'I will arise' are words spoken by the prodigal son in Luke xv. 18, and Yeats uses here this archaic expression, a type of language he soon abandoned. In a letter dated 30 November 1922, Yeats, looking back to 'Innisfree', told some schoolgirls that 'A couple of years later I would not have written that first line with its conventional archaism — "Arise and go" — nor the inversion in the last stanza', though in that same letter Yeats also admitted that 'Innisfree' was 'my first lyric with anything in its rhythm of my own music'.

There is a timelessness about the poem. Even though we know that Yeats was prompted to write the poem in a London Street in 1888, the only contemporary detail in the poem is 'pavements grey'. All other descriptions – the clay and wattle cabin, the bean-rows and bee hive, the birdsong cannot – date the poem to a particular century or age.

The long line gives the poem a stately, leisured tone: the opening words are formal, the repetition of 'go', the Latinate structure, for example, of line 2 (Yeats does not say 'I will build a small cabin there, made of clay and wattles'), the repeated 'there' in line 3, 'peace' in line 5, 'dropping' in line 6, and the very regular end-rhyme all create a very elevated, heightened, musical expression of longing. The voice is deliberate rather than casual.

The poem imagines Innisfree so vividly that the description dominates the poem. Everything, at first, is future tense: 'I will arise . . .'; 'will I have there'; 'I shall have some peace there . . .', but the world of Innisfree is so convincingly portrayed that the poet ends with the present tense. Though Yeats is standing on the 'pavements grey', he hears the lake water lapping. So deep is his sense of longing that he hears it deep in his heart.

Colour, sounds, textures combine to make the world of the poem. If there is a feeling of immediacy, of 'now', the present moment, in stanza 1, there is a sense of a never-ending time in the middle stanza, when Yeats describes the regular rhythm of the day, from dawn to noon to midnight. The eye sees only beauty; the ear hears only beautiful sounds.

The final stanza of the poem is atmospheric in its evocation of the sound of lake water and the contrast between Lough Gill and the London roadway or grey pavements is striking. Line 10 is an excellent example of how alliteration and assonance can achieve such effect:

> I hear **la** ke water **la** pping with l**o**w sounds by the sh**o** re

Yeats was in his early twenties when he began working on this poem. He wrote it in London, but it illustrates how Yeats's heart was in Ireland and how the imagination can create the ideal.

September 1913

This is a public poem prompted by a public event and Yeats is expressing a personal opinion in public. The title is factual and roots the poem in a particular time in Irish history. Yeats was deeply disillusioned by the Irish, especially the wealthy middle class, who had refused to support the housing of the Hugh Lane pictures and in general were mercenary, small-minded and without vision.

The opening stanza is scathing and ironic. The people he addresses are portrayed in an ugly light. They are without dignity or beauty; they are miserly and money, for them, is equated to prayer:

> What need you, being come to sense,
> But fumble in a greasy till
> And add the halfpence to the pence
> And prayer to shivering prayer, until
> You have dried the marrow from the bone?

Line 6 is deeply ironic:

> For men were born to pray and save

Yeats does not believe that men should give their lives to cautious praying and saving, saving their souls or saving their money or both. Perhaps Yeats intended to pun on pray/prey? These middle-class hoarders are, in the academic Alexander Davis's words, 'caught within an economy that, however much it breeds or saves, results in a form of death'.

An ideal Irishman, for Yeats, is John O'Leary and it is against such a figure that all others are measured. A romantic Ireland is an Ireland whose people are fired with ideas and idealism. In 1913, Yeats felt that there was no such energy or fiery optimism within the people; there were no individuals who would inspire and lead Ireland:

> Romantic Ireland's dead and gone,
> It's with O'Leary in the grave.

Yeats's tone is bitter and dismissive at the outset. The language is crisp, the images vivid. It is, in Eavan Boland's words, a poem of 'political disillusion' in which 'Yeats laments the loss of the Ireland he associated with the Fenian leader John O'Leary.' Boland also points out that part of the poem's power is in Yeats's use of the iambic tetrameter, a four foot, four stress line. It's the ballad metre, a very old form which is powerful in the telling of a story. Boland says that Yeats used it 'for the kind of poem which has a forceful argument but not a complicated idea behind it' and the poet has 'a lot of music, incantation and repetition'.

The idea is simple and straightforward: Yeats is deeply disappointed and disillusioned with the present and he compares the Ireland of now with the Ireland of the past. Having named John O'Leary, Yeats then opens up the past and offers a wide historical perspective to include Irish heroes over centuries and generations.

The simple word 'Yet' at the beginning of stanza 2 signals a different tone. Here, Yeats recognises a different kind of Irish man and regrets their passing. There were others, who, like John O'Leary, were willing to give their lives to Ireland.

> Yet they were of a different kind,
> The names that stilled your childish play

Here, Yeats does acknowledge that these heroes, their very names, once 'stilled' their 'childish play'; in other words, Ireland's past heroes once impressed, but the people of 1913 have, in Irish academic Terence Brown's words, 'lost their childhood capacity for wonder'. Once they were in awe of these heroic names; they were 'stilled'.

> Those heroes from the past were selfless and reckless:
> They have gone about the world like wind,
> But little time had they to pray
> For whom the hangman's rope was spun

The image of the wind catches the power and force of their commitment; the image of the rope being spun captures a sense of inevitability and destiny and sacrifice. And what Yeats emphasises here is the difference between them and those who are now so preoccupied with praying and saving. The colloquial, heartfelt, exasperated utterance in line 14:

> And what, God help us, could they save?

This highlights Yeats's despair, the implication being that those who died for Ireland were so giving that they were incapable of saving anything. What the academic Terence Brown calls the 'heady refrain' is repeated:

> Romantic Ireland's dead and gone,
> It's with O'Leary in the grave.

This gives the poem a momentum. The poet Eavan Boland identifies the rhymes and 'that strong artillery' of short lines' as qualities which make it 'a very catchy poem'. It is 'a bitter, cantankerous' poem, says Boland, but it is also a poem, she points out, which is very traditional and disciplined in its form.

The third stanza focuses on particular events and individuals whose story became Ireland's story. The Wild Geese, in their thousands, fought passionately for a cause; Edward Fitzgerald, Robert Emmet and Wolfe Tone lived and died for Ireland. The naming of names here gives the poem an energy and authenticity. Yeats's tone is incredulous ('Was it for this. . . . For this . . . For this . . .') and admiring. He names them with respect and admiration. These names from the history books focus the mind and Yeats's condemnation of the present is all the more strong.

The question asked in lines 17–22 is rhetorical:

> Was it for this the wild geese spread
> The grey wing upon every tide;
> For this that all that blood was shed,
> For this Edward Fitzgerald died,
> And Robert Emmet and Wolfe Tone,
> All that delirium of the brave?

In other words, the answer is implied and the repeated 'this' is indicative of Yeats's disappointment and disillusionment with the times.

Their passion and dedication is summed up in the line:

> All that delirium of the brave?

This is very different from the poem's opening line with its ironic reference to 'sense'. The poem measures sense against madness, caution against delirium and the fumbling, shivering individual versus the romantic hero. The structure of the poem also strengthens the poet's argument. Yeats first presents his reader with the dull and narrow present against a colourful and heroic past and by so doing emphasises Ireland's loss.

Having considered the present and the past, 'September 1913', in its final stanza, imagines a different present. Yeats asks how would those heroes be received if they were living now:

> Yet could we turn the years again
> And call those exiles as they were
> In all their loneliness and pain,
> You'd cry, 'Some woman's yellow hair
> Has maddened every mother's son':

Such heroic men would be mocked and denigrated, says Yeats, by the modern Irish middle class. Their noble motives would be misinterpreted and debased. Their 'delirium of the brave', their devotion, would be reduced to their infatuation with Ireland but belittled here in the image of a 'woman's yellow hair'.

Line 30 portrays Ireland's romantic visionaries as selfless and giving:

> They weighed so lightly what they gave.

They did not measure or weigh up what it was they were so willing to give. Their generosity of spirit did not allow them to view their lives in a calculating way.

The unforgettable refrain takes a different form in the closing lines. With John O'Leary, Romantic Ireland died; the others are also dead and perhaps it is best that they are 'in the grave'. Yeats's bitter, angry tone has given way to acceptance. Ireland has had a gloriously heroic past; the present is uninspiring; the future is not even mentioned.

The Wild Swans at Coole

The poem's title announces a natural grandeur: wild swans on Coole Lake in the west of Ireland is essentially a romantic image. Yeats wrote the poem in 1916, when he was fifty-one, and Yeats's own mood matches the autumn mood. The day is dying, the year is dying and the opening lines capture both the beauty and the sadness of autumn:

> The trees are in their autumn beauty,
> The woodland paths are dry,
> Under the October twilight the water
> Mirrors a still sky

The image of the trees is a stately, dignified one; the world is still; the rhythm is slow, the mood meditative. The poet observes in a detached, almost impersonal way:

> Upon the brimming water among the stones
> Are nine-and-fifty swans.

Counting is a mechanical activity but the 'nine-and-fifty' in this instance might prompt an emotional response in that fifty-eight of the swans are possibly paired and one is without a mate. Swans are magnificent and Michael Schmidt sums up their qualities when, speaking of the wild swans in Yeats's poem, he says that: 'They're natural, beautiful, powerful; most important, they return, they have a noble freedom and a noble permanence'.

Yeats's sadness is revealed indirectly in the first stanza in his being drawn towards twilight and the season, but stanza 2 introduces a more direct, personal note:

> The nineteenth autumn has come upon me
> Since I first made my count;
> I saw, before I had well finished,
> All suddenly mount
> And scatter wheeling in great broken rings
> Upon their clamorous wings.

Biographical detail tells us that when Yeats first visited Coole Park nineteen years before he was deeply depressed by his unhappy love affair with Maud Gonne. Now, at fifty-one, he is reminded of that earlier sorrow, a sorrow that has increased in the intervening years. The mood changes with the abrupt, sudden, unexpected movement of the swans. The strong, active verbs 'mount', 'scatter', the adjectives 'great broken' and 'clamorous' fill the poem with sound and serve as a striking contrast to the silence and stillness of stanza 1.

Yeats's description of himself in relation to the passing of time is passive in the line 'The nineteenth autumn has come upon me'; it is as if the years weigh upon him. The swans are active, powerful and filled with energy.

In the third stanza, the poet speaks of the great change in his life between his first visit to Coole and this visit. He is at his most personal:

> I have looked upon those brilliant creatures,
> And now my heart is sore.
> All's changed since I, hearing at twilight,
> The first time on this shore,
> The bell-beat of their wings above my head,
> Trod with a lighter tread.

He speaks of 'my heart', how 'All's changed'.
The sound of the swans' wings can be heard in that atmospheric line:

> The **bell-beat** of **their wings** above **my head**

This line has a strong and regular beat. Yeats remembers how nineteen years ago, when he first heard their bell-beat, he trod more lightly, his heart lifted.

For Yeats the swans represent or symbolise tireless continuity ('Unwearied still'), togetherness ('lover by lover'), youth ('their hearts have not grown old'), passion. What Yeats says indirectly here is that he himself is weary, old, alone. Passion and conquest will stay with the swans forever.

The final stanza offers a tranquil, calm picture of the wild swans upon the brimming water once again. Two words – 'Mysterious, beautiful' – sum them up:

> But now they drift on the still water,
> Mysterious, beautiful

And the poem ends with Yeats acknowledging that the swans will continue to delight. Their love will continue; others will witness it, even if Yeats will not:

> Among what rushes will they build,
> By what lake's edge or pool
> Delight men's eyes when I awake some day
> To find they have flown away?

Terence Brown says of these closing lines that Yeats imagines the swans 'in their freedom, flown away, leaving him'. Yeats is left with a heavier heart and in Brown's words 'the changes experienced in a personal autumn will be superseded by those of winter'.

An Irish Airman Foresees his Death

Yeats here is writing in the voice of a persona, that of thirty-seven year old Major Robert Gregory, who died in action on the Italian front in 1918. There is a tone of certainty and determination, a feeling of the inevitable from the outset. In the writer Stephen Booth's words, 'Yeats here presented a concise but evocative image of the war in the skies' and, according to Booth, 'There is a feeling that the speaker of the poem is already a partly disembodied spirit, a soul about to begin its "dreaming back"'.

Yeats is writing from hindsight, but Gregory did die in battle and this allows Yeats to allow his persona to speak with foresight. The four-foot line, the tetrameter, is used throughout, and this, together with the regular rhyme, gives the poem an urgency. From the poem's opening words:

> I know that I shall meet my fate

there is a sense of an individual confronting his destiny; that doom is his destiny is clear from the poem's title. The Irish airman is caught up in a war, but there is confusion in his thinking: he fights with the British against the Germans but claims that his real affiliation is with his native Galway. He does not hate the Germans; he does not love Britain. That he associates himself with a particular, local place and its people helps to create an image of Gregory as an unassuming and sympathetic man.

The pronoun 'I' is used six times in the opening four lines and is only used once again towards the end of the poem. This emphasis on himself gives way to a consideration of his allegiances, false and true; the repetition of 'My' reveals his true commitment. It also allows him to examine the reasons for his involvement in the war. Those whom he cares most about will be unaffected by the outcome:

> No likely end could bring them loss
> Or leave them happier than before.

This leads him to admit his reason for becoming an airman. First he rejects the more obvious reasons – 'law', 'duty', 'public men', 'the cheering crowd' – and then the speaker presents us with the haunting romantic explanation:

> A lonely impulse of delight
> Drove to this tumult in the clouds

The poem ends with a calculated, clear, understanding mind at work: 'I balanced all, brought all to mind' – the very balance of the lines acting out the balanced decision. The choice was a considered one, though it began as 'an impulse of delight'. The past and the future are seen as 'a waste of breath', the immediate repetition of the phrase stressing the futility felt. 'This life' is the life of young Major Robert Gregory. Losing one's life in battle is one thing, but that the speaker loses his life because he is drawn to a tumult in the clouds colours the experience differently. The final word in the poem is Gregory's final moment – 'death'.

Easter 1916

This poem is remarkable for many reasons, not least because it shows us that Yeats was not afraid to admit that he was wrong, that he could change his mind. In 'September 1913' he denounced the middle class for their cautious selfishness and argued that Romantic Ireland was 'dead and gone'; in 'Easter 1916' he takes that back and admits that he misjudged them. The Easter Rising was an apparent failure but signalled the beginning of modern Ireland and the making of a Republic. Yeats was not in Ireland at the time of The Rising and in a letter to Lady Gregory, dated 11 May 1916, he spoke of the 'Dublin tragedy' as 'a great sorrow and anxiety' and of how he 'had no idea that any public event could so deeply move me'. In that same letter, he confessed that 'I am very despondent about the future' and that he was 'trying to write a poem on the men executed – "terrible beauty has been born again"'.

The poem begins with a Dublin streetscape in which the poet passes those who were to fight in The Easter Rising and sacrifice their lives for Ireland. The backdrop is grey but their faces in the street are animated and 'vivid':

> I have met them at close of day
> Coming with vivid faces
> From counter or desk among grey
> Eighteenth-century houses.

These men and women have done their day's work, but they have within them a passion and enthusiasm for a cause that became clear when the rebellion took place. Their jobs and lives, it would seem, are routine; they work in shops or offices ('counter or desk') and there is no real understanding between Yeats and these people:

> I have passed with a nod of the head
> Or polite meaningless words,
> Or have lingered awhile and said
> Polite meaningless words

The deliberate repetition of 'polite meaningless words' captures the distance between him and them. The mood is bland, conventional, superficial. The mention of 'Eighteenth-century houses' is not only a background detail but it could also symbolise the British presence in Dublin. These houses were built for the colonists (Merrion Square, for example, was laid out in 1762 and by the end of the eighteenth century Dublin could boast very fine public and private buildings). Yeats makes clear his misreading of the situation when he confesses that, on meeting these men, he privately thought of some 'mocking tale or gibe' to entertain his companion at the club:

> And thought before I had done
> Of a mocking tale or a gibe
> To please a companion
> Around the fire at the club

Yeats tells this story against himself; he is honest in his portrayal of himself in a bad light and he clearly underestimated these people whom he met or passed in the street. There was some contact between the two worlds but it was essentially 'polite' and 'meaningless'. Yeats was convinced that he and his friends at the club were living among fools:

> Being certain that they and I
> But lived where motley is worn

The club becomes, in the poem, a symbol of privilege and separateness; the club is also frequently seen as a very English institution and Yeats with his background was closer to such a world than to those whom he passed on the streets of Dublin. In Terence Brown's words: 'The opening movement of "Easter 1916" magnanimously acknowledges how wrong he had been in thinking that the martyrs and he himself had inhabited a world of drab inconsequentiality, which would not change'.

The poem, which began in a matter-of-fact way, presents the reader with a powerful and paradoxical image by the end of its first stanza. It becomes a recurring image and one which captures Yeats's conflicting emotions. It becomes a key idea within the poem at a whole:

> All changed, changed utterly:
> A terrible beauty is born.

The line used in 'Easter 1916' is the trimeter, a speechlike, three foot line, with a simple and insistent rhyme scheme (abab). The subject matter of the poem is revolution, disturbing, chaotic events, but the form Yeats chose allows him to offer a measured, careful, considered exploration of these dramatic events and their consequences.

The division of the poem into four stanzas of 16-, 24-, 16-, 24-line sections matches, as Helen Vendler notes, the first day of The Rising, 24 April 1916.

The poem on the page therefore memorialises the day and the year (and indeed the month – April is the fourth month and there are four stanzas: 24/4/16), in a very deliberate way.

In stanza 2 and following, Yeats speaks individually of those who were active in the rebellion. First Countess Markiewicz. The phrase 'ignorant good-will' captures her supposed well-intentioned but uninformed nature and Yeats laments how her sweet voice grew shrill through political activism and argument. Patrick Pearse, Thomas MacDonagh and John MacBride are also featured in stanza 2. The rebels, who were only given anonymous 'vivid' faces in stanza 1, are now given qualities and attributes. Patrick Pearse is spoken of in his role as educator and poet:

> This man had kept a school
> And rode our wingèd horse;

Thomas MacDonagh, a fellow-poet and academic, his helper and his friend:

> Was coming into his force;
> He might have won fame in the end,
> So sensitive his nature seemed,
> So daring and sweet his thought.

Yeats's attitude towards John MacBride is more complex. As Maud Gonne's husband, he was jealous of him and the break-up of the marriage in 1905 is probably hinted at in the words 'bitter wrong'. She left MacBride on the grounds of 'cruelty, infidelity and drunkenness'. And yet Yeats admits that MacBride too must be included here:

> This other man I had dreamed,
> A drunken, vainglorious lout.
> He had done most bitter wrong
> To some who are near my heart,
> Yet I number him in the song.

Echoing an earlier idea where the times were viewed as clownish ('motley is worn'), Yeats highlights the reality of the uprising when he speaks of how MacBride and others gave themselves to the cause:

> He, too, had resigned his part
> In the casual comedy

Easter 1916 was neither terrible nor beautiful but gave birth to a complex 'terrible beauty'. MacBride himself was changed from 'drunken, vainglorious lout' and he was changed utterly:

> He, too, has been changed in his turn,
> Transformed utterly:
> A terrible beauty is born.

With stanza 3, line 41, Yeats introduces the symbol of the stone. Like 'terrible beauty', the stone heart is also paradoxical. The stone in the stream stands for resistance, persistence, and the stone heart could also symbolise the individual choked with hatred. It has also been pointed out that Yeats studied the work of the Celtic scholar Ernest Renan. Renan's work examines how the Celts once worshipped stones and the stone, therefore, could be interpreted to symbolise Irish belief. The single-mindedness of the revolutionaries seems to be summed up in lines 41–44:

> Hearts with one purpose alone
> Through summer and winter seem
> Enchanted to a stone
> To trouble the living stream.

The contrast between movement and stillness, between stasis and flux, is central here. If the living stream is time, the constant sense of change and unpredictability is captured in the imagery of the following lines:

> The horse that comes from the road,
> The rider, the birds that range
> From cloud to tumbling cloud,
> Minute by minute they change;
> A shadow of cloud on the stream
> Changes minute by minute;
> A horse-hoof slides on the brim,
> And a horse plashes within it;
> The long-legged moor-hens dive,
> And hens to moor-cocks call

Taken on their own these lines are remarkable for their constant movement, excitement, action, danger, unrest. A key word here is 'changes' (line 50) which, unlike the finality of 'changed' elsewhere in the poem (lines 15, 38, 79), implies possibility, potential, fluidity, and expresses Yeats's hope for progress without blood sacrifice. Details are sensuously evoked – 'tumbling cloud'; 'horse-hoof slides'; 'plashes'; 'dive'; 'hens to moor-cocks call' – and the repeated 'Minute by minute' gives the passage an immediate and living quality. Within 'Easter 1916', this passage, ostensibly describing the life of a stream, becomes an image for history and the deeds of humankind. There is uncertainty but there is also possibility. The stone, however, is static, inflexible, an inert presence. Is Yeats suggesting that those who sacrificed their lives are permanent presences in the living flow of time but that it need not have been like this? A diversity of life surrounds the stone; the stone is but one thing, one part of the stream, but the fanaticism of the rebels allows them to think and talk about only one thing. This third stanza offers neither judgement nor interpretation, but the stone in the stream becomes a simple and powerful image of political events.

'Easter 1916' explores the nature and meaning of heroism and Yeats reaches no one conclusion in the poem. He says what he thinks and what he feels; he asks questions; he wonders if it was needless to die. At line 56, however, Yeats seems to suggest that their sacrifice cannot be ignored when he says that 'The stone's in the midst of all' and the image of the stone heart begins, in fact, at the very centre of the poem on line 41.

Even the judgement with which Yeats begins the fourth and final stanza is qualified. If your sacrifice is too long, it can turn your heart to stone:

> Too long a sacrifice
> Can make a stone of the heart

What began as an almost comic world of noddings and superficial exchanges in the street changes and becomes a serious poem in which Yeats now marks their deaths. In death they are united by their heroic deed; their deaths have elevated them to a different order. Yeats, however, does not speak of their achievement; he does not dwell on how their deaths did not immediately achieve their aim.

The mystery of their sacrifice and death and how much must be sacrificed is impossible to understand:

> Too long a sacrifice
> Can make a stone of the heart.
> That is heaven's part

It is up to heaven to judge and he refuses to do so, but Yeats says that it is 'our' part to offer comfort. There is a tenderness in the image of mother and child but, unlike the sleeping child, the rebels are dead. The comparison of rebels to children, however, trivialises their gesture, according to Irish academic Declan Kiberd: 'The rebels (he implies) were children, and children are not full moral agents'. It is, therefore, an image of false comfort

> To murmur name upon name,
> As a mother names her child
> When sleep at last has come
> On limbs that had run wild

and Yeats recognises it as such:

> What is it but nightfall?
> No, no, not night but death

Then Yeats asks the startling question:

> Was it needless death after all?

And the poem becomes overtly political:

> Was it needless death after all?
> For England may keep faith
> For all that is done and said.

This is a reference to The Bill for Home Rule for Ireland which had been passed in 1913 but shelved at the beginning of the First World War. The poet, however, does not dwell on what the future might bring:

> We know their dream; enough
> To know they dreamed and are dead

But the unsettling question

> And what if excess of love
> Bewildered them till they died?

prompts the reader to think of wasted sacrifice, wasted lives. However, Yeats ends on a very authoritative and confident note. In the very act of making the poem, Yeats is granting these revolutionaries a permanent place in Ireland's history and in Irish poetry:

> I write it out in a verse—
> MacDonagh and MacBride
> And Connolly and Pearse
> Now and in time to be,
> Wherever green is worn,
> Are changed, changed utterly:
> A terrible beauty is born.

Here it is the men who are changed. The roll call of rebel names and descriptions in the first two stanzas and in stanza 4 becomes in its own way the living stream that flows by the stone. Yeats's act of naming them gives the poem a powerful resonance and The Rising, John Wilson Foster suggests, is 'like a stone in the midst of Irish history'.

Whether they were foolish and whether they died needlessly are no longer significant considerations. Yeats transforms the rebels into charismatic, immortal figures. He misread their vivid faces and had mocked them as 'motley'-clad players in a 'casual comedy', but by the poem's end they are tragic heroes. In the opening lines of the poem, he admitted to speaking 'polite, meaningless words', something a poet should never do. By the poem's closing lines, he has written profound, complex words which honour those who gave their lives for Ireland.

Writing in 1916, some months after the Easter Rising, Yeats said: '"Romantic Ireland's dead and gone" sounds old-fashioned now. It seemed true in 1913, but I did not foresee 1916. The late Dublin Rebellion, whatever one can say of its wisdom, will long be remembered for its heroism. "They weighed so lightly what they gave," and gave too in some cases without hope of success'.

The Second Coming

'September 1913' and 'Easter 1916', as evident from their titles, focus on particular events in time. 'The Second Coming' offers a very different temporal perspective, that of thousands of years. Here Yeats imagines Christ returning to earth, but in his stead there comes a slouching beast. The setting is different also in that there are no particular Irish references. The poem takes place, as it were, on a vast, world stage and it was written in 1919, at the end of the Great War. The absence of end-rhyme is appropriate in a poem that speaks of chaos and disorder.

The poem may have been prompted by a particular catastrophe, but the anarchy Yeats speaks of is not specified. The poem begins with a general sense of disorder, disconnectedness, break-down, a catalogue of disasters:

> Turning and turning in the widening gyre
> The falcon cannot hear the falconer;
> Things fall apart; the centre cannot hold;

The 'Turning', 'turning', 'widening' of line 1 charts an image of things spinning out of control and captures what Yeats feared: the collapse of civilisation. Yeats believed that history moves in cycles of birth-growth-decline-death and that the twentieth century would witness the collapse of Western civilisation.

Stephen Coote says, of the poem's opening lines, that 'The pitiless turning of the gyres has brought the democratic and self-effacing Christian period to a terrible climax. Now "The Second Coming is at hand". Far from being, as Christians believe, the period which will see the thousand-year rule of the godly, this era would be, Yeats thought, drawing on the deepest resources of his imagination, an aristocratic, physical, assertive and occult period of frightening primeval energies'.

> Mere anarchy is loosed upon the world,
> The blood-dimmed tide is loosed, and everywhere
> The ceremony of innocence is drowned.

The dramatic and active words – 'Turning and turning', 'fall apart', 'loosed' (repeated), 'drowned' – conjure up a chaotic, uncontrolled scene. The falcon is seen to circle further and further away from the falconer and this has been interpreted to mean that man has lost contact with Christ. Terence Brown reminds us that 'The Second Coming' has been seen as 'a prophetic anticipation of the monstrous unfolding of twentieth-century world history' but that the poem need not refer to a second coming in the Christian sense but to the birth of a deity.

The picture painted in the first stanza is one of anarchy. The pure and simple have been destroyed ('drowned') and the 'blood-dimmed tide', a tidal wave clouded or stained with blood, is an image of bloodshed on a vast scale. The first stanza ends with Yeats's opinion of humanity. Those who are 'best' (leaders, intellectuals?) have no energy or driving force or commitment and the 'worst' are fired with hatred and violence:

> The best lack all conviction, while the worst
> Are full of passionate intensity.

The second and longer stanza imagines the second coming. Yeats is so disillusioned with the present that he is certain that the birth of a new order is at hand:

> Surely some revelation is at hand;
> Surely the Second Coming is at hand.
> The Second Coming!

The tone of conviction, amazement and fear is clearly sensed and then slowly and dramatically the poet summons up a powerful image, not of the infant Christ who came and transformed the Greco-Roman civilisation, but of a sphinx-like creature with a blank and pitiless gaze:

> Hardly are those words out
> When a vast image out of *Spiritus Mundi*
> Troubles my sight

The desert landscape, the burning sun, the birds of prey and the darkness are harsh, unattractive, and the rough beast that the poet imagines will replace the divine child.

The movement in the opening lines of the poem changes in the poem's closing lines, from 'turning' and 'widening' to 'Reel', 'rocking', 'Slouches'. The beast moves slowly, while above are the contrasting frenzied movements of the desert birds:

> somewhere in sands of the desert
> A shape with lion body and the head of a man,
> A gaze blank and pitiless as the sun,
> Is moving its slow thighs, while all about it
> Reel shadows of the indignant desert birds.

This rough beast marks an end and a beginning. Yeats later said that the 'brazen winged beast' in 'my poem "The Second Coming" was 'associated with laughing, ecstatic destruction' and that 'Our civilisation was about to reverse itself, or some new civilisation about to be born from all that our age had rejected...; because we had worshipped a single god it would worship many.'

'The darkness drops again' may be an image of the dark, uncertain future. But Yeats is certain of one thing, that the birth of Christ and the Christian era would eventually lead to the present nightmare:

> but now I know
> That twenty centuries of stony sleep
> Were vexed to nightmare by a rocking cradle

In the final lines of this strange, haunting, powerful poem, Yeats, according to Seamus Deane, is asking if the rough beast can find 'a Bethlehem in which it can be born again as the demonic?' It is a poem whose symbolism will prompt many interpretations, meanings or understandings. Sixteen years after writing the poem, Yeats wrote to a friend and claimed that 'it foretold what was happening'. He was referring to the political barbarism throughout Europe. In Seamus Deane's words, the second coming 'became known as Fascism'.

Sailing to Byzantium

Yeats, in his poetry, often speaks in a voice that addresses public events but there are also poems where Yeats withdraws from the world and explores more personal themes. 'September 1913' is a public utterance; 'The Wild Swans at Coole' and 'Sailing to Byzantium' are preoccupied with his personal life, his disappointments, his growing old, his longing.

The title suggests a stately, graceful journey to an ancient and beautiful place. In Robert Pinsky's words, it 'denotes process'. 'Sailing', here, is a beautiful, timeless concept (substitute any other mode of transport and the image is somehow less attractive) and Byzantium, for Yeats, was an ideal place. The journey is an imagined, metaphorical one.

Yeats rejects Ireland in the opening line. Its strong, direct, dismissive tone is registered immediately in the first word. Yeats chose 'That' rather than 'This', distancing himself further from a country where he is no longer at ease. Ireland, here, symbolises the natural, temporal world; that country, therefore, is more the land of youth than Yeats's actual birthplace:

>That is no country for old men.

The country is teeming with youth and vitality and if the opening stanza read as follows

>The young
>In one another's arms, birds in the trees

>The salmon-falls, the mackerel-crowded sea,
>Fish, flesh, or fowl, commend all summer long

it would present a very attractive life-enhancing picture of young love and the never-ending riches of the natural world. It is old age, however, and the neglect of man's creative spirit by the young that cause Yeats to 'sail' to Byzantium. He dismisses Ireland but at the same time admits that it is attractive.

Though the first stanza begins and ends with negatives ('no country'; 'all neglect') there is, in the bird and fish, a sense of beginning. The salmon leap up-river in spring and the mackerel-crowded seas suggest energy and abundance.

A harsh, realistic, sombre note is struck in the striking description of fish, flesh and fowl as:

>Those dying generations.

In the midst of life, they are in the midst of death; they are 'caught' or trapped, but the 'young/ In one another's arms' are unaware of their mortality. Their lives are sensual, not intellectual, but the young will grow old too:

>Whatever is begotten, born and dies

The magnificent monuments of unageing intellect are neglected by the young and dying; ironically what they neglect is something outside of time and beyond time. Their lives are transient; the works of art are not.

The ageing Yeats realises that he is growing old, that old age is inevitable, but that art will allow him to escape this imperfect world and enter an immortal one. He wrote the poem in September 1926 when he was 61.

In stanza 2, Yeats focuses on himself and the reality of old age. He paints a grim picture:

> An aged man is but a paltry thing,
> A tattered coat upon a stick

Youth and its sensual music are no more and therefore Yeats believes it all the more important that the soul within the ageing body should sing out. Old age is empty and meaningless:

>   unless
> Soul clap its hands and sing, and louder sing
> For every tatter in its mortal dress

The soul defies its ageing, mortal body; the phrase 'and sing, and louder sing' gathers momentum through repetition and its strong sounds contrast with 'paltry', 'tatter'. The image of the soul clapping its hands is simple, childlike, spontaneous, delightful. This soul-singing, however, is best learned by studying great works of art; there is no way to learn to sing except by studying:

> Nor is there singing school but studying
> Monuments of its own magnificence

In stanza 1, the monuments of unageing intellect were being neglected by the young; it is vital that the old pay attention to such works for it is through art that their souls will achieve immortality. The stanza ends with the image of Yeats in old age, having made the journey to Byzantium, a journey of the imagination.

In stanzas 3 and 4, Yeats imagines himself in the holy city, a city of art, of magnificent monuments to the creative imagination and spirit. The tone is reverential and one of longing:

> O sages standing in God's holy fire
> As in the gold mosaic of a wall,
> Come from the holy fire, perne in a gyre,
> And be the singing-masters of my soul.

The soul is what is essential. The work of art (such as the gold mosaic) is the soul's creation and, if studied, such a work allows the viewer to enter the immortal world of art. Stanza 3 contrasts the heart and soul, the body and spirit, the sensual and the intellectual. Yeats speaks of his heart as sick with desire, his body as a broken, confused animal:

> Consume my heart away; sick with desire
> And fastened to a dying animal
> It knows not what it is; and gather me
> Into the artifice of eternity.

Though these are intensely personal lines ('my soul', 'my heart', 'gather me'), the reality of old age and the longing expressed in them are emotions that the reader can identify with.

By stanza 4, the poet imagines that he has been gathered 'into the artifice of eternity'. The natural world is left behind and the world evoked is ornate, privileged, ceremonious:

> Once out of nature I shall never take
> My bodily form from any natural thing,
> But such a form as Grecian goldsmiths make
> Of hammered gold and gold enamelling
> To keep a drowsy Emperor awake;
> Or set upon a golden bough to sing
> To lords and ladies of Byzantium
> Of what is past, or passing, or to come.

In 'The Lake Isle of Innisfree', Yeats longed to be part of the natural world. In 'Sailing to Byzantium', the natural world is rejected and he summons up an elegant civilisation. The 'birds in the tree' of line 2 become a bird of hammered gold and gold enamelling in line 28. The sensual music of stanza 1 has been rejected; Yeats rejects transience and sings of 'what is past, or passing, or to come'.

The immortal work of art is created by mortal man. The artist makes the gold mosaic; the Grecian goldsmith creates the bird; the old man makes the poem. The artist is mortal but art embodies or gives expression to man's soul and, in so doing, man becomes immortal. The very poem on the page becomes Yeats's monument of unageing intellect. 'Sailing to Byzantium' is, in Eavan Boland's words, 'a poem infatuated with the power of the imagination' and it shows us the imagination triumphing over the 'dying animal'. The vocabulary illustrates this tension between the two: 'dying' versus 'unageing'; 'tattered' versus 'Monuments'; 'gold mosaic' versus 'dying animal'; 'bodily form' versus 'hammered gold'.

And Boland also says: 'Yeats goes to Byzantium and there he hopes to enter the culture of art which will save him from the flux of life. He's not going to take his bodily form from any natural thing; he's going to become a work of art; he's going to become, in other words, what he himself can create – an immortal and timeless object'. The poem condemns 'the way in which man himself has been created' but 'celebrates what man can create'.

Though Eavan Boland thinks 'The Circus Animals' Desertion' is Yeats's greatest poem, she says: 'if I were to be asked which, in my opinion, is the best managed, best, most clearly written of all Yeats's poems, this ['Sailing to Byzantium'] is the one. It's not the most powerful; it's not the most haunting. But it has a wonderful command from stanza to stanza. There are only four stanzas, yet every one of them is a sort of magic box which you open to find out more. And the line lengths are beautifully managed.'

In a poem which praises and celebrates the importance of art, it is fitting that its form and structure are in themselves superb examples of a work of art. It is 'decorated' and 'artificial', as Eavan Boland described it.

Whenever we read we instinctively come up with a summary. This is a preliminary and important step and Elder Olson sums up 'Sailing to Byzantium' as follows: 'an old man faces the problem of old age, of death, and of regeneration, and gives his decision. Old age, he tells us, excludes a man from the sensual joys of youth; the world appears to belong completely to the young, it is no place for the old; indeed an old man is scarcely a man at all – he is a tattered coat upon a stick. But the young are so wrapped up in their sensuality that they are ignorant utterly of the world of the spirit. Hence if old age frees a man from sensual passion, he may rejoice in the liberation of the soul; he is admitted into the realm of the spirit; and his rejoicing will increase according as he realises the magnificence of the soul. But the soul can best learn its own greatness from the great works of art; hence he turns to those great works, but in turning to them, he finds that these are by no means mere effigies, or monuments, but things which have souls also; these live in the noblest element of God's fire, free from all corruption; hence he prays for death, for release from his mortal body; and since the insouled monuments exhibit the possibility of the soul's existence in some other matter than flesh, he wishes reincarnation, not now in a mortal body, but in the immortal and changeless embodiment of art.'

A paraphrase, obviously, cannot do justice to the poem being paraphrased but it does highlight the poem's special qualities and clarifies our thinking regarding not only what the poet says but more importantly how he says it.

The Stare's Nest by My Window

This is the sixth poem in a seven-poem sequence and the main title, 'Meditations in Time of Civil War', is an overtly political one. 'The Stare's Nest by My Window' is a political poem but its dominant image is a natural one, bees and birds, bees building and birds looking after the young in a nest.

The opening lines capture a sense of building up and breaking down:

> The bees build in the crevices
> Of loosening masonry, and there
> The mother birds bring grubs and flies.

Things are falling apart ('loosening masonry'), but there is also a sense of continuity. The poet speaks of 'My wall' and the repeated 'loosening' emphasises decay and destruction, but he also speaks of how the bees and the birds create. The poem begins with this activity of the world of nature and the man-made world is crumbling; the stanza ends with a plea that is repeated at the end of all the subsequent stanzas:

> Come build in the empty house of the stare.

Here, Yeats is addressing the honey-bees and creates what Eamon Grennan calls 'a context of maternal nurturing power in a context of violence and decay'. The birds' nest is now empty but Yeats, in wishing the bees to build a hive within the nest, is wishing for one positive, natural, instinctive life-force to replace another.

'The life that goes on' says Eamon Grennan, 'is a natural process independent of history, a gift of grace to the speaker'. But the speaker is fearful and uncertain. There is a feeling of claustrophobia, imprisonment, danger, helplessness, in stanza 2:

> We are closed in, and the key is turned
> On our uncertainty; somewhere
> A man is killed, or a house burned,
> Yet no clear fact to be discerned

He spoke of 'My Window', 'my wall' and now, though he speaks in the plural, 'We', meaning him and his family, the focus is still intensely private. The public world beyond the walls of Thoor Ballylee is a world of death and violence. Punctuation fragments the lines, but the final line is long and flowing when the speaker returns to his original prayer to the honey-bees:

> Come build in the empty house of the stare.

The third stanza lists the facts and there is a strong feeling of unrest. The speaker does not analyse nor does he offer judgement or solution but, against the backdrop of barricades and death, he returns to his hope and wish:

> Come build in the empty house of the stare.

The poet feels helpless. A detail such as 'Last night' brings the reality of the present moment alive, but all he can do is to renew his plea for nature to offer an image of the positive. The nest once contained birds. Now 'empty' captures the silence and the loss. He does not request the stares or starlings to return but asks for the bees to build there instead.

Yeats looks back in the final stanza and confesses how:

> We had fed the heart on fantasies,
> The heart's grown brutal from the fare

Everything springs from our own hearts and yet dreams have hardened the heart. In line 9, Yeats felt that there was 'no clear fact to be discerned' but he does end with the admission that hatred is now a stronger force than love. He addresses the honey-bees again, but this time an even stronger tone is captured in the expressive 'O':

> O honey-bees,
> Come build in the empty house of the stare.

This poem was written at Thoor Ballylee in 1922 and focused on a particular episode in Irish history and yet it achieves a relevance and universality today. Violence seems to be a permanent part of life, but the longing for a counterforce, for some fruitful activity, is also vital.

In Memory of Eva Gore-Booth and Con Markiewicz

Naming people in his poetry is frequent in Yeats. His life became the raw material for his art and his poems therefore chart his life, private and public. The lengthy and proper title lends the poem a dignity and formality. In this elegy he remembers the Gore-Booth sisters. Yeats had met them in 1894. He was thirty-one and they were in their twenties. He wrote the poem in late 1927; Yeats was sixty-two and the two sisters were dead. Eva died in 1926 and Constance died in August 1927.

Though their lives were troubled and difficult, in the opening lines Yeats remembers the two sisters in their youthful beauty. Like Lissadell itself, the lines are bathed in evening sunlight. The fine house, elegance and refinement are captured in the 'Great windows' and silk kimonos:

> The light of evening, Lissadell
> Great windows open to the south,
> Two girls in silk kimonos, both
> Beautiful, one a gazelle.

Each descriptive line presents a new different image from the past. Though distant and long ago, Yeats does not use a verb to distance the scene further. Instead, the images live again in memory.

The tranquillity and beauty are soon shattered at line 5. The poem shifts suddenly from past to more recent present and the change of mood is conveyed in the move from calm, summer evening light to harsh, autumn storms. 'But' signals this sudden and dramatic change:

> But a raving autumn shears
> Blossom from the summer wreath

The harshness of 'raving' and Yeats's use of the present tense ('shears') are forceful, and the image of the 'Blossom from the summer's wreath' suggests something beautiful and elegantly created. And all this is destroyed.

Their lives beyond Lissadell are portrayed as grim. Within eight lines, the poem has moved from elegant room to prison cell:

> The older is condemned to death,
> Pardoned, drags out lonely years
> Conspiring among the ignorant.

Yeats does not expand on their political involvement or campaigning but he regrets their involvement. 'Conspiring among the ignorant' and 'Some vague Utopia' suggests that Yeats did not believe in their social and political work; Eva's 'withered old and skeleton-gaunt body' symbolises for Yeats the futility of their efforts:

> I know not what the younger dreams—
> Some vague Utopia—and she seems,
> When withered old and skeleton-gaunt,
> An image of such politics.

Yeats leaves the harsh reality of their lives and returns to the beautiful world with which the poem began. The sisters are dead but Yeats speaks of them as if they are still alive, which of course, they are in his imagination:

> Many a time I think to seek
> One or the other out and speak
> Of that old Georgian mansion, mix
> Pictures of the mind, recall
> That table and the talk of youth,
> Two girls in silk kimonos, both
> Beautiful, one a gazelle.

The present is obliterated. Within stanza 1, the troubling, unsettling memory is framed by two gloriously beautiful ones. The world of Lissadell, with its civilised atmosphere, which Yeats wanted to return to, predominates.

The second stanza differs from the first in many respects. There are no golden, glowing images. The tone is tender at first. He addresses their ghosts, knowing that their deaths would bring them understanding and wisdom:

> Dear shadows, now you know it all

He looks at their lives and their strong convictions. He speaks of their struggle or fight as weakness ('All the folly of a fight'); they involve themselves with wrong or right issues, but the suggestion is that their involvement was unworthy of them and he gently laments that the only enemy these two innocent and beautiful girls had was time:

> The innocent and the beautiful
> Have no enemy but time

Yeats then speaks to these shades directly. He asks them to 'Arise and bid me strike a match'. The particular details of stanza 1 (house, setting, clothing, prison cell, conversation) now give way, in stanza 2, to one powerful symbol. Yeats imagines himself being told by these two women, who gave their lives to public causes, to set the world and time itself ablaze. The conflagration is a mighty, dangerous, destructive force. He imagines the great fire raging until such a time when the wise realise the significance of it:

> Arise and bid me strike a match
> And strike another till time catch;
> Should the conflagration climb,
> Run till all the sages know.

In the final sentence, the two girls, both beautiful, and Yeats are united as 'We'. He speaks of how they created something valuable and special and he speaks it with triumph:

> We the great gazebo built

However, he denounces those ('They') for resenting 'us' (the Gore-Booths, Yeats and others of their cultural inheritance):

> They convicted us of guilt

Those others felt that the privileged, ascendancy class should feel guilt for being who they are. Yeats, in a dramatic flourish, asks the shades once again to

> Bid me strike a match and blow.

This complex stanza is difficult to tease out but Yeats's imagination here is actively involved in honouring the memory of the Gore-Booth sisters. There was a beauty and a nobility in their lives but they never realised their dream. They worked with the common people but Yeats seems to say that he wishes that 'Dear shadows' would bid him bring about an end to everything.

A. Norman Jeffares says of this poem that it is 'an elegy for lost beauty, lost youth, the lost battle with time as well as a condemnation of the choices the sisters made about their lives'. But the closing lines also express a deep desire to bring about a change, in the dramatic image of the all-consuming conflagration. The mood is no longer elegiac but visionary and determined. The pleading tones – of 'Bid me strike...', 'And strike another...' – are a passionate expression of Yeats's admiration for everything Eva Gore-Booth and Con Markiewicz of Lissadell stood for.

Swift's Epitaph

Yeats had great admiration for Jonathan Swift and he considered Swift's epitaph 'the greatest . . . in history'. Yeats identified with the proud and solitary Swift and an Anglo-Ireland that both belonged to. Yeats translates Swift's Latin but line 1 is Yeats's own variation. The image of sailing in the first line offers an image of stately and dignified departure but, at the heart of the epitaph, is the sense of how Swift is now free from all anger and hatred that had been directed at him when he lived. This self-portrait by Jonathan Swift emphasises a fierce independence. The challenging tone of

> Imitate him if you dare
> World-besotted traveller

implies that Swift himself had travelled vast distances, intellectually and imaginatively, and that he could not be equalled. The epitaph's final line sums up his life's work. The commanding, confident tones in such a short piece and the compression of thought are impressive.

An Acre of Grass

This is Yeats at seventy-one. He begins with a calm, quiet, ordered description of his life at Riversdale in Rathfarnham. 'Picture and book' sum up his lifelong interest in art and literature. It is spacious – 'An acre of green grass/ For air and exercise' – but he realises that he is growing old in body. The references to 'midnight', 'old' house, the silence and absence of movement ('nothing stirs but a mouse') all create a picture of Yeats at 'life's end'.

In stanza 2, he speaks of how he is content ('My temptation is quiet') but also of how his own creative powers, the imagination and the mind, are failing him:

> Neither loose imagination,
> Nor the mill of the mind
> Consuming its rag and bone,
> Can make the truth known.

Here, he captures both the liberating ('loose imagination') and the workaday, mechanical nature ('mill of the mind') of the creative process. Though it is in the everyday and ordinary ('rag and bone') that truth can be found, he no longer seems to be able to capture and communicate that truth in his poetry.

The mood of quiet contemplation with which the poem began now changes dramatically at line 13. He defiantly breaks into an intense expression of desire:

> Grant me an old man's frenzy,
> Myself must I remake

He calls on Timon, Lear, William Blake and Michael Angelo, characters imagined and real, to inspire him. Yeats finds himself in need of their raging, death-defying energies. The word 'frenzy' and Blake beating upon the wall or Michael Angelo's mind piercing the clouds are powerful images of men forever searching, forever exploring.

When Yeats says 'Grant me an old man's frenzy', he is calling perhaps upon the Muse, the source of poetic inspiration. He wishes for the loose imagination and the mill of the mind to allow him, at the end of his life, full expression. The poem ends with a striking image of the force and power of the nature of man's mind. If 'inspired by frenzy', the effect is such that 'An old man's eagle mind' can 'Shake the dead in their shrouds'. The 'eagle mind' is an image of a sharp, focused mind. The poem, which began with an air of quiet acceptance, almost defeatism, ends with a rallying call by Yeats for renewed creative energies. Though 'An Acre of Grass' is one of Yeats's last poems, it is a poem that clings to life.

Politics

The title might lead one to expect a poem on civil government and its administration (in Greek, *polítikos* is citizen). Instead, Yeats dismisses politics in a mocking voice and longs instead for youth and love. The old man is distracted by 'that girl standing there' and he asks how a topic such as international politics could hold his attention.

The poem's theme is easily grasped: that the big, apparently important public events are not as important in the end as the universal experience of love. The questioning tone in the opening lines turns to mockery ('here's a travelled man', 'there's a politician'), then doubt ('maybe what they say is true/ Of war's and war's alarms') and eventually to longing:

> But O that I were young again
>
> And held her in my arms!

The rhyming even-numbered lines give the poem a rhythm and power and in two sentences Yeats gives his reader big and challenging ideas.

In her 1992 novel, *Jazz*, Toni Morrison says something similar: 'Whatever happens, whether you get rich or stay poor, ruin your health or live to old age, you always end up back where you started: hungry for the one thing everybody loses—young loving.'

from Under Ben Bulben V

Yeats was a formalist and this poem, appropriately, is in heroic couplets. In *The Making of a Poem*, Mark Strand and Eavan Boland identify the heroic couplet, with its progressing rhyme scheme (aabbcc, etc.), as 'a form in which a high subject matter could be written'. Yeats lived at a time when many poets (T.S. Eliot for example) favoured Free Verse, but he rejected this technique. If you look at Yeats's poetry, it is clear that he favoured traditional forms in metre, stanza structure, rhyme. In section V of 'Under Ben Bulben', Yeats begins in an authoritative, commanding voice in which he tells Irish poets to learn and practise a formal poetry, not 'the sort now growing up/ All out of shape from toe to top'. It is a proud rallying call for Irish poets to honour and continue their tradition and inheritance. Yeats calls on Irish poets to create for the people of Ireland an heroic and spiritual ideal. He speaks dismissively of those who have no sense of ceremony and history:

> Their unremembering hearts and heads
> Base-born products of base beds.

Yeats has been accused of snobbishness and of looking down on 'Base-born products', but he was also passionate about Ireland and its future. He includes the lowly and the privileged, the peasantry and the country gentlemen in his vision of Ireland; he includes the ascetic and the sensuous, Ireland's religious legacy and the randy laughter of porter drinkers. He is therefore inclusive rather than exclusive and wants Irish poets to write of all aspects of Irish life. Nor should we forget our long and troubled history:

> Sing the lords and ladies gay
> That were beaten into the clay
> Through seven heroic centuries.

His confidence, pride and patriotism are unquestionable:

> Cast your mind on other days
> That we in coming days may be
> Still the indomitable Irishry.

So is his belief in the power of poetry. He is addressing the present but it is only in remembering the past, that present and past can be understood, and the future made possible. This poem is a formal farewell. He completed the poem in September 1938 and it is not unlike a last will and testament. He died the following January.

from Under Ben Bulben VI

This is a stark and prophetic poem. The mood is solemn. The tone is once again authoritative and commanding, the heroic couplet fitting. Personal history is evoked and Yeats's individual, unconventional personality clearly emerges. Though his ancestor was a clergyman, he manages to cherish and break with that tradition. He wishes to be buried in Drumcliff churchyard but there is to be:

> No marble, no conventional phrase

The unconventional words on the tombstone, Yeats's own epitaph, challenge the reader to view life and death realistically. The poem's first section referred to a ghostly, supernatural horseman which Yeats heard about as a boy. Perhaps Yeats, in the closing line, is expressing his fearlessness of death; it could also be interpreted that the man on horseback who might pass by Yeats's grave should not concern himself with death but continue with the business of life.

The "new" poetry course was first examined in 2001. Below are the eight poets prescribed, each year, since then. Names in bold indicate the poets on the exam paper that particular year. [In 2009, a Paper II exam paper was inadvertently handed out to a group of pupils when they ought to have been given Paper I. The four prescribed poets were seen by that group and as a result a substitute Paper II was sat on a Saturday morning and at a cost of one million euros. Originally the paper carried Larkin, Longley, Mahon and Rich. In the substitute paper, Longley was replaced by Montague.]

2001 **Bishop** Boland Dickinson Heaney **Keats Larkin Longley** Shakespeare.

2002 **Bishop Boland** Dickinson Heaney Keats Larkin **Longley Shakespeare**.

2003 Bishop **Donne Frost Heaney** Hopkins Mahon **Plath** Yeats.

2004 Dickinson Frost Heaney **Hopkins Kavanagh Mahon Plath** Wordsworth.

2005 **Boland Dickinson Eliot** Heaney Kavanagh Longley Wordsworth **Yeats**.

2006 **Bishop Donne** Eliot **Hardy** Hopkins **Longley** Plath Yeats.

2007 Bishop Donne **Eliot Frost** Kavanagh **Montague Plath** Yeats.

2008 Boland **Donne** Frost **Larkin Mahon** Montague Plath **Rich**.

2009 **Bishop Keats** Larkin [Longley*] Mahon **Montague*** Rich **Walcott**.

2010 Boland **Eliot Kavanagh** Keats Longley **Rich** Walcott **Yeats**.

2011 **Boland Dickinson Frost** Hopkins Kavanagh Rich Wordsworth **Yeats**.

2012 Boland Heaney Frost **Kavanagh Kinsella Larkin** Plath **Rich**.

2013 **Bishop Hopkins** Kinsella **Mahon Plath** Rich Shakespeare Wordsworth.

2014 Bishop **Dickinson** Heaney Kinsella **Larkin** Mahon **Plath Yeats**.

2015 Dickinson Donne **Frost Hardy Montague Ní Chuilleanáin** Plath Yeats.

2016 **Bishop Dickinson Durcan Eliot** Larkin Ní Chuilleanáin Plath Yeats.

2017 **Bishop Boland Donne** Durcan Eliot Hopkins **Keats** Plath.

2018 Boland Durcan **Frost** Hopkins Keats **Larkin Montague Ní Chuilleanáin**.

2019 **Bishop** Heaney Hopkins **Kennelly** Lawrence Ní Chuilleanáin **Plath Yeats**.

2020 **Boland Dickinson** Durcan Frost Lawrence Ní Chuilleanáin **Rich Wordsworth**.

2021 Bishop Boland Durcan Frost Heaney Hopkins Keats Plath.

2022 Bishop Dickinson Keats Kennelly Lawrence Rich Wordsworth Yeats.

2023 Bishop Dickinson Donne Kavanagh Mahon Meehan Rich Yeats.

Questions from Past Papers

Elizabeth Bishop

- 'Bishop makes skillful use of a variety of poetic techniques to produce poems that are often analytical but rarely emotional.'

Discuss the extent to which you agree or disagree with the above statement. Develop your response with reference to the poems by Elizabeth Bishop on your course. [2019]

- 'From the poetry of Elizabeth Bishop that you have studied, select the poems that, in your opinion, best demonstrate her skilful use of language and imagery to confront life's harsh realities.'

Justify your selection by demonstrating Bishop's skilful use of language and imagery to confront life's harsh realities in the poems you have chosen. [2017]

- 'Bishop uses highly detailed observation, of people, places and events, to explore unique personal experiences in her poetry.'

Discuss this statement, supporting your answer with reference to the poetry of Elizabeth Bishop on your course. [2016]

- 'Bishop's carefully judged use of language aids the reader to uncover the intensity of feeling in her poetry.'

To what extent do you agree or disagree with the above statement? Support your answer with reference to the poetry of Elizabeth Bishop on your course. [2013]

- 'Elizabeth Bishop poses interesting questions delivered by means of a unique style.'

Do you agree with this assessment of her poetry? Your answer should focus on both themes and stylistic features. Support your points with the aid of suitable reference to the poems you have studied. [2009]

- 'Reading the poetry of Elizabeth Bishop.'

Write out the text of a talk that you would give to your class in response to the above title.
Your talk should include the following:
- Your reactions to her themes or subject matter.
- What you personally find interesting in her style of writing.

Refer to the poems by Elizabeth Bishop that you have studied. [2006]

- 'The poetry of Elizabeth Bishop appeals to the modern reader for many reasons.'

Write an essay in which you outline the reasons why poems by Elizabeth Bishop have this appeal. [2002]

- 'Introducing Elizabeth Bishop.'

Write out the text of a short presentation you would make to your friends or class group under the above title. Support your point of view by reference to or quotation from the poetry of Elizabeth Bishop that you have studied. [2001]

Emily Dickinson

- Discuss how Dickinson's unique approach to language, and the balance between beauty and horror in her imagery, help to relieve some of the darker aspects of her poetry.

Develop your response with reference to the poems of Emily Dickinson on your course. [2020]

- 'Dickinson's use of an innovative style to explore intense experiences can both intrigue and confuse.'

Discuss this statement, supporting your answer with reference to the poetry of Emily Dickinson on your course. [2016]

- 'The dramatic aspects of Dickinson's poetry can both disturb and delight readers.'

To what extent do you agree or disagree with the above statement? Support your answer with reference to both the themes and language found in the poetry of Emily Dickinson on your course. [2014]

- 'Emily Dickinson's original approach to poetry results in startling and thought-provoking moments in her work.'

Give your response to the poetry of Emily Dickinson in the light of this statement. Support your points with suitable reference to the poems on your course. [2011]

- What impact did the poetry of Emily Dickinson make on you as a reader?

Your answer should deal with the following:
- Your overall sense of the personality of the poet
- The poet's use of language/imagery

Refer to the poems by Emily Dickinson that you have studied. [2005]

John Donne

- 'Donne's poetry can be simultaneously playful and challenging both in style and content.'

To what extent do you agree or disagree with this statement? Support your answer with reference to the poetry of John Donne on your course. [2017]

- Write an introduction to the poetry of John Donne for new readers.

Your introduction should cover the following:

- ◆ The ideas that were most important to him.
- ◆ How you responded to his use of language and imagery.

Refer to the poems by John Donne that you have studied. [2006]

- 'Why read the poetry of John Donne?'

Write out the text of a talk that you would give, or an article that you would submit to a journal, in response to the above title. Support the points you make by reference to the poetry of John Donne on your course. [2003]

Patrick Kavanagh

- In your opinion, is Kavanagh successful in achieving his desire to transform the ordinary world into something extraordinary?

Support your answer with suitable reference to the poems on your course. [2012]

- 'Aspects of Kavanagh's poetry could be seen as dated and irrelevant, but his unique poetic language has enduring appeal.'

Do you agree with this assessment of his poetry? Support your points with suitable reference to the poetry of Patrick Kavanagh on your course. [2010]

- Imagine you were asked to select one or more of Patrick Kavanagh's poems from your course for inclusion in a short anthology entitled, 'The Essential Kavanagh'.

Give reasons for your choice, quoting from or referring to the poem or poems you have chosen. [2004]

Derek Mahon

- 'Mahon uses language and imagery to transform personal observations into universal reflections.'

Write your response to this statement with reference to the poems by Derek Mahon on your course. [2013]

- 'Derek Mahon explores people and places in his own distinctive style.'

Write your response to this statement supporting your points with the aid of suitable reference to the poems you have studied. [2008]

- 'Speaking of Derek Mahon ...'

Write out the text of a public talk you might give on the poetry of Derek Mahon. Your talk should make reference to the poetry on your course. [2004]

Paula Meehan

This is the first time that Paula Meehan's poetry has been prescribed for the Leaving Certificate examination.

Adrienne Rich

- Discuss how Rich makes effective use of a variety of characters, often in dramatic settings, to probe both personal issues and wider social concerns in her poems.

Develop your response with reference to the poetry of Adrienne Rich on your course. [2020]

- 'Rich's poetry communicates powerful feelings through thought-provoking images and symbols.'

Write your response to this statement with reference to the poems by Adrienne Rich on your course. [2012]

- 'Adrienne Rich explores the twin themes of power and powerlessness in a variety of interesting ways.'

Write a response to the poetry of Adrienne Rich in the light of this statement, supporting your points with suitable reference to the poems on your course. [2010]

W.B. Yeats

- 'Yeats's poetry is both intellectually stimulating and emotionally charged.'
Discuss the extent to which you agree or disagree with the above statement. Develop your response with reference to the themes and language evident in the poems by W. B. Yeats on your course. [2019]

- 'Yeats uses evocative language to create poetry that includes both personal reflection and public commentary.'
Discuss this statement, supporting your answer with reference to both the themes and language found in the poetry of W. B. Yeats on your course. [2014]

- 'Yeats can be a challenging poet to read, both in terms of style and subject matter.'
To what extent do you agree with this statement? Support your answer with suitable reference to the poetry on your course. [2011]

- 'Yeats's poetry is driven by a tension between the real world in which he lives and an ideal world that he imagines.'
Write a response to the poetry of W.B. Yeats in the light of this statement, supporting your points with suitable reference to the poems on your course. [2010]

- Write an article for a school magazine introducing the poetry of W.B. Yeats to Leaving Certificate students. Tell them what he wrote about and explain what you liked in his writing, suggesting some poems that you think they would enjoy reading. Support your points by reference to the poetry by W.B. Yeats that you have studied. [2005]

The Unseen Poem
Part II

Part II

Approaching the Unseen Poem

Every poem, to begin with, is an unseen poem. When approaching a poem, it is useful to ask some very basic questions, such as: Who is speaking in the poem? What is being said? What prompted the poet to write the poem? What struck you first about this particular poem? What do you think of the opening? The Ending? Does the poet use unusual words, images or repetition?

The following is an outline of a step by step approach to the unseen poem on the page.

The shape of the poem on the page

This is often the very first thing you will notice about the text. Certain forms are recognised immediately, for example the fourteen-line sonnet or the sestina. Other poems may have a less definite shape, and that is also an important aspect of those poems. George Herbert (1593–1633) used very specific designs in some of his poems:

Easter Wings

Lord, who createdst man in wealth and store,
Though foolishly he lost the same,
Decaying more and more
Till he became
Most poor:
With thee
O let me rise
As larks, harmoniously,
And sing this day thy victories:
Then shall the fall further the flight in me.

My tender age in sorrow did begin;
And still with sicknesses and shame
Thou didst so punish sin,
That I became
Most thin.
With thee
Let me combine,
And feel this day thy victory;
For, if I imp my wing on thine,
Affliction shall advance the flight in me.

A modern writer who uses the same device is the American poet John Hollander.
His poem 'Swan and Shadow' would lose its impact if it were printed as follows:

Dusk Above the water hang the loud flies Here O so gray
then What a pale signal will appear When Soon before its shadow
fades Where Here in this pool of opened eyes. . .

This is how it should be:

Swan and Shadow

Dusk
Above the
water hang the
loud
flies
Here
O so
gray
then
What   A pale signal will appear
When   Soon before its shadow fades
Where   Here in this pool of opened eye
In us   No Upon us As at the very edges
of where we take shape in the dark air
this object bares its image awakening
ripples of recognition that will
brush darkness up into light
even after this bird this hour both drift by atop the perfect sad instant now
already passing out of sight
toward yet untroubled reflection
this image bears its object darkening
into memorial shades Scattered bits of
light   No of water Or something across
water   Breaking up No Being regathered
soon   Yet by then a swan will have
gone   Yes out of mind into what
vast
pale
hush
of a
place
past
sudden dark as
if a swan
sang

Shape here is so obviously of particular importance, but every poem has been shaped in a special way by means of line number, line length, rhyme and so on. Shakespeare wrote a 154 sonnet sequence; when Romeo and Juliet meet for the very first time in Shakespeare's play, they speak a sonnet between them. Elizabeth Bishop's 'The Prodigal' consists of two sonnets.

The Title

After the look of the poem on the page, the title is the next thing to be noticed. The American poet Emily Dickinson wrote 1,775 poems, but gave none of them titles. However, most poems have a title. What does the choice of title tell us about the poem? When we get to know the poem better we can then think about how effective and suitable the title is. Michael Longley's poem 'Carrigskeewaun' celebrates the place of the title, but each stanza is also given a title.

Consider the following titles. What do they reveal, or not reveal, suggest, imply, announce? Does the title win the reader's attention?

'The Dream of Wearing Shorts Forever' (Les Murray); 'Finale' (Judith Wright); 'Red Roses' (Anne Sexton); 'Red Sauce, Whiskey and Snow' (August Kleinzahler); 'Death of an Irishwoman' (Michael Hartnett); 'Hitcher' (Simon Armitage); 'Fifteen Million Plastic Bags' (Adrian Mitchell); 'For Heidi with Blue Hair' (Fleur Adcock); 'Wanting a Child' (Jorie Graham); 'SOMETHING FOR EVERYONE!!!' (Peter Reading); 'Phenomenal Woman' (Maya Angelou); 'The Hunchback in the Park' (Dylan Thomas); 'Depressed by a book of Bad Poetry, I walk Toward an Unused Pasture and Invite the Insects to Join me' (James Wright); 'Logan' (Catherine Phil MacCarthy); 'Ode on a Grecian Urn' (John Keats); 'Love' (George Herbert and Eavan Boland); 'The Armadillo' (Elizabeth Bishop); [r-p-o-p-h-e-s-s-a-g-r] (E E Cummings); 'Tea at the Palaz of Hoon' (Wallace Stevens); 'Church Going' (Philip Larkin); 'The Black Lace Fan My Mother Gave Me' (Eavan Boland); 'From a Conversation During Divorce' (Carol Rumens)

Language/Vocabulary

The language of poetry is the language of the age in which the poem is written. If someone today wrote a poem using 'thee' and 'thou' it would not convince; if someone today wrote exactly as Keats did, that poem would be dismissed as inauthentic. The poet writes in a language different from his or her predecessors and the poet today is less restricted in terms of subject matter. There is no word today, no emotion, no topic deemed unsuitable for poetry. Sylvia Plath once said that she wanted to get the word 'toothbrush' into a poem, meaning that she felt that there was nothing too ordinary or mundane for the poet to write about.

Yet the magic of poetry is such that each of the poets in this collection – though they span four centuries and all write in English – has a distinctive, unique voice. Their choice of words is part of this unique quality.

Ask yourself how you would describe a poet's vocabulary, his or her choice of words? This may be difficult to do at first. The task is easier if you look at opposites: is the language unusual or ordinary? Formal or colloquial? Does the poet invent new words? And, if so, what does this tell us about the poet? Is the language concrete or abstract? Are the words drawn from Anglo-Saxon, Latin, Anglo-Irish? Are there words on the page from the world of Greek Myth / Science / The Bible? Are there particular words that you would associate with particular poets? And how is the language of poetry different from the language of prose?

The following illustrates some interesting differences between the language of prose and the language of poetry. The first is a newspaper article which, according to his biographer Lawrance Thompson, inspired Robert Frost's poem 'Out, Out—'. The second is the poem itself. A discussion of the similarities and differences between the two should sharpen an awareness of language.

Sad tragedy at Bethlehem
Raymond Fitzgerald, a Victim of fatal accident

Raymond Tracy Fitzgerald, one of the twin sons of Michael G. and Margaret Fitzgerald of Bethlehem, died at his home Thursday afternoon, March 24, as a result of an accident by which one of his hands was badly hurt in a sawing machine. The young man was assisting in sawing up some wood in his own dooryard with a sawing machine and accidently hit the loose pulley, causing the saw to descend upon his hand, cutting and lacerating it badly. Raymond was taken into the house and a physician was immediately summoned, but he died very suddenly from the effect of the shock, which produced heart failure . . .

(From *The Littleton Courier*, 31 March 1901)

'Out, Out —'

The buzz saw snarled and rattled in the yard
And made dust and dropped stove-length sticks of wood,
Sweet-scented stuff when the breeze drew across it.
And from there those that lifted eyes could count
Five mountain ranges one behind the other
Under the sunset far into Vermont.
And the saw snarled and rattled, snarled and rattled,
As it ran light, or had to bear a load.
And nothing happened: day was all but done.
Call it a day, I wish they might have said
To please the boy by giving him the half hour
That a boy counts so much when saved from work.
His sister stood beside them in her apron
To tell them 'Supper'. At the word, the saw,
As if to prove saws knew what supper meant,
Leaped out at the boy's hand, or seemed to leap —

He must have given the hand. However it was,
Neither refused the meeting. But the hand!
The boy's first outcry was a rueful laugh,
As he swung toward them holding up the hand
Half in appeal, but half as if to keep
The life from spilling. Then the boy saw all —
Since he was old enough to know, big boy
Doing a man's work, though a child at heart —
He saw all spoiled. 'Don't let him cut my hand off —
The doctor, when he comes. Don't let him, sister!'
So. But the hand was gone already.
The doctor put him in the dark of ether.
He lay and puffed his lips out with his breath.
And then—the watcher at his pulse took fright.
No one believed. They listened at his heart.
Little — less— nothing! — and that ended it.
No more to build on there. And they, since they
Were not the one dead, turned to their affairs.

The importance of vocabulary is also clearly seen in the following two poems.
They share the same title and they both say something similar. One was written
– the original spelling is retained – at the beginning of the sixteenth century (and
supposedly tells of Thomas Wyatt's sorrow on being forsaken by women friends,
including Anne Boleyn, who left him for Henry VIII); the other was first published in
1979.

They flee from me, that somtime did me seke

They flee from me, that somtime did me seke
With naked fote stalkyng within my chamber.
Once have I seen them gentle, tame, and meke,
That now are wild, and do not once remember
That sometyme they have put them selves in danger,
To take bread at my hand, and now they range
Busily sekyng in continuall change.
   Thanked be fortune, it hath bene otherwise
Twenty tymes better: but once especiall,
In thinne aray, after a pleasant gyse,
When her loose gowne did from her shoulders fall,
And she me caught in her armes long and small,
And therwithall, so swetely did me kysse,
And softly sayd: deare hart, how like you this?
It was no dreame: for I lay broade awakyng.
But all is turnde now through my gentlenesse,
Into a bitter fashion of forsakyng:

And I have leave to go of her goodnesse,
And she also to use newfanglenesse.
But, sins that I unkyndly so am served:
How like you this, what hath she now deserved?

– Thomas Wyatt (1503–42)

They flee from me that sometime did me seek

At this moment in time
the chicks that went for me
in a big way
are opting out;
as of now, it's an all-change situation.
The scenario was once,
for me, 100% better.
Kissing her was viable
in a nude or semi-nude situation.
It was How's about it, baby?
Her embraces were relevant
and life-enhancing.

I was not hallucinating.
But with regard to that one
my permissiveness
has landed me in a forsaking situation.
The affair is no longer on-going.

She can, as of now, explore new parameters
How's about it? indeed!
I feel emotionally underprivileged.
What a bitch!
(and that's meaningful).

– Gavin Ewart (1916–95)

Punctuation

All poets are wordsmiths and punctuation is an aspect essential to poetry. Sometimes its absence is deliberate, as in the poems by Emily Dickinson. The frequent use of the full-stop will naturally slow down a line. In his poem 'Laertes', Michael Longley uses only one full-stop and that is at the end because, in his own words, he 'sustained the sentence from the first word right the way through'. Philip Larkin's 'MCMXIV' is also a one-sentence poem.

The full-stop, comma, colon, exclamation mark, question mark, dash, bracket, ellipsis and italics are just some examples of punctuation and their use are important aspects of a writer's style. You will meet with all of these in the prescribed poems. If you are aware of their importance and significance when you come to read the ten Emily Dickinson poems on your course, for example, consider the significance of how each poem ends: two with a full-stop, seven with a dash, one with a question mark. A poem that ends with a full-stop achieves a sense of closure; the dash often creates the opposite effect.

Rhyme

Rhyme, for centuries, has been one of the most distinguishing characteristics of poetry, though poetry without a regular rhyming scheme is not necessarily a poem without music. Blank verse, which is unrhymed iambic pentameter, for example, achieves rhythm and cadence without end rhyme. Internal rhyme and cross rhyme are also important features in poetry.

The run-on line is deceptive in that often a very rigorous and regular rhyming scheme is not apparent. 'Child of Our Time' by Eavan Boland has a very disciplined and regular end rhyme, but Boland's mastery of rhythm and the flowing line is such that a careless reader might think that the poem has no rhyming scheme.

Rhythm

Rhythm is movement. We are all familiar with rhythm. The individual day, the seasons of the year, the sound of the sea all have their own rhythm or movement. The Dublin poet Paula Meehan believes that our sense of rhythm dates from the time spent in the womb – the regular heartbeat of the mother and our own heartbeat give us an inbuilt rhythmic pattern.

Cadence

Cadence, a musical term, is difficult to define, yet it is easily recognised. A dictionary definition speaks of the rise and fall of words. If you consider the following short extracts, you can hear this rising, falling sound and it is a very effective means of capturing a mood:

> Brightness falls from the air,
> Queens have died young and fair,
> Dust hath closed Helen's eyes.

> (from 'Song' by Thomas Nashe, 1567–1601)

It was evening all afternoon.
It was snowing
And it was going to snow.

(from 'Thirteen Ways of Looking at a Blackbird'
by Wallace Stevens, 1879–1955)

Only the groom, and the groom's boy,
With bridles in the evening come.

(from 'At Grass' by Philip Larkin, 1922–85)

The cadence here creates a mood: in the first an elegiac feeling, in the second a melancholy one, the third a peaceful, tranquil one. The sounds of the words, the arrangement of the words in the line, the use of repetition, for example, create these cadences.

Line break and line length

These are other important aspects of the total impact of the poem. It would be a worthwhile and interesting exercise to think about line break in a poem you are not already familiar with. Here are two poems called by William Carlos Williams minus capital letters, punctuation, line break. How do you think it ought to be arranged on the page?

the red wheelbarrow

so much depends upon a red wheelbarrow glazed with rain water beside the white chickens

to a poor old woman

munching a plum on the street a paper bag of them in her hand they taste good to her they taste good to her they taste good to her you can see it by the way she gives herself to the one half sucked out in her hand comforted a solace of ripe plums seeming to fill the air they taste good to her

The poet Denise Levertov says that 'there is at our disposal no tool of the poetic craft more important, none that yields more subtle and precise effects, than the linebreak if it is properly understood'. Levertov illustrates her point by taking four lines from the William Carlos Williams poem 'To a Poor Old Woman', mentioned above, in which the old woman has been eating plums:

They taste good to her
They taste good
to her. They taste
good to her.

Each word here has a special emphasis because of its place in the line. If Williams had written of the plums that:

> They taste good to her
> They taste good to her
> They taste good to her

it would be a very different and less effective piece. Levertov's commentary (see below) on the four lines from Williams is worth reading, for it shows a mind keenly alert to the power of language.

But first, look again at the four lines that Williams wrote:

> They taste good to her.
> They taste good
> to her. They taste
> good to her.

Levertov observes: 'First the statement is made; then the word good is (without the clumsy overemphasis a change of typeface would give) brought to the center of our (and her) attention for an instant; then the word taste is given is given similar momentary prominence, with good sounding on a new note, reaffirmed – so that we have first the general recognition of well-being, then the intensification of that sensation, then its voluptuous location in the sense of taste. And all this is presented through indicated pitches, that is, by melody, not by rhythm alone.'

The nuts and bolts of poetic language belong in the study of metre, which is the study of sound patterns and measured sounds. Every syllable is long sounding or short and the way such sounds are arranged is an intrinsic part of poetry. When you come to read Shakespeare's sonnets, you will discover that each one is written in a five foot line, each foot consisting of one unaccented syllable followed by an accented one (the iambic pentameter). This is not as complicated as it sounds. The glossary at the back of this book provides a detailed note on metrics.

Imagery

If you say the words traffic-jam, strobe lighting, town, river, hillside, elephant, images form one after the other in your mind, all in a matter of seconds. Many of the words in the English language conjure up an image on their own. Every noun does, for example. However, there is a difference between the image prompted by the word 'tiger' and the phrases 'roaring like a tiger', and 'he's a tiger'. Here tiger becomes simile and metaphor. Symbol is another familiar and powerful technique and symbol occurs when something in the poem such as a tiger in a cage is both actual and means something beyond itself. For example, a caged animal is just that, but it can also stand for the death of freedom. 'The Armadillo' in Elizabeth Bishop's poem of the same name is both actual and symbolic.

And in 'The Harvest Bow' Seamus Heaney writes of how the bow made by his father is an actual object, but it also becomes a symbol of his father's life and work as a farmer, the season itself, and a work of art.

Tone

What is being said and how it is being said are very important. Think for a moment of the sentence: 'Please leave the room'. Tone, or the attitude of the speaker, can make a huge difference here. First try saying that sentence four different ways simply by emphasising a different word each time. Then, if you introduce a note of anger or exhaustion or apathy or urgency into your voice, the sentence takes on a different meaning. In poetry, tone is the attitude the poet/speaker has towards the listener or reader. Tone can be formal or casual/off-hand, serious or tongue-in-cheek, superior or prayer-like, profound or simple and so on.

Mood

A tone can create a mood or atmosphere. Mood is the feeling contained within the work and the feeling communicated to the reader. In 'Sonnet 29' by Shakespeare, the mood at first is one of loneliness and dejection. The speaker feels worthless: 'I all alone beweep my outcast state'. However, the mood is triumphant and exultant in the closing couplet. Shakespeare, remembering his friend and the love that they share, feels an immense emotional richness. In Eavan Boland's poem 'This Moment', the mood throughout is one of expectation and mystery.

Allusion

This is when one writer refers to another writer's work, either directly or indirectly. When an allusion is used, it can enhance or enlarge a topic or it can serve as an effective contrast. When Keats mentions 'the sad heart of Ruth' in 'Ode to a Nightingale', he is referring to a sorrow from a very different time. The moment in the Bible and the moment that the poem focuses on are brought together, one enriching the other, through allusion.

Onomatopoeia

Listen out for the sounds. Read the poem aloud and the onomatopoeic words will clearly reveal themselves. Keats's 'Ode to a Nightingale' contains one of the finest examples of words imitating the thing they describe: 'The murmurous haunt of flies on summer eves'.

Other Aspects To Keep In Mind

Beginnings and Endings

Think about the following examples of opening and closing lines. What do these openings reveal to us of the poets? The situation in which they find themselves? Their tone/mood? Does the poet use the run-on line or punctuation in an interesting way?

Beginnings

'This Italian earth is special to me
because I was here in a war
when I was young and immortal.'

– Harvey Shapiro, 'Italy 1996'

The sunset's slow catastrophe of reds
and bruised blues
leaches the land to its green and grey.

– Robin Robertson, 'Tryst'

That God-is
Light smile of your arms
One second before
I'm in them.

– Ruth Padel, 'Being Late to Meet You at the Station'

never in all my life have I seen as handsome a rat as you.

– Christopher Logue, 'Rat, O Rat . . .'

Endings

And I let the fish go.

– Elizabeth Bishop, 'The Fish'

Never such innocence again.

– Philip Larkin, 'MCMXIV'

To the children, to a bewildered wife,
I think 'Sorry Missus' was what he said.

– Michael Longley, 'Wounds'

And reaching into my pocket in Dublin for busfare home
I found handfuls of marvellous, suddenly worthless coins.

– David Wheatley, 'Nothing to Declare'

For thy sweet love remembered such wealth brings,
That then I scorn to change my state with kings.

– William Shakespeare 'Sonnet 29'

Responding to the Unseen Poem

A Blessing

Just off the highway to Rochester, Minnesota,
Twilight bounds softly forth on the grass.
And the eyes of those two Indian ponies
Darken with kindness.
They have come gladly out of the willows   5
To welcome my friend and me.
We step over the barbed wire into the pasture
Where they have been grazing all day, alone.
They ripple tensely, they can hardly contain their happiness
That we have come.   10
They bow shyly as wet swans. They love each other.
There is no loneliness like theirs.
At home once more,
They begin munching the young tufts of spring in the darkness.
I would like to hold the slenderer one in my arms,   15
For she has walked over to me
And nuzzled my left hand.
She is black and white,
Her mane falls wild on her forehead,
And the light breeze moves me to caress her long ear   20
That is delicate as the skin over a girl's wrist.
Suddenly I realise
That if I stepped out of my body I would break
Into blossom.

James Wright (1927–80)

It is important that we re-read the poem a few times. A poem usually consists of sentences or sections and, having read the poem through several times, it might be useful to approach the poem a sentence or a line or two at a time.

The shape of the poem seems to be irregular. There is no obvious rhyming scheme. The poem contains twelve sentences, some long and flowing, others equally effective because they are short. The lines are of uneven length and the final line is the shortest.

Wright calls his poem 'A Blessing' not '*The* Blessing', which would imply something more specific. If the moment that he writes about is 'a' blessing, it means that there are other such moments also. The blessing experienced in this particular moment, however, is the particular focus of this poem. A blessing has religious and holy connotations and it is a special moment for the poet, though the setting is not a place associated with a conventional religious experience.

The poem begins in a matter-of-fact way – 'Just off the highway' – and the American city and state are named. A 'highway' suggests reinforced concrete, the man-made, busyness, speed, but the second line is soft and natural and beautiful, capturing, as it does, a world 'Just off the highway'. It is twilight, a time of fading light and shadows; the quaint, old-fashioned phrase 'softly forth' contains gentle sounds and the grass contrasts with the highway itself.

The use of the word 'And' at the beginning of line 3, which is also the beginning of a new sentence, leads us further into the poem. The first thing that Wright tells us about the ponies is that their eyes 'darken with kindness' and that they are Indian (Native American) ponies. Their mystery and their nature are conveyed in the words 'darken' and 'kindness'; that they are Indian might be significant. Modern America as symbolised by the highway is very different from the Native American traditions.

'Gladly' and 'welcome' suggest how Wright feels as both he and his friend are approached by the ponies.

The human and the animal world meet when 'We step over the barbed wire'. Wright speaks of the ponies being alone. Their happiness is vividly conveyed in a phrase: 'They ripple tensely'.

There is no sound mentioned. The image Wright uses – 'They bow shyly as wet swans' – is elegant and graceful and beautiful. The three short sentences in lines 11–12, each following the other, are effective. They are both the poet's accurate observation and his conclusions:

> They bow shyly as wet swans. They love each other.
> There is no loneliness like theirs.

The loneliness that the poet speaks of here is a different kind of loneliness, a loneliness that does not frighten or destroy.

The moment passes and the ponies are 'At home once more', happy to be visited and happy to feel at ease 'munching the young tufts of spring in the darkness', a phrase that contains sensuous, evocative details.

The final part of the poem, the last three sentences, focuses on the speaker. 'I', absent from the poem so far, is now used four times. 'I would like to hold the slenderer one in my arms' is Wright's response when his left hand is nuzzled ('ripple';'munching';'nuzzle' add to the sensuousness of the experience). It is clearly a very personal and beautiful moment that the poet is recording. He moves from the very emotional/subjective response to objective description in the lines:

> She is black and white,
> Her mane falls wild on her forehead

He then returns to the intense emotion of 'the light breeze moves me to caress her long ear'. The image of the 'skin over a girl's wrist' is echoing the earlier image of the swans. Both are graceful and slender and delicate. The moment of insight comes and it comes 'suddenly':

> Suddenly I realise
> That if I stepped out of my body I would break
> Into blossom.

The final image is inspired by the natural world and, just as a blossom unfolds naturally and beautifully, Wright, in choosing this image, is giving us a very vivid description of a complex, metaphysical/spiritual moment. It is a poem of longing and here the word 'break', so often associated with destruction, is used with opposite effect. The word 'break' is also placed appropriately at the line break.

●

The above is but a beginning. However, gradually, with each re-reading, you can enter more fully into the poem. If, for example, you focus on the mood of the poem would one word sum up the mood or does the mood change and how would you describe that changing mood? What is the dominant mood of this poem?

Are the verbs or adjectives or sound of particular importance? What if the images were removed? What would the poem lose?

Your own response to a poem on the page should focus on **Theme** and **Technique**. Hundreds of poems may share a similar theme, but every true poet has his or her own individual way of viewing and expressing an idea, his or her own individual way of mastering technique.

Sample Answer on the Unseen Poem

Your response need not be long, but it must be personal. You must engage with the text. And quote little details throughout your answer to support the points you make. The examiner is told to watch out for FOUR things: the candidate's awareness of the poem's

- **Pattern** (or structure)
- **Imagery** (the word pictures painted by the poet and the impact/effect such images have on you, the reader)
- **Sensuousness** (the world as evoked or brought to life through sight, smell, hearing, taste, touch)
- **Suggestiveness** (what personal thoughts, ideas, feelings are prompted by this particular poem)

And, yes, the first letter of the four aspects listed here, as outlined by the Examinations Commission, form an unfortunate and unforgettable acronym: P.I.S.S. But there you go. Did the powers that be think of that at the time?

Here is a poem that could appear as an Unseen Poem and there follows an answer written in exam conditions that earned twenty marks out of twenty.

In this poem, Alistair Elliot celebrates the ordinary things in life.

A Northern Morning

It rained from dawn. The fire died in the night.
I poured hot water on some foreign leaves;
I brought the fire to life. Comfort
spread from the kitchen like a taste of chocolate
through the head-waters of a body,
accompanied by that little-water-music.
The knotted veins of the old house tremble and carry
a louder burden: the audience joining in.

People are peaceful in a world so lavish
with the ingredients of life:
the world of breakfast easy as Tahiti.
But we must leave. Head down in my new coat
I dodge to the High Street conscious of my fellows
damp and sad in their vegetable fibres.
But by the bus-stop I look up: the spring trees
exult in the downpour, radiant, clean for hours:
This is the life! This is the only life!

Question

Write a personal response to this poem, highlighting aspects of it that you liked and/or disliked.

Answer

(Written by Bethany Hart, a Leaving Cert pupil in exam conditions)

On first reading this poem, I did not particularly like it but when I looked closer, the poem opened itself to me, and I can now see that it is intelligent, lyrical and atmospheric. I think the first three lines have a beautiful rhythm; the words are mostly monosyllabic and Elliot creates a steady pace, which suits the relaxed mood of the poem. I liked the image of pouring 'hot water on some foreign leaves' because I found it quirky and different. It seems that in order to celebrate the ordinary things in life, the poet is exaggerating and lyricising them so that making a cup of tea sounds like a beautiful song.

I like how the poet uses rich images such as 'a taste of chocolate' and 'I brought the fire to life' to create a warm atmosphere. The poem is very sensuous in this way; the poet wants to engage his reader's senses with these images.

In the second stanza the poet brings a contrast to the warm feeling previously created. He comments on the happiness that the human race experiences 'with the ingredients of life', describing the world as 'lavish' and 'the world of breakfast as easy as Tahiti'. It seems to me that the poet wants us to return to basics and appreciate the little things. He describes the people around him as 'damp and sad', which not only contrasts with the previous stanza but also with the statement that 'people are peaceful in a world so lavish'. I think the poet is commenting on the fact that possessions do not affect how long happiness lasts.

The final moment in the poem is my favourite moment. It is a sentence of complete exultation and celebration. Elliot describes 'the spring trees' in the 'downpour', as at their best, at their highest, at the moment when the rain is feeding them and bringing life to them. I think he means to tell us that we should be like these spring trees and exult in the things that make us 'radiant' and bring us life.

© Bethany Hart 2011

Appendices/Glossary

Part III

Contents	Page

Appendix I

Responding to a Poem – Some Exercises and Strategies

Some Questions to Ask

- Who is speaking? (the poet/a persona/an inanimate object/an animal?)
- What is being said?
- What occasion prompted the poem/why was it written?
- How does the poem begin?
- How does it end? (Write down the opening and closing lines and comment on the style)
- Which line/section captures the gist of the poem?
- Which image is the most effective/striking/memorable?
- What struck you first about a particular poem?
- What struck you while re-reading the poem?
- Comment on the shape of the poem.
- Are the lines regular in length?
- Comment on the stanza divisions.
- Does the poem belong to a particular genre? – sonnet/sestina/ballad/lyric/ epic/ode...?
- Comment on the punctuation in the poem. What would the page look like if only the punctuation remained? (e.g. poet's use of question marks, dashes, commas, and where these occur in the line)
- Ask if the poet uses (i) alliteration (ii) assonance (iii) onomatopoeia (iv) end-rhyme (v) internal rhyme (vi) metaphor (vii) simile (viii) repetition (ix) rhyme scheme (x) run-on lines.
- Comment on the title of the poem.
- If you were to paint this poem, what colours would you use?
- If this poem were a piece of music, how would you describe it? Which musical instrument(s) would suit it best?
- Draw three pictures or images that you see with your mind's eye when reading or thinking about this poem.
- Say from which source the poet has drawn these images – from nature, art, mythology, science . . .
- Which is the most important word/line in the poem? Justify your choice.

Some General Guidelines

- You will need to know the poems well if you are to discuss them and write about them intelligently and in detail. You cannot read these poems too often. When you've made them your own, then you will have the confidence of your own thoughts and opinions about the texts.

- If you know the poems in your head and in your heart, then you will be able to summon up the necessary detail when discussing an aspect of the work. Another way of entering into a close relationship with the text is to write the poems out for yourself. Professor Helen Vendler, of Harvard University, says: 'I know no greater help to understanding a poem than writing it out in longhand with the illusion that one is composing it – deciding on this word rather than another, this arrangement of its masses rather than another, this prolonging, this digression, this cluster of senses, this closure.'

- If you read through the collected poems of any poet, it is as if you are looking at, as Wallace Stevens puts it, a globe upon the table. It is a complete and unique world. For example, the poems by John Donne on your course (and they include his finest work) are by a distinctive voice. If we were given an unsigned poem by Donne, we should be able to recognise some of the characteristics which make his poetry memorable and unique: vocabulary, sentence structure, the poetic form, thematic preoccupations and so on.

Appendix II

How to Write a H1 Answer

We all have a lot of faff and fluff and nonsense in our heads. However, whatever else you can say about the poetry on your course, you have to admit that it is intelligent. And having *intelligent* things to think about and discuss is a *good* thing. Think positive from the outset. It's the only way to go.

Every year, poor unfortunates sit down to mark hundreds and hundreds of Leaving Certificate English exam scripts. First, they've had to drive up or down or across to Athlone to collect the scripts, then drive home with a boot full of paper and, secondly, they must then mark and mark and mark, and finish the lot to a deadline. How do they do it? And what is the biggest complaint year after year? What do most English examiners say afterwards? Well, more often than not, it is, 'If only the candidates answered the question . . .' There's definitely a market out there for the T-shirt that reads, 'Answer the bloody question!' It would serve as a useful *aide-memoire*.

It is truly extraordinary, frustrating and disappointing that so many Leaving Cert candidates, again and again, ignore or misinterpret a question's main topic or focus. This is an exam and, therefore, you really must do what you are invited to do. Suppose you love the poetry of Joe Bloggs and could write a brilliant five-page essay on the imagery in that poet's work, and the question on the exam paper invites you to discuss the tone and mood in Joe Bloggs's poetry. Then you simply *must* focus on tone and mood, and nothing else. Obviously, the images may convey or capture a mood, but you must adapt your material on the day of the exam and think things through all over again.

Prepare. Prepare. Prepare.

Someone said, 'If you don't know it, you can't say it.' This means that you simply have to know the poems – five or six per poet at Higher Level. Otherwise, you haven't a chance. Ideally, you should read the poems repeatedly until you know them well in your head and in your heart. One of the best things you can do is to write out the poems in your own handwriting. This, of course, is a really stupid thing to do if you do it without thinking. But if you take every poem, line by line, and write out every word, your relationship with that poem will be an up-close-and-personal one. Pay attention to what you are doing. You will notice such details as line length, the choice of words, how the poem is punctuated, the use of similes, repetition, etc. Obviously, some lines are more important than others; some lines are well worth quoting if you want to illustrate a point you are making.

You might also have read a biographical note on the poet you are studying. This is undoubtedly useful, but watch that you don't just lob in a biographical detail for the sake of it. Again, in the exam hall, you must decide what is *relevant* to the question you are answering. For example, if you are writing an answer on, say, 'Eavan Boland and the world of her poetry', it is significant and worth mentioning that she and her husband moved to the suburbs in the early 1970s and that they have called Dundrum home ever since. And it is also worth quoting Declan Kiberd's remark that Boland 'is one of the very few Irish poets to describe with any kind of fidelity the lives now lived by half a million people in the suburbs of Dublin.' Or if you're writing on Wordsworth and exploring how he saw nature as a guide and guardian, it could be mentioned that Wordsworth's mother died when he was eight and his father when he was thirteen. Likewise, if you are focusing on Emily Dickinson's eccentric, unique style it might be relevant to say that her poems, when first published, were altered to make them look less odd or extraordinary.

When you think about any poet, ask yourself:

- What makes that particular poet unique?
- What does that poet say?
- How does that poet say it?

Bear the following in mind:

- *What* the poet says is the poet's **theme**.
- *How* the poet is saying it is **style**.

Most questions allow for a discussion and analysis of both what is being said and how it is being said.

Glossary of Literary Terms

ACROSTIC: this is when the first letter in each word at the beginning of a line or stanza spells out a word, name or title. For example:

Man
Is
Never
Dead

ALLEGORY: the word allegory comes from Greek *allos*, 'other', and *agoreuein*, 'to speak'. In literature, an allegory is a work which has a surface meaning and another, deeper, meaning; in other words it can be read at two levels. An example would be George Orwell's *Animal Farm*. It is a story about a group of animals and can be read as such, but it also charts certain events in Eastern European and Russian politics.

ALLITERATION: when two or more words in close connection begin with the same letter or sound and affect the ear with an echoing sound. Examples include the childhood doggerel, 'Betty bought a bit of butter but the butter Betty bought was bitter'. Dickinson uses alliteration as in 'Berries of the Bahamas – have I –/But this little Blaze . . .'; or Larkin in 'The Whitsun Weddings' - 'A slow and stopping curve southwards we kept'; or Seamus Heaney's 'to the tick of two clocks'.

ALLUSION: this is when a writer deliberately introduces into his/her own work recognisable elements from another source. This may be a reference to a well-known character, event, or place or to another work of art. For example, in her poem 'Love', Eavan Boland never names Virgil's Aeneas but the reader is expected to identify 'the hero . . . on his way to hell' as an allusion to Book VI of *The Aeneid*.

AMBIGUITY: when language is open to one or more interpretations based on the context in which it occurs. Ambiguity can be intentional or unintentional. An example would be the opening line of Keats's 'Ode on a Grecian Urn': 'Thou still unravished bride of quietness' – where the word 'still' can mean 'without movement, silent' or 'as before, up to the present time'.

ANAGRAM: this is when a rearrangement of the letters in one word or phrase results in a new word or phrase, as in 'listen' into 'silent', 'now' into 'won'.

ANAPHORA: when a word or phrase is repeated for effect at the beginning of lines, clauses or sentences. The Bible contains many examples, as in the Book of Ecclesiastes: 'A time to be born, and a time to die. A time to plant, and a time to pluck up that which is planted.' In Shakespeare's Sonnet 66, ten of the fourteen lines begin with 'And'.

ANTITHESIS: in Greek, 'antithesis' means 'opposition'. Antithesis occurs when contraries are placed side by side, as in T.S. Eliot's 'We are the hollow men/We are the stuffed men' from 'The Hollow Men'; or Samuel Johnson's 'Marriage has many pains, but celibacy has no pleasures'; or in Shakespeare's Sonnet 116 'Whose worth's unknown, although his height be taken'.

ARCHAISM: in Greek, the word means 'old-fashioned', and an archaism is when a writer or speaker deliberately uses a word or phrase no longer in current use, for example, 'oft', 'morn', 'thy'. Keats's use of 'faery' in 'Ode to a Nightingale' is an example.

ARCHETYPE: the word comes from Greek meaning 'original or primitive form' and archetypes can take the form of symbols, characters, images or events which we respond to in a deep and meaningful way. For example fire, the dark, the sun, the father, the mother, snake, birth, death, the young man setting out on a journey, the young man from the country first arriving in the city all come under the heading archetype.

ASSONANCE: in Latin, 'assonare' is 'to answer with the same sound'. Assonance is when vowel sounds are repeated in a sequence of words close to each other. For example, in W. B. Yeats: 'I hear lake water lapping with low sounds by the shore'.

AUBADE: in French, 'aubade' means 'dawn'. The aubade is a celebratory morning song or a lament that two lovers must part.

BALLAD: a simple and memorable song that tells a story in oral form through narrative and dialogue. It is one of the oldest forms of literature and was originally passed on orally among illiterate people. Ballads often tell of love, courage, the supernatural. Ballads usually are written in four-line stanzas with an abcb rhyme, and often have a refrain. The first and third lines are usually four stress iambic tetrameter, the second and fourth lines are in three stress iambic trimeter. For example:

> There lived a wife at Usher's Well
> And a wealthy wife was she
> She had three stout and stalwart sons,
> An sent them o'er the sea.

Other examples of ballad include Keats's 'La Belle Dame sans Merci' and the anonymous 'Frankie and Johnny'.

BLANK VERSE: this is unrhymed iambic pentameter and is often used in long poems and dramatic verse. One of the earliest examples of blank verse in English is to be found in Henry Howard Surrey's translation of Virgil's *Aeneid*, which was published in 1540. Shakespeare, Milton, Wordsworth, Robert Frost all wrote in blank verse.

CADENCE: the word 'cadence' means 'the fall of the voice' and refers to the last syllables in a pattern of words. Cadence is difficult to define, and yet it is easily identified or, more accurately, easily heard. When Philip Larkin writes at the end of 'At Grass

> With bridles in the evening come

we know that the sounds have been arranged in a particularly effective way on the page. For example, he puts the verb at the end which is not usual in English (it is a Latin form), but the effect is musical and beautiful and very different from 'Come with bridles in the evening', which says exactly the same thing. Cadence is found especially in Biblical poetry, free verse, prose poetry. Ezra Pound in *Make It New* (1934) urged poets to 'compose in the sequence of the musical phrase, not in sequence of a metronome'.

CAESURA: a caesura is a pause which usually occurs in the middle of a line and is caused by rhyme, punctuation or syntax. For example, Boland uses the caesura for effect in the closing lines of 'The Pomegranate':

> The legend will be hers as well as mine.
> She will enter it. As I have.
> She will wake up. She will hold
> the papery flushed skin in her hand.
> And to her lips. I will say nothing.

CARICATURE: from an Italian word meaning 'to exaggerate'. When a character's personality or physical feature is portrayed in a distorted manner, the result is a caricature. The cartoonist's work is almost always a caricature.

CLICHÉ: a phrase which has through overuse become familiar and jaded. The word cliché originally referred to a plate used in printing which produced numerous identical copies. Clichés were once original and interesting uses of language but now, though it is difficult to do so, they are best avoided. Examples include 'a clear blue sky', 'go haywire', 'hard as a rock', 'stand up and be counted', 'tough as nails'.

CLIMAX: climax comes from a Greek word meaning ladder and a climactic moment is one when there is intensity. In a Shakespearean play, for example, there is often a climax in Acts III and V, when the audience's interest is at its height. In Shelley's sonnet 'Ozymandias' the lines 'My name is Ozymandias, King of Kings,/Look on my Works, ye Mighty, and despair!' form a climax.

CLOSURE: the way a poem, novel, play, etc. ends and how the author achieves the sense of an ending. For example, Shakespeare in his sonnets uses a rhyming couplet; Philip Larkin in 'The Explosion' places a single line between eight three-line stanzas.

COMPARATIVE LITERATURE: the study of the relationships and similarities between different literatures by writers from different nations or peoples – e.g. you can read *Great Expectations* by Charles Dickens and *Cat's Eye* by Margaret Atwood and examine and analyse both as 'coming of age' novels or *Bildungsroman* (an upbringing or education novel) – one about a boy in the nineteenth-century in England, the other about a girl growing up in Canada in the twentieth century. Ian Reed states that 'Unless we compare things, we cannot see things either wholly or fully'; and Michael Lapidge says: 'The comparative approach is instinctive to human intelligence. From our very infancy we learn by comparing like with like, and by distinguishing the like from the nearly like, and the other.'

CONCEIT: conceit comes from a Latin word meaning 'to seize' and the literary conceit occurs when a writer expresses an idea in which an interesting connection is made between two distinct things. For example, when a writer compares his state of love to that of a ship in a storm or when John Donne (1572–1631) likens the souls of two lovers to a compass:

> If they be two, they are two so
>   As stiffe twin compasses are two,
> Thy soule, the fixt foot, makes no show
>   To move, but doth, if the other doe.

Dr Johnson described the conceit most associated with the seventeenth-century Metaphysical poets as 'a kind of *discordia concors* [a harmony of opposites]; a combination of dissimilar images, or discovery of occult resemblances in things apparently unlike . . . The most heterogeneous ideas are yoked by violence together'. In Seamus Heaney's poem 'Valediction', the poet uses the conceit of a ship at sea to express his own inner feeling.

COUPLET: two lines of rhymed or unrhymed verse which follow the same metre. Eavan Boland's 'The War Horse' is written in couplets. The heroic couplet is made up of iambic pentameter lines which rhyme in pairs.

CRITICISM: the evaluation, interpretation and discussion of a work

CROSS RHYME: (or interlaced rhyme) this occurs when a word at the end of a line rhymes with a word in the middle of a following line.

ECPHRASIS: also spelt *ekphrasis* (meaning 'description' in Greek); it is a poem that describes a work of art, e.g. Keats's 'Ode on a Grecian Urn' or Bishop's 'Poem' or Derek Mahon's 'Courtyards in Delft'.

ELEGY: elegy comes from the Greek word meaning lament. The elegy is usually a long, formal poem that mourns the dead. Gray's 'Elegy in a Country Churchyard' is one of the more famous. Also, Whitman's elegy for Abraham Lincoln, 'When Lilacs Last in the Dooryard Bloom'd' and W. H. Auden's 'In Memory of W.B. Yeats'.

ELISION: this occurs when a syllable is omitted or when two syllables are slurred together to form one. For example, in Shakespeare's sonnet:

> Th' expense of spirit in waste of shame

Or in Elizabeth Bishop's 'Questions of Travel':

> blurr'dly and inconclusively

END RHYME: this is when the words at the end of lines rhyme.

ENJAMBMENT: also known as the run-on line, enjambment occurs when a line ending is not end stopped but flows into the following line. For example these lines from Michael Longley's 'The Greengrocer':

> He ran a good shop, and he died
> Serving even the death-dealers
> Who found him busy as usual
> Behind the counter, organised
> With holly wreaths for Christmas,
> Fir trees on the pavement outside.

EPIGRAM: a short witty well-made poem. Coleridge defined the epigram as follows and the definition is itself an epigram.

> 'What is an epigram? A dwarfish whole
> Its body brevity, and wit its soul'

Another example would be the epigram called 'Coward' by A. R. Ammons: 'Bravery runs in my family.'

EPIPHANY: a moment of illumination, beauty, insight. For example, the closing lines of Elizabeth Bishop's 'The Fish' or the final stanza of Seamus Heaney's 'Sunlight'.

EYE RHYME: (also known as sight-rhyme) eye-rhyme occurs when two words or the final parts of the words are spelled alike, but have different pronunciations as in 'tough/bough', 'blood/mood'.

FEMININE ENDING: (also known as 'light ending') the feminine ending is an unstressed syllable at the end of a regular metrical line and is added for its musical quality. This feminine ending makes for a falling foot.

FEMININE RHYME: words of two (or more) syllables which rhyme. Shakespeare's sonnets 20 and 87 use feminine end rhymes throughout.

FOOT: a metrical unit of measurement in verse and the line can be divided into different numbers of feet as follows:

one-foot line	:	monometer
two-foot line	:	dimeter
three-foot line	:	trimeter
four-foot line	:	tetrameter
five-foot line	:	pentameter
six-foot line	:	hexameter
seven-foot line	:	heptameter
eight-foot line	:	octameter

Once a line is divided into feet, each foot can then be identified as containing a distinctive metrical pattern. For example, if a foot contains one weak and one strong stress (U –) that foot is an iamb or an iambic foot. If there are five iambic feet in a line, it is known as an iambic pentameter. The following are the most common forms of metrical foot – the stress pattern is given and an example:

iamb (iambic)	:	∪ – (hello)
rochee (trochaic)	:	– ∪ (only; Wallace; Stevens)
anapest (anapestic)	:	∪ – (understand)
dactyl (dactylic)	:	– ∪ ∪ (suddenly; Emily; Dickinson)
spondee (spondaic)	:	– – (deep peace)

FREE VERSE: on the page, free verse is unrhymed; it often follows an irregular line length and line pattern and is unmetered. Free verse depends on rhythm, repetition or unusual typographical and grammatical devices for effect.

FULL RHYME: (also known as perfect rhyme or true rhyme) when the sound or sounds in one word are perfectly matched by the sounds in another. For example, soon and moon, thing/spring, mad/bad, head/said, people/steeple, curious/furious, combination/domination.

HAIKU: the word 'haiku' in Japanese means 'starting verse', and the haiku is a sixteenth-century Japanese form of lyric poem of seventeen syllables in three lines of five, seven and five syllables respectively. Originally, the haiku had to follow certain rules: it had to have nature imagery, a reference to a season, a reference to a religious or historical event; had no rhyme; had to create an emotional response in the reader; and it had to capture the essence of its theme in an insight. The seventeenth century Japanese poet Basho wrote many fine haikus. Here are some modern ones:

1.1.87
Dangerous pavements.
But I face the ice this year
With my father's stick.
– Seamus Heaney

This is a haiku.
Five syllables and then foll
ows seven. Get it?
– John Cooper Clarke

To write a haiku
 In seventeen syllables
Is very diffic.
 – John Cooper Clarke

HALF RHYME: (also called slant-rhyme, near-rhyme, off-rhyme, half-rhyme, partial rhyme, imperfect rhyme) half-rhyme occurs when two words have certain sound similarities, but do not have perfect rhymes. Half-rhymes often depend on the same last consonant in two words such as 'blood' and 'good' or 'poem' and 'rum'. Emily Dickinson, Hopkins, Yeats, Dylan Thomas, Elizabeth Bishop and many other poets use half-rhyme.

HYPERBOLE: in Greek, the word 'hyperbole' means 'an overshooting, an excess' and hyperbole is the deliberate use of exaggeration or overstatement for dramatic or comic effect. For example, in 'The Daffodils' Wordsworth is using hyperbole in 'Ten thousand saw I at a glance'. The opposite of hyperbole is litotes.

IAMB: the iamb is a metrical foot made up of one unaccented syllable followed by an accented one (‿ –). The word 'today' or 'forget' or 'hello' are examples of the iamb.

IAMBIC PENTAMETER: the word pentameter is Greek for five measures and is used to describe a line of verse containing five metrical feet. The iambic pentameter is the most commonly used meter in the English language and there's a very simple reason for this: the length of an iambic pentameter line is the length of time most of us can hold our breath. Blank verse, which Shakespeare used in his plays, is unrhymed iambic pentameter. There is a old girls' skipping chant which goes 'I must, I must, I must, improve my bust' and it is a perfect example of iambic pentameter. So too is a sentence such as 'You make me sick, you make me really sick' or 'My birthday is the twenty-sixth of May'. The iambic pentameter could be represented as follows:

> daDA daDA daDA daDA daDA or (‿ – | ‿ – | ‿ – | ‿ – | ‿ –)

Obviously, when you read a line of iambic pentameter, you do not exaggerate the stress, just as we do not exaggerate the stress on a vowel sound in our everyday speech. In the poem, however, the underlying structured pattern creates a music and a flow that is heard in the ear. If you look at and read lines such as the following from Eavan Boland's 'The Pomegranate', you will see and hear them as iambic pentameters:

> I climb the stairs and stand where I can see (line 26)

> The rain is cold. The road is flint-coloured (line 43)

Not every line in a poem that is written in iambic pentameter will follow the iambic pentameter pattern. If that were the case, the sequence of stresses could have a crippling effect. The rule for poets seems to be that they will use a rule, knowing that it can be broken or abandoned when necessary. The best judge, in the end, is the ear rather than a book on metrics.

IMAGE: in literature, an image is a picture in words, and similes, metaphors and symbols all offer the reader word-pictures as in

> 'his brown skin hung in strips
> like ancient wallpaper,
> and its pattern of darker brown
> was like wallpaper:
> shapes like full-blown roses . . .'
> – Elizabeth Bishop 'The Fish'

'. . . where the ocean
Like a mIghty animal
With a really wicked motion
Leaps for sailor's funeral . . .'
– Stevie Smith 'Deeply Morbid'

Ezra Pound defined the image as 'an intellectual and emotional complex in an instant of time' and this definition reminds us that the image involves the head and the heart. Our intellect creates the picture and our emotions are also involved in determining our response to it, and all of this takes place in an instant of time. Single words such as 'snow', 'rat', 'velvet', 'isolation' and so on present us with images of our own making. The poet, in creating a successful image, allows the reader to see something in a new and interesting way.

IMAGERY: the pictures presented in a work of literature which communicate more fully the writer's intention. For example, the predominant imagery in a play by Shakespeare may be light and darkness and these images become powerful ways of portraying characters, moods, the play's structure.

IN MEDIAS RES: in Latin, the phrase means 'in the middle of things', and, when a work is said to begin immediately or abruptly and without introduction, then it is said to begin *in medias res*. For example, Seamus Heaney's poem 'St Kevin and the Blackbird':

And then there was St Kevin and the blackbird.

INTERNAL RHYME: this is a rhyme which occurs within the line to create a musical or rhythmical effect, as in Elizabeth Bishop's 'Filling Station', where 'taboret' (American pronunciation) and 'set' and the repeated color form an internal rhyme:

Some comic books provide
the only note of *color* —
of certain *color*. They lie
upon a big dim doily
draping a tabor**et**
(part of the s**et**), beside
a big hirsute begonia.

INTERTEXTUALITY: the term was coined by Julia Kristeva in 1966. It refers to the interdependence of literary texts; any one text does not exist in isolation, but is linked to all the texts which have gone before. All texts define themselves against other texts, either through differences or similarities.

IRONY: there are two kinds of irony: verbal irony, when something is said and the opposite is meant; and irony of situation, the classic example being the story of Oedipus.

KENNING: a word invention frequently found in Old Norse and Anglo-Saxon or Old English in which two ideas are joined to form a condensed image. For example, 'whale road' or 'swan's path' for sea; 'sky-candle' for the sun. Gerard Manley Hopkins uses kennings in his poetry, calling the kestrel a 'windhover', for example.

LITOTES: litotes is the technique whereby you say something positive by contradicting a negative. A famous example is when Saint Paul said of Rome: 'I am a citizen of no mean city'; in other words he is saying that he is a citizen of a magnificent and great city. If you say of someone that he/she is not bad-looking' you are using litotes.

LYRIC: from the Greek word for lyre, a stringed musical instrument. The lyic poem was originally sung and accompanied by the lyre. Lyric now means a personal, concentrated, musical, short poem. Helen Vendler says 'Lyric is the genre of private life: it is what we say to ourselves when we are alone.' Examples include Ben Jonson's 'Song: To Celia', 'Fern Hill' by Dylan Thomas, Michael Longley's 'Amish Rug'.

MASCULINE RHYME: when stressed monosyllabic words rhyme.

METAPHOR: when a direct link is made between two things without using 'like' or 'as'. Metaphors are often more powerful than similes. 'You're an angel' is more effective than 'You're like an angel'; 'He blazed a trail through the town' is a metaphor which gives a vivid image of a person directly compared to fire – colourful, exciting, dangerous.

METRE: the word metre comes from the Greek word for measure and there are different ways of identifying the metre in a poem:
   (a) by the number of stressed syllables in a line: STRONG-STRESS METRE
   (b) by the number of stressed and unstressed syllables in a line: ACCENTUAL-SYLLABIC METRE
   (c) by the number of syllables in a line: SYLLABIC METRE
   (d) by the duration of short and long syllables in a line: QUANTITATIVE METRE
Do not worry overmuch about the technicalities of metre. I. A. Richards compared metre in a poem to a frame around a painting. It is obviously important but the poem can be appreciated and understood without a thorough knowledge of every technical term in the book. Metre can appear too artificial if overemphasised. When you speak or write, you do not always plan a metrical pattern in your speech, yet the words you speak and the order in which you speak them often make for an effective sound-pattern. The metrical pattern is important, but your ear and your command of language allow you to communicate effectively. In poetry, metre is very important; it is one of poetry's most distinguishing features.

METRICS: the composing or study of the rhythmic pattern in verse. The theories relating to these.

MOOD: this is the feeling contained within a poem and the feeling communicated to the reader. If someone walked into a room containing several people and angrily shouted at you to 'Get out of here at once!', the TONE of voice used would be an ANGRY, COMMANDING one and the MOOD within the room might be one of UNEASE. Do not confuse TONE and MOOD. Tone has to do with the expressing of an attitude; mood has to do with feeling.

MOTIF: motif comes from Latin and means 'to move'. Motif means a theme, a technique, an event, a character which is developed and repeated in a work. For example, in Shakespeare's *Macbeth*, light and darkness become a motif. In literature in general, there are certain motifs such as the *Carpe Diem* (Seize the Day) motif, which means to make the most of a situation. In Michael Longley's poetry, the relationship between father and son, be it between Longley and his own father or that between Odysseus and Laertes, becomes a motif.

MYTH: a story of strange, unusual, supernatural happenings of unknown authorship which was passed on to future generations in an effort to explain origins and natural events.

NEAR RHYME: (also known as slant-rhyme, partial-rhyme, oblique-rhyme, half-rhyme) near-rhyme occurs when two words sound approximately the same and are placed within the poem for musical effect. Emily Dickinson frequently used near-rhyme such as in 'song'/'tongue'.

NEGATIVE CAPABILITY: a phrase used by John Keats (1795–1821) in a letter dated 21 December 1817; it refers to a power of sympathy and a freedom from self-consciousness. In the letter he wrote that the true poet is one who is 'capable of being in uncertainties, Mysteries, doubts, without any irritable reaching after fact and reason'. Keats, by way of illustration, spoke of a sparrow picking among the gravel outside his window, and his observation of the sparrow was so intent and interested that he became that sparrow.

OBJECTIVE CORRELATIVE: the term was first used by Washington Allston in 1850 in *Lectures on Art* and later by T. S. Eliot in his study of *Hamlet*. The phrase refers to how the objective or external world can produce an emotion in the viewer; how there is a correlation between the object and the viewer. Similarly, if a writer uses certain details, descriptions in his/her work, a specific emotional response will be evoked in the reader.

OCTAVE/OCTET: an eight-line stanza. In a Petrarchan sonnet, the fourteen lines are divided into octet and sestet. The octet often poses a question and this is answered in the sestet.

ODE: a poem of celebration and praise. John Keats wrote some of the most famous odes in the English language.

ONOMATOPOEIA: in Greek, 'onomatopoeia' means 'the making of a name' and onomatopoeia refers to words whose sounds imitate what is being described. For example, 'buzz', 'slap', 'cuckoo', 'gargle'.

OTTAVA RIMA: an Italian eight-line stanza in iambic pentameter with an abababcc rhyming scheme.

OXYMORON: (in Greek, the word means foolishness) oxymoron refers to a figure of speech in which contradictory and opposite aspects are linked. It is similar to paradox, but the oxymoron is contained within a phrase, the paradox within a statement. Examples of oxymoron include 'cruel kindness' and 'thunderous silences'.

PALINDROME: in Greek the word palindrome means 'running back again'. A palindrome is a word, a line of verse or a sentence which reads the same way backwards and forwards: e.g. 'Dad'; 'noon'; 'Madam, I'm Adam'; 'Was it a cat I saw?'. The following refers to Napoleon: 'Able was I ere I saw Elba'. Other examples are: 'Sums are not set as a test on Erasmus'; and 'A man, a plan, a canal – Panama!'

PARADOX: a paradox is when language expresses a truth in what seems, at first, to be a contradiction. For example, Wordsworth's 'The child is father of the man' or Shakespeare's line in *Julius Caesar*: 'Cowards die many times before their deaths'.

PARODY: this is when a well-known work is deliberately imitated in a mocking or humorous way. The reader is expected to be familiar with the original work, if the parody is to be effective.

PATHETIC FALLACY: this term was coined by John Ruskin in 1856 and it refers to the writer's technique of attributing human feeling or behaviour to nature. For example, in 'Lycidas' John Milton says of the flowers 'And Daffadillies fill their cups with tears'.

PATHOS: the word *pathos* in Greek means 'suffering' or 'passion'. Pathos is a deep, sympathetic feeling which the writer summons up in the reader or audience. The final line of Seamus Heaney's poem, 'Mid-term Break' is an example: 'A four foot box, a foot for every year.'

PENTAMETER: this is a line of poetry which is made up of five metrical feet. The iambic pentameter (ᴗ –/ᴗ –/ᴗ –/ᴗ –/ᴗ –) is the most commonly used meter in the English language.

PERIODS OF ENGLISH LITERATURE: the following is an outline of the periods into which English literature has been divided by literary historians, though the exact dates sometimes vary:

450 – 1100	Old English or Anglo-Saxon period
1100 – 1500	Middle English or Medieval English period
1500 – 1660	The Renaissance
1558 – 1603	Elizabeth the First's reign Elizabethan
1603 – 1625	Jacobean (after James I)
1625 – 1649	Caroline age
1649 – 1660	Commonwealth period/Puritanism
1660 – 1798	Neo–Classical period
1660 – 1700	The Restoration
1700 – 1745	Augustan Age (the Age of Pope)
1745 – 1798	Age of Sensibility (the Age of Samuel Johnson)
1798 – 1832	Romantic Period
1832 – 1901	Victorian period
1901 – 1914	Edwardian
1910 – 1936	Georgian
1914 – 1970s	Modern English
c. 1970s –	Postmodern

PERSONA: in Latin, the word *persona* means person or mask, and the persona is the speaker in a work such as poem or play who is different from the poet or playwright. The list of characters in a play used to be given under the heading *Dramatis Personae* (the dramatist's persons). In Michael Longley's poem 'Self-Heal' and in 'Wedding-Wind' by Philip Larkin, the voice is that of a female persona.

PERSONIFICATION: this occurs when a writer gives human qualities to inanimate objects or abstractions. For example, if one said that the clouds were in a rage that would be personification.

POETIC LICENSE: when rules are broken, when facts are ignored, when logic is abandoned all for the sake of the overall effect. Emily Dickinson abandons conventional grammatical rules with poetic license. Or Eavan Boland mixes Greek and Latin names in her reference to the myth of Ceres and Proserpine/Demeter and Persephone.

PUNCTUATION: in Latin, the word *punctus* means 'to point' and punctuation indicates speed, flow, emphasis, direction, the emotional charge of language and so on. The following are the more familiar forms:

comma	,	a slight pause
semicolon	;	a longer pause or a division between clauses
colon	:	a long pause; introduces a list, explanation or quotation
full-stop	.	indicates a full stop at the end of a sentence; also used at the end of certain abbreviated words (e.g. Prof. and ad. but not Mr because Mr in the abbreviated version ends with the same letter as the word in full does)
ellipsis	...	indicates that something is missing or is being omitted
dash	–	used to indicate a break in a sentence or elsewhere
hyphen	-	connects compound words
quotation marks	' '	are used to indicate quoted material

	" "	indicate a quotation within a quotation or something of a false or spurious nature
slash	/	indicates a line ending
exclamation mark	!	used for emphasis or to express emotion
question mark	?	suggests puzzlement, confusion, a need for information
parentheses	( )	used in an aside
brackets	[ ]	indicates an editorial comment
italics	*italics*	used for emphasis, foreign words

PUN: a play upon words alike or nearly alike in sound, but different in meaning. A famous example is the dying Mercutio's line in *Romeo and Juliet* (III i): 'Ask for me tomorrow and you shall find me a grave man.'

QUATRAIN: in French, 'quatrain' means a collection of four, and quatrain, in English, refers to a poem or stanza of four lines, usually with alternating rhyming schemes such as abab, aabb, abba, aaba, abcb.

REPETITION: repeated sounds, words, structures is a feature of all poetry to a lesser or greater degree. Repetition has many effects such as emphasis, music, surprise, predictability. Paul Durcan's use of repetition in 'Going Home to Mayo, Winter, 1949' or Elizabeth Bishop's use of repetition in the closing lines of 'The Fish' are significant and effective.

RHYME: when a sound is echoed creating a music and order within the work.

RHYME SCHEMES:

Couplet	aa
Triplet	aaa
Ballad stanza	abab
Limerick	aabba
Ottava Rima	abababcc

RHYTHM: the work in Greek means 'flowing'. Rhythm refers to how the words move or flow.

ROMANTICISM: Romanticism and the Romantic Movement belong to a period in English Literature in the late eighteenth century and the beginning of the nineteenth. Some date the beginning of the movement from the beginning of the French Revolution in 1789; others from 1798 when Wordsworth and Coleridge published *Lyrical Ballads*. The movement ended in the 1830s (Victoria became queen in 1837). The movement began as a reaction to the formality and restraint of neo-classicism in the preceding age. The Romantic Movement focused on the individual's feelings and imagination. The child was valued for its innocence and society was regarded as a corrupting influence. The Romantic poet wrote about his own thoughts and feelings (Wordsworth, speaking of *The Prelude*, said that 'it was a thing unprecedented in literary history that a man should talk so much about himself') and celebrated nature over city life and civilisation. Samuel Johnson, in the eighteenth century, had said that 'The man who is tired of London is tired of life'; the Romantics often found their inspiration in nature.

RUN-ON LINE: this is the same as enjambment. See above.

SARCASM: not to be confused with IRONY, sarcasm is a crude and obvious method of expressing apparent praise when the opposite is meant.

SENSIBILITY: the sensitivity and quality of a person's mind, the capacity of feeling or emotion.

SENTIMENTALITY: an expression of feeling which is excessive, indulgent, immature.

SESTET: a group of six lines, usually the final six lines in a sonnet where the fourteen line poem is divided into eight (octet) and sestet.

SESTINA: a complicated poetic form in which the poem consists of six stanzas of six lines each followed by three-line stanza. The same six end-words occur in each of the first six stanzas and form a definite pattern. The final stanza also contains the six key-words. Elizabeth Bishop's 'Sestina' is an example.

SIMILE: from the Latin word for 'like', the simile is a figure of speech in which one thing is compared to another, using the words 'like', 'as', 'as if'. For example:

> When I was small I swallowed an awn of rye.
> My throat was like standing crop probed by a scythe.
> – Seamus Heaney 'The Butter-Print'

SONNET: a fourteen line poem, usually in iambic pentameter.

STREAM OF CONSCIOUSNESS: the phrase was invented by the nineteenth-century American psychologist William James to describe the writer's attempt to imitate or capture every thought, impression, memory, feeling and so on in an individual consciousness, as they happen. The most famous example of stream of consciousness is found in the closing forty pages of James Joyce's *Ulysses*. Here Joyce has entered into Molly Bloom's consciousness. Her thoughts and ideas flow through the reader's mind, and Joyce abandoned all conventional punctuation to give the passage immediacy. Here is an excerpt:

> I love flowers Id love to have the whole place swimming in roses God of heaven theres nothing like nature the wild mountains then the sea and the waves rushing then the beautiful country with fields of oats and wheat and all kinds of things and all the fine cattle going about that would do your heart good to see rivers and lakes and flowers all sorts of shapes and smells and colours springing up even out of the ditches primroses and violets nature it is as for them saying theres no God I wouldnt give a snap of my two fingers for all their learning why dont they go and create something I often asked him atheists or whatever they call themselves go and wash the cobbles off themselves first then they go howling for the priest and they dying and why why because theyre afraid of hell on account of their bad conscience ah yes I know them well who was the first person in the universe before there was anybody that made it all who ah that they dont know neither do I so there you are they might as well try to stop the sun from rising tomorrow the sun shines for you he said the day we were lying among the rhododendrons on Howth head in the grey tweed suit and his straw hat the day I got him to propose to me yes first I gave him the bit of seedcake out of my mouth and it was leapyear like now yes 16 years ago my God after that long kiss I near lost my breath . . . . .

STYLE: the manner of writing or speaking, e.g. the way a writer uses words may be direct or convoluted or vague or inaccurate or florid . . . . 'Style most shows a man, speak that I may see thee' (Ben Jonson)

SUBJECT MATTER: this refers to the actual material spoken of in the work. For example, a poet might write about a cluttered room which is the subject matter of the poem, but the theme of the poem could be the confusion felt because a relationship has ended. In Elizabeth Bishop's poem 'Filling Station', the subject matter is an oily, dirty, petrol (gas) station but the poem's theme is human endeavour, dignity, love.

SUBLIME: in Latin, this means high, lofty, elevated. The sublime in literature refers to moments of heightened awareness, intense feeling. The closing lines of James Wright's poem 'A Blessing' are sublime.

SURREALISM: Surrealism is a movement in art and literature which sought to release and express the creative potential of the unconscious mind. It frequently contains the irrational juxtaposition of images. The Uruguayan-born French writer Isidore Lucien Ducasse's (1846–1870) description of 'the chance meeting on a dissecting-table of a sewing machine and an umbrella' has been frequently quoted as a definition of surrealism. Salvador Dali's paintings are examples. The surreal is literally 'above the real'. In writing, the surreal occurs when conventional modes are broken, and dreamlike or nightmarish or seemingly unrelated images are juxtaposed. In Michael Longley's poem 'The Linen Workers', the opening lines have a surreal quality: 'Christ's teeth ascended with him into heaven:/ Through a cavity in one of his molars/The wind whistles; he is fastened for ever/By his exposed canines to a wintry sky.'

SYMBOL: a symbol is a word, phrase or image which represents something literal and concrete, but also suggests another source of reference. In everyday life, a piece of coloured cloth is just that, but that same cloth can be a country's flag. It is both object and symbol. Similarly in literature: in Shakespeare, the King is a male character, but he is also the symbol of power, authority and God's presence on earth. The use of symbol is a powerful device because of its rich, complex associative qualities. In Michael Longley's poem 'The Civil Servant', the smashing of the piano is a symbolic act.

SYNAESTHESIA: in Greek, *synaesthesia* means 'to feel or perceive together', and it is when one sensory perception is expressed in terms of a different sense. For example, when an image is experienced through two senses at the same time, as in:

> a loud red coat
> purple stained mouth

SYNECDOCHE: this is a figure of speech in which a part stands for the whole. For example, 'sail' stands for ship; 'hired hands' or 'all hands on deck' means hired persons.

TETRAMETER: the word *tetrameter* in Greek means four measures and the tetrameter is a four foot, four stress line. These feet can be iambic, trochaic and so on. The iambic tetrameter is the second most widely used form in English poetry, the most common being the iambic pentameter.

THEME: theme comes from a Greek word meaning 'proposition', and the theme of a work is the main or central idea within the work. Theme should be distinguished from subject matter. For example, the subject matter of Philip Larkin's 'Church Going' is visiting churches, but the theme of the poem is our natural fascination with religion, its power, effect and future.

TONE: the tone is the attitude conveyed by the writer. From the writer's tone of voice, the reader can identify the attitude of the writer towards his/her subject matter and/ or audience. A tone can be reverent, angry, disrespectful, cautious, dismissive, gentle, reserved, slangy, serious.

TRIMETER: the word *trimeter* in Greek means 'three measures' and the trimeter line is a three foot line. The trimeter is used in nursery rhymes and in many songs, such as Sir Thomas Wyatt's 'I will and yet I may not'.

TROCHEE: the trochee is a two syllable foot. The first syllable is long or stressed, the second is short and unstressed (‿ –). Examples are 'pushing', 'running'. It is known as the falling foot, opposite to the iambic foot, which is a rising foot.

VERSE: verse comes from the Latin word 'to turn' or 'a line or row of writing'. Verse can now refer to a line in a poem, a stanza, a refrain or a passage from the Bible. Verse can also refer to an entire poem based on regular meter or a poem that is lacking in profundity.

VILLANELLE: the word comes from Italian *villanella*, a rustic song or dance. At first, a villanelle was called such because of its pastoral subject and the use of a refrain. Later, the villanelle followed a strict pattern and became a poem of five three-line stanzas and a concluding quatrain, with only two rhymes throughout. The intricate rhyming scheme is as follows: aba, aba, aba, aba, aba, abaa. Examples of the villanelle are Dylan Thomas's 'Do Not Go Gentle Into That Good Night' and 'One Art' by Elizabeth Bishop.

VOICE: this is the distinctive utterance of a writer; it is the sounds we hear when we read or listen to the poem. In other words, a writer's ability to use words in such a way that a reader can recognise that writer's unique quality. T. S. Eliot identified three voices in poetry:

1. the poet in silent meditation
2. the poet addressing an audience
3. the voice of a dramatic character or persona created by the poet

The publishers would like to thank the following for permission to reproduce copyright material in this book.

Poems

'Death of a Field', 'Cora, Auntie', 'Prayer for the Children of Longing' and 'Hearth Lesson' by Paula Meehan (*Painting Rain*, 2009) is reprinted here by kind permission of Carcanet Press Limited, Manchester, UK.

Dedalus Press for kind permission to use the artwork for Meehan's 2020 publication *As If By Magic* and the following poems by Paula Meehan 'Buying Winkles', 'The Pattern', 'The Statue of the Virgin at Granard Speaks', 'My Father Perceived as a Vision of St Francis'.

'The Red Wheelbarrow' and 'To a Poor Old Woman' by William Carlos Williams from *The Collected Poems: Volume I*, 1909-1939 ©1938 is reprinted here by kind permission of Carcanet Press Limited, Manchester, UK.

"The Voice You Hear When You Read Silently" from *NEW & SELECTED POEMS* by Thomas Lux. Copyright © 1997 by Thomas Lux. Reprinted by permission of Houghton Mifflin Harcourt Publishing Company. All rights reserved.

Penguin Random House for *The Complete Poems* by Elizabeth Bishop. Published by Chatto and Windus. Reprinted by permission of The Random House Group Limited © 2004.

THE POEMS OF EMILY DICKINSON: READING EDITION, edited by Ralph W. Franklin, Cambridge, Mass.: The Belknap Press of Harvard University Press, Copyright © 1998, 1999 by the President and Fellows of Harvard College. Copyright © 1951, 1955 by the President and Fellows of Harvard College. Copyright © renewed 1979, 1983 by the President and Fellows of Harvard College. Copyright © 1914, 1918, 1919, 1924, 1929, 1930, 1932, 1935, 1937, 1942 by Martha Dickinson Bianchi. Copyright © 1952, 1957, 1958, 1963, 1965 by Mary L. Hampson.

'Grandfather', 'After the Titanic', 'Ecclesiastes', 'As It Should Be', 'Rathlin', 'Day Trip to Donegal', 'A Disused Shed in Co. Wexford', 'The Chinese Restaurant in Portrush', 'Antarctica', 'Kinsale' by kind permission of the author and The Gallery Press, Loughcrew, Oldcastle, County Meath, Ireland from *New Collected Poems* (2011) and *New Selected Poems* (2016).

'Shancoduff' and 'A Christmas Childhood' by Patrick Kavanagh are reprinted from *Collected Poems*, edited by Antoinette Quinn (Allen Lane, 2004). The poetry of Patrick Kavanagh is reprinted by kind permission of the Trustees of the Estate of the late Katherine B. Kavanagh, through the Jonathan Williams Literary Agency.

'A Blessing' from *The Branch Will Not Break* © 1963 by James Wright. Published by Wesleyan University Press and reprinted with permission.